THE SELECTED WRITINGS

OF SIR EDWARD COKE

EDWARD COKE

THE SELECTED WRITINGS

AND SPEECHES OF

Sir Edward Coke

Volume Two

EDITED BY

STEVE SHEPPARD

LIBERTY FUND

INDIANAPOLIS, INDIANA

© 2003 Liberty Fund, Inc.

Frontispiece and cover art:
volume I: Reproduced courtesy of the Right Honourable
the Earl of Leicester and the Holkham Estate.
volume II: Collection of the Editor.
volume III: Corbis-Bettmann.

08   07   06   05   04   03   P   5   4   3   2   1

Library of Congress Cataloging-in-Publication Data

Coke, Edward, Sir, 1552–1634.
[Selections. 2003]
The selected writings and speeches of Sir Edward Coke
edited by Steve Sheppard.
p.   cm.
Includes bibliographical references and index.
ISBN 0-86597-313-X (pbk.: alk. paper)
1. Law—England.
I. Sheppard, Steve, 1963–
II. Title.
KD358.C65   2003
349.42'092—dc22   2003061935

ISBNs:
0-86597-313-X   volume I
0-86597-314-8   volume II
0-86597-441-1   volume III
0-86597-316-4   set

Liberty Fund, Inc.
8335 Allison Pointe Trail, Suite 300
Indianapolis, Indiana 46250-1684

Contents to Volume II

D. The Fourth Part of the *Institutes*

II

Coke's Speech and Charge at the Norwich Assizes

In 1606, Coke was sitting as justice in the Court of Assizes in Norwich. As was the custom, he charged the grand jury with the forms of crime it should consider in bringing indictments, but he particularly suggested the jurors should be concerned with official misconduct. The charge was recorded and published by Robert Pricket in London in 1607 under the title *The Lord Coke His Speech and Charge. With a Discoverie of the Abuses and Corruption of Officers.* Coke realized the charge was politically volatile, and it appears he was criticized at court, so, in the preface to his Seventh Part of the *Reports,* published in 1608, he repudiated the publication of the charge as misrepresenting his comments and being full of errors. See p. 164.—*Ed.*

(Preface, written by Robert Prickett)
To The Right Honourable the Earle of Exceter,
Knight of the most Honorable order of the Garter:
and one of the Lordes of his Majesties most Honorable privie Counsel.
R. P. wisheth all encrease of Honor
and endlesse happinesse.[1]

May it please your Hon. The observation which this world begets, may teach experience truly to report, that *Love* and *Charity* are for the most part growne so cold, even in the hotest Sun-shine of our *Profession,* as that despised *Povertie,* though addicted to the *Religious exercise* of endevors commendable, is in the best employment (which seemes with greatest *Favor* to *smile* upon his *Hope*) so coldly recompensed, as that *poore unpitied dejected miserable Povertie* knowes neither *Meanes* nor *Place* how or where to warme it selfe.

Unhappie I, in this best time of greatest happines, who being as I am a Poore dispised, hated, scorned, and unrespected *Souldier* so unfortunate as no commended meanes, though many used, with confirmation both of *love* and *Loyaltie,* can bee of power from dispayres *Gulfe,* to raise a *Spirit*

---

1. [*Ed.:* The Reader should note that the Preface is that of the reporter, and not, obviously, the words of Coke himself. It is reprinted here owing to Coke's later disavowal of the printing, which may well have met with his initial approval.]

drowned, in worst of misery: but were I not indeered unto those by heaven made mine, who are indeed, to me, their life, more deare from whom there is no way to run, unlesse in me, selfe being be disolved, I would assuredly by heavens assistance in some honest *War* with use of *Armes,* give to my life so long as I should live, a living maintenance: but now *Immured* in my native home, unseperably *Yoakt*[2] with leane-fact povertie. I have experience to conclude that as it is most certaine *Pax procreat Bellum,*[3] so is it no lesse true, that a confirmed *Peace, Non amat Filios belli,*[4] untill she hath need of them.

In this estate not knowing how to mend my selfe, *Religions* Lawe shall make my resolution honest, & though *Rerum conditionem mutare non possum,*[5] yet I will have power to say *Hoc possum magnum sumere animam et viro forti dignum,*[6] with patience therefore shal my grieved thoughts joyfully be thrown upon my makers providence by whose assistance I will still resolve with a constant Bosome to persist in the prosecution of commended deedes, for this I know *Spes mea, Christo vivens, Est vivere ut semper vivam.*[7]

And thus, my Honorable Lord, having breathed forth a sight unto the grace of your compassionate respect: I humbly crave your Honor will vouchsafe, to patronize in this little booke (by me collected) not my owne but the words of that reverend and learned *Judge,* the Lord *Coke,* who at his coming to *Norwich,* did at the *Assises* there upon the bench, deliver a charge so exelent as that it worthyly deserves to bee continued in perpetuall memorie, which being thus prodused to a publique view, I hope it shall unto our *Publickeweale* remaine a worthy presedent, wherein *Romes* champions may with shame decerne their long continued shamefull practices, *Puritans* & *Sismatickes* learne to knowe with what *Injustice* they disturbe the happinesse of our most happie peace, our *Justices,* inferior officers, *Jurors,* and Commons generally, may in this booke find out commended *documents,* and *instructions* profitable as wel directing how to govern as to be governed: all which particulars the learned *Judge* hath wisely handled with such plau-

---

2. [*Ed.:* yoked.]
3. [*Ed.:* Peace begets war.]
4. [*Ed.:* does not love the sons of war.]
5. [*Ed.:* I cannot alter the condition of things.]
6. [*Ed.:* I may undertake this great [work], worthy of a spirited and mighty man.]
7. [*Ed.:* My hope, oh living Christ, is so to live that I may live for ever.]

sible *Oratorical* wisedomes eloquence, as that when I heard him speake, I thought the *Poet* had just cause to say, *Prospera lux orritur linguisque; animisque; favete: Nam dicenda bono sunt bona verba die.*[8] If therefore in this following worke my Memory hath given a true instruction to my pen, I hope my labour shalbe accounted profitable, when it administers a publique benefit.

Thus Right Hon., *Earle,* what I have herein performed, together with my most unworthy selfe, I humbly referre unto your Honoured wisedomes consideration, remaining as I will alwayes rest,

> Your Honours in all humblenesse
> of Dutie.
>   R. P.

The Lord Coke,

the Preface to his Charge given at the Assises houlden in Norwich,
the fourth of August, 1606.

Because I perceive the time hath more swiftly passed then I did expect: my strife and labour with my selfe, hath bin in my selfe to abreviate what I purpose to speak. And though my speech shall principally bee directed to you of the Jurie, which are sworne: yet for that I know the scope and summe of my endevours are solely dedicated to Gods glory and my countries publicke benefit, I hope that all my words shall extend unto the generall good of all these here present; unto whom they are spoken. For I do purpose in my course, as it were with a finger to point out those growing and groning evils, which doe not only for the present time disturb & hurt our Publique Weale, *but doe also strive, and that with a most dangerous force to deface, ruin, & utterly subvert the Honors of our auncient name, & our now* Great Brittaines Monarchie. *But before the substance of my intended speech receives his purposed begining, I think it not amisse first to begin with my selfe, and of my selfe to speake thus much.*

There was a certaine young Romane, *whose youth so directed his labours, with industrious care to attaine to knowledge by the reading and study of good letters,*

---

8. [*Ed.:* The longed-for day is dawning; be favorable with your tongue and minds. Ovid, *Fast.* 1.71.]

as that the Senat *of* Rome *amongst themselves determined to make that yong man a Judge: thereby with honored reputation to recompence the travels of his youth, & to give encouragement unto other* Romane *Citizens by their good endevors to attain unto like estate & credit in the government of* Romes Publique Weale.

It happened that shortly after the determination by the Consuls & Senat *agreed upon, the yong man upon whom the place of a Judge should be conferred, comming unto the knowledge therof, fell presently into a deepe consideration with himselfe about the force & Office of that worthy place wherunto he should be called. And first considered that in his owne opinion, he was most unfit: sufficiently to execute the substantiall and somtimes dangerous (though most commended duties) properly belonging to so great a dignity. For this yong* Roman *having many Friends, Kinsfolkes, & Allies, some of them of such Rancke & Place, in the authority of government, as that their love or hate could not aptly draw unto it selfe a light or trivial respect (amongst whom) this young man thoght that comming to be a* Judge; *time might unhappely produce some such occation wherin his sentence, in the place of* Judgement, *might give distaste, procure enimies, loose Friends & gaine suspect of hatefull partialitie. From which corrupt & most impoysoned evill, thogh this yong* Roman *did never so much desire, to stand cleared, yet* Judging *amongst Friends, & Kinsfolks, he should assuredly (as he thought) by some detractors, be therof suspected.*

The Romaine Cittizen *having thus unto himselfe presented divers Obsticles and Objections, which could not in his owne sence receive sufficient contradiction, he resolved by no meanes to take upon him the place & person of a* Judge: *but did use all his Friendes and greatest power of meanes to perswade the* Senate, *to alter their determination concerning him and to bestow so great an Office on some other, that might more worthily deserve the same.*

Whilest this young man continued in a discontented passion, with purpose to desire some good advice, he goeth unto a faithfull friend of his, whom he acquainted with what the Senate purposed, and how loath he was to undertake so high an Office as to be a Judge. His friend upon hearing the cause, presently concluded, that hee had great reason to shun the execution of such an Office, in the discharge where of, so much danger rested. For (said he) Cave ne sis Judex inter Amicos *because* inter Amicos Judicare[1] *Amongst friends to judge, is a thing nothing more dangerous. And therefore be constantly advised, that in any wise he should refuse*

---

1. [*Ed.:* Beware that you be not a judge between friends, [because] to judge between friends.]

such honor, though offered unto him: and rather be contented with a meane and privat life, then in such a place to be imployed; in which he should assuredly loose old friends, and get new enemies.

This yong man (though thus by his friend advised, and in himselfe resolved never to take upon him any such, as he accounted dangerous dignitie) yet when he understood, that the Senat would not be altered in their purpose, but that by them the place was decreed unto him, he then determined with himselfe, to trie the counsell of some other friend, whose Judgement and Experience might beare some generall note, in directing the high affaires to the State belonging. And in this purpose he went unto a certain Nobleman, whose prudent wisdome had oft bin used in businesse of most weighty consequence: unto whom, when he had laid open his mind, shewed his griefe, and signified the Senats pleasure. The noble Gentleman with pleasant, yet grave alacritie of spirit (seasoned with the soundnesse of a learned and understanding wisedome) did most powerfully advise, that this young man should cheerefully accept so worthy an Office, being so freely bestowed upon him. And that he should by no means seeme to neglect the gracious clemencie of supreme authoritie. Nor in any sort account it dangerous amongst friends to judge: for in the Office and execution of Judgement, he that is a Judge (Desinet esse Amicus[2]) ceaseth to be a friend: for in the manner of judgement, no acquaintance, no griefes, no friends, no remembrance of fore-passed present, or hope of future friendship must direct the thoughts of him that is a Judge. All that on judgements seat is done, must be, because justice commaunds the doing thereof, and that with no other affection, but onely because it is just. And therefore said this Noble Gentleman unto his friend, arme thy selfe, in the constancie of a conscionably uprightnes, and be noe longer loath to execute the Honorable Office of a Judge, *but in thy love to* Romes Common-wealth, *dedicate thy laboures to her publique benifit.*

By the grave and sage advice of that Honored Lord, this yong man was perswaded contrarie to his former purpose, with humble thankfulnes to accept that Office, which the Senate *without any meanes of his, was pleased freelie to bestowe upon him: and yer genrallie made shew as if he ment the contrarie and soddainlie preparing a sumptuous Feast, unto which he envited all his Friends, Kinsfolke, and familiar acquintance, seeming that in regard he did rather choose to leave his Countrie, then to take upon him the Office of a* Judge: *he had provided a*

---

2. [*Ed.:* ceases to be a friend.]

Banquet or Feast, to Banquet with his Friends before his departure: and in some solemne maner would take leave of them all. Who being, as they thought, to this end assembled: did sorrowfully expect the occasion of their griefe, by the departure of their friend, which when the yong man perceived, he spake thus unto them.

It is true that I purpose as I must, to take my leave of you all, and to be a stranger to my dearest friends, and nearest Allies: I must forget all former friendships, and my most familiar Acquaintance, I must accompt as greatest strangers unto me; Thus must I depart from you, & yet continue amongst you, for by the love, power & authoritie of the Senate, *I am appointed to be a Judge, and in the seate of Justice, I must forget the remembrance of your former friendships and acquaintance, and onely in the person of a Judge, with respect to keepe my conscience cleare, I must with equitie & uprightnes, justly administer justice unto you all. And this is my cause, by the love & favour of my greatest maister King* James, *in whose royall and gratious disposition I am,* (Sinè precationè, vel precatio,[3] *without price or request, freely called unto this great Office, by the favour of my King) Unto whose service, my life, and all I have is humbly bound, by him, and by his gratious Clemency, I am thus sent to bee a* Judge *amongst my Kinsfolkes and familiar friends, even in bosome of my native Country.*

I must therefore as the young Romaine *did, take leave of all former Acquaintance, & do that which is just unto all Estates and Degrees, without partialitie. Which dutie (by Gods permission and assistance) I will faithfully performe, so long as God and my King shall please: that in this place I be employed in the uprightnesse and equitie of Judgement, shall all my performance entirely consist. The contrarie whereof shall (as I hope) neither be desired nor expected. And thus much for my selfe.*

¶ Here followeth the words of his Charge in Order.

As concerning the manner and Method of my charge, I will for order and memorie sake, extract or draw forth all that I purpose to speak, from five words in his Majesties Commission contained: the words are these; *Quis, Quibus, Quid, Quomodo,* and *de Quibus.*[1] *Quis,* from whom the *Commission* commeth; *Quibus,* to whom it is directed; *Quid,* what it concerneth; *Quomodo,*

---

3. [*Ed.:* without payment or seeking.]

1. [*Ed.:* who, to whom, what, how, and concerning what things.]

how it ought to be executed; and *de Quibus,* of who, and of what causes, wee are to enquire by vertue of the *Commission* unto us graunted: and this last, *De Quibus* is of all the rest the greatest.

As touching the first word, *Quis,* whom, or from whom our *Commission* commeth, that is, from the Imperiall Majestie of Great Brittaines Monarchie, our dread Lord, and Soveraigne, *King James,* the lawfull Heyre unto our King-domes Throne: whose Princely Scepter is his proper owne, by a most royall and lineall discent. It is his Commission, by whose powerfull authoritie we are now and at all times commaunded to doe him service: for the awfull sway of his Soveraigne government doth, ought, and must injoyne all his subjects to a due subjection and obedience; for he is over us the Lords annointed, and in these his Realmes and Dominions, in all Causes, & over all Persons, as well Ecclesiasticall as Civile, next under Christ Jesus our supreame Governour. Unto his Highnesse then let our lives submission bend; let our faiths loyaltie dedicate it selfe unto his vertues praise: and for the long continuance of his Majesties most happie, powerfull, and victorious Rule, let all good subjects pray.

Now that I have spoken from whom our Commission commeth, the next word which doth direct my worke is, *Quibus,* To whom it is directed, that is, To us his Majesties *Justices* of Assise, to whome by vertue of the *Kings* Com-mission is given such power, as that in the administration of Justice wee doe represent the person of our *King:* So as if in the time of the Assises one shall strike another in the presence of the Judge, be it no more then a blow on the eare, the Law provid`eth, That the offendor shall loose his hand, wherewith hee gave the stroake, because the offence was done as in the presence of the Prince: For the Law hath so much care to protect the person of a Judge: As that if a *Justice* of Assise shall happen by any in his Circuit to be slaine, the Law adjudgeth it to bee *Lese Crimen Majestatis,*[2] An offence done against the Majestie of the King, and is punishable, as in cause of Treason.

To shew the worthinesse of our Place and Office, you shall understand, that the Kings Majestie at his Coronation is sworne to doe Justice unto all his Subjects, which in his owne Person it is impossible to performe. And therfore his Highnesse is constrayned by his Ministers, Deputies, Justices, and Judges, to administer Justice unto all his people. Men therfore (in such place em-

---

2. [*Ed.:* crime of lèse-majesté (treason).]

ployed) ought with wonderous care, & conscionable diligence to discharge
the trust in them reposed: for unto them, & into their hands, is (as it were)
delivered the Kings owne Oath; because, what he is sworne unto, must be by
them in his behalfe performed. See then the dignity of the Justices and Judges
of Assizes, *Assignavimus vos Justiciaries nostros.* We have assigned you our
Justices, and you may administer Justice unto our Subjects. Thus by the Kings
Commission the Kings owne Oath is put into our hands: and at this instant
(in the place and person of a Judge) my Soveraignes Oath into my hands is
put: I (though his unworthie Subject) am by his gracious clemencie Authorized
(as in his owne person) according to his owne Oath, to administer Justice
unto you his Subjects: Which duty (by Gods assistance) as I have vowed, I
will faithfully performe: For if any (with a Kings Oath trusted) shall be so
vilde, as to falsifie their trust, such offence is more then Capitall.

The Place of a Judge then, the greater that it is, so much the more should
their care be, to discharge the same, upon whom so weighty an Office and
Honorable Authoritie is bestowed.

From whom our *Commission* commeth, and to whom it is directed, hath
bin briefely specified: I will now proceed, and shew out of this word *Quid,*
what is in the *Commission* contained. Briefely therefore, it is that bounded
limit, in which solely doth consist the strength of our authoritie; beyond which
compasse we are commaunded not to passe: For it appointeth unto us the
Justices of Assises, what it is that wee must execute, as well in causes betwixt
partie and partie, as also the *King* and partie depending. So as wee are not
onely to heare, judge, and determine, such Causes of Controversie, as shall
by Writ of *Nisi prius*[3] bee tryed, but also to examine, acquit, or condemne
all such Prisoners, as shall for any offence against his Majestie bee brought
before us, to receive their Tryall. So that by vertue of our *Commission* wee
have authoritie, as in the person of our Soveraigne, to judge in causes, that
doe concerne the life and death of the Subject.

That our Commission then is very Large, Ample, and Absolute, contayning
in it selfe a powerfull Authoritie, may by your selves bee judged. And to the
end, that Justice may by us receyve the more full sound and perfect Execution,
Our Commission, when it hath largely described unto us what wee may doe
therein, it then most sweetely doth Appoint, Limit, and Commaund. What

3. [*Ed.:* A Court sitting with a jury.]

manner of doing we must use in those thinges appointed to bee done, so that it dooth not onely give unto us authoritie, what to execute, but dooth also lay downe unto us the manner how our Authoritie must bee executed, and to the understanding here of, my next word *Quomodo* doth direct it selfe.

Wee then, the *justices* of Assises and Gaole Deliverie, are by his Majestie appointed to administer justice unto his Subjects; but *Quomodo,* how, not according to our owne Will, Conceit, or Opinion, but *Secundum Legem & Consuetudinem Moduli Anglicani,*[4] According to the Lawe, Custome, and Manner of England: Which Lawe, Custome, and Manner must bee executed with Knowledge, judgement, understanding, and Equitie. For wee must know our selves, and Place wherein wee are: Wee must Knowe and understand each cause before us brought, and according to our Knowledge and understanding, wee must uprightly Judge, according to Equitie, without (in the least sort) beeing drawne, by respecting eyther Person or Profite, to beare a Partiall Hand in the Execution of Judgement.

Partialitie in a Judge, is a Turpitude, which doth soyle and stayne all the Actions done by him. A Judge that will bee Partiall, will receive a Bribe, and such an one cannot by any meanes bee just, in his manner of Judging. Brybes, and Partiall dealyng dooth defile the Puritie of Justice, with great suspected Evill: For a *Judge,* if but in some things he be knowne to take a Bribe, or be approved Partiall, he leaveth no one Action done by him, free from the like suspect. A *Judge* that for a Bribe will speake, and but once execute a Justice purchased, all his words & Actions for ever after may justly bee suspected, though never so uprightly done or spoken.

A *Judge* must uprightly, with an equall and indifferent eare and minde fully heare and understand each cause before hee judgeth; otherwise, it is not possible that justice should bee justly executed: And to judge in a point of difference, hearing but one partie speake, is assuredly to be unjust; for this sentence is directly true: *Qui Judicat causam parte inaudita altera, Æquum licet, Statuat, Judex iniquus est:*[5] Who judgeth a cause for the one partie, not hearing the other, though what he doth, may stand to be upright, yet is the Judge unjust.

---

4. [*Ed.:* According to the law and custom of the manor of England. [Note: the original editor substitutes "manoriae," or manor, for "Moduli," or Manner.]]

5. [*Ed.:* Whoever gives judgment in a cause without hearing the other side, even if he decides fairly, is an unfair judge.]

Our auncient Fathers did in their Pictures and Emblemes oftentimes enclose
a very great and substantiall wisedome: Justice (as you know) useth ever to
bee painted with a Sword in the one hand, and a paire of Scales or Ballance
in the other; thereby signifying, That Justice never strikes her Stroke, till first
the cause be weighed in the Ballance; her Blow comes not, until the weight
of the Cause to be tried, hath by an upright hand equally received sufficent
triall: for then she knoweth rightly how to strike her stroke and not before:
when the glory of her dignity shall receive perfectious Honor, as wel by pro-
tecting the Good, as in punishing the Bad.

Mee thinkes, that oftentimes when I ryde by the way, I see the Effects of
Justice rightlie resembled, when I behold a River with a silver currant, bounded
in her equall course, with what just proportion shee doth disperse her streames,
without bewraying any little rage of intemperate violence. But if the passage
of that streame bee stopt; then how like a raging Sea, shee over-flowes her
banckes: and that then by an unresisted force, the Meadowes, humble Vallies,
weake and low growne Shrubs are drowned up; enduring a recure-lesse wracke,
whilest Hilles & Mountaines stand safe from feare of harme. Even so it fareth
with us: The equall course of Justice being stayed, the poore & meaner sort
of people they are overwhelmed with wrongs oppression, whilest great and
wealthy men, like Hilles and Mountaines, buyld their Stations sure, being
freed from any cause of griefe: Justice with-held, only the poorer sort are those
that smart for it.

Justice unto all estates doth measure an even proportion to rich and poore,
her met-wand keepes an equall length, being sealed with the testimonie of an
upright conscience. To Kings, Rulers, Judges, and Magistrates, this sentence
is proper: *Vos Dii estis;*[6] you are Gods on earth: when by your execution of
Justice and Judgement, the God of heaven is by your actions represented: but
if by us, that so are called *Gods,* Justice and Judgement be perverted; it will
be heavy for our soules, when we shall dye like men.

Briefly, the office of a Judge, is patiently to heare each party speake soberly;
to answere or object, directly; to see (as neere as may bee possible) each truth
substantially prooved: And then to Judge with an upright heart according to
Justice and Equitie: Never in any one thing preferring Conclusion, before a
conscionable, wise, and judiciall Consideration. In which uprightnesse, the

6. [*Ed.:* You are Gods.]

execution of Justice used by the Right Honourable (my most worthie Pred-ecessor) in this place shall be an Example, which I will desire to follow.

Of all the Morall vertues, Justice *(Queene like)* is enthroned: for unto her onely is a Throne ascribed, because her Execution doth neerest represent Heav-ens eternall Deitie. Justice and Mercie are inseparable Vertues; Mercie and Judgement, as it was Righteous King *Davids,* and lately our good Queenes, heavenly *Elizabeth:* so it is nowe vertuous King *James* his Song, in whose princely breast Mercie and Judgement are most gloriously united. And to the end, that I his Subject, and in his place his Substitute, and you his Subjects may execute Justice as wee ought, I will nowe out of my last word, *de Quibus,* declare unto you, of whom, and of what Causes wee are to enquire, that Justice and Judgement may thereby receive a more cleare and powerfull Execution.

Those then of whome wee are in the first place to enquire, are such, by whome our *King* is most disobeyed, his State disturbed, and Kingdomes threat-ened: Whereof (if you consider) it will be evident, That all those growing and desperate attempting evils, by which, wee are most prowdly menaced and afflicted, doe principally proceed from three sorts of Recusants living amongst us. Of all which, the *Popish* Recusant is the most dangerous with our *English Romanists* will I therefore at the first begin, and in the discription of their Actions and practises, I doe desire that my wordes may bee entertained with your best Attention.

Our Worldes Admired *Queene, Renowned Elizabeth,* did (as you know) in the beginning of her Raigne, change the State of Religion in this Kingdome in her first Parlament, by the consent of her Lordes Spirituall and Temporall, being especially by the Lord of Heaven directed, *Error, Popish blindnesse,* and Faithlesse *Constitutions* grounded upon Humaine *Traditions* were extinct. And Religions Puritie according to the Law of Faith, was Reestablished, being built upon the unremoved foundation, of the alone Authenticke word *Canonicall.* The bookes of the old and newe Testament, from the trueth whereof, shee did alwayes direct the course of her so happie and Tryumphant Government.

Notwithstanding, the Change of Religon, it cannot bee denyed. That for the first tenne yeeres, of her Majesties Raigne, the estate of *Romaine Catholique* in *England* was Tollerable, though some were Committed in the beginning of her Comming to the Crowne, yet none but those whose precedent Actions, had caused the faith of their Allegience to remaine doubtfull, and so was the manner of their commitment mixed with such gratious Clemencie. As that they rather endured a favourable restraint, then any straight or rigorous imprisonment, But as well those so restrayned, as generally all the Papists in this Kingdome, not any of them did refuse to come to our Church, and yeeld their formall Obedience to the Lawes Established. And thus they all Continued, not any one refusing to Come to our Churches, during the first tenne yeeres of her Majesties government. And in the beginning of the eleventh yeere of her Raigne, *Cornewallyes, Beddingfield* and *Silyarde* were the first Recusants. They absolutely refusing to come to our Churches. And untill they in that sort began the name of *Recusant,* was never heard of amongst us.

In the beginning of the eleventh yeere, when three *Recusants* were onely in this Kingdome to bee found. In the same yeere, *Pope Impius,* though abusively surnamed *Pius Quintus,* his Hellishnes was informed by some of our *English Jesuits,* that such was the number of *Romaine Catholiques* here in *England,* as that if his Horriblenesse would denounce an Excommunication against the *Queene* there was in this Realme and Kingdome, a power *Catholical* which would presently upon an instant be in redinesse, to enter into open hostilitie with force sufficient to depose, and utterly to supplant her Highnes; and to reestablish the *Romaine* faith.

Pope Impius of that name the firste, upon the Information specified the better to sever his hope in his good meaning to this Kingdome, presently plotteth with the *King of Spaine* for a suddaine Invasion upon the present Excommunication of the *Queene.* And to this end one *Robert Rodulphy* a gentleman of *Florence,* was sent by the *Pope,* under colour of Marchandize, to sollicit a Rebellion amongst us. And gave order unto him for the receiving of one hundred and fiftie thousand Crownes, to set forward this Attempt. And *Phillip* King of *Spaine,* by the instance of the *Pope,* had determined to send the *Duke* of *Alna* into *England,* with all his forces in the Low Countries To Assist some great men amongst us, who were by the *Pope* Sollicited, to be the principall Agents in a most Rebellious enterprise, unto whome some of the one hundred and fiftie Thousand Crowns was delivered, and some other part sent into *Scotland* for the like effect.

Thus as you have heard even at the same time, when her Majesty the late *Queene,* delt most mercifully with the *Papists,* did the *Pope* with them conspire to worke her Ruyne, & this Kingdomes Overthrowe, secretly complaning how on sodaine they might bring upon us Distructions, Spoyle, and generall Desolation, when our then *Soveraigne* that *Queene* of *Vertue,* knowing Shee had diserved no such evill, did not in the least sort suspect any such danger.

The Pope having as he thought surely Established the foundation of his hopes; Hee then Denounced the Excommunication against the *Queene* which was not unto her selfe made knowne, untill the intended Rebellion in the *North* brake forth, a little before Christmas, in the yeere 1569, being the twelfth yeere of her Highnesse Raigne. And then it was knowne, that the *Pope* had Excommunicated her *Majestie.* And thereby freed her Subjects as the *Bull* imported, from their Subjection and Obedience. But God was pleased that the *Popes Bull* was so Bayted, as that the Rebellion by it procured, was sodainly suppressed; For the *Pope* whose labour is to defend Lies, was himselfe deceived with a lie, for the strength of the *Papists* here not being such as hee was enformed, The true harted Protestants taking parte with their Soveraigne, did quickly Cutt the Throats of our *English Romaines,* dryving some of the heads of that Rebellion, unto a shamefull flight, and brought the rest by our Lawes *Justice,* to a shamefull death.

Her Majestie in the thirteenth yeere of her Raigne, having made the Law before specified, the very next yeere following, out Commeth *Sanders Booke de Visibili Monarchya,*[7] wherein he plainely seteth downe how the *Pope* had sent one *Morton* and *Web,* two Priests before the said Rebellion to the Lords & Gentlemen in the *North,* to Excite them, with their followers, to take up Armes, signifying unto them the *Popes* Commandement: Alleadging, That her Majestie being excommunicated, Her Subjects were released from their Obedience. And therefore he doth Directly Justifie the sayd *Commotion.* Ascribing the evill successe thereof to the late publishing of the saide Excommunication. Because it was not generally knowne, untill the yeere after it was Denounced. When *Felton* had set it upon the *Bishop* of *Londons* gate. Affyrming that if it had bin published the yeere before, or when the Rebells were in Armes, they had assuredly prevailed against the *Queene,* and executed the saide Sentence at the same time, for her deposinge from the Crowne.

Thus Trayterously with more then Brazen Insolence, did that Traytor *Sanders* spitt out his poysoned venim. Thereby desiring to Corrupt the hearts of her highnes Subjects, and to make them fit for a newe Rebellion, which course by him taken, was Immitated by *Parsons,* & many others to the like effect. Who ceased not by there Hereticall and Lying Pamphlits, with most Trayterous impudencie, to abuse her Majestie and the *State.* And not thus contented, in the yeere one thousand five hundred seventie and nine, *Stukely* assisted by

7. [*Ed.:* Of Visible Monarchy.]

Sanders, and other *Catholiques,* both *English, Irish,* and *Italian,* with the *Popes* Commission, entred into *Ireland.* The *Pope* himselfe, in the furtherance of that Course sending thither certaine forces upon his owne Charge, Whilest all that time, her Majestie that *Queene* of mercie was so farre from being moved, as that with Patience, shee endured all these Injuries, onely inforcing that one Lawe, which as you have heard, shee most Justly made against them.

Whilest *Ireland* by the *Popes* procurement remained in Combustion. It happened that, *Pius Quintus* dyed, and *Gregorie* the thirteenth succeeded in his place, who presently Reneweth his Predecessors former *Bull,* and denounced her Majestie to bee Excommunicated, with *Intimation* of all other particulers in the former *Bull* mentioned, which done, there was by him sent over into *England. Campion* and *Parsons,* they came unto us in the yeere one thousand five hundred and eightie, their comming was to Alienate the hearts of her Majesties Subjects, from their due obedience. And to make a partie strong to depose the *Queene,* Joyning with the *Pope, and King of Spaine,* by whome there was then an intended preparation against us. But the Attempts and practises of them both at that instant fayling in *England. The Pope as a Temporall Prince,* displayeth his Banner in *Ireland,* with purpose to deprive her *Highnes.* First from that Kingdome, and then by degrees to depose her from this. Notwithstanding so mild was the proceedings of her Majestie against them, as that there were in the space of Tenne yeers, not much above twelve persons, that were by the Justice of her Lawes adjudged to die, and the most of them *Semenaries,* and all of them Convicted in causes of Treason.

Her Majestie when shee heard of the second Excommunication, and had seene what followed in her Kingdome upon the first. Shee was then in all Christian Pollecie enjoyned to prevent the successe of dangers imminent. Her Highnesse therefore, in the yeere one thousand five hundred eightie and one, caused a Proclamation to bee made for the calling home of her Subjects from beyond the Seas, such especially as were Trayned up in the Seminaries, perceiving that they learned nothing there but disloyaltie, & Treason. And presently after this her Proclamation, shee called a Parliament, wherein a Lawe was agreeable in effect to the sayd Proclamation, enforced with a penaltie of death, for any *Jesuite* or *Seminary* Priest, to repayre into *England,* and for any to receive or intertaine them, shee would willingly that those of such profession, should keep themselves without the Limits of her Kingdome.

But if against her will, they would come into her Land to sow the seed of Sedition, and Rebellion amongst her Subjects, and to lay, their plots how to supprize her life, and to make a way for Forraigne Enemies with bloodie handes to enter uppon her Dominions. And by Hostill Invasion to bring her Kingdomes to distruction, and to expose her people unto the Slaverie of a servile yoake, What shoulde her Majestie lesse have done in the prevention of such a Lamentable evill, but to hang up them that were the principall Actors in so bloodie and Tragecall a Tyranny.

From the yeere eighty one, to eightie eight, her Majestie was not free from Continual *Traiterous* and *Rebellious* practises, desperately attempted against her life, or intended subvertion of her Kingdome. First the *Popes* forces being over-throwne in *Ireland, the Pope and King of Spaine,* presently joyned with the *Duke of Guise,* for the executing of a most desperate disignment against her Majestie. *Arden* and *Someruilde,* would have layd vyolent handes upon her sacred person. *Doctor Parrie,* intended the like villanie. *Northumberland* revolted from his Obedience. *Mendoza* the *Jesuite,* and others of that Crue or Sect, appointed by the *Pope* to order and Mannage these develish designments.

In the yeare eightie, to forerunne the purposed *Spanish Invasion,* against which time *Campion, Parsons, Haywoode,* and all the *Jesuites* and *Seminaries,* had so besturred themselves. There is certaine bookes printed beyond the Seas, sent hither into *England,* thereby to prepare the hearts of our people, to Joyne with *Spaine,* and to take up armes against their Soveraigne, with perswasions grounded upon this position. Viz. That in all warres which may happen for Religion: every Catholike man is joyned in conscience to imploy his person and forces by the Popes direction, that is, how far, when, where, & how either at home or abroad, he may and must breake with his temporall Soveraigne, and that upon paine of deadly sinne. Upon a foundation so diabolical: What fruits other then devillish can be expected? And yet, do but further note how damnable a spirit is in their bookes and writings bewrayed.

All the Papists in this kingdome, were most violently perswaded, that upon the Spanish invasion, they should all joyne their greatest force with Spaine. It was in them accounted an error of conscience, want of courage, and effeminate dastardie, that they had suffered her Majestie almost thirtie yeares to raigne over them. They were threatned with Excommunication, and utter ruine, both of themselves and their posteritie, if they did any longer obey and defend, or acknowledge her highnes to be their Queene or superior, and did not foorthwith joyne their forces to the Spaniards. And to the end, that this most godlesse, trayterous, inhumane and unnaturall appointment, by subjects to their lawfull annointed Soveraigne, and native countrey, might receive the better acceptance; There was used a most insinuating, though faithlesse manner of perswasion, guilded over with a seeming shew of Holinesse: (For thus, our English Romane Catholikes were promised) That in the king of Spaines armie, there were diverse Priests readie to serve everie mans spirituall necessitie, by confession, counsell, and all consolation in Christ Jesus, and that they should be so assisted by the blessed patrons, both in heaven, and in earth, with the gard of all Gods holy Angels, with our blessed Saviour in the soveraigne Sacrament, and with the dailye, most holy Oblation of Christs owne deare body and bloud. As that it could not fall out otherwise, but that they should assuredly prevaile: Herby may the world perceive in what Angelike manner of brightnesse Popish doctrine can suite treasons damnable, even as blacke as hell.

You have heard what preparation was provided by the Pope and Papists, for the furtherance of Spaines intended invasion, we will now proceed to matter of action. And but call to our remembrance (that ever to bee remembred) powerfull worke of God: for our deliverance in the yeare 88. The king of Spanes Armado, that admirable, and warlike navie, so well furnished with valiant souldiers, and all munition fit for warre, when suddenly we were in danger by a Potent enemie to be surprised, when her late Majesties Royall Navie, was scarily put foorth to sea. And the best ships of strength not fully furnished with shot and powder, as was necessarie in so weightie a businesse: yet to the never dying glory of a maiden Queene, such was her princely power, although at sea but in part unprovided, as that by the love and grace of heavens eternall providence, her Majestie by a most noble Battell at sea, even in the presence of her kingdoms Territories, did utterly disperse and overthrow, that surnamed invincible Spanish navie, so that not any Spaniards floate, (unlesse brought captive could arrive) upon her Englands shoare. Nor but verie few of their so much admired fleete of shippes, returned to their native home. Thus did God on Queene *Elizabeth* bestow a glorious victorie, even in the despite of Pope, Papist, trayterous Jesuits, Seminaries, Monkes, Friers, and all the rablement of that Antichristian Sec.

The power of Spaine, was brought against us, by the procurement of our English Papists, and what recompence was intended for them, in the charitie of their catholike profession may appeare, by that which the Duke of *Medina Sidonia* affirmed, which was, *That both Catholickes and Heretikes that came in his way, should be all one to him, his sword could not discerne them, so he might make way for his master, all was one to him.* Thus did Papists, as still they doe, desire to worke our downefall in the certaintie of their owne destruction.

God having shewed his love to our late Queene and kingdome, by that wonderfull deliverance before described: The Pope to further his accustomed indevours, practised with Spaine, about a new invasion, and the better to bring his purpose to passe: *Parsons,* that auncient Jesuite, and most notorious traytor, under the Pope, chiefe governour of all the Jesuits, (principall enemies to *Jesus,*) was placed in the Spanish Court, by whose perswasion there was a new *Seminarte* erected at *Valedolyde,* from whence in three yeares, there was sent thirteene priests into England, to prepare a passage for the new intended invasion. Whereupon in the yeare 1591. a Proclamation went forth for the apprehending of all such Priests or Seminaries, as should come from Spaine. Because their intention was knowne unto the State here. But to the end the Divell (the Pope I should say) might want no instrument for the effecting of murthers, treasons, and rebellions, by *Parsons* procurement, more Seminaries were erected in Spaine, (and England still troubled with Romes trayterous disciples. But the new invasion being twise set on foote, God did so warre against their purposes, as that their prepared Navie was at sea, dispersed by stormes, so as most of them endured shipwracke.

That expectation failing, then was the Infant of Spaine intituled to the Crowne of *England:* (and to that end, sundry bookes divulged) Queene *Elizabeth* was by them accounted a tyrant: more tyrannicall then *Nero, Decius, Dioclesion, Maxentius,* or any the greatest persecutors of the Christians: Not thus contented, from the yeare 88. to the yeare 99. there were continual treasons practised against the Royall person of her late Majestie, *Patricke, Collen, Lopez, Torke, Williams, Squire,* all attempting to murther her Highnesse.

All these attempts, plots, projects, & trayterous stratagems, taking no effect. Then was there from the Pope a new Bull sent, wherby the Papists were commaunded to use a formall maner of obedience, until they might grow to be a strength sufficiently strong to depose the Queene. Which expectation once accomplished, then had they power by the said Bull to take up armes against her. Thus they never left continuall practising, untill a little before her Majesties death: about which time, by some of the principall *Agents,* in the last most horrible treason, there was complotted another Spanish invasion: For the accomplishing wherof, the yonger *Winter* was a messenger unto the King of Spaine, and *Gujdo Fawkes* unto the Pope, and a third was imployed to the Archduke.

The King of Spaine at that time beeing our enemie, entertained *Winters* motion, with most kinde acceptance, protesting that the English Catholiks should bee as deare unto him, as his home-borne *Castillians,* and in love to the intended businesse, vowed in the word of a King to defend their safety, (all which, as souldiers say, with pollicie in warre he might do) beeing then our enemy. But it is a matter cleane out of my *Element,* and therefore I will dispute no further about it: But the Counsell of Spaine holding a conference about the mannaging of the plot by *Winter* layd. It was objected that there would be want of horse for such a businesse. Whereupon *Winter* undertaketh to furnish them with a certaine number, and receiveth gold to that end. At last the purposed designement being embraced with a generall consent, a souldier standing by, being some Commander, a Captaine, or such like, ruffles out this souldier like Latine, *Nunc temptus pro nobis erit aliquid obtinere: [Now shall it be time for us to get something].* But in the middest of this intended preparation, it happened, that her Majestie Royall, and most gracious *Elizabeth* died: And our now Imperiall Soveraigne King *James,* did both inherite her kingdomes and her vertues.

His Majestie beeing with peace established in his royall seate, the king of Spaine would no longer embrace his former purposed appointment: Nor would consent, that any thing should against a king be plotted, with whom he never had warre: Nor by whom he never received any injurie. So as our Papists were in that behalfe dismissed of their expected hope: and enforced to seeke out some other meanes; and now I will betray a secret (I am sure not generally knowne.) In the discourse whereof I doe desire attention.

Pope *Clement* the ninth, who was accounted the last best of many Popes, (all notwithanding being naught.) He understanding Spaines purpose, as before is specified, concerning an invasion, supposing that the *Queene* might die before that businesse tooke effect: And foreseeing unto whom these kingdomes should of right descend, sent secretly a Bull into England, which was so closely concealed, amongst our Papistes here, as that her Majestie in her life time knewe not thereof. (For if she had) I am sure, that by reason of mine employment neare unto her: I should have heard if she had knowne any such thing. But assuredly both her selfe, and the *State,* were ignorant thereof.

But now this Bull being brought to light (which my selfe have seen & read) it importeth thus much *quando contingeret illam miserimam Elizabetham mortuam esse.*[8] That when that miserable wench Elizabeth should happen to dye, *Tunc nos volumus.*[9] Then we will, that all and every of you, do use your best

---

8. [*Ed.:* when the miserable woman Elizabeth should happen to die.]
9. [*Ed.:* then we will that you.]

& uttermost endevors *quo basunque modes et vis*[10] by what strength or meanes
so ever to keepe out the Scottish Hereticke, that in any wise he may not be
admitted to the kingdome of England, unlesse he would reconcile himselfe
to Rome, *and hold his crowne of the Pope, and conforme himselfe and all his
subjects to the religion of the Romane Church.* This *Bull* until Garnet was taken,
slept in *England,* beeing filled with a most proud, scornfull and Trayterous
boldnesse.

When that *miserimam faeminam*[11] *Miserable* woman or *wench Elizabeth*
shall dye, had the *Papall* proud usurper, no other attribute to bestowe upon
a *Queene* then *Miserable wench?* shee lived Renowned thorough all the Corners
of the worlde, shee ruled in peace, beloved of all her Subjects, unlesse those
infected with the *Romane Leprosie,* shee was admired, & feared, confronting
all oppositions, with undoubted confidence, shee was a Prince potent enough,
to defend her Kingdomes and to helpe her Neighbours beeing oppressed with
glorious victorie she beat Spaine from off her coasts, and rifled him in the
bosome of his owne kingdome, wrapping his townes and shippes in cloudes
of fire and smoake. She swaied the Roiall Scepter of her kingdomes government
with triumphant victorie maintaining peace amongst her people, even in the
worlds dispight, 44 yeares her unmatched wisdome, and unconquered prowes
crowned her the *Peereles wonder* of her sexe: she liv'd and died a Queene, her
life beloved, and her death lamented: And yet for all this, was she no more
in the Popes account, then a *miserable wench.* Let the Popes pride sinke to
hell: whilest heavens *Elizabeth* (whose blessed soule from earth to heaven is
taken) doth, and shall with *God and Christ* for ever live in the heavenly glorie
of eternall happinesse.

Pope *Clement* the ninth, having by his Bull, as before specified, given commaundement that the Papists should by all meanes howsoever withhold our
now Soveraigne from his lawfull right. (And notwithstanding that *Rebellious
Commission,*) his Majestie being with great joy peaceably enstalled. *Peersie* &
Catesby went unto their great Provinciall *Garnet,* & of him enquired, whether
the king being as he was already established, they might by vertue of the Popes
Bull, use any meanes to supplant or depose him, considering they were not
of force to withstand his comming at the first. And *Garnet* answered, that
undoubtedly they might, whereupon they presently resolved to put in exe-

10. [*Ed.:* by whatever means and ways.]
11. [*Ed.:* miserable woman.]

cution that most horrible powder treason, the like whereof, untill that time, was never to the world reported.

Some are of opinion, that if a tolleration of religion had bin admitted unto the Papists: that then no such bloudie stratagem should by any of them have bene practised. But if you shall consider the tenor of the Popes Bull, you may then perceive, that their request of indifferent Tolleration was but a colourable pretence in them. For that might not have served the turnes: For they were enjoyned to worke his Majesties overthrow, unlesse hee would reconcile him-selfe to *Rome,* hold his Crown of the Pope, and conforme himselfe and all his subjects to the Religion of the *Roman Church:* It is not then a toleration only which they seeke, nor could they have beene contented therewith (al-though so much shall never be graunted unto them.) They may therefore easily despaire of the rest (though they the Pope and the Divell) doe never so much conspire to bring their Hell-borne practises to passe.

As touching the last horred treason, by inhuman savages complotted: I knowe not what to speake, because I want words, to describe the trayterous, detestable, tyrannicall bloudy, murtherous villany of so vilde an action. Onely this had their horrible attempt taken place. This *Sea Invyronde ylande,* the beauty, and wonder of the world. This so famous and farre renown'd great *Brittains Monarchy,* had at one blowe endured a recoverlesse ruine, beeing overwhelmed in a sea of bloud, all those evils, should have at one instant happened, which would have made this happiest kingdome of all kingdomes, the most unhappy. Our conquering Nation, conquered in her selfe: her faire and fertile bosome, beeing by her owne native (though foule unnatural chil-dren) torne in peeces, should have beene made a scorne to all the nations of the earth. This so well planted, pleasant, fruitfull worlds, accounted *Edens paradise,* should have beene by this time, made a place disconsolate, a wast and desert wildernesse, generally overrunne with heards of bloud-desiring wolves. This so well govern'd, Populous, potent Monarchy, had in one mo-ment beene left without either *King, Queene, Prince, State, Nobility, Law, Justice,* or any strength of government, sodainly had we then beene throwne not onely to the cruelty of civill warre, that too too murtherous *Domestick* spoyling enemie: But also even in that instant generally have beene exposed unto the all-devouring hand of forraine Enemies, in our Congregations, the songs of *Syon* had no more been sung: But in their steed had bin brought unto us the songs of *Gehenna* set from *Rome:* that *Sathans* synagogue, all our best-freedomes liberty, had by this bene turn'd into the worst bondage of most slavish servitude: *Papists, Romane Catholickes* that would have wrought all our destructions thus; Should not justice, justly then commaund their actions chiefly to be enquired of.

If what hath bene spoken, be unto your memories committed, you may then consider, that from the eleventh yeare of Queene *Elizabeths* Raigne, untill the third yeare of our now Soveraignes government, the Papists have continually labored to advance the supremacy of the *Romane Church,* which to accomplish they have contended thirty foure years, in which time they have not omitted to practise Treasons and Rebellions onely amongst us here at home. But have also complotted to bring upon us *Forraine Invasions,* & that from time to time, so soone as they were dismissed of one hope, they presently set a foote some other project: both at home and abroad: and still being by the love and mercy of GOD towards us continually prevented: At last, taking counsell with hell, and *Sathan,* they had practised a most hellish attempt. wherein their Divellishnesse brought it selfe nearest to the nature of the Divell, making fire and brimstone the instruments of our destruction. And though the principall Actors of that evill, have thereby themselves destroyed: yet the former experience of their continuall attempting may give us warning, that they will not yet sease to attempt, and though that *Jesuites* and *Seminaries* have beene the principall Agents in all the severall complotted treasons, and that the Papists amongst us cannot generally be accused, yet thus much I must say, those persons, and that Religion whereby *Jesuites* and *Seminaries* are received, protected and concealed, are equally to be accounted daungerous, for were there not such receivers amongst us, *Romes* state, Traytors would not so fast come, swymming from *Tyber* hither to arrive at *Tyborne.* Onely I conclude, therefore, that if in great *Brittaine,* there were no Papists, this *Monarchy* should be as free from treason as any Nation in the world.

But now deare Contrimen, seeing you have heard what godlesse and dangerous practises have continually by *Romes* favorites beene plotted against us. I desire that with attention you will understand what it is (as they say) for which with such vehemency they contend. The world is made believe, that the advancement of Religion is the onely cause for which they strive, wherein they joyne themselves unto the *Pope,* because there is no religion good, but that which is by the *Pope* allowed, wherein my purpose is to binde all Papists unto their owne assertion.

That *Pius Quintus*[12] whome those of their side doe account to have beene

---

12. [*Ed.:* Pope Pius the Fifth.]

a good *Pope* (though by false perswasions too much misled) before the time of his excommunication against Queene *Elizabeth* denounced, sent his letter unto her Majestie, in which hee did allow the *Bible,* and Booke of *divine service,* as it is now used amongst us, to bee authenticke, and not repugnant to truth. But that therein was contayned enough necessary to salvation, (though there was not in it, so much as might conveniently bee) and that hee would also allowe it unto us, without chaunging any parte: so as her Majestie would acknowledge to receive it from him the *Pope,* (and by his allowance) which her Majestie denying to do, she was then presently by the same Pope excommunicated: And this is the truth concerning Pope *Pius Quintus,* as I have faith to God and men. I have oftentimes heard avowed by the late *Queene* her owne wordes: And I have conferred with some *Lordes* that were of greatest reckoning in the *State,* who had seene and read the letter, which the Pope sent to that effect: as have bene by me specified. And this upon my credit, as I am an honest man, is most true.

By this then all our *English Papistes,* either *Jesuites* or *Seminaries* may learne to knowe that it is not Religion that they strive for, but onely to maintaine the *Antichristian* head of *Romes* usurpt supremacie. And if there bee in this presence any *Romane Catholickes,* or so manie of this nation, as shall heare of that which hath now beene spoken, I entreate them, as my deare and loving Countrey men, that they will no longer bee seduced, by any living spirite sent from Rome, the Pope, whom they beleeve, hath himselfe allowed, that in our Church, *We have a doctrine of Faith and Religion, sufficiently necessarie to Salvation:* Deere Countreymen, wee have then enough, and neede not the helpe of anie Pope, Sythence all the Papistes generally came unto our Churches before our late *Queene Elizabeth* was excommunicated.) Against our *Dread Soveraigne* there is no Excommunication denounced. In Gods name, then let us joyne in our prayers, and Sacraments, and performe a due obedience to God, and to our *King,* as wee are all of one Nation, so let us be all of one *Church,* and *Christ* beeing onely our head, let us all desire as in one sheepfolde, to be the sanctified members of his glorious bodie.

If there be any Papists so foolish, and altogether reasonlesse, as to expect that in time his Majestie may be drawne to such alteration, or Tolleration: as they desire, I will them assuredly to know, they hope in vaine, for his Majestie is, and ever hath beene confidently resolved, in matter of *Religion,* to continue the selfe same order and profession, which he now professeth. Whereof I will give you an instance, Since the time of the *Earle of Northumberlands* Imprisonment, there was amongst his papers found a letter, which was objected against him in *Starre Chamber*, when himselfe was called unto his answere: The letter was directed to the *Kings Majesty*, that now is, as he was then *King* of *Scotland*. In which amongst other things, the *Earle* had advised his *Highnesse* not to desire to bee proclaimed Heire apparant to this *Crowne*, nor proclaime *Prince Henry* to be the *Prince of Wales*, But to stay the time, untill the *Queenes* death. And that then he would resolve at his comming to admit unto the *Catholicks* a Tolleration for their religion, which he requested, because the Papists did put some trust in him, to Sollicit that businesse in their behalfe. This letter beeing read, his Majesties owne answer was shewed: (Till that time, by Gods owne hand preserved) to signifie unto the world his religious un-removed confidence. To the first parte of the *Earles* letter, his *Highnesse* an-swered, that he had no contrary purpose, but to attend *Gods* leasure. And for his motion concerning the *Catholicks* tolleration, he was purposed to come unto this kingdome in peace. But as touching matter of Government, he was resolved never to alter anything, either in *Church* or *State*. His Majesties most noble and *Kingly* resolution, not enduring then to temporize under any pretext of humane pollicy. Can it now be thought, that his *Highnes* will be removed in matter of Religion, from that Station whereupon his Soules salvation stand-eth built.

Such Papists (as notwithstanding the impossibility of their hope will still remaine perverse) despising to be admonished: Let them know for certainty, that the lawes concerning them, shall receive a most strict and severe execution, you therfore of the jury, ought to be very carefull in that businesse. And all the justices in their severall Limits, are in their allegiance to the *King*, bound in conscience to use all diligence so to observe the Papists, as that unto their houses, there bee not any *Jesuites* or *Seminaries* intertayned. For there practise, is to Alienate the hearts of our *English* Subjects, from the obedience to their soveraigne. In which imployment, though the Jesuites bee most notorious, yet I account the *Seminarie* Priests more dangerous; Because their estimation stealeth to it selfe a better opinion in the hearts of the simple. Notwithstanding, all their worke is directed to one and the selfe same end; If all good subjects then shall desire the administration of *Justice*, according to the Lawes estab-lished: they may either be converted or supplanted. By whome our subversion, and utter supplanting hath so often times beene attempted. I therefore leave them, their actions and proceedings to be judged off, and carefullie to be lookt into, by your most mature consideration and best diligence, least that our too

too much conveniencie, doth yet untimely bring uppon us some dangerous mischief. Them and their actions therfor are principally in the first place to be enquired of, and that with such regard as their cunning may by no meanes outreach the meaning of the Statute Law inacted for their punishment, wherin though there be as much concluded, as the wisedome of our state could devise, in the prevention of any future evill, yet as I heare the *Pope* hath already granted such dispensation, as that by their hellish sophistrie of equivocating, they may take a course wherein to deceive our hope of there amendment, but in Gods name let the law provided, receive a just and faithfull execution, & then doubt not, but their faithlesse Popish policie shall be sufficiently prevented. And that in time the most sacred person of Gods anointed King, whome *Pope Clement* the ninth, could proudly dare to tearm the scottish *Heritike,* shall underneath his Princely foot tread downe Romes faithlesse *Papall* proud and Antichristian heresy, & now in hells despight, vertuous King *James* being the *Emperiall* Majesty of great *Brittaines Monarchy,* the strength of whose establisht awfull government, makes the proudest Territories & most strong foundation of earths Babilonde to shake, I doubt not but in his royall selfe and his most blest posterity, as is already by force of his commaunding power, not without just cause fearfully suspected, the destruction of the scarlet whore shall be made certaine to her, and her adulterates, when they together shall bee with wrath destroyed for the accomplishing of which most glorious worke, let all true beleeving protestants, like faithfull subjects to their lawfull *Soveraigne* yeelde there best obedience to his highnesse lawes, and thus much concerning Romane *Catholikes.*

Those that you are in the second place to enquier of, are a second manner of Recusants, though nothing so dangerous as the *Popish recusant* is, yet are they a Sect not to be tollerated in any *Monarchyall* government. They are a certaine Brotherhood, which can indure no *Bishops:* The originall founder of their schisme, as they now professe, it hath (as some of them say) turnd an *Apostatate,* to his first profession, in so much as they are ashamed of his name, and will by no meanes in their fraternity be derived from him, yet they remaine knowne to the world, by the name of *Brownings.* The most part of them are simple, & Illiterate people. And they together with those of that sorte, which seeme to have learning, are as all the rest, onely arrogant, and wilfully perverse, fitter to be reformed by punishment, rather then by argument: And though their ignorance understands not what they doe, yet doe their endeavours strive to shake in sunder the whole frame of our *Emperiall* government, for if (as they desire) the forme of our *Civill Lawes* were abrogated, Then should our *Common Law,* and it of necessity fall togither. For they are so *woven* and *incorporated* each in other, as that without the one, the other cannot stand: for example.

An action Reall, beeing brought at *common* Law, in Bar thereof Bastardy is pleaded, our *common* Law can then proceed no further, untill by the *civill* Law the matter of Bastardy be determined, So is it in the right of a *Womans* Dowre, and in the tryall of *Wills;* In all these, and diverse others without the Assistance of the *civill* Law, the *common* Law hath no power to determine. If then the *civill* Law must of necessity remain, it is no lesse necessary that the judges therof should be continued.

And againe without the grave assembly of our Reverend *Bishops,* his Majesties high court of parliament, should be unfurnished, no law being there enacted, but that which is by the *King,* his Lords spirituall and temporall confirmed. These therefore that would have no *Bishops* amongst us, do in their desires strive, from his highnes, and the dignity of his State, to pluck the right hand of government, and as much as in them lyeth to break in sunder, the golden frame of just *Authority* for if no *Bishops,* then no *Lawes,* if no *Lawes,* no *King;* and to this height doth their presumption clime, although their ideot blindnes seems as if they did not understand so much, the mischiefe of their schisme is most unsufferable: For never was there a nation knowne to flourish having a *Monarchie* in the kingdome, and a *Mallachie* in the Church. And therfore you of the Jurie faile not to enquire of all such Sectaries and present them.

It is therefore the faithfull Protestant, that only sets the *Crowne* upon our Soveraignes head, & holds it up so fast, as no opposition can make it shake. And by their loyall hands will *Heaven* be pleased, to keep it safe from falling, which Mercy in the most *Royall issue* now established, God for christs his sake confirme unto us, so long as Sun & Moon endureth.

The last sort of Recusants, though troublesome, (yet in my conscience the least dangerous) are those which do with too much violence, contend against some ceremonies used in the Church, with whose indirect proceedings, in mine owne knowledge, his Majestie is not a little grieved. But I will hope (as his *Highnesse* doth) that in time, they will grow wise enough to leave their foolishnesse, and consider that ceremonies not against the Analogie of Faith, nor hindering Faiths devotion, are no such bug-beares as should scar them from the exercises of divine duties, nor cause them to disturbe the peace of our Church, whose government is more consonant to Scripture then all the best reformed Churches at this day in the world. You of the Jurie faile not therefore to enquire of their abuses, which doe delay to conforme themselves unto the lawes obedience, that such of them as doe growe insolent, may not goe unpunished: And thus much concerning our three sorts of *Recusants.*

Thus having touched these growing evills, which beeing well considered, doe cry for justice against themselves, threatning (if not suppresse) To make our *Commonwealth* to grone under the burthen of inforced calamity. I will now, from them proceed unto those growing enormities, whose ungovernd height is already to such imperfection grown, as that the justice of this king-domes government, receiveth scandall by their meanes, and the publick *weale* grieved by unjust oppression.

I heare a generall complaint against the multiplicity of ecclesiasticall courts, and that causes are in them continued longer then an upright and orderly proceeding would necessarily inforce, by meanes wherof, his Majesties good subjects, do receive losse, and are much hindred, by there so often constrayned attendance. But in this Diocesse, I hope the occasion of any such complaints, shall no more be heard of, Because I speake before those reverend Magistrates, the Lord Bishop, and the Chancelour of that dioces being then present upon the bench, in whose authority consisteth sufficient power to reforme those abuses already complained upon, I will therfore insist no further, few words content the wise, what I have spoken, I know is heard by an approved wise-dome.

As touching the pennall Statutes for the punishing of any unreverent de-meanure in Churches, or violence offered to the ministers, or quarrelling stryk-ing, or drawing of any weapon in Church, or Church yard, I know they be ordynary matters, given in every charge. And therfore you are not ignorant of the Lawes in that case made and provided: I will therfore in respect of the shortnesse of the time, onely point out unto you some severall officers, whose actions not beeing sufficiently looked into, many abuses are committed, which do passe unpunished.

Our common wealth, Receives much injurie by our *Escheators,* who by abusing their commission, doe most intollerable wrong, to many of his Maj-esties good Subjects, for an *Escheator* will come into the country, and beeing informed of an honest yeoman deceased, be it that his Lands, be not above the yearly value of forty or fiftie Pounds, & leaving an heire behind him, an inquiry shall bee made, by what evidence every acre of ground is holden, and finding but one peece, for which an expresse evidence cannot bee shewed, for that particular parcell, Then by a jury to that end Summoned by the *Escheator,* that peece of ground must be adjudged to be held in *Capite.* And so an office beeing found: all the whole inheritance must bee taynted, and the yong heire a warde to the *King,* who then beeing presently Begged by some one or other, by then hee hath compounded for his wardship, sued out his livery, and then perhaps marryed to one starke naught, or not worth any thing, the yong heire shall bee lest just worth so much, and no more: And this (as I thinke) is a most lamentable thing. God forbid that every man should be inforced by such course, to prove his right in every particular acre of ground which he hath. For many particular peeces are oft included in one evidence, without being distinguished by severall names. So that it is impossible, but by such course, as the *Escheator* takes, lands that never held in *Capite,* must needs be brought in compasse of such *Tenure.* And againe, the intent of the Law, for the benefit of the *king,* looketh only to Manors, Lands, and Tenements of great value, without having respect to such petty things. Where an heire to cleare the incumbrance, must overthrow his estate, loose his inheritance, and be undone for ever. But this notwithstanding, so the *Escheator* may have his part, in the spoile, he careth not to use any indirect corruption. You of the jurie therefore for the good of your selves and yours, carefully looke to the proceedings used in this case, and such abuse as you shall find therein, let it be presented. And such as shall bee found offendors, they shall know, that we have lawes to punish them. For proofe whereof, I would you could find out some, of whom there might be made an example: But if you will be content to let the *Escheator* alone, and not looke unto his actions, he will bee contented by deceiving you, to change his name, taking unto himselfe the two last syllables, only with the *Es* left out: and so turne *Chetor.*

We have then an excellent *Officer,* surnamed the *Clarke* of the *Market,* concerning whose office, for mine owne part, I see not the necessitie thereof, considering the Justices of peace in their severall limmits, are at every Sessions to enquire of, and to punish all those abuses which are by the Clarke of the market continued, under shew of reformation. For he will come downe and call before him all waights and measures, and where a fault is found, there must a Fee be payd, which is devided betwixt him and the Informer: So the offendor payes for his offence, to the end it might be continued, but not reformed. And thus the Clarke of the market by receiving bribes, enricheth himselfe, by abusing his Majesties lawes, and wronging his Subjects. It was

once my hap to take a Clarke of the market in these trickes: But I advanst
him higher then his fathers sonne; by so much as from the ground to the
toppe of the Pillorie. If you of the Jurie will therefore have a care to find out
these abuses, by Gods grace they shall not goe unpunished. For we have a
Coyfe, which signifies a *Scull:* whereby in the execution of Justice, wee are
defended against all oppositions, bee they never so violent.

There is a certaine ruffling officer, which will seeme to command much by
the authoritie of his Commission. And he wilbe known to be a Purveyor.
Some of which officers, if they can find nothing to be dealing with, they will
purvey mony out of your purses: if you will suffer them. But know there is
no mony to be purveyed, unlesse by the high way side, and any Purveyor that
shall take such course, is but in his passage the high way to the *gallowes.*

But to speake of that, which may by them bee lawfully done, admit a
Purveyor commeth downe with Commission, to take up timber for the *Kings*
use; What timber is it then that he must take: He cannot come and pull downe
any timber in my house, what then? May he go into any of my woods which
I purpose to preserve, and there marke out of my best timber, and inforce me
to suffer it to be felled, and carried away at the kings price? No, There is not
any such authoritie granted unto him. But only thus, If I have any timber
felled, which I purpose to sell: then may the Purveyor (the King having use
of timber) come and make choise of what trees he will. For there is great
reason, that in such case the king should first be served. But if any of you do
desire to preserve your timber growing, be not scared with a Purveyors warrant:
Nor do not preserve the standing of your trees by bribing any one of them.
The dignitie of his Majesties prerogative *Royall* is not used to enforce his
subjects to indure wrong. But the rust being scoured off, which abused time,
hath cast upon it, then will the glorie thereof shine in the perfection of an
uncorrupted brightnesse. You of the Jurie therfore looke into the abuses done
by *Purveyors,* and present them.

Resides these spoken of. There is also a Salt peterman, whose Commission
is not to breake up any mans house or ground without leave. And not to deale
with any house, but such as is unused for any necessarie imployment by the
owner. And not to digge in any place without leaving it smooth and levell:
in such case as he found it. This Salt-Peter man under shew of his authoritie,
though being no more then is specified, will make plaine and simple people
beleeve, that hee will without their leave breake up the floore of their dwelling

house, unlesse they will compound with him to the contrary. Any such felow, if you can meete with all, let his misdemenor be presented, that he may be taught better to understand his office: For by their abuse the countrey is often times troubled.

There is another troublesome fellow called a *Concealer,* who is indeed little better then a plaine *Cosioner,* and would in many things be proved so, if well looked unto, there be many Statute lawes to prevent the occurrence of his mischiefe, give him not a peny for any of his claimes or titles: For they are meere illusions, and like himselfe not worth any thing.

There be 4 sorts of people, whom if you observe, you shall find not any of them to thrive. I have alwayes knowne them little better then beggers, and may easily be knowne by these names. A *Concealer* of whom I have spoken: unto whom is rightly joyned a *Promooter,* a *Monopolitan,* and an *Alcumist:* The *Promooter* is both a *begger* and a *knave,* and may, if well looked unto, in the part of an *Informer* (For many abuses) by your information eyther be well punished or reformed. Their Office, I confesse, is necessarie. And yet it seldome happeneth, that an honest man is imployed therein: yet there is some hope, that by punishing their abuses, they may at the last bee made honest against their wils. In which imployment, you of the Jurie shall do well to use a respective diligence.

As touching the *Monopolitane,* hee for the most part useth at a deare rate to pay for his foolishnes: For some of that profession, have bene so wise, to sell twentie, thirtie, or perhaps fortie pound land a yeare, and bestow most part of the money in purchasing of a *Monopolie:* Thereby to anoy and hinder the whole *Publicke Weale* for his owne privat benefit: In which course he so well thriveth, as that by toyling some short time, either in *Starch, Vineger,* or *Aquavitae,* he doth in the end thereby purchase to himselfe an absolute beggerie, and for my owne part, their purposes and practises considered, I can wish unto them no better happinesse.

But then our golden Foole the *Alcumist,* he will be striving to make Gold and Silver, untill he leaves himselfe not worth a pennies weight in either of both. I will not deny, but to understand the nature, quintessence, & spirit of the *Minerals,* out of them to extract a *Metaphisicall* and *Paracelsian* manner of Physicke, may according to *art* be commendable, but by the studie of *Alcumie,* to desire to turne imperfect mettals into Gold and Silver, such labour I account ridiculous: And oftentimes by those of this *Camicall Science* is Fellony

comitted: For by any imperfect commixture, to use multiplication, either in
Gold or Silver, is directly Fellonie by *Statute Law:* you of the Jurie are therefore
to enquire of such offendors, and present them.

Because I must hast unto an end, I wil request that you will carefully put
in execution the *Statute* against *Vagarants:* Since the making whereof, I have
found fewer theeves, and the *Gaole* lesse pestered then before.

The abuse of *Stage players,* wherewith I find the Countrey much troubled,
may easily be reformed: They having no Commission to play in any place
without leave: And therefore, if by your willingnesse they be not entertained
you may soone be rid of them.

You are also concerning *Innes* and *Alehouses* diligently to observe what the
Statute Lawe determineth. As also to keep the orders set down by my *honorable
predecessor,* concerning which, there is now by the appointment of the *Lords*
of the *Counsel,* certaine *Briefes* to be delivered unto all the *Justices* in their
severall *Limmits.* And assuredly, if you of the Jurie, pettie *Constables, Chiefe
Constables,* and *Justices* of Peace, would together; labour that the *Lawes* carefully
Enacted for our good, might receive a a due and just execution, abuses would
then bee reformed, *God* and our *King* faithfully served and honored. And the
tranquillitie of our *Publicke weale* preserved: which so great happinesse, that
it may the better be accomplished, I would request, that all imployed in any
place of authoritie, would have an speciall care to suppresse that root of evill,
from whence all mischiefs do proceed, and that is *Idlenes:* For idle persons
are those of whome the *Psalme* speaketh, *They doe wickedly all the day long,
they imagine wickednesse upon their beds, the imaginations of their hearts are evill
continually,* and such for the most part are all those, given over to an idle
deposition: who by their wickednes do make themselves worse then beasts:
For, *Homo malus infinitis modis plura mala perpetraverit quam bestia,* an evill
man by an infinit manner committeth more evill then a beast. For the reformation of which dangerous evill: you shall do well to have an especiall eye
unto the company that frequent *Taverns, Innes, Alehouses, Bowling allies,* and
such like thriftlesse places of resort, where you shall find *Tradesmen,* and *Ar-
tificers,* which have no other meanes whereby to live, then onely the lawfull
use of their *Science,* or *Manuall profession.* And yet such is their unthriftie
idlenesse, as they will spend their time and labors profit, at some, or all the
places before recited: whilest their wives and children sit at home and weepe,
wanting necessarie maintenance: Those of such condition, let them be enquired of and presented: For were the Justice of the Lawe rightly executed

uppon such offendors (they receiving condigne punishment for their offence) would be inforced to betake themselves unto a better course of life, and live as becometh good Subjects in the list of a more commended obedience.

Of that idle company, you shall also finde some of our accounted *Gallants* young *Gentlemen,* upstarts, perhaps honest yeomens sonnes, that by their intemperate *Ryote,* love to spend their inheritance before they come to inherit, and being questioned for their chargeable and expensive manner of living, they will bravely answer that they spend nothing but their owne: And will seeme as if they scorn'd to be reformed by *admonition* or *authority.* The law provideth a course whereby to teach such vain & idle *royoters* so to spend, that they may keepe their own: For when by their misdemenor all their owne is spent; Then their next course is to live upon the goods of others: and then at last, such Gallants turning starke theeves, do make their last period at the *Gallowes,* reaping to themselves, by an untimely death, the fruit of idlenesse.

There is also a sort of idle seeming *Gentlemen,* whom if you do observe, you shall find them walking with a gray hound in a slip, or a birding peece upon their necke, and they forsooth will make a path over the *Statute Lawe,* and into any mans *Groundes, Lordshippes,* or *Liberties,* passe and repasse at their pleasure: As if it were lawfull for everie Fellow to keepe a *Graye hound,* and to hunt, when and where he listeth, or as if a birding peece were no *Gunne,* and so not included in the Statute made against *Gunnes.*

But if you would finde out those Fellowes, and present them, they shall be taught to knowe themselves: And that the wisedome of a *Kingdomes state,* in the framing of a *Statute Law,* could not be deluded by a vaine and shallow brain'd idlenesse of their ridiculous Foolery. Let them be therfore punished whose misdemenor in this case offendeth.

The better to prevent the *Ryotous* expence of unthriftie idlenesse, you shall do well to have a speciall care unto the *Statute* for *Apparell,* by the neglect whereof too much abuse is nourished.

As touching all the abuses last recited, have great respect to punish one abuse, in which all our idle *Gallants* and disordered disolutes do desire to swim, untill themselves, and their whole *estate* do sinke, in the *Slymie dregs of Swinelike drunkennes,* to *drunkards* therefore have especiall heed, you know the *Lawe* provideth for their *punishment,* & were such *offendors* duly *presented, Indited, Fined,* & *imprisoned,* they may by such good meanes be in time haply *refined* from that *contagious evill,* their continuall amisse, beeing continually with *Justice* punished, to the utter suppressing of such vile occasion: From whence as from *Hels* mouth flames forth, *Ryoats, murthers, man-slaughters, quarrels, fightings, whoredemes,* and *presumptuous blasphemies,* all proceeding from that sinke of sin, in whose sick healths is *dronke* the bodies *Surfiting,* and the *Soules damnation.* In this, as in all the rest of the abuses specified, use your best indeavors for the furtherance of a setled *Reformation,* according to the *Lawes established:* For you must know, that *Vita &, vigor Juris, in execucione consistit,* The life and strength of the Laws, consisteth in the execution of them: For in vaine are just lawes Inacted, if not justly executed.

And now my loving *Countrey men,* because I would that all which I have spoken, may receive a profitable remembrance. I will thus conclude, *Similes* and *Comparisons* doe best confirme our understanding: and do fastest cleave unto the memorie; my conclusion therefore, shall consist upon this one *Similitude.*

There was a certain man, who having a great account to make unto a mightie *King,* made triall of his best Friends, that might accompany him, in that dangerous journey, and not forsake him untill his account were made. This man upon his Inquisition found one friend that would go with him a great part of the way, but then forsake him. And that was his (*Riches.*) Some other Friends he found that would goe with him untill he came in sight of the *Kings* pallace, but then they would also leave him and beare him company no further, all these Friends were his *wife* and *children,* that would follow him to his grave. But at last, he found one Friend that would go with him into the presence of the *King,* and not forsake him, untill he had seene his account made and for ever beare the greatest part with him, either in woe, or happinesse, and this Friend was his *Conscience;* Deare Countrymen betwixt *God* and your *Consciences* therefore, make your peace, for he is the *King,* unto whom all of us must make a strickt account of all our actions done. This then considered, such would be our care, as *God* and our *King* should be obeyed, and our peace in this life, and in the world to come preserved. Unto which eternall grace be we all in *Jesus Christ* committed.

FINIS.

III

Excerpts from the Small Treatises

These books were of neither the influence nor the breadth of the *Institutes*. The only one to be published in Coke's life was the *Entries*, a pleading manual. The others, dealing with specific problems of property law, were published from his manuscripts posthumously, separately and also in a single binding of *Law Tracts*, in 1764.—*Ed.*

A. Book of Entries

The Book of Entries was first published in 1614 under the title *A Booke of Entries. Containing Perfect and Approved Presidents of Counts, Declarations, Informations, Pleints.* It is the only treatise, other than the First Part of the *Institutes,* that Coke published during his lifetime. It was the result of Coke's careful study and use of pleading, which exercised a strong influence on the outcome of law cases. The *Entries* enjoyed some success but later became only one among several competing manuals containing pleadings from Coke's *Reports.*—*Ed.*

Epigrams from the Title Page:

Cicero Rhetor. Lib. 4.
Rerum omnium imperiti, qui unius cujusque; rei de rebus ante gestis exampla petere non possunt, hi per imprudentiam facillime deducuntur in fraudem: at hi qui sciunt quid aliis acciderit, facile ex eorum eventibus suis possunt rationibus providere.[1]

Vir bonus est quis?
Qui Consulta patrum, qui Leges juraque servat.[2]

Periculosum existimo quod doctorum virorum non comprobatur exemplo.[3]

Deo duce εὑρηκα.[4]

1. [*Ed.:* People who are inexperienced in everything, and are unable to seek out precedents of what has been done before in every case, are most easily deceived through imprudence; but those who know what has happened to others may easily from their fortunes prepare themselves for their own affairs. (Cicero, *Rhetorica ad Herennium,* iv. 13, 30).]

2. [*Ed.:* Who is a good man? It is he who preserves the decisions of our forefathers, the statutes and laws.]

3. [*Ed.:* I consider anything dangerous which is not proved by the example of learned men.]

4. [*Ed.:* Led by God, I have found it (eureka).]

The Preface of Sr. Edward Coke, Knight

Lord Chiefe Justice of England of Pleas Before the King Himselfe to be
Holden Assigned, and One of the Lords of His Majesties Most Honorable
Privie Councell.

Deo, Patriæ, Tibi.[5]

He that duly considereth (learned Reader) the Theoricke and Practique parts
of the laws of England, that is, the Knowledge in universalities, and the Practise
in particulars, shall find that most aptly to be applied to this profession that
long since was spoken of another, *Ars longa, vita brevis, studium difficile, occasio
præceps, experimentum periculosum.*[6] A learned man in the lawes of this realme
is long in making, the student thereof, having *sedentariam vitam*[7] is not commonly long lived, the study abstruse and difficult, the occasion sodaine, the
practise dangerous. Many have written of the former part, onely one of the
later, unlesse you will account that auncient little treatise called *Les novel Tales*,
or *Novæ narrationes*, to be one; and yet the Active part is as necessarie as the
Speculative, for *usus & experientia dominantur in artibus;*[8] and certain it is,
that no art can be perfectly attained unto by reading without use and exercise.
What auayleth the Serjeant or Apprentice the general knowledge of the laws,
if he know not withall the forme and order of legall proceedings in particular
cases, and how to plead and handle the same soundly, and most for his Clients
advauntage? Good pleading hath three excellent qualities, that is to say (as
Littleton saith) it is Honorable, Laudable, and Profitable: Honorable, for he
cannot be a good pleader, but he must be of excellencie in judgement, *Honor
est præmium excellentiae:*[9] Laudable for the fame and estimation of the professor, *Laus est sermo elucidans magnitudinem scientiæ:*[10] And profitable for three
respects: first, for that good pleading is *Lapis lidius*[11] the touchstone of the

---

5. [*Ed.:* To God, to the country, to you.]

6. [*Ed.:* Professional skill takes a long time, whereas life is short, study difficult, favourable opportunity
slippery, experiment dangerous.]

7. [*Ed.:* a sedentary life.]

8. [*Ed.:* In acquiring professional skill, use and experience are the rule.]

9. [*Ed.:* Honour is the prize of excellence.]

10. [*Ed.:* A discourse explaining the greatness of knowledge is a matter for praise.]

11. [*Ed.:* The touchstone.]

true sence of the law: secondly, to the Client whose good cause is often lost or long delayed for want of good pleading, for herein is *occasio praeceps & experimentum periculosum*[12] lastly, to the professor himselfe, who being for skill therein exalted above others, *tanquam inter viburna Cupressus*[13] it cannot be unto him but exceeding profitable. It is true, that of ancient time Judges gave no way to nice and overcurious exceptions to formes of counts or pleadings; nay before the raigne of king Edw. 3. they sometimes gave too much way to the neglect of legall formes in pleading, and that made Sir *William de Thirning* chiefe Justice of the Court of Common Pleas to say in 12. *Hen.* 4. 19. *Que devant le raigne del Roy Edw. 3. le manner de pleder no fuit forsque feeble, eyant regard que fuit unques puis in temps de cel Roy.*[14] And I am of opinion, that the neglect of essentiall formes would bring in ignorance and confusion: yet doe I well allow, that men should not be fined *pro non pulchre' placitando,*[15] or as some Records say *pro stultiloquio,*[16] because the same have beene forbidden by acts of Parliament, *videlicet Marlebridge cap.11. Westm. 1. cap.* 8. and 1. *Edw. 3. cap.* 8. *Vide Registr'* 179. 13. *Edw.* 1. *tit Attachment* 8. & *F.N.B.* 270. *Inter placita de Banco, termin' Mich. ann. 5. Hen. 3. incipiente Rot' 10. Dors. Essex. Radulphus de Bardfield qui narravit pro germano filio Turoldi, in misericordia pro stultiloquio:*[17] which and many other Records doe prove, that the fine in those dayes was set vpon the Councellor and not upon the Client; for it was not holden just that the Client should be fined for the Councellors fault, and that had beene to have added affliction to the afflicted, *videlicet*[18] to fine the Client for erronious pleading, who therefore lost his cause. And Sir *Robert de Wilby* in Anno 24. *Edw. 3. fol.* 48. speaking to the Councellors at the barre, *Ieo ay vieu le temps, que si vous vibes plead un erronious plea, que vous alastes al prison.*[19]

12. [*Ed.:* opportunity slippery and experiment dangerous.]

13. [*Ed.:* as great as a cypress among the brushwood.]

14. [*Ed.:* That before the reign of King Edward III the manner of pleading was but weak, having regard to the fact that it never was afterwards in the time of that king.]

15. [*Ed.:* for not pleading finely.]

16. [*Ed.:* for miskenning (speaking badly).]

17. [*Ed.:* Among the pleas of the Bench for Michaelmas term beginning in the fifth year of Henry III, on the dorse of roll 10: Essex. Ralph of Bardfield who counts on behalf of the natural son of Turold, in mercy for miskenning.]

18. [*Ed.:* that is to say.]

19. [*Ed.:* I have seen the time when, if you had pleaded an erroneous plea, you would have gone to prison.]

And even as he that hath a long journey upon weightie affaires that require present dispatch, especially *si via fit salebrosa, saxis aspera, sentibus obducta, gurgitibus intercisa, torrentibus rapida &c.*[20] would be glad of a sure guide that by approved experience could lead him in the right way, both to avoyd dangers, and to come with speed to his journeys end; So the professor of the Law (that is presently to plead his Clients cause, which many times is full of obscuritie and difficultie, in the pleading whereof if there be found errour, though the right be good, the cause quaileth) will (I persuade my selfe) be glad of this Booke, contayning many excellent Presidents of Counts, Pleadings, and all other matters fitting almost everie particular Case that can fall out; which being upon mature deliberation sifted, examined, and approved in the highest Courts of Justice, *videlicet* the Chauncerie, Kings Bench, Common Pleas, and Exchequer, may serve for well experienced guides in his Clients cause, to conduct him in such a way as his Client may avoid daunger, and attaine to his desired end.

What reverence hath beene given by the most reverend Sages of the law to judiciall Presidents, appeareth (amongst many others) in *Ellice Case in 39. H. 6. fol. 30.* where the opinion of learned *Prisot* chiefe Justice of the Court of Common Pleas, and other Justices, was, That in a writ of *Mesne, quele pl' covient de fine force de surmitter le tenure inter le mesne & Seignior paramout en son Count, ou auterment il ne serra bone: & puis quant* Prisot *avoit demaund de les prothonotaries le forme de les novel Tales, & ensement que ils avoyent view que les Tales ne fesoyent mention de nultenure in tiel case, & que cest forme avoiet touts foits este use, ils ne voillont chaunger cest use, nient obstant que lour opinion fuit al contrarie,* Quia non valet ratio contra experimentum.[21]

No man can be a compleat Lawyer by universalitie of knowledge without experience in particular cases, nor by bare experience without universalitie of knowledge; he must be both speculative & active, for the science of the laws, I assure you, must joyne hands with experience. *Experientia* (saith the great

---

20. [*Ed.:* if the way is made full of roughness, uneven with rocks, overgrown with thorns, cut through by abysses, rushing with torrents, etc.]

21. [*Ed.:* that the plaintiff must of necessity set out in his count the tenure between the mesne and the lord paramount, or else it is not good: but later, when Prysot (C.J.) had asked the prothonotaries the form in the *Novae Narrationes,* and (they said) they had seen that the *Narrationes* did not mention any tenure in such cases, and that this form had always been used, they (i.e. the judges) would not change that usage, even though their opinion was to the contrary.]

Philosopher) *est cognitio singularium, ars vero universalium.*[22,23] The learned
Sages of the law doe found their judgement upon legall reason and judiciall
President; the one they find in our bookes of yeres and termes, the other out
of records formerly examined and allowed: These two, Reason and President
are *clarissima mundi lumina,*[24] whereby all the wise men of the world are
directed: But in these dayes of many it may be justly said, *Quod statim sapiunt,
statim sciunt omnia, neminem verentur, imitantur neminem, ipsi sibi exempla
sunt.*[25] But it is safe for the Client and for the Councellor also (if he respect
his conscience) to follow Presidents formerly approved and allowed, and not
to trust to any new frame carved out of his owne invention, for *Nihil simul
inventum & perfectum est.*[26]

The former Booke of Entries being published at that time when the Authour
was beyond the Seas (as in his Preface he confesseth) could not so exactly and
perfectly be done (though it be, for many Presidents therein, verie profitable
and of good use) as if he had bin at the fountaines head it selfe, and might
have had conference with the grave Judges, and well experiensed Prothonotaries, Officers, and Clarkes.

In this Booke six things are worthie of observation. First, that none of the
Presidents herein have bin by any published heretofore. 2. That they are of
greater authoritie and use, and fitter for the moderne practise of the law, for
that they be for the most part of later times, and principally, of the raigne of
our late Soveraigne Ladie of ever blessed memorie Queene Elizabeth, and of
his most excellent Majestie the King that now is. 3. That for thy further satisfaction (learned Reader) everie President hath a true reference to the Court,
yeare, terme, number-roll, and record, where the President it selfe is to be
found. 4. In this worke are contayned the records of divers of the cases which
in the nine former parts of my Commentaries I have published, with a certaine
reference to the report it selfe. 5. Here shall you find Presidents adjudged upon
Demurrer, wherein lye hidden many matters of Law and excellent points of
learning, which being never reported, here is for thy better light (studious

22. [*Ed.:* Experience is knowledge of particular things, nay rather the art of general things.]

23. [*Ed.:* Aristotle's *Metaphysics,* book 1.]

24. [*Ed.:* the clearest lights of the world,]

25. [*Ed.:* That they are wise straight away, know everything instantly, respect no one, copy no one, set
their own precedents.]

26. [*Ed.:* Nothing is invented and perfected at the same time.]

Reader) a short touch given of the reasons and causes whereupon they were adjuged. Lastly, there is an exact and plaine table of Titles, without perplexed and intricat divsions or subdivisions or tedious referments, everie mans owne method and observation in reading, being ever the best and readiest of all others for himselfe. Read these Presidents (learned Reader) and reape in this faire and large field, the delectable and profitable fruits of reverend Experience and Knowledge; which you may doe with greater ease, for that more easily shall you learne by patterne than by precept: and they have beene so painfully and diligently weeded, as it cannot be sayd, that in this fruitfull field,

Infœlix lolium aut steriles dominantur avena.[27]

Your true and faithfull friend

EDW. COKE.

---

27. [*Ed.:* Barren tares or rather wild oats have dominion.]

B. The Compleat Copyholder

The *Compleat Copyholder,* first published in 1630, is a textbook post-humously built from Coke's manuscript notes on the ancient estate, the copyhold. Copyholds were one of the most basic tenancies, usually held by villeins, small tenant farmers on manors, or great estates, who paid in rents in money or in kind to their landlords. Their interests were not conveyed by indenture, deed, or by the other grants that specified their protections in their lands. Rather they were written on a list, literally, copied into a court roll. The rights and duties of copyholders were limited but controlled primarily by the custom specific to each manor. Coke was among the first to attempt to state the rights and powers essential to all copyholds, and his cases, treatment of copyhold in the First *Institute,* and treatment in this volume allowed considerably greater protection for the working agricultural poor than had been given before. — *Ed.*

Sec. XXXIII.

| Customes are defined to be a Law, or Right not written, which being es- [68] tablished by long use, and the consent of our Ancestors, hath been, and is daily practised.

Custome, Prescription, and usage, how-I-soever there be correspondency [69] amongst them, and dependancy one on the other, and in common speech, one of them is taken for another, yet they are three distinct things; Custom and Prescription differ in this. 1. Custom cannot have any commencement since the memory of man, but a Prescription may, both by the Common Law, and the Civill: and therefore where the *Statute.* 1.*H*.8. saith, that all actions popular; must be brought within three yeares after the offence commited; whosover offendeth against this *Statute,* and doth escape uncalled for three

Custome, Prescription, and Usage, how they differ.

yeares, he may be justly said to prescribe an immunity against any such Action.
2. A Custome toucheth many men in generall; Prescription, this, or that man
in particular: and that is the reason why Prescription is personall, and is alwayes
made in the name of some person certaine, and his Ancestors, or those whose
estate he hath; but a Custome having no person certaine in whose name to
prescribe, is therefore called and alledged after this manner. In such a Borough,
in such a Manor, there is this or that Custome. And for usage, that is the
efficient cause, or rather the life of both; for Custome and Prescription lose
[70]   their being, if usage faile. Should I goe about to make a Cata-|-logue of severall
Customes, I should with *Sisiphus, saxum volvere,*[1] undertake an endlesse peece
of worke, therefore I will forbeare, since the relation would be an argument
of great curiositie, and a taske of great difficultie. I will onely set down a briefe
distinction of Customes, and leave the particulars to your owne observation.
Customes are either Generall or Particular. Generall, which are part of the
Common law, being currant through the whole Common-wealth, and used
in every County, every City, every Towne, and every Manor. Particular, which
are confined to shorter bounds and limits, and have not such choice of fields
to walke in, as generall Customes have. These particular Customes are of two
sorts, either disallowing what generall Customes doe allow, or allowing what
generall Customes doe disallow, as for example sake. By the generall Customes
of Manors it is in the Copiholders power to sell to whom he pleaseth, but by
a particular Custome used in some places, the Copyholder, before he can
inforce his Lord to admit any one to his Copihold, is to make a proffer to
the next of the blood, or to the next of his Neighbors *ab oriente solis,*[2] who
[71]   giving as much as the partie to whom the Surrender was made, should I have
it: so on the other side by the generall Customes of Manors, the passing away
of Copyhold land by Deede, for more than for one yeare without licence, is
not warranted; yet some particular customes in some Manors doe it: so by
the generall Customes of Manors, Presentments, or any other act done in the
Leete, after the moneth expired, contrary to the Statute of *magna Charta,* and
31. *E.* 3. are voyd; yet by some particular Customes, such acts are good, and
so in millions of the like, as in the sequell of this discourse shall be made
manifest. And therefore, not to insist any longer in dilucidating this point,

1. [*Ed.:* Roll a stone [with] Sisyphus,]
2. [*Ed.:* sun from the east.]

let us in few words learne the way how to examine the validity of a Custome: For our direction in this businesse, we shall doe well to observe these fixed Rules, which will serve us for exact tryall. 1. Customes and Prescriptions ought to be reasonable, and therefore a Custome that no Tenant of the Manor shal put in his Cattell to use his common in *Campis seminatis:*[3] after the Corne severed, untill the Lord have put in his Cattell, is a voyd Custome, because unreasonable, for peradventure the Lord will never put in his Cattell, and then the Tenants shall lose their profits: so if the Lord will prescribe that he hath such a Custome with-l-in his Manor, that if any mans beasts be taken by him [72] upon his Demesnes damage Fesant, that he may detaine them untill the owners of the beasts give him such recompence for his harmes, as hee himselfe shall request; this is an unreasonable Custome, for no man ought to be his owne Judge. 2. Customes and Prescriptions ought to be according to common right, and therefore if the Lord will prescribe to have of every Copyholder belonging to his Manor, for every Court he keepeth a certaine summe of money, this is a void prescription, because it is not according to common Right, for hee ought for Justice sake to doe it *Gratis;*[4] but if the Lord prescribe to have a certaine Fee of his Tenants, for keeping an extraordinary Court, which is purchased onely for the benefit of some particular Tenants, to take up their Copyholds and such like; this is a good prescription, and according to common right. 3. They ought to be upon good consideration, and therefore if the Lord will prescribe that whosoever passeth through the Kings High way which lyeth through his Manor, should pay him a peny for passing, this prescription is voyd, because it is not upon a good consideration; but if he will prescribe to have a peny of every one l that passeth over such a bridge within his Manor, [73] which bridge the Lord doth use to repaire, this is a good prescription, and upon a good consideration. So if the Lord will prescribe to have a fine at the marriage of his Copyholder, in which Manor the custome doth admit the husband to be Tenant by the curtesie, or the seme Tenant in Dower of a Copyhold, this prescription is good, and upon a good consideration; but in such Manors, where these estates are not allowed, the Law is otherwise. 4. They ought to be compulsary, and therefore if the Lord will prescribe that every Copyholder ought to give him so much every moneth to beare his charges

---

3. [*Ed.:* in sown fields.]
4. [*Ed.:* freely.]

in time of warre, this prescription is void; but to prescribe they ought to pay so much money for that purpose, is a good prescription; for a payment is compulsary, but a gift is Arbitrary at the voluntary liberty of the giver. 5. They ought to be certaine; and therefore, if the Lord will prescribe that whensoever any of his Copyholders dye without heire, that then another of the Copyholders shall hold the same lands for the yeere following, this prescription is void, for the incertainty; but if the Lord will prescribe to have of his Copy-

[74]   holders, 2 d. an Acre Rent, in time of warre | 4 d. an Acre, this prescription is certain enough. 6. They ought to be beneficiall to them that alledge the prescription; and therefore if the Lord prescribeth that the custome hath alwayes beene within the Manor, that what distresse soever is taken within his Manor, for any common persons cause, is to be impounded for a certaine time within his pound; this is no good prescription, for the Lord is hereby to receive a charge, and no commoditie: but if the prescription goeth further, that the Lord should have for every beast so impounded a certaine summe of money, this is a good prescription. If we desire to be more fully satisfied in the generall knowledge of prescriptions and Customes, wee shall finde many Maximes, which make very materiall for this purpose, amongst which I have made choyse of these three, as most worthy of your observation. 1. Things gained by matter of Record onely, cannot be challenged by prescription, and therefore no Lord of a Manor can prescribe to have fellons goods, fugitives goods, Deodands and such like; because they cannot bee forfeited untill it appeare of Record: but waves, estraies, wreckes, and such like may be challenged by prescription, because they are gained by usage, without matter of

[75]   Record. | 2. A custome never extendeth to a thing newly created; and therefore if a Rent be granted out of Gavel-kind Land, or land in *Borough-English,* the rent shall descend, according to the course of the Common Law, not according to the Custome. If before the *Statute.* 32. *H.* 8. Lands were deviseable in any Borough, or City by speciall Custome; A Rent granted out of these Lands, was not deviseable by the same Custome; for what things soever have their beginning since the memory of man, Custome maintaines not. If there be a Custome within a Manor, that for every house or cottage two shillings Fine shall be paid, if any Tenant within these liberties maketh two houses of one, or buildeth a new house, hee shall not pay a fine for any of these new houses; for the Custome onely extendeth to the old. So if I have Estovers appendant to my house, and I build a new house, I shall not have Estovers for this new built house upon this ground. It hath been doubted, if a man by Prescription

hath course of water to his Fulling-mill, he converting these into Corne-mills, whether by this conversion, the Prescription is not destroyed, in regard that these Corne-mills are things newly created; but because the qualitie of the thing, and not the substance is altered; | therefore this alteration is held in- sufficient to overthrow the Prescription; for if a man by Prescription hath Estovers to his house, although they alter the Roomes and Chambers in the house, as by making a Parlour where there was a Hall, *vele converso*,[5] yet the Prescription stands still in force: and so if by Prescription I have an ancient Window to my Hall, and I convert this into a Parlor, yet my neighbours upon this change cannot stoppe my Window; *Causa qua supra*.[6] 3. Customes are likewise taken strictly, though not alwayes literally. There is a Custome in *London,* that Citizens and Freemen may devise in Mortmayne: A Citizen that is a Forreiner, cannot devise by this Custome. An Infant by the Custome of *Gavelkind,* at the age of fifteene, may make a Feoffment; yet he cannot by the Custome make a Will at that age to passe away his Land; to make a Lease, and a Release, which amounteth to a Feoffment. If there be any custome that copyhold-lands may be leased by the Lord, *vel per Supervisor, vel deputatum supervisoris:*[7] This Custome giveth not power to the Lord, to authorize any by his last Will and Testament, to keepe a Court in their owne name, and to make Leases, *Secundum consuetudinem Manerii:*[8] but these Customes I have this strict construction, because they tend to the derogation of the Common Law; yet they are not to be confined to literall interpretation; for if there be a Custome within any Manor, that Copyhold Lands may be granted in *Feodo simplici,*[9] by the same Custome they are grantable to one, and the heires of his body, for life, for yeeres, or any other estate whatsoever; because, *Cui licet quod majus, non debet quod minus est non licere;*[10] so if there be a Custome that copyhold lands, may be granted for life; by the same Custome they may be granted, *Durante viduitate,*[11] but not *e converso,*[12] because an estate during

[76]

[77]

5. [*Ed.:* or conversely,]
6. [*Ed.:* For the above reason.]
7. [*Ed.:* or by the surveyor, or the surveyor's deputy:]
8. [*Ed.:* According to the custom of the manor:]
9. [*Ed.:* In fee simple,]
10. [*Ed.:* If a greater thing is permissible for someone, a lesser thing ought not to be impermissible;]
11. [*Ed.:* During widowhood,]
12. [*Ed.:* conversely,]

Widdowhood, is lesse than an estate for life. Before the *Statute* of 32. *H.* 8. Lands in certaine Boroughs were devisable by Custome: By the same Custome was *implicitie*[13] waranted, authorizing Executors to sell Lands devisable. Now with your patience, I will onely point at the manner of pleading of Customes, I finde a foure-fold kinde of Prescribing.

1. To prescribe in his Predecessours, as in himselfe, and all those whose estate he hath.

[78]   2. To prescribe generally, not tying his Prescription to place, or person, as where a Chiefe Justice prescribeth, that it hath been | used, that every Chiefe Justice may grant Offices; or where a Sergeant prescribeth, *Quod talis habetur consuetudo,*[14] that Sergeants ought to be impleaded by originall Writ, and not by Bill.

3. To Prescribe in a place certaine.

4. To Prescribe in the place of another.

The first sort of these Prescriptions, a Copyholder cannot use, in regard of the imbecillity of his estate; for no man can Prescribe in that manner, but onely Tenants in Fee simple, at the Common Law.

The second sort of these may be used sometimes by Copyholders in the pleading of a generall Custome, but in alledging of a particular Custome, a Copyholder is driven to one of the last, and as occasion serveth, he useth sometimes the one, sometimes the other. If he be to claime Common, or other profit in the soyle of the Lord, then he cannot Prescribe in the name of the Lord, for the Lord cannot Prescribe to have Common or other profit in his owne soyle; but then the Copyholder must of necessitie Prescribe in a place certaine, and alleadge, that within such a Manor, there is such a Custome, that all the Tenants within that Manor, have used to have Common in such a place, parcell of | the Manor: but if he be to claime common, or other profit in the soyle of a stranger, then he ought to prescribe in the name of his Lord, saying, that the Lord of the Manor, and all his Ancestors, and all those whose estate he hath, were wont to have a Common in such a place for himselfe, and his Tenants at will, &c.

[79]

---

13. [*Ed.:* [*implicite*] impliedly.]
14. [*Ed.:* that there is such a custom (as follows).]

C. Little Treatise
on Baile and Mainprize

The *Little Treatise*, first published in 1635 shortly after Coke's death, augments Coke's discussions of criminal procedure in the Second and Third Parts of the *Institutes*. Bail and mainprize were the two methods by which a sheriff or other officer of a court could be required to set free the person detained. Bail was used primarily for a person arrested or imprisoned on suspicion of a crime, but mainprize could be used in other situations, and it required the delivery of the person detained into the custody of someone who promised to deliver the detainee for a later hearing. — *Ed.*

The Conclusion with Advertisment.

The end and scope of this little Treatise is, (under correction of those of better judgement) to set forth what the Law of the Realme doth require touching Baile and Maineprize: A necessary thing (in mine opinion) for such as be Justices of the peace, to be knowne: for as he that standeth upon plaine & sure ground, although he should be borne of rage and tempest to the ground, yet might hee without danger rise of himselfe againe: so hee that hath the administration of Justice, and in all his occasions is guided and directed by the rule of the law, neither abusing his authority, nor exceeding his Commission, standeth on a sure ground, which will beare him up at all seasons: *Sapientis est cogitare* (saith Cicero) *tantum esse permissum quantum commissum & creditum.*[1] And good was the Counsell (as those that follow it finde) who-

---

1. [*Ed.*: A wise man bears in mind that only so much is permitted as is committed and entrusted to him.]

soever gave it, (*videlicet*)[2] exceede not the Commission: And albeit it is truely said, that *Judicium est legibus & non exemplis:*[3] And as the Logician saith, *Exempla demonstrant, non probant;*[4] yet undoubtedly it is a great contentment and satisfaction to an honest minde and a good conscience, especially in cases that concerne the life and liberty of a man, to follow the president of grave and reverend men: how beit for as much as all good Lawes are instituted, and made for the repelling of those evils that most commonly happen: For *ad ea quae frequentius accidunt jura ad prantur,*[5] and principally doe respect the generall peace and profit of the people: and therefore we use to say, that a mischiefe is rather to be suffered then an inconvenience: That is to say, that a private person should be punished or damnified by the rigour of the Law, then a general rule of the Law should be broken to the generall trouble and prejudice of many. It is therefore very necessary, that the Law and discretion should bee Concomitant, and the one to be an accident inseparable to the other, so as neither Law without discretion, least it should incline to rigour, nor discretion without Law, least confusion should follow, should bee put in use: my meaning hereby, is not to allow of every mans discretion that sitteth on the seate of Justice: (for that would bring forth a monstrous confusion) But I meane that discretion, that ariseth upon the right discerning, and due consideration of the true and necessary circumstances of the matter: and as wee commonly use to say, that Common Law is nothing else but common reason; and yet we meane thereby nothing lesse, then that common reason where-with a man is naturally endued, but that perfection of reason which is gotten by long and continuall study: so in associating discretion so neare to Law, it is not meant to preferre it to that society: each mans discretion, which commonly rather deserveth the name of affection and selfe-will, then of discretion indeed: but that discretion onely we allow of in this place, that either grave and reverend men have used in such cases before, or rise of the circumstances of the matter: (as is aforesaid) As for example, being not also impertinent to the matter of our Treatise, if it were a question, whether in an appeale of Maine, the defendant were to bee let to Baile, or Maineprize, or no. It is

---

2. [*Ed.:* that is to say.]

3. [*Ed.:* One ought to judge according to the laws and not according to precedents:]

4. [*Ed.:* Precedents illustrate but do not prove;]

5. [*Ed.:* laws are adapted to those things which occur frequently,]

necessary to be examined, whether the manner of the Maine were horrible or hainous: for the defendant may be denied Baile and Maineprize: whether the same were done upon a suddaine affray, or of the plaintiffes assault, or against the intent of the defendant, &c. For the defendant may bee let to baile: and this I take to be a lawfull discretion, for to that end is the booke, reason of the booke in 6. H. 7. fo. 2. where in an appeale of Maine, the Justices of the Kings Bench denied the defendant to bee bailed; for that upon the examination of the matter, it appeared to be most cruel and horrible, and therefore in respect of the abhominable hainousnes of the same, the Justices would not suffer the defendant to be bailed: and with this agreeth the opinion of Bract. in the 2. treatise of his 3. booke ca. 8. *Appellati vero de morte hominis, & de pace & plagis periculosis saltem capiantur, et in prisonam detru antur, et ibi custodiantur, donec per Dominum Regem per Pleg' dimittantur, vel per Judicem deliberantur, &c.*[6] whereby I note that he saith, *plag' periculosis,*[7] insinuating a difference *inter plagas periculosas, & minus periculosas,*[8] in that he saith, *Donec per Dominum Regem per pleg' demittantur,*[9] it is to bee understood, untill by that Court the offence be determined and judged, they bee let to Baile, and this particular may suffice to the resolution of the generall.

To conclude, the Authour of all wisedome and true knowledge, thought it requisite, that those that were Judges of the earth, should bee both wise and learned, whom I beseech God to blesse with his true knowledge and wisedome.

FINIS.

6. [*Ed.:* But only those who are accused of homicide, and breach of the peace, and giving dangerous wounds, shall be taken and put in prison, and detained there, until they are released by the lord king on bail (lit. by pledge) or delivered by a judge, etc.]

7. [*Ed.:* dangerous wounds,]

8. [*Ed.:* between dangerous and non-dangerous wounds,]

9. [*Ed.:* Until they are released by the lord king on bail.]

IV

Excerpts from the
Institutes

The *Institutes of the Lawes of England* is a comprehensive and vast project which Coke apparently contemplated as a whole prior to publishing his first volume, the great *Commentary upon Littleton*, in 1608. While Coke's *Institutes* is roughly patterned on the Justinian *Institutes*, its namesake, the organization of Coke's work bears little resemblance to that of Justinian's. The four parts of Coke's work cover matters of property, statutes, crimes, and courts. The first two parts are in the forms of glosses on earlier texts, and the last two parts are effectively treatises inventorying the examples of their respective genre. Although Coke had apparently written components of the latter three parts while he was on the bench, having, as he says in his preface below, completed much of them by 1608, portions of these works seem to have been completed in the later 1610s and 1620s, after his dismissal as chief justice. Only the first part appeared during his lifetime, being published in 1608 and going rapidly through new editions. The manuscripts for the other three parts were among the papers seized by the Crown while Coke lay dying, and they were published only after the manuscripts were restored to Coke's son by Parliament during the Commonwealth.— *Ed.*

A. The First Part of the *Institutes*

Thomas de Littleton was a Justice of Common Pleas in the later half of the fifteenth century, serving from 1466 to 1481. He wrote a textbook of property law, *Tenures,* during a time of considerable political unrest; the War of the Roses ran throughout his time on the bench. Dramatically updating a book of the same name then already a century old itself, Littleton's *Tenures,* perhaps appearing about 1470, was a comprehensive treatise on the estates by which land could be held, as well as on the procedures for transfers of interest in land. The feudal property system was then at its peak, and the heart of its economy was the complicated system by which various people held an interest in land in return for services to others; Littleton's book brought considerable clarity to the area, and it remained the leading treatise for over a century.

By Coke's day, Littleton's treatise was, however, beginning to age quickly. Coke glossed the text, section by section, providing annotations of later cases and statutes that modified or applied ideas in Littleton's text. More important, perhaps, he added a trove of ideas on related matters, often matters only casually related to the text he had before him. His commentary includes observations on the nature of law, the practice and study of law, and of man in general, as well as of the particular problems Littleton had placed in each section.

Coke upon Littleton soon became the essential tool for the study of the law. Its mastery was required of every law student for the next century and a half. The difficulty of the task for a fledgling lawyer was notorious, but the rewards were seen by most students as well worthwhile. A fine illustration of the point is in the experience of young Joseph Story, long before he became a U.S. Supreme Court justice or a law professor. In 1799, his tutor, Samuel Sewell, required him to read "the intricate, crabbed, and obsolete learning of *Coke on Littleton,*" a task he found, initially, quite over-

whelming. "I took it up, and after trying it day after day with very little success, I sat myself down and wept bitterly. My tears dropped upon the book, and stained its pages." With tenacity, though, he began "to see daylight, ay and to feel that I could comprehend and reason upon the text and the comments. . . . The critical period was passed; I no longer hesitated."
— *Ed.*

Epigrams from the Title Page:

Quid te vana juvant miserae ludibria chartae?
Hoc lege, quod possis dicere jure meum est.[1]
Martial.

Major haereditas venit unicuique; nostrum à Jure, et Legibus, quàm à Parentibus.[2]
Cicero.

1. [*Ed.:* What pleasure do you find in the empty sham of a wretched sheet? Read this, so you may say [of it] 'It is mine by right' [adapted from Martial, *Epigrams,* 10.4].]
2. [*Ed.:* A greater inheritance comes to everyone from our law and legislation than from their parents.]

THE FIRST PART OF THE INSTITUTES OF THE LAWES OF ENGLAND: OR A COMMENTARY UPON *LITTLETON*, NOT THE NAME OF THE AUTHOR ONLY, BUT OF THE LAW IT SELFE.

The Preface.
Deo, Patriae, Tibi.[1]
Proemium.[2]

Our Author, a Gentleman of an ancient and faire descended Family de Littleton, tooke his name of a Towne so called, as that famous chiefe Justice Sir John de Markham, and divers of our Profession and others have done.

The name and degree of our Author.

Thomas de Littleton Lord of Frankley, had issue Elizabeth his only child, and did beare the Armes of his Ancestors, *viz.* Argent, a Chevron betweene three Escalop shels Sable. The bearing hereof is verie ancient and honourable, for the Senators of Rome did weare bracelets of Escalop shels about their armes, and the Knights of the Honourable Order of S. Michael in France[3] do weare a coller of Gold in the forme of Escalop shels at this day. Hereof much more might be said, but it belongs unto others.

His Armes.

With this Elizabeth married, Thomas Westcote Esquire, the Kings servant

---

1. [*Ed.:* To God, to the country, to you.]
2. [*Ed.:* The Preface.]
3. Instituted by *Lewis* the eleventh, King of France, *9.E.4.*

Thomas Westcote.

in Court, a Gentleman anciently descended, who bare Argent, a Bend betweene two Cotisses Sable, a Bordure engrayled Gules, Bezantie.

But she being faire and of a noble spirit, and having large possessions and inheritance from her Ancestors de Littleton, and from her mother the daughter and heire of Richard de Quatermains, and other her Ancestors, (ready meanes in time to worke her owne desire) resolved to continue the honour of her name (as did the daughter and heire of Charleton with one of the sonnes of Knightly, and divers others) and therefore prudently, whilest it was in her owne power, provided by Westcotes assent before marriage, that her issue inheritable should be called by the name of de Littleton. These two had issue foure sons, Thomas, Nicholas, Edmund and Guy, and foure daughters.

Our Author bare his Mothers surname.

Thomas the eldest was our Author, who bare his fathers Christian name Thomas, and his mothers surname de Littleton, and the armes de Littleton also; and so doth his posteritie beare both name and armes to this day.

Camden[4] in his Britannia saith thus; Thomas Littleton alias Westcote, the famous Lawyer[5] to whose Treatise of Tenures the Students of the Common Law are no lesse beholding, than the Civilians to Justinians Institutes.

The dignitie of this faire descended Family de Littleton hath growne up together, and spread it selfe abroad by matches with many other ancient and honourable Families, to many worthy and fruitfull branches, whose posteritie flourish at this day, and quartereth many faire Coats, and[6*] enjoyeth fruitfull and opulent inheritances thereby.

He was of the Inner Temple, and read learnedly upon the Statute of *W.2. De donis conditionalibus,*[7] which we have. He was afterward called *ad statum & gradum Servientis ad Legem,*[8] and was Steward of the Court of the Marshalsey of the Kings houshold, and for his worthinesse was made by King *H.6.* his

Kings Serjeant.

Serjeant,[9] and rode Justice of Assise the Northern Circuit, which places he held under King *E.4.* untill he in the sixth yeare of his reigne constituted him

---

4. *Camden.*

5. Psal 92.II. The just shall flourish like the Palme tree, and spread abroad like the Cedars in Libanus.

6. *The best kind of quartering of Armes.

7. [*Ed.:* An English statute that converted fee-simple conditional estates to fee-tails, rendering them inalienable.]

8. [*Ed.:* of the office and rank of Serjeant at law,]

9. Rot. Pat. 33. H. 6. part 15 M. 16. Mich. 34. H.6. fol. 3. a.

one of the Judges of the Court of Common Pleas,[10] and then he rode North-amptonshire Circuit. The same King in the 15. yeare of his reigne, with the Prince, and other Nobles and Gentlemen of ancient bloud, honoured him with Knighthood of the Bath.[11]

Judge of the Com-mon Pleas.

Knight of the Bath.

He compiled this Book when he was Judge, after the fourteenth yeare of the reigne of King *E.4.* but the certain time we cannot yet attain unto, but (as we conceive) it was not long before his death, because it wanted his last hand, for that Tenant by Elegit, Statute Merchant, & Staple, were in the table of the first printed Booke, and yet he never wrote of them.[12]

When hee wrote this Booke.

Our Author in composing this Work had great furtherance, in that he flourished in the time of many famous and expert Sages of the Law. Sir Richard Newton,[13] Sir John Prisot,[14] Sir Robert Danby,[15] Sir Thomas Brian,[16] Sir Pierce Arderne,[17] Sir Richard Choke,[18] Walter Moyle,[19] William Paston,[20] Robert Danvers,[21] William Ascough,[22] and other Justices of the Court of Common Pleas: And of the Kings Bench, Sir John June,[23] Sir John Hody,[24] Sir John Fortescue,[25] Sir John Markham,[26] Sir Thomas Billing,[27] and other excellent men flourished in his time.

The de-ceased of his Con-temporar-ies.

And of worldly blessings I account it not the least that in the beginning of my study of the Lawes of this Realme, the Courts of Justice, both of Equitie & of Law, were furnished with men of excellent Judgement, Gravitie, and

---

10. *Rot. Pat. 6. E. 4.* Parte 1. M.15.
11. *15. E. 4.*
12. *14. E. 4. tit. Garranty 5.* Litt. Sect. 692. 729. & 730.
13. He died 27. *H. 6.*
14. He died 39. *H. 6.*
15. Died 11. *E. 4.*
16. Died 16. *H. 7.*
17. Died 7. *E. 4.*
18. Over lived our Author.
19. Survived him also.
20. Died 23. *H. 6.*
21. Survived our Author.
22. Died 33. *H. 61.*
23. Died 18. *H. 6.*
24. Died 20. *H. 6.*
25. Removed 1. *E. 4.*
26. Removed 8. *E. 4.*
27. Died 21. *E. 4.*

Wisdome; As in the Chancerie, Sir Nicholas Bacon, and after him Sir Thomas
Bromley. In the Exchequer Chamber, the Lord Burghley, Lord high Treasurer
of England, and Sir Walter Mildemay Chancellor of the Exchequer. In the
Kings Bench, Sir Christopher Wray, and after him Sir John Popham. In the
Common Pleas, Sir James Dyer, and after him Sir Edmund Anderson. In the
Court of Exchequer, Sir Edward Saunders, after him Sir John Jefferey, and
after him Sir Roger Manwood, men famous (amongst many others) in their
severall places, and flourished, and were all honoured and preferred by that
thrice noble and vertuous Queene Elizabeth of ever blessed memorie. Of these
reverend Judges, and others their Associates, I must ingenuously confesse, that
in her reigne I learned many things which in these Institutes I have published:
And of this Queene I may say, that as the Rose is the queene of flowers, and
smelleth more sweetly when it is pluckt from the branch: so I may say and

Queene
Elizabeth.

justifie, that shee by just desert was the Queene of Queenes, and of Kings
also, for Religion, Pietie, Magnanimitie, and Justice; who now by remembrance thereof, since Almightie God gathered her to himselfe, is of greater
honour and renowne, than when she was living in this world. You cannot
question what Rose I meane; for take the Red or the White, she was, not
onely by royall descent, and inherent Birthright, but by Rosiall Beautie also,
heire to both.

And though we wish by our labours (which are but *Canabula Legis*,[28] the
cradles of the Law) Delight and Profit to all the Students of the Law, in their
beginning of their study, (to whom the first part of the Institutes is intended)
yet principally to my loving friends, the Students of the honourable and worthy

Inner Tem-
ple. Clif-
fords Inne.
Lyons
Inne.

Societies of the Inner Temple, and Cliffords Inne, and of Lyons Inne also,
where I was sometime Reader. And yet of them more particularly to such as
have been of that famous University of Cambridge, *Alma mea mater*.[29] And
to my much honoured & beloved Allies & Friends of the Counties of Norfolke,
my deare & native Country; and of Suffolke, where I passed my middle age;
& of Buckinghamshire, where in my old age I live. In which Counties, we
out of former Collections compiled these Institutes. But now returne we againe
to our Author.

His mar-
riage.

He married with Johan one of the daughters and coheires of William Burley

28. [*Ed.:* the cradles of the law.]
29. [*Ed.:* My alma mater.]

of Broomescroft Castle in the Countie of Salop, a Gentleman of ancient descent, and bare the Armes of his Family, Argent, a Fesse Checkie Or and Azure, upon a Lion Rampant Sable, armed Gules. And by her had three sons, Sir William, Richard the Lawyer, and Thomas.

His issue.

In his lifetime, he, as a loving Father and a wise man, provided matches for these three sons, in vertuous and ancient Families, that is to say, for his son Sir William, Ellen Daughter and Coheire of Thomas Welsh Esquire, who by her had issue Johan his onely childe, married to Sir John Aston of Tixall Knight: And for the second wife of Sir William, Mary the Daughter of William Whittington Esquire, whose posteritie in Worcestershire flourish to this day. For Richard Littleton his second son, to whom he gave good possessions of inheritance, Alice daughter and heire of William Winsbury of Pilleton-hall in the Countie of Stafford, Esquire, whose posteritie prosper in Staffordshire to this day. And for Thomas his third son, to whom hee gave good possessions of inheritance, Anne daughter and heire of John Botreaux Esquire, whose posteritie in Shropshire continue prosperously to this day. Thus advanced he his posteritie, and his posteritie by imitation of his Vertues have honoured him.

The establishment of his posteritie by the matches of his three sonnes, with Vertue & good Bloud.

He gave possessions of inheritance to his younger sons, for their better advancement.

He made his last Will & Testament the 22. day of August in the 21. yeare of the reigne of King Edward the fourth, whereof he made his three sons, a Parson, a Vicar, & a Servant of his Executors, & constituted supervisor thereof, his true & faithfull friend John Alcock Doctor of Law, of the famous University of Cambridge, then Bishop of Worcester, a man of singular Pietie, Devotion, Chastitie, Temperance, & Holinesse of life, who amongst other of his pious & charitable works, founded Jesus College in Cambridge, a fit and fast friend to our honourable & vertuous Judge.

His last Will.

His Executors.

His Superviser.

He left this life in his great & good age, on the 23. day of the month of August, in the said 21. yeare of the reigne of King Edward the fourth: For it is observed for a speciall blessing of Almighty God, that few or none of that profession die *Intestatus & improles*[30] without Will & without Child; which last Will was proved the 8. of November following in the Prerogative Court of Canterbury, for that hee had *Bona notabilia*[31] in divers Dioceses. But yet our Author liveth still *in ore omnium juris prudentium.*[32]

His age.

His departure.

---

30. [*Ed.:* intestate and without issue.]

31. [*Ed.:* Notable goods; property worthy of notice, or of sufficient value to be accounted for.]

32. [*Ed.:* in the mouth of all lawyers.]

Littleton is named in *1.H.7.* and in *21.H.7.*[33] Some do hold, that it is no error either in the Reporter or Printer; but that it was Richard the son of our Author, who in those daies professed the Law, and had read upon the statute of *West. 2.*[34] *quia multaper malitiam,*[*35,36] unto whom his Father dedicated his Book; And this Richard died at Pilleton hall in Staffordsh. in *9.H.8.*

His Sepulchre.
   The body of our Author is honourably interred in the Cathedrall Church of Worcester, under a faire Tomb of Marble, with his statue of portraiture upon it, together with his own match, & the matches of some of his Ancestors, and with a memoriall of his principall titles, and out of the mouth of his statue proceedeth this praier, *Fili Dei miserere mei,*[37] which he himselfe caused to be made and finished in his life time, & remaineth to this day. His wife Johan Lady Littleton survived him, and left a great inheritance of her Father, and Ellen her Mother, daughter & heire of John Grendon Esquire, and other her Ancestors, to Sir William Littleton her son.

When this Worke was published.
   This Work was not published in print, either by our Author himselfe, or Richard his son, or any other, untill after the deceases both of our Author, and of Richard his son. For I finde it not cited in any Booke or Report, before Sir Anthony Fitzherbert cited him in his *Natura Brevium;*[38] who published that Booke of his *Natura Brevium* in *26.H.8.*[39] Which Work of our Author, in respect of the excellencie thereof, by all probabilitie should have beene cited in the Reports of the reignes of *E.5. R.3. H.7.* or *H.8.* or by S. Jermyn in his Booke of the Doctor and Student, which he published in the three and twentieth yeare of *H.8.* if in those dayes our Authors Booke had beene printed.

Nota.
   And yet you shall observe, that Time doth ever give greater authoritie to Works and Writings that are of great and profound learning, than at the first they

When this Work was first imprinted.
had. The first impression that I finde of our Authors Booke was at Roan in France by William le Tailier (for that it was written in French) *Ad instantiam,*[40]

33. 1. H. 7. fol. 27. 21. H. 7. fol. 32.h.
34. H. 2. 2. cap.12.
35. [*Ed.:* Because many through malice . . . (the opening words of the Statute of Westminster II, c. 12).]
36. See *Littleton Sect. 749.*
37. [*Ed.:* Son of God, have mercy on me.]
38. [*Ed.: The Nature of Writs.*]
39. *F.N.B. 212.c.*
40. [*Ed.: at the instance of.*]

Richardi Pinson, at the instance of Richard Pinson the Printer of King *H.8.* before the said Book of *Natura Brevium* was published; and therefore upon these and other things that we have seene, wee are of opinion, that it was first printed about the foure and twentieth yeare of the reigne of King *H.8.* since which time hee hath beene commonly cited, and (as he deserves) more and more highly esteemed.

He that is desirous to see his picture, may in the Churches of Frankley and Hales Owen see the grave and reverend countenance of our Author, the outward man, but he hath left this Booke, as a figure of that higher & nobler part, that is, of the excellent and rare endowments of his minde, especially in the profound knowledge of the fundamentall Lawes of this Realme. He that diligently reads this his excellent Work, shall behold the childe and figure of his minde, which the more often he beholds in the visiall line, and well observes him, the more shall he justly admire the judgement of our Author, and increase his owne. This only is desired, that he had written of other parts of the Law, and specially of the rules of good pleading (the heart-string of the Common Law) wherein hee excelled: for of him might the saying of our English Poet be verified; *His Picture. The figure of his Minde.*

> *Thereto he could indite and maken a thing,*
> *There was no Wight could pinch at his writing.*[41]

So farre from exception, as none could pinch at it. This skill of good pleading he highly in this Work commended to his sonne, and under his name to all other Students sons of his Law. He was learned also in that Art, which is so necessarie to a compleat Lawyer, I meane Logick, as you shall perceive by reading of these Institutes, wherein are observed his Syllogismes, Inductions, and other arguments; and his Definitions, Descriptions, Divisions, Etymologies, Derivations, Significations, and the like. Certaine it is, that when a great learned man (who is long in making) dieth, much learning dieth with him.[42] *Good pleading. Logicke.*

That which we have formerly written, that this Book is the ornament of the Common Law, and the most perfect and absolute Work that ever was written in any humane Science; and in another place,[43] that which I affirmed *The commendation of his Worke.*

41. *Chaucer.*
42. *Seneca.*
43. *Lib. 2. fo. 67. Epist. 10. li. 10.*

and tooke upon me to maintaine against all opposites whatsoever, that it is
a Work of as absolute perfection in his kinde, and as free from errour as any
book that I have knowne to be written of any humane learning, shall to the
diligent and observing Reader of these Institutes be made manifest, and we
by them (which is but a Commentarie upon him) be deemed to have fully
satisfied that, which we in former times have so confidently affirmed and
assumed. His greatest commendation, because it is of greatest profit to us, is,
that by this excellent Work, which he had studiously learned of others, he
faithfully taught all the professors of the Law in succeeding ages. The victorie
is not great to overthrow his opposites, for there was never any learned man
in the Law, that understood our Author, but concurred with me in his commendation: *Habae enim justam venerationem quicquid excellit;*[44] For whatsoever excelleth hath just honour due to it. Such as in words have endevoured
to offer him disgrace, never understood him, and therefore we leave them in
their ignorance, and wish that by these our Labors they may know the truth,
and be converted. But herein we will proceed no further: For, *Stultum est
absurdas opiniones accuratius refellere,*[45] It is meere folly to confute absurd opinions with too much curiositie.

    And albeit our Author in his three Books cites not many authorities, yet
he holdeth no opinion in any of them, but is proved and approved by these
two faithfull witnesses in matter of Law, Authoritie, and Reason. Certaine it
is, when hee raiseth any question, and sheweth the reason on both sides, the
latter opinion is his owne, and is consonant to Law. We have knowne many

Nota.

of his cases drawne in question, but never could find any judgement given
against any of them, which we cannot affirme of any other Booke or Edition
of our Law. In the reigne of our late Soveraigne Lord King James of famous
and ever blessed memorie, it came in question upon a demurrer in Law,[46]
whether the release to one trespasser should be available or no to his companion, Sir Henry Hobart that honourable Judge and great Sage of the Law,
and those reverend and learned Judges, Warburton, Winch, and Nichols his
companions, gave judgement according to the opinion of our Author, and
openly said, That they owed so great reverence to Littleton, as they would

---

44. Cicero [*Ed.:* for whatsoever excels has a just veneration.]
45. *Aristotle.* [*Ed.:* It is foolish to refute absurd opinions with minute care.]
46. Mich. 13. Jac. in Communi Banc. inter Cock & Ilnours.

not have his Case disputed or questioned: and the like you shall finde in this part of the Institutes. Thus much (though not so much as his due) have we spoken of him, both to set out his life, because he is our Author, and for the imitation of him by others of our Profession.

We have in these Institutes endevoured to open the true sense of every of his particular Cases, and the extent of everie of the same either in expresse words, or by implication, and where any of them are altered by any latter Act of Parliament, to observe the same, and wherein the alteration consisteth. Certaine it is, that there is never a period, nor (for the most part) a word, nor an &c. but affordeth excellent matter of learning. But the module of a Preface cannot expresse the observations that are made in this Worke, of the deepe Judgement and notable Invention of our Author. We have by comparison of the late and moderne impressions with the originall print, vindicated our Author from two injuries; First, from divers corruptions in the late and moderne prints, and restored our Author to his owne: Secondly, from all additions and incroachments upon him, that nothing might appeare in his worke but his owne.

What is endevoured by these Institutes.

Our hope is, that the young Student, who heretofore meeting at the first, and wrastling with as difficult termes and matter, as in many yeares after, was at the first discouraged, as many have beene, may by reading these Institutes, have the difficultie and darknesse both of the Matter, and of the Termes & words of Art in the beginnings of his study facilitated & explained unto him, to the end he may proceed in his study cheerfully, and with delight; and therefore I have termed them Institutes, because my desire is, they should institute and instruct the studious, and guide him in a ready way to the knowledge of the nationall Lawes of England.

The benefit of these Institutes.

Wherefore called Institutes.

This part we have (and not without president) published in English, for that they are an Introduction to the knowledge of the nationall lawes of the Realme; a work necessary, and yet heretofore not undertaken by any, albeit in all other professions there are the like. Wee have left our Author to speake his owne language, & have translated him into English, to the end that any of the Nobilitie, or Gentrie of this Realme, or of any other estate, or profession whatsoever, that will be pleased to read him & these Institutes, may understand the language wherein they are written.

Wherefore published in English.

I cannot conjecture that the generall communicating of these Lawes in the English tongue can worke any inconvenience, but introduce great profit, seeing that *Ignorantia Juris non excusat,* Ignorance of the Law excuseth not. And

Regula.

herein I am justified by the wisdome of a Parliament; the words whereof be,[47] *That the Lawes and Customes of this Realme the rather should be reasonably perceived and knowne, and better understood by the tongue used in this Realme, and by so much everie man might the better governe himselfe without offending of the Law, and the better keepe, save, and defend his heritage and possessions. And in divers Regions and Countries where the King, the Nobles, and other of the said Realme have beene, good governance and full right is done to everie man, because that the Lawes and Customes be learned and used in the Tongue of the* *Regula.* *Countrey:* as more at large by the said Act, and the purview thereof may appeare: *Et neminem oportet esse sapientiorem Legibus,*[48] No man ought to be wiser than the Law.

And true it is that our Books of Reports and Statutes, in ancient times were written in such French as in those times was commonly spoken and written by the French themselves. But this kind of French that our Author hath used

Our Authors kinde of French. is most commonly written and read, and verie rarely spoken, and therefore cannot be either pure, or well pronounced. Yet the change thereof (having been so long accustomed) should be without any profit, but not without great danger and difficultie: For so many ancient Termes and words drawne from that legall French, are growne to be *Vocabula artis,* Vocables of Art, so apt & significant to expresse the true sense of the Lawes, & are so woven into the lawes themselves,[49] as it is in a manner impossible to change them, neither ought legall termes to be changed.

In Schoole Divinitie, and amongst the Glossographers and Interpreters of the Civill and Canon Lawes, in Logick and in other liberall Sciences, you shall meet with a whole Army of words, which cannot defend themselves *in Bello Grammaticali,* in the Grammaticall Warre, and yet are more significant, compendious, and effectuall to expresse the true sense of the matter, than if they were expressed in pure Latine.

Wherefore called the first part. This Worke wee have called The first part of the Institutes, for two causes: First, for that our Author is the first booke that our Student taketh in hand. Secondly, for that there are some other parts of Institutes not yet published, (*viz.*) The second part being a Commentarie upon the Statute of *Magna*

47. 36. E. 3. *cap. 25.*
48. [*Ed.:* No one ought to be wiser than the laws.]
49. 36. E.3. ubi supr.

Charta, Westm. I. and other old Statutes. The third part treateth of Criminall causes and Pleas of the Crowne: which three parts we have by the goodnesse of Almightie God already finished. The fourth part wee have purposed to be of the Jurisdiction of Courts; but hereof we have onely collected some materialls towards the raising of so great and honourable a Building. Wee have by the goodnesse and assistance of Almightie God brought this twelfth Worke to an end: In the eleven Bookes of our *Reports* wee have related the opinions and judgements of others; but herein we have set downe our owne.

Before I entred into any of these parts of our Institutes, I acknowledging mine owne weaknesse and want of judgement to undertake so great Workes, directed my humble Suit and Prayer to the Author of all Goodnesse and Wisdome, out of the Booke of *Wisdome;* [50] *Pater & Deus misericordiae, da mihi fedium tuarum assistriceur sapientiam, mitte eam de Coelis sanctis tuis & à sede magnitudinis tuae, ut mecum sit & mecum laboret, ut sciam quid acceptum sit apud te;* Oh Father and God of mercie, give me wisdome, the Assistant of thy seats; Oh, send her out of thy holy Heavens, and from the seat of thy Greatnesse, that shee may be present with mee and labour with mee, that I may know what is pleasing unto thee, *Amen.*

Our Author hath divided his whole Worke into three Bookes: In his first he hath divided Estates in Lands and Tenements, in this manner; For; *Res per divisionem melius aperiuntur.* [51,52]

Our Author dealt onely with the Estates and termes abovesaid; Somewhat Wee shall speake of Estates by force of certaine Statutes, as of Statute Merchant, Statute Staple, and *Elegit,* [53] (whereof our Author intended to have written) and likewise to Executors to whom lands are devised for payment of debts, and the like.

I shall desire, [54] that the learned Reader will not conceive any opinion against any part of this painfull and large Volume, untill hee shall have advisedly read over the whole, and diligently searched out and well considered of the severall Authorities, Proofes, and Reasons which wee have cited and set downe for warrant and confirmation of our opinions thorowout this whole worke.

---

50. Lib. Sap. ca. 9. Vers. 4.10.

51. Bracton.

52. [*Ed.:* Things are opened better by division.]

53. [*Ed.:* "He has Chosen"; a writ of execution for a debt.]

54. *Regula. Incivile est, parte una perspecta, totare non cognita, de ea judicare.* [*Ed.:* It is improper to scrutinize one part without knowing the whole and from that to reach a conclusion.]

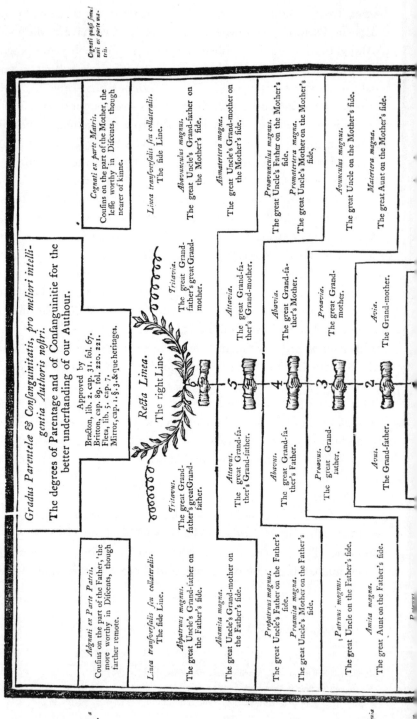

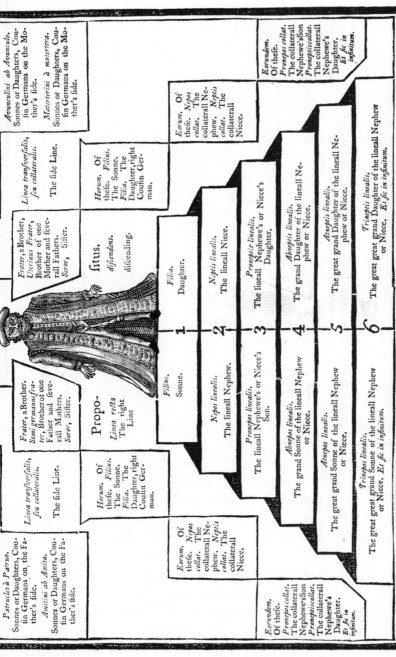

Place this next before Folio 18. b.

A Figure of the division of Possessions.

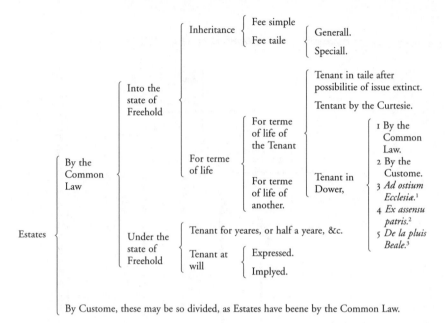

By Custome, these may be so divided, as Estates have beene by the Common Law.

1. [*Ed.:* At the door of the church.]
2. [*Ed.:* By or with the consent of the father, another form of Dower.]
3. [*Ed.:* of the most fair, another form of Dower.]

Mine advice to the Student is, That before hee read any part of our Commentaries upon any Section, that first he read againe and againe our Author himselfe in that Section, and doe his best endevours, first of himselfe, and then by conference with others, (which is the life of Study) to understand it, and then to read our Commentarie thereupon, and no more at any one time, than he is able with delight to beare away, and after to meditate thereon, which is the life of reading. But of this Argument we have for the better direction of our Student in his Study, spoken in our Epistle to our first Booke of *Reports*.

And albeit the Reader shall not at any one day (doe what he can) reach to the meaning of our Author, or of our Commentaries, yet let him no way discourage himselfe, but proceed; for on some other day, in some other place, that doubt will be cleared. Our Labours herein are drawne out to this great Volume, for that our Author is twice repeated, once in French, and againe in English.

Section 1
Fee Simple

| Tenant in Fee simple is hee which hath Lands or Tenements to hold to him and his heires for ever. And it is called in Latine, *Feodum Simplex*, for *Feodum* is the same that Inheritance is, and *Simplex* is as much to say, as lawfull or pure. And so *Feodum simplex* signifies a lawfull or pure Inheritance. For if a man would purchase lands or tenements in fee simple, it behoveth him to have these words in his purchase, To have and to hold to him and to his Heires: for these words (his Heires) make the Estate of the Inheritance. For if a man purchase Lands by these words, To have and to hold to him for ever; or by these words, To have and to hold to him and his Assignes for ever: in these two cases hee hath but an estate for terme of life, for that there lack these words (his Heires) which words onely make an Estate of Inheritance in all Feoffments and Grants.

"Tenant,"

In Latine *Tenens,* is derived of the verb *Teneo* and hath in the Latin five significations.[1] 1. It signifies the estate of the Land, as when the Tenant in a *Praecipe* of land pleads, *Quod non tener,*[2] etc. this is as much as to say, That hee hath not seisin of the Freehold of the Land in question. And in this sense doth our Author take it in this place: & therefore he saith, tenant in fee simple is hee which hath lands to hold to him & his heires. 2. It signifieth the Tenure of the service whereby the lands & tenements beene holden, and in this sense it is said in the Writ of right, *Quae clamat tenere de te per liberum seruitium, &c.*[3] And in this signification hee is called a Tenant or holder,[4] because all the lands & tenements in England in the hands of subjects, are holden mediately or immediately of the King. For in the law of England we have not properly, *Allodium,*[5] That is,[6] any Subjects Land that is not holden, unlesse you will take *Allodium,* for *Ex. solido,* as it is often taken in the Booke of Domesday: and tenents in Fee simple are there called *Alodarii* or *Aloarii,* And he is called

---

1. Vide Sect. 85.
2. [*Ed.:* that he does not hold, etc.]
3. [*Ed.:* which he claims to hold of you by free service, etc.]
4. 8. H. 7. 12. 18. E. 3. 35. 24. B. 3. 65, 66. 44 E. 3. 5. 48. E. 3. 9.
5. [*Ed.:* a free inheritance. The word appears Danish in origin, from the Lex Salica.]
6. Mir. des Just. c.1. sect. 3. Customes de Normandy, cap. 28.

a Tenant, because hee holdeth of some superior Lord by some service.[7] And therefore the King in this sense cannot be said to be a Tenant, because hee hath no superior but God Almightie; *Praedium domini: regis est directum dominium cuius nullus Author est nisi Deus.* And[8] as Bracton saith, *Omnis quidem sub eo, & ipse sub nullo, nisi tantum sub Deo.* The posessions of the King are called *Sacra patrimonia.* & *Dominica Coronae Regis.* But though a Subject hath not properly *Directum,*[9] yet hath hee *utile Dominium.*[10] Of these Tenants our Author, speaketh in his second Booke. Also Tenere signifieth performance, as in the Writ of Covenant, *Quod teneat conventionem,* that is, That he hold or performe his Covenant. And likewise it signifieth to be bound, as it is said in everie common Obligation, *teneri & firmiter obligari.*[11] Lastly, It signifieth to deeme or judge, as in 38. Ed. 3c. 4. It shall be holden for none (that is) judged or deemed for none, and so wee commonly say, it is holden in our Bookes. And these severall significations doe properly belong to our Tenant in Fee simple. For he hath the estate of the Land, he holdeth the land of some superiour Lord, and is to performe the services due, and thereunto he is bounden by doome and judgement of Law. Of the severall estates of Land, our Author treateth in his first booke, and beginneth with Fee simple, because all other estates and interests are derived out of the same.

"Fee Simple."

Fee commeth of the French *Fief,* (i)[12] *praedium beneficiarium,*[13] and legally signifieth Inheritance, as our Author himselfe hereafter expoundeth it. And Simple is added, for that it is descendible to his heires generally, that is, simply, without restraint to the heires of his body, or the like. *Feodum est quod quis tenet ex quacunque causa, sive sit tenementum, sive redditus, &c.* In Domesday it is called *Feudum.* (a)[14] Of Fee simple, it is commonly holden, that there be

---

7. Le st. de 16. R. 2. cap. 5. 14-El.y. 313. a 1 Co. 47. in Alton Woods case.

8. Bract. lib. 1. cap. 8.

9. [*Ed.:* control.]

10. [*Ed.:* control of the use.]

11. [*Ed.:* duty of holding and rents.]

12. Brit. fo. 83. 207, 208. Fleta lib. 5. cap. 5 & cap. 8. Bract. lib. 4. 263. lib. 3 Domesday. Mir. des Just cap. 2. sect. 15. 17. Bract. lib. 2. cap. 5. 6. 7. Brit. cap. 84. fol 89. Flet. lib. 3. cap. 2. 8 & 9. & lib. 5. cap. 5.

13. [*Ed.:* benefit of the estate.]

14. (a) Bract. fo. 263. & 207. Pl. Com. in Wals. cas. 7. H. 4. 46. 8. H. 4. 15. 18 H. 8. b. 27. Ass. 33.

three kinds, viz. fee simple absolute, fee simple conditionall, and fee simple qualified, or a base fee. But the more genuine and apt division, were to divide fee, that is, Inheritance, into three parts, viz. Simple as absolute, Conditionall, and qualified or base. For this word (Simple) properly excludeth both conditions and limitations, that defeat or abridge the fee.* [15] Hereby appeareth, that fee in our legall understanding signifieth, that the land belongs to us & our heires, in respect whereof the owner is said to be seised in fee, and in this sense the King is said to be seised in fee. (b)[16] It is also taken, as it is holden of another by service, and that belongeth onely to the Subject; *Item dicitur feodum alio modo eius qui alium feoffat, & qod quis tenet ab alio, ut si sit qui dicat, talis tenet de me tot feoda per servitium militare.* And Fleta saith, *Poterit unus tenere in feodo quoad servitia, sicut dominus capitalis, & non in Dominico, alius in feodo & dominico, & non in servitio, sicut libere tenens alicuius*[17] (c)[18] And therefore if a stranger claims a Seigniorie, and disteine and avow for the service, the Tenant may plead, That the Tenancie is *extra feodum, &c.* of him (that is) out of the Seigniorie, or not holden of him that claimeth it, but he cannot plead *Hors de fon fee,* unlesse he take the tenancie, that is, the state of the Land upon him. Of fee in the first sense our Author treateth in this first Booke; and as is taken in the second sense, in his second booke: and of the third you shall read in our Author, Sect. 13, 643, 644, 645. and plentifully in our books quoted in the margent.

"Lands or Tenements."

Here is to be observed, That a man may have a fee simple in three kinds of hereditaments, viz. Reall, Personall, and Mixt: Reall, as Lands and Tenements, whereof our Author here speaketh: Personall, King Edward the first in the

18. Ass 5. 18 E.3. 46. 24. E. 3. 2 8. 9. E. 4. 18. 16. H. 7 4. d. 106. 3. Account 56.22 R. 2 Disc. 50. 12 E. 4. 3. 15 E. 4. 8. Dy. 8 E1. 252, 253. 12 H.8.8. 4 H.7.2. The Case of a person which hath a qualified fee, see in the title of Desc.

15. (*) Vide sect 4.

16. (b) Bract. lib. 4 fo. 263. Flet. lib. 5. cap.5. Brit. fo. 205.207.

17. [*Ed.:* Fee is also spoken of in another way, in respect of one who enfeoffs another, and that which he holds of another, as where one says, such a person holds of me so many fees by knight-service. (And Fleta saith). One may hold in fee with respect to the services, like a chief lord, and not in defense demesne; and another may hold in fee and demesne and not in service, like those holding freely of another.]

18. (c) 2 Ass. p. 4. 12. Ass. 38 12. E. 3. tit Hors de son fee. 28. 28. Ass. 41. 7. H. 4. 30. 2. H. 6. 1.

thirteenth yeare of his Reigne,[19] *Concessit Edmundo fratri suo charissimo, quod ipse & haeredes sui habeant ad requisitionem suam in Cancellaria nostra & haer-* [2 a] *edum nostrorum Justi-\-ciarios ad placita forestarum quas idem Frater noster habet ex dono domini Regis Henrici parris nostri secundum assiss. forestae tenend; &c.*[20] In this case the grantee and his heires had a personall inheritance in making of a request to have Letters patents of Commission to have Justices assigned to him to heare and determine the pleas of the forrests, and concerneth neither lands or tenements. And so it is if an Annuity be granted to a man and his heires, It is a fee simple personall, *& sic de similibus.* And lastly hereditaments mixt both of the realty and personality. As the Abbot of Whitbie in the County of Yorke having a forrest of the gift of William of Percie founder of that Abby, and by the Charters of King John and of other his progenitors, King Henry the third did grant[21] *Abbati & conventui de Whitbye quod ipsi & eorum successores in perpetuum habeant viridarios suos proprios de libertate sua de Whitb. eligend' de cetero in pleno com' Eborum prout moris est ad responsiones & presentationes, faciend' de transgressionibus quas amodo fieri continget de venatione infra metas forestae suae de Whitbye quam habent ex donatione Willi. de Percey, & Alani de Percey, filii ejus, & redditione & concessione domini Johan. quondam regis Angliae patris nostri & confirmatione nostra coram justiciariis nostris itinerantibus ad placita forestae in partibus illis & non alibi sicut viridarii forestae nostrae hujusmodi responsiones & presentationes facere debent, & consueverunt. Et si contingat aliquos forinsecos qui non sunt de libertate predictorum Abbatis & conventus transgressionem facere de venatione infra metas forestae predictae quos predicti viridarii attachiare non possunt: Volumus & concedimus pro nobis & heredibus nostris quod hujusmodi transgressores per Justicarios forestae nostrae ultra Trentam attachientur ad praesentationem viridariorum praedict. ad respondendum, inde coram justiciariis nostris itinerantibus ad placita forestae nostrae in partibus illis cum ibid. ad placitandum venerint prout secundum assisam & consuetudinem forestae fuerint faciend.*[22]

19. Rot. pat. 13. E. 1.

20. [*Ed.:* Granted to Edmund, his dearly beloved brother, that he and his heirs should have, at their request in the Chancery of us and our heirs, justices to hold pleas of the forest according to the assize of the forest, which our same brother has by the gift of the lord King Henry our father, etc.]

21. Ro. Pat. an. 47. H. 3. Itin. Pickering. 8. E. 3. Ro. 42.

22. [*Ed.:* To the abbot and convent of Whitby, that they and their successors thenceforth for ever should

Which Charter was pleaded upon the Claime made by the Abbot of Whitbye before Willoughby, Hungerford, and Hanbury, Justices in Eire in the forrest of Pickering, which Eire began Anno 8.Edw.3. And these before them were allowed. And when the King createth an Earle of such a county or other place, To hold that dignity to him and his heires, This Dignity is personall, and also concerneth lands and tenements. But of this matter more shall be said in the next Chapter, Sect. 14. & 15.

"Called in Latine, *feum sinplex*, for *Feodum* is the same that Inheritance is,"

Here[23] Littleton himselfe teacheth the signification of *feodum;* according to that which hath bin said, which onely is to be applied to fee simple pure and absolute. And this and all his other interpretations of words and Etymologies throughout all his three bookes (wherein the studious Reader will observe many) are perspicuous, and ever *per notiora & nunquam ignotum per ignotius,*[24] and are most necessary, for *ignoratis terminis ignoratur & ars.*[25,26]

"*Simplex* is as much to say, as lawfull or pure."

Hereof hee treateth onely in this place. And Litt. saith well, that *Simplex idem est quod purum. Simplex enim dicitur quia sine plicis; & purum dicitur, quod*

---

have their own verderers to be chosen from their liberty of Whitby in the full county assembly of York, as is customary, to make answers and presentments of trespasses which should hereafter occur in hunting within the bounds of his forest of Whitby, which they have by the gift of William de Percy and Alan de Percy his son, and by the render and grant of the lord John, our father, late king of England, and by our confirmation, before our justices in eyre for pleas of the forest in those parts, and not elsewhere, just as the verderers of our forest ought and are accustomed to make such answers and presentments. And if it should happen that any outsiders, who are not of the liberty of the aforesaid abbot and convent, commit any trespass in hunting within the bounds of the aforesaid forest, whom the aforesaid verderers cannot attach, we will and grant for ourself and our heirs that such trespassers shall be attached by the justices of our forests beyond the Trent, at the presentment of the aforesaid verderers, to answer there before our justices in eyre for pleas of our forest in those parts, when they come there to plead, as to what should be done in accordance with the assize and custom of the forest.]

23. Bract. lib. 4 cap. 9. fo. 263. Brit. cap. 32. & 79.

24. [*Ed.:* using careful observation and never overlooking those things one does not know.]

25. [*Ed.:* if the terms are not understood, the art itself is not understood.]

26. For interpretation of words and Etymologies, Vid. Sect. 9. 18. 95. 116. 119. 135. 154 164. 174. 184. 186. 194. 204. 234. 267. 268. 332. 337. 424. 520. 592. 645. 689. 733.

est merum & solum sine additione. Simplex donatio & pura est ubi nulla addita est conditio siue modus, simplex enim datur quod nullo additamento datur.[27,28]

"a lawfull or pure Inheritance."

And therefore it is well said,[29] *quod donationum alia simplex & pura, quae nullo jure civili vel naturali cogente, nullo precedente metu vel interveniente ex mera gratuitaque libertate donantis procedit, & ubi nullo casu velit donator ad se reverti quod dedit, alia sub modo conditione vel ob causam, in quibus casibus non proprie sit donatio cum donator, id ad se reverti velit, sed quedam potius feodalis dimissio, alia absoluta & larga, alia stricta & coarctata sicut certis heredibus quibusdam a successoribus exclusis, &c.*[30] And therefore seeing fee simple is *hereditas legitima vel pura,*[31] it plainly confirmeth that the division of fee is by his authority rather to be divided as is aforesaid than fee simple. And he saith well in the disjunctive *legitima vel pura,* for every fee simple is not *Legitimum.* For a disseisor, abator, intruder, usurper &c. have a fee simple, but it is not a lawfull fee. So as every man that hath a fee simple, hath it either by right or by wrong. If by right, then he hath it either by purchase or discent. If by wrong, then either by disseisin, intrusion, abatement, usurpation, &c. In this Chapter he treateth onely of a lawfull fee simple, and divideth the same as is aforesaid.

"For if a man would purchase."

Persons capable of purchase who have ability to grant.

Persons capable of purchase are of two sorts, persons naturall created of God, as I. S. I. N. &c. and persons incorporate or politique created by the policy

---

27. Bract. lib. 2. cap. 39. fo. 92. 62. b. lib. 4. cap. 28. Fleta. lib. 3. cap. 8. Bract. lib. 2. cap. 5, &c. Britt. cap. 34.

28. [*Ed.:* Simple is the same as pure. And simple is so called because it is *sine plicis* (without folds); and something is called pure when it is absolute and single, without addition. A simple and pure donation is where no condition or qualification is added; for something is given simply when it is given with no addition.]

29. Fleta, lib. 3. ca. 3. Plowd. 58.b.

30. [*Ed.:* One kind of gift is simple and pure, not constrained by civil or natural law, with no fear preceding it or intervening, which proceeds from the pure and gratuitous liberality of the giver, and where the donor does not wish the thing given to revert to himself in any situation; another is qualified, upon condition, or for a cause, in which cases it is not properly a donation, since the donor wishes it to revert to him, but rather a certain feudal demise; another is absolute and large; another strict and forced, as when it is to certain heirs, excluding others from the succession, etc.]

31. [*Ed.:* a lawful or pure inheritance.]

of man, (and therefore they are called bodies politique) and these be of two sorts, viz, either sole, or aggregate of many: againe aggregate of many, either of all persons capable, or of one[32] person capable, and the rest incapable or dead in law, as in the Chapter of Discontinuance, Sect. 57. shall be shewed. Some men have capacitie to purchase, but not abilitie to hold.[33] Some capacity to purchase and abilitie to hold, or not to hold, at the election of them or others. Some capacity to take and to hold. Some neither capacity to take nor to hold. And some specially disabled to take some particular thing.

If an alien Christian or infidell purchase houses, lands, tenements, or hereditaments to him | and his heires, albeit he can have no heires, yet he is of capacitie to take a fee simple but not to hold. For upon an office found, the king shall have it by his prerogative, of whomsoever[34] the land is holden. And so it is if the alien doth purchase land and die, the law doth cast the freehold and inheritance upon the King. If an alien purchase any estate of freehold in houses, lands, tenements, or hereditaments, the King upon office found shall have them. If an alien be made Denizen and purchase lands and die without issue, the lord of the fee shall have the escheat, and not the King.[35] But as to a lease for yeares, there is a diversitie betweene a lease for yeares of a house for the habitation of a marchant stranger being an alien, whose king is in league with ours, and a lease for yeares of lands, meadowes, pastures, woods, and the like. For if he take a lease for yeares of lands, meadowes, &c. upon office found, the king shall have it. But of a house for habitation he may take a lease for yeares as incident to Commercety, for without habitation hee cannot merchandize or trade. But if he depart, or relinquish the realme, the king shall have the lease. So it is if he die possessed thereof, neither his Executors or administrators, shall have it, but the king: for he had it only for habitation as necessary to his trade or traffique, and not for the benefit of his Executor or adminstrator. But if the alien be no merchant, then the king shall have the lease for yeares, albeit it were for his habitatation, and so it is if he be an alien enemie. And all this was so resolved by the Judges assembled together for that purpose in the case of Sir James Croft, Pasch. 29. of the reigne of Queene Elizabeth.[36] Also if a man commit felony, and after purchase lands and after

[2 b]

32. Vid. Sect. 57.
33. 11. Eliz. Dier 283. 11. H. 4. 20 & 26. 7. E. 4. 29.
34. 32. Hen. 6. 23. Pl. Com. 483.
35. 5. Mar. Br. tit. Denizen. 22.
36. Pasch. 29. Eliz. in Sir James Croft's case. 49. Ass. pl. 2. 49. E. 3. 11.

is attainted, he had capacitie to purchase but not to hold it, for in that case
the Lord of the fee shall have the Escheat. And if a man be attainted of felony,
yet he hath capacity to purchase to him and to his heires, albeit he can have
no heire, but he cannot hold it, for in that case the king shall have it by his
prerogative, and not the Lord of the fee, for a man attainted hath no capacity
to purchase (being a man *civiliter mortuus*[37]) but onely for the benefit of the
king, no more than the alienee hath. If any sole Corporation or aggregate of
many, either Ecclesiasticall or temporall (for the words of the statute be *Si
quis religiosus vel alius*[38]) purchase Lands or Tenements in fee, they have capacity to take but not to retaine (unlesse they have a sufficient Licence in that
behalfe) for within the yeare after the alienation, the next Lord of the fee may
enter, and if he doe not, then the next immediate lord from time to time to
have half a yeare, and for default of all the mesne Lords, then the king to have
the land so aliened for ever, which is to be understood of such inheritance as
may be holden. But of such inheritances as are not holden, as Villeins, rents
charges, commons, and the like, the king shall have them presently by a favourable interpretation of the statute. An Annuity granted to them is not
mortmaine,[39] because it chargeth the person onely. Some have said that it is
called mortmaine *Manus mortua, quia possessio corum est immortalis, manus
propossessione, & mortua pro immortali*,[40] and the rather for that by the lawes
and statutes of the realme, all Ecclesiastiall persons are restrained to alien.[41]
Others say it is called *manus mortua per Antiphrasin*,[42] because bodies politique
and corporate never die. Others say that it is called Mortmaine by resemblance
to the holding of a mans hand that is ready to die, for that he then holdeth
he letteth not goe till he be dead. These and such others are framed out of
wit and invention, but the true cause of the name, and the meaning thereof,
was taken from the effects, as it is expressed in the statute it selfe,[43] *per quod
quae servitia ex hujusmodi feodis debentur, & quae ad defensionem regni ab initio*

---

37. [*Ed.*: Civilly dead; dead in the view of the law.]

38. [*Ed.*: If any religious or other person.]

39. Magna Charta. cap. 36. 7. E. 1. stat. 2. de. religiosis. W. 2. 13. E. 1. cap. 33. 15. R. 2. cap. 5. 23. H.
3. Ass. p. 17. Brit. fo. 32. Fleta, lib. 3. cap. 4. &. 5. 19. E. 2. tit. Vil. 1 34. 29. E. 3 Ibid. 13. 21. E. 3. 5. 4.
H. 6. 9. 19. H. 66. 3. 65. 3. E. 4. 14. 19. E. 3.

40. Mortm. 8. 34. H. 6. 37. 19. H. 6. 63. (plowd. 502.a.) 7. E. 4. 14. [*Ed.*: dead hand, because the
possession thereof is immortal, 'hand' meaning the possession, and 'dead' meaning immortal.]

41. Pl. Com. 193. in Wroteslyes case.

42. [*Ed.*: dead hand, by antiphrasis.]

43. Le statut de Religiosis. 7. E. 1. st. 2.

provisa fuerunt indebite subtrahuntur & capitales domini eschaetas suas amit-tunt,[44] so as the lands were said to come to dead hands as to the Lords, for that by alienation in Mortmaine, they lost wholly their escheats, and in effect their knights services for the defence of the Realme, Wards, Marriages, Reliefes, and the like, and therefore was called a dead hand, for that a dead hand yeeldeth no service.

I passe over Villeins or Bondmen, who have power to purchase lands, but not to reteyne them against their Lords, because you shall reade at large of them in their proper place in the Chapter of Villenage.

An infant or minor (whome we call any that is under the age of 21 yeares) have without consent of any other, capacity to purchase, for it is intended for his benefit, and at his full age he may either agree thereunto, and perfect it, or without any cause to be alleged, Waive or disagree to the purchase, and so may his heires after him, if he agree not thereunto after his full age.

A man of non sane memory may without the consent of any other, purchase lands, but hee himselfe cannot waive it, but if he die in his madnesse, or after his memory recovered without agreement thereunto, his heire may Waive and disagree to the state, without any cause shewed, and so of an Ideot. But if the man of non sane memory, recover his memory, and agree unto it, it is una-voydable.

If an Abbot purchase lands to him and his successors without the consent of his Covent, he himselfe cannot Waive it, but his successor may upon just cause shewed,[45] as if a greater rent were reserved thereupon than the value of the land, or the like, but he cannot Waive it unlesse it be upon just cause, *et sic de similibus praelatus Ecclesiae suae conditioné meliorare potest, deteriorare nequit.*[46] And in another place he saith,[47] *Est enim Ecclesia ejusdem conditionis, quae fungitur vice minoris.*[48]

| But no Simile holds in everie thing, according to the ancient saying,   [3 a]
Nullum simile quatuor pedibus currit.[49] (a)[50] An hermaphrodite may purchase

---

44. [*Ed.:* whereby the services which are owed from such fees, and which were originally provided for the defence of the realm, are unduly withdrawn, and the chief lords lose their escheats.]

45. 41.43. Ass. p. 23.

46. [*Ed.:* a prelate of the church may improve the condition of his church but not worsen it.]

47. Bract. lib. 2. fo. 12. &. 32.

48. [*Ed.:* A church also is in the same condition, because it has the status of a minor.]

49. [*Ed.:* No simile runs upon four feet.]

50. (a) 1. H. 7. 16. 7. H. 4. 17. 18. H. 6. 8. 9. E. 3. 30 15. E. 4. fol. 1. b. 27. H 8. 24.

according to that Sex which prevaileth. A feme covert cannot take any thing of the gift of her husband, but is of capacitie to purchase of others without the consent of her husband. And of this opinion was Littleton in our Books, and in this Booke Sect 677. but her husband may disagree thereunto, and divest the whole estate, but if he neither agree nor disagree, the purchase is good; but after his death, albeit her husband agreed thereunto, yet shee may without any cause to be alleaged waive the same, and so may her heires also, if after the decease of her husband she her selfe agreed not thereunto.

(b)[51] A wife (Uxor) is a good name of Purchase, without a Christian name, and so it is, if a Christian name be added and mistaken, as Em for Emelya, &c. for *utile per inutile non vitiatur*.[52] But the Queene, the Consort of the King of England, is an exempt person from the King by the Common Law, and is of abilitie, and capacitie to purchase and grant without the King. Of which see more at large, Sect. 206.

(c)[53] The Parishioners or Inhabitants, or *probi homines* of Dale, or the Church wardens, are not capable to purchase lands, but goods they are, unlesse it were in ancient time when such grants were allowed.

(d)[54] An ancient grant by the Lord to the Commoners in such a waste, that a way leading to their Common should not be streightened, was good, but otherwise it is of such a grant at this day. (e)[55] And so in ancient time a grant made to a Lord, & *hominibus suis tam liberis quam nativis*,[56] or the like, was good, but they are not of capacitie to purchase by such a name at this day. But yet at this day if the King grant to a man to have the goods and cattels *de hominibus suis,* or *de tenentibus suis,* or *de residentibus, infra feodum, &c.*[57] it is good, for there they are not named as purchasers or takers, but for another mans benefit, who hath capacitie to purchase or take. (f)[58] And regularly it

51. (b) A name of purchase. 2. H. 4. 25. 11. H. 5. 8. 46. E. 3. 22. 12. Ass. 18. 30. E. 3. 18. F. N. B. 97. a. 1. Ass. 11. 13. Estoppel. 231.

52. [*Ed.:* The useful is not vitiated by the useless.]

53. (c) 12. H. 7. 8. 37. H. 6. 30. 10. H. 4. 3. b.

54. (d) 32. E. 3. barre 261.

55. (e) 33. E 3. grant 83. 18. E. 3. 50. 12. Ass. 35. 14. H. 6. 12. 34. Ass. p. 11. 40. Ass. p. 21.

56. [*Ed.:* and to his men, both freemen and niefs (serfs).]

57. [*Ed.:* of his men, (or) of his tenants, (or) of residents within the fee, etc.]

58. (f) Bract. lib. 4. tract. 1. ca. 20. Britton fol 121. 122. 3. E. 3. 78. 25. E. 3. 43. 26. Ass. 61. 30. Ass. 16. 46. E. 3. 22. 39. E. 3. 17. 3. H. 6. 25. 19. H. 6. 2. 30. H. 6. 1. 34. H. 6. 19. 11. H. 4. 27. 9. E. 4. 29. 5. E. 4 46. 65. 14. H. 7. 11. 20. Eliz. Dier 259. 8. E. 3. 436. 20 3. 25. 1. H. 4. E3. 5. H. 6. 26. 19. H. 6. 2. 34. H. 6. 19. 5 E. 4. 55. 27. H. 8. 11. 1. H. 5. 5 18. E. 3. 32. 27. E. 3. 85. 8. E. 3. 427. 7. H. 6. 29. 9 H. 5. 9.

is requisite that the Purchaser be named by the name of Baptisme and his surname, and that speciall heed bee taken to the name of Baptisme, for that a man cannot have two names of Baptisme as he may have divers surnames. (g)[59] And it is not safe in writs, pleadings, grants, &c. to translate surnames into Latine. As if the surname of one be Fitzwilliam, or Williamson, if he translate him to filius Willi. if in truth his father had any other Christian name than William, the Writ, &c. shall abate, for Fitzwilliam or Williamson is his surname whatsoever Christian name his father had, therefore the Lawyer never translates surnames. And yet in some cases, though the name of Baptisme be mistaken, (as in the case before put of the wife) the grant is good.

So it is if lands be given to Robert Earle of Pembroke where his name is Henry, to George Bishop of Norwich, where his name is John, and so of an Abbot, &c. for in these and the like cases there can be but one of that Dignitie or name. And therefore such a grant is good, albeit the name of Baptisme be mistaken. If by Licence lands be given to the Deane and Chapter of the holy and individed Trinitie of Norwich, this is good, although the Deane bee not named by his proper name, if there were a Deane at the time of the grant, but in pleading he must shew his proper name. And so on the other side, If the Deane and Chapter make a Lease without naming the Deane by his proper name, the Lease is good, if there were a Deane at the time of the Lease, but in pleading the proper name of the Deane must be shewed, and so to the Booke of 18.Edw.4. to be intended for the same Judges in 13.Edw.4. held the grant good to a Mayor, Alderman, and Commonaltie, albeit the Mayor was not named by his proper name, but in pleading it must be shewed, as it is there also holden. If a man be baptized by the name of Thomas, and after at his Confirmation by the Bishop he is named John, he may purchase by the name of his Confirmation. And this was the case of Sir Francis Gawdye, late chiefe Justice of the Court of Common Pleas, whose name of Baptisme was Thomas, and his name of Confirmation Francis, and that name of Francis by the advice of all the Judges in Anno 36.Hen.8. hee did beare, and after used in all his purchases and grants. (h)[60] And this doth agree with our ancient

---

59. (g) 40. E. 3. 22. Fitzwilliam. 24 E. 3. 64. Fitzjohn. 39. E. 3. 24. Fitzrobert. 27. E. 3. 85. tit. grant, 67. 18. E. 323, 24. 18. E. 4. 8b. 14. H. 7. 31. 32. 13. E. 4. 8. 5. E. 3. Vouch 179. 37. E. 3. 85. where the proper name is mistaken.

60. (h) 22. R. 2. briefe. 936. 12. R. 2. foeffments 58. 9. E. 3. 14. 46. E. 3. 21. 3. H. 6. 26. 34. H. 6. 19. 1. H. 7. 29. 5. E. 2 briefe. 741. 14. H. 7. 11.

Bookes, where it is holden that a man may have divers names at divers times, but not divers Christian names. And the Court said, that it may be that a woman was baptized by the name of Anable and fortie yeares after she was confirmed by the name of Douce, and then her name was changed, and after she was to be named Douce, and that all purchases, &c. made by her by the name of Baptisme before her Confirmation remaine good, a matter not much in use, nor requisite to be put *in ure,* but yet necessarie to be knowne. (i)[61] But purchases are good in many cases by a knowne name, or by a certaine description of the person without either surname, or name of Baptisme, as *Uxori I. S.* as hath beene said, or *primogenito filio,* or *secundo genito filio, &c.* or *filio natu minimo I.S.* or *seniori puero,* or *omnibus filiis* or *filiabus I.S.* or *omnibus liberis seu exitibus* of I.S. or to the right heires of I.S.[62]

(k)[63] But if a man doe infranchise a Villeine, *cum tota sequela sua,*[64] that is not sufficient to infranchise his children borne before, for the incertaintie of the word *sequela.* (l)[65] But regularly in Writs, the Demandant or Tenant is to be named by his Christian name and Surname, unlesse it be in cases of some Corporations or Bodies politique.

[3 b] ǀ (a)[66] A bastard having gotten a name by reputation may purchase by his reputed or knowne name to him and his heires, although he can have no heire but of his body. A man makes a lease to B. for life, remainder to the eldest issue male of B. & the heires males of his body. B. hath issue a bastard son, he shall not take the remainder, because in Law he is not his issue,[67] for *qui ex damnato coitu nascuntur inter liberos non computentur.*[68] And as Littleton saith, A bastard is *quasi nullius filius*[69] & can have no name of reputation as

---

61. (i) 17. E. 3. 29. 18. E. 3. 59. 30. E. 3. 18. 11 H. 4. 84. Pl. Com. 525. 21. R. 2. devise 41. E. 3. 19. 15. E. 3. Counter-Plea de Vouch. 43. 35. Ass. 13. 37. H. 6. 30. 11. E. 4. 2. 7. H. 4. 5. 40. E. 3. 9. 37. H. 8. Bru Nosme 40.

62. [*Ed.:* as "to the wife of I.S." as hath beene said, or "to the firstborn son, or second son," etc. or "to the youngest son of I.S." or "elder son," or "to all the sons and daughters of I.S." or "to all the children and issue of I.S." or to the right heires of I.S.]

63. (k) 15. H. 7. 14.

64. [*Ed.:* with his whole family.]

65. (l) 8E. 3. 437. 29. E. 3. 44 19. E. 4 11. 21 E. 4. 19. 7. H. 6. 29.

66. (a) 39. E. 3. 11. 24. 17. E. 3. 42. 35. Ass. 13. 41. E. 3. 19.

67. Vide sect. 118.

68. [*Ed.:* whoever is born of a guilty union shall not be reckoned among the children.]

69. [*Ed.:* as it were, the son of no one.]

soone as he is borne. (b)[70] So it is if a man make a lease for life to B. the remainder to the eldest issue male of B. to bee begotten of the body of Jane S. whether the same issue be legitimate or illegitimate. B. hath issue a bastard on the body of Jane S. this son or issue shall not take the remainder, for (as it hath beene said) by the name of issue, if there had beene no other words he could not take, and (as it hath beene also said) a bastard cannot take, but after hee hath gained a name by reputation, that hee is the sonne of B. &c. (c)[71] And therefore he can take no remainder limited before he be borne, but after he be borne, and that he hath gained by time a reputation to be knowne by the same of a son, then a remainder limited to him by the name of the sonne of his reputed father is good. But if he cannot take the remainder by the name of issue at the time when hee is borne hee shall never take it. And so it seemeth, and for the same cause, if after the birth of the issue, B. had married Jane S. so as hee became Bastard eigne,[72] and had a possibilitie to inherit, yet he shall not take the remainder.

Persons deformed having humane shape, ideots, mad men, lepers, deafe, dumb, and blinde, minors, and all other reasonable creatures have power to purchase and retaine lands or tenements. (d)[73] But the Common Law doth disable some men to take any estate in some particular things: As if an office either of the grant of the King or Subject which concernes the administration, proceeding, or execution of Justice, or the Kings revenue, or the Common-wealth, or the interest, benefit, or safetie of the subject, or the like; if these, or any of them be granted to a man that is unexpert, and hath no skill and science to exercise or execute the same, the grant is meerely void, and the partie disabled by Law, and incapable to take the same, *pro commodo regis & populi,*[74] for only men of skill, knowledge, & abilitie to exercise the same are capable of the same to serve the King & his people. (e)[75] An infant or minor is not capable of an office of Stewardship of the Court of a Mannor either in

---

70. (b) So it was resolved. M. 38 & 39. Eliz. in Bre. de errore, for land in Portington in Come. Salop.

71. (c) 39. E. 3. 11. 24. 35. Ass. 13. 41. E. 3. 10. 17. E. 3. 42. (6. Co. 66.)

72. [*Ed.:* A son whose birth precedes his parents' marriage.]

73. (d) S. E. 4. tit. office & officer. Bro. 48. vinters case. 5. Mar. Dier. fo. 150. b. and Scroggs case. (Hob. 148.)

74. [*Ed.:* for the advantage of the king and the people.]

75. (e) M. 40. & 41. Eliz. in the King's Bench between Scamler an Walters.

possession or reversion. (f)[76] No man though never so skilfull and expert, is capable of a judiciall office in reversion, but must expect untill it fall in possession. And see Sect. 378. where bargaining or giving of money, or any manner of reward, &c. for offices there mentioned, shall make such a purchaser incapable thereof, which is worthy to bee knowne, but more worthy to be put in due execution.

Some are capable of certaine things for some speciall purpose, but not to use or exercise such things themselves. As the King is capable of an office, not to use, but to grant, &c.

A monster borne within lawfull matrimony, that hath not humane shape cannot purchase much lesse retaine any thing. (g)[77] The same Law is *de professis & mortuis seculo,* for they are *civiliter mortui,*[78] whereof you shall read at large in his proper place, Sect. 200.

"purchase."

In Latine *Perquisitum* of the Verbe *Perquirere,* Littleton describeth it in the end of this Chapter in this manner, Item, purchase *est appel le possession de trés outenèments que home ad per son fait, ou per son agreement, a quel possession il neavient per title de discent de nul de ses ancesters, ou de ses cosens mes person fait dem.*[79] So as I take it, a purchase is to be taken, when one commeth to lands by conveyance or title, and that disseisins, abatements, intrusions, usurpations, and such like estates gained by wrong, are not said in Law purchases, but oppressions and injuries.

Note that purchasers of lands, tenements, leases, and hereditaments for good and valuable consideration, shall avoyd all former fraudulent and covinous conveyances, estates, grants, charges & limitations of uses, of or out of the

---

76. (f) 11. co 2. in Auditor Curle's case. Vide Sect. 378. 1. H. 7. 31.

77. (g) Bract. lib. 5 fo. 421. 415. Britt. cap. 22. 39. Fleta lib. 6. cap. 41. I. E. 3. 9. 44. E. 3. 4. 3. H. 6. 24. 21. R. 2. Judgement 263. 7. H. 4. 2. 14. H. 8. 16 Doct. & Stud. 141. Pl. Com. fo 47. Britt. cap. 33.

78. [*Ed.:* of those who have been professed and are dead to the world (for they are) civilly dead,]

79. [*Ed.:* Also, purchase is called the possession of lands or tenements that a man has by his deed or agreement, to which possession he does not come by title of descent from any of his ancestors or of his kinsmen; but by his own deed.]

same, (h)[80] by a Statute made since Littleton wrote, whereof you may plainly and plentifully read in my Reports, to which I will adde this case, I. C. had a Lease of certaine lands for 60 yeares if hee lived so long, and forged a Lease for 90 yeares absolutely, and he by Indenture reciting the forged Lease for valuable consideration bargained, and sold the forged Lease: and all his interest in the land to R. G. It seemed to me that R. G. was no purchaser within the Statute of 27 Eliz. for he contracted not for the true & lawfull interest, for that was not knowne to him, for then perhaps hee would not have dealt for it, and the visible and knowne tearme was forged, and although by generall words the true interest passed notwithstanding he gave no valuable consideration nor contracted for it. And of this opinion were all the Judges in Serjeants Inne in Fleetstreet.

(i)[81] In ancient time when a man made a fraudulent feoffment it was said, *quod posuit terram illam in brigam,*[82] where *brigam* doth signifie wrangle, contention, or intricacie, for fraud is the mother of them all. (k)[83] And on the other side, purchases, estates, and contracts may be avoyded since Littleton wrote by certaine Acts of Parliament against Usurie above ten in the hundred, in such manner and forme as by those Acts is provided. Which Statutes are well expounded in my books of Reports which may be read there. To them that lend money my caveat is, that I neither directly nor indirectly, by art, or cunning invention, they take above ten in the hundred, for they that seeke by fleight to creepe out of these Statutes, will deceive themselves, and repent in the end. [4 a]

"Purchase Lands."

Littleton here and in many other places putteth Lands but for an example, for his rule extendeth to Seigniories, Rents, Advowsons, Commons, Estovers, and other hereditaments of what kinde or nature soever.

Lands and other things to be purchased.

80. (h) 27. Eliz. cap. 4. 13. Eliz. cap. 5. 3 co. 80. 82 83. Twine's case. 5. co. 60. Gooche's case, 6 co. 72. Burrel's case, 11. co. 74. Pasch. 12. Ja. inter Jones pl. and Sir Rich. Groobham def. in ejectione firmae in evidence al Jurie.
81. (i) Hill. 18. E. 3. coram Rege in Thesaur.
82. [*Ed.:* that he placed his land in a wrangle.]
83. (k) 37. H. 8. cap. 6. 13.Eliz. cap. 8. 5. Co. 69. Burtun's case, Eodem, lib. 7 Claiton's case.

"Land."

Terra,[84] Land in the legall signification comprehendeth any ground, soile or earth whatsoever, as Meadowes, Pastures, Woods, Moores, Waters, Marshes, Furses and Heath, *Terra est nomen generalissimum, & comprehendit omnes species terrae,*[85] but properly *Terra dicitur à terendo, quia vomere teritur,*[86] and anciently it was written with a singler, and in that sense it includeth whatsoever may bee plowed, and is all one with *arvum ab arando.*[87] It legally includeth also all Castles, Houses, and other buildings: for Castles, Houses, &c. consist upon two things, viz. land or ground, as the foundation and structure thereupon, so as passing the land or ground, the structure or building thereupon passeth therewith.[88] Land is anciently called *Fleth,* but land builded is more worthy than other land, because it is for the habitation of man, and in that repeat hath the precedencie to be demanded in the first place in a *Praecipe,* as hereafter shall be said. And therefore this element of the Earth is preferred before the other elements; first and principally, because it is for the habitation and resting place of man, for man cannot rest in any of the other elements, neither in the Water, Aire or fire. For as the Heavens are the habitation of Almightie God, so the Earth hath he appointed as the Suburbs of Heaven to be the habitation of man; *Coelum coeli Domino, terram autem dedit filiis hominum.*[89] All the whole Heavens are the Lords, the earth hath he given to the children of men. Besides, everie thing as it serveth more immediately or more meerely for the food and use of man (as shall be said hereafter) hath the precedent dignitie before any other. And this doth the earth, for out of the earth commeth mans food, and bread that strengthens mans heart, *Confirmat cor hominis,* and Wine that gladdeth the heart of man,[90] and Oyle that makes him a cheereful

---

84. Pl. Com 168 b & 170. a & 151. 4.co. 87 b. Lutterel's case. 4. E. 3. 161 & 6. E. 3. 283. 8. E. 3. 377. Temps. E. 1. Briefe. 811. 28. 14. 8. Dyer, 47.

85. [Ed. *Terra* (land) is an extremely general noun and comprehends all species of land.]

86. [Ed. *Terra* (land) is so called from *terendo* (wearing down) because it is worn down by the plough.]

87. [*Ed.: arvum* (a ploughed field) (is derived) from *arando* (ploughing).]

88. * Tr. 7. E. 3. coram Rege Northampt. In Thesaur.

89. Psal. 115. 16. [*Ed.:* The heaven, even the heavens, are the Lord's; but the earth he has given to the children of men.]

90. Psal. 104. 15.

countenance. And therefore *Terra olim Ops mater dicta est quia omnia hac opus habeant ad vivendum.*[91] And the Divine agreeth herewith, for he saith,[92] *Patriam tibi & nutricem, & matrem, & mensam, & domum posuit terram Deus, sed & sepulchrum tibi hanc eandem dedit.*[93] Also the waters that yeeld fish for the food and sustenance of man are not by that name demandable in a *Praecipe,* but the land whereupon the water floweth or standeth is demandable (as for example) *viginti acr' ter' aqua coopert',*[94] and besides the earth doth furnish man with many other necessaries for his use, as it is replenished with hidden treasures, namely with Gold, Silver, Brasse, Iron, Tinne, Lead, and other metals, and also with great varietie of precious stones, and many other things for profit, ornament and pleasure. And lastly, the earth hath in Law a great extent upwards, not only of water as hath beene said, but of aire and all other things even up to Heaven, for *cujus est solum ejus est usque ad coelum,* as it is holden, 14.Hen.8.fo.12. 22.Hen.6.59. 10.Edw.4.14. Regist. origin and in other bookes.

And albeit land, whereof our Author here speaketh, be the most firme and fixed inheritance, and therefore it is called *solum, quid est solidum,*[95] and fee simple the most highest and absolute estate that a man can have, yet may the same at severall times be moveable;[96] sometime in one person, and *alternis vicibus*[97] in another, nay sometime in one place, and sometime in another. As for example, if there be 80 acres of meadow which have been used time out of minde of man, to be divided betweene certain persons, and that a certaine number of acres appertaine to everie of these persons, as for example, to A. 13. acres to be yearely assigned and lotted out,[98] so as sometime the 13. acres lye in one place, and sometime in another, and so of the rest. A. hath a moveble fee simple in 13. acres, and may be parcell of his Mannor, albeit they have no certaine place, but yearly set out in severall places, so as the number onely is

---

91. [*Ed.:* Earth was once called the abundant mother, because all things have to live therefrom.]

92. Chrysost. Hom. 30.

93. [*Ed.:* God gave you the earth as your homeland and nurse, and mother, and food (lit. table), and home, and even gave the same to you for your burial.]

94. [*Ed.:* twenty acres covered with water]

95. [*Ed.: solum* (soil), because it is *solidum* (solid).]

96. Vid. sect. 59. wherein this case liverie shall be made.

97. [*Ed.:* at alternate times.]

98. Vid. sect. 648. How these 13 acres may be charged.

certaine, and the particular acres or place wherein they lye after the yeare incertaine. And so it was adjuged in the Kings Bench upon an especiall verdict.[99]

If a partition be made betweene two Coparceners of one and the selfe-same land, that the one shall have the land from Easter untill Lammas to her and to her heires, and the other shall have it from Lammas till Easter to her and her heires, or the one shall have it the first yeare, and the other the second yeare *alternis vicibus,* &c. there it is one selfe-same land wherein two persons have severall inheritances at severall times. So it is if two Coparceners have two severall Mannors by descent, & they make partition, that the one shall have the one Mannor for a yeare, and the other the other Mannor for the same yeare, and after that yeare, then he that had the one Mannor shall have the other, & *sic alternis vicibus* for ever, and albeit the Mannors be severeall, yet are they certaine, and therefore stronger than Bridgewaters case, so as this doth make a Division of states of inheritances of lands, viz. Certaine or un-moveable whereof Littleton here speaketh, and incertaine and moveable,[100] whereof these three cases for examples have beene put. Wherein it is to bee noted, that the possession is not onely severall, but the inheritance also.

[4 b]
By what
names, &c.
lands, &c.
shall passe.

| It is also necessarie to bee seene by what names lands shall passe. (a)[101] If a man hath twentie acres of land, and by Deed granteth to another and his heires, *vesturam terrae,*[102] and maketh Liverie of seisin *secundum formam cartae,*[103] the land it selfe shall not passe, because hee hath a particular right in the land, for thereby he shall not have the houses, timber trees, mines and other reall things parcell of the Inheritance, but he shall have the vesture of the land, (that is) the Corne, Grasse, Underwood, Swepage, and the like; and hee shall have an Action of trespasse, *quare clausum fregit.*[104] (b)[105] The same

---

99. Hill, 34. Eliz Rot. 489. in trans inter Weldon & Bridgewater in Banco Regis Temps. E.1. tit. partition 21. F.N.B. 62. L. Vide l Co. fo.87. per Walmsl. F. N. B. 62. K.

100. Vide sect. 114. where advowsons, &c. may be appendent and in gros.

101. (a)Vide sect. 289. 14. H. 8. 6. 4. Hen. 7. 3. 10. H. 7. 24. 11. H. 7. 21. 14. H. 7. 4. 6. 21. H. 7. 36. 77. 9. H. 6. 52. 37 H. 6. 35. 22. E. 4. barre 116. 11. H. 4.90. 18. E. 3. Execution. 56. 4 E. 3.48. 8 E. 3. 13. 9. Ass. p. 12. 38. E. 3. 24.

102. [*Ed.:* The vesture of the land; that is, the corn grass underwood, sweepage and the like.]

103. [*Ed.:* According to the form of the charter (deed).]

104. [*Ed.:* Wherefore he broke the close.]

105. (b) Bract. fo. 222. 17. E. 3. 75. 39. H. 6. 38. II. Eliz. Dy. 285.

Law, if a man grant *herbagium terrae,* hee hath a like particular right in the land, and shall have an Action *quare clausum fregit,* but by grant thereof and liverie made, the soile shall not passe, as is aforesaid. (c)[106] If a man let to B. the herbage of his woods, and after grant all his lands in the tenure, possesion, or occupation of B. the woods shall passe, for B. hath a particular possession and occupation, which is sufficient in this case, and so it was resolved. (d)[107] So if a man be seised of a River, and by Deed doe grant *separalem piscariam*[108] in the same, and maketh liverie of seisin *secundum forman cartae,* the soile doth not passe nor the water; for the Grantor may take water there, and if the river become drie, hee may take the benefit of the soile, for there passed to the Grantee but a particular right, and the liverie being made *secundum forman cartae,* cannot enlarge the grant. (e)[109] For the same reason, if a man grant *aquam suam,* the soile shall not passe, but the Pischarie[110] within the water passeth therewith. And land covered with water shall be demanded by the name of so many Acres *aqua coopert*[111] whereby it appeareth that they are distinct things. (f)[112] So if a man grant to another to dig turves[113] in his land; and to carrie them at his will and pleasure, the land shall not passe, because but part of the profit is given, for trees, mines &c. shall not passe. (g)[114] But if a man seised to lands in fee by his Deed granteth to another the profits of those lands, to have and to hold to him and his heires, and maketh liverie *secundum formam cartae,* the whole land it selfe doth passe, for what is the land but the profits thereof, for thereby vesture, herbage, trees, mines, and all whatsoever parcell of that land doth passe.

(h)[115] By the grant of the Boillourie of salt, it is said that the soile shall passe, for it is the whole profit of the soile, And this is called *Saliva* of the

---

106. (c) Pasch, 12. Ja. inter Dockwray & Points in evidence al Jury in Banke le Roy.

107. (d) Vide Sect. 279. Bract. fo. 208. 40. E. 3.45. Pl. Com. 154. 10. H. 7. 24. 28. 7. H. 7. 13. 18. H. 6. 29. 34. H. 6. 43. 20 H. 6. 4. 18. E. 4. 4. 4. E. 3. 48. l. E. 3. 4. 32. E. 3. Scir. fac. 100. 22. E. 4. barre 116. 12. H. 3. Ass. 427. 34. Ass. 11. 13. E. 3. tit. Entrie 57. 20. E. 3. Briefe 685. W. 2. c. 24.

108. [*Ed.:* a several fishery.]

109. (e) Tr. 11. R. 2. in tresp. nient. Imprimee ne abridg. 11. H. 7.4.

110. [*Ed.:* fishing rights]

111. [*Ed.:* covered with water.]

112. (f) 7. E. 3. 34. 2 5. Ass. 9. 10. 7. Ass. 9.

113. [*Ed.:* turf]

114. (g) 45. E. 3. tit. foeffments et faits 90. 14. H. 8 6. Pl. Com. 541. b. F.N.B. 8. 12. E.3. Dower 90.

115. (h) Ass. p. 12. 9. E. 3. 443. 466. Domesday. 7. R. I. int. fines in Thesaur.

French word *Salure* for a Salt-pit, and you may read *de Saliva* in Domesday, and *Selda,* signifieth the same thing: (i)[116] & where you shall read in Records *de lacerta in profunditate aque salse,*[117] there *lacerta* signifieth a fathome. A man seised of divers acres of wood, grants to another *omnes boscos suos,*[118] all his woods, not onely the woods growing upon the land passe, but the land it selfe, and by the same name shall bee recovered in a *Praecipe,* for *Boscus* doth not onely include the trees, but the land also whereupon they grow.

(k)[119] The same Law if a man in that case grant *omnes boscos suos crescentes,*[120] &c. yet the land itselfe shall passe, as it hath been adjudged.[121] *Frassetum* signifieth a wood, or ground that is woodie. (l)[122] If a man hath a wood of Elder trees containing 20. acres, and granteth to another 20. *acras alneti* (with an N not a V) the wood of Elders, and the soile thereof shall passe, but no other kinde of woods shall passe by that name. *Alnetum est ubi alni arbores crescunt.*[123],[124] And *Sullings* are taken for Elders. (m)[125] *Salicetum* doth signifie a wood of wilowes, *ubi salices crescunt,*[126] these trees in our Books are called *Sawces.*[127] *Selda,* is a wood of Sallowes, Willowes, or Withies. A brackie ground is called *Filecetum, ubi filices crescunt.*[128] A wood of Ashes is called *Fraxinetum, ubi fraxini crescunt,*[129] and passeth by that name, and *Lupulicetum* where hops grow, and *Arundinetum,* where reeds grow. Some say that *Dene* or *Denne,* whereof *Dena* commeth, is properly a valley or dale. *Denasylvae,* and the like. (n)[130] *Drofden,* or *Drufden,* or *Druden,* signifieth a thicket of wood in a valley,

---

116. (i) Int. inquisit apud Launcast. anno 6. E. 1 in Thesaur. Mich 1 H. 5. coram Rege Rot. 3.in Thesaur.

117. [*Ed.:* of a fathom in the depth of the salt water.]

118. [*Ed.:* all his woods.]

119. (k) Tr. 7. Eliz. in Banco regis 5. co. 11. Ives case. 14. H. 8. 1. 46. E. 3. 22. 28. H. 8. Dyer. 19. 32. H. 8. Br reservat. 39. 7. E. 6. Dyer 79.

120. [*Ed.:* all his woods growing etc.]

121. Glanvil. lib-8. cap. 3.

122. (l) Domesday Regist. F.N.B. 2.

123. [*Ed.:* an *alnetum* (elder wood) is where elder trees grow.]

124. Hill 14. E. 3. coram Rege Lanc. in Thesaur.

125. (m) 8. E. 2. Wast. III. 7. Ass. 18. 11. Ass. p. 13. 41. E. 3. Wast, 82.

126. [*Ed.:* where willows grow.]

127. *Inter inquisit. apud Lanc. in com. Cornubie coram Justic. Aud. anno 6. E. I. in Thesaur. the B. of Exceters case.

128. [*Ed.:* where ferns grow.]

129. [*Ed.: fraxinetum* (ash grove), where ashes grow.]

130. (n) Domesday.

for *Druf* or *Dru,* signifieth a thicket of wood, and is often mentioned in Domesday. And sometimes *Dena* or *Denna* signifieth, as *Villa* and *Denne,* a towne.

(o)[131] *Cope* signifieth a hill, & so doth *Lawe,* as *Stanlawe* is *Saxeus collis.*[132] (p)[133] *Howe* also signifieth a hill. And *Hope combe,* and *Stow* are valleyes, & so doth *Clough.* And *Dunham* or *Duna,* signifieth a hill or higher ground, and therefore commonly the townes that end in *Dun,* have hills or higher grounds in them, which we call *Downes.* It commeth of the old French word *Dun.*

(q)[134] In our Latine a wood is called *Boscus, Grava* signifieth a little wood, in old Deeds, and *Hirst* or *Hurst* a wood and so doth *Holt* and *Shawe. Twaite* signifieth a wood grubbed up, and turned to arable. *Stethe* or *Stede,* betokeneth properly a banke of a River, and many times a place, as *Stowe* doth, and *Wic,* a place upon the Sea shore, or upon a River. *Lea* or *Ley* signifieth pasture.

(r)[135] If a man doth grant all his pastures, *Pasturas,* the land it selfe imployed to the feeding of beasts doth passe, and also such pastures or feedings, as he hath in another mans soile. *Leswes* or *Lesues* is a Saxon word, and signifieth pastures. (s)[136] Between *Pastura* and *Pascuum,* the legall difference is that *Pastura* in one signification containeth the ground it selfe called pasture, and by that name is to be demanded. *Pascuum* feeding, is wheresoever cattell are fed, of what nature soever the gound is, and cannot be demanded in a *Praecipe* by that name.

(t)[137] If a man grant *omnia prata sus,* all his meadowes; the land it selfe of that kinde passe, & *dicitur pratum quasi paratum,* because it groweth *sponte* without maintenance. (u)[138] A man grant *omnes brueras suas,* the soile where heath doth grow passeth, and may be demanded by that name | in a *praecipe,* [5 a] it is derived from *bruyer* a French word for heath, and it is called *Ros* in the British tongue.

---

131. (o) Camden 460. 151.

132. [*Ed.:* a stone hill.]

133. (p) Pasch. 44. E. 3. coram Rege in Thes.

134. (q) Hill, 13. E. 2. Lanc. coram Rege. in thesaur Camden Britt. 247. Rot. Par. 18 E. 1. 8. Evesque de Carlisle's case.

135. (r) Pl. Com. 169. a. 4. E. 2. Briefe. 792. 793. 3. E. 3. 86. 4. E. 4. 1. 27. H. 8. 12.

136. (s) 20. Ass. pl. 9.

137. (t) Pl. Com. 169a. 13. E.3 Briefe. 241. 33. E. 3. Entrie. 80.

138. (u) Domesday. F.N.B. 2. Regist.

Roncaria or *Rancaria* signifieth land full of brambles & briers, and is derived of *Roucier* the French word which signifieth the same, & as much as *senticetum.* (a)[139] By the grant of *omnes Juncarias* or *joncarias,* the soile were rushes do grow, doth passe, for *Lonc* in French is a Rush, whereof *Joncaria* commeth. (b)[140] A man grant *omnes Ruscarias suas,* the soile where *ruscii.* kneholme, or butchers pricks or broome doe grow, shall passe, and so in the verse in the Register it is called, but in F.N.B. fol. 2. in the verse, *Pischaria* is put in stead of *Ruscaria.* And *Jampna*[141] commeth of *lonc* and *nower,* a waterish place, and is all one in effect with *Joncaria.* Hee that granteth *omnes mariscos suos,* all his fennes or marish grounds doe passe. *Mariscus* is derived of the French word *mares* or *marets;* the Latine word for it, is *palus* or *locus paludosus. Mora* is derived of the English word Moore and signifieth a more barren and un-profitable ground than marshes, dangerous for any cattell to goe there, in respect of myrie and morish soyle, neither serves it for getting of turves there: (c)[142] you shall read in Record, that such a man *perquisuit trescent. acr. maretti,* &c. this word *maretrum* is derived of *mare* the sea, and *tego,* and properly signifieth a moorish and gravelly ground, which the sea doth cover and over-flow at a full sea, and lyeth betweene the high water marke, and the low water marke, *infra fluxum & refluxum maris.* By grant of these particular kindes, the land of these particular kindes onely doe passe, but as hath beene said by the grant of land in generall, all these particular kindes, and some others doe passe. *Non mihi si centum linguae sint oraque centum, Omnia terrarum per-currere nomina possem.* And therefore let us turne our eye to generall words, which doe include lands of severall sorts and qualities. (d)[143] By the name of an Honor, which a subject may have, divers mannors and lands may passe. So by the name of an Isle, Insula, many mannors, lands and tenements may passe.

139. (a) Regist. 1. E. 3. 4. F.N.B. 2.

140. (b) 16. Ass. p. 2. Register.

141. Jampna.

142. (c) Pasch. 41. E. 3. coram. Rege Lincoln. rot. 28.

143. (d) Mag. Chart. c. 31. Walingford Nott. Bolon. Lanc. &c. Trin. 33. E. 1. coram Rege in Thes. honor de Huntingdon. Mich. 9. E. 1. Coram Rege in Thes. 8. E 2. Ass 377. 26. Ass. p. 60. 6. E. 3. 56–47. E. 3. 21. honor de Pevevevel. 49. E.3.3. 24. honor de Egles. 9. H. 6. 27. 36. H. 8. Dyer 58. Honor de Glouc. F.N.B. 265. honor Abbath. de Merle. 5. E. 4. 129. 7. H. 6. 39. 1. E. 3. 4. &c. 13. E. 3. jurisdict. 23. 4. co. 88. Lutterel's case. 5. H. 7. 9. 14. H. 4. in recordo longo. 8. H. 4. Pl. Com. 168. 8. H. 7. 1. 4. E. 4. 16.

Holme or *hulmus* signifieth an Isle or fenny ground. *[144] A Commote is a great Seigniory, & may include one or divers mannors; (e)[145] By the name of a castle, one or more mannors may be conveyed, & *è converso,* by the name of a mannor, &c., a castle may passe. In Domesday I read *Comes Alanus habet in suo castellatu 200. maneria, &c. praeter castellarium habet 43. maneria,* and in that booke a castle is called *castellum,* and *castrum,* and *domus defensibilis,* and *mansus muralis.* (f)[146] But note by the way, that no subject can build a castle or house of strength embattelled, &c. or other fortress defensible, called in Law by the names aforesaid, and sometimes *domus kernellatae,* or *Carnel-latae, imbattellatae, tenellatae, machecollatae, mese, carnelet,* &c without the licence of the King, for the danger which might ensue, if everie man at his pleasure might do it. And they be called imbattlements, because they are defences against battles in assaults. *Tenellare* or *tanellare,* is to make holes or loopes in walls to shoot out against the Assailants. *Machecollare* or *machecoulare,* is to make a warlik device over a gate or other passage like to a grate through which scalding water, or ponderous, or offensive things may be cast upon the assaylants. But to returne to the matter from whence upon this occasion we are fallen.

By the name of a towne *Villa,* a mannor may passe. In Domesday, *Alodium* (in a large sense) signifieth a free mannor and *Alodiarii* or *Alodarii,* Lords of the same, and *Lannemanni* there signifie lords of a mannor, having *socam & sacam de tenentibus & hominibus suis.*[147] (g)[148] And by the name of a Mannor, divers townes may passe, *quod olim dicebatur fundus nunc manerium dicitur,*[149] by the name of a *ferme* or *fearme firma,* houses, lands, and tenements may passe, and *firma* is derived of the Saxon word *feormian,* to feed or releeve, for in ancient time they reserved upon their Leases, cattell and other victuall & provision for their sustenance. (h)[150] Note a fearme in the North parts is called

---

144. *13. E. 3. jurisdict.23.

145. (e) 26. Ass. 54. 29. E. 3. 15. 29. H. 6. travers 4. Bract. fo 434 1 E. 3. 4. 5 H. 7. 9. 3. E. 2. Avowry 188. 37. H. 6. 26. 18. H. 6. 11. Lib. rub. sca. fo. 18.

146. (f) In veter. Mag. Cart. cap. escheatriae fol. 162. Britton. cap. 20. Rot. Parliam. 45. E. 3. nu. 34. 6. H. 4. nu. 19. 1. E. 4. cap. 1. Rot. Parliam. 1. E. 3. 2. pars. AlanoCharleton. 22. E. 3. 2. pars. Thoma Barkley &c.

147. [*Ed.:* soke and sake (the lord of the manor's right to hold court and compel attendance) of their tenants and men.]

148. (g) Lamb. exposit. verb. ferme. Pl. Com. 195.

149. [*Ed.:* what was once called *fundus* (farm) is now called a manor.]

150. (h) Pl. Com. 169. Regist. 227. b. eject. firmae.

a *Tacke,* in Lancashire a *Fermeholt,* in Essex a *Wike.* But the word *fearme,* is the generall word, and anciently *fundus* signified a fearme and sometime land. (i)[151] Lands making a Knights fee, shall passe by the grant of a Knights fee *de uno feodo militis.*[152]

(k)[153] *Unum solinum* or *solinus terrae* in Domesday book containeth two plow Lands and somewhat lesse than an halfe, for there it is said, *Septem Solini,* or *Solina terrae sunt 17. carucat'. Una hida seu carucata terrae* which is all one as a plow land, viz. as much as a plough can till, fullery also signifieth a plow-land. *Una virgata terrae,* a yard land, the Saxons called it *Girdland,* and now the G. is turned to a Y. as in some Countries 10. in some 20. in some 24. in some 30. &c. (l)[154] *Una bovata terrae,* an oxgange, or an oxgate of land, is as much as an oxe can till. (m)[155] But *carucata terrae* and *bovata terrae,* are words compound, and may containe meadow, pasture, and wood, necessarie for such tillage. *Jugum terrae* in Domesday, containeth halfe a plow-land. And by all these names in the reign of Richard the first lands were usually demanded and long after.

(n)[156] By the name of a *Grange, Grangia* a house or edifice, not onely where corne is stored up like as in barnes, but necessarie places for husbandrie also, as stables for hay and horses, and stables and styes for other cattell, and a curtilage, and the close wherein it standeth shall passe, and it is a French word, and signifieth the same, as we take it.

(o)[157] *Stagnum,* in English a poole, doth consist of water and land, and there-[5 b] fore by the name of | *Stagnum* or a poole, the water and land shall passe also. (a)[158] In the same manner *Gurges,* a deepe pit of water, a gors or gulfe consisteth of water and land, and therefore by the grant thereof by that name, the soile doth passe, and a praecipe doth lye thereof, & shall lay his esplées in taking

151. (i) 17. E. 3. fo. 8. 5. E. 3. 213. 16. E. 3. bre. 165. 12. E. 2. bre. 814.

152. [*Ed.:* of one knight's fee.]

153. (k) 4. E. 3. 161. 6. E. 3. 283. 2. E. 3. 5. 35. H. 6. 29. Pl. Com. 168. 7. Ass. 8. 11. Ass. 13. Lamb. expos. verb. Hyda & virgat. terrae. Glanvil. lib. cap. Domesday. Bract. lib. 2. cap. 26, 27, & lib. 5. fol. 434. Regist. 72.

154. (l) 5. E. 3. fine 49. 13. E. 3. fine 67. 39. H. 6. 8. 4. E. 3. 159. 8. E. 3. 377. Bracton fol. 180. 269–431. 5. H. 3. Droit. 66. Pl. Com. 168.

155. (m) 13. E. 3. bre. 241. 2. E. 3. 57. temps. E. 1 bre. 811. Pl. Com. 168.

156. (n) Pl. Com. 169. Linwood. 44. E. 3. 21. 4. E. 3. 32.

157. (o) 4. E. 3. tit. feoffments & faits 79. 14. E. 3. Formedon. 34. 34. Ass. pl. 11.

158. (a) 13. E. 3. 4. 4. E. 3. 143. 8. E. 3. 381. 10. E. 3. 482. 13. E. 3. entry, 57. F. N. B. 191. b.

of fishes, as Breames and Roches. In Domesday it is called *guort, gort* & *gors*   Domesday.
plurally, as for example, *de 3. gorz. mille anguillae.*

(b)[159] So it is of a Forest, Parke, Chase, vivarye, and Warren in a mans owne
ground, by the grant of any of them, not onely the privilege, but the land it
selfe passes, for they are compound. In the book of Domesday, that is called
lewad and *leuga,* and *lewed,* and *lewe,* which in Latine is called *leuca.*

(c)[160] *Stadium,* or *ferlingus sive ferligum,* or *quarentena terrae,* is a furlong
of Land, and is as much as to say, a furrow long, which in ancient time was
the eighth part of a mile, and land will passe by that name. And some hold,
that by that name land may be demanded. And *de ferlingis* & *quarentenis,* you
shall read divers times in the booke of Domesday, and there you shall read   Domesday.
In insula Rex habet unum frustrum terrae unde exeunt sex vomeres.[161] *Nota*
frustrum signifieth a parcell,[162] (d)[163] *Warectum* or *wareccum,* or *varectum,* doth
signifie fallow; *Terra jacet ad Warectum,* the land lyeth fallow: but in truth the
word is *vervactum, quasi vere novo victum seu subactum, terra novalis seu requieta,*
quia alternis annis requiescat.[164] (e)[165] *Tam culta novalia.*[166] (f)[167] By the grant
of a messuage, or house *mesuagium,* the orchard, garden and curtilage doe
passe, and so an acre or more may passe by the name of a house. It is derived
of the French word *mese.* (g)[168] In Domesday, a house in a City or Burrough,
is called *haga;* other houses are called there *mansiones, mansurae,* & *domus,*
(h)[169] and in an ancient plea concerning Feuersham in Kent, *hawes* are interpreted to signifie *mansiones.* In Normans French it is called *mesiul* or *mesuil:*
Bye signifieth a dwelling, *bye* an habitation, and *byan* to dwell.

159. (b) Temps E. 1. bre. 861. 4. E. 3. 5. 10. H. 7. 30. 44. E. 3. 12. 43. E. 3. 24. 35. H. 6. 55. 3. H. 6. 2.
Domesday, Bracton lib. 4. fo. 235. Int adjudicat. coram Rege. p. 39. E. 3. lib. 2. fo. 95. in Thesaur.

160. (c) 40. Ass. 38. 4. H. 6. 14. 35. E. 1. ca. 6. Anno 10. E. 1. inter fines in Thesaur. Ferlingus terrae
continet 32. acras.

161. Frustrum. 16. E. 3. tit. comon. 9.

162. [*Ed.:* In the island the king has one piece (*frustrum*) of land whence come six ploughs.]

163. (d) Mich. 8. H. 3. incipien. 9. Coram Rege. Warr. Ro. 6.

164. [*Ed.: vervactum* (fallow), meaning, as it were, newly *vere victum* (truly gained) or worked, newly
ploughed or refreshed land, because in alternate years it rests.]

165. (e) Virg. Eclog. 1. a.

166. [*Ed.:* newly cultivated land.]

167. (f) Bract. 211. 233. 22. E. 4. trans 140. Pl. Com. 168. 171. 23. H. 8. Br. feoffments 53. 9. Ass. p. 21.
35. H. 6. 44. Pl. Com. 169.

168. (g) Domesday.

169. (h) Pasch. 30. E. 1. cortam Rege Kanc. in Thesaur. Statut. de extent. manerii Domesday.

It is to be noted, that in Domesday there be often named *bordarii seu borduanni, cosces, coscet, cotucami, cotarii,* are all in effect bores or husbandmen, or cotagers, saving that *bordarii,* which commeth of the French word *borde* for a cottage, signifieth their bores holding a little house with some land of husbandry bigger than a cottage, and *coterelli* are meere cottagers, *qui cotagia & curtilagia tenent.*[170]

Villani in Domesday (often named) are not taken there for bondmen, but had their name *de villis,* because they had fermes, and there did worke of husbandry for the Lord, and they were ever named before *bordarii,* &c. and such as are bondmen are called there *servi.*

(i)[171] *Coleberti* often also named in Domesday signifieth Tenants in free socage by free rent, and so it is expounded of record. *Radmans* and *Radchemisters,* (*Rad,* or *rede,* signifieth firme and stable) there also often named, these are *liberi tenentes qui arabant & herciebant ad curiam domini, seu falcabant, aut metebant,*[172] because their estates are firme and stable, and they are many times called *Sochemans* and *sokemanni* because of their plough service.

Dreuchs signifieth free tenants of a Mannor there also named. *Taini* or *thaini mediocres* were free holders, and sometime called *milites regis,* and their land called Tainland, and there it is said, *haec terra T.R.E. fuit Tainland, sed postea conversa in Reveland.*[173] (k)[174] But *thainus regis* is taken for a Baron, for it is said in an ancient Author, *Thainus regis proximus comiti est, & ibidem mediocris thainus, & alibi Baro sive thainus.*[175] *Berquarium* or *Bercaria* commeth of *Berc,* an old Saxon word, used at this day for barkes or rindes of trees, and signifieth a Tanhouse, or a heath house, where barkes or rindes of trees are laid to tan withall, and *Berquarij* are mentioned in Domesday. It signifieth also, and more legally a sheepe coat, of the french word *Bergerie.*

(l)[176] By *Vaccaria* in Law is signified a Dairy house, derived of *vacca* the

---

170. [*Ed.:* who are tenants of the cottage and curtillage.]

171. (i) Int. placita coram domino Rege Mich. 10. E. 3. Rot. 26. Lamb. exposit. verb. Thanus.

172. [*Ed.:* free tenants who ploughed and harrowed to the lord's court, or reaped, or harvested.]

173. [*Ed.:* the king's knights . . . this land in the time of King Edward was theign-land, but is now converted into reeve-land.]

174. (k) Lib. Rub. cap. 15. &. cap. 41. & 76. W. 2. c. 46. 7. H. 438. Lib. d'Entries tit. Ass. Corps. Pol. 2.

175. [*Ed.:* The king's theign is next to an earl, and a middle theign there, and elsewhere a baron or theign.]

176. (l) 7. H. 4. 38. Fleta. lib. 2. cap. 35. Domesday. 10. R. 1. Inter fines.

cow. In Latine it is *Lactarium* or *Lactitium,* and *vaccarius* is mentioned in Domesday. And Fleta maketh also mention of *porcaria* a swinestye.

The content of an Acre is knowne, the name is common to the English, German, and French. In legall Latine it is called *Acra,* which the Latinists call *iugerum.* In Domesday it is called *Arpen prati, sylvae, &c. 10. R.I. inter fines, Acra in Cornwall continet 40. perticatas in longitudine & 4. in latitudine, & quaelibet perticata de 16. pedibus in longitudine.*[177]

(m)[178] By the grant of a Selion of land, *Selio terrae,* a ridge of land which containeth no certainty, for some be greater and some be lesser, and by the *grante de una porca,* a ridge doth passe, *Selio* is derived of the French word *Sellon* for a ridge.

(n)[179] By the grant *de centum libratis terrae,* or *50. libratis terrae* or *centum solidatis terrae &c.*[180] land of that value passeth, and so of more or lesse, and in ancient time by that name it might have beene demanded. (o)[181] And many things may passe by a name, that by the same name cannot be demanded by a *praecipe* (for that doth require more prescript forme) but whatsoever may be demanded by a *praecipe,* may passe by the same name by way of grant.

(p)[182] *Frythe* is a plaine betweene woods, and so is *lawnd* or *laund, Combe, hope, dene, glyne, hawgh, howgh* signifieth a Vally. *Howe, hoo, knol, law, peu,* and *cope* a hill. *Ey, Ing* and *worth* signifieth a watry place or water. *Falesia* is a banke or hill by the sea-side, it commeth of *falaize,* which signifieth the same: of all these you shall read in ancient bookes, charters, deeds, | and records,   [6 a] and to the end that our student should not be discouraged for want of knowledge when he meeteth with them *(nescit enim generosa mens ignorantiam pati)*[183] wee have armed him with the signification of them, to the end he may proceed in his reading with alacritie, and set upon, and know how to worke into with delight these rough mines of hidden treasure.

177. [*Ed.:* An acre in Cornwall contains forty perches in length and four in width, and every perch is sixteen feet in length.]

178. (m) 9. E. 39.Temps. E. 1. Br. 866. Mich. 30. E. 1. coram Rege. Glouc. in Thesaur.

179. (n) Bract. fo. 377. 431. 43. E. 3. 27 Regist. fo. 1. 94 248. 249. F.N.B. fo. 87. F. I.

180. [*Ed.:* of a hundred librates (pound's-worth) of land, or fifty librates (pound's-worth) of land, or a hundrd solidates (shilling's-worth) of land.]

181. (o) Regula.

182. (p) 7 R. 1 Inter fines Sussex.

183. [*Ed.:* for a noble mind cannot bear ignorance.]

(m)[184] By the name of *Minera,* or *Fodina plumbi,* &c.[185] the land itself shall passe in a grant if it liverie be made, and also be recovered in an *assise, & sic de similibus.*[186]

By the grant of a fould course or the like, lands and tenements may passe. (n)[187] *Tenementum,* Tenement is a large word to passe, not onely lands and other inheritances which are holden, but also offices, rents, commons, profits apprender out of lands and the like, wherein a man hath any franktenement, and whereof he is siesed ut *de libero tenemento.* But *haereditamentum,*[188] hereditament, is the largest word of all in that kinde, for whatsoever may be inherited is an hereditament, be it corporeall or incorporeall, reall or personall or mixt.

(o)[189] A man seised of lands in fee hath divers Charters, deeds & evidences, or maketh a feoffment in fee, either without warrantie, or with warrantie onely against him and his heires, the purchaser shall have all the Charters, deeds and evidences, as incident to the Lands, *& ratione terrae,*[190] to the end he may the better defend the land himselfe, having no warrantie to recover in value, for the evidences are as it were the sinewes of the land, and the feoffor being not bound to warrantie hath no use of them. But if the feoffor be bound to warrantie, so that he is bound to render in value, then the defence of the title at his perill, and therefore the feoffee in that case shall have no deeds that comprehend warrantie, whereof the feoffor may take advantage. Also he shall have such Charters as may serve him to deraigne the warrantie paramount; Also hee shall have all deeds and evidences, which are materiall for the maintenance of the title of the land, but other evidences which concerne the possession, and not the title of the land, the feoffee shall have them.

184. (m) 17. E. 3. 7. 43. E. 3. 35. b. Regist. 65. 10. H. 7. 21. Pl. Com. 191. 195. Bract. 211 326.

185. [*Ed.:* A mine of lead.]

186. [*Ed.:* as of freehold.]

187. (n) 45. E. 3. Vouchee 72. 33. E. 3. Grant 102 11. H. 6. 22. 27. 14. E. 4. 4. 20. Ass. p. 9. 3. E. 419. 11. H. 7. 25.

188. [*Ed.:* as of a free tenement.]

189. (o) Lib. fo. 1 & 2 in Seign. Buckhursts case. 44. E. 3. ll b. 39. E. 3. 17. a. 19. H. 6 65. b. 4. H. 6. a. 10. E. 4. 9 b. 18. E. 4. 14. 15. 6. H. 7. 3. b. H. 7. 33. a.]

190. [*Ed.:* and by reason of land.]

"To have and to hold."

These two words doe in this place prove a double signification, viz., *a ayer* to have an estate of inheritance of lands descendible to his heires, and *tener* to hold the same of some superior land.

There have been eight formall or orderly parts of a deed of feoffment,[191] viz. 1. the premisses of the deed implied by Littleton. 2. the habendum, whereof Littl. here speaketh. 3. the tenendum mentioned Littleton, 4. the Reddendum, 5. the Clause of warrantie, 6. the *In cujus rei testimonium,* comprehending the sealing, 7. The date of the deed containing the day, the moneth, the yeare, and stile of the King, or of the yeare of our Lord. (p)[192] Lastly, the clause of *hiis testibus,*[193] and yet all these parts were contained in verie few and significant words, (q)[194] *Haec fuit candida illius aetatis fides et simplicitas, quae pauculas lineis omnia fidei firmamenta posuerunt.*[195]

The office of the premisses of the deed is twofold. First, rightly to name the feoffor and the feoffee. And secondly, to comprehend the certaintie of the lands or tenements to be conveyed by the feoffment, either by expresse words, or which may by reference be reduced to a certaintie; for, *certum est quod certum reddi potest.*[196] The habendum hath also two parts, viz. first, to name againe the feoffee, and secondly to limit the certaintie of the estate. The Tenendum at this day where the fee simple passe, must be of the chiefe lords of the fee. And of the Reddendum more shall be said in his proper place, in the Chapter of Rents.[197] Of the Clause of warantie more shall be said in the chapter of warranties. *In cujus rei testimonium sigillum meum apposui*[198] was added, for the Seale is of the essentiall part of the deed. The date of the deed many times Antiquitie omitted, and the reason thereof was, for that the limitation of prescription or time of memorie did often in processe of time change,

---

191. Vid. Sect. 40. & 370. 371 many things de cartis & Factis, Fleta lib. ca. 14. Britton 100. 101. Bracton lib. 5. fo. 396. a. 399. 38. H. 6. 33. 36. Pl. Com. Wrotesleyes case, fol. 96.]

192. (p) Vid.Throgmortons case. Pl. Com.

193. [*Ed.:* these being witnesses.]

194. (q) Lib. 6. fo. 43. in sir Anthony Mildmayes case, Vid. sect. 278.

195. [*Ed.:* Such was the innocent faith and simplicity of that age, that all the points of an agreement were put into a few lines.]

196. [*Ed.:* something is certain if it can be made certain.]

197. Brit. fo. 101.

198. [*Ed.:* In witness whereof I have set my seal.]

and the law was then holden that a deed, bearing date, before the limited time of prescription was not pleadable, and therefore they made their deeds without date, to the end they might alleage them within the time of prescription. And the date of the deeds was commonly added in the reiqne of Henry the second and Edward the third and so ever since.

And sometime Antiquitie added a place, as *Datum apud D.*[199] which was in disadvantage of the feoffee, for being in generall, hee may alleage the deed to be made where he will. And lastly, Antiquitie did adde, *hiis testibus* in the continent of the deed after the *In cujus rei testimonium,*[200] written with the same hand that the deed was, which witnesses were called, the Deed read, and then their names entered. (r)[201] And this is called charter land, and accordingly the Saxons called it *Bockland,* as it were bookeland. Which clause of *hiis testibus* in subjects deeds continued until and in the reigne of Henry the eighth but now is wholly omitted. And it appeareth by the ancient Authors and authorities of the Law; that before the Statute of 12. Edw.2.ca.2. Processe should be a market against the witnesses named in the deed, *testes in carta nominatos,*[202] (s)[203] and that the same Statute was but an affirmance of the Common Law, which not being well understood, hath caused varietie of opinions in our bookes. But the delay therein was so great, and some times (though rarely) by exceptions against those witnesses, which being found true; they were not to be sworne at all, neither to be joyned to the Jurie, nor as witnesses, (t)[204] as if the witnesse were infamous, for example, if he attainted of a false verdict, [6 b] or of a conspiracie at the | suit of the King, or convicted of perjurie, or of a Premunire, or of forgerie upon the Statute of 5. Eliz. cap. 14. and not upon the Statue of 1 Hen. 5. cap. 3. or convict of felony, or by judgement lost his cares, or stood upon the pillorie or tumbrell, or beene *stigmaticus* branded,

199. [*Ed.:* given (or dated) at D.]

200. [*Ed.:* in witness whereof.]

201. (r) Lamb. exposit. verb. terra ex scripto. Vid. Fortescue cap. 32. see the second part of the Institut. cap. 38. 12. E. 2. c. 2. see the second part of the Institutes. Marlbr. cap. 6. & cap. 14.

202. [*Ed.:* the witnesses named in the charter.]

203. (s) Brit fo. 65. 101. 11. E. 3. Proces. 170. 6. H. 3. Proces. 209. 8. H. 3. Proces. 210. 4. E. 2. gard. 119.

204. (t) Mirror ca. 4. sect. de infamies & perjurie. Glanvil. lib. 2. cap. 15. Bract. lib. 5. fol. 288. 292. Brit. fo 134. 135. 101. Fleta lib. 5. ca 21. 8. E. 2. Ass. 396. 2. E. 3. 22. 24. E. 3. 34. 43. E. 3. conspir. 11. 27. Ass. 29. 33. H. 6. 55 H. 6. 30.

or the like, whereby they become infamous for some offences, *quae sunt minoris culpae sunt majoris infamiae.*[205] (c)[206] If a Champion in a Writ of right become recreant or coward, he thereby loseth *liberam legem,*[207] and thereby becomes infamous, and cannot be a witnesse, for regularly he that loseth *liberam legem,* becommeth infamous, and can be no witness. Or if the witnesse be an Infidell, or of non sane memorie, or not of discretion, or a partie interessed, or the like. (d)[208] But often-times a man may be challenged to be of a Jurie, that cannot be challenged to be a Witnesse, and therefore though the Witnesse be of the nearest alliance, or kindred, or of counsell, or tenant, or servant to either partie, (or any other exception that maketh him not infamous, or to want understanding, or discretion, or a partie in interest) though it be proved true, shall not exclude the witnesse to be sworn, (e)[209] but he shall be sworne, and his credit upon the exceptions taken against him left to those of the Jurie, who are triers of the fact, insomuch as some Bookes have said, that though the witnesse named in the Deed be named a Disseisor in the writ, yet hee shall be sworne as a witnesse to the deed. (f)[210] A Witnesse amongst others named in a deed was outlawed, and no Processe was awarded against him by the Statute, because he was *extra legem,*[211] and an outlawed person cannot be an Auditor. And the Court in some bookes have said, that they have not seene witnesses challenged, which is regularly to be understood with the limitations above-said, but such as are returned to be of a Jurie, are to be challenged for the causes aforesaid for outlawrie, and divers other causes (for the which a witnesse cannot be challenged) and such Processe against witnesses banished. But seeing the witnesses named in a Deed shall be joyned to the Inquest, and shall in some sort joyne also in the verdict (in which case if Jurie and Witnesses finde the Deed that is denied to be the Deed of the partie, the adverse partie is barred of his attaint, because there is more than twelve that affirme the verdict.) It is reason that in that case of joyning, such exception shall be taken

---

205. [*Ed.:* [To lose] one's free law (called the Villainous judgement).]
206. (c) Fortescu. cap. 26. Pat. 55. H. 3. m. 3. Stanf. Pl. Cor. 174. a.
207. [*Ed.:* free law.]
208. (d) Fortescu. ca. 25.
209. (e) 22. Ass. 12. &c. 41. 23. Ass. 11. 19. E. 2. tit. Ass. 40.
210. (f) 34. E. 1. Proces. 208.
211. [*Ed.:* Out of the law; out of the protection of the law.]

against the Witnesse as against one of the Jurie, because he is in the nature of a Juror. (a)[212] And therefore to put one example, if he be outlawed in a personall action he cannot be joyned to the Jurie, but yet that is no exception against him to exclude him to be sworne as a Witnesse to the Jurie. And the reason of all this is, for that if he with others should joyne in verdict with the Jurie in affirmance of the Deed, the partie should be barred of his Attaint. But note, there must be more than one witnesse, that shall bee joyned to the Inquest. And albeit they joyne with the Jurie, and finde it not his Deed, notwithstanding this joyning, the partie shall have his attaint, for it is a maxime in law, (b)[213] That Witnesses cannot testifie a negative, but an affirmative. And if one of the witnesses named in the Deed be one of the panell, he shall be put out of the panell, and all these secrets of law doe notably appeare in our bookes.

To shut up this point, it is to be knowne (c)[214] that when a triall is by witnesses, regularly the affirmative ought to be proved by two or three witnesses, as to prove a summons of the Tenant, or the challenge of a Juror, and the like. But when the triall is by verdict of 12. men, there the judgement is not given upon witnesses, or other kinde of evidence, but upon the verdict, and upon such evidence as is given to the Jurie they give their verdict. And Bracton saith there is *probatio duplex, viz. viva.*[215] as by witnesses *viva voce,* and *mortua,*[216] as by deeds, writings, and instruments. And many times Juries, together with other matter, are much induced by presumptions, whereof there be three sorts, viz. violent, probable, and light or temerarie. *Violenta praesumptio* is many times *plena probatio,*[217] as if one be run thorow the body with a sword in a house whereof he instantly dieth, and a man is seene to come out of that house with a bloudy sword, and no other man was at that time in the house. *Praesumptio probabilis* moveth little, but, *Praesumptio levis seu temeraria,*[218] moveth not at all. So it is in the case of a Charter of feoffment,

212. (a) 34. E. I. tit.proces 208 II. Ass. p. 19. 20. 12. Ass. p. 1. 12. 41. 18. Ass. p. 11. 22. Ass. 15. 23. Ass. 15. 40. Aff. 23. 48. Ass. p. 5. 21. H. 6. 30. [*Ed.:* Note: the 1639 edition's note lettering is used here, but it is erratic.]

213. (b) 48. E. 3. 30. 12. H. 6. fo. 6. 2. 50. E. a. 16. 43. E. 3. 32. 12. H. 4. 9. 19. E. 2. Ass. 408. Pasch. 14. E. 3. Coram rege Devon. in Thesaur. Fleta lib. 6. cap. 6. F.N.B. 106. b. & 97. c.

214. (c) Mirror ca. 3. Pl. Com. fo. 10. Bract. lib. 5 fo. 400.

215. [*Ed.:* proof is of two kinds, that is to say, living.]

216. [*Ed.:* with the living voice; by word of mouth, and dead.]

217. [*Ed.:* Full proof (that is, proof by two witnesses).]

218. [*Ed.:* A light or random presumption.]

if all the witnesses to the Deed be dead (as no man can keepe his witnesses alive, & time weareth out all men) then violent presumption which stands for a proofe is continuall and quiet possession,[219] for *ex diuturnitate temporis omnia praesumuntur solemniter esse acta,*[220] also the Deed may receive credit,[221] *per collationem sigillorum, scripturae, &c. & super fidem cartarum mortuis testibus erit ad patriam de necessitate currendum.*[222]

Note, it hath beene resolved by the Justices, that a wife cannot be produced either against or for her husband,[223] *quia sunt duae animae in carne una,*[224] and it might be a cause of implacable discord and dissention between the husband and the wife, and a meane of great inconvenience, but (d)[225] in some cases women are by Law wholly excluded to beare testimony, as to prove a man to be a Villeine, *mulieres ad probationem status hominis admitti non debent.*[226] It was also agreed by the whole Court (e)[227] that in an Information upon the Statute of usurie, the partie to the usurious contract shall not be admitted to be a witnesse against the Usurer, for in effect hee should be *testis in propria causa,*[228] and should avoyd his owne bonds and assurances, and discharge himselfe of the money borrowed, and though hee commonly raise up an Intormer to exhibit the Information, yet *in rei veritate*[229] he is the partie. And herewith in effect agreeth Brit-l-ton, that be that challengeth a right in the thing in demand, cannot be a witnesse, for that he is a partie in interest. But now let us returne to that from the which by way of digression (upon this occasion) we are fallen.

[7 a]

And the ancient Charters of the King which passed away any franchise or

---

219. Fleta lib. 6. ca. 33. 8. E. 3 290. 39. E. 3. 21. 5.

220. [*Ed.:* From length of time (after lapse of time) all things are presumed to have been done in due form.]

221. Glanvil. lib. 10. ca. 12. Fleta lib. 6. ca. 33.

222. [*Ed.:* by the addition of seals, writing, etc.; and upon the credit of charters with dead witnesses it will be necessary to have recourse to the country (i.e., jury).]

223. Pasch. 10. Ja. in Com. Banco upon the stat. of Bankrupts.

224. [*Ed.:* because they are two souls in one flesh.]

225. (d) Fleta, lib. 2. ca. 44. 13. E. 1. tit. Vill. 36. 37. 19. E. 2. Ibid. 32.

226. [*Ed.:* women ought not to be admitted to prove the status of a man.]

227. (e) Tr. 8. Ja. in Com. banco. Smithes case. In evidence upon an information upon the statute of Usury. Brit. fol. 134.

228. [*Ed.:* a witness in his own cause.]

229. [*Ed.:* in truth.]

revenue of any estate of inheritance, had ever this clause of *hiis testibus*[230] of the greatest men of the Kingdome, as the Charters of creation of Nobilitie, yet have at this day: when *hiis testibus* was omitted, and when *teste me ipso*,[231] came in into the Kings grants, you shall read in the second part of the Institutes, Mag. Charta, cap. 38. I have tearmed the said parts of the Deed, formall or orderly parts, for that they be not of the essence of a Deed of feoffment, for if such a Deed be without *premisses, habendum, tenendum, reddendum* clause of warrantie,[232] the clause of *In cujus rei testimonium*,[233] the Date, and the clause of *hiis testibus,* yet the Deed is good. (f)[234] For if a man by Deed give lands to another, and to his heires without more saying, this is good, if he put his Seale to the Deed, deliver it, and make liverie accordingly. (g)[235] So it is if A. give lands, to have and to hold, to B. and his heires, this is good, albeit the feoffee is not named in the promisses. And yet no well advised man will trust to such Deed, which Law by construction maketh good *ut res magis valeat*,[236] but when forme and substance concurre, then is the Deed faire and absolutely good. The sealing of Charters and Deeds is much more ancient than some, out of error, have imagined, for the Charter of the King Edwyn, brother of King Edgar, bearing Date *Anno Domini* 956, made of the land called Jecklea in the Isle of Ely, was not onely sealed with his owne Seale (which appeareth by these words, *Ego Edwinus gratia Dei totius Britannicae telluris Rex meum donum proprio sigillo confirmavi)*[237] but also the Bishop of Winchester put to his Seale, *Ego Aelfwinus Winton Ecclesiae divinus speculator proprium sigillum impressi.*[238] And the Charter of King Offa, whereby he gave the Peterpence, doth yet remaine under Seale. But no King of England, before, or since the Conquest, sealed with any seale of Armes, before King Richard

---

230. [*Ed.*: these being witness.]

231. [*Ed.*: witness myself; a solemn formula of attestation by the sovereign, used at the conclusion of charters, and other public instruments, and also of original writs out of chancery.]

232. [*Ed.*: warranty is an English word.]

233. [*Ed.*: In testimony whereof.]

234. (f) Mirror ca. 1. sect. 6 &. and cap. 5. sect. 1: Glanvil. lib. 10. ca. 12. Bract. lib. 5. fol. 396. Flet. li. 6. c. 32. Brit. f. 66.

235. (g) Vid. Tearmes of the Law, verb. faits. Vid. Glanvil. lib. 10. c. 12. Mirr. c. 1. sect. 3. & c. 3.

236. [*Ed.*: that the thing should rather prevail.]

237. [*Ed.*: I, Edward, by the grace of God king of all the land of Britain, have confirmed my gift with my own seal.]

238. [*Ed.*: I, Ælfwin, God's overseer of the church of Winchester, have stamped my own seal.]

the first but the Seale was the King sitting in a chaire on the one side of the Seale, and on horse backe on the other side in divers formes. And King Richard the first sealed with a Seale of two Lyons, for the Conqueror for England bare two Lyons, and King John in the right of Aquitaine (the Duke whereof bare one Lyon) was the first that bare three Lyons, and made his Seale accordingly, and all the Kings since have followed him. And King Edward the third in anno 13. of his reigne did quarter the Armes of France with his three Lyons, and took upon him the title of King of France, and all his Successors have followed him therein.

In ancient Charters of feoffment there was never mention made of the deliverie of the Deed, or any liverie of seisin indorsed, for certainly the witnesses named in the Deed, were witnesses of both: and witnesses either of deliverie of the Deed, or of liverie of seisin by expresse tearmes was but of latter times, and the reason was in respect of the notorietie of the feoffment. And I have knowne some ancient deeds of feoffment having liverie of seisin indorsed suspected, and after detected of forgerie. As if a Deed in the stile of the King name him *Defensor fidei*[239] before 13.Henry the eighth or Supreme head before 20.Henry the eighth at what time hee was first acknowledged supreme head by the Clergie, albeit the King[240] used not the stile of Supreme head in his Charters, &c. till 22.Henry the eighth or King of Ireland, before 33.Henry the eighth at which time he assumed the title of the King of Ireland, being before that called Lord of Ireland, it is certainly forged, & *sic de similibus.*[241]

And some have observed, that Grace was attributed to King Henry the fourth.[242] Excellent Grace to King Henry the sixth Majestie to King Henry the eighth and before, the King was called, Soveraigne Lord, Liege Lord, Highnesse and Kingly Highnesse, which in Latine in legall proceedings is called *Regia Celsitudo,* as the beginning of the petition of right to the King is, *Humillimè supplicavit vestrae Celsitudini regiae, &c,*[243] and the like. And upon this occasson it shall not be impertinent, seeing it is part of the formall Deed, to set downe the severall stiles of the Kings of England since the Conquest.

239. [*Ed.:* Defender of the faith.]

240. 21. H. 8 cap. 15.

241. [*Ed.:* and likewise of similar things.]

242. Vid. 2. H. 4. ca. 15. where Royall Majestie is attributed to the King, and Crimen Laesae Majestatis far more ancient.

243. [*Ed.:* Royal highness . . . Humbly supplicates unto your royal highness, etc.]

William the Conquerour commonly stiled himselfe *Willielmus Rex,* and sometimes *Willielmus Rex Anglorum.* And the like did William Rufus, and sometimes *Willielmus Dei gratia Rex Anglorum.*[244]

Henry the first, *Henricus Rex Anglorum,* and sometimes *Henricus Dei gratia Rex Anglorum.*[245]

Mawde the sole daughter and heire of Henry the first wrote, *Matildis Imperatrix Henrici Regis filia & Anglorum Domina.*[246] Divers of whose creations and grants I have seene.

King Stephen used the stile that King Henry the first did.

Henry the second, Fitz Emprice omitted *Dei gratia,* and used this stile, *Henricus Rex Angliae, Dux Normanniae, & Aquitaniae, & Comes Andegaviae,*[247] hee having the Duchie of Aquitaine, and Earledome of Poitiers in the right of Elianor his wife heire to both: And the Earledomes of Anjow, Tournie, and Maine, as sonne and heire to Jeffery Plantagenet by the said Mawde his wife, daughter and sole heire of King Henry the first. She was first married to Henry the Emperour, and after his death to the said Jeffery Plantagenet. Which Duchie of Aquitaine doth include Gascoinge and Guian.

King Richard the first used the stile that Henry the second his father did, yet was hee King of Cyprus, and after of Jerusalem, but never used either of them.

[7 b] I King John used that stile, but with this addition *Dominus Hiberniae,*[248] and yet all that hee had in Ireland was conquered by his father King Henry the second which title of *Dominus Hiberniae,* hee assumed, as annexed to the Crowne, albeit his father, in the 23. yeare of his reigne, had created him King of Ireland in his life time.

King Henry the third stiled himselfe as his father King John did, untill the 44. yeare of his reigne, and then he left out of his stile *Dux Normanniae, & Comes Andegaviae,* and wrote onely *Rex Angliae, Dominus Hiberniae, & Dux Aquitaniae.*

King Edward the first stiled himselfe in like manner as King Henry the third his father did, *Rex Angliae, Dominus Hiberniae, & Dux Aquitaniae.* And

---

244. [*Ed.:* William, by the grace of God king of the English.]
245. [*Ed.:* Henry, by the grace of God king of the English.]
246. [*Ed.:* Maud the Empress, daughter of King Henry, and lady of England.]
247. [*Ed.:* Henry, king of England, duke of Normandy and Aquitaine, and earl of Anjou.]
248. [*Ed.:* Lord of Ireland.]

so did King Edward the second during all his reigne. And King Edward the third used the selfe same stile untill the 13. yeare of his reigne, and then hee stiled himselfe in this forme, *Edwardus Dei gratia Rex Angliae & Franciae, & Dominus Hiberniae,* leaving out of his stile *Dux Aquitaniae.* He was King of France, as sonne and heire of Isabel wife of King Edward the second daughter and heire of Philip le Beau King of France, he first quartered the French Armories with the English in his great Seale, *Anno Domini 1338. & regni sui 14.*

King Richard the second and King Henry the fourth used the same stile that King Edward the third did. And King Henry the fifth untill the 8. yeare of his reigne continued the same stile, and then wrote himselfe, *Rex Angliae, Haeres & Regens Franciae, & Dominus Hiberniae,* and so continued during his life.

King Henry the sixth wrote,[249] *Henricus Dei gratia Rex Angliae et Franciae, & Dominus Hiberniae;* this King being crowned in Paris King of France used the said stile 39. yeares, till hee was dispossessed of the Crowne by King Edward the fourth who after he had reigned also about ten yeares, King Henry the sixth was restored to the Crowne againe, and then wrote, *Henricus Dei gratia Rex Angliae, & Franciae, & Dominus Hiberniae ab inchoatione regni sui 49. & receptionis regiae potestatis primo.*[250]

King Edward the fourth Richard the third and Henry the seventh stiled themselves, *Rex Angliae & Franciae, & Dominus Hiberniae.*

King Henry the eighth used the same stile till the tenth yeare of his reigne, and then hee added this word (*Octavus*) as *Henricus octavus Dei gratia, &c.* In the 13. yeare of his reigne hee added to his stile *Fidei Defensor.* In the 22. yeare of his reigne, in the end of his stile hee added, *Supremum Caput Ecclesiae Anglicanae.*[251] And in the 23. yeare of his reigne hee stiled himselfe thus, *Henricus octavus Dei gratia Angliae, Franciae & Hiberniae Rex, Fidei Defensor, &c. & in terra Ecclesiae Anglicanae & Hiberniae supremum caput.*[252]

King Edward the sixth used the same stile, and so did Queene Mary in the

---

249. Vid. Rot. Parliam. anno 1. H. 6. nu. 15. he was stiled Rex Franciae & Angliae & Domimus Hiberniae.

250. [*Ed.:* Henry, by the grace of God king of England and France, and lord of Ireland, in the forty-ninth year since the beginning of his reign and in the first year of his resumption of the royal power.]

251. [*Ed.:* Supreme Head of the Church of England.]

252. [*Ed.:* Henry the eighth, by the grace of God king of England, France, and Ireland, defender of the faith, etc., and supreme head in earth of the Church of England and Ireland.]

beginning of her reigne, and by that name summoned her first Parliament, but soone after omitted *Supremum Caput*. And after her marriage with King Philip, the stile not withstanding that omission was the longest that ever was, viz. Philip and Mary by the grace of God King and Queene of England and France, Naples, Jerusalem and Ireland, Defenders of the faith, Princes of Spaine and Cicily, Archdukes of Austria, Dukes of Millaine, Burgundy and Brabant, Countees of Hasburgh, Flanders and Tyroll. And this stile continued till the fourth and fifth yeare of King Philip and Queen Mary, and then Naples was put out, and in place thereof both the Cicilies put in, and so it continued all the life of Queene Mary.

I need not mention the stile of Queene Elizabeth, King James, nor of our Soveraigne Lord King Charles, because they are so well knowne, and I feare I have beene too long concerning this point, which certainly is not unnecessarie to be knowne for many respects. But to shew the causes and reasons of these alterations would aske a Treatise of itselfe, and doth not sort to the end that I have aimed at. And now let us returne to the learning of Charters and Deeds of Feoffments and Grants.

Verie necessarie it is that Witnesses should bee underwritten or indorsed, for the better strengthening of Deeds, and their names (if they can write) written with their owne hands. For Liverie of seisin see hereafter Sect. 59.[253] and for Deeds, Sect. 66. and of Conditionall Deeds see our Author in his Chapter of Conditions. And now let us proceed to the other words of our Author.

"To him and to his Heires."

Haeres, in the legall understanding of the Common Law,[254] implyeth that he is *ex justis nuptiis procreatus,* for *haeres legitimus est quem nuptiae demonstrant,*[255] and is he to whom lands, tenements, or hereditaments by the act of God, and right of blood doe descend of some estate of inheritance, for *Solus Deus haeredem facere potest non homo: dicuntur autem haereditas & haeres ab haerendo,*

253. Liverie of seisin incident to a feoffment. Vid. sect. 59.
254. Mirr. cap. 2. sect. 15. Bract. lib. 2. fol. 62 b. Flet lib. 6. cap. 1 & 54. & lib. 1. c. 13. Glanvil. lib. 7. cap. 1. & capa. 12. & 13.
255. [*Ed.:* begotten of a rightful marriage (for) he is a lawful heir whom marriage points out as such; who is born in wedlock.]

*quod est arctè insidendo, nam qui haeres est, haeret, vel dicitur ab haerendo quia
haereditas sibi haeret, licet nonnulli haeredem dictum velint quod haeres fuit, hoc
est dominus terrarum, &c. quae ad eum preveniunt.*[256]

A monster which hath not the shape of mankinde, cannot be heire or inherit
any land, albeit it be brought forth within marriage, (a)[257] but although hee
hath deformitie in any part of his bodie, yet if he hath humane shape he may
be heire. *Hii qui contra formam humani generis converso more procreantur, ut
si mulier monstrosum, vel prodigiosum enixa, inter liberos non computentur, partus
tamen cui natura aliquantulem ampliaverit vel diminuerit, non tamen supera-
bundanter (ut si sex digitos vel nisi quatuor habuerit) bene debet inter liberos
connumerari. | Si inutilia natura reddidit, ut si membra tortuosa habuerit, non
tamen is partus monstrosus.*[258] Another saith, *Ampliatio seu diminutio membrorum non nocet.*[259] (b)[260] A Bastard cannot be heire, for (as hath beene said
before) *qui ex damnato coitu nascuntur inter liberos non computentur.*[261] Everie
heire is either a male, or female, or an Hemophradite, that is, both male and
female. And an Hermophradite (which is also called Androgynus) shall be
heire, either as male or female, according to that kinde of the sex which doth
prevaile. *Hermaphradita, tam masculo, quàm foeminae comparatur secundum
praevalescentiam sexus incalescentis.*[262] And accordingly it ought to be baptized.
See more of this matter, Sect. 35.

(c)[263] A man seised of lands in fee hath issue an Alien that is borne out of

[8 a]

---

256. [*Ed.:* Only God may make an heir, not man. *Haereditas* (inheritance) and *haeres* (heir) are so called
from *haerendo* (adhering), that is, firmly sticking, either because he who is an heir adheres or because the
inheritance adheres to him who is the heir, even though many would like to be called heir, that is, lord
of the lands etc. which have come to him.]

257. (a) Bract. lib 5. fol. 437. 438. Brit. cap. 66. fol. 167. & cap 83. Fleta. lib. 1. cap. 5.

258. [*Ed.:* Those who are born without human form shall not be considered children, as for instance
when a woman gives birth to something monstrous or unnatural. But if nature has added or subtracted
a little something, provided it not be excessive (for instance, if the offspring has six fingers, or four), he
shall rightly be considered a child. If nature has rendered something useless, for instance if the offspring
has twisted limbs, he shall not on that account be considered a monster.]

259. [*Ed.:* Those who are born of an unlawful intercourse are not reckoned among the children.]

260. (b) Vid. Sect 188. 399. Bract. lib. 2. fol. 92. Brit. fo. Fleta lib. 2 ca. 5. & 1. 6. c. 8. Fleta ubi supra.
3. R. 2. Entr. cong. 38.

261. [*Ed.:* whoever is born of a guilty union shall not be reckoned among the children.]

262. [*Ed.:* A hermaphrodite shall be treated either as male or as female according to the prevalence of
the sex when warmed.]

263. (c) Mirror ca. 1. ca. 3. sect. ca. 5 sect. Bract. lib. 5. fol. 415. 427. Britt. fo. 29. Fleta lib. 6. ca. 47.

the Kings ligeance, he cannot be heire, *propter defectum subjectionis,*[264] albeit hee be borne within lawfull marriage. If made Denizen by the Kings Letters Patents, yet cannot hee inherit to his father or any other. But otherwise it is if hee be naturalized by Act of Parliament, for then hee is not accousted in Law *Alienigena,* but *Indigena.* But after one be made Denizen, the issue that hee hath afterwards shall be heire to him, but no issue that he had before. If an Alien commeth into England and hath issue two sonnes, these two sonnes are *Indigenae* subjects borne, because they are borne within the Realme. And yet if one of them purchase lands in fee, and dieth without issue, his brother shall not be his heire, for there was never any inheritable blood betweene the father and them, and where the sonnes by no possibilitie can be heire to the father, the one of them shall not be heire to the other. See more at large of this matter, Sect. 198.

If a man be attainted of treason, or felony, although he be borne within wedlocke, hee can be heire to no man, nor any man heire to him *propter delictum,*[265] for that by his attaindor his blood is corrupted. And this corruption of blood is so high, as it cannot absolutely be salved, and restored but by Act of Parliament,[266] for albeit the person attainted obtaine his Charter of pardon, yet that doth not make any to be heire whose blood was corrupted at the time of the attainder, either downeward or upward. (d)[267] As if a man hath issue a sonne before his attainder, and obtaineth his pardon, and after the pardon hath issue another sonne, at the time of the attainder, the blood of the eldest was corrupted, and therefore he cannot be heire. But if he dye living his father, the younger sonne shall be heire, for he was not in esse at the time of the attainder, and the pardon restored the blood as to all issues begotten afterwards. But in that case if the eldest sonne had survived the father, the younger sonne cannot be heire; because he hath an elder brother which by possibilitie might have inherited, but if the elder brother had beene an Alien, the younger sonne

---

13. E. 3. br. 677. 25. E. 3. de natis ultra mare. 31. E. 3. Cosinage 5. 42. E. 3. 1. 11. H. 4 26. 14. H. 4 19. 20. 3. H. 6. 55. 22. H. 6. 38. 9. E. 4. 7. lib. 7. fo. 1. in Calvins case.

264. [*Ed.:* for want of subjection.]

265. [*Ed.:* on account of wrongdoing.]

266. 1. E. 3. 4. 6. E. 3. 55. 27. E. 3 77. 3. E. 2. discent. Br. 64. 31. E. 1. discent. 17. 46. E. 3. Petition 20. 26. Ass. pl. 2. 49 Ass. pl. 4. 29. Ass. pl. 11. 9. H. 5. 9.

267. (d) Stanf. pl. cor. 195. 196. Bracton lib. 3. fo. 132. 133. 276. & lib. 5. fo. 374. Britton fo. 215. b. Fleta lib. 1. ca. 28.

should be heire, for that the Alien never had any inheritable blood in him. See more plentifully of this matter, Sect. 646, 647.

If a man hath issue two sonnes, and after is attainted of treason, or felony, and one of the sons purchase lands and dieth without issue, the other brother shall be his heire, for the attainder of the father corrupteth the lineall blood only, and not the collaterall blood betweene the brethren, which was vested in them before the attainder, and each of them by possibilitie might have beene heire to the father, and so hath it beene adjudged, (*)[268] but other wise in the case of the Alienee, as hath beene said. (e)[269] But some have holden that if a man after he be attainted of treason or felony have issue two sonnes; that the one of them cannot be heire to the other, because they could not be heire to the father, for that they never had any inheritable blood in them.

(f)[270] One that is borne deafe and dumbe may be heire to another, albeit it was otherwise holden in ancient time. And so if borne deafe, dumbe, and blinde, for *in hoc casu, vitio parcitur naturali*,[271] but contract they cannot. Ideots, leapers, mad men, outlawes in debt, trespasses, or the like, persons excommunicated, men attainted in a praemunire, or convicted of heresie, may be heires.

(g)[272] If a man hath a wife, and dieth, and within a verie short time after the wife marrieth againe, and within nine monethes hath a childe, so as it may be the childe of the one or of the other. Some have said, That in this case the childe may chuse his father, *quia in hoc casu filiatio non potest probari*,[273] and so is the Booke to be intended, for avoyding of which question and other inconveniences, this was the Law before the Conquest, *Sit omnis vidua sine marito duodecim mensibus, & si maritauerit perdat dotem*.[274]

(h)[275] A man by the Common Law cannot be heire to goods or Chattels,

268. (*) In the Exchequer Mic. 40. & 41. Eliz. in le Case de Hobby.

269. (e) Bract. lib. 4. fol. 130. Britton fol. 15. Fleta lib. 1. cap. 58.

270. (f) Bract. lib. 5. fol. 421. 430. 434. lib. 2. fol. 12. Fleta lib. 6. ca. 39. 47. 14. H. 3. Bre. 877. 32. E. 3. Age 8. 10. E. 3. 535. 18. E. 3. 53. 13. E. 3 Ley 49.

271. [*Ed.*: in this case he suffers from a natural deficiency.]

272. (g) 21. E. 2. 29 Panorollus nova rep. 485, &c. Opus eximium 48. b. Lambard de priscis Anglorum legibus 120. 72. acc.

273. [*Ed.*: because in this case the affiliation cannot be proved.]

274. [*Ed.*: Let every widow be unmarried for twelve months, and if she marries she should lose her dower.]

275. (h) Bract. lib. 4. ca. 9. fol. 265. lib. 2. fo. 62. b. Fleta lib. 6. ca. 1. Lib. 8. fo. 54. Syms case.

for *haeres dicitur ab haereditate.*[276] (i)[277] If a man buy divers fishes, as Carps, Breames, Tenches, &c. and put them in his pond, and dyeth, in this case the heire shall have them, and not the Executors, but they shall goe with the inheritance, because they were at libertie and could not be gotten without industrie, as by nets, and other engines, otherwise it is if they were in a trunke or the like. Likewise Deere in a Parke, Coneyes in a Warren, and Doves in a Dove-house, young and old shall goe to the heire. (k)[278] But of ancient time the heire was permitted to have an Action of debt upon a bond made to his Ancestor and his heires, but the Law is not so holden at this day. Vid. Sect. 12.

(l)[279] It is to be noted that one cannot be heire till after the death of his Ancestor, hee is called *haeres apparens,* heir apparent.

[8 b]   I In our old Bookes and Records there is mention made of another heire, viz. *haeres astrarius* so called of *Astre,* that is, an harth of a house, because the Ancester by conveyance hath set his heire apparent, and his family in a house and living in his lifetime, of whom Bracton saith thus, (a)[280] *item esto quod haeres sit astrarius, vel quod aliquis antecessor restituat haeredi in vita sua haereditatem, & se dimiserit, videtur quod nullo tempore jacebit haereditas, & ideo quod nec relevari possit, nec debet, nec relevium dari.*[281] (b)[282] For the benefit and safetie of right heires *contra partus suppositos,* the Law hath provided remedy by the Writ *De ventre inspiciendo,*[283] whereof the rule in the Register is this; *Nota si quis habens haereditatem duxerit aliquam in uxorem & postea moriatur ille sine haerede de corpore suo exeunte, per quod haereditas illa fratri ipsius*

276. [*Ed.:* heir is so called from inheritance.]

277. (i) Mich. 36. & 37. El. Rot. 25. Inter Gray. & Paulet in the Kings Bench. Stanford 25. b. 18. E. 4. 8. 22. Ass. 25. 18. H. 8. 2.

278. (k) 13. E. 3. det. 135. 139. 140. 47. E. 3. 23. 25. E. 3. fol. 43. 26. E. 3. fo. Vid. for an heirelome haereditarium or principalius, sect. 12.

279. (l) Mirror ca. 1. sect. 3.

280. (a) Bract. lib. 2. fo 85. Heref p. 8. E. 1. Ro. 80. de Banco. Mirror cap. 2. sect. 18. Britton 151. b.

281. [*Ed.:* Suppose the heir is *astrarius* (found on the hearth), or that some ancestor in his lifetime restores his inheritance to the heir and renounces his own interest; it seems that the inheritance will never lie vacant and therefore that it cannot and ought not to be taken up, nor any relief given.]

282. (b) Registr. fo. 227. Bracton lib. 2. fo. 69. Britton fol. 165. Fleta lib. 1. ca. 14.

283. [*Ed.:* Writ to inspect the belly, where a woman feigned to be pregnant, to see whether she was with child.]

defuncti descendere debeat, & uxor dicit se esse praegnantem de ipso defuncto cum non sit, habeat frater, & haeres breve de ventre inspiciendo.[284] It seemeth by Bracton and Fleta which followed him, that this Writ doth lye, *Ubi uxor alicujus in vita viri sui se praegnantem fecit cum non sit, vel post mortem viri sui se praegnantem fecit cum non sit ad exhaeredationem veri haeredis, &c. ad quaerelam veri haeredis per praeceptum domini regis, &c.*[285] which is to be understood according to the rule of the Register: when a man having lands in fee simple dieth, and his wife soone after marrieth againe, and faines her selfe with childe by her former husband, in this case though she be married, the Writ *De ventre inspiciendo* doth lye for the heire. But if a man seised of lands in fee (for example) hath issue a daughter, who is heire apparent, she in the life of her father cannot have this writ for divers causes; first, because she is not heire, but heire apparant, for as hath beene said, *nemo est haeres viventis,*[286] and this Writ is given to the heire to whom the land is descended. And both Bracton and Fleta saith, that this Writ lieth *Ad quaerelam veri haeredis,*[287] which cannot be in the life of his Ancestor, and herewith agreeth Britton and the Register.[288] Secondly, the taking of a husband in the case aforesaid being her owne act, cannot barre the heire of his lawfull Action once vested in him. Thirdly, the Law doth not give the heire apparant any Writ, for it is not certaine whether he shall be heire, *solus Deus facit haeredes.*[289] Fourthly, the inconvenience were too great if heires apparent in the life of their Ancestor should have such a Writ to examine and trie a mans lawfull wife in such sort as the Writ *De ventre inspiciendo* doth appoint, and if she should be found to be with child, or suspect, then shee must bee removed to a Castle and there safely

284. [*Ed.:* Note that if anyone having an inheritance takes someone to wife, and afterwards dies without an heir begotten of his body, so that the inheritance ought to descend to the brother of the deceased, and the woman says she is pregnant by the deceased, when she is not, the brother and heir shall have a writ *de ventre inspiciendo* (for inspecting the belly).]

285. [*Ed.:* where someone's wife claims to be pregnant in the lifetime of her husband, when she is not, or after her husband's death claims to be pregnant, when she is not, to the disinheritance of the true heir, etc., at the suit of the true heir by command of the lord king, etc.]

286. [*Ed.:* No one can be heir during the life of his ancestor.]

287. [*Ed.:* at the suit of the true heir.]

288. Britton fo. 165. b. Regist. ubi supra.

289. [*Ed.:* God alone makes the heir.]

kept untill her deliverie, and so any mans wife might be taken from him against the Laws of God and man.[290]

The words of the Writ *De ventre inspiciendo* make this evident, *Rex Vic. salutem, monstravit nobis A. quod cum R. quae fuit uxor Clementis B. praegnans non sit, ipsa falsò dicit se esse praegnantem de eodem Clemente, ad exhaeredationem ipsius A. desicut terra quae fuit ejusden C. ad ipsum A. jure haereditario descendere debeat tanquam ad fratrem & haeredem ipsius se si praedict. R. prolem de eo non habuerit, &c.*[291] But this rather belongs to the Treatise of originall Writs, and therefore thus much herein shall suffice.

And it is to be observed that everie word of Littleton is worthy of observation, first (Heires) in the plurall number, for if a man give land to a man & to his heire in the singular number, he hath but an estate for life, for his heire cannot take a fee simple by descent, because he is but one, and therefore in that case his heire shall take nothing. Also observable is this conjunctive (Et), for if a man give lands to one, To have and to hold to him or his heires, hee hath but an estate for life for the uncertaintie. (Se, suis)[292] If a man give land unto two, To have and to hold to them two & *haeredibus* (c)[293] omitting *suis,* they have but an estate for life for the uncertaintie, whereof more hereafter in this Section. But it is said, if land be given to one man, & *haeredibus,* omitting *suis,* that notwithstanding a fee simple passeth, but it is safe to follow Littleton.

(d)[294] "and his Assignes."

Assignee commeth of the verbe *assigno.* And note there bee Assignes in Deed, and Assignes in Law, whereof see more in the Chapter of Warrantie, Sect. 733.

---

290. Vid. Bracton, Britton & Fleta ubi supra. Registr. ubi supra. Bracton and Fleta ubi supra hare (ad exhaereditationem.)

291. [*Ed.:* The king to the sheriff, etc. greeting. A. has shown to us that, whereas R., who was the wife of Clement B., is not pregnant, she falsely says that she is pregnant by the same Clement, to the disinheritance of the selfsame A., inasmuch as land which was the selfsame Clement's ought to descend to him the said A. by hereditary right as his brother and heir, if the aforesaid R. should have no issue by him, etc.]

292. [*Ed.:* his.]

293. (c) 10. H. 6. 7. 22. H. 6. 15. Pl. Com. 28. b. 22. E. 4 16. 2. H 4. 13. 20 E. 3. br. 377

294. (d) Lib. 5 fo. 96. 97. Britt. fo. 28. H. 8. Dyer. Pl. Com. 287, 288. [*Ed.:* Lib. 5 is 5 Coke *Reports.*]

"these words (his Heires) which words onely make an Estate of Inheritance in
all Feoffments and Grants."

(e)[295] *Si autem facta esset donatio, ut si dicam, do tibi talem terram, ista donatio
non extendit ad haeredes sed ad vitam donatoria, &c.*[296] (f)[297] Here Littleton
treateth of purchases by naturall persons, and not of Bodies politique or corporate; (g)[298] for if lands be given to a sole Body politique or corporate, (as
to a Bishop, Parson, Vicar, Master of an Hospitall, &c.) there to give him an
estate of inheritance in his politique or corporate capacitie, hee must have
these words, To have and to hold to him and his successors, for without these
words *Successors,* in these cases there passeth no inheritance, for as the heire
doth inherit to the Ancestor, so the Successor doth succeed to the Predecessor,
and the Executor to the Testator. (h)[299] But it appeareth here by Littleton,
that if a man at this day give lands to IS and his Successors, this createth no
fee simple in him, for Littleton speaking of naturall persons saith that these
words (his heires) make an estate of inheritance in all Feoffments and Grants,
whereby he excludeth these words (his successors.) (i)[300] And yet if it be an
ancient grant it must be expounded as the Law was taken at the time of the
grant. (k)[301] A Chantrie Priest incorporate tooke a Lease to | him and his   [9 a]
successors for a hundred yeares, and after tooke a release from the Leasor to
him and his successors, and it was adjudged that by the release he had but
an estate for life, for he had the Lease in his naturall capacitie for it could not
goe in succession, and (his successors) gave him no estate of inheritance for
want of these words (his heires.) (l)[302] If the King by his Letters Patents giveth

295. (e) Bract lib. 2. ca. 39 fo. 92. b. Br ca. 39 fo. 99. b. Fleta lib. 6. ca. 1. 2. & lib. 3. cap. 2. 20. H 6.
35. 36. 19. H. 6. 17. 22. 74. 2. E. 4. 16. b. 4. E. 6 Pl. Com. 26.

296. [*Ed.:* If a gift is made in this way, as if I say, I give you such and such land: this gift does not
extend to heirs but only to the life of the donor, etc.]

297. (f) Vid. sect. 413.

298. (g) 7 E. 3. 25. Vid. sect. 686. 25. E. 3. 35. Bract. lib. 2 fo. 62. b. Vid. sect. 413.

299. (h) Pl. Com. 242. Seignior Berkleyes case.

300. (i) Vid. Britt. fo. 86. 121. & 130. 17. E. 3. 5. b. 33. H. 6. 22. 10. H. 7. 13. 14. 9. H. 7 11. 16. H. 7.
9. 15. E. 4. 10. 14. H. 6. 12. 35. H 6. 54. 24. Ass. 14. 40 Ass. 21. Tr. 5. E. 3. Rot 4 in Scaccario. 3. E. 3. 32.
7. E. 3. 40. 11. H. 4. 84. 12 H. 4. 12. 18 E 3. Conusans 39. b. 5 E. 4. 121. 38. E. 3. 4. Lib. 9 fo. 28. in Case
de Abb. de Strata Marcella.

301. (k) Hil. 21. Eliz. Dyers manuscript, Inter Ansley & Johnson in Com. Banco.

302. (l) 18. H. 6. 11. b. &c. adjudge.

lands *Decano & Capitulo, habendum sibi & haeredibus & successoribus suis,*[303] In this case albeit they be persons in their naturall capacitie to them and their heires, yet because the Grant is made to them in their politique capacitie, it shall enure to them and their successors. And so if the King doe grant lands to I. S. *Habendum sibi & successoribus sive haeredibus suis,*[304] this Grant shall enure to him and his heires.

(m)[305] B. having divers sonnes and daughters, A. giveth lands to B. *& Liberis suis, et a lour heires,*[306] the father and all his children doe take a fee simple joyntly by force of these words (their heires) but if hee had no childe at the time of the feoffment, the childe borne afterward shall not take.

These words (his heires) doe not onely extend to his immediate heires, but to his heires remote, and most remote, borne and to be borne, (n)[307] *Sub quibus vocabulis (haeredibus suis) omnes haeredes propinqui comprehenduntur, & remoti, nati, & nascituri.*[308,309] And *haeredum appellatione veniunt haeredes haeredum in infinitum.*[310] And the reason wherefore the Law is so precise to prescribe certaine words to create an estate of inheritance, is for avoyding of uncertaintie, the mother of contention and confusion.

There be many words so appropriated, as that they cannot be legally expressed by any other word, or by any periphrasis, or circumlocution: Some to estates of lands, &c. as here and in (a)[311] other places of our Author. In this place these words *tantsolement,* not *solement* alone, but *tantsolement* all onely, i. *solummodo,*[312] or *duntaxat* are to be observed; (b)[313] Some to Tenures; (c)[314] Some to persons; (d)[315] Some to offences; (e)[316] Some to formes of or-

303. [*Ed.:* to a dean and chapter, to have unto them and their heirs and successors.]

304. [*Ed.:* to have unto him and his successors or his heirs.]

305. (m) 15. E. 3. tit. Counterplea de Voucher 43. 37. H. 6. 30. 11. E. 4. 1.

306. [*Ed.:* and his children.]

307. (n) Fleta lib. 3. cap. 8.

308. Pl. Com. 163.

309. [*Ed.:* Under which words 'his heirs' are comprehended all the heirs, whether near or remote, born or about to be born.]

310. [*Ed.:* under the appellation 'heirs' come the heirs of heirs, and so on infinitely.]

311. (a) Sect. 17. 62. 133.

312. [*Ed.:* all only.]

313. (b) Sect. 156. 161.

314. (c) Sect. 184.

315. (d) Sect. 190. 194. 746.

316. (e) Sect. 9. 67. 194. 204. 234. 236. 241. 405. 485. 478. 651. 655. 646. 620. 614. 637. 674. 692.

iginall Writs either for recoverie of right, or removing, or redresse of wrong, (f)[317] Some to warrantie of land. These have I touched for examples, I leave others to the studious Reader to observe, and adde, holding this for an undoubted veritie, that there is no knowledge, case, or point in Law, seeme it of never so little account, but will stand our Student in stead at one time or other, and therefore in reading, nothing to be pretermitted.

"make an Estate."

Status dicitur à stando,[318] because it is fixed and permanent. The Isle of Man, which is no part of the Kingdome, but a distinct Territorie of it selfe, hath beene granted by the great Seale to divers subjects and their heires. (g)[319] It was resolved by the Lord Chancellor, the two chiefe Justices and chiefe Baron, that the same is an estate descendible according to the course of the Common Law, for whatsoever state of inheritance passe under the great Seale of England, it shall be descendible according to the rules, and course of the Common Law of England.

"in all Feoffments and Grants."

Here hee giveth the feoffment the first place, as the ancient and most necessarie conveyance, both for that it is solemne and publike, and therefore best remembered and proved, (*)[320] and also for that it cleareth all disseisins, abatements, intrussions, and other wrongfull or defensible estates, where the entrie of the Feoffor is lawfull, which neither Fine, Recoverie, nor Bargaine and sale by Deed indented and inrolled doth. And here is implyed a division of Fee, or Inheritance, viz. (h)[321] into corporeall (as Lands and Tenements which lye in Liverie) comprehended in this word Feoffment, and may passe by Liverie by Deed, or without Deed, which of some is called *Haereditas corporata,*[322]

317. (f) Sect. 733.

318. [*Ed.: status* (estate) is so called from *stando:* (being established).]

319. (g) Tr. 40. Eliz. in le Countee de Derbyes case, by the Lo. Chancellor, les 2. chiefe Justices, & chiefe Baron.

320. (*) Vide sect. 49. & 66.

321. (h) Mirror c. 2. sect. 15. & c. 5. sect. 1. Bract. lib. 2. fo. 53. 366. 368. Fleta lib. 3. ca. 1. 2. 15. Britt. 84. 87. a. & fol. 63. 101. 102. 141. 142. agreeth herewith. Pl. Com. 171. Hill. & Grange.

322. [*Ed.:* incorporate inheritance.]

and incorporeall, (which lye in Grant, and cannot passe by Liverie, but by
Deed, (as advowsons, Commons, &c. and of some is called *Haereditas in-
corporata*) and, by the deliverie of the Deed, the Freehold, and Inheritance
of such Inheritance, as doth lye in Grant, doth passe) comprehended in this
word Grant. And the Deed of incorporeate inheritances doth equall the Liverie
of corporeate. And therefore Littleton saith, in all feoffments and Grants,
Hereditas, alia corporalis, alia incorporalis: Corporalis est, quae tangi potest &
videri, incorporalis quae tangi non potest, nec videri.[323,324]

Feoffment *is derived of the word of Art* Feodum,[325] *quia est donatio feodi,*[326]
for the ancient Writers of the Law called a feoffment *donatio,* of the verbe *do*
or *dedi,* which is the aptest word of feoffment. And that word Ephron used,[327]
when he enfeoffed Abraham, saying, I give thee the field of Machpelah over
against Mamre, and the Cave therein I give thee, and all the trees in the field
and the borders round about, all which were made sure unto Abraham for a
possession, in the presence of many witnesses.

By a feoffment the corporeate fee is conveyed, and it properly betokeneth
a conveyance in fee, as our Author himselfe hereafter saith, in his Chapter of
Tenant for life. And yet sometime improperly it is called a feoffment when
an estate of freehold onely doth passe, *Done est nosme generall plus que nest*
feoffment, car done est generall a touts choses moebles & nient moebles, feoffment
est riens forsque del soyle.[328] And note there is a difference *inter cartam &*
[9 b] *factum,*[329] for | *carta* is intended a Charter which doth touch inheritance, and
so is not *factum* unlesse it hath some other addition.

Grant, *Concessio,* is properly of things incorporeall, which (as hath been

---

323. Mirror cap. 5. sect. 1. Britton cap. 34.

324. [*Ed.:* An Inheritance is the succession to every right which the deceased had. Inheritance is either
corporeal or incorporeal; corporeal is that which can be touched and seen, incorporeal that which cannot
be touched or seen.]

325. For the Antiquitie of Feoffments see the second part of the Institutes, Marlebridge ca. 4. 8. E. 3.
24. 18. H. 6. 24. 39. H 6. 39.

326. Genesis 23. [*Ed.:* because it is a gift of the fee.]

327. Vide sect. 57. Britton cap. 34. 44. E. 3. 41. See more of feoffment, sect. 60. See of factum, Sect.
259.

328. [*Ed.:* 'Done' (or grant) is the general name, more of which is feoffment, because *done* is general
to all things mobile, feoffment is of nothing not attached to the soil.]

329. [*Ed.:* Gift is a general name, which is more than feoffment, because 'gift' is general in respect of
all things movable and immovable, whereas feoffment is of nothing but the soil.]

329. [*Ed.:* between a charter and a deed.]

said) cannot passe without Deed.[330] And here it is to be observed (that I may speake once for all) that everie period of our Author in all his three Bookes containes matter of excellent learning, necessarily to bee collected by implication, or consequence, for example hee saith here, that these words (his heires) make an estate of inheritance in all feoffments and grants, he expressing feoffments and grants, necessarily implyeth, that this rule extendeth not, first, to Last Wills and Testaments, for thereby, (i)[331] as he himselfe after saith, an estate of inheritance may passe without these words (his heires) (k)[332] As if a man devise 20. acres to another, and that he shall pay to his Executors for the same ten pound, and hereby the Devisee hath a Fee simple by the intent of the Devisor, albeit it be not to the value of the land. (l)[333] So it is if a man devise lands to a man *imperpetuum,* or to give, and to sell, or *in feodo simplici,* or to him and to his Assignes for ever. In these cases a Fee simple doth passe by the intent of the Devisor, but if the devise be to a man and his Assignes without saying (for ever) the Devisee hath but an estate for life. (m)[334] If a man devise land to one & *sanguino suo,*[335] that is a Fee simple, but if it be *Semini suo,*[336] it is an estate taile.

(n)[337] Secondly, that it extendeth not to a Fine *sur conusans de droit come ceo que il ad de son done,*[338] by which a fee also may passe without this word (heires) in respect of the height of that fine, and that thereby is implyed that there was a precedent gift in fee.

Thirdly, nor to certain Releases, and that three manner of wayes, (o)[339] first when an estate of inheritance passeth and continueth, as if there be three Coparceners or Joyntenants, and one of them release to the other two, or to one of them generally without this word (heires) by Littletons owne opinion

---

330. Lib. 3. f. 63. in Lincolne College case.

331. (i) Litt. lib. 3. c. de Attorn. sect. 5. 8. 6. 4. E. 6. Estates Br. 78. 26. H. 8. Testaments 18. 22 Eliz. Dier 371. Temps H. 8. tit. Conscience. Br. 25.

332. (k) 21. E. 3. 16. 34. H. 6. 7. 19 H. 8. 9. lib. 3. fo. 21. in Borastons case lib. 6. f. 16. 17. lib. 10. fo. 67.

333. (l) vide sect. 585.

334. (m) Mich 40. & 41. Eliz. in Error Int. Downhall & Catesby adjudge. Brooke tit. taile 21.

335. [*Ed.:* and his blood.]

336. [*Ed.:* to his seed.]

337. (n) Lib. 1. fo. 100. Shelleyes case 42. E. 3. 7. 19. H. 6. 17. b. 22. b. Pl. Com. 248.

338. [*Ed.:* upon an acknowledgement of right, as that which he has of his gift.]

339. (o) Litt. lib 2. ca. Tenant. common sect. 304, 305. cap. Atrorn. sect. 37. 4. Dier. Eliz. 263.

they have a Fee simple as appeareth hereafter. 2. By release (p)[340] when an estate of inheritance passeth and continueth not, but is extinguished, as where the Lord releases to the Tenant, or the Grantee of a rent, &c. release to the Tenant of the land generally all his right, &c. hereby the Seigniorie, rent, &c. are extinguished for ever, without these words (heires.) 3. (q)[341] when a bare right is released, as when the Disseisee release to the Disseisor all his right, he need not (saith our Author in another place) speake of his heires. But of all these, and the like cases, more shall be treated in their proper places. 4. Nor to a Recoverie, A. seised of land suffereth B. to recover the land against him by a common recoverie where the judgement is *quod praedictus B. recuperet versus praed'. A. tenementa praedicta cum pertin',*[342] yet B. recovereth a fee simple without these words (heires) for regularly everie Recoveror recovereth a fee simple. 5. Nor to a creation of Nobilitie by Writ, for when a man is called to the Upper House of Parliament by Writ, he is a Baron and hath inheritance therein without the word (heires) yet may the King limit the generall state of inheritance created by the Law and Custome of the Realme to the heires males, or generall, of his body by the Writ, as he did to Bromflete who in 27. H. 6:[343] was called to Parliament by the name of the Lord *Vescye,* &c. with the limitation in the Writ to him and the heires males of his body, but if he be created by Patent, he must of necessitie have these words (his heires) or the heires males of his body, or the heires of his body, &c. otherwise he hath no inheritance. The first creation of a Baron by patent that I finde was of John Beauchampe of Holte created Baron by patent in 11. R. 2. for Barons before that time were called by Writ. And it is to be observed that of ancient times Earles, &c. were created by girding them with a sword, and nominating him Earle, &c. of such a Countie or place, and this with a calling of him to Parliament by Writ, by that name was a sufficient creation of inheritance.

But out of this rule of our Author, the Law doth make divers exceptions *(Et exceptio probat regulam)*[344] for sometime by a feoffment a Fee simple shall

---

340. (p) Litt. lib. 3. c. Releases. sect. 479. 480. 20 H. 6. 17. 19. H. 6. 17. 22.

341. (q) Litt. cap. Releases. sect. 467.

342. [*Ed.:* that the aforesaid B. should recover against the aforesaid A. the aforesaid tenements with the appurtenances.]

343. 27. H. 6. Lo. Vescies case.

344. [*Ed.:* And the exception proves the rule.]

passe without these words (his heires.) For example, first, (r)[345] if the father
enfeoffe the son, To have and to hold to him and to his heires, and the son
infeoffeth the father as fully as the father infeoffed him, by this the father hath
a Fee simple, *quia verba relata hoc maxime operantur per referentiam ut in esse
videntur.*[346] (s)[347] Secondly, in respect of the consideration, a Fee simple had
passed at the Common Law without this word (heires) and at this day an
estate of inheritance in taile, as if a man had given land to a man with his
Daughter in frank marriage generally, a Fee simple had passed without this
word (heires) for there is no consideration so much respected in Law, as the
consideration of marriage, in respect of alliance and posteritie. (t)[348] Thirdly,
if a Feoffment or Grant bee made by Deed to a Mayor and Communaltie or
any other Corporation aggregate of many persons capable, they have a Fee
simple without the word (Successors) because in judgement of the Law they
never dye. (u)[349] Fourthly, in case of a sole Corporation a Fee simple shall
sometime passe without this word (Successors) as if a feoffment in fee be made
of land to a Bishop, To have and to hold to him in *libera eleemosyna,*[350] a Fee
simple doth passe without this word (Successors.) (w)[351] And so if a man give
lands to the King by Deed inrolled, a Fee simple doth passe without these
words (Successors or Heires) because in judgement of Law the King never
dieth. Fifthly, in Grants sometimes an Inheritance shall passe without this
word (heires) (x)[352] as if partition be made between Coparceners of lands in
Fee simple, and for oweltie of partition the one grant a rent to | the other   [10 a]
generally, the Grantee shall have a Fee simple without this word (heires) because the Grantor hath a Fee simple in consideration whereof he granted the
rent. *Ipsae etenim leges cupiunt ut jure regantur.*[353] Sixthly, by the Forrest Law
if an Assart[354] bee granted by the King at a Justice seat (which may be done

---

345. (r) 39. Ass. 12. 41. E. 3. tit. Feoffments & Faits 254 14 H. 4. 13. 34. E. 3. Avowrie 258.

346. [*Ed.:* words which are referred to (in an instrument) have as much force by reference as if they were in being (i.e. in the instrument itself).]

347. (s) Vide sect. 17 12. H. 4. 19. in Formdon.

348. (t) 8. E. 3. 27. 11. H. 7. 12. 22. E. 4. 11. H. 4. 84. 2. H 4. 13.

349. (u) 19. H. 6. 74. 20. H. 6. 36.

350. [*Ed.:* in free alms (frankalmoin).]

351. (w) Pl. Com. Lo. Berkleyes case.

352. (x) 29. Ass. 25. 15. H. 7. 14. 2. H. 7. 5. 11. H. 4. 3 21. E. 1. 21. Ass.

353. [*Ed.:* The laws themselves require that they should be governed by law.]

354. [*Ed.:* The rights to stunt forest trees so they will die and then to work the newly arable land.]

without Charter) to another *Habendum & tenendum sibi imperpetuum*[355] he hath a Fee simple without this word (heires) (y)[356] for there is a speciall Law of the Forrest, as there is a Law Marshall for wars, and a Marine Law for the Seas. (z)[357] And this rule of our Author extendeth to the passing of estates of inheritances in exchanges, releases, or confirmations that ensure by way of enlargement of estates, warranties, bargaine and sales by Deed indented and inrolled, and the like, in which this word (heires) is also necessarie, for they doe tantamount to a feoffment or grant, or stand upon the same reason that a feoffment or grant doth, for like reason doth make like Law, *Ubi eadem ratio, ibi idem jus.*[358] And this is to be observed thorowout all these three Bookes, that where other cases fall within the same reason, our Author doth put his case but for example, for so our Author himselfe in another place[359] explaneth it, saying, *Et memorandum que en totus auters cases coment que ne sont icy expressment moves & specifies si sont en semblable reason sont en semblable ley.*[360] And here our Author is to bee understood to speake of heires when they are inheritable by discent, for they are capable of land also by purchase, and then the course of descent is sometime altered, as if lands of the nature of Gavelkind be given to B and his heires having issue divers sons, all his sons after his desease shall inherit, but if a lease for life be made, the remainder to the right heires of B. and B. dieth, his eldest son only shall inherit, for hee onely to take by purchase is right heire by the Common Law. So note a diversitie betweene a purchase and a descent, but where the remainder is limited to the right heires of B. it need not to be said, and to their heires, for being plurally limited it includeth a Fee simple, and yet it resteth but in one by purchase.

Out of that which hath beene said it is to be observed, that a man may purchase lands to him and his heires by ten manner of conveyances, (for I speake not here of Estoppels.) First, by Feoffment: Secondly, by Grant (of

---

355. [*Ed.:* to have and to hold unto him for ever.]

356. (y) 40. H. 7. 7.

357. (z) 22. E. 3. 3. 45. E. 3. 20. 9. E. 2. 21 Lib. 4. f. 121. Bustards case. Vide Sect. 465 469. 610. 19. H. 6. 17. 22. 19. E. 2 garr. 85

358. [*Ed.:* Where the same reason exists, there the same law prevails.]

359. Sect. 301.

360. [*Ed.:* And remember that in all other cases, even if they are not here expressly moved and specified, if they are within the same reasoning they are the same in law.]

which two our Author here speaketh.) Thirdly, by Fine, which is a feoffment of record. Fourthly, by common Recoverie, which is a common conveyance, and is in nature of a feoffment of record. Fifthly, by Exchange, which is in nature of a Grant. Sixthly, by Release to a particular Tenant. Seventhly, by Confirmation to a particular Tenant, both which are in nature of Grants. Eighthly, by Grant of a reversion or remainder with attornment of the particular Tenant, of all which our Author speaketh hereafter.[361] Ninethly, by bargaine and sale by Deed indented and inrolled ordained by Statute since Littleton wrote. Tenthly, by Devise by custome of some particular place, as hee sheweth hereafter, and since he wrote; by Will in writing, generally by authoritie of Parliament.

What words are apt words for a Feoffment or Grant, *vide* Sect. 531.[362] Our Author speaketh of Feoffments and Grants, whereby is implyed lawfull conveyances, and therefore this rule extendeth not to Disseisins, Abatements, or Intrusions into lands or tenements, or to usurpations to Advowsons, &c. in which cases estates in Fee simple are gained by the act and wrong of the Disseisors, Abators, Intruders and Usurpers, and if a disseisin, abatement, or intrusion be made to the use of another, if *cey que use* agreeth thereunto in pays by this bare agreement he gaineth a Fee simple without any liverie of seissin or other ceremony.

Section 2
Fee Simple

And if a man purchase land in fee simple and dye without issue, hee which is his next cosen collaterall of the whole bloud, how farre so ever hee bee from him in degree, may inherit and have the land as heire to him.

Littleton sheweth here who shall bee heire to lands in Fee simple, for he intendeth not this case of an estate taile, for that he speaketh of an heire of the whole bloud, for that extendeth not to estates in taile as shall bee said hereafter in this Chapter, Sect. 6.

---

361. 27. H. 8. ca. 16. 32. H. 8. ca. 2. 34. H. 8. ca. 5.
362. Sect. 531. 37. Ass. p. 38. Ass. p. 9. 12. E. 4. 9. & c.

"his next cosen collaterall."

Neither excludeth hee brethren or sisters because hee hath a speciall case concerning them in this Chapter, Sect. 5. and in his Chapter of Parceners, but
[10 b] this is intended | where a man purchaseth lands and dieth without issue, and
having neither brother nor sister, then his next cosin collaterall shall inherit.[1]
So as here is implyed a divisson of heires, viz. lineall (who ever shall first inherit)
and collaterall, (who are to inherit for default of lineall.) For in descents it is
a maxime in Law *quod linea recta semper praefertur transversali.*[2] Lineall descent
is conveyed downward in a right line, as from the grandfather to the father,
from the father to the sonne, &c. Collaterall descent is derived from the side
of the lineall, as grandfathers brother, fathers brother, et.[3] *Prochein cousin collateral enheritera*[4] doth give a certaine direction to the next cosin to the son,
and therefore the fathers brother and his posteritie shall inherit before the
grandfathers brother and his posteritie. *Et sic de caeteris,* for *propinquior excludit
propinquum, & propinquus remotum, & remotus remotiorem.*[5]

Upon this word (*Prochein*) I put this case. One hath issue two sonnes A.
and B. and dieth, B. hath two sonnes C. and D. and dieth. C. the eldest son
hath issue and dieth: A. purchaseth lands in Fee simple and dieth without
issue, D. is his next cosin, and yet shall not inherit, but the issue of C. for
hee that is inheritable is accounted in Law next of bloud. And therefore here
is understood a division of next, viz. next, *jure repraesentationis,*[6] and next,
jure propinquitatis[7] that is, by right of representation and by right of propin-
quitie.[8] And Littleton meaneth of the right of representation, for legally in
course of descents he is next of bloud inheritable. And the issue of C. doth
represent the person of C. and if C. had lived he had beene legally next of
bloud. And whensoever the father if he had lived, should have inherited, his

1. Glanvil. lib. 7. ca. 3. 4 Bract. lib. 2. c. 30. fo. 65. Britton cap. 119. Fleta lib. 6. cap. 1. & 2.

2. [*Ed.:* that the direct line is always preferred to the transverse.]

3. Bract. lib. 2. cap. 30. fo 64. Fleta lib. 5. cap. 5 & lib. 6. ca. 1. & 2. Britton ca. 119. Mirror 11. ca. 1. sect. 3. 30. Ass. p. 47.

4. [*Ed.:* next cousin (or first cousin), collateral heir]

5. [*Ed.:* And so of the rest, for the nearer excludes the near, and the near the remote, and the remote the more remote.]

6. [*Ed.:* by right of representation.]

7. [*Ed.:* by right of proximity.]

8. 19. R. 2 tit. gar. 100.

lineall heire by right of representation shall inherit before any other, though another be *jure propinquitatis* neerer of bloud. And therefore Littleton intendeth his case of next cosin of bloud immediately inheritable. So as this produceth another division of next bloud, viz. immediately inheritable, as the issue of C. and mediately inheritable as D. if the issue of C. die without issue, for the issue of C. and all that live be they never so remote shall inherit before D. or his line,[9] and therefore Littleton saith well *de quel pluis long degree que il soit.*[10] And here ariseth a diversitie in Law betweene next of bloud inheritable by descent and next of bloud capable by purchase. And therefore in the case before mentioned if a Lease for life were made to A. the remainder to his next of bloud in fee. In this case as hath beene said D. shall take the remainder, because he is next of bloud and capable by purchase, though he be not legally next to take as heire by descent.

Section 3
Fee Simple

But if there be father and son, and the father hath a brother that is uncle to the son, and the son purchase land in fee simple, and die without issue, living his father, the uncle shall have the land as heire to the son, & not the father, yet the father is neerer of bloud; because it is a maxime in Law, That inheritance may lineally descend, but not ascend. Yet if the son in this case dye without issue, and his uncle enter into the Land as heire to the sonne (as by Law hee ought) and after the uncle dieth without issue, living the father, the father shall have the land as heire to the uncle, & not as heire to his sonne, for that he commeth to the land by collelaterall discent & not by lineal ascent.

"yet the father is neerer of bloud,"[1]

And therefore some doe hold upon these words of Littleton that if a Lease for life were made to the sonne the remainder to his next of bloud, that the father should take the remainder by purchase, and not the uncle, for that Littleton saith the father is next of bloud, and yet the uncle is heire. As if a

---

9. 3. Ass. p. 47.

10. [*Ed.:* of however remote a degree he be.]

1. 5. Edw. 6. tit. Administr. Br. 47. Ratcliffes case ubi sup. See after in the Chapter of Socage.

man hath issue two sonnes, and the eldest sonne hath issue a sonne and die, a remainder is limited to the next of his bloud, the younger son shall take it, yet the other is his heire.

(p)[2] "it is a maxime in Law, That inheritance may lineally descend, but not ascend."

[11 a]   Maxime, i.e. a sure foundation or ground of Art, and a | conclusion of reason so called (q)[3] *quia maxima est ejus dignitas & certissima authoritas, atque quod maxime omnibus probetur,*[4] so sure and uncontrollable as that they ought not to be questioned. (r)[5] And that which our Author here and in other places calleth a Maxime, hereafter he calleth a Principle, and it is all one with a Rule, a common ground, *Postulatum* or an *Axiome,* and it were too much curiositie to make nice distinctions betweene them. And it is well said in our Bookes, (s)[6] *nest my a disputer lancient principles del ley.*[7] I never read any opinion in any booke old or new against this Maxime, but onely in lib. rub. where it is said, (t)[8] *si quis sine liberis discesserit, pater aut mater ejus in haereditatem succedat, vel frater & soror si pater & mater desint, si nec hos habeat, soror patris vel matris & deinceps qui propinquiores in parentela fuerint haereditario succedant, & dum virilis sexus extiterit, & haereditas abinde sit, foemina non haereditat.*[9] But all our ancient Authors and the constant opinion ever since doe affirme the maxime.

By this maxime in the conclusion of his case, onely lineall ascention in the right line is prohibited, and not in the collaterall, (u)[10] *Quaelibet haereditas*

---

2. (p) Pl. Com. 293. b. Osbornes case.

3. (q) Pl. Com. 27. b.

4. [*Ed.:* because a maxim is of the same worthiness and most certain authority as something which is completely proved to everyone.]

5. (r) Sect. 90. f. 48.

6. (s) 12. Hen. 4. Glanvill lib. 7.cap. 1. Bract lib. 2. cap. 29.

7. [*Ed.:* the ancient principles of our law are not to be disputed.]

8. (t) Lib. Rub. cap. 70.

9. [*Ed.:* If anyone dies without children, his father and mother succeed to the inheritance, or the brother and sister if there are no father and mother, and if he does not have those then the sister of his father or mother, and thereafter those who are next in the *parentela* (ancestral line) succeed; and so long as there is someone of the male sex who may have the inheritance, a woman does not inherit.]

10. (u) Britt. ca. 119. Fleta lib. 6. ca. 1. Numb. ca. 27. Ratcliffes case ubi supra.

naturaliter quidem ad haeredes haereditabiliter descendit, nunquam quidem na-
turaliter ascendit, descendit itaque jus quasi ponderosum quod cadens deorsum
recta linea vel transversali, & nunquam reascendit ea via qua descendit post mor-
tem antecessorum, à latere tamen ascendit alicui propter defectum haeredum in-
ferius provenientium;[11] so as the lineall ascent is prohibited by Law, and not
the collaterall. And in prohibiting the lineall ascent, the Common Law is
assisted with the Law of the twelve tables.

Here our Author for the confirmation of his opinion draweth a reason and
a proofe (as you have perceived) from one of the maximes of the Common
Law: Now that I may here observe it once for all, his proofes and arguments,
in these his three bookes, may be generally divided into two parts, viz. from
the Common Law and from Statutes, of both which, and of their severall
branches I shall give the studious Reader some few examples, and leave the
rest to his diligent observation.

For the Common Law his proofes and arguments are drawn from twentie
severall fountaines or places.

(a)[12] First, from the Maximes, Principles, Rules, Intendment and Reason
of the Common Law, which indeed is the rule of the Law, as here, and in
other places our Author doth use.

(b)[13] Secondly, from the bookes, records, and other authorities of Law cited
by him, *Ab authoritate, & pronunciatis.*[14]

(c)[15] Thirdly, from originall Writs in the Register, *à rescriptis valet argu-*
mentum.[16]

(d)[17] Fourthly, from the forme of good pleading.

(e)[18] Fifthly, from the right entrie of Judgements.

---

11. [*Ed.:* An inheritance naturally descends to the heirs by way of inheritance, but never naturally ascends. For the right descends like a weight falling downwards in the direct or transverse line, and it never re-ascends in the same path by which it descends after the death of ancestors, but sometimes ascends collaterally to someone by reason of the want of heirs below.]

12. Sect. 5. 8. 90. 96. 52. 53. 57. 59. 65. 99. 130. 146. 156. 169. 178. 231. 293. 302. 352. 360. 376. 377. 396. 410. 440. 441. 346. 347. 462. 431.

13. (b) Sect. 20. where a number other are quoted.

14. [*Ed.:* of authority and proclamation]

15. (c) Sect. 67. 132. 170. 234. 241. 263. 613. 614.

16. [*Ed.:* from writing if sound argument.]

17. (d) Sect. 58. 170. 183. 369.

18. (e) Sect. 248. 249.

(f)[19] Sixthly, *à praecedentibus approbatis & usu,* from approved Precedents and Use.

(g)[20] Seventhly, *à non usu,* from not use.

(h)[21] Eighthly, *ab artificialibus argumentis, consequentibus & conclusionibus,* artificiall arguments, consequents and conclusions.

Ninthly, (i)[22] *à communi opinione jurisprudentium,* from the common opinion of the Sages of the Law.

Tenthly, (k)[23] *ab inconvenienti,* from that which is inconvenient.

Eleventhly, (l)[24] *à divisione,* from a division, *vel ab enumeratione partium,* from the enumeration of the parts.

Twelfthly, (m)[25] *à majore ad minus,* from the greater to the lesser, or (n)[26] from the lesser to the greater, (o)[27] *à simili,*[28](p)[29] *à pari.*[30]

13. (p)[31] *Ab impossibili,* from that which is impossible.

14. (q)[32] *A fine,* from the end.

15. [33] *Ab utili vel inutili,* from that which is profitable or unprofitable.

16. (r)[34] *Ex absurdo,* for that thereupon shall follow an absurditie, *quasi à surdo prolatum,*[35] because it is repugnant to understanding and reason.

17. (s)[36] *A natura & ordine naturae,* from nature or the course of nature.

[11 b] | 18. (t)[37] *Ab ordine religionis,* from the order of Religion.

---

19. (f) sect. 88. 74. 76. 145. 332. 371. 372. 445.

20. (g) 108. 733.

21. (h) sect. 170. 264. 283. 302. 429. 464. 629. 633. 686. 340. 418. 613. 686. 739.

22. (i) sect. 697. 59. 104. 288. 332. 478.

23. (k) Sect. 87. where many others are quoted.

24. (l) sect. 13. where many more are quoted, but see chiefly. sect. 281.

25. (m) sect. 438. 439. 441.

26. (n) sect. 18.

27. (o) 301. &c.

28. [*Ed.:* from the similar.]

29. (p) 291. 298. 409. &c.

30. [*Ed.:* from the equal.]

31. (p) 129. 440. [note, this note is mis-designated "p" duplicating the sequence, in the first edition.]

32. (q) sect. 46. 194.

33. sect. 360.

34. (r) sect. 722.

35. [*Ed.:* As if uttered by a deaf-mute.]

36. (s) sect. 114. 223. 129. 211. 107. 108.

37. (t) Sect. 202.

19. (u)[38] *A communi praesumptione,* from a common presumption.

20. (w)[39] *A lectionibus jurisprudentium,* from the readings of learned men or Law. From Statutes his arguments and proofes are drawne.

1. (x)[40] From the rehearsall or preamble of the Statute.

2. By the body of the Law diversly interpreted.

Sometime by other parts of the same Statute, which is *benedicta expositio, & ex visceribus causae.*[41]

(y)[42] Sometime by the reason of the Common Law. But ever the generall words are to bee intended of a lawfull Act, (z)[43] and such interpretation must ever be made of all Statutes, that the innocent or he in whom there is no default may not be damnified.

"in Law,"

There be divers Lawes within the Realme of England. As first (a)[44] *Lex Coronae,* the Law of the Crowne.

2. (b)[45] *Lex & consuetudo Parliamenti. Ista lex est ab omnibus quaerenda, à multis ignorata, à paucis cognita.*[46]

3. (c)[47] Lex naturae, the Law of nature.

4. (d)[48] *Communis Lex Angliae,* the Common Law of England sometime called *Lex terrae,* intended by our Author in this and the like places.

5. (e)[49] Statute Law, Lawes established by authoritie of Parliament.

6. (f)[50] *Consuetudines,* Customes reasonable.

38. (u) Sect. 440.

39. (w) Sect. 481.

40. (x) Sect. 13. &c. Sect. 731. 692. 635. 633. 441. 103. 193. 154. 140. a.

41. [*Ed.:* a blessed exposition, and from the innermost parts of the cause.]

42. (y) Sect. 464.

43. (z) Sect. 731. 685.

44. (a) 17. Edw. 3. Rot. parl. nu. 19. 25. Edw. 3. cap. I. Regist. inter Unra regia, 61. &c.

45. (b) Commonly spoken of in Parliament Rols.

46. [*Ed.:* The law and custom of parliament. This law is to be sought out by everyone, but is unknown to many, and known to very few.]

47. (c) 13. Edw. 4. 9. Lib. 7. Calvins case, Pl. Com. Sharingtons case.

48. (d) This Law appeareth in our Bookes and judiciall Records.

49. (e) These are of record in Rolls of Parliament.

50. (f) Whereof you shall read in our Author, and in our Bookes.

7. (g)[51] *Jus belli,* The Law of Armes, Warre, and Chivalrie, *in republica maximè conservanda sunt jura belli.*[52]

8. (h)[53] Ecclesiasticall or Canon Law in Courts in certaine Cases.

9. (i)[54] Civill Law in certaine cases not onely in Courts Ecclesiasticall, but in the Courts of the Constable and Marshall, and of the Admiraltie, in which Court of the Admiraltie is observed, *la ley Olyron,* anno 5. of Richard the first, so called, because it was published in the Isle of Olyron.

10. (k)[55] *Lex forestae,* forest Law.

11. (l)[56] The Law of Marque or reprisail.

12. (m)[57] *Lex mercatoria,* Merchant, &c.

13. (n)[58] The Lawes and Customes of the Isles of Jersey, Gernesey, and Man.

14. (o)[59] The Law and priviledge of the Stannaries.

15. (p)[60] The Lawes of the East, West, and middle Marches, which are now abrogated.

But here of this is little taste for our Student, that he may be capable of that which hee shall read concerning these and others in Records, and in our Bookes, and orderly observe them, shall suffice.

"and his uncle enter into the Land."

For if the Uncle in this case doth not enter into the land, then cannot the father inherit the land, for there is another maxime in Law herein implyed. (q)[61] That a man that claimeth as heire in fee simple to any man by descent

---

51. (g) Rot. Parl. 2. Ric. 2. nu. 3. 13. Ric. 2. ca. 2.

52. [*Ed.:* In a state the laws of war are to be especially upheld.]

53. (h) Lib. 7. Candries case articul. super cartas, &c.

54. (i) 37. Hen. 6. Fortese. cap. 32. 13. Hen. 4. 4. 28. H.8. ca. 15.

55. (k) Carta de Foresta, &c. the Eires of the Forests.

56. (l) 27. Edw. 3. ca. 17. Wi.ca.23. 4. Hen. 5. cap. 7.

57. (m) Mirror des Justic. c. 1. Bract. 334–444. Fleta lib. 2. ca. 51. 52. &c. 5. Edw. 3. 11.38. Edw. 3. 27. Edw. 3. 7. cap. 8. Fortesc. 32. F. N. B-117. 13. H. 4.9. Rot. parl. 6. Hen. 4. nu. 43. 10 Hen. 7. 16. 47. Edw. 3. 21. 30. E.1. Account. 127. Carta Mercatoria 31. E. 1. Rot. patent.

58. (n) Mich. 41. Edw. 3. coram Rege in Thesaur. 12. E. 3. 5b. Hen. 8. fol. 5. Rot. pat. an. 20. E. 1. lib. 7. Calvins case, fol. 21. Regist. fol. 22.

59. (o) 50. Edw. 2. Rot parl. 50. Edw. 3. Rot. patent. &c.

60. (p) 31. Hen. 6 ca. 3. 4. Ia. c. 1.

61. (q) 11. Hen. 4. 11. 10. Ass. 27. 34. Ass. p. 20. 19. E. 2. Quar. imped. 177. 45. Edw. 3. 13. 40. Ass. p. 6.

must make himselfe heire to him that was last seized of the actuall freehold and inheritance. And if the Uncle in this case doth not enter, then had he but a freehold in Law, and no actuall freehold, but the last that was seized of the actuall freehold was the sonne to whom the father cannot make himselfe heire, and therefore Littleton saith, *Et son uncle enter en la terre (sicome denoit per la ley)*[62] to make the father to inherit, as heire to the uncle. (r)[63] Note, that true it is that the uncle in this case is heire, but not absolutely heire, for if after the descent to him the father hath issue a sonne or daughter, that issue shall enter upon the Uncle. (f)[64] And so it is if a man hath issue a sonne and daughter, the sonne purchaseth land in fee and dieth without issue, the daughter shall inherit the land, but if the father hath afterward issue a sonne, this sonne shall enter into the Land as heire to his brother, and if he hath issue a daughter and no sonne, she shall be coparcener with her sister.

"as by Law hee ought."

These words as a key doe open the secrets of the Law, for hereupon it is concluded, that where the Uncle cannot get an actuall possession by entrie or otherwise, there the father in this case cannot inherit. And therefore if an Advowson[65] be granted to the sonne and his heires, and the sonne dye without issue, and this descend to the uncle, and he dye before he doth or can present to the Church, the father shall not inherit, because he should make himselfe heire to the son, which hee cannot doe. And so of a rent and the like. But if the uncle had presented to the Church, or has seisin of the rent, there the father should have inherited. For Littleton putteth his case of an entrie into land but for an example, If the sonne make a Lease for life, and die without issue, and the reversion descend to the uncle, and he die, the reversion shall not descend to the father, because in that case he must make himselfe heire to the sonne. A. infeoffe the sonnes with warrantie to him and his heires, the sonne dies, the uncle enters into the Land and dies, the father if he be impleaded shall not take advantage of this war-l-rantie, for then he must vouch A. as heire to his sonne, which hee cannot doe for albeit the warrantie de- [12 a]

---

62. [*Ed.:* And his uncle enters in the land (as by the law he ought).]
63. (r) 11. Ass. p. 6. Doct. & Stud. 12b. 22. H. 6. 35.
64. (s) 19. Hen. 6. 61.
65. [*Ed.:* the right to present a church or benefice; a patronage.]

scended to the uncle, yet the uncle leaveth it as he found it, and then the father by Littletons *(devoit)*[66] cannot take advantage of it. For Littleton, Sect. 603. saith that warranties shall descend to him that is heire by the Common Law,[67] and Sect. 718. hee saith that everie warrantie which descends, doth descend to him that is heire to him which made the warrantie by the Common Law, which proveth that the father shall not be bound by the warrantie made by the son, for that the father cannot be heire to the son that made the warrantie.[68] And a warrantie shall not goe with tenements, whereunto it is annexed, to any especiall heire but alwaies to the heire at the Common Law. And therefore if the uncle be seised of certaine lands, and is disseised, the son release to the disseisor with warrantie, and die without issue, this shall bind the uncle, but if the uncle die without issue, the father may enter, for the warrantie cannot descend upon him. So if the sonne concludeth himselfe by pleading concerning the tenure and services of certaine lands, this shall bind the uncle, but if the uncle die without issue, this shall not bind the father, because he cannot be heire to the son, and consequently not to the Estoppell in that case:[69] but if it be such an Estoppell as runneth with the land, then it is otherwise.

Section 4
Fee Simple

And in case, where the sonne purchaseth Land in Fee simple, and dyes without issue, they of his bloud on the fathers side shall inherit as heires to him, before any of the bloud on the mothers side. But if hee hath no heire on the part of his father, then the land shall descend to the heires on the part of the mother. But if a man marrieth an inheretrix of lands in Fee simple, who have issue a son, and die, and the sonne enter into the tenements, as sonne and heire to his mother, and after dies without issue, the heires of the part of his mother ought to inherit, and not the heires of the part of the father. And if hee hath no heire on the part of the mother, then the Lord of whom the land is holden, shall have the land by Escheat. In the same manner it is, if lands descend to the sonne,

---

66. [*Ed.:* Ought]
67. Vid. sect. 603 718.
68. Vid. sect. 735. 736. 737.
69. 35. Hen. 6. 33. John Crook's case.

of the part of the father, and hee entreth, and afterwards dies without issue, this Land shall descend to the heires on the part of the father, and not to the heires on the part of the mother. And if there bee no heire of the part of the father, the Lord of whom the Land is holden shall have the land by Escheat. And so see the diversitie, where the sonne purchaseth lands or tenements in Fee simple, and where hee commeth to them by descent on the part of his mother, or on the part of his father.

By this it appeareth[1] that our Author divideth heires into heires of the part of the father; and into heires of the part of the mother. (a)[2] And note it is an old and true Maxime in Law, that none shall inherit any lands as heire, but onely the bloud of the first Purchaser, for (*)[3] *refert à quo fiat perquisitum,*[4] As for example, Robert Coke taketh the daughter of Knightley to wife and purchaseth lands to him and to his heires, and by Knightley hath issue Edward, none of the bloud of the Knightleys though they be of the bloud of Edward shall inherit, albeit hee had no kindred but them, because they were not of the bloud of the first purchaser, viz. of Robert Coke.

(b)[5] "they of his bloud on the fathers side."

Here it is to be understood, that the father hath two immediate blouds in him, viz. the bloud of his father, and the bloud of his mother, both these blouds are of the part of the father. (c)[6] And this made ancient Authors say, that if a man be seised of lands in the right of the wife, and is attainted of felony, and after hath issue, this issue should not inherit his mother, for that he could derive no bloud inheritable from the Father. And both these blouds of the part of the Father must bee spent | before the heire of the bloud of the [12 b] part of the mother shall inherit, wherein ever the line of the male of the part

---

1. Vid. Sect 354. an excellent point.

2. (a) Pl. Com. Sir Edward Clere's case 47.

3. (*) Fleta lib. 6. ca. 1. 2. &c. Bracton lib. 2. fol. 65. 67. 68. 69. &c. Britton ca. 119. 24. Edw. 3. 50. 36. Edw. 3. 29. 30. 38. 49. Edw. 3. 12. 49. Ass. p. 4. 12. Edw. 4. 14. Pl. Com. 445. & 450. 7. Edw. 6. Dyer 6. 24. Edw. 3. 24. 37. Ass. 4. 40. Edw. 3. 9. 42. Edw. 3. 10. 45. Edw. Releases, 28. 7. Hen. 5. 3. 4. 8. Ass. 6. 35. Ass. 2. 5. Edw. 4. 7. 3. Hen. 5. 21. Hen. 7. 33. 40. Ass 6. Ratcliffs case lib. 3. fol. 42.

4. [*Ed.:* it refers to the person from whom a purchase is made.]

5. (b) Bracton, ubi supra. Fleta, ubi supra. Britton, ca. 118. 119. Pl. Com. 445. Clere's case. Tr. 19. Edw. 1. in Banco Rot. 25. Lincoln. Will. Seels case.

6. (c) Britton, fol. 15. fleta, lib. 1. ca. 18. Pl. Com. 445. 446. &c. Clere's case.

of the father, (that is) the posteritie of such male, bee they male or female, (who ever in descents are preferred) must faile before the line of the mother shall inherit, (d)[7] and the reason of all this is for that the bloud of the part of the father is more worthy, more neere in judgement of Law, than the bloud of the part of the mother.

"before any of the bloud on the mothers side."

And it is to be observed,[8] that the mother hath also two immediate blouds in her, (viz.) her fathers bloud, and her mothers bloud. Now to illustrate all this by example. Robert Fairefield Sonne of John Fairefield and Jane Sandie, take to wife Anne Boyes Daughter of John Boyes and Jane Bewpree, and hath Issue William Fairefield who purchaseth lands in fee. Here William Fairefield hath foure immediate blouds in him, two of the part of his father, viz. the bloud of the Fairefields, and the bloud of the Sandies, and two of the part of his mother; viz. the bloud of the Boyses, and the bloud of the Bewprees, and so in both cases upward *in infinitum.*

Now admit that William Fairefield die without issue, first the bloud of the part of his father, viz. of the Fairefields, and for want thereof the bloud of the Sandies (for both these are of the part of the father) if both these faile, then the heires of the part of the mother of William Fairefield shall inherit, viz. first the bloud of the Boyses, and for default thereof the bloud of the Bewprees.

It is necessarie to be knowne in what cases the Heire of the part of mother shall inherit, and where not. If a man be seised of lands as Heire of the part of his mother, and maketh a feoffment in fee, and taketh backe an estate to him and to his heires, this is a new purchase, and if hee dieth without issue, the heires of the part of the father shall first inherit. If a man so seised maketh a feoffment in fee upon condition,[9] and die, the heire of the part of the father which is the heire at the Common Law shall enter for the condition broken, but the heire of part of the mother shall enter upon him, and enjoy the land. (m)[10] A man so seised maketh a feoffment in fee reserving a rent to him and

---

7. (d) 19. Ric. 2. garr. 100.

8. Britton ca. 118. 119. Fleta lib. 6. ca. 2.

9. 5. Hen. 7. 24.

10. (m) 7. Hen. 6. 4. Lib. 1. fol. 100. Shelleyes case. [note: the note designations here leap to "m."]

to his heires, this rent shall goe to the heires of the part of the father; but (n)[11] if he had made a gift in taile, or a lease for life reserving a rent, the heire of the part of the mother shall have the reversion, and the rent also, as incident thereunto, shall passe with it; but the heire of the part of the mother shall not take advantage of a condition annexed to the same, because it is not incident to the reversion, nor can passe therewith. (o)[12] If a man had been seised of a mannor as heire on the part of his mother, and before the Statute of *Quia emptores terrarum,*[13] had made a feoffment in fee of parcell to hold of him by rent and service, albeit they be newly created, yet for that they are parcell of the mannor, they shall with the rest of the mannor descend to the heire of the part of the mother, *quia multa transeunt cum universitate quae per se non transeunt.*[14] If a man hath a rent secke of the part of his mother, and the tenant of the land | granteth a distresse to him and his heires, and the Grantee dieth, the distresse shall goe with the rent to the heire of the part of the mother as incident or appurtenant to the rent, for now is the rent secke become a Rent charge.   [13 a]

(p)[15] A man so seised as heire on the part of his mother maketh a Feoffment in Fee to the use of him and his heires, the use being a thing in trust and confidence shall insue the nature of the land, and shall descend to the heire on the part of the mother. (q)[16] A man hath Seigniorie as heire of the part of his mother, and the Tenancie doth escheat, it shall goe to the heire of the part of the mother. If the heire of the part of the mother of land whereunto a Warrantie is annexed is impleaded and Vouche, and judgement is given against him, and for him to recover in value, and dieth before execution (r)[17] the heire of the part of the mother shall sue execution to have in value against the Vouchee, for the effect ought to pursue the cause, and the recompence shall ensue the losse.

---

11. (n) 5. Edw. 2, tit. Arowry, 207.

12. (o) 5. E. 2, Arowry 207.

13. [*Ed.:* name of statute of 1290.]

14. [*Ed.:* because many things pass when aggregated with something else which do not pass by themselves.]

15. (p) 5. Edw. 4. 4. lib. 1. fol 100. Shelleyes case. 27. Hen. 8. Dyer Buckenhams case. 32. Hen. 8. gard. Brook 93, 13. Hen. 7. 6.

16. (q) 16. E. 3. age. 46.

17. (r) Pl. Com. 292. & 515. See more on this in the chapter of Warranties.

If a man giveth lands to a man, to have and to hold to him and his heires on the part of his mother, yet the heires of the part of the father shall inherit, for no man can institute a new kinde of inheritance not allowed by the Law, and the words (of the part of his mother) are void, as in the case that Littleton putteth this Chapter. If a man giveth lands to a man to him and his heires males, the Law rejecteth this word males, because there is no such kinde of inheritance, whereof you shall read more in his proper place.

If a man hath issue a sonne, and dieth, and the wife dieth also, lands are letten for life, the remainder to the heires of the wife, the sonne dieth without issue, the heires of the part of the father shall inherit, & not the heires of the part of the mother, because it vested in the son as a Purchaser. And the rule of Littleton holdeth as well in other kinde of Inheritances, as in Lands and Tenements. (f)[18] And therefore if there be Lord, *feme mesne*,[19] and Tenant, and the Mesne binde her selfe and her heires by her Deed to the acquitall of the Tenant, the Mesne take husband, the Tenant by his Deed granteth to the husband and his heires, that hee or his heires shall not bee bound to acquitall, the husband & wife have issue, and die, this issue, being bound as heire to his mother, shall not take benefit of the said grant of discharge, for that extends to the heires of the part of the father, and not to the heires of the part of the mother, and therefore the heire of the part of the mother was bound to the Acquitall. And thus much for the better understanding of Littleton's Cases concerning the heire of the part of the mother shall suffice.

"But if a man marrieth an inheretrix."

Here there is another maxime, (t)[20] That whensoever Lands doe descend from the part of the mother, the heires of the part of the father shall never inherit. And likewise when Lands descend from the part of the father, the heires of the part of the mother shall never inherit. *Et sic paterna paternis, et è converso, materna maternis.*[21] For more manifestation hereof, and of that which hereafter shall be said touching Descents, see a Table in the end of this Chapter.

18. (s) 38. Edw. 3. 12.

19. [*Ed.:* an intermediate tenancy held by a woman.]

20. (t) 39. Edw. 3. 29. 49. Edw. 3. 12.

21. [*Ed.:* And so from the father's side to the father's heirs, and, conversely, from the mother's side to hers.]

"shall have the land by Escheat"

(u)[22] Escheat, *Eschaeta* is a word of art, and derived from the French word *Eschear (id est) cadere, excidere* or *accidere,* and signifieth properly when by accident the Lands fall to the Lord of whom they are holden, in which Case wee say the Fee is escheated. And therefore, of sonne, Escheats are called *excadentiae, or teriae excadentiales* (w)[23] *Dominus vero capitalis loco haeredis habetur quoties per defectum vel delictum extinguitur sanguis sui tenentis, loco haeredis & haberi poterit, nisi per modum donationis sit reversio cujusque tenementi.* And Ockam (who wrote in the reigne of Henry the second) treating of Tenures of the King, saith, *Porro eschaetae vulgo dicuntur, quae decedentibus hiis quae de Rege tenent, &c. cum non existit ratione sanguinis haeres ad fiscum relabuntur.*[24] (x)[25] So as an Escheat doth happen two manner of wayes, *aut per defectum sanguinis,* i.e for default of heire, *aut per delictum tenentis,* i.e. for felony, and that is by judgement three manner of wayes, *aut quia suspensus per collum, aut quia abjuravit regnum, aut quia utlegatus est.*[26] And therefore, they which are hanged by Martiall Law, *in furore belli* forfeit no Lands: and so in like Cases Escheats by the Civilians are called *Caduca.*

(y)[27] The father is seised of Lands in fee holden of I.S. the son is attainted of high treason, the father dieth, the Land shall escheat to I.S. *propter defectum sanguinis,* for that the father dieth without heire. And the King cannot have the Land because the sonne never had any thing to forfeit. But the King shall have the Escheat of all the Lands whereof the person attainted of high treason was seised, of whomsoever they were holden.

---

22. (u) Vide sect. 130. Glanvill lib. 7. cap. 17. Bract. lib. 3. fol. 118. Fleta lib. 5. cap. 5. & lib. 3. cap. 10. Britton ca 37. & cap. 119. F. N. B. 100. Tr. 19. E. 1. in Banco Rot. 25.

23. (w) Fleta lib. 6. cap. 1. Ockam cap. quod non absolvitur, &c.

24. [*Ed.:* The chief lord takes the place of an heir whenever the blood of his tenant is extinguished by default (i.e. of kin) or misconduct. And he to whom the reversion of the tenement was made by the condition of the gift shall take the place of the heir. . . . Formerly those things were called escheats which, on the death of those who hold of the king etc., when there is no heir by reason of blood, go back to the fisc.]

25. (x) Pl. Com. Dame Hales case.

26. [*Ed.:* either for defect of blood . . . or through the wrongdoing of the tenant . . . because he has been hanged by the neck, or has abjured the realm, or has been outlawed.]

27. (y) Pl. Com. in Nichols case.

(z)[28] In an Appeale of Death or other felony, &c. processe is awarded against the Defendant and hanging the processe the Defendant conveyeth away the land, and after is outlawed, the conveyance is good and shall defeat the Lord of his Escheat, but if a man be indited of felony, and hanging the processe against him, hee conveyeth away the Land, and after is outlawed, the Conveyance shall not in that case prevent the Lord of his Escheat. And the reason of this diversitie is manifest: For in the case of the Appeale, the Writ containeth no time when | the felony was done, and therefore the Escheat can relate but to the Dutlawrie pronounced. But the inditement containeth the time when the felony was committed, and therefore the Escheat upon the Outlawrie shall relate to that time. Which cases I have added, to the end the Student may conceive, that the observation of writs, Inditements, Processe, Judgements, and other Entries, doth conduce much to the understanding of the right reason of the Law.

[13 b]

Of this word *(Eschaeta)* here used by our Author, commeth (a)[29] *Eschaetor,* an ancient Officer so called, because his office is properly to looke to Escheats, Wardships, and other casualties belonging to the Crowne. In ancient time there were but two Escheators in England, the one on this side of Trent, and the other beyond Trent, at which time they had Subescheators. But in the reigne of Edward the second, the Offices were divided and severall Escheators made in everie Countie for life, &c. and so continued untill the reigne of Edward the third. And afterwards by the statute of 14 Edw. 3. it to enacted by authoritie of Parliament, that there should be as many Escheators assigned, as when king Edward the third came to the Crowne, and that was one in every Countie, and that no Escheator should tarrie in his office above a yeere, and by another Statute to be in office but once in three yeeres, the Lord Treasurer nameth him.

And hereof also commeth *Eschaetria,* which signifieth the Escheatership, or the office of the Escheater. But now let us heare what our Author will further say unto us.

28. (z) 38. Edw. 3. f. 37. 30. Hen. 6. 5. Bract. 1., tit. de Forf. Staunf. pl. cor. 192. and according to this diversitie was it resolved in 5. Hen. 6. as it appeareth by my Lord Diers Manuscripts.

29. (a) Mirror ca. 1. sect. 5. 5 1. Hen. 3. statutum de Scac. Britton fo 23. 34. Flet. lib. 1. cap. 36. & lib. 2 cap. 34. 35. Regist. 301. his Oath 18. Edw. 1. Rot. Parl. Part. 21. Edw. I. Rot. 1. 29. Edw. I. stat. de Eschaetoribus. 14. Edw. 3. c. 8. 28. Edw. 1. ca. 18. F. N. B. 100. c. Stamf. Praer. 81. 1. Hen. 8. ca. 4. 3. Hen. 8. ca. 2. Capitula Eschaetriae in Vet. Magna Carta, fo. 160. 161. &c.

"And so see the diversitie."

This kinde of speech is often used by our Author, and doth ever import matter of excellent observation, which you may finde in the Sections noted in the margent.[30]

And it is to be well observed, that our Author saith, *Sil nad ascun heire, &c. la terre eschaetera.*[31] In which words is implyed a diversitie (as to the Escheat) between Fee simple absolute, which a naturall body hath, and Fee simple absolute which a body politique or incorporate hath. (b)[32] For if land holden of I. S. be given to an Abbot and his Successors: In this case if the Abbot and all the Convent die, so that the body politique is dissolved, the Donor shall have againe this land, and not the Lord by Escheat. And so if land be given in Fee simple to a Deane and Chapter, or to a Major and Commonaltie, and to their Successors, and after such body politique or incorporate is dissolved, the Donor shall have againe the land, and not the Lord by Escheat. And the reason and cause of this diversitie is, for that in the case of a body politique or incorporate the Fee simple is vested in their politique or incorporate capacitie created by the policie of man, and therefore the Law doth annex a condition in Law to everie such gift and grant; That if such body politique or incorporate be dissolved, that the Donor or Grantor shall re-enter, for that the cause of the gift or grant faileth, but no such condition is annexed to the estate in Fee simple vested in any man in his naturall capacitie, but in case where the Donor or Feoffor reserveth to him a Tenure, and then the Law doth imply a Condition in Law by way of Escheat. Also (as hath been said) no Writ of Escheat lyeth but in the three cases aforesaid, and not where a body politique or incorporate is dissolved.

Section 5
Fee Simple

Also if there bee three brethren, and the middle brother purchaseth lands in Fee simple, and dye without issue, the elder brother shall have the Land by

---

30. Sect. 147. 149. 248. 289. 417. 667. &c.
31. [*Ed.*: If he has no heir, etc., the land will escheat.]
32. (b) 7. Edw. 11. 12. Fitz. N. B. 33. g. Edw. 3. 16. 17. Edw. 2. Stat. de templariis.

descent, and not the younger, &c. And also if there be three brethren, and the youngest purchase lands in Fee simple, & die without issue, the eldest brother shall have the land by descent & not the middle, for that the eldest is most worthy of bloud.

Now commeth our Author to the descent between brethren, which hee purposely omitted before. *Discent, descensus* commeth of the Latine word *descendo*, and, in the legall sense, it signifieth, when lands doe by right of bloud fall unto any after the death of his Ancestors: or a descent is a meanes whereby one doth derive him title to certaine lands, as heire to some of his Ancestors. And of this, and of that which hath beene spoken doth arise another division of estates in fee simple, viz. every man that hath a lawful estate in fee simple, hath it either by descent, or purchase.

[14 a] | "The eldest is most worthy of bloud."

It is a maxime in Law that the next of the worthiest bloud shall ever inherit, as the male and all descendant from him before the female, and the female of the part of the father before the male or female of the part of the mother, &c. because the female of the part of the father is of the worthiest blud. (c)[1] And therefore among the males the eldest brother and his posteritie shall inherit lands in Fee simple, as heire before any younger brother, or any descending from him, because (as Littleton saith) hee is *pluis digne de sanke. Quod prius est dignius est, and qui prior est tempore prior est jure. Si quis plures filios habuerit, jus proprietatis primo descendit ad primogenitum, eò quòd inventus est primo in rerum naturâ.*[2] In King Alfreds time Knights fees descended to the eldest sonne, for that by division of them between males the defence of the Realme might be weakened, but in those dayes Socage fee was divided betweene the heires males, and there with agreeth Glanvill.[3] *Cùm quis haerēditatem habens moriatur, &c. si plures reliquerit filios, tunc distinguitur utrùm ille fuerit miles, sive per feodum militare tenens, aut liber Sockmannus, quia si*

---

1. (c) Britton cap. 119. Bract. lib. 2. cap. 30. 277. 279. 2. E. 3. 26. 3. Eliz. Dyer 138 Stanford praer. 52. 58. 3. E. 1. tit. avowrie. 235. 28 E. 3. discent. &c. Bra. lib. 4. 211. Fleta lib. 6. cap. 2. Glanvill lib. 7. cap. 1. Mirror cap. 1. sect. 3.

2. [*Ed.:* That which is earlier is more worthy, [and] he who is first in time is stronger in law. If someone has several children, the right of property descends to the firstborn, because he is the first in being.]

3. Glanvill lib. 7. cap. 3. & ca. 1. Vide Pl. Com. 2 29b.

miles fuerit aut per militiam tenens, tunc secundum jus regni Angliae primogenitus filius patri succedit in toto, &c. si verò fuerit liber Sockmannus, tunc quidem dividetur haereditas inter omnes filios, &c.[4] But hereof more shall be said hereafter in his proper place.

Section 6
Fee Simple

Also it is to bee understood, that none shall have land of Fee simple by descent as heire to any man, unlesse hee be his heire of the whole bloud, for if a man hath issue two sonnes by divers venters, and the elder purchase lands in Fee simple, and dye without issue, the younger brother shall not have the land, but the uncle of the elder brother, of some other his next cosin shall have the same, because the younger brother is but of halfe bloud to the elder.

No man can be heire to a Fee simple by the Common Law, (d)[1] but hee that hath *sanguinem duplicatum,* the whole bloud, that is, both of the father and of the mother, so as the halfe bloud is no bloud inheritable by descent, because that hee that is but of the halfe bloud cannot be a compleat heire, for that hee hath not the whole and compleat bloud, and the Law in descents in Fee simple doth respect that which is compleat and perfect. And this maxime doth not onely hold where lands (whereof Littleton here speaketh) are claimed or demanded as heire, (e)[2] but also in case of appeale of death: for if one brother be slaine, the other brother of the halfe bloud shall never have an appeale (albeit hee shall recover nothing therein either in the realtie or personaltie) because in the eye of the Law hee is not heire to him.[3] Also this rule extends to a warrantie, as our Author himselfe elsewhere holdeth.

---

4. [*Ed.:* When someone who has an inheritance dies etc., if he leaves several children, then a distinction is to be made as to whether he was a knight, or held by a knight's fee, or a free sokeman, because if he was a knight or a tenant in chivalry then according to the law and custom of England the firstborn son succeeds the father in everything, etc., whereas if he was a free sokeman then the inheritance is divided amongst all the sons, etc.]

1. (d) Bract. lib. 4. 279b idem lib. 2. fo. 65. Britton cap. 119. I. E. 3. 19 John Giffords case. 31. E. 3 Conterpl. de voucher 88. 40. As.6. 4.2. Formd. 49. Vid. Ratcliffes case, lib. 31 fol. 40. 41.

2. (e) 7. E. 4. 15.

3. Sect. 737.

Section 7
Fee Simple

And if a man hath issue a son and a daughter by one venter, and a son by another venter, & the son of the first venter purchase lands in fee and dye without issue, the sister shal have the land by descent as heire to her brother, & not the younger brother, for that the sister is the whole bloud of her elder brother.

[14 b]　　This is put for an example to illustrate that which hath | beene said, and needeth no explanation. And herewith agreeth Britton.[1]

Section 8
Fee Simple

And also where a man is seised of lands in Fee simple, & hath issue a sonne and daughter by one venter, and a son by another venter, and dye, and the eldest son enter, and dye without issue, the daughter shall have the land, & not the younger son, yet the younger son is heire to the father but not to his brother, but if the elder sonne doth not enter into the land after the death of his father but dye before any entry made by him then the younger brother may enter & shall have the land as heire to his father: but where the elder son in the case aforesaid enters after the death of his father, & hath possession there the sister shall have the land, Because *Possessio fratris de feodo simplici facit sororem esse haeredem.*[1] But if there be 2. brothers by divers venters, and the elder is seised of land in fee, & die without issue, & his uncle enter as next heire to him, who also dye without issue, now the younger brother may have the land as heire to the uncle, for that he is of the whole bloud to him, albeit hee be but of the halfe bloud to his elder brother.

"seised of lands in Fee simple,"

These words exclude a seisin in Fee taile, albeit he hath a Fee simple expectant. (f)[2] And therefore if Lands bee given to a man and his wife, and to the heires

---

1. Britton cap. 119.

1. [*Ed.:* The brother's possession of an estate in fee simple makes the sister to be heir.]

2. (f) 24. E. 3.24.30. 31. E.g. Count de Vouch. 83. 32. E. 3. tit. Voucher. 37. Ass. p. 4. 40. E. 3.9. 42. E. 3. 10. 39. E. 3. 10. fol. 13. 7. H. 5. 3.

of their two bodies, the remainder to the heires of the husband, and they have issue a sonne, and the wife dyeth, and hee taketh another wife, and hath issue a sonne, the father dieth, the eldest sonne entreth, and dyeth without issue, the second brother of the halfe bloud shall inherit, because the eldest sonne by his entrie was not actually seised of the fee simple, being expectant but onely of the estate taile. And the rule is, that *Possessio fratris de feodo simplici facit sororem esse haeredem,* and here the eldest sonne is not possessed of the Fee simple but of the estate taile. And where Littleton speaketh onely of Lands (g)³ yet there shall bee *Possessio fratris* of an use, of a seigniorie, a rent, an advowson and of other hereditaments.

"and the eldest son enter,"

(h)⁴ These words are materially added when the father dies seised of lands in fee simple, for if the eldest sonne doth not in that case enter, then without question the youngest | son shall be heire, because as it hath beene said before [15 a] regularly hee must make himselfe heire to him that was last actually seised (or to the purchaser) and that was to the father where the eldest sonne did not enter. And therefore Littleton addeth that the son is heire to the father. (i)⁵ But when the eldest sonne in this case doth enter, then cannot the youngest sonne being of the halfe bloud bee heire to the eldest, but the land shall descend to the sister of the whole bloud. Yet in many cases albeit the sonne doth not enter into lands descended in Fee simple, the sister of the whole bloud shall inherit, & in some cases where the eldest sonne doth enter, yet the younger brother of the halfe bloud shall be heire.

(k)⁶ If the father maketh a Lease for yeares, & the Lessee entreth & dieth, the eldest son dieth during the tearme before entrie or receipt of rent, the younger sonne of the halfe bloud shall not inherit but the sister, because the possession of the Lessee for yeares, is the possession of the eldest son, so as he is actually seised of the Fee simple, and consequently the sister of the whole bloud is to bee heire. The same Law it is if the lands be holden by Knights

---

3. (g) 5. E. 4. fo. 7. Pl. Com. fo. 58. in Wimbishes case.
4. (h) 10. Ass. 17. 34. Ass. 10. 31. E. 3. Count de Vouchee 88. 32. E. 3. tit. Vouch. 94.
5. (i) 11. H. 4. 11. 40. E. 3. 30. 41. E. 3. 13. 40. Ass. p. 6. Ratcliffes case, lib. 3. fol. 41.
6. (k) 5. E. 4.7 h. 3. H. 7.5. 8. Ass. p. 6. 45. E. 3. tit. Releases, 28.

service, and the eldest sonne is within age, and the Gardian entreth into the lands. And so it is if the Gardian in Socage enter.

But in the case aforesaid, if the father make a lease for life or a gift in taile, and dieth, and the eldest sonne dieth in the life of Tenant for life or Tenant in taile, the younger brother of the halfe bloud shall inherit, because the Tenant for life or Tenant in taile is seised of the Freehold, and the eldest sonne had nothing but reversion expectant upon that Freehold or estate taile, and therefore the youngest sonne shall inherit the land as heire to his father, who was last seised of the actuall Freehold. And albeit a rent had beene reserved upon the lease for life, and the eldest sonne had received the rent and died, yet it is holden by some[7] that the younger brother shall inherit because the seisin of the rent is no actuall seisin of the Freehold of the land. But 35. Ass. pl. 2. seemeth to the contrarie, because the rent, issueth out of the land and is in lieu thereof, wherein the onely question is, whether such a seisin of the rent be such an actuall seisin of the land in the eldest sonne as the sister may in a Writ of right make herselfe heire of this land to her brother. But it is cleere that (l)[8] if there be a *bastard eigne,* and *mulier puisne,*[9] and the father maketh a Lease for life or a gift in taile be reserving a rent and dye, and the bastard receive the rent and dye, this shall barre the mulier, for the reason of that standeth upon another maxime as shall manifestly appeare in his apt place, Sect. 399.

"seised of lands,"

(m)[10] But in this case if the eldest sonne doth enter and get an actuall possession of the Fee simple, yet if the wife of the father be indowed of the third part and the eldest sonne dyeth, the younger brother shall have the reversion of this third part notwithstanding the elder brothers entrie, because that his actuall seisin which hee got thereby was by the endowment defeated. But if the eldest sonne had made a lease for life, and the Lessee has endowed the wife of the father, and tenant in dower had died, the daughter should have had

---

7. 7. H. 5. 34. per Halls & Logdington. 35. Ass. p. 2.

8. (l) 14. E. 2. Bastard 26. Vid. Sect. 399.

9. [*Ed.:* When a man has a bastard son, and afterwards marries the mother and by her has also a legitimate son, the elder son is "bastard eigne," and the younger son is "mulier puisne."]

10. (m) 7. H. 5. 2. 3. 4i.

the reversion, because the reversion was changed and altered by the Lease for life, and the reversion is now expectant on a new estate for life.

"enter"

Hereupon the question groweth, whether if the father be seised of divers severall parcels of lands in one Countie, and after the death of the father the sonne entreth into one parcell generally, and before any actuall entrie into the other dieth, this generall entrie into part shall vest in him an actuall seisin in the whole, so as the sister shall inherit the whole. And this is a *Quaere* in 21. Hen. 7. 33. a.[11]

| And some doe take a diversitie when an entrie shall vest, or devest an   [15 b] estate, that there must be severall entries into the severall parcels, but where the possession is in no man, but the Freehold in Law is in the heire that entreth, there the generall entrie into one part reduceth all into his actuall possession. And therefore if the Lord entreth into a parcell generally for a Mortmaine, or the Feoffor for a condition broken, or the Disseisee into parcell generally, the entrie shall not vest nor devest in these or like cases, but for that parcell. But when a man dies seised of divers parcels in possession, and the Freehold in Law is by a Law cast upon the heire, and the possession in no man, there the entrie into parcell generally seemeth to vest the actuall possession in him in the whole. But if his entrie in that case be speciall, viz. that he enter onely into that parcell and into no more, there it reduceth that parcell only into actuall possession.

"man is seised of lands"

What then is the Law of a Rent, Advowson, or such things that lye in grant? (g)[12] If a Rent, or an Advowson doe descend to the eldest sonne, and hee dieth before he hath seisin of the Rent, or present to the Church, the Rent or Advowson shall descend to the youngest sonne, for that he must make himselfe heire to his father, as hath been oftentimes said before. The like Law is of Offices, Courts, Liberties, Franchises, Commons of inheritance, and such like.

11. 21 H. 7. 33n.
12. (g) 19. F. 2. Quare imped. 177. 3. H. 7. 5.

(h)[13] And this case differeth from the case of the Tenant by the Courtesie, for there if the wife dieth before the rent day, or that the Church become voyd, because there was no laches or default in him, nor possibilitie to get seisin, the Law in respect of the issue begotten by him will give him an estate by the Courtesie of England. But the case of the descent to the youngest sonne standeth upon another reason, viz. to make himselfe heire to him that was last actually seised, as hath beene said.

"in Fee simple"

(i)[14] For halfe bloud is not respected in estates in taile, because that the issues doe claime in by descent, *per formam Doni*,[15] and the issue in taile is ever of the whole bloud to the Donee.

(k)[16] "Possessio fratris de Feodo simplici facit sororem esse haeredem."

Hereupon foure things are to bee observed, everie word almost being operative and materiall. First, That the brother must be in actuall possession: For *Possessio est quasi pedis positio*.[17] Secondly, *De feodo simplici*,[18] exclude estates in taile. Thirdly, *Facit sororem esse haeredem*.[19] So as (l)[20] *Soror est haeres facta*,[21] and therefore some act must be done to make her heire, and the younger sonne is *haeres natus*,[22] (m)[23] if no act be done to the contrarie. And albeit the words be *Facit sororem esse haeredem*, yet this doth extend to the issue of the sister, &c. who shall inherit before the younger brother. Fourthly, Of Dignities whereof no other possession can be had but such as descend (as to be a Duke, Marquesse, Earle, Viscount, or Baron) to a man and his heires, there can be

---

13. (h) 7. E. 3. 66. tit. bar. 293. 3. H. 7.5.
14. (i) 8. E. 3. 11. 40. E. 3. 12. Ratcliffes case, lib. 3. F. 41.
15. [*Ed.:* by the form of the gift; by the designation of the giver and not by the operation of law.]
16. (k) Bracton lib. 2. fo. 65. & lib. 4 fol. 279. Britton cap. 119. Flet. li. 6. c. 1. 24 E. 3. 30.
17. [*Ed.:* Possession is, as it were, the position of the foot.]
18. [*Ed.:* of fee simple.]
19. [*Ed.:* causes the sister to be heir.]
20. (l) Ratcliffes case, lib. 3. fol. 42.
21. [*Ed.:* the sister is the born heir.]
22. [*Ed.:* an heir born.]
23. (m) Britton cap. 119.

no possession of the brother to make the sister to inherit, but the younger brother being heire (as Littleton saith) to the father, shall inherit the Dignitie inherent to the bloud, as heire to him that was first created noble.

And you shall understand that concerning Descents there is a Law, parcell of the Lawes of England, called *Jus Coronae*,[24] and differeth in many things, from the generall Law concerning the subject.[25] As for example, The King in any suit for any thing that pertaines to the Crowne shall not shew in certaine his cosinage as a subject shall doe, or as be himselfe shall doe for things touching his Dutchie. (n)[26] And in the case of the King, if he hath issue a sonne, and a daughter by one venter, and a sonne by another venter, and purchaseth lands and dieth, and the eldest son enter and dieth without issue, the daughter shall not inherit these lands, not any other Fee simple lands of the Crowne, but the younger brother shall have them. Wherein note that neither *possessio fratris* doth hold of lands of the possessions of the Crowne, nor halfe bloud is no impediment to the descent of the lands of the Crowne, as it fell out in experience after the decease of King Edward the sixth to the Queene Marie, and from Queene Marie to Queene Elizabeth, both which here were of the halfe bloud, and yet inherited not onely the Lands which King Edward or Queene Marie purchased, but the ancient Lands parcell of the Crowne also.

A man that is King by descent of the part of his mother,[27] purchase lands to him and his heires and dye without issue, this land shall descend to the heire of the part of the mother, but in the case of a subject, the heire of the part of the father shall have them.

So King Henry the eighth purchased lands to him and his heires, and died having issue two daughters, the Lady Mary, and the Lady Elizabeth, after the decease of King Edward, the eldest daughter Queene Mary did inherit only, all his lands in Fee simple. For the eldest daughter, or sister of a King shall inherit all his Fee simple lands. So it is if the King purchaseth Lands of the custome of Gavelkinde, and dye having issue divers sons, the eldest son shall onely inherit these lands. And the reason of all these cases is, for that the qualitie of the person doth in these and many other like cases alter the descent,[28]

24. [*Ed.:* Law of the Crown.]
25. 6. H. 4. 2.
26. (n) 24 H. 6. fol. 34. Pl. Com. sol. 245. 25 E. 3. ca. *de natis ultra mare.*
27. Pl. Com. ubi supra.
28. Pl. Com. fol. 247.

so as, all the Lands and possessions whereof the King is seised in *jure Coronae,* shall *secundum jus Coronae,* attend upon and follow the Crowne, and therefore to whomsoever the Crowne descend, those Lands and possessions descend also, for the Crowne and the Lands whereof the King is seised in *jure Coronae,* [16 a] are concomitantia.[29] If the | right heire of the Crowne be attained of treason, yet shall the Crowne descend to him, and *eo instante* (without any other reversall) the attainder is utterly avoided, as it fell out in the case of Henry the seventh.[30] (o)[31] And if the King purchase lands to him and his heires, he is seised thereof in *jure Coronae, è fortiori,*[32] when he purchases land to him his heires and successours.

But hereof this little taste shall suffice.

Section 9
Fee Simple

And it is to wit, that this word *(inheritance)* is not only intended where a man hath Lands or Tenements by descent of inheritage, but also everie Fee simple or taile which a man hath by his purchase may be said an inheritance, because his heires may inherit him. For in a Writ of right which a man bringeth of land that was of his owne purchase, the Writ shall say, *Quam clamat esse jus & haereditatem suam.*[1] And so shall it be said in divers other Writs which a man or woman bringeth of his owne purchase, as appeares by the Register.

"And it is to wit"[2]

This kind of speer is used twice in this Chapter, and oftentimes by our Author in all his three Bookes, and ever teacheth us some rule of Law, or generall or sure leading point, as you shall perceive by reading, and observing of the same, which for the ease of the studious Reader I have observed.

---

29. [*Ed.:* concomitant.]
30. Pl. Com. 238. 1. H. 7. fol. 4
31. (o) 43. E. 3. fol. 20.
32. [*Ed.:* (by) law of the Crown, and so it follows.]
1. [*Ed.:* Which he claims to be his right and inheritance.]
2. Sect. 45, 46. 57. 59. 80. 100. 146. 164. 170. 184. 229. 243. 259. 274. 280. 293. 300. 305. 419. 420. 421. 489. 632. 697. 749.

"Quam clamat esse jus & haereditatem suam."

(a)[3] Here our Author declareth the right signification of this word (inheritance.) And true it is, that in the Writ of right Patent, &c. *Quando Dominus remittit Curiam suam,*[4] The words of the Writ be, *Quam clamat esse jus & haereditatem suam.* And in the *Praecipe in capite,* in a *Cui in vita,*[5] (b)[6] when the Defendant claimeth by purchase, the Writ is *Quam clamat esse jus & haereditatem suam.* And with Littleton agreeth the Register, fol. 4. & 232. and the Booke in 49 Edw. 3. 22. against sodaine opinions 7. Hen. 4. 5. 10. Hen. 6.9. 39. Hen. 6.38. Pl. Com. Wimbethes case 47. And yet in 7. Hen. 4.5. which is the Booke of the greatest weight, Sir. William Thirning Chiefe Justice of the Common Bench (as it seemeth doubting of it) went into the Chancerie to enquire of the Chancerie men the forme of the Writ in that case, and they said that the forme was both the one way and the other, so as thereby the opinion of Littleton is confirmed, and the Booke in 6. Edw.3. fol.30. is notable,[7] for there in an Action of waste the Plaintife supposed, that the Defendant did hold *de haereditate sua,*[8] and it is ruled, that albeit the Plaintife purchased the reversion, yet the Writ should serve. And there it is said, It hath beene seene, that in a *Cui in vita,* the Writ was, which the Demandant claimed as her right and inheritance, when it was her purchase. And so this point wherein there might seeme some contrarietie in bookes is manifestly cleared. But in the Statute of West. 2. cap. 5.[9] *de haeredite uxorum* by construction of the whole Statute is taken onely for the wives inheritance by descent, and not by purchase, as appeareth in 1. Edw. 2. tit. *Quare imped.* 43. 35. Hen. 6. 54. F. N. B. 34.b.[10]

There be some that have an inheritance (c)[11] and have it neither by descent, nor properly by purchase, but by Creation, as when the King doth create any man a Duke, a Marquesse, Earle, Viscount, or Baron to him and his heires,

---

3. (a) Sect. 732. Bract. Lib. 2. fo. 62. b. Fleta, lib. 6. cap. 1.

4. [*Ed.:* when the lord has waived his court.]

5. [*Ed.:* A writ in Chancery to protect a tennant-in-chief who has been dispossesed of his lands.]

6. (b) Regist. fol. 1, 2. Regist. Fo. 4. 232. 49E.3. 22. 7H. 4. 5. 10H. 6. 38. 6 E. 3. 30. Pl. Com. Wimbeshe's case, 47. & 58. b.

7. 6. E. 3. 30.

8. [*Ed.:* of his inheritance.]

9. W. 2. ca. 5.

10. I. E. 3. tit. quare Imped. 43. 35. H. 6. 34. F. N. B. 34 b.

11. (c) Lib. 6. fol. 5a. 53. Countes de Rutlands case, lib. 8. fol 16. 17. the Princes case.

or to the heires males of his bodie, &c. hee hath an inheritance therein by Creation. A man may have an inheritance in title of Nobilitie and Dignitie three manner of wayes, that is to say, by Creation, by Descent, and by | Prescription. By Creation two manner of ordinarie wayes (for I will not speake of a Creation by a Parliament) by Writ, and by Letters Patents. Creation by Writ is the ancienter way, and here it is to be observed; that a man shall gaine an inheritance by Writ. King Richard the second created John Beauchampe de Holte Baron of Kedermister by his Letters Patents, bearing date the 10. of October, anno regni sui II. before whom there was never any Baron created by Letters Patents, but by Writ. And it is to bee observed, that if hee bee generally called by Writ to the Parliament, he hath a Fee simple in the Barony without any words of inheritance. But if he be created by Letters Patents, the state of inheritance must be limited by apt words, or else the grant is void. If a man be called by Writ to the Parliament, and the Writ is delivered unto him, and he dieth before he commeth and sits in Parliament, whether he was a Baron or no? And it is to be answered that he was no Baron, for the direction and deliverie of the Writ to him maketh not him Noble; for the better understanding whereof it is to be knowne that the words of the Writ in that case are, *Rex, &c. E. B. de D. Chivalier salutem. Quia de advisamento & assensu concilii nostri pro quibusdam arduis & urgentibus negotiis statum & defensionem regni nostri Angliae, &c. concernentibus quoddam Parliamentum nostrum apud Civitatem Westm. à 21. Octob. proxim. futuro teneri ordinavimus, & ibid. vobiscum & cum Praelatis, Magnatibus & Proceribus dicti regni nostri colloquium habere & tractatum, vobis in fide & ligeancia quibus nobis tenemini firmiter injungendo mandamus, quod consideratis dictorum negotiorum arduitate, & periculis imminentibus cessante excusatione quacunque, dictis die & loco personaliter intersitis nobiscum & cum Praelatis, Magnatibus, & Proceribus supradictis, super dictis negotiis tractatur' vestrumque consilium impensur', &c.*[12,13] And this Writ

12. [*Ed.:* The king, etc. to E. B. of D., knight, greeting. Because, by the advice and consent of our council, we have ordained our certain parliament to be held at Westminster on the twenty-first day of October next coming, for certain arduous and urgent business concerning the estate and defence of our realm of England, there to have discussion and treaty with you and with the prelates, great men and peers of our said realm: we, firmly enjoining, command you upon the faith and allegiance which you bear unto us, considering the arduousness and imminent dangers of the said business, that you, leaving aside all excuses whatsoever, be there personally at the said day and place with us and with the prelates, great men and peers mentioned above, to treat and give your advice upon the said business, etc.]

13. Lib. 6. fol. 52. 53. Countesse of Rutlands case, 8. H. 6. 10. 48. E. 3. 30. 35. H. 6. 46. Pl. Com. 223.

hath no operation or effect untill hee sit in Parliament, and thereby his bloud is ennobled to him and his heires lineall, and thereupon a Baron is called a Peere of Parliament. (d)[14] And if issue be joyned in any action, whether he be a Baron, &c. or no, it shall not be tried by Jurie, but by the Record of Parliament, which could not appeare unlesse hee were of the Parliament. Therefore a Duke, Earle, &c. of another Kingdome, are not to bee sued by those names here, for that they are not Peeres of our Parliament. And albeit the Creation by Writ is the ancienter, yet the Creation by Letters Patents is the surer, for hee may bee sufficiently created by Letters Patents, and made Noble, albeit hee never sit in Parliament.

(e)[15] And it is to be observed that Nobilitie may bee granted for terme of life, by act in Law without any actuall Creation; as if a Duke take a wife, by the intermarriage shee is a Duchesse in Law, and so of a Marquesse, an Earle, and the rest, and in some other case. And there is a diversitie betweene a woman that is Noble by Descent, and a woman that is noble by marriage. (f)[16] For if a woman that is Noble by Descent, marrie one that is under the degree of Nobilitie, yet remaineth Noble still; but if shee gaine it by marriage, shee loseth it, if shee marrie under the degree of Nobilitie, and so is the rule to be understood, *Si mulier nobilis nupserit ignobili desinit esse nobilis.*[17] (g)[18] But if a Dutchesse by marriage marrieth a Baron of the Realme she remaineth a Dutchesse and loseth not her name, because her husband is Noble, *&c de caeteris.*[19]

And as an estate for life may be gained by marriage, so may the King create either man or woman Noble for life (h)[20] but not for yeares, because then it might goe to Executors or Administrators. The true division of persons is, that everie man is either of Nobilitie, that is, a Lord of Parliament of the upper House, or under the degree of Nobilitie, amongst the Commons, as Knights,

---

14. (d) 35. H. 6 46. 48. E. 2.30b. 43. Ass. p. 6. 22. Ass. p. 24. Regist. 287. 11. E. 3. breve 472. 20. E. 4. 6.

15. (e) Lib. 6. fol. Countes de Rutlands case, 2. H. 6. 11. 22. Ass. 24. 12. E. 3. breve 254. 3. H. 4. 19. 11. H. 4. 25. Vide Fleta lib. 6. ca. 10.

16. (f) Lib. 4. fol. 118. Actons case, Tempore Mariae Reginâ. Brooke nosme de dignitie 69. 14. H. 6. 18. 2. H. 6. 11.

17. [*Ed.:* If a noblewoman marries someone who is not noble, she ceases to be noble.]

18. (g) 22. H. 6. 52.

19. [*Ed.:* and likewise of the rest.]

20. (h) Lib. 9. fol. 97. 98. Sir George Reynels Case.

Esquires, Citizens and Burgesses of the lower House of Parliament, commonly called House of Commons, and he that is not of the Nobilitie is by intendment of Law among the Commons.

"as appeares by the Register"

Which booke in the Statute of West. 2. ca. 24. is called *Registrum de Cancellaria,* because it containeth the formes of Writs at the Common Law that issue out of the Chancerie, *tanquam ex officina justiciae.*[21] There is a Register of originall Writs, and a Register of judiciall Writs, but when it is spoken generally of the Register it is meant of the Register originall. For the antiquitie and excellencie of this Booke, see in my Preface to the eighth part of my Commentaries. This excellent Booke our Author voucheth divers times in these Bookes, and so doth he divers other Authorities in Law of severall kindes, but with this observation, that he citeth no Authoritie, but when the case is rare or may seeme doubtfull, which appeareth in this, that he putteth no Case in all his three Bookes but hath warrant of good Authoritie in Law. For he knew well the rule,[22] that *perspicua vera non sunt probanda.*[23] And the like observation its made of Justice Firzherbert in his Booke of *Natura Brevium,* that he never citeth Authoritie, but when the Case is rare or was doubtfull to him. The Authorities which our Author hath cited in his three Bookes I have collected.

Section 10
Fee Simple

[17 a] I And of such things whereof a man may have a Manuell occupation, possession or receipt, as of lands, Tenements, Rents, and such like, there a man shall say in his Count Countant and Plea Pleadant, that such a one was seised in his demesne as of fee, but of such things which do not lye in such Manuall occupation, &c. as of an Advowson of a Church and such like, there he shall say, that hee was seized as of fee, and not in his Demesne as of fee. And in Latine it is in one Case, *Quod talis seisitus fuit in dominico suo ut de feodo,*[1] and in the other Case, *Quod talis seisitus fuit, &c. ut de feodo.*

21. [*Ed.:* as from the workshop of justice.]
22. Vide sect 88. 97. 96. 101. 157. 234. 308. 383 412. 480 433. 514. 643. 644. 657. 660. 692. 701. 729.
23. [*Ed.:* Plain truths need not be proved.]
1. [*Ed.:* that such and such was seised in his demesne as of fee.]

"In his Count Countant."

In Count Countant. Count, i.e. *narratio* commeth of the French word *Conte* which in Latine is *Narratio,* and is vulgarly called a Declaration. The originall writ is according to his name *Breve,* briefe & short, but the Count which the Plaintife or Demandant make is more narrative & spacious and certaine both in matter & in circumstance of time and place, to the end the defendant may be compelled to make a more direct answer; so as the writ may be compared to Logicke and the Count to Rhetoricke, and it is that which the Civilians call a Libell. And in that ancient booke of the Mirror of Justices,[2] Lib. 2. cap. des Loiers, Contors are Serjants skilfull in Law, so named of the Count as of the principall part, and in Wil. 2. ca.29.[3] hee is called Serjant Counter.

"in his Plea Pleadant."

Placitum. Here Littleton teacheth good pleading in this point, of which in his third Booke and Chapter of Confirmation, Sect. 534. hee thus saith, *Et saches mon sits que est un des pluis honorables, laudables, & profitable choses en nostreley, de auer le science de bien pleader en actions reals & personels, & pur ceo, ieo toy counsaile especialment de metteraton courage, & cure de ceo apprender.*[4] And for this cause this Word *Placitum* is derived *à placendo, quia bene placitare super omnia placet,*[5] and it is not as some have said, so called *per Antiphrasin, quia non placet.*[6]

"seised."[7]

Seisitus commeth of the French word *seisin, i. possessio,* saving that in the Common Law *seised,* or *seisin* is properly applyed to Freehold, and possessed

---

2. Mirror des Justices.

3. W. 2. cap. 39.

4. [*Ed.:* And know, my son, that it is one of the most honorable, laudable and profitable things in our law to have the knowledge of pleading well in actions real and personal, and therefore I advise you especially to employ your effort and care in learning it.]

5. [*Ed.: placitum* (plea) (is derived) from *placendo* (pleasing), because pleading well pleases above all.]

6. [*Ed.:* by antiphrasis, because it does not please.]

7. Bract. lib. 4. fol. 253. Idem lib. 5. fol. 372. Britton fol. 205. 206. Fleta lib. 5. cap. 5. Stanf. praer. 8.

or possession properly to goods and chattels; although sometime the one is used in stead of the other.

"in his demesne as of fee, *In Dominico suo ut in feodo.*"[8]

Dominicum is not onely that inheritance, wherein a man hath proper dominion or ownership, as it is distinguished from the lands which another doth hold of him in service, but that which is manually occupied, manured, and possessed, for the necessarie sustentation, maintenance and supportation of the Lord and his houshold, and savoureth *de domo,* of the house, either *ad mensam,* for his or their board and sustentation, or manually received (as Rents) for bearing and defraying of necessarie charges publike or private. Of these (saith our Author) he should plead, that he is seised *in dominico suo ut de feodo, i.e. de feodo dominicali, seu terrâ dominicali, seu redditu dominicali,*[9] which is as much to say as Demeyne or Demaine, of the hand, i. manured by the hand, or received by the hand, and therefore he calleth it manuall occupation, possession or receipt. And in Domesday[10] Demeane land is called Inland, as for example, *4. bovatas terrae de Inland, & 10. bovatas in servitio.*[11]

"in such Manuall occupation, &c."

[17 b]   There is nothing in our Author but is worthy | of observation. Here is the first (&c.) and there is no (&c.) in all his three Bookes (there being as you shall perceive verie many) but it is for two purposes. First it doth imply some other necessarie matter. Secondly, that the Student may together with that which our Author hath said, inquire what authorities there be in Law that treat of that matter, which will worke three notable effects: First, it will make him understand our Author the better: Secondly, it will exceedingly adde to the Readers invention. And lastly, it will fasten the matter more surely in his memorie, for which purpose I have for his case in the beginning set downe in these Institutes, the effect of some of the principall authorities in Law, as

---

8. Pl. Com. fol. 191. Wrote sleys case.
9. [*Ed.:* in his demense as of fee, that is, of a demense fee, or demesne land, or demesne rent.]
10. Domesday.
11. [*Ed.:* four bovates (each 12–15 acres) of 'inland' (i.e. demesne) land, and ten bovates in service.]

I conceive them concerning the same. In this place the (&c.) implyeth possession or receipt, and such other matter as appeareth by my notes in this Section. As for the Authorities of Law, you shall finde the effect of them in this Section, and the like of the rest of the (&c.) which you shall finde in the Sections hereafter mentioned, omitting those (for avoyding of tediousnesse) that either are apparent, or which are explained in some other places, viz. Sect. 20. 48. 102. 108. 120. 125. 136. 137. 146. 149. 154. 164. 166. 167. 168. 177. 179. 183. 184. 194. 200. 202. 210. 211. 217. 220. 226. 233. 240. 242. 244. 245. 248. 262. 264. 269. 270. 271. 279. 320. 322. 323. 325. 326. 327. 329. 330. 335. 336. 341. 347. 348. 349. 350. 352. 355. 356. 359. 364. 365. 374. 375. 377. 381. 384. 389. 393. 395. 397. 399. 401. 402. 410. 417. 428. 433. 447. 449. 464. 470. 471. 477. 483. 489. 500. 501. 522. 532. 552. 553. 556. 558. 562. 578. 591. 592. 593. 594. 603. 613. 624. 625. 630. 632. 634. 637. 638. 648. 659. 660. 661. 669. 687. 693. 700. 718. 745. 748. 749. All which I have observed and quoted here once for all, for ease of the studious Reader.

"*ut de feodo,*"[12]

Where (ut) is not by way of similitude, but to be understood positively that he is seised in fee.[13] And so it is where one pleads a descent to one *ut filio & haeredi,*[14] that is, to Io.S. that is sonne and heire, & *sic de caeteris,*[15] where *(ut) denotat ipsam veritatem.*[16]

"as of an Advowson"

Of an Advowson (i)[17] wherein a man hath as absolute ownership and propertie as hee hath in Lands or Rents, yet hee shall not plead, that hee is seised in *Dominico suo ut feodo,* because that inheritance, favouring not *de domo,*[18] cannot either serve for the sussentation of him and his houshold, nor any thing can bee received for the same for defraying of charges. And therefore

12. [*Ed.:* As of fee.]
13. Briton 205. 206. optime. Fleta lib. 6. cap. 5. Idem lib. 3. cap. 15.
14. [*Ed.:* as son and heir.]
15. [*Ed.:* and likewise of the rest.]
16. [*Ed.: ut* (as) denotes the truth itself.]
17. (i) 7. E. 3. 63. 24. E. 3. 74. 34. H. 6. 34. 19. E. 3. Quar, imp. 154. Mirror cap. 2. sect. 17. [*Ed.:* "Advowson" is the right to control a church or beneficence.]
18. [*Ed.:* Desmesne as of his fee . . . control.]

hee cannot say, that hee is seised thereof *in dominico suo de feodo,* whereby it appeareth how the Common Law doth detest Simony, and all corrupt bargaines for presentations to any Benefice, but that (k)[19] *idonea persona* for the discharge of the Cure should be presented freely without expectation of any thing; nay, so cautious is the Common Law in this point that the Pl. in a *Quare impedit* should recover no damages for the losse of his presentation untill the Statute of West 2.cap.5. And that is the reason that Gardian in Socage (l)[20] shall not present to an Advowson, because hee can take nothing for it, and by consequent hee cannot account for it. And by the Law hee can meddle with nothing that hee cannot account for it. (m)[21] And in a Writ of right of Advowson, the Patron shall not alleage the explees or taking of the profits in himselfe, but in his Incumbent. And hereby the old Bookes shall bee the better understood, viz. Bracton, lib. 4. tract.3. cap. nu. 5. *Est autem dominicum quod quis habet ad mensam, & proprie, sicut sunt Boordlands Anglice.* And Fleta lib. 5.ca.5. *Est autem dominicum proprie terra ad mensam assignata. Dominicum etiam dicitur ad differentiam ejus quod tenetur in servitio.*[22] But of an Advowson and such like hee shall plead, that hee is seised *de advocatione ut de feodo & jure.*[23]

"Advowson."

Advocatio, signifying an advowing or taking into protection, is as much as *jus patronatus.* Sir William Herle in 7. Edw. 3. fol. 4.[24] saith, that it is not long past, that a man did known what an Advowson was, but when a man would grant an Advowson hee granted, *Ecclesiam* the Church, and thereby the Advowson passed, Vide 45. Edw. 3. 5.[25] But surely the word is of greater antiquitie,

19. (k) Lib. 6. fol 51. Boswels case.

20. (l) 8. E. 2 Presentment al Eglise 10. 7. E. 3. 39. 27. E. 3. 89. 29. E. 3. 5. 31. E. 3. Estoppel 240.

21. (m) 7. E. 3. 63. Bracton 263. 372. Flera lib. 5. cap. 5.

22. [*Ed.:* Demense is what someone has to (supply) the table (i.e. to provide food), and for his own use, as 'board-lands' are in English. . . . Demesne is land set aside to (supply) the table, for his own use. It is also called demesne to distinguish it from what someone holds in service.]

23. [*Ed.:* of the advowson as of fee and right.]

24. 7. E. 3. 4.

25. 45. E. 3. 1.

for in the Register there is an originall Writ *de recto Advocationis,* and in the originall Writ of Assise *de darreine presentment* the Patron is callen *Advocatus.* (n)[26] Vide Wil. 2. ca.5. And so doth (o)[27] Bracton call him. *Advocatus autem dici poterit ille ad quem pertinet jus advocationis alicujus, ut ad Ecclesiam prae-sentet nomine proprio & non alieno.*[28] And (p) Fleta lib. 5. cap.14.[29] agreeth herewith almost *totidem verbis: Advocatus est ad quem pertinet jus advocationis alterius Ecclesiae, ut ad Ecclesiam nomine proprio non alieno possit praesentare.*[30] And (q)[31] Britton cap. 92. The Patron is called *Avow,* and the Patrons are called *Advocati,* for that they bee either Founders, or Maintainers, or Bene-factors of the Church either by building, donation, or increasing of it, in which respect they were also called *Patroni,* and the Advowson *jus patronatus.*

And it is to be understood that there is a great (r)[32] diversitie *inter advo-cationem medietatis Ecclesiae, &c. & medietatem advocationis Ecclesiae.*[33] And of their severall remedies for the same, For the Advowson of the moytie is when there be severall Patrons, and two severall Incumbents in one Church, the one of the one moytie thereof, and the other of the other moytie, and one part as well of the Church as of the Towne allotted to the one, and the other part thereof to the other, and in that case each Patron if he be disturbed shall have a *Quare impedit, quod permittat ipsum praesentare idoneam personam ad medietatem Ecclesiae.*[34]

But if there be two Coparceners, and they do agree to present by turne, each of them in truth hath but a moytie of the Church, but for that there is but one Incumbent, if either of them bee disturbed she shall have a *Quare impedit, &c. praesentare idoneam personam ad Ecclesiam;*[35] for that there is

[18 a]

26. (n) W. 2. ca. 5
27. (o) Bract. lib. 4. fo. 240.
28. [*Ed.:* He to whom the right of advowson belongs may be called the avowee (patron), since he may present to the church in his own name and not in someone else's.]
29. (p) Fleta lib. 5. cap. 14.
30. [*Ed.:* In so many words: A patron is he to whom appertains the right of presentation to a church, in such a manner that he may present to such a church in his own name, and not in the name of another.]
31. (q) Britton cap. 92.
32. (r) 33. H. 6. 11. b. per Prisot: 14. H. 6. 15. per Newton. 31. E. 1 droit 68. 69. F.N.B. 31 b. Lib. 10. 135. 136. R. Smiths case. 45. E 3. Fines 41. 45. E. 3. 12. 17. E. 3. 78. 17. E. 2. Dower 163.
33. [*Ed.:* between an advowson of a moiety of a church, and a moiety of the advowson of a church.]
34. [*Ed.:* That he permit him to present a suitable parson to the moiety of the church.]
35. [*Ed.:* to present a suitable parson to the church.]

but one Church and one Incumbent, and so of the like. But in (s)[36] the said case of the Coparceners one of them shall have a writ of right of Advowson *de medietate advocationis,*[37] for in truth she hath but a right to a moytie, but in the other case where there be two Patrons and two Incumbents in one Church, each of them shall have a writ of right of Advowson *De advocatione medietatis.*

And as there may (as hath beene said) be two severall Parsons in one Church, so there may be two that may make but one parson in a Church. (t)[38] Britton saith, *Si ascun Esglise soir done a divers persons per un sole avowe nul ne sepura pleadre per assise de juris utrum ne nul estre implede sauns lautre, &c.*[39] And therewith agreeth Fleta. (u)[40] *Item licet aliqua Ecclesia divisa fuerit inter duos, sive bona sua habeant communia sive separata, dum tamen unicum habeant advocatum nullus eorum sine alio agere poterit vel implacitari.*[41] And Fitzh. saith[42] that two Prebendaries may be one Parson of a Church, who shall joyne in a *Juris utrum,*[43] so as one Rectorie may be annexed to two severall Prebends, and both of them make but one Parson. But where one is Parson of the one moytie of a Church, and another of the other moytie, as hath been said, there one of them shall have a *juris utrum* against the other, and in the Writ shall name him *persona medietatis Ecclesiae, &c.* But for avoyding of suspicion of curiositie if we should proceed any further[44] herein, we will attend what Littleton will further teach as.

36. (s) Britton fol. 235. 31. E. I. droit. 68. 97. F.N.B. 31. b. 5. 33. 5. H. 7. 8. 17. E. 3. 38. 75. 76. 7. E. 327. 8. E. 3. 425. 22. Ass. p. 33. 14. H 4 10. 33. E. 3. Quare. imp. 196.

37. [*Ed.:* of the moiety of an advowson.]

38. (t) Britton fo. 235.

39. [*Ed.:* If any church is given to various persons by one sole avowee (patron), no one may plead by assize of *juris utrum* and none of them may be impleaded without the other.]

40. (u) Fleta lib. 5. ca. 19.

41. [*Ed.:* Even if some church is divided between two, whether they have their goods in common or separately, nevertheless so long as they have one advowson neither of them may sue or be impleaded without the other.]

42. F.N.B. 49. o.

43. [*Ed.:* An abolished writ which lay for the parson of a church whose predecessor had alienated the lands and tenements thereof.]

44. F. N. B. 49. p.

Section 11
Fee Simple

And note that a man cannot have a more large or greater estate of inheritance than Fee simple.

This doth extend as well to Fee simples conditionall & qualified as to Fee simples pure and absolute. For our Author, speaketh here of the amplenesse and greatness of the estate, and not of the perdurableness of the same. And he that hath a Fee simple conditionall or qualified, hath as ample and great an estate as hee that hath a Fee simple absolute, so as the diversitie apeareth between the quantitie and qualitie of the estate.

From this state in Fee simple, estates in taile, and all other particular estates are derived, and therefore worthily our Author beginneth his first Book with Tenant in Fee simple, for *à principalioribus seu dignioribus est inchoandum.*[1]

"cannot have a more large or greater estate."

For this cause two (a)[2] Fee simples absolute cannot be of one and the selfe-same land. If the King make a gift in taile, and the Donee is attainted of treason, in this case the King hath not two simples in him, viz. the ancient reversion in Fee, & A Fee simple determinable upon the dying without issue of Tenant in taile, but both of them are consolidated and conjoyned together, and so it is if such a Tenant in taile both convey the land to the King his heires and successors, the King hath but one estate in Fee simple united in him, and the Kings grant of one estate is good, and so was it adjudged in the Court of Common Pleas. And yet in severall persons by act in Law, a reversion may bee in Fee simple in one, and a Fee simple determinable in another by matter *Ex post facto;* as if a gift in taile made to a Villeine, and the Lord enter, the Lord hath a Fee simple qualified, and the Donor a reverssion in fee, but if the Lord infeoffe the Donor, now both Fee simples are united, and he hath but one Fee simple in him: but one Fee simple cannot depend upon another

---

1. [*Ed.:* One should begin with the principal or more worthy matters.]

2. (a) Pl. Com. 3 9. &c 248. 19. H. 8. Dier 4. 29. H. 8. Dier 33. 16. Eliz. Dier 330. 2. Marie Dier 107. Austens case. Pa. 33. Eliz. Rot. 108. In Quar. imp. between the Queene Pl. and the Bishop of Lincolne, Hussey and others Def. 15. E. 4. 6. 8.

by the grant of the partie, as if lands be given to A. so long as B. hath heires of his body the remainder over in fee, the remainder is voyd.

Section 12
Fee Simple

Also purchase is called the possession of lands or tenements that a man hath by his deed or agreement, unto which possession hee commeth not by title of descent from any of his Ancestors, or of his Cousins, but by his owne deed.

[18 b] Purchase in Latine is either *acquisitum,* of the verb *acquiro,* for so I find it in the originall Register 243. *In terris vel tenementis quae | viri & mulieres conjunctim acquisiverunt, &c.* Bracton,[1] calleth it *perquisitum;* and by (b)[2] Glanvill it is called *quaestus* or *perquisitum.*

A purchase is always intended by title, and most properly by some kinde of conveyance either for money or some other consideration, or freely of gift: for that is in Law also a purchase. But a descent, because it commeth meerely by act of Law, is not said to be a purchase, and accordingly the makers of the act of Parliament in I. Hen. 5. ca. 5[3] speaketh of them that have lands or tenements by purchase or descent of inheritance. And so it is of an Escheat or the like, because the inheritance is cast upon, or a title vested in the Lord by act in Law and not by his owne deed or agreement, as our Author here saith, Like Law of the state of Tenant by the Courtesie, Tenant in Dower or the like. But such as attaine to lands by meere injurie and wrong, as by disseisin, intrusion, abatement, usurpation, &c. cannot be said to come in by purchase, no more than Robbery, Burglary, Pyracy or the like can justly be termed purchase.

If a Nobleman, Knight, Esquire, &c. be burried in a Church, and have his Coat armor and Pennions with his armes, and such other ensignes of honour as belong to his degree or order set up in the Church, or if a grave stone or tombe be laid or made, &c. for a monument of him. (c)[4] In this case albeit the freehold of the Church be in the Parson, and that these be annexed to the freehold, yet cannot the Parson or any take them or deface them, but he

---

1. Bracton lib. 2. fol. 65. [*Ed.:* As to land, it may be held by men and women, jointly acquired.]
2. (b) Glavnill lib. 7. cap. I. Brit. c. 33. fo. 84 & 121.
3. Pl. Com. Wimbishes case 47.b. 1. H. 5. ca. 5.
4. (c) 9. H. 4. 24.

is subject to an action to the heire, and his heires in the honour and memorie of whose Ancestor they were set up. And so it was holden, Mic. 10. Ja.[5] And here with agreeth the Lawes (d)[6] in other Countries. Note this kinde of inheritance: and some hold that the wife or Executors that first set them up may have an action in that case against those that deface them in their time. And note that in some places chattels as heire-loomes, (as the best bed, table, pot, pan, cart, and other dead chattels movable) may goe to the heire, and the heire in that case may have an action so; for them at the Common Law, and shall not sue for them in the Ecclesiasticall Court, but the heire-loome is due by Custome and not by the Common Law. And the (e)[7] ancient jewels of the Crowne are heire-loomes and shall descend to the next Successor, and are not devisable by testament.

An heire-loome is called *principalium* or *haereditarium*.[8]

Consuetudo hundredi de Stretford in Com' Oxon' est quod haeredes ten'torum infra hundredum praedictum existen' post mortem antecessorum suorum habebunt, &c.[9] principalium, Anglice an heire-loome, *viz. De quodam genere catallor', utensilium, &c. optimum plaustrum, optimam carucam, optimum ciphum, &c.*[10]

Our Author hath not spoken of parcencers in this Chapter, for that he hath particular Chapters of the same.

Gradus parentelæ, &c.[11]

Section 21
Fee Tail, part 2

| And all these Entailes aforesaid be specified in the said Statute of W. 2. Also there bee divers other estates in taile, though they bee not by expresse words specified in the said Statute, but they are taken by the equitie of the same Statute.   [24 a]

5. Mich. 10. Ja obiter in Com. banc in Pyms case.

6. (d) B. Cassanaeus fol. 13. Conc. 29. 30. E. 3. 2. & 3. 39. E. 2. 6. 9. 10. I. H. 5 tit Executors 108 tit. Descent Br. 43. 9. E. 4. 15. Madam Wiches case.

7. (e) Vide 28. H. 8. 24.

8. [*Ed.:* principal [or] hereditary thing.]

9. Int. adjudicata coram Rege Tr. 41. E. 3. lib. 2 fol 104. in Thesaur. Sect. 241. 242. &c.

10. [*Ed.:* The custom of the hundred of Stretford in the country of Oxford is that the heirs of tenements within the aforesaid hundred, after the death of their ancestors, have [and have been accustomed since time immemorial to have] a principal, in English 'heirloom', that is to say, from whatever kind of chattels, utensils, etc., the best cart, the best plough, the best cup, etc.]

11. [*Ed.:* The degrees of relationship, etc.]

As if lands be given to a man, and to his heires males of his body begotten, in this case his issue male shal inherit, and the Issue female shall never inherit, and yet in the other entailes aforesaid, it is otherwise.

"And all these Entailes aforesaid be specified in the said Statute of *W*[estmister].2."

And so it appeareth by the said statute. *Auxy sont divers auters estates en le taile, &c.* And herewith agreeth Carbonels Case, 33. Edw. 3. titulo Taile 5.

That the cases of the statute are set downe but for examples of estates tailes generall and speciall, and not to exclude other estates taile 3. Edw. 3. 32. 18. Ass. p. 5. 13. Edw. 3. 46. 1. Mar. Dyer 46. Pl. Com. Seignior Barkleys case, fo. 251.[1] For, *Exempla illustrant, non restringunt legem.*[2]

[24 b] | "equitie."

Is a construction made by the Judges, that cases out of the letter of a statute yet being within the same mischiefe, or cause of the making of the same, shall bee within the same remedie that the Statute provideth; And the reason hereof is for that the Law-maker could not possibly set downe all cases in expresse termes, *Aequitas est convenientia rerum quae cuncta coaequiparat, & quae in paribus rationibus paria jura & judicia desiderat.* And againe, *Aequitas est perfecta quaedam ratio quae jus scriptum interpretatur & emendat, nulla scripturâ comprehensa, sed solum in vera ratione consistens. Aequitas est quasi aequalitas.*[3] *Bonus Judex secundum aequum & bonum judicat, & aequitatem stricto juri praefert. Et jus respicit aequitatem.*[4]

"As if lands be given to a man, and to (f)[5] his heires males of his body begotten, in this case his issue male shall inherit, and the Issue female shall never inherit, &c."

This shall be explaned afterward, Sect. 24.

1. 3. E. 3. 32 18. E. 3. 46. 18. Ass. p. 5. 1. Mar. Di. 46. Pl. Com. 251.

2. [*Ed.:* Examples illustrate, but do not restrain, the law.]

3. Bract. lib. 4 fol. 186.

4. [*Ed.:* Equity is the assemblage of things that make equality among all people, and that in equal parts through reason brings law and a desirable judgment. . . . Equity is the perfection of that reason that interprets and improves the written laws; no written law can be understood but that it consists of true reason. Equity is nearly equality. The good judge (is one who) follows equity and good decision and prefers strictly equitable decisions. And the law seeks equity.]

5. (f) 18. Ass. p. 5. 18. E. 3. 46. 33. E. 3, Taile 5. 3. E. 3. 32. Il. Com. Seigniour Barkleys case. 1. Mar. Dy. 46. V. Sect. 24.

Section 69
Tenant at Will, part 2

| Also if a house be letten to one to hold at will, by force whereof the Lessee [56 a] entreth into the house, & brings his householdstuffe into the same, and after the Lessor puts him out, yet hee shall have free entrie, egresse and regresse into the said house, by reasonable time to take away his goods and Utensils. As if a man seised of a mese in fee simple, fee taile, or for life, hath certain goods within the said house, and makes his Executors, and dieth, whosoever after his decease hath the house, his Executors shall have free entrie egresse and regresse to carrie out of the same house the goods of their testator by reasonable time.

"if a house be letten to one to hold at will,"

The reason of this is evident upon that which hath beene said before.

"house."

or Mai-l-son, called in Legall Latine *Messuagium,* containeth (as hath beene [56 b] said) the Buildings, Curtelage, Orchard, and Garden.

Cottage, *Cotagium* is a little house without land to it. (a)[1] See 31. Eliz. cap. I and Cottagers in Doomesday Booke are called *Cotterelli:* and in ancient Records *Haga* signifieth a house. If a man hath a house neer to my house, and hee suffereth his house to be so ruinous, as it is like to fall upon my house, (b)[2] I may have a writ *De domo reparanda,*[3] and compell him to repaire his house. But a Praecipe lieth not *de domo,* but *de messuagio.*[4]

"by reasonable time"

(c)[5] This reasonable time shall be adjudged by the discretion of the Justices, before whom the cause dependeth; and so it is of reasonable fines, customes, and services, upon the true state of the case depending before them; for rea-

---

1. (a) 31. El. ca. 1. in Doomesday.
2. (b) Reg. 153. F.N.B. 127. 4. E. 2. Vouch 244. Six acres of land may be parcell of a house.
3. [*Ed.:* A writ by which one tenant in common could compel his cotenant to contribute towards the repair of common property.]
4. [*Ed.:* [not] for a house [but] for a messuage.]
5. (c) 22. E. 4. 27. 34. H. 6. 40.

sonableness in these cases belongeth to the knowledge of the Law, and therefore to be decided by the Justices. (d)[6] *Quam longum esse debet non definitur in jure, sed pendet ex discretione Justiciariorum:*[7] And this being said of time, the like may be said of things incertaine, which ought to be reasonable; for nothing that is contrarie to reason, is consonant to Law.

(e)[8] "As if a man seised of a mese[9] in fee simple, fee taile,"

This is so evident as it needeth no explaination.

Section 80
Tenant by the Verge, part 3

[62 a]   I And so it is to be understood, that in divers Lordships, and in divers Manors, there be many and divers customes, in such cases as to take tenements, & as to plead, and as to other things and customes to bee done, and whatsoever is not against reason, may well be admitted and allowed.

"be many and divers customes,"

This was cautiously set downe, for in respect of the varietie of the customes in most Mannors, it is not possible to set downe any certaintie, only this incident inseparable everie custome must have, viz. that it be consonant to reason, for how long soever it hath continued, if it bee against reason, it is of no force in Law.

"against reason,"

This is not to be understood of everie unlearned mans reason, but of artificiall and legall reason warranted by authoritie of Law: *Lex est summa ratio.*[1]

---

6. (d) Bract. li. 2. ca. 5a. 5b.

7. [*Ed.:* How long reasonable time ought to be is not defined by law, but depends upon the discretion of the judges.]

8. (e) 2. H. 6. 15. 21. H. 6. 30.

9. [*Ed.:* house and its appurtenances.]

1. [*Ed.:* Law is the perfection of reason.]

Section 96
Escuage, part 2

I But it appeareth by the pleas and arguments made in a plea upon a Writt of
detinue of a writing obligatorie brought by one *H. Gray. T.7.E.3.* that it is not
needfull for him which holdeth by Escuage to goe himselfe with the King if
hee will finde another able person for him conveniently arrayed for the warre
to goe with the King. And this seemeth to be good reason. For it may be that
hee which holdeth by such services is languishing, so as hee can neither goe nor
ride. And also an Abbot or other man of Religion, or a feme sole, which hold
by such services, ought not in such case to goe in proper person. And Sir *William
Herle* then chief Justice of the common place said in this plea, that Escuage
shall not bee granted, but where the King goes himselfe in his proper person.
And it was demurred in judgment in the same plea, whether the 40. dayes should
bee accounted from the first day of the muster of the Kings host made by the
Commons, and by the commandement of the King, or from the day that the
King first entred into *Scotland.* Therefore inquire of this.

TR. 7. E. 3. &c.[1] This is the first booke at large that our Author hath cited
and it is to be observed that this point is not debated in the said booke, but
onely it is there admitted, and yet is good authoritie in law, for our Author
saith that it appeareth by this booke, now both by Littleton himselfe, and by
the booke of 7. Edw. 3. it is apparant that albeit the tenure is that hee which
holdeth by a whole knights fee ought to be with the King, &c. to doe a corporall
service, yet he may finde another able man to doe it for him.

By the Statute of Magna Charta, cap. 20. it is provided, that no knight that
holdeth by Castle-gard shall bee distreined to give money for the keeping of
the Castle, *Si ipse eam facere voluerit in propria persona sua vel per alium probum
hominem faciet si ipse eam facere non possit propter rationabilem causam.*[2]

Some have thought that hee that holds by Escuage is taken by the equitie
of this statute that speaketh onely of Castle-gard, but it is holden that this
statute is but an affirmance of the common law. For where that Act saith,
(propter rationabilem causam)[3] that reasonable cause is referred to the tenants

---

1. Tr. 7. E. 3. fol.29.
2. [*Ed.:* if he will perform it in his own person, or by some other good man if for reasonable cause he
is unable to do it himself.]
3. [*Ed.:* for reasonable cause.]

owne discretion and choyce, and the cause is not materiall or issuable no more than in the case that Littleton here putteth, as hereafter appeareth. And I would advise our Student, that when he shall be enabled and armed to set upon the yeere bookes, or reports of Law, that hee be furnished with all the whole course of the Law, that when hee heareth a case vouched and applyed either in Westminster Hall, (where it is necessarie for him to be a diligent hearer, and observer of cases of Law) or at readings or other exercises of learn-

[70 b] ing, hee may find | out and reade the case so vouched, for that will both fasten it in his memorie, and bee to him as good as an exposition of that case, but that must not hinder his timely and orderly reading, which (all excuses set apart) he must binde himselfe unto, for there bee two things to be avoided by him, as enemies to learning, *praepostera lectio,*[4] and *praepropera praxis.*[5] But let us now heare what our author will say:

"And this seemeth to be good reason."

Here Littleton sheweth three reasons wherefore the Tenant should not be constrained to doe his service in person.

First, It may be the Tenant is sicke, so as he is neither able to goe nor ride. And ever such construction must be made in matters concerning the defence of the Realme or common good, as the same may be effected and performed. To the former disabilitie may be added where a Corporation aggregate of many, as Deane and Chapter, Mayor and Communaltie, &c. or an Infant being a Purchaser, for these also must finde an able man. But it may be objected that in these particular Cases the Tenant might finde a man, but not when hee himselfe is able without all excuse or impediment. To this it is answered, that *Sapiens incipit à fine.*[6] And the end of this service is for defence of the Realme, and so it be done by an able and sufficient man, the end is effected.

Secondly, Seeing there are so many just excuses of the Tenant, it were dangerous, and tending to the hindrance of the service, if these excuses should

---

4. [*Ed.:* preposterous reading.]
5. [*Ed.:* premature practice.]
6. [*Ed.:* A wise man begins with the last.]

be issuable *Multa in jure communi contra rationem disputandi pro communi utilitate introducta sunt.*[7]

Lastly, both Littleton and the Booke in the 7. Edw. 3, giveth the Tenant power, without any cause to be shewed to finde an able and sufficient man, and oftentimes *Jura publica ex privato promiscue decidi non debent.*[8]

"an Abbot or other man of Religion,"

Note that if the King had given Lands to an Abbot and his Successours to hold by Knights Service, this had beene good, and the Abbot should doe homage and finde a man., &c. or pay Escuage, but there was no Wardship or Reliefe or other Incident belonging thereunto. And though the Law saith that this was a Mortmaine, that is, that they held fast their Inheritances, yet if the Abbot with the assent of his Covent, had conveyed the land to a natural man and his heires, now Wardship and Reliefe & other Incidents belonged of common right to the Tenure. And so it is, if the King give Lands to a Mayor and Communaltie, and their Successours to be holden by Knights Service. In this case the Patentees (as hath beene said) shall doe no homage, neither shall there be any Wardship or Reliefe, onely they also shall finde a man, &c. or pay Escuage. But if they convey over the lands to any naturall man and his heires, now Homage, Ward, Marriage, and Reliefe, and other Incidents belong hereunto. And yet this possibilitie was *remota potentia,*[9] but the reason hereof is, *Cessante ratione legis cessat ipsa lex,*[10] the reason of the immunitie was in respect of the Body politique, which by the conveyance over ceaseth, which is worthy of observation.

And it is to be observed, that everie Bishop in England hath a Barony, and that Barony is holden of the King *in Capite,*[11] and yet the King can neither have Wardship or Reliefe.

If two Joyntenants be of Land holden by Knights Service, if one goeth with the King, it sufficeth for both, and both of them cannot be compelled to goe, for by their Tenure one man is onely to goe.

---

7. [*Ed.:* Many things have been introduced into the common law, with a view to the public good, which are inconsistent with sound reason.]

8. [*Ed.:* Public Rights ought not to be decided promiscuously with private.]

9. [*Ed.:* a remote possibility.]

10. [*Ed.:* When the reason of the law ceases, the law itself ceases,]

11. [*Ed.:* in chief,]

If the Tenant peravaile goeth, it dischargeth the Mesne, for one Tenancie shall pay but one Escuage.[12]

"or other man of Religion,"

Here this word (Religion) is taken largely, viz. not onely for regular, or dead persons, as Abbots, Monks, or the like; But for secular persons also, as Bishops, Parsons, Vicars, and the like, for neither of them are bound to goe in proper person. For *nemo militans Deo implicet' secularibus negotiis.*[13]

"languishing,"

So it may be said of an Ideot, a mad man, a leper, a man maimed, blinde, deafe, of decrepit age, or the like.

"or a feme sole,"

Seeing that a feme sole, that cannot performe Knights Service, may serve by deputie, it may bee demanded wherefore an Heire male being within the age [71 a] of 21 | yeeres may not serve also by Deputie, being not able to serve himselfe.

To this it is answered, that in cases of Minoritie, all is one to both sexes, viz. if the Heire male be at the death of the Ancestor under the age of one and twentie, or the Heire female under the age of 14. they can make no Deputie, but the Lord shall have wardship as an incident to the Tenure: therefore Littleton is here to be understood of a feme sole of full age, and seised of land holden by Knights Service either by purchase or descent.

"conveniently arrayed for the warre."

So as here are foure things to be observed.
First, (as hath beene said) that he may finde another.
Secondly, that he that is found must be an able person.
Thirdly, he must be armed at the costs and charge of the Tenant, and herein

---

12. 6. H. 3. Avowrie 242. F.N.B. 83. 84.
13. [*Ed.:* No one serving God should be wrapped up in secular affairs.]

is to be noted, *Quod non definitur in jure*,[14] with what manner of Armor the Souldier shall be arrayed with, for time, place, and occasion doe alter the manner and kinde of the Armour.

Fourthly, he must have such Armour, as shall be necessarie, and so appointed in readinesse.

Ferdwit is a Saxon word,[15] & *significat quietanciam murdri in exercitu.*[16] *Worscot* is an old English word and signifeth *Liberum esse de oneribus armorum.*[17]

It is truly said, *Quod miles haec tria curare debet, corpus ut validissimum & pernicissimum habeat, arma apta ad subita imperia, caetera Deo, & imperatori curae esse.*[18]

Sapiens non semper it uno gradu, sed una via, non se mutat sed aptat. Qui secundos optat eventus, dimicet arte non casu. In omni conflictu non tam prodest multitudo quam virtus.[19,20]

Est optimi ducis scire & vincere, & cedere prudenter tempori. Multum potest in rebus humanis occasio, plurimum in bellicis.[21,22]

Quid tam necessarium est quam tenere semper arma quibus tectus esse possis.[23,24] But I will take my leave of these excellent Authors of Art Militarie, and referre them to those that professe the same, and will returne to Littleton.

"muster."

I finde this word in the Statute of 18. Hen. 6. cap. 19. and the ancient Militarie Order is worthy of observation, for before and long after that Statute, when

---

14. [*Ed.:* That it is not defined in law.]

15. Fleta lib, I. cap. 42.

16. [*Ed.:* and it signifies an acquittal of murder in battle.]

17. [*Ed.:* To be free of the burdens of arms.]

18. Livius. [*Ed.:* That a knight ought to care for three things: that he should have a stout and agile body, arms apt to be taken up for the empire, [and thirdly] to take care for God and the emperor.]

19. Vegetius.

20. [*Ed.:* The wise man does not always go with one step, but goes one way; does not change himself, but adapts.]

21. Polybius.

22. [*Ed.:* It is for the best leader to understand and conquer, and prudently to give way to opportunity. Chance has much influence on human affairs, even more in war.]

23. Vegetius.

24. [*Ed.:* What is so needful as always to bear arms, with which you may be protected?]

the King was to be served with Souldiers for his warre, a Knight or Esquire of the Countrey, that had Revenues, Farmers and Tenants would covenant with the King by Indenture inrolled in the Exchequer to serve the King for such a terme for so many men (specially named in a List) in his warre, etc. an excellent institution that they should serve under him, whom they knew and honoured, and with whom they must live at their returne, these men being mustered before the Kings Commissioners, and receiving any part of their wages, and their names so recorded, if they after departed from their Captaine within the Terme, contrarie to the forme of that Statute, it was felony. But now that Statute is of no force, because that ancient and excellent forme of militarie course is altogether antiquated: but latter Statutes have provided for that mischiefe.[25]

To muster is to make a shew of Souldiers well armed and trained before the Kings Commissioners in some open field. *Ubi se ostendentes praeludunt proelio.*[26] In Latine it is *censere, seu lustrare exercitum.*[27]

By the Law before the Conquest Musters and shewing of Armour should be *Uno eodem die per universum regnum, ne aliqui possint arma familiaribus & notis accommodare, nec ipsi illa mutuo accipere, ac justitiam Domini Regis defraudare, & Dominum Regem & Regnum offendere.*[28,29]

Concerning the point in Law, demurred in judgement, in 7. Edw. 3, here mentioned by our Author: The Law accounteth the beginning of the fortie dayes after the King entreth into the forraine Nation, for then the warre beginneth, and till he come there, he and his host are said to goe towards the warre, and no militarie service is to be done, till the King and his Host come thither.

"Sir William Herle."

A famous Lawyer constituted Chiefe Justice of the Common Pleas by Letters Patents dated, 2. *die Martii anno 5. E. 3.* It appeareth by Littleton, and by the

---

25. Lib. 6. fol. 27. the Souldiers case.

26. [*Ed.:* Where by showing themselves they make a prelude to battle.]

27. [*Ed.:* to assess or review the army.]

28. Lamb. fol. 135. b.

29. [*Ed.:* On one same day throughout the realm, so that no one should be able to lend arms to his servants and friends, nor to borrow them, and defraud the lord king's justice and offend the king and the realm.]

Record that he was a Knight, against the conceit of those, that thinke, that the chiefe Justices of the Court of Common Pleas were not knighted till long after.

Our Student shall observe that the knowledge of the Law is like a deep Well out of which each man draweth according to the strength of his understanding. He that reacheth deepest, he seeth the amiable and admirable secrets of the Law, wherein, I assure you, the Sages of the Law in former times, (whereof Sir William Herle was a principall one) have had the deepest reach. And as the Bucket in the depth is easily drawne to the uppermost part of the water, (for *Nullum elementum in suo proprio loco est grave),*[30] but take it from the water, it cannot be drawne up but with great difficultie. So albeit beginnings of this studie seeme difficult, yet when the Professor of the Law can dive into the depth, it is delightfull, easie, and without any heavie burthen, so long as he keepe himselfe in his owne proper element.

| "Justice."

In Glanvil hee is called *Justicia in ipso abstracto,*[31,32] as it were Justice it selfe, which appellation remaines still in English and French, to put them in minde of their dutie and functions. But now in legall Latine they are called *Justiciarii tanquam justi in concreto,*[33] and they are called *Justiciarii de Banco, &c,*[34] and never *Judices de Banco, &c.*

"Common Bank (place)"

Banke is a Saxon word, and signifieth a Bench or high seat, or a Tribunall, and is property applyed to the Justices of the Court of Common Pleas, because the Justices of that Court set there as in a certaine place: for all Writs returnable into that Court are *Coram Justiciariis nostris apud Westmon*[35] or any other certaine place where the Court set, and Legall Records tearme them *Justiciarii*

---

30. [*Ed.:* No element in its own place is heavy.]
31. Glanvile lib. 2. cap. 6. &c.
32. [*Ed.:* Justice, in its abstract form.]
33. [*Ed.:* Justices, just men as it were in concrete form.]
34. [*Ed.:* Justices of the Bench, etc.]
35. [*Ed.:* Before our justices at Westminister.]

de Banco. But Writs returnable into the Court called the Kings Bench, are *Coram nobis (i. Rege) ubicunque fuerimus in Anglia.*[36] And all judiciall Records there are stiled *Coram Rege.* But for distination sake it is called the Kings Bench,[37] both because the Records of that Court are stiled (as hath beene said) *Coram Rege,* and because Kings in former times have often personally set there. For the antiquitie of the Court of Common Pleas they erre, that hold that before the Statute of Magna Charta there was no Court of Common Pleas, but had his Creation by, or after that Charter: for the learned know, that in the six and twentieth yeere of Edward the Third, the Abbot of B. in a Writ of Assize, brought before the Justices in Eire claimed Conusance and to have Writs of Assize, and other originall Writs out of the Kings Court by prescription, time out of minde of man, in the raignes of Saint Edmond, and Saint Edward the Confessor before the Conquest. And on the behalfe of the Abbot were shewed divers allowances thereof in former times in the Kings Courts, and that King Henry the first confirmed their usages, and that they should have Conusance of Pleas, so that the Justices of the one Bench, or the other, should not intermeddle. And the Statute of *Magna Charta,* erecteth no Court, but giveth direction for the proper jurisdiction thereof in there words. *Communia Placita non sequantur Curiam nostram, sed teneantur in aliquo certo loco.*[38] And properly the Statute saith, *non sequantur,* for that the Kings Bench did in those dayes follow the King *ubicunque fuerit in Anglia,* and therefore enacteth that Common Pleas should be holden in a Court resident in a certaine place. In the next Chapter of *Magna Charta* (made at one and the same time) it is provided:[39] *Et ea quae per eosdem (s. justiciarios itinerantes) propter difficultatem aliquorum articulorum terminari non possunt, referantur ad Justiciarios nostros de Banco, & ibi terminentur.*[40] And in the next to that, *Assisae de ultima praesentatione semper capiantur coram Justiciariis de Banco, & ibi terminentur.*[41]

36. [*Ed.:* before ourself (that is, the king) wheresoever we shall then be in England.]

37. 26. Ass. p. 24. 4. E. 3. fo, 19. Bracton lib. 3. fol. 105b. Britton fol. I. & 2 Fleta lib. 2. cap. 2. Mirror. cap 5 Sect. 1. Fortescue cap. 51. See in the preface to the third part of my Reports.

38. [*Ed.:* Common pleas shall not follow our court but shall be held in some certain place.]

39. Mirror. cap. 5. sect. 2. Fleta lib. 2. cap. 54.

40. [*Ed.:* And those things which cannot be determined before them (that is, the justices in eyre), on account of the difficulty of some points, shall be referred to our justices of the Bench and determined there.]

41. [*Ed.:* Assizes of darrein presentment shall always be taken before the justices of the Bench, and determined there.]

Therefore it manifestly appeareth, that at the making of the Statute of *Magna Charta,* there were *Justiciarii de Banco,* which all men confesse to be the Court of Common Pleas. And therefore that Court was not created by or after that Statute. For the Authoritie of this Court, it is evident by that which hath beene said, that it hath jurisdiction of all Common Pleas. But let us returne to Littleton.

"demurred in judgment."

A Demurrer commeth of the Latine word *Demorari,* to abide, and therefore hee which demurreth in Law, is said, he that abideth in Law, *Moratur,* or *Demoratur in lege.*[42] Whensoever the Counsell learned of the partie is of opinion, that the Court or Plea of the adverse partie is insufficient in Law, then he demurreth or abideth in Law, and referreth the same to the judgment of the Court, and therefore well saith Littleton here, *demurre en judgement,* the words of a Demurrer being *Quia narratio, &c. materiaque in eadem contenta minus sufficiens in lege existit, &c,*[43] and so of a Plea, *Quia Placitum, &c. materiaque in eodem contenta minus sufficiens in lege existit, &c. unde pro defectu sufficientis narrationis sive placiti, &c. petit judicium, &c.*[44] But if the Plea be sufficient in Law, and the matter of fact be false, then the adverse partie taketh issue thereupon, and that is tried by a Jurie, for matters in Law are decided by the Judges, and matters in fact by Juries, as elsewhere is said more at large.

Now as there is no issue upon the fact, but when it is joyned betweene the parties, so there is no Demurrer in Law, but when it is joyned, and therefore when a Demurrer is offered by the one partie as is aforesaid, the adverse partie joyneth with him, (for example) saith, *Quod Placitum praedictum, &c. materiaque in eodem contenta bonum & sufficiens in lege existunt, &c. & petit judicium,*[45] and thereupon the Demurrer is said to be joyned, and then the Case is argued by Councell learned of both sides, and if the points be difficult, then it is argued openly by the Judges of that Court,[46] and if they or the greater

---

42. [*Ed.:* he dwells or demurs in law.]

43. [*Ed.:* which count, etc., and the matter contained in the same, is insufficient in law, etc.]

44. [*Ed.:* because the plea, etc., and the matter contained in the same, is insufficient in law, etc., wherefore for want of a sufficient count (or plea), etc. he prays judgment, etc.]

45. [*Ed.:* that the aforesaid plea, and the matter contained in the same, are good and sufficient in law, etc.; and he prays judgment.]

46. Vid. Bract. lib. 5. fo. 352.b.

part concurre in opinion, accordingly judgment is given, and if the Court be
equally divided, or conceive great doubt of the Case, then may they adjourne
it into the Exchequer Chamber, where the Case shall be argued by all the
Judges of England,[47] where if the Judges shall be equally divided, then (if none
of them change their opinion) it shall be decided at the next Parliament by
a Prelate, two Earles, and two Barons which shall have power and commission
of the King in that behalfe, and by advice of themselves, the Chancellor,
[72 a]   Treasurer, the Justices of | the one Bench and the other, and other of the
Kings Councell, as many and such as shall seeme convenient, shall make a
good judgment, &c.[48] And if the difficulty be so great as they cannot determine
it, then it shall be determined by the Lords in the upper house of Parliament.
See the statute, for it extends not onely to the case abovesaid, but also where
judgements are delayed in the Chancery, Kings bench, Common bench, and
the Exchequer, the Justices assigned, and other Justices of Oyer and Terminer,
sometime by dificulty, sometime by divers opinions of Justices, and sometime for other causes. (a)[49] Before which Statute, if judgements were not given
by reason of difficulty, the doubt was decided at the next Parliament, (which
then was to be holden once every yeere at the least) (b)[50] *Si autem talia nunquam
prius evenerint, & obscurum & difficile sit eorum judicium, tunc ponatur judicium in respectum usque ad magnam curiam, ut ibi per concilium curiae terminentur.*[51] But hereof thus much shall suffice. (r)[52] He that demurreth in
Law confesseth all such matters of fact as are well and sufficiently pleaded. If
there be a demurrer for part and an issue for part, the more orderly course is
to give judgement upon the demurrer first, but yet it is in the discretion of
the Court to try the issue first if they will. After demurrer joyned in any Court
of Record, the Judges shall give judgement according as the very right of the

---

47. 14. E. 3. cap. 5. statute. 1.

48. Rot. Parlia. 14. E. 3. ca. 3. a proceeding in Sir John Stantons case upon difficultie in the Court of
Common Pleas. Vide Britton fol. 41. 21. E. 3. 37. 38. 39. E. 3. 1. 21. 35. 40. E. 3. 34. 13. H. 4. 3. 4.

49. (a) 4. 3. c.14.

50. (b) Bracton lib. 1 cap.2. nu. 7. Brit. fol. 41. I. E. 3. 7. 8. 2. E. 3. 5. 7.

51. [*Ed.:* But if such things have never happened before, and their judgment is obscure and difficult,
then the judgment shall be put in respite until the great court, and there they may be determined by advice
of the court.]

52. (c) 17. E. 3. 50. 6. 47. E. 3. 13. 14. 5. H. 7. 1. 13. b. 4. 7. b. Pl. Com. 85. 411. 172. 48. E. 3. 15. 2. R.
2. inquest. 2. 38. E. 3. 25. 11. H. 4. 5. 75. 3. E. 4. 2.

cause and matter in Law shall appeare, without regarding any want of forme in any Writ, Returne, Plaint, Declaration, or other pleading Proces, or course of proceeding, except those only which the party demurring shall specially and particularly set downe and expresse in his demurrer. (a)[53] Now what is substance and what is forme you shall reade in my Reports.

And in some cases a man shall alleage special matter, and conclude with a Demurrer, (b)[54] as in an action of trespasse brought by I.S. for the taking of his horse, the defendant pleads that he himselfe was possessed of the horse until he was by one I. S. dispossessed, who gave him to the plaintife, &c. the plaintife saith that I. S. named in the barre, and I. S. the plaintife were all one person, and not divers; and to the plea pleaded by the defendant in the manner, he demurred in Law and the Court did hold the plea and demurred good, for without the matter alleaged he could not demurre. Now as there may be a demurrer upon counts and pleas, so there may be of Aid prier, Voucher, Receipt, waging of Law, and the like. (c)[55] By that which hath beene said it appeareth, that there is a general demurrer, that is, shewing no cause, and a speciall demurrer which sheweth the cause of his demurrer. Also by that which hath beene said, there is a demurrer upon pleading, &c. and there is also a demurrer upon evidence. (d)[56] As if the plaintife in evidence shew any matter of Record, or Deeds, or Writings, or any sentence in the Ecclesiasticall Court, or other matter of evidence by testimony of witnesses, or otherwise, whereupon doubt in Law ariseth, and the defendant offer to demurre in Law thereupon, the plaintife cannot refuse to joyne in demurrer no more than in a demurrer upon a count, replication, &c. and so *E converso,* may the plaintiff demurre in Law upon the evidence of the defendant.

But if evidence for the King in an Information or any other suit be given, and the Defendant offer to demurre in Law upon the Evidence, the Kings counsell shall not be inforced to joyne in Demurrer:[57] but in that case, the Court may direct the Jury to finde the speciall matter.

53. (a) Lib. 3. fol. 57.Linc. Coll. case Lib. 5. fol. 74.Wymeke case. Lib. 10. fol. 88.usque. 9th. Doctor Leyfields case.

54. (b) 12. E. 4. 7. 31. E. 3. estoppel. 244 33. H. 6. 9. 10. 22. E. 4. 50. I. H. 7. 21.

55. (c) 14 H. 4. 31. 37. H. 6.6.

56. (d) Lib. 5. fol. 104. 2. Bakers case.

57. (e) 38. H. 8. Dyer.53.

"in judgment."

For the signification of this word, Vide Sect. 366.

Section 108
Knight's Service, part 6

[80 b] | Note, it hath been a question, how these words shall bee understood. (*Si parentes conquerantur.*)[1]

And it seemeth to some who considering the Statute of *Magna Charta,* which willeth, *Quod haeredes maritentur absque disparagatione, &c.*[2] Upon which, this Statute of *Merton* upon this point is founded, that no action can be brought upon this Statute, insomuch as it was never seene or heard, that any action was brought upon the Statute of *Merton* for this disparagement against the Gardian for the matter aforesaid, &c. And if any action might have been brought for this matter, it shall bee intended that at some time it would have been put in ure. And note that these words shall bee understood thus, *Si parentes conquerantur, id est, si parentes inter eos lamententur,*[3] which is as much to say, as if the Cousins of such Infant have cause to make lamentation or complaint amongst themselves, for the shame done to their Cousin so disparaged, which in manner is a shame to them, then may the next Cousin to whom the inheritance cannot descend, enter and ouste the Gardein in Chivalrie. And if he will not, another cousin of the Infant may doe this, and take the issues & profits to the use of the Infant, & of this to render an account to the Infant when he comes to his full age: or otherwise the Infant within age may enter himselfe & ouste the Gardein, &c. *Sed quaere de hoc.*[4]

"the Statute of Magna Charta,"[5]

[81 a] Though it be in forme of a | Charter, yet being granted by assent and authoritie of Parliament, Littleton here saith it is a Statute.[6]

---

1. [*Ed.:* if the relatives complain.]
2. [*Ed.:* that heirs shall be married without disparagement etc.]
3. [*Ed.:* if the relatives complain, that is, grumble among themselves.]
4. [*Ed.:* but query concerning this.]
5. 9. H. 3.
6. Vide Lib. 8. the Princes case.

This Parliamentarie Charter hath divers appellations in law. Here it is called Magna Charta, not for the length or largenesse of it (for it is but short in respect of the Charters granted of private things to private persons now adayes being *(Elephantinae Chartae*[7]*)* but it is called the great Charter in respect of the great weightinesse and weightie greatnesse of the matter contained in it in few words, being the fountaine of all the fundamentall lawes of the Realme, and therefore it may truly be said of it, that it is *magnum in parvo*. It is in our Bookes called *Charta libertatum*,[8] *et Communis libertas Angliae*, or *Libertates Angliae. Charta de liberratibus, Magna Charta, &c.* And well may the Lawes of England be called *Liberrates, quia liberos faciunt*.[9] *Magna fuit quondam magnae reverentia Chartae.*[10]

This Statute of Magna Charta, is but a confirmation or restitution of the Common Law, as in the Statute called *Confirmatio chartarum*,[11] *Anno* 25. Edw. 1.[12] it appeareth by the opinion of all the Justices; and in 5. Hen. 3. tit. Mord. 53.[13] Magna Charta is there vouched, for there it appeareth, that King John had granted the like Charter of renovation of the ancient Lawes

This Statute of Magna Charta hath beene confirmed above thirty times and commanded to bee put in execution, By the Statute of 25. Edw. 1. c. 2 judgements[14] given against any points of the Charters of Magna Charta or Charta de Forests are adjudged void. And by the Statute of 42. Edw. 3. cap. 3.[15] If any Statute bee made against either of these Charters it shall be voyd.

---

7. [*Ed.:* Elephantine Charter.]

8. Bracton, 414. & 291. Fleta, lib. 2. cap. 48. & lib. 3. cap. 3. Mirror, cap. 2. § 18. Britton, fol. 177. b.

9. [*Ed.: libertates* (liberties), because they make men *liberos* (free).]

10. [*Ed.:* Great was once the reverence of Magna Carta (the great charter).]

11. [*Ed.:* The Confirmation of the charters, a statute accepting Magna Carta as the Common Law, and declaring void judgements contrary to it.]

12. 25. Edw. 1.

13. 5. Hen. 3. Mord. 53. Math Paris, 246. 276. 248.

14. 25. Edw. 1. cap. 2.

15. 42. Edw. 5. cap. 1.

"considering the Statute of Magna Charta, Upon which, this Statute of Merton upon this point, is founded. *Quod haeredes maritentur absque disparagatione,*"[16] "founded,"

So as Magna Charta is the foundation of other Acts of Parliament. This Act extendeth as well to females as to males.

"no action can be brought upon this Statute, insomuch as it was never seene or heard . . . &c. And if any action might have been brought for this matter, it shall bee intended that at some time it would have been put in ure."

Hereby it appeareth how safe it is to be guided by judiciall presidents the rule being good,[17] *Periculosum existimo quod benorum virorum non comprobatur exemplo.*[18] And as usage is a good Interpreter of Lawes, so non usage where there is no example is a great intendment, that the Law will not beare it; for saith Littleton, If any Action might have beene grounded upon such matter, it shall be intended that sometime it should have beene put in ure. Not that an Act of Parliament by non User can be antiquated or lose his force, but that it may be expounded or declared how the Act is to be understood.

"*Si parentes conquerantur,*"

Of this sufficient hath beene said before.

"if the Cousins"[19]

Here Littleton expoundeth Parents to be his Cousins, under which name of Cousins Littleton includeth Uncles and other Cousins, who when the Father is dead are *in loco parentum.*[20]

---

16. [*Ed.:* that heirs shall be married without disparagement,]

17. Vide Petitiones coram Domino Rege in Parliamento, fol. 3. 18. Hen. 6. 39. Hen. 6. 39. per Ashton 6. Eliz. Dier, 229. 23. Eliz. Dier. Nullum breve de errore de judicio in 5. port, quia nullum breve repetitur. 3. Edw. 3. 50. 11. Hen. 4. 7. & 38.

18. [*Ed.:* I consider that dangerous which is not approved by the example of good men.]

19. Vide Le statute de Marlebridge, cap. 27. In custodia parentum.

20. [*Ed.:* In the place of a parent; instead of a parent; charged with a parent's rights, duties, and responsibilities.]

"have cause to make lamentation,"

Note if they have cause to make, lamentation on, it sufficeth, though they complaine.

"for the shame done to their Cousin."

For when their Cousin is disparaged in his marriage, it is not onely a shame and infamie to the heire, but in him to all his bloud and kindred.

"then may the next Cousin to whom the inheritance cannot descend, enter and ouste the Gardein in Chivalrie."

This is worthy the observation, for the words of the Statute are generall, *Secundum dispositionem parentum,* and the construction thereof shall be according to the reason of the Common Law, for the next Cousin, to whom the inheritance cannot descend, shall enter and ouste the Gardian, and shall be in place of a Gardian, as it is in case of a Gardian in socage.[21]

"And if he will not, another cousin of the Infant may doe this."

Still pursuing the reason of the Common Law in case of Gardian in Socage.

"and take the issues & profits to the use of the Infant, &c."

This is so evident as it needeth no explaination.

"or otherwise the Infant within age may enter himselfe & ouste the Gardein."

If none of the Cousins aforesaid will enter, then the heire himself may enter. In all which the reason of the Common Law is pursued. But what if the heire be disparaged, and the next of kin doth enter, and when the heire commeth to 14 hee agreeth to the marriage; yet shall not this give any advantage to the Lord, for that he had lost the Wardship before.

21. [*Ed.:* according to the disposition of the relatives.]

Section 138
Frankalmoin, part 5

[97 a] | Also if it be demanded, if tenant in frankmarriage shall doe fealtie to the donor or his heires before the fourth degree be past, &c. it seemeth that he shall, for he is not like as to this purpose to tenant in frankalmoigne, for tenant in frankalmoign by reason of his tenure shall doe divine service for his Lord, (as is said before) and this he is charged to doe by the Law of holy Church, and therefore he is excused and discharged of fealty, but tenant in frankmarriage shal not doe for his tenure such service, and if he doth not fealty, he shall not doe any manner of service to his Lord neither spirituall nor temporall, which would be inconvenient and against reason, that a man shall be tenant of an estate of inheritance to another, and yet the Lord shall have no manner of service of him, and so it seemes he shall doe fealty to his Lord before the fourth degree be past. And when he hath done fealty, he hath done all services.

"which would be inconvenient."[1]

An argument drawne from an inconvenience, is forcible in Law, as hath been
[97 b]   obser-l-ved before, and shall be often hereafter. *Nihil quod est inconveniens, est licitum.*[2,3] And the law that is the perfection of reason, cannot suffer any thing that is inconvenient.

It is better, saith the laws,[4] to suffer a mischiefe (that is pecultar to one) than an inconventence that may prejudice many: See more of this after in this Chapter.

Note, the reason of this diversity, betweene Frankalmoigne and Frankmarriage, standeth upon a maine maxime of Law, that there is no land, that is not holden by some service spirituall or temporall, and therefore the donee in Frankmarriage shall doe realty, for otherwise he should doe to his Lord no service at all, and yet it is Frankmarriage, because the Law createth the service of Fealty for necessity of reason, and avoiding of an inconvenience. But tenant in Frankalmoigne both spirituall and divine service, which is within the said

---

1. V. Sect. 87. 139. 201. 269. 440. 478. 655. 722
2. [*Ed.:* Nothing that is inconvenient is lawful.]
3. 40. Ass. 27.
4. Littleton fo. 50. b. 42. Edw. 3. 5. 28. Edw. 3. 395. 20. Hen. 6. 28.

Maxime and therefore the Law will not cohort him to doe any temporall service. See the next session.

"and against reason,"

And this is another strong argument in Law, *Nihil quod est contra rationem est licitum.*[5] For reason is the life of the Law, nay the common Law it selfe is nothing else but reason, which is to be understood of an artificiall perfection of reason, gotten by long study, observation, and experience, and not of every mans naturall reason, for, *Nemo nascitur artifex.*[6] This legall reason, *est summa ratio.*[7] And therefore if all the reason that is dispersed into so many severall heads were united into one, yet could he not make such a Law as the Law of England is, because by many successions of ages it hath been fined and refined by an infinite number of grave and learned men, and by long experience growne to such a perfection, for the government of this Realme, as the old rule may be justly verified of it, *Neminem oportet esse sapientiorem legibus:*[8] No man (out of his owne private reason) ought to be wiser than the Law, which is the perfection of reason.

Section 170
Tenure in Burgage, part 9

| And note that no custome is to bee allowed, but such custome as hath bin used   [113 a]
by title of prescription, that is to say, from time out of minde. But divers opinions have beene of time out of minde, &c. and of title of prescription, which is all one in the Law. For some have said, that time of minde should be said from time of limitation in a Writ of right, that is to say, from the time of King *Richard* the first after the Conquest, as is given by the Statute of Westminster the first, for that a Writ of right is the most highest Writ in his nature that may be. And by such a writ a man may recover his right of the possession of his Ancestors, of the most ancient time that any man may by any writ by the Law, &c. And in so much that it is given by the said Estatute, that in a writ of right none shall

---

5. [*Ed.:* Nothing that is against reason is lawful.]
6. [*Ed.:* No one is born an artificer.]
7. [*Ed.:* is the highest reason.]
8. [*Ed.:* No man ought to be wiser than the laws:]

be heard to demand of the seisin of his Ancestors of longer time, than of the time of King *Richard* aforesaid, therefore that is proved, that continuance of possession, or other customes & usages used after the same time is the title of prescription, and this is certaine. And others have said, that well and truth it is, that seisin and continuance after the limitation, &c. is a title of prescription, as is aforesaid, and by the cause aforesaid. But they have said that there is also another title of prescription that was at the Common Law, before any estatute of limitation of writs, &c. And that it was where a custom or usage, or other thing hath beene used, for time whereof mind of man runneth not to the contrary. And they have said that this is proved by the pleading: where a man will plead a title of prescription of custome hee shall say that such custome hath been used from time whereof the memory of men runneth not to the contrary, that is as much to say, when such a matter is pleaded, that no man then alive hath heard any proofe of the contrary, nor hath no knowledge to the contrary, & insomuch that such title of prescription was at the common law, & not put out by an estatute, *Ergo,* it abideth as it was at the common law, & the rather, insomuch that the said limitation of a writ of right, is of so long time passed, *Ideo quaere de hoc.*[1] And many other customes and usages have such ancient Boroughs.

"prescription,"

Prescription is a title taking his substance of use and time allowed by the Law; [113 b] *Prescriptio est titulus ex usu & tempore substantiam | capiens ab authoritate Legis.*[2] In the Common Law a prescription which is personall is for the most part applied to persons, being made in the name of a certaine person and of his Ancestors, or those whose estate he hath, or in bodies politique or corporate, & their Predecessors, for as a naturall body is said to have Ancestors, so a body politique or corporate is said to have Predecessors. And a custome which is locall is alleaged in no person, but laid within some Mannor or other place. As taking one example for many, J. S. seised of the mannor of D. in[3] fee prescribeth thus: That J. S. his Ancestors, and all those whose estate he hath in the said Mannor, have time out of minde of man had and used to have Common of pasture, &c. in such a place, &c. being the land of some other,

---

1. [*Ed.:* Therefore query concerning this.]

2. [*Ed.:* Prescription is a title based on usage and time [for] taking something with authority of law.]

3. 12. Edw. 4. 1. 2. Mariae, Br. Preascr. 100. 6. Edw. 6. Dier 71. 14. Edw. 3 Bar. 277. 43. Edw. 3. 32. 7. Hen. 6. 26. 22. Hen. 6. 14 16. Edw. 2. tit. Presc. 53. 45. Ass. 8. 40. Ass. 27. 41. 21. Edw. 4. 53. 54.

&c. as pertaining to the said Mannor. This properly we call a prescription. A custome is in this manner: A Coppyholder of the Mannor of D. doth plead, that within the same Mannor, there is and hath been such a custome time out of mind of man used, that all the Coppyholders of the said Mannor have had and used to have Common of pasture, &c. in such a wast of the Lord, parcell of the said Mannor, &c. where the person neither doth or can prescribe, but alleageth the custome within the Mannor. But both to customes and Prescriptions, these two things are incident inseparable, viz. Possession, or usage; and Time. Possession must have three qualities, it must be long, continuall, and peaceable, *Longa, continua, & pacifica:* For it is said,[4] *Transferuntur dominia sine titulo & traditione, per usucaptionem s. per longam, continuam, & pacificam possessionem. Longa, i.e. per spatium temporis per legem definitum,* of which hereafter shall bee spoken, *Continua dico ita quod non sit legitime interrupta.* | *Pacificam dico, quia si contentiosa fuerit, idem erit quod prius, si*   [114 a] *contentio fuerit justa. Ut si verus Dominus statim cum intrusor vel disseisor ingressus fuerit seisinam, nitatur tales viribus repellere, & expellere, licet id quod inceperit perducere non possit ad effectum, dum tamen cum defecerit diligens sit ad impetrandum & prosequendum. Longus usus nec per vim, nec clam, nec precario,* &c.[5,6]

If a man prescribeth to have a rent, and like-wise to take a Distresse for the same, it cannot be avoided by pleading, that the rent hath beene alwayes paid by cohersion, albeit it began by wrong.[7]

"a title of prescription."

Seeing that prescription maketh a title, it is to be seene, first to what things a man may make a title by prescription without charter. And secondly, how it may be lost by interruption.

---

4. Bract. fo. 51. 52.

5. [*Ed.:* Ownership is transferred without title and delivery by usucaption, that is, by long, continuous and peaceful possession. Long, that is, for a period of time defined by law. I say 'continuous', [that is], provided it is not lawfully interrupted. I say 'peaceful', because if there is a dispute, the result will be as before, if the dispute is rightful: as where the true owner immediately after an intruder or disseisor has entered into seisin tries to repulse and expel them with force, even though he is unable to perfect what he has begun, provided that he is diligent in beginning and prosecuting the attempt. Long use neither by force, nor by stealth, nor by permission, etc.]

6. Bract fol. 222. b.

7. 13. Edw. 4. 6.

For the first, as to such franchises and Liberties as cannot bee seised or forfeited, before the cause of forfeiture appeare of Record,[8] no man can make a title by prescription because that prescription being but an usage in pais, it cannot (*)[9] extend to such things as cannot bee seised nor had without matter of Record: as to the goods and chattels of Traitors, Felons, Felons of them-selves, Fugitives, of those that be put in exigent, Deodands, Conusance of

[114 b] Pleas, to make a Corporation, to have a Sanctuarie, to make a Coro-|-ner, &c. to make Conservators of the peace, &c.

(c)[10] But to Treasure Trove, Waifes, Estraies, Wrecke of sea, to hold Pleas, Courts of Leets, Hundreds, &c. Infange thiefe, Outfange thiefe, to have a Parke, Warren, Royall fishes, as Whales, Sturgions, &c. Faires, Markets, Franke foldage, the keeping of a Goale, Toll, a Corporation by prescription, and the like, a man may make a Title by usage and prescription only without any matter of Record, (*)[11] Vide Sect. 310. where a man shall make a Title to lands by prescription.

But is to be observed (f)[12] that although a man cannot as is aforesaid pre-scribe in the said Franchise to have *Bona & catalla proditorum, felonum, &c.*[13] yet may they and the like be had obliquely or by a meane by prescription; for a Countie Palatine may be claimed by prescription, and by reason thereof to have *Bona & catalla proditorum, felonum, &c.*

As to the second, by what meanes a Title by prescription or custome, may be lost by interruption;[14] It is to be knowne that the title being once gained by prescription or custome, cannot be lost by interruption of the possession for 10. or 20. yeeres, but by interruption in the right, as if a man have had a Rent or Common by prescription, unity of possession of as high and per-durable estate is an interruption in the right.

---

8. 21. Hen. 6. Prescrip. 44. 21 Edw. 4. 6. 1. Hen. 23. 9. Hen. 7. 11. 20. 7. Hen. 6. 45. 6. Edw. 3. 32. 42. 45. Edw. 3. 2 2. Edw. 4. 26.

9. (*) Fleta lib. 1. cap. 25. Brit. fo. 6. & 15. 44. Ass. p. 8 49. Edw. 3. 3. Saunf. Pl. Cor. 21. 51. Lib. 5. co. 109. 110 Lib. 9. co. 29.

10. (c) 22. Edw. 3. Coron. 241. Hen. 7. 11. 20. 18. Hen. 6. prescrip. 45. 11. Hen. 4. 10. 21. Hen. 7. 33. 9. Edw. 4. 12. 39. 3. 35. 46. Edw. 3. 6. 11. Hen. 6. 25 F.N.B. 91. 1. Hen. 7. 24. Stanf. pl. Cor. 38 44. Edw. 3. 4 22. Edw. 4. 43. 14. 3. Edw. 3. Brook prescript. 57. 44. Ass. pl.

11. (*) 8. Hen. 6. 16.

12. (f) 12. Edw. 4. 16. 32. Hen. 6. 25 12. Eliz. Dier 288. 289

13. [*Ed.:* The goods and chattels of traitors, felons, etc.]

14. 11. Edw. 3. tit. issue 40.

In a Writ of Mesne the Plaintife made his title by prescription,[15] that the Defendant and his Ancestors had acquited the Plaintife & his Ancestors, and the Terre tennant time out of minde, &c. the Defendant tooke issue, that the Defendant & his Ancestors had not acquited the Plaintife & his Ancestors & the Terre tenant, and the Jurie gave a speciall verdict, that the Grandfather of the Plaintife was enfeoffed by one Agnes and that Agnes and her Ancestors were acquited by the Ancestors of the Defendant time out of minde before that time, since which time no acquitall had been, and it was adjudged and affirmed in a Writ of error, that the Plaintife should recover his Acquitall, for that there was once a title by prescription vested, which cannot be taken away by a wrongfull Cesser to acquite of late time, and albeit the verdict had found against the letter of the issue, yet for that the substance of the issue was found, viz. a sufficient title by prescription, it was adjudged both by the Court of Common Pleas, and in the Writ of error by the Court of Kings Bench for the plaintife, which is worthy of observation. So a *Modus decimandi*[16] was alleaged[17] by prescription time out of minde for tithes of lambs, and thereupon issue joyned, and the Jurie found that before 20 yeeres then last past there was such a prescription, and that for these 20 yeeres, he had paid tithe lambe *in Specie,* and it was objected, first, That the issue was found against the Plaintife, for that the prescription was generall for all the time of prescription, and 20 yeeres faile thereof. 2. That the partie by payment of tithes *in Specie* had waived the prescription or custome. But it was adjudged for the Plaintife in the prohibition, for albeit the *Modus decimandi* had not beene paid by the space of 20 yeeres, yet the prescription being found, the substance of the issue is found for the Plaintife. And if a man hath a Common by prescription, and taketh a lease of the land for 20 yeeres, whereby the Common is suspended, after the yeeres ended, he may claime the Common generally by prescription, for that the suspension was but the possession, and not to the right, and the inheritance of the Common did alwayes remaine, and when a prescription or custome doth make a title of inheritance (as Littleton speaketh) the partie cannot alter or waive be the same *in pais.*

---

15. 15. Edw. 3. tit. judgement 133. 14. Edw. 3. ibid. 155.

16. [*Ed.:* a modus (i.e. a customary or covenanted scheme) for tithing.]

17. Mich. 43. & 44 Eliz. in a prohibition betweene Nowell pl. and Hicks Vicar of Edmunton defendant in the Kings bench.

"time out of minde, &c. and of title of prescription, which is all one in
the Law,"

So as the time prescribed or defined by Law is, time, whereof there is no
memorie of man to the contrary. (c)[18] *Omnis quaerela, & omnis actio injuriarum
limitata intra certa tempora.*[19]

"time of limitation."

Limitation as it is taken in Law is a certaine time prescribed by Statute, within
the which the Demandant in the action must prove himselfe or some of his
Ancestors to be seised.

"in a Writ of right,"

In (f)[20] ancient time the limitation in a Writ of Right was from the time of
Henry the first whereof it was said, *à tempore Regis Henrici senioris.*[21] After
that by the Statute of (g)[22] Merton the limitation was from the time of Henry
the Second and by the Statute (h)[23] of West. I. the limitation was from the
time of Richard the First. And this is that limitation that Littleton here speaketh of, whereof in the Mirror in reprose of the Law it is thus said, (i)[24] *Abusion
est de counter cy longe temps dount nul ne poet testmoigner de vieu & de oyer que
ne dure my generalment ouster 40. ans.*[25]

[115 a] | Time of limitation is twofold, First, in Writs, and that is by divers Acts
of Parliament.[26] Secondly, To make a title to any Inheritance, and that (as
Littleton here saith) is by the Common Law.

---

18. (e) Bracton fo. 314

19. [*Ed.:* Every lawsuit and every action for wrongs is limited within certain periods.]

20. (f) Regist. 158 Bracton fo. 373. 5. Ass. p. 2. 34. Hen. 6. 40

21. [*Ed.:* from the time of King Henry the elder.]

22. (g) Stat. de Mert. 20 Hen. 3. ca. 8

23. (h) West 1. an. 3. Edw. 1. c. 8 Vide W. 2. 13. Edw. 1. ca. 46

24. (i) Mirror ca. 5. sect 1.

25. [*Ed.:* It is an abuse to count of such a long time ago that no one may bear witness of sight and hearing, which generally does not last beyond forty years.]

26. Glanvil li. 13. ca. 3. & 34. Mirror, ca. 5. Sect. 4. Fleta. 1. 2. c. 38. & li. 4. c. 5. Britton fol. 79. 82. Bracton lib. 2. fol. 52. & fol. 179. 253. 373.

Limitation of times in Writs are provided by the said Statute of Merton, and after by the said Statute of West. I. which Littleton here citeth, and which was in force when he wrote, but is since altered by a profitable and necessary Statute (k)[27] made Anno 32. Hen. 8. and by that Act, the former limitation of time in a Writ of Right is changed and reduced to threescore yeeres next before the Teste of the Writ, and so of other actions, as by the statute at large appeareth. But it is to be observed that this Act of 32. Hen. 8. extendeth (l)[28] not to a *Formedon*,[29] in the *Discender*,[30] nor to the Services of Escuage, Homage, and Fealtie, for a man may live above the time limited by the Act: neither doth it extend to any other service, which by common possibility may not happen or become due within sixty yeeres; as to cover the hall of the Lord, or to attend on his Lord when he goeth to warre, or the like, nor where the seisin is not traversable or issuable, neither doth it extend to a Rent created by Deed,[31] nor to a Rent reserved upon any particular estate, for (m)[32] in the one case the Deed is the title, and in the other the reservation, nor to any writ of Right of advowson, *Quare impedit*,[33] or Assise of *Darreine presentment*[34] (for there was a Parson of one of my Churches that had been Incumbent there above fifty yeeres, and died but lately) or any Writ of Right of Ward, or ravishment of Ward, &c. but they are left as they were before the Statute of 32. Hen. 8.[35] But hereof thus much for the better understanding of Littleton shall suffice.

"from the time of King Richard the first."

[36] And that was intended from the first day of his reigne, for (from the time) being indefinitely, doth include the whole time of his reigne, which is to be observed.

27. (k) 32. Hen. 8. cap. 2. see the second part of the Institutes. Merton, c. 8.
28. (l) Mich. 10. & 11. Eliz. Dier 278. Fitzwilliams cafe.
29. [*Ed.:* Writ to recover entailed property.]
30. [*Ed.:* Writ used by the issue in tail to recover entailed property.]
31. Lib 4. fol. 10. & 11. Bevils case.
32. (m) Lib 8 fo. 65. Sir Wil. Fosters case.
33. [*Ed.:* Writ to enforce a patrons right to fill a vacant benefice.]
34. [*Ed.:* Writ of assise that allows a person with right of advowdson to determine who had the right to fill a benefice and recover damages in another's interference with this right.]
35. 1. Mar. Parliam. 2. cap. 5. Vide 17 Edw. 3. 11. Pl. Com 371.b.
36. Vide 34. Hen. 6. 36.

"a Writ of right,"

Breve de recto,[37] As writ of Right, so called, for that the words in the Writ of Right are, *Quod fine dilatione plenum rectum teneas.*[38]

"title of prescription that was at the Common Law, . . . from time whereof the memory of men runneth not to the contrary."[39]

Docere oportet longum tempus, & longum usum illum, viz. qui excedit memoriam hominum, tale enim tempus sufficit pro jure.[40]

"any proofe of the contrary,"

For if there bee any sufficient proofe of Record or writing to the contrarie, albeit it exceed the memorie, or proper knowledge of any man living, yet is it within the memorie of man: for memorie or knowledge is twofold First, By knowledge by proofe, as by Record or sufficient matter of writing.[41] Secondly, by his owne proper knowledge. A Record or sufficient matter in writing are good memorialls, for *Litera scripta manet.*[42] And therefore it is said, when we will by any record or writing commit the memory of any thing to Posterity, it is said *tradere memoriae.*[43] And this is the reason that regularly a man cannot prescribe or alleage a Custome against a Statute, because that is matter of Record, and is the highest proofe and matter of Record in Law. But yet a man may prescribe against an Act of Parliament, when his Prescription or Custome in saved or preserved by another Act of Parliament.

There is also a diversity betweene an Act of Parliament in the negative and in the affirmative, for an affirmative Act doth not take away a custome as the Statutes of Wills of 32 and 34. Hen. 8. doe not take away a Custome to devise

---

37. [*Ed.:* A writ of right, or license for a person ejected out of an estate, to sue for the possession of it.]

38. [*Ed.:* That without delay you hold full right.]

39. Bract. lib. 4. fol. 230. Fleta lib. 4. cap. 24.

40. [*Ed.:* It is necessary to explain long time, and this long usage, that is to say, something which exceeds memory of men, for such time suffices for law.]

41. 28. Ass. 25. 38. Ass. 18. 45. Edw. 3. 26. 5. Hen. 7. 10. 8. Hen. 7. 7. 11. Hen. 7. 21. Dier. 23. Eliz. 273.

42. [*Ed.:* Written words last.]

43. [*Ed.:* to hand on in memory.]

Lands, as it hath beene often adjudged. Moreover, there is a diversitre betweene Statutes that be in the negative, for if a Statute in the negative be declarative of the ancient Law, that is in affirmance of the Common Law, there as well as a man may prescribe or alleage a Custome against the Common Law, so a man may doe against such a Statute, for as our Author saith, *Consuetudo, &c. privat communem legem.*[44] As the Statute of Magna Charta provideth,[45] that no Leet shall be holden but twice in the yeere, yet a man may prescribe to hold it oftener, and at other times, for that the Statute (n)[46] was but in affirmance of the Common Law.

So the Statute (o)[47] of 34. Edw. 1. provideth that none shall cut downe any trees of his owne within a Forrest without the view of the Forrester: but inasmuch as this Act is in affirmance of the Common Law, a man may prescribe to cut downe woods within a Forrest without the view of the Forrester. And so was it adjudged in 16. Eliz. in the Exchequer by Sir Edward Sanders Chiefe Baron, and other the Barons of the Exchequer, as Sir John Popham Chiefe Justice of the Kings Bench reported to me.

In the Eire of the Forrest of Pickering before Willoughby, Hungerford and Hanbury, Justices Itinerants there, Anno 8. Edw. 3. I read (p)[48] a claime made by Henry de Percy, Lord of the Manor of Semor within the said Forrest, the Forresters, Verderours, and Regarders found his claime to be true, viz. *Quod praedictus Henricus de Percy, & omnes antecessores sui tenentes | maneriū prae-* [115 b] *dictum à tempore quo non extat memoria & sine interruptione aliquali tenuerunt praedictū manerium cum pertinentiis extra regardum Forestae, & habuerunt Woodwardū portantem arcū & sagittas ad praesentandū praesentanda de venatione tantum, &c. & habuerunt in boscis suis de Semere forgeas, & mineras, & amputârunt, dederunt, & vendiderunt boscum suum infra manerium praedictum sine visu forestariorum pro voluntate sua, & fugarunt & ceperunt Vulpes, Lepores, Capriolos, &c. sicut idē Henricus Percy superius clamat.*[49] Which claime by pre-

44. [*Ed.:* Custom, etc., supersedes the common law.]

45. Magna Charta cap. 35.

46. (n) 6. Hen. 7. 2. 8. Hen. 4. 34. 12. Hen. 7. 18. 31. Hen. 6. leet. 11. 18. Hen. 6. 13.

47. (o) 34. Edw. 1. tit. forest. Rast. 1. Edw. 3. cap. 2.

48. (p) Itin. pickering ann. 8. Edw. 3. Rot. 38.

49. [*Ed.:* That is to say, that the aforesaid Henry de Percy, and all his ancestors as tenants of the aforesaid manor, from time out of mind and without interruption, have held the aforesaid manor with the appurtenances outside the regard of the forest, and have had a woodward bearing a bow and arrows to make

scription, and found as is aforesaid the Justices doubted onely of two points. The first forasmuch as the said Mannor was within the limits of the Forrest, it should not onely be *Contra assisam Forestae*,[50] (o) for his Woodward to beare Bow and Arrowes, where by Law he ought to beare but an Hatchet and no Bow nor Arrowes within the Forrest, but also *de facili cedere possit in destructionem ferarum, &c.*[51] and therefore doubted whether it might be claimed by prescription. Their second doubt was concerning *fugationem, & captionem Capriolorum in boscis suis praedictis, eo quod est bestia venationis Forestae, & transgressores inde convicti finem facerent ut pro transgressione venationis*,[52] & for that difficultie the claime was adjourned into the Kings Bench. But of the other parts of the Prescription no doubt at all was made: and the like had beene allowed in the same Eire, as in the case of Thomas Lord Wake at Lydell, and of Gilbert of Acton, in the same Eire, Rot. 37. and of others.

"this is proved by the pleading."

Note one of the best arguments or proofes in Law is drawne from the right entries or course of pleading, for the Law it selfe speaketh by good pleading, and therefore Littleton here saith, It is proved by the pleading, &c. as is pleading were *ipsius legis viva vox*.[53]

"insomuch that such title of prescription was at the common law, &c."

Note all the prescriptions that were limited from a certaine time were by Act of Parliament, as from the time of Henry the First which was the first time of limitation set downe by any Act of Parliament, and so from the reigne of Richard the First &c. But this prescription of time out of memory of man

---

presentment of what ought to be presented concerning hunting alone etc., and have had in their woods of Semer forges and mines, and have cut down, given and sold their wood within the aforesaid manor at their will, without the view of the foresters, and have chased and taken foxes, hares, rabbits, etc., as the same Henry has above claimed.]

50. [*Ed.:* Against the assize of the forest.]

51. [*Ed.:* he might easily go in destruction of the wild beasts, etc.]

52. [*Ed.:* chasing and taking of roes in their aforesaid woods, inasmuch as [a roe] is a beast of venison of the forest, and trespassers convicted thereof shall make fine as for a trespass to venison,]

53. [*Ed.:* the living voice of the law itself.]

was (as Littleton here saith) at the Common Law, and limited to no time. Also here is implyed a maxime of the Law, viz. That whatsoever was at the Common Law, and is not ousted or taken away by any Statute, remaineth still.

"common law."

The Law of England in divided, as hath beene said before, into three parts, the Common Law, which is the most generall and ancient Law of the Realms; of part whereof Littleton wrote; 2. Statutes or Acts of Parliament; and 3. particular Customes (whereof Littleton also maketh some mention) I say particular, for if it be the generall Custome of the Realme, it is part of the Common Law.

The Common Law hath no controller in any part of it, but the high Court of Parliament, and if it be not abrogated or altered by Parliament, it remaines still, as Littleton here saith, The Common Law appeareth in the Statute of Magna Charta and other ancient Statutes (which for the most part are affirmations of the Common Law) in the originall writs, in judiciall Records, and in our bookes of termes and yeers. Acts of Parliament appeare in the Rols of Parliament, and for the most part are in print. Particular customes are to be proved.

Section 199
Villenage, part 18

| The fourth is, a man who by judgement given against him upon a Writ of   [129 b] *Praemunire facias, &c.*[1] is out of the Kings protection, if hee sue any action, and the tenant or the defendant shew all the Record against him, hee may aske judgement if hee shall be answered; for the Law and the Kings writs be the things by which a man is protected and holpen, and so, during the time that a man in such case is out of the Kings protection, hee is out of helpe and protection by the Kings Law, or by the Kings writ.

---

1. [*Ed.:* Writ against one who introduces a foreign power into the kingdom. Used to regulate the activities of Roman Catholics.]

"*Praemunire.*"

Some hold an opinion that the writ is called a *Praemunire,* because it doth fortifie *Jurisdictionem jurium regiorum Coronae suae*[2] of the Kingly Lawes of the Crown against foreine jurisdiction,[3] and against the usurpers upon them, as by divers Acts of Parliaments appeare. But in truth it is so called of a word in the Writ; for the words of the Writ be, *Praemunire facias praefatum A.B. &c. quod tunc sit coram nobis, &c.*[4] where *Praemunire* is used for *praemonere,* and so do divers interpreters of the Civill and Canon Law use it, for they are *praemunit* that are *praemoniti.* By the Statutes before quoted in the margent you shall perceive what statutes were made before Littleton wrote, and what have beene ordained since to make offences in danger of a *Praemunire.*

"out of the King's protection,"

[130 a]

The judgement in a *Praemunire* is[5] that the Defendant shall be from thenceforth out of the king's protection, and his Lands and Tenements, goods and chattels | forfeited to the king, & that his body shall remaine in prison at the Kings pleasure. So odious was this offence of *Praemunire,* that a man that was attained of the same, might have beene slaine by any man without danger of Law, because (k)[6] it was provided by Law, that a man might do to him as to the Kings enemy, and any man may lawfully kill an enemy. But Queene Elizabeth and her Parliament,[7] liking not the extreme and inhumane rigor of the

2. [*Ed.:* the jurisdiction of the royal rights of the crown.]

3. For Statutes, Vid. 35. E. 1. stat. de Carlile. 25. E. 3. c. 22. 25. E. 3 stat. de provisors, 27. E. 3. c. 1. 38. E. 4 ca. 3. 2. R. 2. ca. 3. R. 2. c. 3. 12. R. 2. c. 5. 16. R. 3. c. 5. 2. H. 4 c. 3. & 4. 6. H. 4. ca. 1. 24. H. 8. c. 12. 25. H. 8. c. 19. 20. 26. H. 8. c. 16 1. Eliz ca. 1. 5. Eliz ca. 1. 5. Eliz ca. 13. Eliz. ca. 1. 2. 8 27. Eliz. c. 2. 39. Eliz c. 18. For Presidents, Vide Mich. 19 E. 3. coram Rege in Thesaur. Pasch. 44. E. 3. ibid. Melbornes case. Mich. 38. H. 6. ibid. The case of Rich Beauchamp and others. Hil. 25. H. 8. coram Reg. The case of Nic. Bishop of Norwich. Trin. 36. H. 8. Rot. 9. Coram Rege. The case of the Bishop of Bangor. Mich. 26 & 27. El. coram Rege, Perrot against D. Bevance & others. Booke of Entries, fo. 429. & 430 & ibid. Mich. 9. H. 7. f. 23.

4. [*Ed.:* Cause the said A. B. to be warned, etc. to be before ourself, etc.]

5. Booke cases, 21. E. 3. 40. b. 18. H. 68 9. E. 4. 2. 35. E. 3. 7. 24. H. 8 tit. Pramunire 16. 10. H. 4. 12. 27. E. 3. 84. 6. H. 7. 14 44. E. 3. 36. 11. H. 7. tit. Praemunire, P. 5. 17. H. 7. Justice Spillmans in Turberviles case Kilwey, fo. 195. Doct & Stud. lib. 2. cap. 32 Brooke, tit. Praemunire 21. Temps. E. 6. Bishop Barloes case.

6. (k) 24. H. 8. Brooke Coron. 196.

7. 5. Eliz. ca. 1 Hil. 12. Eli. Trugins case resolved per les Justices, 7. H. 4. 20. Simon Beverleys case.

Law in that point, did provide that it should not be lawfull for any person to slay any person in any manner attainted in or upon any *Praemunire,* &c. Tenant in taile is attainted in a *Praemunire,* he shall forfeit the land but during his life, for albeit the Stature of 16. R.2. ca.5. enacteth that in that case their lands and tenements, goods and chattels, shall be forfeit to the King, that must be understood of such an estate as he may lawfully forfeit, and that is during his own life. And these generall words doe not take away the force of the Statute *De donis conditionalibus,* but he shall forfeit all his Fee simple lands, states for life, goods and chattels, and so was it resolved in Trudgins case.

"for the Law and the King's writs."

There bee three things as here it appeareth whereby every subject is protected, viz. *Rex, Lex, & Rescripta Regis,* the King, the Law, and the Kings Writs. The Law is the rule, but it is mute; The King judgeth by his Judges, and they are the speaking Law, *Lex loquens.* The processe and the execution which is the life of the Law consisteth in the Kings Writs. So as he that is out of the protection of the King cannot be aided or protected by the Kings Law, or the Kings Writ, *Rex tuetur legem, & lex tuetur jus.* (1)[8] Besides, men attainted in a *Praemunire* every person that is attained of high treason, petit treason or felony, is disabled to bring any action, for he is (*)[9] *Extra legem positus,*[11] and is accounted in Law *Civiliter mortuus.*[12]

Protection: Generall, Particular.[10]

It is to be understood that there is a generall protection of the King whereof Littleton here speaketh, and this extends generally to all the Kings loyall Subjects, Denizens and Aliens within the Realme, whose offences have not made them uncapable of it, as before it appeareth. And there is a particular protection by Writ, which is one of the Kings Writs that Littleton here speaketh of. This particular protection is of two sorts, one, to give a man an immunitie or freedome from actions or suits, the second, for the safety of his person, servants and goods, lands and tenements whereof he is lawfully possessed from violence, unlawfull molestation or wrong. The first is of right, and by Law; the second are all of grace, (saving one) for the generall protection implyeth as

---

8. (l) 4. E. 4. 8. 1. E. 4. 1. b 30. E. 3. 4. 8. Eliz. Dier 24
9. (*) Mich. 9. E. 3. coram Rege Rot. 84. Warw.
10. [*Ed.:* Of the Generall, vid. li. 7 Calvins case per totum.]
11. [*Ed.:* He who is placed out of the Law,]
12. [*Ed.:* dead in the view of the law.]

much. Of the first sort some are *Cum clausula (volumus),* so called because
the Writ hath this word *(volumus)* in it, viz. *Volumus quod interim sit quietus
de omnibus placitis & querelis, &c.*[13] And the other a protection *Cum clausula,
(nolumus)* so called for the like reason. Of protections *Cum clausula (volumus)*
for staying of pleas and suites there be foure kinds, viz. *Quia profecturus*[14] (so
called by reason they are part of the words of the Writ) 2. *Quia moraturus*[15]
(so named for distinction for the like cause) 3. *Quia indebitatus nobis existit*[16]
of the matter. 4. When any sent into the Kings service in warre is imprisoned
beyond Sea. The former are for staying of actions and suits in generall. The
third is for staying of suits of the subject for debts and duties due by the Kings
debtor to them. Of the fourth you shall reade hereafter in this place. For the
former two these nine things are to be observed. First, for what cause they
are to be granted. 2. For what persons they are allowable. 3. A threefold time
is to be considered, viz. the time of the purchase of them, the time of the
continuance of them, and the time when they shall be cast. 4. In what place
the service is to be performed. 5. In what actions these protections are allowable.
6. Under what seale and to whom they are directed. 7. Who is to allow, or
disallow of them. 8. By whom they are to be cast and in what manner. 9.
How upon just cause they may be repealed or disallowed. I must but point
at these matters, to make the studious reader capable of them, and referre him
to the Books and other Authorities at large being excellent points of learning.

As to the first, it is of two natures, the one concerns services of war, as the
Kings souldier, &c. the other wisdome and counsell, as the Kings Ambassador
or Messenger *Pro negotiis regni,* both these being for the publique good of the
Realme, private mens actions and suits must be suspended for a convenient
time; for *Jura publica anteferenda privatis;*[17] and againe, *Jura publica ex privatis
promiscue decidi non debent,*[18] (a)[19] And the cause of granting of the protection
must be expressed in the protection, to the end it may appeare to the Court

---

13. [*Ed.:* with a *volumus* (we will) clause . . . that is to say, we will that in the meantime you shall be
quit of all pleas and plaints, etc.]

14. [*Ed.:* [a writ of protection] because he is about to go.]

15. [*Ed.:* [a writ of protection] because he is remaining.]

16. [*Ed.:* because he is indebted to us.]

17. [*Ed.:* Public rights are to be preferred to private.]

18. [*Ed.:* Public rights ought not to be decided promiscuously with private.]

19. (a) 39. H. 6. 39. 3. H. 6 tit. protection 2. 13. R. 2 ca. 16.

that it is granted *Pro negotiis regni & pro bono publico,*[20] (b)[21] or as some others say, *pur le common profit del realme.*[22] And Britton saith, *Nostre service, sicome estre en nostre force, & le defence de nous & de nostre.* people, &c.[23,24] A man in execution *in salva custodia*[25] shall not be delivered by a Protection.

(c)[26] To the second these protections are not allowable onely for men of full age, but for men within age, and for women, as necessarie attendants upon the Camp, and that in three cases, *Quia lotrix, seu nutrix, seu obstetrix.*[27]

(d)[28] Corporations aggregate of many are not capable of these two protections, either *Profecturae,* or *Moraturae,*[29] because the Corporation itselfe is invisible, and resteth onely in | consideration of Law. (c)[30] Protection for the   [130 b] Husband shall serve also for the Wife.

(f)[31] Albeit the Vouchee, Tenant by resceit, Preier in aid, or Garnishee bee no parties to the Writ, yet before they appeare, a Protection may be cast for them, because when the Demandant grants the Vouchor or receit in judgement of Law they are made privie, but if the Demandant counterplead the Vouchor or receit, then untill it be adjudged for them, and so they privie in Law, a Protection cannot be cast for them. And so it is of the Garnishee, a Protection may be cast for him at the day of the returne of the *Scire facias.*[32] (g)[33] No Protection can be cast for the Demandant or Plaintife because the Tenant or Defendant cannot sue a Resommons, or a Re-attachment, but the Plaintife onely that sued out the sommons or attachment, &c. must sue also the re-

---

20. [*Ed.:* For the business of the realm and the public good,]

21. (b) Mirror, cap 3. Sect. 23. Britton,281. Fleta lib. 6 cap. 7. 8. &c. Bracton.

22. [*Ed.:* for the common profit of the realm.]

23. [*Ed.:* Our service, as, to be in our force, and the defence of ourself and our people, etc.]

24. 5. Marie Dyer 162

25. [*Ed.:* in safe custody.]

26. (c) 19. H. 6. 51. 30. E. 3. 21 F. N. B. 28. 1. 11. E. 3. Rot. par. 3. part for the Countesse of Warwick.

27. [*Ed.:* Because she is a laundress, or a nurse, or a midwife.]

28. (d) 30. E. 3. 1. 21. E. 4. 36. 31. H. 3. 97.

29. [*Ed.:* Profit . . . persistence [literally, lingering].]

30. (e) 35. H. 6. 3. 43. E. 3. 23 48. E. 37 4. H. 5. protection, 107

31. (f) 45. H. 3. protect. 37. 3 H. 6. 18. 30. 8. H. 6. 10 9. H. 6. 36. 40. E. 3. 18 32. E. 3 protect. 54. 21 E. 3. 14. H. 4. 16. 45. E. 3 tit. protect. 40. 14. E. 3 protect. 66.

32. [*Ed.:* Writ to the sheriff to require another to show cause why the plaintiff should not have the benefit of a matter of record, such as a judgment for a letter patent.]

33. (g) 24. E. 3. 26. 47. E. 3. 5 5. H. 5. 5. 38. E. 3. 1. F. N. B 28. g. 20. R. 2. Protect. 106 22. H. 6. 28. 9. H. 6 36. 45. E 3. 36. 17. E. 3. 24. 25. E. 3. 43. 24. E. 3. 26. 13. E. 3. protection 71. 1 4. E. 3. ib. 65. 63. 20. E. 3. ibid. 84

sommons or re-attachment. And so it is of an Actor in nature of a Plaintife, &c. and the Garnishee after appearance, and an avowant, and the like. (h)[34] An Officer of the Kings receit, or any other Officer in any Court of Record, whose attendance is necessary for the Kings service, or administration of Justice being sued, cannot have a Protection cast for him.

(i)[35] In every action or plea, reall or mixt, against two (where a Protection doth lie) a Protection cast for the one doth put the plea without day for all. So it is in debt, detinue, and account. But in trespasse, or in any action in nature of trespasse, which is in Law severall, where every one may answer without the other, there a Protection cast for the one shall serve for him onely, unlesse they joyne in pleading, or if they plead severall pleas, and one *Venire facias*[36] is awarded against all, there a Protection cast for one, shall put the plea without day for all, and therefore in former times the Plaintife used to sue out severall *Venire facias* in those cases for feare of a Protection, &c.

(k)[37] As to the threefold time, First, a Protection *profecturae,* regularly must not be purchased hanging the plea, but this faileth when he goeth in the Kings service in a Voyage royall; and that is twofold, either touching warre, and that onely is when the King himselfe or his Lieutenant, that is *prorex* goeth, or when any goeth in the Kings ambassage, *Pro negotio regni,*[38] or for the marriage of the Kings daughter or the like, this also is called a Voyage royall. But a Protection *Moraturae*[39] may be purchased, and cast *pendente placito.*[40]

(l)[41] Regularly a Protection cannot be cast, but when the partie hath a day in Court, and when if he made default, it should save his default: therefore

---

34. (h) 7. H. 4. 3. a

35. (i) 9. E. 3. protect. 80 81 32. E. 3. ibid. 55. 16. E. 2. ib. 77. 13. E. 3. ibid. 90 41. E. 3 ib 95. 41. E. 3. 32. 42. E. 3. 9 5. H. 5. 7. 3. H. 4. 15. 2. R. 2 protect. 45. 43. E. 3. ib. 31 2. H. 6. 22. 21. H 6. 41. 38 E. 3. 12. 7. H. 6. 21. 33. B. 3. protect. 116. 4. H 4. 4. 29 E. 3 41. 45. E. 3. 24. 28. 11 E. 4. 7. F. N. B. 28. K.

36. [*Ed.:* A writ to summon the venire of potential jurors.]

37. (k) 3. H. 6. pro. 2. 39. H. 6. 30. 44. E. 3. 12. 13. R. 2 ca. 16. 3. H. 4. 16. 11. H. 4 7. 7. E4. 27. 28. H. 6. 1. 17. H. 6. protect. 56 10. E. 3. 54. 13. E. 3. amerciament. 18. li. 7. fo. 7. 8 Calvins case. 13. R. 2. c. 16

38. [*Ed.:* For negotiations for the King.]

39. [*Ed.:* [because] he is remaining,]

40. [*Ed.:* while a plea is pending.]

41. (l) 4 H. 6. 22. 17. E. 3. 76 33. E. 3. tit protect. 115 34. E. 3. ibi. 124. 27. E. 3. 79 29 E. 3. protect. 85. 88. 2. E. 4. 15. 19. E. 3. protect. 82. 79 13. E. 3. ib. 72. 9. E. 3. 21. 3. id. 6. 55. 4. H. 6. 22. 11. H. 6. 14. 14. H. 6. 22. 21. H. 6. 10. 27. H. 6. 4. 28. H. 6. 1 35. H. 6. 58. 44. E. 3. 2. 16 48. E. 3. 8. 7. H. 4. 5. 14. H. 4 23. 27. E. 3. 78.

when execution is to be granted against body, lands, or goods, no Protection can be cast; because the Defendant hath no day in Court. If a protection be cast at the *Nisi prius*[42] for one, if before the day in banke it be repealed by *Innotescimus*,[43] yet because it was once well cast, it shall save his default, but if the Protection be disallowed, either for variance, or that it lay not in the Action, or the like, there it shall turne to a default.

(m)[44] If a man hath a Protection, notwithstanding plead a plea, yet at another day of continuance after that a Protection may be cast, so at a day after an Exigent, but after appearance he cannot cast a Protection in that Terme untill a new continuance be taken.

(n)[45] Thirdly, no Protection, either *Profecturae* or *Moraturae,* shall indure longer than a yeer and a day next after the *teste* or date of it. And so it is of an *Essoigne de service le Roy.*[46] If a Protection beare *teste 7. die Januarii,* and have allowance *pro uno anno,*[47] the resommons, re-attachment or regarnishment may be sued 8. *Januarii* the next yeere, and yet that is the last day of the yeere.

And where Britton treating of an Essoigne beyond the *Graecian* Sea in a Pilgrimage, &c. saith thus, (o)[48] *Ascun gent nequident se purchasent nos letters de protection patents durable a un an, on a 2.ou a. 3. ans, & jalameyns font attorneys generals, ausi per nos letters patents: & ceux font bien & sagement, car nul grand Seignior ne chivalier de nostre realme ne doit prender chemyn sauns nostre conge, car issent poet le realme remainer disgarny de fort gente.*[49]

Three things are hereupon to be observed, First, that this was a protection of grace, whereof more shall be said hereafter. Secondly, that it was for the safetie of the great men of the realme, and that they should make general Attorneyes, so as no actions, or suits should be, thereby stayed. Thirdly, (by

---

42. [*Ed.:* The "nisi prius" courts tried issues of fact before a jury and one presiding judge.]

43. [*Ed.:* We make known.]

44. (m) 22. E. 3. 4. 16. E. 3 protect. 47. 44. E. 3. 16. 3. E. 3. amerciament. 18. 35. E. 3 Protection 123

45. (n) 39. H. 6. 39. F. N. B 28. Fleta lib. 6. cap. 8 Temps E. 1 grand cap. 26

46. [*Ed.:* essoin of the king's service.]

47. [*Ed.:* for one year.]

48. (o) Brit. fo. 282. 283. & 280 Fleta lib. 6. cap. 8. accord.

49. [*Ed.:* Some people have purchased letters of protection from us to last for a year, or two, or three years, and are nevertheless general attorneys, also by our letters patent; and these do well and wisely, for no great lord or knight of our realm can go away without our leave, for in that way the realm could remain unprovided with men of that sort.]

the way) that great men could not passe out of the Realme without the Kings licence. (p)[50] A Protection granted to one, &c. untill he be returned from Scotland, was disallowed for the incertaintie of the time.

(q)[51] To the fourth, the Protection as well *Moraturae* as *Profecturae* must be regularly to some place out of the Realme of England, and that must be to some certaine place, as *super salva custodia Caliciae, &c.*[52] and not to Carlisle or Wales, which are within the Realme, or the like. But it may be to *Ireland* or *Scotland,* because they are distinct Kingdomes; or to *Calice, Aquitaine,* or the like. But a Protection, *Quia moratur super altum mare,*[53] will not serve, not only because (as some thinke) that *mare non moratur,*[54] but for the incertaintie of the place, and for that a great part of the sea is within the Realme of England.

(r)[55] To the fifth. In some actions, Protections shall not be allowed by the Common Law, & in some actions they are ousted by Act of Parliament, Actions at the Common Law, as all Actions that touch the Crowne, as Appeales of
[131 a] Felony, and Appeales of Mayhem. (f)[56] So | where the King is sole partie no Protection is to be allowed, in like manner in a *Decies tantum,*[57] where the King and the Subject are Plaintifes, but in late Acts of Parliament, Protections in personall actions are expressly ousted. A Protection may be cast against the Queene the Consort of the King.

(t)[58] In a writ of Dower *unde nihil habet,*[59] no protection is allowable, because the Demandant hath nothing to live upon. Otherwise it is in a writ of right of Dower.[60] Likewise in a *Quare impedit,*[61] or Assise of *Darreine pre-*

---

50. (p) 1. E. 3. 25

51. (q) 7. Co. 8. Calvins case. 7. E. 4. 29. F. N. B. 38 c. g. h 7. H. 4. 14. 19 H. 6. 35 38. H6. 3. 32. H. 6. 3. R. 2 Rot. Parliament nu. 21. 22 E. 4. protect. 18. 8. R. 2. ibi. 125. 11. H. 4. 57. regist. judic. 14. 36. H. 6. tit. protect. 27. 6. R. 2. ibid. 14 Regist. orig. 88. saepe.

52. [*Ed.:* upon the safeguard of Calais.]

53. [*Ed.:* Because he remains upon the high seas.]

54. [*Ed.:* the sea does not 'remain'.]

55. (r) Bract. lib. 5 139,140 Britton 181. Fleta lib 6. c. 7. 8. &c. 14. E. 2. protect. 109. 34. E. 3. ibid. 122. 19 E. 3. ibid. 78. 33. E. 3 ib. 99 21. E. 3. 13.

56. (s) 10. H. 6. Protect. 105

57. [*Ed.:* Ten times as much (the penalty for a juror who takes money to give a verdict).]

58. (t) 39. H. 6. 39. 43. E. 3. 6 & 32. 27. H. 6. 1. F. N. B 28. 17. E. 3. 23. lib. 4. f. 35 Bozoms case. Bract. li. 5 fo. 139,140.

59. [*Ed.:* from which nothing is held,]

60. [*Ed.:* The form of the writ of dower in which there is a claim to property.]

61. [*Ed.:* Writ to enforce a patron's right to fill a vacant benefice.]

sentment[62] a protection lieth not, for the eminent danger of the laps. Neither lieth a Protection in an Assise of *Novel disseisin,*[63] because it is *festinum remedium,*[64] to restore the Dissesee to his freehold, whereof he is wrongfully and without judgement disseised. (u)[65] In a *Quare non admisit;*[66] a Protection is not allowable, because it is grounded upon the *Quare impedit,* and the like in a Certificate upon Assise for the like reason, and *sic de similibus.*[67] A protection, *Quia profecturus*[68] is not allowable (as hath beene said) in any Action commenced before the date of the Protection, unlesse it bee in a Voyage Royall. (w)[69] An Infant is vouched, and at the *Pluries venire facias,*[70] a Protection was cast for the Infant, and disallowed, because his age must be adjudged by the inspection of the Court.

(x)[71] By act of Parliament no Protection shall be allowed in an attaint. (But at the Common Law a Protection for one of the Petite Jurie had put the plea without day for all) nor in an Action against a Gaoler for an escape, nor for victuals taken or bought upon the voyage or service, nor in pleas of Trespasse, or other contract made or perpetrated after the date of the same Protection.

(y)[72] In a writ of Error[73] brought by an Infant upon a fine levied, the Plaintife sued a *Scire facias* against the Conusee, for whom a Protection was cast, and the Court examined the age of the Plaintife, and by inspection adjudged him within age, and recorded the same, and then allowed the Protection, and this can be no mischiefe to the Plaintife, whereupon it followeth, that albeit the Plaintife dieth afterwards before the fine reversed, yet after his age adjudged and recorded, his heirs shall in that case reverse the fine for the nonage of his

62. [*Ed.:* An action to recover a benefice presented to a clerk, but usurped by a presentation by a spurious patron.]

63. [*Ed.:* Writ of assise which lay for the recovery of lands or tenements, where the claimant had been lately disseised.]

64. [*Ed.:* A speedy remedy,]

65. (u) 15. E. 3. tit. protection 52. 12. E. 3. ibid 69 31. E. 1. ibid. 112

66. [*Ed.:* Writ against a bishop who refuses to admit a clerk to a benefice.]

67. [*Ed.:* likewise concerning similar things.]

68. [*Ed.:* A writ of protection.]

69. (w) 19. E. 2 protect. 111 32. E. 3. ibid. 54

70. [*Ed.:* Writ for several to appear.]

71. (x) 23. H. 8. c. 3. 34. E. 1 protection 38. 7. H. 4. c. 4 1. R. 2. cap 8.

72. (y) 21. E. 3. 24. 31. E. 3 protect. 97. 1. 5. E. 4. 50 35. H. 6. 43. 46. 8. E. 4. 8 19. E. 3. 22. 13. E. 3. protect. 3. 73.

73. [*Ed.:* Writ sought to cure a matter of record based on a mistake.]

Ancestor. (a)[74] And so it was resolved in the case of *Kekewiche* in a writ of Error brought by him by the opinion of the whole Court of the Kings Bench, otherwise it is, if the Plaintife dieth before his age inspected.

(b)[75] Note in judiciall Writs, which are in nature of Actions, where the partie hath day to appeare and plead, there Protection doth lie, as in Writs of *Scire facias* upon Recoveries, Fines, Judgements, &c. albeit by the Statute of W.2. Essoignes and other delayes be ousted in writs of *Scire facias,* yet a Protection doth lie in the same. So it is in a *Quid Juris clamat,*[76] and the like. But in Writs of Execution,[77] as *Habere facias seisinam, Eleit, Execution upon a Statute, Capias ad satisfaciendum, Fieri facias,*[78] and the like, there no Protection can be cast for the Defendant, because he hath no day in Court, and the Protection extendeth only *ad placita & querelas,*[79] and must be allowed by the Court, which cannot bee but upon a day of appearance.

(c)[80] In a writ of Disceit brought against him that obtained and cast a Protection upon an untrue surmise in delay of the plaintife, that protection is allowable. In an Action brought upon the Statute of Labourers a Protection doth lye, *& sic de similibus.*[81]

(d)[82] To the sixth, no Writ of Protection can be allowed unlesse it be under the great Seale, (*)[83] and it is directed generally.

(e)[84] To the seventh, the Courts of Justice where the Protection is cast, are to allow, or disallow of the same, be they Courts of Record, or not of Record, and not the Sherife, or any other Officer or Minister.

(f)[85] To the eighth, the Protection may be cast either by any stranger, or by the partie himselfe, an Infant, Feme Covert, a Monke, or any other may

74. (a) Pasch. 12. Ja. regis in the Kings Bench

75. (b) 13. E. 3. protect. 72 Fleta 1. 2. c. 12. 40. E. 3. 18 48. E. 3. 18. 19. 37. H. 6. 32 21. E. 4. 19. 15. H. 7. 8 47. E. 3. 5. 17. E. 3. 68 14. E. 3. protect. 64 W. 2. cap. 45

76. [*Ed.:* Writ by which a reversion or remanderman may compell the life tenant to acknowledge his estate.]

77. [*Ed.:* Writ to enforce a judgment at the close of a case.]

78. [*Ed.:* Writ of execution for a sheriff to seize and sell property to satisfy a money judgment.]

79. [*Ed.:* to pleas and plaints, etc.]

80. (c) 20. E. 3. protect. 83

81. [*Ed.:* likewise concerning similar things.]

82. (d) 35. H. 6. 2. Artic. Super. Cart. 6. 46. E. 3. petition 19

83. (*) Lib. 2. co. 17. Lanes case. Lib 8. fo. 68. Trollops case. 20. H. 6. 25. 2. E. 4. 4 38. H. 6. 23

84. (e) 43. E. 3. protect. 96

85. (f) 21. E. 4. 18

cast a Protection for the Tenant or Defendant, and this difference there is when a stranger casteth it, and when the Tenant or Defendant casteth it him-selfe. (g)[86] For the Defendant or Tenant casting it, he must shew cause where-fore he ought to take advantage of the Protection, but an estranger need not shew any cause, but that the Tenant or Defendant is here by Protection.

(h)[87] As to the ninth, A protection may be avoided three manner of waies: First, upon the casting of it before it be allowed. Secondly, by repeale thereof after it be allowed: by disallowing of it many wayes, as for that it lyeth not in that Action, or that he hath no day to cast it, or for materiall variance between the Protection and the Record, or that it is not under the great Seale, or the like. (i)[88] Thirdly, After it be allowed by *Innotescimus*,[89] as if any tarrie in the Countrey without going to the service for which he was retained, over a convenient time after that he had any Protection, or repairs from the same service, upon information thereof to the Lord Chancellor, he shall repeale the Protection in that case by an *Innotescimus*. But a Protection shall not be avoided by an Averment of the partie of that case, because the Record of the Protection must be avoided by matter of as high nature.

| (k)[90] There is a clause in the Protection to this effect, *Praesentibus minime*   [131 b]
valituris, si contingat ipsum, &c. a custodia castri praedicti recedere. Or *si con-tingat iter illud non arripere, vel infra illum terminum à partibus transmarinis redire.*[91] Whereupon there be two conclusions to be observed.

First, That though the protection be allowed by the Court for a yeere, yet if it be repealed by an *Innotescimus* that the Resommons or Re-attachment shall be granted upon the Repeale within the yeare, for the Protection that was allowed had the said clause in it. And of that opinion be our later Bookes, and the Repeale by *Innotescimus* should serve for little purpose, if the Law should not be taken so.

86. (g) 38. H. 6. 23
87. (h) 44. E. 3. 12. 47. E. 3. 6
88. (i) 13. R. 2. c. 16. 11. H. 4 70. 7. H. 6. 22. 22. H. 6. 50 30. H. 6. 3. 19. H. 5. 35 21. E. 4. 20. 1. H. 6. 6. 42 E. 3. 9. 44. E. 3. 2. 39. E. 3 4. 5. 20. E. 3. protect. 86 34. E. 3. ibid. 119
89. [*Ed.*: Certification of a writing not filed in the Record.]
90. (k) 44. E. 3. 4. 12. 47. E. 3. 6 34. E. 3. protect. 119 28. H. 6. 34. H. 6. 22 30. H. 6. 3. 32. H. 6. 4
91. [*Ed.*: The presents to be of validity if he happens to withdraw from guarding the aforesaid castle [or] if that journey happens not to take place, or if he comes back from overseas within that term.]

Secondly, That albeit he that had the Protection either *Moraturae* or *Pro-fecturae,* returne into England, and haply be arrested and in prison, yet if he came over to provide Munition, Habiliments of warre, victuals, or other nec-essaries, it is no breach of the said conditionall clause, nor against the Act of 13. Richard 2. cap. 16. for that in judgement of Law comming for such things are of necessitie for the maintenance of the warre, *moratur,* according to the intention of the Protection and Statute aforesaid. And thus much of the two first Protections, *Cum clausula volumus, Protecturae* and *Moraturae.*[92]

(l)[93] As to the third Protection, *Cum clausula volumus,* the King by his Prerogative regularly is to be preferred in payment of his dutie of debt by his Debtor before any Subject, although the Kings debt or dutie be the latter, & the reason hereof is, for that *Thesaurus Regis est fundamentum belli, & fir-mamentum pacis.*[94] And thereupon the Law gave the King remedy by Writ of Protection to protect his Debtor, that he should not be sued or attached untill hee paid the Kings debt, but hereof grew some inconvenience, for to delay other men of their suits, the Kings debts were the more slowly paid. And for remedie thereof (m)[95] it is enacted by the Statute of 25.E.3. that the other Creditors may have their actions against the Kings Debtor and to proceed to Judgement, but not to Execution unlesse he will take upon him to pay the Kings debt, and then he shall have Execution against the Kings Debtor for both the two debts.

This kinde of Protection hath (as it appeareth) no certaine time limited in it. But in some cases the subject shall be satisfied before the King (n)[96] for regularly whensoever the King is intitled to any fine or duty by the suit of the partie, the party shall be first satisfied, as in a *Decies tantum,*[97] And so if in Action of Debt the Defendant deny his Deed, and it is found against him he shall pay a fine to the King, but the Plaintife shall be first satisfied, and so in all other like cases. And so it is in Bills preferred by subjects in the Star-

92. [*Ed.:* with the *volumus* (we will) clause, [namely], *profecturae* (those about to go) and *moraturae* (those remaining).]

93. (l) Registrum 281. b F. N. B. 28. b 33. H. 8. c. 29. in the praeamble. 41. E. 3. tit. Execution 38. 18. E. 3. ibid. 56 27. E. 3. 88. b 4. E. 4. 16. 3. Eliz. Dier. 197 Rot. pat. 27. E 3. part. I m. 2.

94. [*Ed.:* The king's treasure is the foundation of war and the firm support of peace.]

95. (m) 25. E. 3. cap. 19

96. (n) 41. E. 3. 15. 17. E. 3. 73 29. E. 3. 13. 4. E. 4. 16.

97. [*Ed.:* Penalty for a juror who sells the vote or verdict.]

chamber, their costs and damages (if any be) shall be answered before the Kings fine, as it is daily in experience.

The fourth protection, *Cum clausula volumus,* is when a man sent into the Kings Service beyond Sea is imprisoned there, so as neither Protection, *Profecturae* or *Moraturae,* will serve him, and this hath no certaine time limited in it, (o)[98] whereof you shall read at large in the Register, and F.N.B.

(p)[99] Now are we at length come to Protections, *Cum clausula nolumus,* All which saving one, are of grace, and as hath beene said are implyed under the generall protection, for as Fitzherbert saith, every loyall subject is in the Kings Protection. Of these Protections of grace, you shall not read much in our yeere Books, because they stayed no Actions or Suits; (q)[100] Of the divers formes, of these you shall read at large in the Register, and F.N.B. which were too long and needlesse to be here recited.

The Protection *Cum clausula nolumus,* that is, of right, is, that every spirituall person may sue a Protection for him and his goods, and for the fermors of their lands and their goods, that they shall not be taken by the Kings Purveyor, not their carriages or chattels taken by other Ministers of the King, which Writ both recite the Statute of 14.E.3.

Of these Protections I cannot say any thing of mine owne experience, for albeit Queene Elizabeth maintained many warres, yet she granted few or no Protections, and her reason was, that he was no fit subject to be imployed in her service, that was subject to other mens actions, lest she might be thought to delay Justice.

Section 342
Conditional Estates, part 17

| And therefore it wil be a good & sure thing for him that will make such feoffment in morgage, to appoint an especiall place where the money shall be payd, and the more speciall that it bee put, the | better it is for the feoffor. As if A. infeoffe B. to have to him and to his heires, upon such condition, That if A. pay to B. on the Feast of Saint *Michael* the Arch-Angell next comming,   [211 b]

[212 a]

---

98. (o) Regist. saepe. F. N. B. 28. c.

99. (p) Vide lib. 7. fol. 8. 9. Calvins case.

100. (q) Register 280, c. F. N. B. 29. A. B. C. D. E. F. G. H. Register 280 Statut. de 14. E. 3 F. N. B. 30. A.

in the Cathedrall Church of Saint *Pauls* in London, within foure houres next before the houre of Noone of the same feast, at the Rood loft of the Rood of the North doore, within the same Church, or at the Tombe of Saint *Erkenwald,* or at the doore of such Chappell, or at such a pillar within the same Church, that then it shall bee lawfull to the aforesaid A. and his heires to enter, &c. In this case he needeth not to seek the Feoffee in an other place, nor to bee in any other place, but in the place comprised in the Indenture, nor to bee there longer than the time specified in the same Indenture, to tender or pay the money to the feoffee, &c.

Here is good counsell and advice given, to set downe in Conveyances every thing in certainty and particularity, for Certainty is the mother of Quietness and Repose, and Incertainty the cause of variance and contentions: and for obtaining of the one, and avoiding of the other, the best meane is, in all assurances to take counsell of learned and well experienced men, and not to trust only without advice, to a Precedent. For as the rule is concerning the state of a mans body, *Nullum medicamentum est idem omnibus,*[1] so in the state and assurance of a mans Lands, *Nullum exemplum est idem omnibus.*[2]

"at the Tombe of Saint *Erkenwald,*"

This Erkenwald was a younger sonne of Anna King of the East Saxons, and was first Abbot of Chersey in Surry which hee had founded, and after Bishop of London, a holy and devout man, and lyeth buryed in the South Ile, above the Quire in Saint Pauls Church, where the Tombe yet remaineth that Littleton speaketh of in this place: he flourished about the yeere of our Lord, 680.

The residue of this Section, and the (&c.) are evident.

Section 366
Conditional Estates, part 41

[226 a] | Also albeit a man cannot in any action pleade a condition which toucheth & concernes a freehold, without shewing writing of this, as is aforesaid, yet a man may be aided upon such a condition by the verdict of 12. men taken at large

1. [*Ed.:* No medicine is the same for everyone,]
2. [*Ed.:* No precedent is the same for all purposes.]

in an assise of *Novel disseisin*,[1] or in any other action where the Justices will take the verdict of 12. Jurors at large. As put the case, a man seised of certaine land in fee, letteth the same land to another for terme of life without deed, upon condition to render to the Lessor a certaine rent, and for default of payment, a re-entrie, &c. by force whereof the lessee is seised as of freehold, and after the rent is behinde, by which the lessor entreth into the land, and after the lessee arraigne an Assise of *Novel Disseisin* of the land against the Lessor, who pleads that he did no wrong nor disseisin, and upon this the Assise is taken; in this case the Recognitors of the Assise may say and render to the Justices their verdict at large upon the whole matter, as to say that the defendant was seised of the land in his demesne as of fee, and so seised, let the same land to the Plaintife for terme of his life, rendring to the lessor such a yeerely rent payable at such a feast, &c. upon such condition, that if the rent were behind at any such feast at which it ought to bee payd, then it should bee lawfull for the Lessor to enter, &c. by force of which lease the Plaintife was seised in his demesne as of freehold, and that afterwards the Rent was behind at such a feast, &c. by which the lessor entred into the land upon the possession of the lessee, and prayed the discretion of the Justices if this bee a disseisin done to the Plaintife or not. Then for that it appeareth to the Justices that this was no disseisin to the plaintife, insomuch as the entrie of the Lessor was congeable on him; the Justices ought to give judgement that the plaintife shall not take any thing by his writ of Assise. And so in such case the lessor shall bee ayded, and yet no writing was ever made of the Condition. For aswel as the Jurors may have conusance of the lease, they also aswell may have conusance of the Condition which was declared & rehearsed upon the lease.

"verdict of 12. men."

Veredictum quasi dictum veritatis, as *judicium est quasi juris dictum.*[2,3] *Et sicut ad quaestionem juris, non respondent juratores, sed judices: sic ad quaestionem facti non respondent judices sed juratores.*[4] For Jurors are to try the fact, and

---

1. [*Ed.:* Writ to recover lands and tenements, where the claimant had been lately disseised.]

2. Lib. 8. fo. 155. Lib. 9 fo. 13. Lib. 11. fo. 10.

3. [*Ed.:* The verdict is the *dictum* of truth, (as) the judgment is the *dictum* of law.]

4. [*Ed.:* And just as for questions of law the jurors do not answer but the judges; thus as for questions of fact the judges do not answer but the jurors do.]

[226 b] the Judges ought to judge according to the Law that riseth upon the | fact, for *Ex facto jus oritur.*[5]

"taken at large."

There bee two kinds of verdicts, viz. one generall and another at large or especiall. As in an Assise of *Novel disseisin* brought by A. against B. the Plaintife makes his plaint, *Quod B. disseisivit cum de 20. acris terrae cum pertinentiis,*[6] the Tenant pleads, *Quod ipse nullam injuriam seu disseisinam praefato A. inde fecit,* &c.[7] the Recognitors of the Assise doe finde *Quod praedict. A. injuste & sine judicio disseisivit praedict. B. de praedict. 20. acris terrae cum pertinent'* &c.[8] This is a generall verdict. The like Law it is if they finde it negatively. And Littleton here putteth a case of a Verdict at large or a speciall Verdict, and it is therefore called a speciall Verdict or a Verdict at large, because they finde the speciall matter at large, and leave the judgment of Law therupon to the Court, of which kinde of Verdict it is said, (l)[9] *Omnis conclusio boni & veri judicii sequitur ex bonis & veris praemissis & dictis Juratorum.*[10]

And though Littleton here putteth his case of a Verdict at large upon a generall issue (which in the case hee puts it was necessary for the Tenant to plead, yet when Issue is joyned upon some speciall point, the Jury, as shall bee said hereafter in this Section, may finde the speciall matter, if it be doubtfull in Law, for as much as doubt may arise upon one point upon the generall issue as upon the generall issue. And as a speciall verdict may be found in
[227 a] Common | Pleas, so may it also bee found in Pleas of the Crowne,[11] or criminall causes that concerne life or member.

A Verdict finding matter incertainely or ambiguously is insufficient, and no judgement shall be given thereupon,[12] as if an Executor plead *Pleinment*

---

5. [*Ed.:* The law arises out of the fact.]

6. [*Ed.:* That B. disseised him of twenty acres of land with the appurtenances,]

7. [*Ed.:* That he committed no tort or disseisin against the said A. therein, etc.]

8. [*Ed.:* That the aforesaid A. unjustly and without judgment disseised the said B. of the aforesaid twenty acres of land with the appurtenances, etc.]

9. (l) Trin. 33. E. 1. Coram Rege Nott. in Thesaur.

10. [*Ed.:* Every conclusion of a good and true judgment follows from good and true premises and the verdicts of jurors.]

11. 43. Ass. 31. Staunf. pl. cor. 164. 165. 3. E. 3. coron. 284 286. 287. 44. E. 3. 44. 41. E. 3. Coron. 451.

12. 40. E. 3. 15. 20. E. 3. amendment. 57. 18. E. 3. 49 in Cessavit. 30. E. 3. 23. 7. H. 4. 39.

administre,[13] and issue is joyned thereupon, and the Jury finde, that the Defendant have goods within his hands to bee administered, but finde not to what value, this is uncertaine, and therefore insufficient.

A Verdict that finds part of the issue, and finding nothing for the residue, this is insufficient for the whole,[14] because they have not tryed the whole issue wherewith they are charged. As if an information or intrusion bee brought against one for intruding into a mesuage, and 100. acres of land, upon the generall issue the Jury finde against the Defendant for the land, but saith nothing for the house, this is insufficient for the whole, & so was it twice adjudged. (m)[15] But if the Jury give a verdict of the whole issue, and of more, &c. that which is more is surplusage, and shall not (a)[16] stay judgement, for *Utile per inutile non vitiatur,*[17] but necessary incidents required by law, the Jury may find.

If the matter and substance of the issue bee found, it is sufficient as Littleton himself sayeth hereafter.[18]

Estoppells which bind the interest of the Land, as the taking of a Lease of a mans owne Land by Deed indented, and the like, being specially found by the Jury, the Court ought to judge according to the speciall matter, for albeit Estoppels regularly must be pleaded and relied upon by an apt conclusion, and the Jury is sworne *ad veritatem dicendam,*[19] yet when they finde *veritatem facti,*[20] they pursue well their oath, and the Court ought to adjudge according to Law. (b)[21] So may the Jury finde a warranty being given in evidence, though it be not pleaded, because it bindeth the right, unlesse it be in a Writ of Right, when the Mise in joyned upon the meere right.

| (c)[22] After the verdict recorded, the Jury cannot vary from it, but before   [227 b]

---

13. [*Ed.:* Fully administered,]

14. 17. E. 3. 47. 18. E. 3. 48. 22. E. 3. 1. 18. H. 3. 56. 15. E. 3. Judgement 58. 2. H. 5. 3. 7. H. 6. 5. 7. E. 4. 24. 28. H. 6. 10.

15. (m) Hill. 25. Eliz. in a writ of Error between Brace and the Queen in the Exchequer Chamber. Mich. 28 & 29 Eliz. inter Gomersal & Gomersal in account in the King's Bench.

16. (a) 32. E. 3. Cessavit. 25.

17. [*Ed.:* The useful is not vitiated by the useless,]

18. Vid. Sect. 484. 485. Vid Sect. 58. 13. H. 3. garr. 26 15. E. 3. Ass. 322. 17. E. 3. 6. 18. Ass. 2. 35. Ass. 8.

19. [*Ed.:* to say the truth,]

20. [*Ed.:* the truth of the fact,]

21. (b) 1. H. 4 6. b. 27. H. 8. 22. b. Pl. Com. 515. Lib. 4. fol. 53. Rawlins case & ibid. Pledols case. Hil 31. Eliz. betweene Sutton & Dicons in the Common Place, the case of the Lease for years by Deed indented. 34. E. 3. Droit 29.

22. (c) 7. R.2 Coron. 108. Plo. Com. Freman's Case, 211. 11. H. 4. 2. 20. Ass. 12. 16. Ass. 16. 22. Ass. 23 5. H. 7. 22.

it be recorded they may vary from the first offer of their verdict, and that verdict which is recorded shall stand: also they may vary from a privy Verdict.

An issue found by Verdict shall alwaise be intended true untill it be reversed by attaint, and thereupon upon the attaint no *Supersedeas* is grantable by Law.[23]

If the Jury after their evidence given unto them at the Barre, doe at their owne charges eat or drink either before or after they be agreed on their Verdict, it in finable,[24] but it shall not avoyd the Verdict: but if before they be agreed on their Verdict, they eat or drink at the charge of the Plaintife, if the Verdict bee given for him, it shall avoyd the Verdict: but if it be given for the Defendant, it shal not avoyd it, & *sic è converso*.[25] (d)[26] But if after they be agreed on their Verdict, they eat or drinke at the charge of him for whom they doe passe, it shall not avoyd the Verdict.

(e)[27] If the Plaintife after evidence given and the Jury departed from the Barre, or any for him, doe deliver any Letter from the Plaintife to any of the Jury concerning the matter in Issue, or any Evidence, or any escrowle touching the matter in issue, which was not given in Evidence, it shall avoyd the Verdict, if it be found for the Plaintife, but not if it be found for the Defendant, & *sic è converso*. But if the Jury carry away any writing unsealed, which was given in evidence in open Court, this shall not avoyd their Verdict, albeit they should not have carryed it with them.

By the Law of England a Jury after their Evidence given upon the Issue, ought to bee kept together in some convenient place, without meat or drinke,[28] fire or candle, which some Bookes (f)[29] call an imprisonment, and without speech with any, unlesse it be the Bailife, and with him onely if they be agreed. After they be agreed, they may in causes between party and party give a Verdict, and if the Court be risen, give a privy Verdict before any of the Judges of the Court, and then they may eat and drinke, and the next morning in open Court they may either affirme or alter their privy Verdict, and that which is given

---

23. [*Ed.:* A writ to stay the proceedings at law.]

24. Pasch. 24. H. 8. of the Report of Justice Spilman in the Kings Bench. 11. H. 4. 17. 35. H. 6. Examin. 17. 29. H. 8. 37. Dyer. 35. H. 8. 55. 4. & 5. Eliz. 218. 14. H. 7. 1. 20. H. 7. 3.

25. [*Ed.:* and likewise conversely.]

26. (d) Pasch. 6. E. 6. in the Common place.

27. (e) 11. H. 4. 16. 17. 3. Mar. Jurors Br. 8. Vide Dyer ubi supra.

28. Pasch. 6. E. 6. ubi supra.

29. (f) 24. E. 3. 75.

in Court shall stand. But in criminall cases of life or member, the Jury can give no privy Verdict, but they must give it openly in Court. And hereby appeareth another division of Verdicts, viz a publique Verdict openly given in Court, and a privy Verdict, given out of the Court before any of the Judges, as is aforesaid.

A Jury sworne and charged in case of life or member,[30] cannot be discharged by the Court or any other, but they ought to give a Verdict. And the King cannot be Non-suit, for he is in Judgement of Law ever present in Court: but a common person may be non-suit.

"in an assise of *Novel disseisin* or in any other action.[31]"

Here it is to be observed, That a speciall Verdict, or at large may be given in any Action, and upon any issue, be the Issue generall or speciall: and albeit there be some contrary opinions in our Bookes, yet the Law is now settled in this poynt.

"by which the lessor entereth."

Here it appeareth that the condition is executed by re-entry, and yet the Lessor after his re-entry shall not by the opinion of Littleton, plead the Condition without shewing the Deed, because he was party and privy to the condition: for the parties must shew forth the Deed, unlesse it be by the act and wrong of his adversary, as hath been said, (m)[32] but an estranger which is not privy to the condition, nor claymeth under the same, as in the cases abovesayd appeareth, shal not after the condition is executed in pleading, be inforced to shew forth the Deed: and by this diversity all the bookes and authorities in law which seeme to bee at variance are reconciled. See also for this matter the Section next following.

---

30. 21. E. 3. 18.

31. W. 2. cap. 30. 7. H. 4. 11. 8. E. 4. 29. 9. H. 7. 13. 23. H. 8 tit. verdict. Br. 85. 11. Eliz. Dier. 283. 284. 3. E. 3. Itinere North. 284, 286 43. Ass. 31. 26. H. 8. 5. 44. E. 3. 44. F. tit. Coron. 94 44. Ass. 17. 45. E. 3. 20. pl. Com. 92. 9. H. 7. 3. Vid. lib 9. 12. 13. Dowmans case. And see there many other authorities. 31. Ass. Pl. 21. 10. H. 4. 9.

32. (m) See more before in this chapter, Sect. 365.

"the Recognitors of the Assise may say."[33]

Here it appeareth that the Jurors may find the fact, albeit the Deed bee not shewed in evidence, and the rather, for that the Condition upon the Livery (as hath been said) is good albeit there be no Deed at all.

"and prayed the discretion of the Justices."

That is to say, They, (having declared the speciall matter) pray the discretion of the Justices, which is as much to say, as, That they would discerne what the Law adjudgeth thereupon, whether for the Demandant or for the Tenant: for as by the authority of Littleton, *Discretio est discernere per legem, quid sit justum,*[34] that is, to discerne by the right line of law, and not by the crooked cord of private opinion, which the vulgar call Discretion: *Si à jure discedas, vagus eris, & erunt omnia omnibus incerta:*[35] and therefore Commissions that authorise any to proceed,[36] *secundum sanas discretiones vestras,*[37] is as much to say, as, *Secundum Legem & consuetudinem Angliae.*[38]

"For as well as the jurors may have conusance."

Hereby it appeareth, That they that have Conusance of any thing, are to have Conusance also all Incidents and Dependants thereupon, for an Incident is a thing necessarily depending upon another.

[228 a]   ❡ If a Deed bee made and dated in a forraine Kingdome, of lands within England, yet if[39] Livery and Seisin be made *secundum formam cartae,*[40] the land shall passe, for it passeth by the Livery.

---

33. 10. Ass. 9. 21. Ass. 28. 17. Ass. 20. 31. Ass. 21 23. Ass. 2. 39. E. 3. 28. 44. E. 3. 22. 10. H. 4. 9. 7. H. 5. 5. 9. E. 4. 26. 18. E. 4. 12. 15. E. 4. 16. 17. 11. H. 7. 22.

34. [*Ed.:* Discretion is to know through law what is just,]

35. [*Ed.:* If you depart from the law, you will go astray, and all things will be uncertain to everybody.]

36. Lib. 10. fo. 4. case de Sewers.

37. [*Ed.:* according to your sane discretions.]

38. [*Ed.:* According to the law and custom of England.]

39. 1. H. 3. 17. in Gracye's case

40. [*Ed.:* According to form,]

Section 372
Conditional Estates, part 47

| The making of an Indenture in the first person is, as in this forme. *To all*   [230 a]
Christian people to whom these presents indented shall come, A. of B. sends greeting
in our Lord God everlasting. Know yee me to have given, granted, and by this my
present Deed indented, confirmed to C. of D. such land, &c. Or thus: *Know all*
men present and to come, that I A. of B. have given, granted, and by this my present
Deed indented, confirmed to C. of D. such land, &c. To have and to hold, &c. upon
Condition following, &c. In witnesse whereof, as well I the said A. of B. as the
aforesaid C. of D. to these Indentures have interchangeably put our Seales. Or thus:
In witnesse whereof I the aforesaid A. to the one part of this Indenture have put my
Seale, and to the other part of the same Indenture, the said C. of D. hath put his
Seale, &c.

Here Littleton sets downe three formes of deeds indented in the first person,
Brevis via per exempla, longa per praecepta.[1] It is requisite for every Student to
get Precidents and approved formes, not onely of deeds according to the example of Littleton,[2] but of Fines, and other Conveyances, and Assurances,
and especially of good and perfect pleading, and of the right entries, and formes
of Judgements, which will stand him in great stead, both while he studies,
and after when he shall give counsell. It is safe thing to follow approved precidents, for *Nihil simul inventum est, & perfectum.*[3]

Section 412
Descents, part 27

| Also it is said that if a man be seised of Lands in fee by occupation in time   [249 a]
of warre, and thereof dyeth seised in the time of warre, and the tenements
descend to his heire, such discent shall not oust any man of his entry, and of
this a man may see in a Plea upon a Writ of Aiel, 7.E.2.

---

1. [*Ed.:* [Learning] by rules is long, but by examples short.]
2. Vide Sect. 371.
3. [*Ed.:* Nothing is invented and perfected at the same moment.]

"by occupation in time of Warre,"

First it is necessary to bee knowne, what shall bee said, Time of peace, *Tempus pacis:*[1] and what shall bee said, *Tempus belli, sive guerrae,*[2] time of warre. *Tempus pacis est quan-|-do Cancellaria & aliae Curiae Regis sunt apertae, quibus lex fiebat cuicunque prout fieri consuevit.*[3,4] And so it was adjudged in the case of Roger Mortimer, and of Thomas Earle of Lancaster. *Utrum terra sit guerrina necne, naturaliter debet judicari per recorda Regis, et eorum, qui curias Regis per legem terrae custodiunt, & gubernant, sed non alio modo.*[5,6]

And therefore when the Courts of Justce be open, and the Judges and Minsters of the same may by Law protect men from wrong and violence, and distribute Justice to all, it is said to be time of peace. So, when by invasion, Insurrection, Rebellions, or such like, the peaceable course of Justice is disturbed and stopped, so as the Courts of Justice bee as it were shut up, *Et silent leges inter arma,*[7] then it is said to be time of war. And the tryall hereof is by the Records, and Judges of the Court of Justice, for by them it will appeare, whether Justice had her equall course of proceeding at that time or no, and this shall not be tried by Jury.

If a man be disseised in time of peace, and discent is cast in time of warre, this shall not take away the entry of the disseisee.

Item tempore pacis, quod dicitur ad differentiam eorum quae fuerunt tempore belli, quod idem est, quod tempore guerrino, quod nihil differt a tempore juris, & injuriae, est enim tempus injuriae, cum fuerunt oppressiones violentae quibus resisti non potest, & disseisinae injustae.[8,9]

[249 b] *(margin)*

---

1. [*Ed.:* Time of peace.]

2. [*Ed.:* Time of war.]

3. Inter brevia de anno 1 E. 3. parte 1. & Pasch. 28 E. 3. inter adjudicata coram rege, lib. 2. fol. 37. in Thesaur. Pasch. 39 E 3. inter adjudicta coram rege in Thesaur. lib. 2. fol. 92.

4. [*Ed.:* Time of peace is when the Chancery and other king's courts are open, whereby the law may be done to everyone in the usual way.]

5. [*Ed.:* Whether a land is at war or not ought naturally to be adjudged by the records of the king and of those who keep and govern the king's courts by the law of the land, but not in any other way.]

6. 14 E. 3. tit. Scire facias, 122. but more fully in the record at large

7. [*Ed.:* And amidst the clash of arms the laws are silent,]

8. [*Ed.:* Also in time of peace, which is so called to distinguish it from time of war, which is the same as wartime, and this is no different from time of right and time of wrong; for it is a time of wrong when there are violent oppressions which cannot be resisted, and wrongful disseisins.]

9. Bracton, lib. 4. fol. 240

So as hereby it also appeareth, that time of peace is the time of law and right, and time of warre is the time of violent oppression, which cannot be resisted by the equall course of Law. And therefore in all reall actions, the expleas, or taking of the profits are laid *Tempore pacis,* for if they were taken *Tempore belli,* they are not accounted of in Law.

"by occupation."

Occupation is a word of Art,[10] and signifieth a putting out of a mans Freehold in time of warre, and it is all one with a disseisin in time of peace, saving that it is not so dangerous, as it appeareth have by Littleton, and therefore the Law gave a writ in that case of *Occupavit,*[11] so called, by reason of that word in the Writ, in stead of *disseisivit,*[12] in the Assise of *Novel dissesin,* if the dessesin had beene done in time of peace, whereby it appeareth,[13] how aptly both in this, and in all other places, Littleton thorow his whole Booke speaketh. But albeit *Occupatio* whereof Littleton here speaketh, is used only in the said Writ, and in none other, (that I can finde or remember) yet hath it been used commonly in Conveyances and Leases, to limit or make certaine precedent words *ad tunc in tenura & occupatione.*[14] But *occupaitio* is applyed to the possession, be it lawfull or on unlawfull; It hath also crept into some Acts of parliament, as 4 H. 7.cap. 19. 39. Eliz. cap. 1 and others, and *occupare,* is sometime taken to conquer.

"and of this a man see in a Plea upon a Writ of Aiel, [year] 7.E.2."

Hereby it appeareth, that ancient termes or yeares, after the example of Littleton, are to bee cited and vouched, for confirmation of the Law, albeit they were never printed, and that of those yeares, those especially of E. 1. H. 3. &c. are worthy of the reading and observation, a great number of which I have sene and observed, which in mine opinion doe give a great light, not onely to the understanding and reason of the Common Law, (which Fitz-

---

10. Ingham cap. de novel disseisin.
11. [*Ed.:* Writ for recovery in peace of land taken during war.]
12. [*Ed.:* out of his land or tenement in time of war.]
13. Lib. 4. fol. 49, 50. Ognel's case.
14. [*Ed.:* then in the tenure and occupation.]

herbert either saw not, or were by him omitted) but also to the true exposition
of the ancient Statutes, made in those times, yet mine advice is, that they be
read in their time: for after our Student is enabled and armed to set on our
yeere Bookes, or reports of the Law, let him reade first the latter reports, for
two causes: First, for that for the most part the latter Judgements and Resolutions are the surest, and therefore it is the best to season him with them
in the beginning, both for the settling of his judgement, and for the retaining
of them in memory. Secondly, for that the latter are more facile and easier to
be understood, than the more ancient: but after the reading of them, then to
read these others before mentioned, and all the ancient Authors that have
written of our Law; for I would wish our Student to be a compleat Lawyer.
But now to returne. As it is in case of discent, so it is in case of presentation,
for no usurpation in time of warre putteth the right Patron out of possession,
albeit the incumbent come in by institution and induction: And time of war
doth not only give priviledge to them that be in warre, but to all others within
the Kingdome, and although the admission and institution be in time of peace,
yet if the presentment were in time of warre, it putteth not the right Patron
out of possission.[15]

Section 464
Releases, part 20

[272 a] | Another cause they alledge, That if such Land bee worth forty shillings a yeare,
&c. then such Feoffor shall bee sworne in Assise and other enquests in Plees
reals, and also in Plees personals, of what great summe soever the Plaintiffe will
declare, &c. And this is by the Common Law of the land, *Ergo* this is for a great
cause, and the cause is, for that the Law will that such feoffors and their Heires
ought to occupie, &c. and take and enjoy all manner of profits, issues, and
revenues, &c. as if the Lands were their owne without interruption of the Feoffees, notwithstanding such Feoffement, *Ergo,* the same Law giveth a privity betweene such Feoffors and the Feoffees upon confidence, &c. for which causes
they have said, That such releases made by such Feoffees upon confidence to
their feoffor or to his heires, &c. so occupying the Lands, shall be good enough:
and this is the better opinion, as it seemeth.

Quære, for this seemeth no Law at this day.

15. 6 E. 3. 41. 7. E. 3 darr. pres. 2. 18 E. 2. quare imp. 175 F. N. B. 31.

By the Statute of 2. Hen. 5. cap. 3. Statute. 2. it is enacted, That in three cases,[1] he that passeth in an Enquest, ought to have Lands and Tenements to the value of fortie shillings, viz. First, Upon tryall of the death of a man. Secondly, in Plea reall betweene party and party. And thirdly, In Plea personall, where the debt, or the dammages in the Declaration amount unto fortie Markes. And it is worth the noting, That the Judges that were at the making of that Statute did construe it by equity: for where the Stature speakes in the disjunctive debt or dammages, they adjudged that where the debt and dammages amounted to forty Markes, that it was within the Statute.[2] Fortescue (f)[3] saith, *Ubi damna vel debitum in personalibus Actionibus non excedunt quadraginta Marcas monetae Anglicanae, hinc non requiritur, quod Juratores in Actionibus hujusmodi tantum expendere possint: habebunt tamen terram vel redditum, ad valorem competentem, juxta discretionem justiciariorum, &c.*[4] And forasmuch as the time of the making of this Statute, the greater part of the Lands in England in those troublesome and dangerous times (when that unhappy controversie betweene the Houses of Yorke and Lancaster was begun) were in use. And the Statute was made to remedy | a mischiefe, that the Sheriffe   [272 b] use to return simple men of small or no understanding, and therefore the Statute provided,[5] That hee should returne sufficient men, and albeit in Law the Land was the Feofees, yet for that they had it but upon trust, and *Cesty que use,*[6] tooke the whole profits, as our Authour here saith, and in equity and conscience the Land was his, therefore the Judges for advancement and expedition of justice, extended the Statute (against the Letter) to *Cesty que use,* & not to the Feoffees.

(n)[7] But note if a man hath a Freehold *pur terme dauter vie,*[8] or is seised in his Wifes right, and is returned on a Jury, yet if after he be returned, *Cesty*

---

1. 28. H. 8. Dy. fol. 9. Vid. W. 2. cap. 38. L'estat. de 21. E. I de juratis penendis in Ass. &c.

2. 9. H. 5. fol. 5.

3. (f) Fortesc. cap. 15.

4. [*Ed.:* Where the damages or debt in personal actions do not exceed forty marks of English money, it is not requisite that the jurors in such actions should be able to spend so much; nevertheless they shall have land or rent to a sufficient value, according to the discretion of the justices, etc.]

5. 15. H. 7. 13. b. 13. H. 7. b. 5. E. 4. 7. a.

6. [*Ed.:* Property held by one for the benefit, or use, of another,]

7. (n) 3. H. 6. 39. Challeng. 19. 21. H. 6. 39.

8. [*Ed.:* for a term measured by the life of another,]

que vie, or his wife die, he may be challenged, and so it is if after the returne the Lands be evicted.

"And this is by the Common Law . . ."

Here three things are to be observed. First, That the surest construction of a State is by the rule and reason of the common Law. Secondly, That uses were at the Common Law. Thirdly, That now seeing the Statute (g)[9] of 27.H. 8.ca. 10. which hath been in enacted since Littleton wrote, hath transferred the possession to the use, this case holdeth not at this day, but this latter opinion before that Statute was good Law, as Littleton here taketh it.

"the same Law giveth a privity . . ."

Hereof it followeth, That when the Law gives to any man any estate or possession, the Law giveth also a privity & other necessaries of the same and Littleton concludeth it with an Illative, *Ergo, mesme la Ley dont privitie,*[10] which is very observable for a conclusion in other cases.

And the (*Quaere*) here made in the end of this Section is not in the Originall, but added by some other, and therefore to be rejected.

Also since Littleton wrote, the said Statute of 2. H. 5. is altered:[11] for where that Statute limited forty shillings, now a later Statute hath raised it to foure pounds, and so it ought to be contained in the *Venire facias.*[12]

Nota,[13] an Use is a Trust or Confidence reposed in some other, which is not issuing out of the Land, but as thing collaterall, annexed in privity to the estate of the Land, & to the person touching the Land, *scilicet,* that *Cesty que use* shall take the profit,[13] and that the Terre-tenant shall make an estate according to his direction. So as *Cesty que use* had neither *Jus in re,*[14] nor *Jus ad rem,*[15]

---

9. (g) 27. H. 8. cap. 10.

10. [*Ed.:* Therefore, the same law gives a privity,]

11. 27. EI. cap. 6.

12. [*Ed.:* Writ to a Sheriff directing him to summon a pool of jurors.]

13. Pl. Com. 352. b. in Delamere's case, & 349. b. Lib. I. fol. 121. 123. 127. 140. in Chudleye's case. Lib. 2. fol. 58. 78 Lib. 6. fol. 64. Lib. 7. fol. 13, 34.

14. [*Ed.:* A right in the thing,]

15. [*Ed.:* A right to the thing,]

but for breach of trust his remedy was only by *Sub poena,* in Chancery: and yet the Judges for the cause aforesaid, made the said construction upon the said Statute.

Now how Jurors shall bee returned both in Common Plees, and also in Plees of the Crowne, and in what manner evidence shall be given to them, and how they shall be kept untill they give their verdict, you may read in Fortescue,[16] & therefore need not to be here inserted.

Section 481
Releases, part 37

| Also to prove that the graund Assise ought to passe for the demandant, in the case aforesaid I have often heard the reading of the statute of West[minster]. 2. which begunne thus: *In casu quo vir amiserit per defaltam tenementum quod fuit jus uxoris suae, &c.*[1] that at the Common Law before the said Statute, if a lease were made to a man for terme of life, the remainder over in fee, and a Stranger by feigned Action recovered against the Tenant for life by default, and after the Tenant dyeth, he in the remainder had no remedie before the Statute, because he had not any possession of the Land.   [280 a]

"I have often heard the reading of the statute of West[minster]. 2."

Here it is to bee observed, of what authority ancient Lectures or Readings upon Statutes were, for that they had five excellent qualities: First, They declared what the Common | Law was before the making of the Statute, as here it appeareth. Secondly, they opened the true sense & meaning of the Statute. Thirdly, their cases were briefe, having at the most one poynt at the Common Law, and another upon the Statute. Fourthly Plaine and Perspicuous, for then the honour of the Reader was to excell others in authorities, arguments, and reasons for proofe of his opinion & for confutation of the objections against it. Fifthly, they read, to suppresse subtill inventions to creepe out of the Statute. But now readings having lost the said former qualities, have lost also their former authorities, for now the cases are long, obscure, and intricate, full of   [280 b]

---

16. Fortesc. cap. 25,26,27.

1. [*Ed.:* In the case where a man loses by default the tenement which was his wife's right etc. . . . (the opening words of the Statute of Westminster II, c. 3).]

new conceits, liker rather to Riddles than Lectures, which when they are opened they vanish away in the smoke, and the Readers are like to Lapwings,[2] who seeme to be nearest their nests when they are farthest from them, and all their study is to finde nice evasions out of the Statute. By the authority of Littleton ancient Readings may be cited for proofe of the Law, but new Readings have not that honour, for that they are so obscure and darke.

"the statute of West[minster]. 2."

Which is the third chapter.

"the remainder over in fee,"

Here is to be observed, that although the Statute speaketh of a Reversion, (a)[3] yet by the authority of Littleton a remainder is within the Statute.

See the Statute of 14. Eliz. cap. 8. which provideth fully for him in the remainder.

"feigned Action."

Feint is a Participle of the French word *Feindre,* which is to feign or falsly pretend, so as a feint Action is a false Action.

"had no remedie before the Statute,"

(b)[4] Here it appeareth by Littleton, That if a man maketh a Lease for life the remainder in fee, and tenant for life suffereth a recovery by default, that he in the remainder should not have a Formedon by the common law: for Littleton saith, That he had not any remedy before the Statute. Neither is there any such writ in that case in the Register, albeit in some Bookes mention is made of such a Writ.

---

2. [*Ed.:* A form of plover known for its erratic manner of flight, and its oft-sold eggs.]

3. (a) 24. E. 3. 35. 28. E. 3. 96. 18. E. 2. Entrie 74. 3. E. 2. Entrie 7. 6. E. 3. 24. 7. E. 3. 54,55 15. E. 4. 15. F. N. B. 217. d. Register 241.

4. (b) W. 2. cap. 5. Vid. 34. E. 3 Formedon 31. 11. E. 3. ibid. 31. 8. E. 3. 59. F. N. B. 217. d. 7. H. 7. 13.

Section 723
Warranty, part 30

| The third cause is, when the condition is such, that if the elder sonne alien,   [379 a]
&c. that his estate shall cease or be void, &c. then after such alienation, &c.
may the Donor enter by force of such condition, as it seemeth, and so the donor
or his heires in such case ought sooner to have the land then the second son,
that had not any right before such alienation; and so it seemeth that such re-
mainders in the case aforesaid are void.

Here it is to bee observed, that part of the condition that prohibiteth the
alienation made by tenant in taile is good in Law, with such distinction as
hath beene before said in the Chapter of Conditions. And the consequent of
the Condition, viz. that the lands should remaine to another, &c. is void in
Law, and by the opinion of *Littleton* the Donor may re-enter for the Condition
broken, for *utile per inutile non vitiatur:*[1] Which being in case of a Condition
for the defeating of an estate, is worthy of observation.

And it is to bee noted, that after the death of the Donor, the Condition
descendeth to the eldest sonne, and consequently his alienation doth extin-
guish the same for ever, wherein the weaknesse of this invention appeareth,
and therefore *Littleton* here saith, that it seemeth that the Donor may re-enter,
and speaketh nothing of his Heires. A man hath issue two sonnes, and maketh
a Gift in taile to the eldest, the Remainder in fee to the puisne, upon condition,
that the eldest shall not make any Discontinuance with Warranty to barre him
in the Remainder, and if he doth, that then the puisne son and his heires shall
re-enter, the eldest make a Feoffment in Fee with Warranty, the father dieth,
the eldest sonne dieth without issue, the puisne may enter, but if the Discontinuance had beene after the death of the father, the puisne could not have
entred. In this case foure points are to be observed. First, as *Littleton* here
saith, the Entrie for the breach of the Condition is given to the father, and
not to the puisne sonne. Secondly, | that by the death of the Father the con-   [379 b]
dition descends to the elder Sonne, and is but suspended, and is revived by
the death of the eldest Sonne without issue, and descendeth to the youngest
Sonne.[2] Thirdly, That the feoffment made in the life of the Father cannot

---

1. [*Ed.:* A useful thing is not vitiated by what is useless,]
2. 41. E. 3. fol.

give away a condition that is Collaterall, as it may doe a right.³ Fourthly, That a Warrantie cannot binde a title of Entrie for a condition broken, (as hath beene said) but if the discontinuance had been made after the death of the Father, it had extinct the condition: Which case is put to open the reason of our authors opinion.

In these last three Sections our Author hath taught us an excellent point of Learning, That when any innovation or new invention starts up, to trie it with the Rules of the common Law, (as our Author here hath done) for these be true Touchstones to sever the pure gold from the drosse and sophistications of novelties and new inventions. And by this example you may perceive, That the rule of the old common Law being soundly (as our Author hath done) applied to such novelties, it doth utterly crush them and bring them to nothing, and commonly a new invention doth offend against many rules and reasons (as here it appeareth) of the common Law, and the antient Judges and Sages of the Law have ever (as it appeareth in our Bookes⁴) suppressed innovations and novelties in the beginning, as soone as they have offered to creepe up, lest the quiet of the common Law might be disturbed: and so have Acts of Parliament done the like,⁵ whereof by the authorities quoted in the margent, you may in stead of many others, upon this occasion take a little taste. But our excellent Author, in all his three Bookes, hath said nothing but *Ex veterum sapientium ore, et more.*⁶

Section 728
Warranty, part 35

| Also it is spoken in the end of the said statute of Glou[cester] which speaketh of the alienation with Warrantie made by the tenant by the courtesie in this forme. Also, in the same manner, the heire of the woman after the death of the father and mother shall not bee barred of action, if hee demandeth the heritage or the marriage of his Mother by writ of Entry,¹ that his father aliened in his mothers time, whereof no fine is levied in the Kings Court. And so by force of

---

3. Vid. Sect. 446.
4. 31. E. 3. Gager deliverance 5. 22. Ass. 12. 38. E. 3. 1. 2. H. 4. 18, &c.
5. (a) I. E. cap. 15. stat. 3. 18. E. 3. cap. 1. & 6. 4. H. 4. ca. 2. 11. H. 6. c. 23. 2. E. 4. cap. 8, &c.
6. [*Ed.:* By the mouth and usage of the wise men of yore.]
1. [*Ed.:* The basic action to recover lands wrongfully held by another.]

the same statute, if the husband of the wife alien the heritage or marriage of his wife in fee with Warrantie, &c. by his Deed in the Countrey, it is cleere Law, that this Warranty shall not bar the heire, unlesse he hath Assets by discent.

"whereof no fine is levied in the Kings Court, &c."

Here are three things worthy of observation concerning the construction of Statutes. First, that (a)[2] it is the most naturall and genuine exposition of a Statute to construe one part of the Statute by another part of the same Statute, for that best expresseth the meaning of the makers.[3] As here the question upon the generall words of the Statute is, whether a fine levied onely by a husband seised in the right of his wife with Warranty shall bar the heire without Assets. And it is well expounded by the former part of the act, whereby it is enacted, that alienation made by Tenant by the curtesie with warranty shall not bar the heire, unlesse assets des-l-cend. And therefore it should be inconvenient [381 b] to intend the statute in such manner, as that he that hath nothing but in the right of his wife should by his fine levied with warrantie barre the heire without assets. And this exposition is *ex visceribus actus*.[4]

Secondly, the words of an act of Parliament must bee taken in a lawfull and rightfull sense, as here the words being (whereof no fine is levied in the Kings Court) are to be understood, whereof no fine is lawfully or rightfully levied in the Kings Court. And therefore (b)[5] a fine levied by the husband alone is not within the meaning of the Statute, for that fine should worke a wrong to the wife, but a fine levied by the husband and wife is intended by the Statute, for that fine is lawfull and worketh no wrong. (c)[6] So the Statute of W.2.c.5. saith *(Ita quod Episcopus Ecclesiam conferat)*[7] is construed, *Ita quod Episcopus Ecclesiam legitimè conferat,*[8] and the like in a number of other Cases in our Bookes. And generally the rule is, *Quod non praestat impedimentum quod de jure non sortitur effectum.*[9]

---

2. (a) Pl. Com. fo. 75. 7. E. 3. 89.

3. Vide Bract. lib. 4. f. 321. Fleta. 5. cap. 34.

4. [*Ed.*: from the innermost part of the act.]

5. (b) Pl. Com. 246. b. Seignior Barkleye's case li. 9. fol. 26. in case del Abbot de Strata mercella.

6. (c) 11. H. 4. 80. 9. E. 4. 12. 21. H. 6. 28. 4. E. 4. 31. 12. H. 4. Formedon 15.

7. [*Ed.*: Provided that the bishop do consecrate the church.]

8. [*Ed.*: Provided that the bishop do lawfully consecrate the church,]

9. [*Ed.*: An impediment which in law gains no effect does not stand.]

Thirdly, that construction must bee made of a statute in suppression of the mischiefe, and in advancement of the remedie, as by this case it appeareth. For a fine levied by the husband only, is within the letter of the Law, but the mischiefe was, the heire was barred of the Inheritance of his mother, by the warranty of his father without Assets, and this act intended to apply a remedy, viz. that it should not barre unless there were assets, and therefore, the mischiefe is to be suppressed, and the remedie advanced, *Et qui haeret in littera, haeret in cortice,*[10] as often before hath beene said.

Epilogue

And know my son, that I would not have thee beleeve, that all which I have said in these Bookes is Law, for I will not presume to take this upon me: But of those things that are not Law, inquire & learne of my wise Masters learned in the Law; notwithstanding albeit that certaine things which are moved and specified in the said Bookes, are not altogether Law, yet such things shall make thee more apt, and able to understand & apprehend the Arguments and the reasons of the Law, &c. For by the Arguments and Reasons in the Law, a man more sooner shall come to the certaintie and knowledge of the Law.

Lex plus laudatur quando ratione probatur.[1]

"I will not presume,"

Here observe the great modestie and mildness of our Author, which is worthy of imitation; for *Nulla virtus, nulla scientia locum suum & dignitatem conservare potest sine modestia.*[2] And herein our Author followed the example of Moses, who was a Judge, and the first Writer of Law, for he was *Mitissimus omnium hominum qui fuit in terris,*[3] as the holy History testifieth of him.

"the Arguments and the reasons of the Law,"

Ratio est anima Legis;[4] for then are we said to know the Law, when we apprehend the reason of the Law, that is, when we bring the reason of the Law

---

10. [*Ed.:* He who sticks to the letter sticks to (only) the bark of the tree.]
1. [*Ed.:* The law is the more praised when it is approved by reason.]
2. [*Ed.:* Without modesty, no virtue, no knowledge, can preserve its place and dignity.]
3. [*Ed.:* The mildest of all men who was in the lands,]
4. [*Ed.:* Reason is the soul of law;]

so to our owne reason, that wee perfectly understand it as our owne, and then and never before, we have such an excellent and inseperable propertie and ownership therin, as wee can neither lose it, nor any man take it from us, and will direct us (the learning of the Law is so chained together) in many other Cases. But if by your studie and industrie you make not the reason of the Law your owne, it is not possible for you | long to retaine it in your memorie. [395 a] And well doth our author couple arguments and reasons together, *Quia argumenta ignota & obscura ad lucem rationis proferunt & reddunt splendida:*[5] and therefore *argumentari & ratiocinari* are many times taken for one. And that our author may not speake any thing without authority (which in these Institutes we have as we take it manifested) his opinion herein also agreeth with that of the learned and reverend Chiefe Justice of the Court of Common pleas. Sir Richard Hankford, (y)[6] *Home ne scavera de quel mettal un campane est, si ne soit bien bate, ne le ley bien conus sans disputation.*[7] And another saith, (*)[8] *Jeo aye dispute cest matter pur la apprender la ley.*[9] So as our author hath made a most excellent Epilogue or Conclusion with a grave advice and counsell, together with the reason thereof, which all students are to know and follow, and with *Scire* and *sequi,*[10] I will conclude our authors Epilogue.

"*Lex plus laudatur quando ratione probatur.*"[11]

This is the fourth time that our author hath cited verses.[12]

When I had finished this worke of the first part of the Institutes, and looked backe and considered the multitude of the conclusions in Law, the manifold diversities between cases & points of learning, the varietie almost infinite of authorities ancient, Constant & Moderne, & withall their amiable & admirable consent in so many successions of ages, the many changes & alterations

5. [*Ed.*: because he brings unknown and obscure arguments to the light of reason and makes them bright:]
6. (y) 11. H. 4. 4. 37.
7. [*Ed.*: One shall not know of what metal a bell is (made) until it well beaten; nor can the law be well known without disputation.]
8. (*) 41. E. 3. 22. Kirton. Vide Sect. 377.
9. [*Ed.*: I have disputed this matter in order to learn the law.]
10. [*Ed.*: to know [and] to follow.]
11. [*Ed.*: The law is the more praised when it is approved by reason.]
12. Vid. Sect. 384. 443. 550.

of the Common Law, & additions to the same, even since our author wrote, by many acts of Parliament, & that the like worke of Institutes had not been attempted by any of our profession whom I might imitate, I thought it safe for me to follow the grave & prudent example of our worthy Author, not to take upon me, or presume that the reader should thinke, that all that I have said herein to be Law: yet this I may safely affirme, that there is nothing herein, but may either open some windowes of the Law, to let in more light to the Student by diligent search to see the secrets of the Law, or to move him to doubt, and withall to enable him to inquire and learne of the Sages, what the Law together with the true reason thereof in these cases is: Or lastly upon consideration had of our old Bookes, Lawes, and Records, (which are full of venerable Dignitie and antiquity) to find out where any alteration hath beane upon what ground the Law hath beene since changed, knowing for certaine, that the Law is unknowne to him that knoweth not the reason thereof, and that the knowne certainty of the Law is the safety of all. I had once intended for the ease of our student to have made a Table to these institutes, but when I considered that Tables and abridegments are most profitable to them that make them, I have left that worke to every Studious Reader. And for a farewell to our Jurisprudent I wish unto him the gladsome light of Jurispidence, the lovelinesse of Temperance, the stabilitie of Fortitude, and the soliditie of Justice.

FINIS

B. The Second Part of the *Institutes*

First published in 1642, *The Second Part of the Institutes of the Lawes of England* was, like Coke's commentary on Littleton, a glossator's project. Coke selected the statutes that then most affected the rights and interests of England and annotated each section of them, not only presenting cases that applied or modified each statute but also describing and amplifying its meaning and application. The most significant of these is undoubtedly his commentary on Magna Carta, which became the essential understanding of its meaning for the next three hundred years.

Magna Carta, as it was signed in 1215, signed again, confirmed, and confirmed again by various kings over the years, was originally a series of concessions to the baronial families and the Church, with some benefits for merchants, townsmen, and the lesser aristocracy. The art of Coke's gloss was, however, to read the terms as they were written, which were in more general words, and to find in them a much more universal set of protections. The form of Magna Carta that Coke set for his text was the form in which Henry III confirmed it, in 1225, primarily because its status as law prior to that time is not so clear as it was after Henry's confirmation of it.

The remaining statutes cover a host of subject matter, particularly interests in land. In that context, though, it is important to see estates in land as much as a constitutional matter as a matter of private law. The relationship among monarch, mesne lord (or an intermediate holder of an estate), tenant, and tenant's servants was the relationship that structured almost all other relationships in the state, including access to Parliament and the courts. The one significant institution outside of that structure ran in a rough parallel, the Church. Statutes dealing with religious matters had an influence that is, perhaps, difficult for the modern mind to grasp. It is at least suggested by the tremendous influence the Church wielded as the largest landlord after the King, a situation that changed only with Henry

VIII's dissolution of the monasteries, and by the Church's control of ecclesiastical offenses, such as heresy, recusancy, or improper use of the sacraments. —*Ed.*

Epigrams from the Title Page:

Jurisperito dixit, In lege quid scriptum est? quomodo legis?
Luc. 10. 26.[1]

Quod non lego, non credo.
August.[2]

Jurisprudentia est juvenibus regimen, senibus
solamen, pauperibus divitiae, & divitibus securitas.[3]

Deo, Patriae, Tibi.
A Proeme to the second Part of the Institutes.

In the first Part of the *Institutes,* following *Littleton* our Guide, we have treated of such parts of the Common Laws, Statutes, and Customes, as he in his three Books hath left unto us. We are in this second Part of the *Institutes* to speak of *Magna Charta,* and many ancient and other Statutes, as in the Table precedent doe appeare.

It is called *Magna Charta,* not that it is great in quantity, for there be many voluminous Charters commonly passed,[1] specially in these later times, longer then this is; nor comparatively in respect that it is greater then *Charta de Foresta,* but in respect of the great importance, and weightinesse of the matter, as hereafter shall appeare: And likewise for the same cause *Charta de Foresta,*

---

1. [*Ed.:* He said unto one learned in the law, what is written in the law? How readest thou? Luke, ch. 10, v. 26.]

2. [*Ed.:* What I do not read, I do not believe. Augustine.]

3. [*Ed.:* Jurisprudence is a discipline for young men, and a solace for old; riches for the poor, and security for the rich.]

1. Marlb. cap. 5. Inspex. 25. Edw. 1. 12. Hen. 3. *Sententia lata super Chartas.* Bract. lib. 3. fol. 291. & lib. 5. fol. 414. Mirror. cap. § Registr. 8 Edw. 3. Itin Pick. Rot. 43. Atons Case. Rot. Pat. 20. Marcii I Edw. 3. de perambulatione for in Coũ Essex Rot. Parl. 22. Edw. 3. nu. 36.

is called, *Magna Charta de Foresta,* and both of them are called *Magnae Chartae libertatum Angliae.*[2]

King *Alexander* was called *Alexander Magnus,* not in respect of the largenesse of his body, for he was a little man, but in respect of the greatnesse of his heroicall spirit, of whom it might be truly said,

Mens tamen in parvo corpore magna fuit;[3]

So as of this Great Charter it may be truly said, that it is *Magnum in parvo.*[4]

And it is also called *Charta libertatum Regni;*[5] and upon great reason it is so called of the effect, *Quia liberos facit:*[6] Sometime for the same cause, *Communis libertas,*[7] and *le Chartre des franchises.*[8]

There be four ends of this Great Charter, mentioned in the Preface, *viz.* 1. The honour of Almighty God, &c. 2. The safety of the Kings Soule; 3. The advancement of holy Church; and 4. The amendment of the Realme: foure most excellent ends, whereof more shall be said hereafter.

The Ends.
Sapiens incipit a fine.[9]

By Charter bearing date the 11. day of *February,* in the 9. yeare of King Henry the third and secondly, by that Charter established by Authority of Parliament then sitting, and so entered into the Parliament Roll; the Witnesses to the said Charter were 31. Lords Spirituall, *viz. Stephen Langton* Archbishop of *Canterbury, E.* Bishop of *London, I. B.* of *Bath, P.* of *Winchester, H.* of *Lincoln, Robert of Salisbury, W.* of *Rochester, W.* of *Worcester, I.* of *Ely, H.* of *Hereford, R.* of *Chicester, William* of *Exeter,* Bishops. The Abbot of *S. Edes,* the Abbot of *S. Albons,* the Abbot of *Battaile,* the Abbot of S. *Augustines* in *Canterbury,* the Abbot of *Evesham,* the Abbot of *Westminster,* the Abbot of *Burghe* S. *Peter,* the Abbot of *Reading,* the Abbot of *Abindon,* the Abbot of *Malmesbury,* the Abbot of *Winchcombe,* the Abbot of *Hyde,* the Abbot of *Certefey,* the Abbot of *Shernborn,* the Abbot of *Cerne,* the Abbot of *Abbotebury,* the Abbot of *Middleton,* the Abbot of *Selbie,* the Abbot of *Cirencester;* And 33. of the No-

By what Authority, and when.

2. [*Ed.:* Great charters of the liberties of England.]
3. [*Ed.:* Nevertheless, great was the mind in the little body;]
4. [*Ed.:* A great thing in a small package.]
5. [*Ed.:* The charter of the liberties of the realm.]
6. [*Ed.:* Because it makes men free.]
7. [*Ed.:* Common liberty.]
8. [*Ed.:* the Charter of liberties.]
9. [*Ed.:* Reason begins with the ends.]

bility, *viz. Hubert de Burgo* Chiefe Justice of *England,* and 32. Earles and Barons, *viz. Randall* Earle of *Chester* and *Lincoln, William* Earle of *Salisbury, William* Earle *Warren, Gilbert* of *Clare* Earle of *Glocester* and *Hertford, William de Ferrars* Earle of *Derby, William Mandevile* Earle of *Essex, H. de Bigod* Earle of *Norffolk, William* Earle of *Albemarle, H.* Earle of *Hereford, John* Constable of *Chester, Robert de Ros, R. Fitzwalter, Robert de Vipount, William de Bruer, R. de Mountfitchet, P. Fitzherbert, William de Aubeine, Robert Gresly, Reignald de Brehus, John de Movenne, J. Fitz-Alen, Hugh de Mortimer, Walter de Beauchamp, William de S. John, Peter de Mololacu, Brian de Lisle, T. de Multon, Richard de Argentein, Jeffrey de Nevill, William Maudint, John de Baalim,* and others.

There were many of the great Charters, and *Charta de Foresta,* put under the Great Seale, and sent to Archbishops, Bishops, and other men of the Clergie, to be safely kept, whereof one of them remain at this day at *Lambeth,* with the Archbishop of *Canterbury.*

The great providence and policy for preservation of it.

Also the same was entred of Record in a Parliament Roll.

And after King Edward the first by Act of Parliament[10] did ordain that both the said Charters should be sent under the Great Seale, as well to the Justices of the Forest, as to others, and to all Sheriffes, and to all other the Kings Officers, and to all the Cities through the Realme, and that the same Charters should be sent to all the Cathedrall Churches, and that they should be read and published in every County four times in the yeare in full County,[11] *viz.* the next County day after the feast of S. *Michael,* and the next County day after *Christmas,* and the next County day after *Easter,* and the next County day after the Feast of S. *John.*

The quality.

It was for the most part declaratory of the principall grounds of the fundamentall Laws of *England,* and for the residue it is additionall to supply some defects of the Common Law; and it was no new declaration: for King *John* in the 17. yeare of his raigne had granted the like, which also was called *Magna Charta,* as appeareth by a Record before this Great Charter made by King Hen. 3.[12]

Home ne suer' Mordanc' apud Westmonasterium des terres in auter Countie,

---

10. 25 Edw. 1. cap. 1.

11. 25. Edw. I. cap. 3. 28. Edw. I. ca. 2. & 17.

12. Mat. Par. fo. 246, 247, 248.

car ceo ser encont' Lestatut de Magna Charta sinon que illa assisa semel interminata fuit coram Justic'.[13,14]

Also by the said Act of 25. E. I[15] (called *Confirm' Chartar'*)[16] it is adjudged in Parliament that the Great Charter, and the Charter of the Forest should be taken as the Common Law.

Soon after the making of this Great Charter, the young King by evill Counsell fell into great mislike with it, which *Hubert de Burgo summus Justiciarius Anglia*[17] perceiving (who in former times had been a great lover, and well deserving Patriot of his Country, and learned in the Laws (for *Rot. claus. II.* Hen. *3. membr. 44.* I finde that he, and many others were Justices *Itinerant* in *5* Hen. *3.*[18] and I have seen a fine levied before him, and sixe other Judges, between *Stephen de Wamcesle,* and the Abbot of *Hales*) yet meaning to make this a step to his ambition (which ever rideth without reines) perswaded and humored the King that he might avoid the Charter of his Father King *John* by duresse, and his own great Charter, and *Charta de Foresta* also, for that he was within age when he granted the same, whereupon the King in the 11. yeare of his raign, being then of full age, got one of the great Charters, and of the Forest into his hands, and by the counsell principally of this *Hubert* his Chiefe Justice, at a Councell holden at *Oxford,* unjustly cancelled both the said Charters, (notwithstanding the said *Hubert de Burgo* was the primier Witnesse of all the temporall Lords to both the said Charters) whereupon he became in high favour with the King, insomuch as he was soon after (*viz.* the 10. of *December,* in the 13. yeare of that King, created to the highest dignity that in those times any Subject had) to be an Earle, *viz.* of *Kent.* But soon after (for flatterers and humorists have no sure foundation) he fell into the Kings heavy indignation, and after many fearfull and miserable troubles, he was justly, and according to Law sentenced by his Peeres in open Parliament, and justly degraded of that dignity which he unjustly had obtained by his

How, and upon what grounds it hath been impugned.

---

13. [*Ed.:* One shall not sue a mort d'ancestor at Westminster for lands in another County, for that would be against the statute of Magna Carta, unless the assize was at the time undetermined before the justices.]

14. Pasch. 5 Hen. 3. tit. Mordaunc' f. 53.

15. Stat. 25. Edw. 1. Confirm. Chart.

16. [*Ed.:* Confirmation of the charters.]

17. [*Ed.:* Hubert de Burgo, Chief Justice of England.]

18. Rot. claus. 11 Hen. 3 membr. 44. 5 Hen. 3.

counsell for cancelling of *Magna Charta,* and *Charta de Foresta.*[19] And the King by his Charter granted, *Quod nos firmiter & integre tenebimus judicium de Huberto de Burgo per Barones dictum;*[20] he was buried in the Frier predicants where *Whitehall* is now built, so as no Monument remains of him at this day.

In this advice *Hubert de Burgo* either dissembled his opinion, or grosly erred (as ever ambitious flattery bedazles the eye, even of them, that be learned) first, for that a King cannot avoid his Charter, albeit he make it when he is within age, for in respect of his royall and politique capacity as King, the Law adjudgeth him of full age. Secondly, it being done by Authority of Parliament, and enrolled of Record, it was strange that any man should think that the King could avoid them in respect he was within age. Thirdly, it was to no end to cancell one where there were so many, or to have cancelled all, when they were of Record in the Parliament Roll, or to have cancelled Roll and all, when they were, for the most part, but declaratories of the ancient Common Laws of *England,* to the observation, and keeping whereof, the King was bound and sworn. What successe those potent and opulent Subjects, *Hugh Spencer* the Father, and Son had, for giving rash and evill counsell to King Edward the second *enconter la forme de la grand Chartre,*[21] I had rather you should read then I should declare.

Exilium turgonis la Spencer patris & filii.[22]

After the making of *Magna Charta,* and *Charta de Foresta,* divers learned men in the Laws,[23] that I may use the words of the Record, kept Schooles of the Law in the City of *London,* and taught such as resorted to them, the Laws of the Realme, taking their foundation of *Magna Charta,* and *Charta de Foresta,* which as you have heard, the King by ill advice sought to impeach.

The King in the 19 year of his raign,[24] by his Writ, commanded the Maior and Sheriffes of *London, Quod per totam Civitatem London clamari faciant & firmiter prohiberi, ne aliquis scholas tenens de legibus in eadem Civitate de caetero ibidem leges doceat, & si aliquis ibidem fuerit hujusmodi scholas tenens, ipsum sine dilatione cessare fac'; Teste Rege, &c. 11. die Decembris, Anno Regni sui decimo*

---

19. Rot. claus. 17 Hen. 3. m. 1. & 2. Rot. Pat. 17 Hen. 2. m. I. à tergo & 12.

20. [*Ed.:* That we shall firmly and wholly keep the judgment given by the barons concerning Hubert de Burgh.]

21. [*Ed.:* against the form of the great charter.]

22. [*Ed.: The Banishment of Hugh de Spencer, father and son.*]

23. Rot. claus. Anno 19 Hen. 3. m. 22.

24. 19 Hen. 3. ubi supra.

nono.[25] But this Writ took no better effect then it deserved, for evill counsell being removed from the King, he in the next yeare, *viz.* in the 20. yeare of his raigne compleat, and in the one and twentieth yeare current, did by his Charter under his great Seale confirme both *Magna Charta,* and *Charta de Foresta,* he being then 29. years old. And after in the 52. yeare of his raigne established and confirmed both the same by Act of Parliament,[26] with the clause, *Quod contravenientes per Dominum Regem, cum convicti fuerint, graviter puniantur.*[27] Hereby shall some opinions and resolutions in our Books be the better understood, which speak of alienations without license before or after 20 Hen. 3.[28] which yeare was named for that the King then confirmed the said great Charter, and in like manner did King Edward the first by Act of Parliament in the 25. year of his raign: and the said two Charters have been confirmed, established, and commanded to be put in execution by 32. severall Acts of Parliament in all.

This appeareth partly by that which hath been said, for that it hath so often been confirmed by the wise providence of so many Acts of Parliament.

And albeit judgements in the Kings Courts are of high regard in Law, and *Judicia*[29] are accounted as *Juris dicta,*[30] yet it is provided by Act of Parliament, that if any judgement be given contrary to any of the points of the great Charter, or *Charta de Foresta,* by the Justices, or by any other of the Kings Ministers, &c. it shall be undone, and holden for nought.[31]

And that both the said Charters shall be sent under the great Seale to all Cathedrall Churches throughout the Realm there to remain, and shall be read to the people twice every yeare.[32]

The highest and most binding Laws are the Statutes which are established by Parliament;[33] and by Authority of that highest Court it is enacted (onely

Of what high estimation it hath been.

---

25. [*Ed.:* That they cause to be proclaimed and firmly prohibited throughout the city of London that no one holding a law school in the same city should from thenceforth teach laws there, and if anyone should keep such schools there, make him stop without delay. Witness the king, etc., on the eleventh day of December in the nineteenth year of his reign.]

26. Marlb. cap. 5. 15 Edw. 4. 13.

27. [*Ed.:* That those contravening, if convicted, shall be grievously punished by the lord king.]

28. 20 Ass. p. 17. 14 Hen. 4. 2, & 3. Bro. Alien. sans license. 10.

29. [*Ed.:* Judgments.]

30. [*Ed.:* Statements of the law.]

31. Confirm. Chart. 25 Edw. 1. ca. 1. & 2. Vet. Mag. Chart. 2. part, fol. 35.

32. 25 Edw. I. ubi supra.

33. 42 Edw. 3. cap. 1. 25 Edw. 1. ubi supra.

to shew their tender care of *Magna Charta,* and *Charta de Foresta) That if any Statute be made contrary to the great Charter, or the Charter of the Forest, that shall be holden for none:* By which words all former Statutes made against either of those Charters are now repealed; And the Nobles and great Officers were to be sworn to the observation of *Magna Charta,* and *Charta de Foresta.*

Magna fuit quondam Magnae reverentia Chartae.[34]

We in this second Part of the *Institutes,* treating of the ancient and other Statutes have been inforced almost of necessity to cite our ancient Authors, *Bracton, Britton,* the *Mirror, Fleta,* and many Records, never before published in print, to the end the prudent Reader may discerne what the Common Law was before the making of every of those Statutes, which we handle in this work, and thereby know whether the Statute be introductory of a new Law, or declaratory of the old, which will conduce much to the true understanding of the Text it selfe. We have also sometime in this and other Parts of the *Institutes,* cited the *Grand Custumier de Normandy,* where it agreeth with the Laws of *England,* and sometime where they disagree, *ex diametro,*[35] being a Book compounded as well of the Laws of *England,* which King *Edward* the Confessor gave them, as he that Commenteth upon that Book testifieth (as elswhere we have noted) as of divers Customes of the Duchie of *Normandie,* which book was composed in the raign of King Henry the third *viz.* about 40. yeares after the Coronation of King *Richard* the first, 3. *Septembris, Anno* 1. of his raign, *Anno Dom.* 1189. about 138. yeares after the Conquest. See that Book *cap.* 22. *fo.* 29. *a.* and the Comment upon the same, & *cap.* 112. In which *Custumier* a great number of the Courts of Justice, of the originall Writs, and of many other of the titles of the Laws of *England,* are not so much as named or mentioned. And seeing we have in these, and other parts of our *Institutes,* cited the Laws and Statutes of divers Kings before the Conquest, and in the Conquerors time, we have thought good for the ease of the Reader, to set down the times wherein those Kings lived, and deceased. *Inas* began to raign *Anno Dom.* 689. and deceased 726. *Aluredus, alias Alfredus, alias Elfredus,* began to raign *Anno Dom.* 872. and deceased 901.[36] Of this *Alured* it is thus written,[37]

---

34. [*Ed.:* Great was once the reverence of the great charter.]
35. [*Ed.:* from the opposite side,]
36. In Historia Eliensi fol. 38. lib. 2.
37. Cl. Caius D. m. Cant.

Aluredus acerrimi ingenii princeps per Grimbaldum & Johannem doctissimos Monachos tantum instructus est, ut in brevi librorum omnium notitiam haberet, totumque novum & vetus Testamentum in eulogiam Anglicae gentis transmutaret (cujus translationis pars nobis feliciter accidit.)[38] This learned King in advancement of Divine and humane knowledge, by the perswasion of those two Monks founded the famous University of *Cambridge. Edwardus,* son of the said *Alured,* began to raign *Anno Dom.* 901. and deceased 924. [a] *Ethelstanus, alias, Adelstane* eldest son of the said *Edward* began to raign *Anno Dom.* 924. and deceased 940. [b] *Edmundus* began to raign *Anno Dom.* 940. and deceased 946. [c] *Edgarus* began to raign *Anno Dom.* 959. and deceased 975. [d] *Etheldredus* began to raign *Anno Dom.* 979. and deceased 1016. [e] *Canutus* began to raign *Anno Dom.* 1016. and deceased 1035. [f] *Edwardus* began to raign *Anno Dom.* 1042. and deceased 1066. [g] *Willielmus Bastardus* began to raign *Anno Dom.* 1066. and deceased 1087.

Some fragments of the Statutes in the raigns of the abovesaid Kings doe yet remain, but not onely many of the Statutes, and Acts of Parliament, but also the Books and Treatises of the Common Laws both in these and other Kings times, and specially in the times of the ancient *Brittons* (an inestimable losse) are not to be found.

It is to be observed that in *Domesday Haroldus,* who usurped the Crown of *England,* after the decease of King *Edward* the Confessor, is never named *per nomen Regis, sed per nomen Comitis Haroldi, seu Heraldi;*[39] And therefore we have omitted him.

In citing of the abovesaid Laws originally written in the Saxon tongue, we have referred you to M. *Lambard,* who accurately and faithfully translated the same into Latin, one page containing the Saxon, and the next the Latin, and is in print (for our manner is not to cite anything, but so to referre the Reader, as he may easily finde it;) *Sed ut unicuique suus tribuatur honos,*[40] all those Statutes in the raigns of all the abovesaid Kings were of ancient time plainly and truly translated into Latin, (whereof we have a very ancient, if not the first Manuscript) which no doubt did not a little abbreviate M. *Lambards* pains.

a *Fortis, sapiens, & fortunatus: Danos expuli: & Angliam in Monarchiam reduxit.*

b *Martir apud Hoxon̄ olim Hegilsdon.*

c *Pacificus, Rex excellentissimus.*

d Named in Domesday. Glouc' Ecclesia de Evesham. Adelredus.

e In Domesday he is ever written *Cnut' Rex.*

f He is ever called in Domesd. *Episcopus S. Edw. Cestr: Rex Edwardus dedit Regi Griffino terram quae jaccbat trans aquam quae De vocatur.*

g He is in Domes. written Willielmus Rex, *vel* Willielmus, *vel* W. Rex.

---

38. [*Ed.:* Alfred, a ruler of the sharpest ingenuity, was so educated by the two most learned monks Grimbald and John that he had brief notes of all books, and translated the whole of the Old and New Testament into English speech (part of which translation happily remains to us).]

39. [*Ed.:* By the name of king, but by the name of Earl Harold, or Herald.]

40. [*Ed.:* But in order to do each of them his honour,]

Upon the Text of the Civill Law, there be so many glosses and interpretations, and again upon those so many Commentaries, and all these written by Doctors of equall degree and authority, and therein so many diversities of opinions, as they do rather increase then resolve doubts, and incertainties, and the professors of that noble Science say, That it is like a Sea full of waves. The difference then between those glosses and Commentaries, and this which we publish, is, that their glosses and Commentaries are written by Doctors, which be Advocates, and so in a manner private interpretations: And our Expositions or Commentaries upon *Magna Charta,* and other Statutes, are the resolutions of Judges in Courts of Justice in judiciall courses of proceeding, either related and reported in our Books, or extant in judiciall Records, or in both, and therefore being collected together, shall (as we conceive) produce certainty, the Mother and Nurse of repose and quietnesse, and are not like to the waves

Regula.   of the Sea, but *Statio bene fida peritis:*[41] for *Judicia sunt tanquam Juris dicta.*[42]

Finis Proemii.[43]

But now let us peruse the Texit selfe.

---

41. [*Ed.:* A trusty harbor for the learned:]
42. [*Ed.:* Judgments are like statements of the law.]
43. [*Ed.:* The end of the Preface.]

Magna Charta,
Edita *Anno nono* H.3.

‖ HENRY, by the Grace of God, King of England, Lord of Ireland, Duke of [1]
Normandy and Aquitaine, and Earl of Anjou, to all Archbishops, Bishops, Abbots, Priors, Earls, Barons, Sheriffs, Provosts, Officers, and to all Bailiffs, and
other our faithful Subjects, which shall see this present Charter, Greeting: Know
Ye, that We, unto the honour of Almighty God, and for the salvation of the
souls of our Progenitors and Successors Kings of England, to the advancement
of Holy Church and amendment of our Realm, of our meer and free will, have
given and granted to all Archbishops, Bishops, Abbots, Priors, Earls, Barons,
and to all Freemen of this our Realm, these Liberties following, to be kept in
our Kingdom of England for ever.

"Henry, by the Grace of God, King of England, &c."

Concerning the Styles of the Kings of England, both before and after this
King, and how often they altered the same, see in the first part of the Institutes,
Sectione prima.[1]

"Archbishops, Bishops, Abbots, Priors, Earls, Barons, &c."

This or the like particular direction, this King and his Progenitors before him
used; and so did Edw. 1. Edw. 2. &c. Edw. 3. King Ric. 2. in his Letters Patents
used a more generall, and compendious direction, viz. *Omnibus ad quos praesentes literae pervenerint, &c.*[2] which direction is used to this day, saving in
Charters of Creation of Dignities, the directions to this day, are *Archiepiscopis,
Episcopis, Ducibus, Marchionibus, &c.* and *hiis testibus,*[3] in the end.

"We, unto the honour of Almighty God, and for the salvation of the souls, of
our Progenitors and Successors Kings of England, to the advancement of Holy
Church and amendment of our Realm."

Here bee foure notable causes of the making of this great Charter rehearsed.
1. The honour of God. 2. For the health of the Kings soul. 3. For the exaltation
of holy Church; and fourthly, for the amendment of the Kingdome.

Note not onely the preamble of this Charter, & of the forest, but the bodies of the Charters themselves are contained in the Charter of King *John,* An. 17. of his reign, *Mat. Par.* Pag. 246. *Quae ex parte maxima leges antiquas & regni consuetudines continebant. pag. 244.*

1. The first Part of the Institutes, *Sect. 1.*
2. [*Ed.:* To all to whom the present letters shall come, etc.]
3. [*Ed.:* to the archbishops, bishops, dukes, marquesses, etc. [and] these being witnesses.]

There be those excellent Laws contained in this great Charter, and digested into 38. Chapters, which tend to the honour of God, the safety of the Kings conscience, the advancement of the Church, and amendment of the King-dome, granted and allowed to all the Subjects of the Realme.

[2] | "our meer and free will."

These words were added, for that King John, as hath been said, made the like Charter in effect, and sought to avoid the same, pretending it was made by duress.

This great Charter is divided into 38. Chapters.

Chapter 1

First, We have granted to God, and by this our present Charter have confirmed, for Us and our Heirs for ever, that the Church of England shall be free, and shall have all her whole Rights and Liberties inviolable. We have granted also, and given to all the Freemen of our Realm, for Us and our Heirs for ever, these Liberties under-written, to have and to hold to them and their Heirs, of Us and our Heirs for ever.

Sanctum Dei,[1] *imprimis, Ecclesiam liberam facio, ita quod nec vendam, nec ad firmam ponam, nec mortuo Archiepiscopo sive Episcopo, vel Abbate aliquid accipiam de dominio Ecclesiae, seu de hominbus ejus, donec successor in eam ingrediatur, et omnes malas consuetudines quibus regnum Angliae injuste opprimebatur, inde au-fero.*[2]

"We have granted to God."

We have graunted to God: when any thing is granted for God it is deemed in Law to be graunted to God, and whatsoever is graunted to his Church for his honour, and the maintenance of his Religion and service, is graunted for and to God; *Quod datum est Ecclesiae, datum est Deo.*[3]

---

1. Inter leges seu Institutiones Regis Hen. 1. Cap. 1.

2. [*Ed.:* What is holy to God, and above all the church I make free, so that I shall neither sell nor farm, nor upon the death of an archbishop or bishop or abbot shall I take anything from the dominion of the church, or from their men, until their successor enters upon it, and I abolish therefrom all evil customs by which the realm of England was unjustly oppressed.]

3. [*Ed.:* That which is given to the Church is given to God.]

And this and the like were the formes of ancient Acts and Graunts, and those ancient acts and graunts must be construed and taken as the Law was holden at that time when they were made.[4]

Here in this Charter, both in the title and in divers parts of the body of the Charter, the King speaketh in the plurall number, *concessimus;*[5] The first King that I read of before him, that in his graunts wrote in the plurall number, was King John, Father of our King Henry the third other Kings before him wrote in the singular number, they used *Ego,*[6] and King John, and all the Kings after him, *Nos.*[7]

"for Us and our Heirs for ever."

These words were added to avoid all scruples, that this great Parliamentary Charter might live and take effect in all successions of ages for ever. More of this word (heires) hereafter in this Chapter: When *Pro nobis, haeredibus & successoribus nostris*[8] came in, shall be shewed in his fit place.

"that the Church of England, &c."

This at the making of this great Charter, extended not to Ireland, nor to any of the Kings forain Dominions; but by the Law of Poynings,[9] made by the Authority of Parliament in Ireland, in *Anno* 11. Hen. 7. all the Laws and Statutes of this Realm of England before that time had or made do extend to Ireland, so as now Magna Charta doth extend into Ireland.

"That the Church of England shall be free."

That is, that all Ecclesiasticall persons within the Realm, their possessions, and goods shall be freed from all unjust ex-l-actions and oppressions, but [3]

---

4. See the first part of the Institutes. *Sect.* 1.

5. [*Ed.:* We have granted.]

6. [*Ed.:* I.]

7. [*Ed.:* we.]

8. [*Ed.:* For ourself, our heirs and successors,]

9. [*Ed.:* This is Poyning's Law, an Irish statute that enforced English statutes there; apparently 10 Hen. 7.]

notwithstanding should yeeld all lawfull duties, either to the King or to any of his Subjects, so as *libera*[10] here, is taken for *liberata*,[11] for as hath been said, this Charter is declaratory of they ancient Law and Liberty of England, and therefore no new freedom is hereby granted, (to be discharged of lawfull tenures, services, rents, and aids) but a restitution of such as lawfully they had before, and to free them of that which had been usurped and incroached upon them by any power whatsoever; And purposely, and materially, the Charter saith *Ecclesia*, because *Ecclesia non moritur*,[12] but *moriuntur Ecclesiastici*,[13] and this extends to all Ecclesiasticall persons of what quality or order soever.

"and shall have all her whole Rights."

That is that all Ecclesiasticall persons shall enjoy all their lawful jurisdictions, and other their rights wholly without any diminution or substraction whatsoever; and *jura sua*[14] prove plainly, that no new rights were given unto them, but such as they had before, hereby are confirmed;[15] and great were sometimes their rights, for they had the third part of the possessions of the Realme, as it is affirmed in a Parliament Roll.

"Liberties inviolable."

Libertates[16] are here taken in two senses. 1. For the Laws of England so called, because *liberos faciunt*,[17] as hath been said. 2. They are here taken for priviledges held by Parliament, Charter or prescription more then ordinary;[18] and in this sense it is taken in the Writ *De libertatibus allocandis*,[19] and in another Writ

---

10. [*Ed.*: free.]
11. [*Ed.*: freed.]
12. [*Ed.*: The Church does not die,]
13. [*Ed.*: Ecclesiastical persons die,]
14. [*Ed.*: their rights.]
15. Rot. Parliam. 4. Ric. 2. Nu. 13.
16. [*Ed.*: Liberties.]
17. [*Ed.*: it makes men free,]
18. Regist. fol. 19. & 262. F. N. B. fo. 229.
19. [*Ed.*: For allowing liberties.]

De libertatibus exigendis in itinere,[20] but it is but *libertates suas,*[21] such as of right they had before; *Jura Ecclesiae publicis aequiparantur.*[22]

Every Archbishoprick and Bishoprick in England are of the Kings foundation, and holden of the King *per Baroniam,*[23] and many Abbots and Priors of Monasteries were also of the Kings foundation, and did hold of him *per Baroniam,* and in this right the Archbishop and Bishops, and such of the Abbots and Priors as held *per Baroniam,* and called by Writ to Parliament, were Lords of Parliament; and this is a right of great honour that the Church, viz. the Archbishop and Bishops now have. *Ecclesia est infra aetatem, & in custodia Domini Regis, qui tenetur jura & haereditates suas manutenere & defendere;*[24] And in other Records it is said,[25] *Ecclesia quae semper est infra aetatem fungitur semper vice minoris, nec est juri consonum quod infra aetatem existentes, per negligentiam custodum suorum exhaeredationem patiantur seu ab actione repellantur.*[26]

They are discharged of purveyance for their own proper goods.[27]

And this was the ancient Common Law, and so declared by divers Acts of Parliament, and there is a Writ in the Register for their discharge in that behalfe:[28] And this is not restrained by the said Act of 27. Hen. 8. for thereby it is provided that the Purveyor shall observe the Statutes for them provided, so as where the Purveyor is prohibited to purvey by any Statute, the said Act of 27. Hen. 8. setteth him not at liberty.

And true it is, that Ecclesiaticall persons have more and greater liberties then other of the Kings Subjects, wherein, so set down all, would take up a whole Volume of it self, and to set down no example, agreeth not with the

---

20. [*Ed.:* For liberties demanded in the eyre.]

21. [*Ed.:* their liberties,]

22. [*Ed.:* The rights of the Church are equivalent to public rights.]

23. [*Ed.:* by a barony.]

24. [*Ed.:* The Church is under age, and in the wardship of the lord king, who is bound to maintain her rights and inheritances.]

25. Glanv. I. 7. c. 1. Bract. lib. 3. fol. 226. 1. 5. fo. 427. TR. 22. Edw. 1. in com. Banc. Rot. Fleta lib. 2.

26. [*Ed.:* The Church, which is always under age, is always in the position of a minor, and it is not consonant with law that those who are under age should suffer a disinheritance or be barred from an action through the negligence of their guardians.]

27. See hereafter c. 21.

28. 14. Edw. 3. cap. 12. stat. 2. 18. Edw. 3. cap. 4. 1 Ric. 2. cap. 3. 8 Edw. 3. fol. 26. Regist. 289. vid. 27 2. Hen. 8. c. 24 vid. postea. c. 21.

Office of an Expositor; therefore some few examples shall be expressed, and the studious Reader left to observe the rest as he shall reade them in our Books, and other Authorities of Law.

If a man holdeth Lands of Tenements, by reason whereof he ought (upon election, &c.) to serve in a temporall office,[29] if this man be made an Ecclesiasticall person within holy Orders, he ought not to be elected to any such office, and if he be, he may have the Kings Writ for his discharge, and the words of the Writ are observable, *Rex, &c. Cum secundum legem & consuetudinem Regni nostri Angliae Clerici infra sacros ordines constituti ad tale officium eligi non debeant, nec hactenus consueverunt, &c.,*[30] and the reason thereof is expressed in the Writ, *Quia juri non est consonum, quod hii qui salubri statu animarum, &c. (in tali loco, &c.) deserviunt, alibi extra (eundem locum) secularibus negotiis compellantur.*[31]

[4]   ¶ By this writ it appeareth that this was the ancient common Law, and custome of England and had a sure foundation,[32] *Nemo militans Deo, implicet se negotiis secularibus, ut ei placeat cui se probavit.*[33] Ecclesiasticall persons have this priviledge that they ought not in person to serve in warre. Also Ecclesiasticall persons ought to be quit and discharged of Tolles and Customes, Avirage, Pontage, Paviage, and the like, for their Ecclesiasticall goods, and if they be molested therefore, they have a writ for their discharge, by which writ it appeareth that this was the ancient Common Law of England.[34] *Rex, &c. cum personae Ecclesiasticae secundum consuetudinem hactenus in regno nostro usitatam, & approbatam; ac ad telonium, paviagium & muragium, &c. de bonis suis Ecclesiasticis alicubi in eodem regno praestand' nullatenus teneantur, &c.*[35]

---

29. Regist. 58. F.N. B. 175.

30. [*Ed.:* The king, etc. Whereas, according to the law and custom of our realm of England, clerks in Holy Orders ought not to be elected to such an office, nor have been accustomed [to be so elected] before now, etc.]

31. [*Ed.:* because it is not consonant with law that those who, for the good estate of souls, etc., should be compelled to serve in secular business (in such a place, etc.) elsewhere outside (the same place).]

32. 2. Timot. c. 2.

33. [*Ed.:* No one serving God should implicate himself in secular affairs, so that he may please him to whom he has pledged himself.]

34. Litt. fol. 20. Regist. fol. F.N.B. 227.

35. [*Ed.:* The king, etc. Whereas ecclesiastical persons, according to the custom used and approved until now in our realm, are in no way liable to pay tolls, pavage and murage, etc. out of their ecclesiastical goods anywhere in the same realm, etc. (Pavage was a toll to maintain roads; murage a fee to maintain walls.)]

If any Ecclesiasticall person be in feare or doubt that his goods or Chattells, or Beasts, or the goods of his farmor, &c. should be taken by the ministers of the King, for the businesse of the King, he may purchase a protection *cum clausula nolumus.*[36,37]

Distresses shall not be taken by Sheriffs or other of the Kings ministers in the inheritance of the Church wherewith it was anciently endowed, but otherwise it is of late purchase.[38]

If any Ecclesiasticall person knowledge a statute Merchant or statute staple or a recognizance in the nature of a statute staple, his body shall not be taken by force of any processe thereupon, and for more surety thereof the writ thereupon to take the body of the conusor is *si laicus sit.*[39]

If a person bee bound in a recognizance in the Chancery or in any other Court, &c. and he pay not the sum at the day, by the Common Law, if the person had nothing but Ecclesiasticall goods, the recognizee could not have had a *levari fac*[40] to the Sheriffe to levie the same of these goods, but the writ ought to be directed to the Bishop of the Dioces to levie the same of his Ecclesiasticall goods.[41]

*[42] In an action brought against a person (wherein a *Capias*[43] lieth) for example, an account, the Sheriffe returns *quod clericus est beneficiatus, nullum habens laicum feodum,*[44] in which he may be summoned, in this case the plaintiffe cannot have a *Capias* to the Sheriffe to take the body of the person, but he shall have a writ to the Bishop to cause the person to come and appeare. But if he had returned *quod clericus est nullum habens laicum feodum,*[45] then is a *Capias* to be granted to the Sheriffe, for that it appeared not by the returne that he had a benefice, so as he might bee warned by the Bishop his Diocesan,

36. [*Ed.:* with the clause *nolumus* (we do not wish).]
37. F.N.B. 29. Regist. 289.
38. See the exposition of the statute of Artic. Cler. cap 9.
39. [*Ed.:* if he be a layman.]
40. [*Ed.:* Writ of execution to the sheriff to seize lands and goods and sell them or collect their rents until the debt is satisfied.]
41. Regist. 300. F.N.B. 266. a. 16. E. 3. proces 165. Regist. judi. 22.
42. (*) 18. Edw. 2. Proc. 205. 9 Edw. 3. 30. 24. Edw. 3. 44. 25. Edw. 3. 44. 29. Edw. 3. 44. 32. Edw. 3. Proces 58. 34. Edw. 3. *Scir. fac.* 153. 45. Edw. 3. 6. 47. Edw. 3. 14. 21. Hen. 6. 16. Regis. judic. 6. *Artic. Cler.* c. 9.
43. [*Ed.:* an arrest warrant.]
44. [*Ed.:* that he is a beneficed clerk having no lay fee,]
45. [*Ed.:* that he is a clerk having no fee,]

and no man can be exempt from justice. See more of this matter Artic. Cleri. cap. 9.

Secundum legem & consuetudinem Regni Angliae clerici in decenna, &c. poni non debeant, vel ea occasione distringi vel inquietari non consueverunt:[46] and Ecclesiasticall persons are not bound to appeare at Tournes or viewes of Frank-pledge.[47,48]

But hereof this little taste shall in this place suffice, with this, that as the over-flowing of waters doe many times make the river to lose his proper chanell, so in times past Ecclesiasticall persons seeking to extend their liberties beyond their true bounds, either lost or enjoyed not that which of right belonged to them.

"We have granted also, and given to all Freemen of our Realm, &c."[49]

These words (*omnibus liberis hominibus regni*[50]) doe include all persons Ecclesiasticall and temporall and temporal incorporate politique or naturall, nay they extend also to villeines, for they are accounted free against all men saving against the Lords.

[51] "these Liberties under-written."

Here it is to be observed that the aforesaid clause that concerned the Church onely, is in favour of the Church generall without any restraint, but this clause that concernes all the Kings subjects hath a restraint by reason of this word (*subscriptas*[52]) which restraineth *libertates* to the 38. Chapters of this great Charter.

46. [*Ed.:* According to the law and custom of the realm of England, clerks ought not to be put into dozins, etc., and are not accustomed to be distrained or vexed by reason thereof. (A dozin managed a frankpledge.)]

47. [*Ed.:* Combinations of ten men, all of whom pledge the good conduct of themselves and their fellows; method of social control imposed on all Saxons after the conquest.]

48. Marlebr. c. 10. Briton. f. 19. B. Fleta. li. 2. c. 45. Rot. brevi. an. 2. Ric. 2. part 2. m. 8.

49. Litt. sect. 189.

50. [*Ed.:* all the free men of the realm.]

51. *See the statute of 34. E. I. de tallagio non conc. cap.4. which is more generall.

52. [*Ed.:* underwritten.]

*53 Note that courts of justice are also called *libertates,* because in them the Lawes of the Realm *que liberos faciunt,*54 are administred.

| "Heirs." [5]

At this time *Haeredes*55 were taken for *Successores*56 and *Successors* for *Haeredes.*

"of Us."

In this place these words are not inserted to make a legall tenure of the King, but to intimate that all liberties at the first were derived from the Crowne.

Chapter 2

If any of our Earls or Barons, or any other, which hold of Us in chief by Knight's Service, die, and at the time of his death his Heir be of full age, and oweth to us Relief, he shall have his inheritance by the old Relief; that is to say, the Heir or Heirs of an Earl for a whole Earldom, by one hundred pound; the Heir or Heirs of a Baron, for an whole Barony, by one hundred marks; the Heir or Heirs of a Knight, for one whole Knight's Fee, one hundred shillings at the most; and he that hath less shall give less, according to the old Custom of the Fees.

"If any of our Earls or Barons."

At this time there was never a Duke, Marquesse, or Viscount in England, for if there had been, they had (no doubt) been named in this Chapter; the first Duke that was created since the Conquest, was Edward the Black Prince, in 11 Edw. 3. Robert de Vere Earle of Oxford, was in the 8. year of Richard the second, created Marquesse of Dublin in Ireland, and he was the first Marquesse that any of our Kings created.[1]

The first Viscount that I finde of Record, and that late in Parliament by

53. ªMich. 17. E. 1. in Com. banc. rot. 221. leic. fee the first part of the Institut. Sect. 1.
54. [*Ed.:* which make men free,]
55. [*Ed.:* Heirs.]
56. [*Ed.:* Successors.]
1. Rot. Parliam. anno 11. Edw. li. 5. fo. 1. in casu principis. Rot. Par. 8. Ric. 2.

that name, was John Beaumont, who in the 18. yeare of H.6. was created Viscount Beaumont.[2]

"Earls."[3]

Dicuntur Comites, viz. quia in Comitatu sive à societate nomen sumpserunt, qui etiam dici possunt Consules a consulendo: Reges enim tales sibi associant ad consulendum & regendum populum Dei, ordinantes eos in magno honore, & potestate, & nomine, quando accingunt eos gladius, ringis gladiorum, &c, gladius autem significat defensionem Regni & Patriae.[4]

"Barons."

Sunt & alii potentes sub Rege qui dicuntur Barones, hoc est, robur belli:[5,6] And where some have thought that *Baro* is no Latin word, we find it in *Tullies* Epistles, *Apud Patronem, Et alios Barones te in maxima gratia posui.*[7] *Galfridus Cornwall tenet manerium de Burford de Rege, per servitium Baroniae,*[8] But it is to be understood, that if the King give Land to one and his heirs, *Tenend de rege per servitium Baroniae,*[9] he is no Lord of Parliament untill he be called by Writ to the Parliament. These which are Earls and Barons have offices and duties annexed to their dignities of great trust and confidence, for two purposes, 1. *Ad consulendum tempore pacis.*[10] 2. *Ad defendendum Regem & Patriam tempore belli.*[11] And prudent Antiquity hath given unto them two ensignes to

---

2. Rot. Pat. 18 H. 6. 12 Febr.

3. Bract. lib. 1. fol. 5. b. Fleta lib. 1. cap. 5. Briton. 68. b.

4. [*Ed.: Comites* (earls) are so called because they take their name from *comitatus* (county or company) or from society (fellowship), who might also be called consuls from counselling; for kings associate such people with themselves in governing and ruling the people of God, investing them with great honour, power and name, when they gird them with swords, sword-belts, etc. For the sword signifies the defence of the realm and the country.]

5. [*Ed.:* There are other powerful men under the king who are called barons, that is, *robur belli* (the strength of war).]

6. Bract. *ubi. supr. l.*

7. Ad Artic. Ep. 5. Inquis. 40. E. 3. [*Ed.:* I have put you in the greatest favor with Patro and the other *barones* (blockheads).]

8. [*Ed.:* Geoffrey of Cornwall holds the manor of Burford of the king by service of a barony.]

9. [*Ed.:* To be held of the king by baronial service.]

10. [*Ed.:* To give counsel in time of peace.]

11. [*Ed.:* To defend the king and the country in time of war.]

resemble, and to put them in minde of their duties;[12] for first they have an honourable and long robe of scarlet resembling Counsell, in respect whereof they are accounted in Law, *De magno concilio Regis*.[13] 2. They are girt with a sword that they should ever be | ready to defend their King and Country: [6] And it is to be observed that in ancient Records the Barony (under one word) included all the Nobility of England,[14] because regularly all Noblemen were Barons, though they had a higher dignity, and therefore of the Charter of King Edward the first in the Exposition of this Chapter hereafter mentioned, the conclusion is, *Testibus Archiepiscopis, Episcopis, Baronibus, &c.*[15] So placed, in respect that *Barones* included the whole Nobility: and the great Councell of the Nobility, when there were besides Earles and Barons, Dukes and Marquesses, were all comprehended under the name *De la Councell de Baronage*.[16,17]

"or any other, which hold of Us in chief"

It is worthy of observation, with what great judgement this Statute concerning reliefe is penned; For by the Act of Parliament called, The Assise of Clarendon, Anno 10. Hen. 2. Anno Domini 1164. it is thus enacted; *Archiepiscopi, Episcopi, & universae personae Regni, qui de Rege tenent in capite, habeant possessiones suas de Rege, sicut Baroniam, & inde respondeant Justiciariis & ministris Regis, & sicut caeteri Barones debent interesse curiae Regis cum Baronibus, &c.*[18] Therefore this Chapter beginneth, *Si quis Comitum, vel Baronum;*[19] So as (as to reliefe of an Earle or Baron) it is not materiall that he hath *Baroniam*, unlesse he be Noble, that is, Earle or Baron, and others being not Noble, but holding in *Capite*,[20] shall pay reliefe according to the Knights fees which he hath. See hereafter Cap. 31. who shall be said to hold in *Capite*.

---

12. Inter record. in Turri 27. Aug. 5. H. 4. the Earle of Northumb. Case, &c.
13. [*Ed.*: Of the king's great council.]
14. Glanv. 1. 9. c. 4.
15. [*Ed.*: Witnessed by the archbishops, bishops, barons, etc.]
16. [*Ed.*: Of the council of baronage.]
17. 5. H. 4. *ubi sup.*
18. [*Ed.*: The archbishops, bishops, and all persons of the realm who hold of the king in chief shall have their possessions of the king as a barony, and shall answer therefore to the king's justices and ministers as other barons ought to do in the king's court with the barons, etc.]
19. [*Ed.*: If any of the earls or barons.]
20. [*Ed.*: In chief.]

"by Knight's Service,"

For this see the first part of the Institutes, Sect. 103. 112, 154, 157, 126, 127. whereunto you may adde this Record following.

Per Assisam Johannes de Moyse, qui est infra, aestatē, implacitat Thom' de Weylaund & Marg' ux' ejus pro uno Messuag.ii. molendinis, iiii. acris prati, & xlii.s. red. in Eastsmithfield ext' Algate.[21] *Ipsi voc' ad war' Rad' de Berners, qui war' & dic' quod nihil clamat nisi custod. eo quod Johannes pater dicti Johannis tenuit de eo praedicta ten' per homag' & servic' vi.d. & inveniendi quendam hominem pro eo in turri London. cum arcubus & sagittis per quadraginta dies tempore guerrae. Johannes dic' quod tenet ten' praed. per homagium & servitium quorundam calcariorum vel vi.d. pro omni servic'. Et sic omittendo multa ex utraque parte manifeste patebit per verd' Jur' & per Jud' Cur' quid in hac ass.*

Veredictum.   *terminatum fuit. Jur' dic' quod praedicta ten' tenent' de praedicto Radulpho per homagium & servic' unius paris calcariorū deauratorum vel sex den'*[*22] *& inven' quend' hominē pro ipso Radulpho in turri Lond. cum arcub' & sagit' per xl. dies*

The Judgement.   *tempore guerrae in boreal' Angulo turris praedicta pro omni servic'.* Et quia compertū est, &c. quod Radulphus cognoscit in responc' quod praedict' herestenere debet eadem ten' per pradict' homag' & servic' praedict' calcar' vel sex denar' & per serjantiā inveniedi unū hominē pro eo in praed' turri per xl. dies, & manifeste liquet quod huōdi minores serjantiae quae debent fieri pro Dominis suis de quibus tenent tenementa sua per alios quā seipsos nullā inde dabunt custodiā eisdē Dominis, nec dare debent licet iidem Domini infra etatem haeredū per negligentiam propinquorum parentū hujusmodi custodias occupaverunt, & iste Radulpus non potest dedicere quod unquā aliquā habuit seisinam de praedict' Custod' nisi per occupationem suam & negligentiam parentum praedict' haeredis antecessoris sui dum infra aetatem fuit, & non alio jure. Considerat' est quod praedict' Johannes rec' inde seis. &c. & damn' Cx.l.iv.s.vii.d. &c. Valor terr' per annum x.x.l.x.d.*[23]

---

21. Hil. 8. E. 1. in Banc. Rot. 86. Midd. Which Record is cited in the first part of the Instit. *Sect. 157. in marg.*

22. *Tr. 17. E. 1. in Banc. Rot. 29. Salop Walt. de, Hoptons Case. Acc.

23. [*Ed.:* By the assize, John de Moyse, who is under age, impleads Thomas de Weylaund and Marg. his wife, for one messuage, two mills, four acres of meadow, and forty-two shillings-worth of rent in East Smithfield without Aldgate. They vouch to warranty Ralph de Berners, who warrants and says that he claims nothing except the wardship, inasmuch as John, father of the said John, held the aforesaid tenements of him by homage and the service of sixpence and finding a certain man for him in the tower of London

See the first part of the Institutes, Sect. 155. & 157. and note the diversitie between such a tenure of the King, for in that case it should be a tenure by Grand-serjanty,[24] and that Grand-serjanty, for the greatest part, is to be done within the | Realme, and Knights service out of the Realme, as Littleton there saith.   [7]

"full age."

See the first part of the Institutes, Sect. 104.

"the old Relief; that is to say, &c."

Concerning the word *Relevium*,[25] vide 1. Part Institut. Sect. 103. It appeareth that the reliefe here set down, is the ancient relief, and was certain at the Common Law; But there had been of long time an heavy incroachment of an incertain reliefe at will and pleasure, which under a fair term was called *rationabile Relevium*,[26] and this Act had just cause to say, *Per Antiquum re-levium*,[27] for in the raign of Hen. 2. Grandfather to Hen. 3. the King exacted

---

with bows and arrows for forty days in time of war. John says that he holds the tenements aforesaid by homage and the service of certain spurs, or sixpence for all service. And so, omitting much on both sides, it will manifestly appear by the verdict of the jury and the judgment of the court what was determined in this assize. The jurors say that the aforesaid tenements are held of the aforesaid Ralph by homage and the service of one pair of gilt spurs or sixpence, and of finding a certain man for the selfsame Ralph in the tower of London with bows and arrows for forty days in time of war, in the north corner of the aforesaid tower, for all service. And because it was found, etc. that Ralph confessed in his answer that the aforesaid heir ought to hold the aforesaid tenement by homage and the aforesaid service of spurs or sixpence, and by the serjeanty of finding one man for him in the aforesaid tower for forty days, etc., and it manifestly appears that such petty serjeanties ought to be performed for their lords, of whom they hold their tenements, by persons other than themselves, no wardship thereof is or ought to be given to the same lords, even if the same lords have occupied such wardships when the heirs were under age through the negligence of their nearest relatives, and Ralph could not deny that he ever had any seisin of the aforesaid wardship except by his occupancy and the negligence of the relatives of the aforesaid heir of his ancestor, while he was under age, and not in another right: it was [therefore] decided that the aforesaid John recover seisin thereof, etc. and damages of £110. 4s. 7d., etc. The value of the land £20. 0s. 10d. a year.]

24. See 11 H. 4. 72. & 24. E. 3. 32.
25. [*Ed.:* Relief.]
26. [*Ed.:* reasonable Relief.]
27. [*Ed.:* By the old relief.]

an incertain reliefe, for so Glanvill saith,[28] who wrote in his time, *De Baroniis vero nihil certum Statutum est, quia juxta voluntatem & misericordiam Domini Regis solent Baroniae Capitales de releviis suis Domino Regi satisfacere.*[29] And Glanvill under the name of Baronies doth include Earledomes also, so the reliefe of all the nobility was taken as incertain at that time, and therefore how necessary it was that the ancient reliefe should be restored is evident.

"that is to say, the Heir or Heirs."

Of this word (heire) see the first part of the Institutes, Sect. 1. whereunto you may adde that which was there omitted, concerning the Antiquity of descents, which the Germanes had agreeable with the ancient Laws of the Britons, continued in England to this day, out of that faithfull and learned Historian, who of the ancient Germanes saith;[30] *Haeredes successoresq; sui cuique liberi, & nullū Testamentum: si liberi non sunt, proximus gradus in possessione, fratres, patrui, avunculi, &c.*[31] Wherein we observe three things. 1. That for Default of children and brethren, the Uncle, &c. and not the Father, or any in the right line ascendent should inherit, but the collaterall onely. 2. That by the Common Law no Testament or last Will could be made of Land. 3. That of ancient time *Successores*[32] were *Synoyma*[33] with *haeredes.*[34] But in this ancient Statute it is pertinently said, *haeres,*[35] and not *successor,* for every Bishop of England hath a Barony, and so had many Abbots and Priors (in respect whereof they were Lords of Parliament) and yet they paid no reliefe, because their successors came to it by succession and not as heire by inheritance; And this Act saith, *Habeat haereditatem suam.*[36] And they are seised in *Jure Episcopatus*

---

28. Glanv. 1. 9. c. 4. Ockham cap. *Quod non absolvitur. Custummer de. Norm. Cap.* 34. and the Comment thereupon.

29. [*Ed.*: Nothing certain is laid down for baronies, because the chief baronies are to make satisfaction to the lord king for their reliefs at the lord king's mercy and pleasure.]

30. *Tacitus de moribus Germanorum.*

31. [*Ed.*: Everyone has his children as his heirs and successors, and no testament; and if there are no children, the next degree in possession, brothers, the father's brothers, uncles, and so forth.]

32. [*Ed.*: Successors.]

33. [*Ed.*: Synonymous.]

34. [*Ed.*: heirs.]

35. [*Ed.*: heirs.]

36. [*Ed.*: Let him have his inheritance.]

Monasterii, &c. de Comitatu integro & de Baronia integra.[37] The Barons in Domesday are accounted amongst the Tenants in Chiefe. Vide Glanv. lib. 9. cap. 6 Magna Charta cap. 31.

It is to be understood that of ancient time (as it evidently appeareth by this Chapter, and by our Books)[38] every Earledome and Barony were holden of the king in Capite, which proveth that both the Dignities of the Earle and the Baron, and the Earldome and Barony were derived from the Crown.[a39] And it is to be known that the fourth part of the yearly valus of an Earledome, a Barony, and the living of a Knight, was the ancient reliefe that this Chapter speaketh of. And for that of ancient time,[b40] a Knights living was esteemed at 20.l. per ann. (which in those dayes was sufficient to maintain the dignity of a Knight) his ancient[c41] relief was 5.l. which is the fourth part of his living by one year.

The yearly value of a Barony was to consist of 13. Knights fees, and a quarter, which by just account amounted to 400. Marks by the year, therefore his reliefe was as is here set down 100. Marks.

See an ancient Manuscript intituled, *De modo tenendi Parliamentum, &c. tempore Regis Edwardi filii Regis Etheldredi, cui quidem modus suit per discretiores Regni cora Willielmo Duce Normannorū & Conquestore & Rege Angliae ipso conquestore hoc tempore praecipiente recitat'& per ipsum approbat', &c.*[42] Of the Authority and Antiquity whereof you may reade in the fourth part of the Institutes Cap. of the Court of Parliament, *Et hic infra.*[43]

Now every Earledome consisted of the value of an entire Barony and an halfe, which amounted to 20. Knights fees amounting to 400.l. per annum, and therefore his ancient reliefe here called *Antiquum relevium,* being the fourth part of the yearly value of his Earledome was 100.l. In that excellent Charter which King H. 1. | made on the day of his Coronation, *Communi* [8]

---

37. [*Ed.:* In right of the bishopric of the monastery, etc. of the whole earldom and of the whole barony.]

38. Bract, lib. 2. fol. 76. a. 84. 16. E. 3. Eschaunge 2. 20. E. 3 Assise. 122. & tit. avowr. 126. 22. E. 3. 18. 18. Ass. Pl. ult. 24. E. 3. 66. nontenure 16. 46. E. 3. forfeit. 18. 10. H. 7. 19. a.

39. *a* See the first part of the Institutes, sect 95. Cambden Brit. 122. Acc.

40. *b* 1 E. 2. cap. 1. 7. H. 6. 15.

41. M. 2. Jac. lib. 11. Metcalfs Case. fol. 33, 34.

42. [*Ed.:* 'Of the manner of holding Parliament, etc.', in the time of King Edward, son of King Æthelred, which 'Manner' was recited before William, duke of Normandy and conqueror and king of England, by command of the conqueror himself at that time, and by him approved, etc.]

43. [*Ed.:* And this [is dealt with] below.]

Concilio & assensu Baronum Regni Angliae[44] amongst other things it is thus contained, *Omnes malas consuetudines, quibus Regnum Angliae opprimebatur, inde aufero, quas malas consuetudines exinde suppono. Si quis Baronum meorum, Comitum, five aliorum, qui de me tenet, mortuus fuerit, haeres suus non redimet terram suam, sicut faciebat tempore fratris mei, sed legitima & justa relevatione relevabit eam, sicut homines Baronum meorum legitima & justa relevatione re-levabunt terras suas a Dominis suis, &c. Legem*[45] *Regis Edw. vobis reddo cum illis emendationibus, quibus Pater meus emendavit consilio Baronum suorum.*[46]

By this Charter it appeareth, 1. that there was a lawfull and just reliefe, to bee paid by the Earle, and Baron, which implyeth a proportionable reliefe according to the value of the living, by reason of this word (*Justa*)[47] which cannot be intended of an uncertaine reliefe, but of the just reliefe, upon the Computation of so many Knights fees contained in the *Modus*,[48] whereunto this Charter hath relation. 2. It appeareth that there was an unjust reliefe, in the time of William Rufus his Brother, which upon search we have found in an ancient Manuscript in the Librarie of Arch-Bishop Parker, which we have seene, and will transcribe, in that Language that we finde it.

De releefe al cunte que al Roy afert 8. chivals enfrenees, & ensebees, & 4. Hauberts & 4. Hawmes & 4. escues, & 4. launces, & 4. espees les aultres, & 4. chaceurs & 4. palefrees à freins eta chevestre.[49]

De reliefe a barun 4. chivals les 2. exfrenes & enseeles & 2. hauberts & 2. hawmes & 2. escus, & 2. espees & 2. launces, & les autres 2. chivals un chaceur & un palfrey a freins & a chevestres.[50]

---

44. [*Ed.:* By the common council and the assent of the barons of the realm of England.]

45. *i. Edw. filii Etheldredi. [*Ed.:* Edward II, the Confessor.]

46. [*Ed.:* All bad customs, whereby the realm of England was oppressed, I take away and from henceforth put down. If any of my barons, earls, or others, who hold of me, should die, his heir shall not redeem his land as was done in the time of my brother but shall take it up with a rightful and just relief, just as the men of my barons take up their lands from their lords with lawful and just relief, etc. I render to you the law of King Edward, with the amendments which my father made by the advice of his barons.]

47. [*Ed.:* Just.]

48. [*Ed.:* Manner.]

49. [*Ed.:* The relief of an earl which belongs to the king: eight horses with bridles and saddles, four hauberks, four helms, four shields, four lances, and four swords. The others, four hunters and four palfreys with bridles and halters.]

50. [*Ed.:* The relief of a baron: four horses, two with bridles and saddles, two hauberks, two helms, two shields, two swords, and two lances. The others, two horses, a hunter and a palfrey, with bridles and halters.]

De reliefe a vavassur a son lige senior doit estre quite per le chival son pier; tiel come il avoit jour de son mort, & per son hawme, & per son escu & per son haubert, & per son lance, & sul fuit disaparaile, que il noust chiual ne arme juste quite per C. sol.[51]

Le relief al villian le meliour avoir que il averad 2. Chivals, 2. Boefs, 2. Vaches durrad a son seignior & puis sont touts les villains in frankpledge.[52]

In K. Canutus time, *Relevatio Comitis fuit 8. equi, 4. sellati, 4. insellati, & galeae 4. & lorice. 4. cum 8. lanceis, & totidem scutis, et gladii.*[53] *4. et*[54] *CC. mancae auri.*[55]

Postea[*56] *thani Regis, qui ei proximus sit, 4. equi, 2. sellati, 2. non sellati. 2. gladii. 4. lancee, et totidem scuta, et galea cum lorica sua, et 50. mancae auri.*[57]

Et: mediocris thani equus cum apparatu suo et arma sua et halstang in Westsexa, &c.[58]

Lastly, this Chapter of Magna Charta is but a restitution and declaration of the ancient Common Law, and that *antiquum relevium* of the Earle, and Baron was certaine; so now joyning both together, this certaine reliefe here set downe is *legitimum, justum & antiquum relevium,*[59] mentioned in the *Modus, &c.*

It is said that there be ancient precedents in the Exchequer, that he that held by a Dukedome, which being valued at two Earles livings, should pay according to the proportionall and just fourth part of his living by yeare, 2co. li. And a Marques that held by a Marquedoome, who should have two Baronies, should pay for his reliefe 200. marks. What the value of the living of

51. [*Ed.:* The relief of a vavasour (vassal to a baron) to his liege lord: he ought to be quit by his father's horse, the one he had on the day of his death, and by his helm, his shield, his hauberk, and his lance, and if he was unequipped so that he had no horse or arms, then he shall be quit by one hundred shillings.]

52. [*Ed.:* The relief of a villein: he shall give his lord the best thing that he had, two horses, two oxen, two cows, and then are all the villeins in frankpledge.]

53. Inter leges Canuti. cap. 97.

54. *CC. marc.

55. [*Ed.:* The relief of an earl was eight horses, four saddled and four unsaddled, four helms, and four hauberks, with eight lances and as many shields and swords, and two hundred gold coins (*mancae*).]

56. *i. Baronis.

57. [*Ed.:* Afterwards the king's theigns, who were nearest to him: four horses, two saddled and two not, two swords, four lances, and as many shields and helms with his hauberk, and fifty gold coins (*mancae*).]

58. [*Ed.:* And the middle theigns one horse with its furniture and his arms and *halstang* in Wessex, etc.]

59. [*Ed.:* lawful, just and ancient relief,]

a Viscount should be, I have not heard, but certaine it is he should pay the fourth part of the yeerely value of his Viscountesdome.

But all this is to be intended, where the King granteth a Dukedome, Marquesdome, Earledome, Viscountesdome, or Barony to hold, as here it is spoken, *de nobis in Capite per servitium militare, viz. De Comitatu integro & de Baronia integra, & qui minus habuerit, minus det secundum antiquam con-suetudiē feodorū.*[60]

[9] | But in some cases the heire of an Earle, or a Baron may pay the reliefe expressed in this statute, albeit he hath not so many knights fees, as is above-said;[61] so if upon the creation of the Earle the King did grant any Mannors, Lands, or Annuity *per Comitatum, & nomine Comitis,*[62] or *sub nomine & honore Comitis,*[63] or the like, he should pay, C. li. for reliefe, and so of the Baron, *mutatis mutandis*[64] for a speciall reservation may derogate from the Common Law.

But otherwise it is, if the Mannors, Lands, or annuity be granted unto the Earle, *ut idem Comes statum & honorem Comitis melius manutenere & supportare possit,*[65] or, *ad sustinendum nomen et onus,*[66] or the like; for then the Earle holdeth not *per Comitatum,* or, *nomine Comitis.*

But now the ancient manner of creation is altered, for now, when the King creates a Duke, a Marques, an Earle, a Viscount, or Baron, he seldome creates a Dukedome, Marquisdome, Earledome, &c. *ad sustinendum nomen & onus,*[67] viz. to grant him Mannors, Lands, tenements, &c to hold of him in chiefe, for commonly upon creations the King grants to them created an annuity; And therefore at this day Noblemen doe pay such reliefes,[68] as other men use to doe, in respect of their tenures, for as the heire of a Knight shall not pay reliefe, unlesse he have a Knights fee, &c. so the heire of an Earle, or Baron,

---

60. [*Ed.:* of us in chief by knight-service, that is to say, for a whole earldom and a whole barony, and whoever shall have less shall give less according to the old custom of the fees.]

61. Com. Mich. 14. E. 3. rot. 8. ex pte rem. Thes. Com. Hil. 25. E. 3. rot 4. ex pte rem. Thef. Com. Hil. 7. H. 4. rot. 2. rot. cart. 36. E. 3. nu. 8. the Earle of Cambridges case.

62. [*Ed.:* by an earldom, and in the name of an earl.]

63. [*Ed.:* under the name and honour of an earl,]

64. [*Ed.:* changing what ought to be changed.]

65. [*Ed.:* so that the same earl might better maintain and support the estate and honour of an earl,]

66. [*Ed.:* to support the name and burden,]

67. [*Ed.:* to support the name and burden,]

68. 6. H. 8. Dier. 2.

shall not pay reliefe by this great Charter, unlesse he hath an Earledome, or Baronie, as is aforesaid.[69]

"one hundred shillings at the most;"

And this was the ancient reliefe for a Knights fee, and so was holden in the reigne of Hen. 2. for Glanvil saith,[70] *dicitur autem rationabile relevium alicujus juxta consuetudinem regni de feodo unius militis per centum solidos,*[71] so as the fee of a Knight at that time was certaine, viz. the fourth part of his living *per annum,*[72] and so ought, as appearreth, the relief of the Nobility to have been in curtainty, though they were not permitted to have it so, which favored of the power of a conqueror to keepe the Nobility under, or to make himselfe the more amiable to them.

"according to the old Custom of the Fees."

This is observable, that these certaine and proportionable rates are according to the ancient custome of reliefes.

[73] A Knight holds land by Grand Serjantie, he is not within this Statute, and therefore shall not pay the reliefe of a Knight declared by this act, but the heire being of full age at the decease of his ancestor, shall pay the value of his lands for one yeere which is his *Primer season.*[74]

But here it is demanded, seeing Littleton saith, that tenure by Cornage, if it be of any other Lord then the King, is Knights service, what reliefe the Heir of such a tenant shall pay, or whether he shall pay any reliefe at all. Littleton in the same place saith, that tenure by Cornage draweth unto it ward, and mariage, and speaketh nothing of reliefe, and by this act reliefe is to be payed according to the quantity of the Knights fee,[75] viz. *De feodo militis integro per*

---

69. 17. E. 2 prer. regis cap. 3.

70. Glanvil lib. 9. cap. 4. lib. 9. fol. 124. Antony Lowes case. Stat. 1. E. 2. de militibus. 1. Part of the Institut. sect. 103. 112. 113. 154. 157. *vide* Bracton *ubi supra.* Britton cap. 69. Fleta. 1. 3. c. 17.

71. [*Ed.:* The reasonable relief of anyone according to the law and custom of the realm is said to be by one hundred shillings for one knight's fee.]

72. [*Ed.:* by the year.]

73. *11. H. 4. 72. b. 1. part of the Institut. sect. 154. 157. Litt. sect. 156.

74. [*Ed.:* Payment due to the Crown by a tenant-in-chief on the accession to the fee.]

75. Mich. 18. E. 1. in Banco rot. 84. Westmerl. & *eodem anno.* rot. 158. Cumberland. 10. Swinborns case *acc. cornagium.*

centum solidos & qui minus habuerit,[76] but a tenure by Cornage hath no such quantities, *nec suscipit majus & minus,*[77] and therefore tenure by Cornage, though it be Knights service, is not within this Statute; Hereof you may read a Record to this Effect.

Inter Johannem Craistoke querentem versus Idoneam de Leybourne quae distrinxit ipsum per averia pro relevio dando, pro terris in Dunston, Brampton yanene which, Eseclyve, et Boulton, *quae valent* C. li. per ann. *quae tenet de ea per homagium et Cornagium. Et ipse dicit quod talis est consuetudo patriae de Westm. quod haeredes post mortem antecessorum suorum debent relevare terras suas dominis de quibus,* &c. *scilicet solvendo pro relevio quantum terrae valent per annum, quae de ipsis dominis tenentur, nisi de minori ipsis dominis possunt satisfacere, unde ipsa advocat captionem pro relevio secundum praedictam consuetudinem,* &c.

Johannes negat talem esse consuetudinem, sed concedit, quod tenet tenementa
[10] *prae-|-dicta per Cornag'xxv. s. vi.d. et dicit quod antecessores sui prius duplicarunt antecessor.ipsius Idoneae solvendoLi.s. Ipsa dicit quod cum Johannes cogn', quod ipse tenet praedicta ten' de ipsa per cornagiū, ad quod hujusmodi relevium mere est accessor', ratione consuet' praedictae. Et dic' quod idem Johannes exigit tale relevium versus tenentes suos in eadem patria a tempore quo non, &c. Et de consuet' uterq', pon' se super patriam. Ideo ven' Jur' in Crō S. Johannis Baptistae, &c. Insuper Idonea dic' quod duplex est tenura in Com' Westmerl. scilicet, una per Albā firmā, et alia per Cornagium.*[78] *Et quod tenentes per Albam firmam post*

---

76. [*Ed.:* For a whole knight's fee by one hundred shillings, and whoever shall have less, less.]

77. [*Ed.:* nor does it admit of greater and less.]

78. [*Ed.:* Between John Craistoke, plaintiff, against Idonea de Leybourne, who has distrained him by cattle for relief to be given for lands in Dunston, Brampton, Yanenewhich, Eseclyve, and Boulton, which are worth one hundred pounds a year, and which he holds of her by homage and cornage. And she says that there is this custom of the region of Westmoreland, that heirs after the death of their ancestors ought to relieve their lands from the lords of whom, etc., that is to say, paying for relief as much as the lands which they hold of the same lords are worth by the year, unless they can satisfy the lords with less; and therefore she avows the taking for relief according to the aforesaid custom, etc.

John denies this to be the custom, but concedes that he holds the aforesaid tenements by cornage of twenty-five shillings and eightpence. And he says that his ancestors paid double, paying the ancestors of the selfsame Idonea fifty-one shillings. She says that, since John has confessed that he holds the aforesaid tenements of her by cornage, to which such relief is purely accessory, by reason of the aforesaid custom; and she says that the same John demanded such relief against his tenants in the same region from time immemorial, etc., (she prays judgment). And each of them puts himself on the country concerning the custom. Therefore let a jury come on the morrow of St. John the Baptist, etc. Idonea further says that

mortem antecessorum suorum debent duplicare firmam suam tantum. Et tenentes per Cornagium post mortem antecess. suorum tenentur reddere valorem terrarum suarum unius anni. Et Johannes e contra dic' quod consuetudo patriae est quod haeredes non solvant nisi duplicando Cornaginm, &c.[79]

Bracton li. 2. fo. 84. cap. 36. nu. 2.[80] *Et imprimis de feodo militari quale sit rationabile relevium antiquum de feodo militari distinguitur in Carta libertatum, cap.2.&c.*[81] And in the same Chapter, nu.7. saith thus, *De serjantiis vero nihil certum exprimitur, quid vel quantum dare debeant haeredes, ideo juxta voluntatem Dominorum Dominis satisfaciant pro relevio, dum tamen ipsi Domini rationem & mensuram non excedant.*[82]

Certain it is, that he that hold by Castle-guard shall pay no Escuage, for Escuage must be rated according to the quantity of the Knights fees,[83] as for a whole Knights fee, or half a Knights fee, &c. and of that nature is not Castle-guard. Littleton treating of Castle-guard, saith,[84] that in all cases where a man holdeth by Knights service, such service draweth to it Ward and Marriage, and speaks not there of relief.

Chapter 3

But if the Heir of any such be within Age, his Lord shall not have the Ward of him, nor of his Land, before that he hath taken of him Homage; and after such an Heir hath been in Ward, when he is come to full Age, that is to say, to the Age of one and twenty years, he shall have his Inheritance without Relief, and without Fine: So that, if such an Heir being within Age, be made

---

tenure in the county of Westmoreland is of two kinds, that is to say, one by blanch-farm (white rent) and the other by cornage; and that the tenants by blanch-farm after their death of their ancestors ought only to double their rent, whereas the tenants by cornage after the death of their ancestors are bound to render the value of their lands for one year. John, to the contrary, says that the custom of the region is that heirs shall not pay more than double the cornage, etc.]

79. *Alba firma Cornagium.*

80. Bract. 1. 2. fo. 84 vide Glanv. l. 7. cap 9. Flet. 1. 3. cap. 17. Brit. fo. 177, 178, &c.

81. [*Ed.:* First, concerning a knight's fee, what is a reasonable old relief for a knight's fee is distinguished in the charter of liberties (Magna Carta), ch. 2.]

82. [*Ed.:* Concerning serjeanties, nothing certain is laid down as to what or how much heirs ought to give, but they shall satisfy the lords according to the will of the lords, provided that the same lords do not exceed a reasonable measure.]

83. Lit. sect. III.

84. Lit. sect. 97. Lit. sect. III.

Knight, yet nevertheless his Land shall remain in the keeping of his Lords, unto the term aforesaid.

"Heir."

This Statute is onely to be intended of an heire male, whereof *haeres*[1] is derived: and who shall be *haeres,* &c. See the first part of the Institutes. lib. 1. sect. 1, 2, 3. *Custumier de Norm.* 99. and the Expositions upon the same.[2]

"before that he hath taken of him Homage."[3]

For homage see the first part of the Institutes. sect. 85. and it is to be observed that in England and France it is called *Homage, Homagium,* and in Italy *Vassalagium.*

Some have thought that these words are to be understood that the heire within age shall not be in Ward untill the Lord hath taken the homage of some of the auncesters of the Ward, so as the auncester of the heire may die in the homage of the Lord: for in a Writ of Ward brought by the Lord, it is a good plea to say that the auncester died not in his homage, and the Statute [11] saith not *Antequam homagium | suum ceperit,*[4] but *homagium*[5] generally; and, say they, if the Lord should receive homage of the heire, he should not be in Ward at all.[6]

But this is not the right intendment of these words, but the Statute meant that the homage should be taken of the heire himselfe, and that for the benefit of the heire and so doth it appear by[a7] our old Books that wrote some after this Statute, and *contemporanea expositio est fortissima in lege,*[8] and so do the words themselves of this Law import, and the reason thereof is notable, which

---

1. [*Ed.:* heirs.]

2. 35 H. 6. 52.

3. See the Custumier de Norm. cap. 29. and the Comment upon the same. & cap. 32 & le Latine Com. sul. 48. b.

4. [*Ed.:* Before he has taken his homage.]

5. [*Ed.:* homage.]

6. 16 E. 3 Relief 6. & 10.

7. *a* Brac. 1. 2. fo. 41. 71, 81, 89, 252. Brit. fol. 171. Fleta, 1. 1. ca. 9 Mirror, ca. 952. Glanvi. lib. cap. 1. & 6. 13 Edw. 1. gard. 136. 31 Edw. gard. 155.

8. [*Ed.:* a contemporaneous exposition is the strongest in law,]

was, that before the Lord should have benefit of Wardship, he should be bound to two things;[b9] To warrant the Land to the heir and to that end the heir might have a Writ, *De homagio capiendo;*[10] 2. To acquit him from service and other duties to be done and paid to all other Lords, both which the Lord was bound to do[c11] as the law was then holden) if the Lord accepted *homage de droit*[12] of his tenant, (in such sort as the Lord is, if he receiveth *homage auncestrel*[13] at this day) but otherwise it is of *homage in fait;*[14,15] *Homagium est juris vinculum, quo quis astringitur ad warrantizandum, defendendum, & acquietandum tenentem suum in seisina versus omnes per certum servitum in donatione nominatum & expressum; & etiam vice versa, quo tenens astringitur ad fidem Domino suo servand: & servitium debitum faciend.*[16,17] We have an ancient Manuscript of a case adjudged in a Writ of Customes and Services betweene Alexander of Poulton, and Robert de Norton, that homage is of an higher nature to divers purposes then escuage. 1.[f18] For that homage bindeth to warranty, which escuage doth not. 2. Homage is so solemne as that it cannot be done again as long as the Tenant that made it liveth, but escuage may be given every other year.[g19] And Littleton saith that homage is the most honourable service, and humble service of reverence, and yet it is true that escuage taking it for service, draweth to it homage.

[h20] But at the Common Law, if a man holding Land by Knights service, had made a gift in frank marriage, and the donee had died, his heir within age, the heir should be in Ward before any homage received, *Quia Dominus*

---

9. *b* Trin. 4. E. 2. fo. 65. b. in Libro meo William St. Quintin's case. Homage auncestel only bindeth to warranty, but homage *in fait* bindeth to acquitall. See the first part of the institutes, sect. 143. fol. 101. Verb. & ad receive homage.

10. [*Ed.:* a writ to compel a lord to receive a tenant's homage.]

11. *c* Tr. 9. E. 2. *Ubi supra.*

12. [*Ed.:* homage of right.]

13. [*Ed.:* Homage held by a tenant and that tenant's ancestors.]

14. [*Ed.:* homage in fact.]

15. *d* Bract. fol. 78. Brit. & Fleta *ubi supra.* 47. E. 3. gar. 99. Temp E. 1. garr. 90.

16. [*Ed.:* Homage is a legal bond whereby someone is constrained to warrant, defend, and acquit his tenant in seisin against all persons by a certain service named and expressed in the gift; and also, conversely, whereby the tenant is constrained to keep faith to his lord and perform the service due.]

17. *e* M. S. in temp. E. 1.

18. *f* See the first part of the institutes, sect. 149.

19. *g* Lit. sect. 35. Sect. 99.

20. *h* 13 H. 3. gar. 42.

non potest capere homagium usque ad tertium haeredem,[21] and this Statute is to be intended where homage was to be received by Law, yet did the Tenant in judgement of Law die in the homage of the Lord, or otherwise he could not be in Ward, a case worthy of great consideration.

[i22] But after when it was resolved for Law, and so held to this day, that homage of it selfe doth not binde the Lord to any warranty or acquitall, unlesse it were homage auncestrell, which either is worne out, or very rare in England at this day; then according to the old rule, *Cessante ratione legis cessat ipsa lex;*[23] The heir cannot binde the Lord to receive homage in this case, but if the tenure be by homage auncestrell there the Lord shall not have the custody of body or land before he receiveth homage of the heire, for that homage bindeth him to warranty and acquitall, and consequently within the reason of this Law.

[k24] Here is to be noted that one within age may doe homage, but he cannot do fealty because that is to be done upon oath. *Hoc observato, quod si minor homagium fecerit nullum tamen juramentum fidelitatis, antequam ad aetatem pervenerit, praestabit.*[25] See more concerning this matter 1. Part. Institut. lib. 2. cap. Homage & Fealty.

"be made Knight."

Be made a Knight; And his tenure of service is called *Servitium militare,*[26] Knights service,[27] and therefore if the King create the heire within age, a Duke, a Marquesse, an Earle, a Viscount or a Baron, yet he shall remain in Ward for his body, but if the heire of a Duke, or of any other of the Nobility be made a Knight, he shall be out of Ward for his body. If the heire in Ward be created a Knight of the Garter, a Knight of the Bathe, a Knight Banneret, or a Knight Bachelor, he shall be out of Ward for his body for that he is a Knight,

---

21. [*Ed.:* Because the lord cannot take homage until the third heir.]

22. *i* 35 H. 6. gard. 72. 14 H. 7. 11. Lit. sect.

23. [*Ed.:* When the reason of the law ceases, the law itself ceases.]

24. *k* Brac. l. 2. fo. 79. See the first part of the Institutes. Lit. lib. 2. cap. homage & fealty.

25. [*Ed.:* Observing this, that if a minor does homage he shall not take any oath of fealty until he comes of age.]

26. [*Ed.:* knight-service.]

27. *l* Lib. 6. fol. 73. Sir Drue Druires case. 15 E. 4. 10. Pl. Com. Ratcliffes case. See hereafter *verbo remaneat.*

and somewhat more, and the Statute speaketh generally, unlesse a Knight, and therefore within the words and meaning of this Law, and the Soveraigne of Chivalry hath adjudged him able to doe Knights service.

And this word *Fiat,*[28] be made, proveth that Knighthood ought to be by creation making, and cannot be by descent.

[m][29] But albeit the heir be made a Knight within age yet is he not freed of the value | of his marriage, for that was vested before in the King, or other Lord, and the King being Soveraigne of Chivalry hath adjudged him of full age, that is, able to doe Knights service to this intent, to free his body from custody, but neither to barre the King or other Lord of the value of the marriage, no more then if he had attained to his full age of 21. years.

[12]

"remain in the keeping of his Lords."[30]

This word (*remaneat*[31]) implieth that this Statute is to be understood onely, where the heir after he be in Ward is made knight within age, for when the heire apparent is made knight within age in the life of the auncester, and the auncester dieth, his heir within age, he shall be out of Ward both for body and Land, because the Soveraign of Chivalry hath adjudged him of full age, and able to do knights service in the life of his auncester, so as in that case no title of Wardship did ever accrew, and there can be no *remanere*[32] or residue, but of that thing that had his essence or beeing.

Chapter 4

The Keeper of the Land of such an Heir, being within Age, shall not take of the Lands of the Heir, but reasonable Issues, reasonable Customs, and reasonable Services, and that without Destruction and Waste of his men, and his goods. And if We commit the custody of any such Land to the Sheriff, or to any other, which is answerable to Us for the Issues of the same Land, and he make De-

---

28. [*Ed.:* be made.]

29. *m* See Sir Drue Druries case. *ubi supra.*

30. Lib. 8. fol. 171. Sir Henry Constables case. 1 5. E. 4. 10. Pl. Com. 267. 2. E. 6 tit. gard. Br. Sir Anthony Browns case. Sir Drue Druries case. *Ubi supra.* Pl. Com. Ratclifs case.

31. [*Ed.:* remain.]

32. [*Ed.:* remainder.]

struction or Waste of those things that he hath in Custody, We will take of him amends and recompence therefore, and the Land shall be committed to two lawful and discreet men of that Fee, who shall answer unto Us for the Issues of the same Land, or unto him whom we will assign. And if We give or sell to any man the Custody of any such Land, and he therein do make Destruction or Waste, he shall lose the same Custody. And it shall be assigned to two lawful and discreet Men of that Fee; who also in like manner shall be answerable to Us, as afore is said.

"Keeper."

A Keeper, some derive the word *à cura & sto, quia custos est is cui cura rei stat custodiend';*[1] and thereupon sometime he is called *Curator,* in French he is called a *Gardien,* so as his name custos doth put him in minde of his office and duty, that is not onely to keep and preserve the Lands and Tenements of the Ward committed to his custody in safety, but also to educate and bring up his ward vertuously, and to advance him in marriage without disparagement. Vide 1. part Institut. Sect. 103. of the cause and end of Wardship; and see the 4 part of the Institut. cap. Court of Wards and Liveries.

"reasonable Issues."[2]

Exitus is derived *ab exeundo,*[3] and signifieth the rents and profits issuing out or comming of the Lands or Tenements of the Ward, which must be taken by the Gardien in reasonable manner, and therefore to *exitus, rationabiles*[4] is added, for that nothing that is unreasonable is allowed by Law.[5]

"reasonable Customs."

That is, things due by custome or prescription, and appendant or appurtenant to the Lands or Tenements in Ward, as advowsons, commons, waste, straie

---

1. [*Ed.:* [some derive *custos* (keeper)] from *cura* (care) and *sto* (I stand), because a keeper is someone who stands to take care of something.]

2. Bract. lib. 7. fol. 87. W. 2. ca. 39. Flet. li. 6. ca. 61. 5 E. 3. 6. 24 E. 3 28, 29.

3. [*Ed.: exitus* (issue) [is derived] from *exeundo* (coming out).]

4. [*Ed.:* reasonable.]

5. Brac. li. 2. fo. 87.

wreck, and the like; also the reaso-l-nable customes, fines, &c. of Tenants in   [13]
Villenage, or by Copy of Court roll where fines be incertain: for though the
customes, duties, fines, or the like be incertain, yet if that which is exacted
or demanded be unreasonable, it is against the Common Law, for this word
(*consuetud'*)[6] and the divers significations thereof see hereafter cap.30.

"reasonable Services."

This also, as appears by Glanvill that wrote in the reigne of Hen. 2. was the
Common Law of England, that incertain services and aides ought to be reasonable; for, saith he,[7] the Lord may *rationabilia auxilia de hominibus suis inde
exigere, ita tamen moderate secundum quantitatem feodorum suorum & secundum
facultates, ne minus gravari inde videantur, vel suum contenementum amittere;*[8,9]
and that which he speaketh there of aids, is to be applied to all incertain services,
customes, fines, or duties.

But it may be demanded, How and by whom shall the said reasonablenesse
in the cases aforesaid be tried? This you may reade in the first part of the
Institutes, Sect. 69.

"and that without Destruction and Waste of his men, and his goods."[10]

For these words, Destruction and Waste, see the first part of the Institutes,
Sect. 67. and the Statute of Gloc. cap. 5.

"And if We Commit, &c."

For this word *commiserimus*[11] vide the first part of the Institutes, Sect. 58. &
531. Here the Committee of the King is taken for him to whom the king

---

6. [*Ed.:* customs.]

7. Glanv. li. 9. c. 8. W. 1. cap. 31. 25 E. 3. cap. 11.

8. [*Ed.:* demand reasonable aids from his men for this purpose, but this must be in moderation according
to the quantity and wealth of their fees, lest they should seem to be oppressed thereby or lose their 'contenement' (property necessary to maintain their position).]

9. Contenementū.

10. Marleb. cap. 17. Mirror. cap. 5. § 2. li. 4. fol. 57.

11. [*Ed.:* we commit.]

committeth the custody of the Land to one or more; by this word *commisimus,* reserving a Rent, *Quamdiu quis alius plus dare voluerit,*[12] and there the king remain Gardien.

"We will take of him amends and recompence therefore."[13]

And this may be upon an office found, or by Writ directed to the Sheriffe to this effect, *Quia datum est nobis intelligi, &c.*[14]

"And if We give or sell to any man the Custody, &c."

In this case the King graunteth, or selleth the very custody itselfe, so as the grauntee or vendee becommeth Guardian in fact: and that this distinction betweene the Committee and Grauntee was by the Common Law, hear what Glanvill saith,[15] *Si verò Dominus Rex aliquam custodiam alicui commiserit, tunc distinguitur utrum ei custodiam pleno jure commiserit ita quod nullum inde reddere computum oportet ad Scaccarium aut aliter: si vero plene ei custodiam commiserit, tunc poterit, &c. negotia sicut sua recte disponere.*[16] King H. 7. graunted a Ward to the Dutches of Buckingham *quamdiu in manibus suis fore contigerit;*[17] And afterwards the King made a speciall Livery, as by Law he might, to the heir within age, and it was adjudged, as Justice Frowick reported, that the Duches was without remedy; but otherwise it had been if the graunt were *durante minore aetate haeredis,*[18] or, *durante minore aetate & quamdiu in manibus nostris, &c.*[19]

But here it may be materially demanded, What if the Committee or Grauntee doth waste, and the King during the minority taketh no amends, what

---

12. [*Ed.:* So long as someone else will give more.]

13. Reg. fo. 72, 73. Brac. li. 2. fo. 47. lib. 4. fol. 317. 20 H. 3. Waste 138. 40 Assis. Pl. 22. lib. intrat. Rast. 616.

14. [*Ed.:* Because it is given to us to understand, etc.]

15. Glanv. li. 7. c. 10.

16. [*Ed.:* If the lord king has committed a wardship to anyone, there is a distinction according to whether he committed to him the full right in that wardship, with no liability to render an account for it at the Exchequer, or not; if he did commit the wardship to him fully, then he may rightfully deal with it as he would his own.]

17. [*Ed.:* so long as it should happen to be in his hands.]

18. [*Ed.:* during the minority of the heir.]

19. [*Ed.:* during the minority and so long as [it should happen to be] in our hands, etc.]

remedy hath the heire after his full age?[20] The answer is, That he shall have an action of Waste, and that by order of the Common Law: and then it is further doubted and demanded, What shall the heire then recover, for the Wardship cannot be lost, seeing the heire is of full age, neither by this Statute nor by the Statute of Gloc.[21] To this the answer is very observable, that seeing that the Wardship cannot be lost, and the Waste, being to the heirs ditherision, ought not to remain unpunished, that the heire shall recover treble damage, for that penalty is annexed to the action of Waste; and therefore if an action of Waste were given against Tenant in tail *apres possibilitie*,[22] generally the plaintife shall recover treble damages, because they are annexed to this suit. But if the king doe take amends, then the heire at full age shall have no action of Waste.

| "he shall lose the same Custody."[23]   [14]

This is understood of the land, and not of the body for the words be *tradatur duobus, &c. qui de exitibus terrae nobis inde respondeant.*[24]

(*)[25] Nota, since this statute of *Magna Charta* divers other statutes against wastes and destructions in the lands of Wards have been made.

At the making of this statute, the King has not any prerogative in the Custodie of the lands of Idiots during the life of the Idiot, for if he had had, this Act would have provided against Wast, &c. committed by the Committee, or assignee of the King to be done in their possessions, as well as in the possessions of Wards, but at this time the gardianship of Idiots &c. was to the Lords and others according to the Course of the Common Law. And Idiots from their nativity were accounted alwayes within age, and therefore the Custodie of them was perpetuall so long as they lived, for that their impotencie was perpetuall. And the Lord of whom the Land was holden, had not a tenant that was able to doe him service. And therefore within the reason of a Custodie

---

20. 7 E. 3. 12,13. 3 E. 2 Waste 3. Registr. 72.

21. 12 H. 4. 3. F. N. B. 59. e. & 60. c. Vide *notabile recordum.* M. 32. F. l. Coram Rege. Rot. 76. Dublin. See hereafter in the Exposition upon the Statute of Gloc. ca. 5.

22. [*Ed.:* after possibility (of issue extinct).]

23. Bracton lib. e. fol. 285. 316. 317. Gloc. cap. 5. Dier 28. H. 8. fol. 25. Britt. fo. 33. 34.

24. [*Ed.:* delivered to two, etc., who shall answer to us therein from the issues of the land.]

25. *W. I. cap. 21. Gloc. cap. 5. Artic. sup. cart. cap. 18. 14. E. 3. cap. 13 36. E. 3. cap. 13.

of a minor or of an heire within age in Case of Wardship. And this appeareth by Fleta,[26] *Solent tutores Idiotarum & stultorum cum corporibus eorum perpetuo, quod lictium fuit & provisum, eo quod se ipsos regere non noverint,*[*27] *nam semper judicabantur infra aetatem: vel quia verumq: plures per hujusmodi custodiam ex haeredationes compatiebantur, provisum fuit. & cōmuniter concessum quod Rex corporū & haereditatū hujusmodi idiotarum & stultorum sub perpetuis custodiam obtineret, dum tamen à nativitate fuerint idiotae & stulti; secus autē si tardae a quocunque Domino tenuerint, & ipsos maritaret, & ex omni exhaeredatione salvaret hoc cum adjecto quod domini feodorum & aliis quorum interfuerit ut servitiis, redditibus & custodiis usque ad legitimam aetatem secundum conditionem feodorum, releviis & hujusmodi nihil juris deperiret.*[28]

But then it is demanded, when was this prerogative given to the King?[29] Certain it is, that the King had it before the statute of 17. E. 2. *de praerogativa Regis,*[30] for it appeareth in our Bookes, that the King had this prerogative, Anno. 3. E. 2. And before that, it is manifest that the King had it before Britton wrote in the raigne of E. 1. as you may read in his booke.[31]

And it is as cleare, that when Bracton wrote[32] (who wrote about the end of the reigne of Hen. 3. that the King had not then this prerogative.

And therefore it followeth, that this prerogative was given to King Edward the first before that Britton wrote, by some Act of Parliament, which is not now extant. And it appeareth by the Mirror of Justices agreeing with Fleta,

---

26. Fleta. lib. 1. cap 10. § Solent.

27. *Nota, the cause of alteration by Act of Parliament. Mirror cap. 1. c. 9 § *En auter maneracc.* Britton. cap. 66. fol. 167. b. acc. 17. E. 2. cap. 9.

28. [*Ed.:* It is the custom for guardians to have the wardship of [the lands of] idiots and fools, with their bodies, in perpetuity, and this has been permissible and lawful in that they do not know how to govern themselves and are always deemed to be under age. However, because several people suffered disinheritance by means of such wardships, it was provided and generally agreed that the king should have the wardship of the bodies and inheritances of such idiots and fools in perpetuity, from whatsoever lords they held [the land], provided nevertheless that they have been idiots and fools from birth—though it is otherwise if they became so later—and that the king should provide them with a marriage and preserve them from all disinheritance, with the proviso that the lords of the fees should not lose any of their rights, nor others who have an interest in the services, rents, and wardships, until the age of majority, according to the nature of the fees.]

29. 3. E. 3. tit. gar. 5.

30. [*Ed.:* Concerning the king's prerogative (the name of the statute).]

31. Britton cap. 66. fol. 167. b.

32. Brac 1. 5. 421. a. Stanf. prerog. ca. 9. fol. 33. 34.

that this prerogative was granted by Common assent, vide. lib. 4. *Beverleys Case* fol. 126.

Chapter 5

The Keeper, so long as he hath the Custody of the Land of such an Heir, shall keep up the Houses, Parks, Warrens, Ponds, Mills, and other things pertaining to the same Land, with the Issues of the said Land; and he shall deliver to the Heir, when he cometh to his full Age, all his Land, stored with ploughs and all other things, at the least as he received it. All these things shall be observed in the Custodies of Archbishopricks, Bishopricks, Abbeys, Priories, Churches, and Dignities vacant, which appertain to Us; except this, that such Custody shall not be sold.

I That this was the Common Law appeareth by Glanvile, who saith,[1] *Restituere* [15] *autem tenentur custodes haereditates ipsis haeredibus inslauratas & debitis acquietatas juxta exigentiam temporis custodiae & quantitatis haereditatis.*[2]

"All these things shall be observed in the Custodies of Archbishopricks, &c."

The Custodie of the temporalties of every Arch-Bishop, and Bishop within the realme, and of such Abbeyes, and Priories, as were of the Kings foundation, after the same became voide, belonged to the king during the vacation thereof by his prerogative:[3] for as the spiritualties belonged during that time to the Deane and Chapter, *de communi jure,*[4] or to some other Ecclesiasticall person by prescription, or composition, so the temporalties came to the King as founder, and this doth belong to the King, being *patronus & protector Ecclesiae,*[5] in so high a prerogative incident to his Crowne, as no subject can claime the temporalties of an Arch-Bishop, or Bishop, when they fall by grant or prescription.[6]

1. Glanvil lib. 7. cap. 9. Fleta li. 1. e. 11. 10. H. 7. 6. & 30 See the 1. part of the Institutes sect. 67.

2. [*Ed.:* Guardians are bound to restore to the selfsame heirs their inheritances, in good condition and free of debts, in proportion to the length of wardship and the size of the inheritance.]

3. See prer. regis, cap. 14. W. 1. cap. 21. Fleta li. 1. c. 11. 14. E. 3. ca. 4. 5 *vide* cap. 33.

4. [*Ed.:* of common right,]

5. [*Ed.:* patron and protector of the church,]

6. adjudged 21. E. 1.

Regula.   But as, *In omni re nascitur res quae ipsam rem exterminat,*[7] unlesse it bee
timely prevented (as the worme in the wood, or the mothe in the Cloth, and
the like) so oftentimes no profession receives a greater blow, then by one of
their owne coat: for Ranulph an ecclesiasticall person, and King William Rufus
his Chaplain, a man *subacto ingenio,*[8] and *profunda nequitia,*[9] was a factor for
the King in making merchandize of Church livings, in as much, as when any
Archbishopricke, Bishopricke, or Monastery became void, first he perswaded
the King to keepe them voide a long time, and converted the profits thereof
sometime by letting, and sometime by sale of the same, whereby the temporalties were exceedingly wasted, and destroyed. Secondly, after a long time
no man was preferred to them *per traditionem annuli & baculi,*[10] by livery of
season, freely, as the old fashion was, but by bargain, and sale from the King
to him, that would give most, by meanes whereof the Church was stuffed
with unworthy, and insufficient men, and many men of lively wits, and to-
wardlinesse in learning despairing of preferment turned their studies to other
professions. This Ranulph, for serving the Kings turnes, was advanced, first,
to be the Kings Chancellour, & after to be Bishop of Duresme, who after his
advancement to so high dignities, made them servants to his sacrilegious and
simoniacall designes. King Henry the first seeing this mischiefe, and foreseeing
the great inconvenience that would follow thereupon, was contented for his
owne time to binde his owne hands, to the end the Church now naked and
bare might receive some comfort, and have meanes to provide things necessary
for their profession, and calling. He thereupon at his Coronation made a
Charter to this effect,[11] *Quia regnum oppressum erat injustis exactionibus, ego
in respectu dei & amore quem erga vos omnes habeo, sanctā Dei Ecclesiam imprimis
liberam fac' ita quod nec vendam, nec ad firmam ponam, nec mortuo Archiepiscopo, sive Episcopo vel abbate, aliquid accipiam de Dominio Ecclesiae vel hominibus ejus, donec successor eam ingrediatur, & omnes malas consuetudines, quibus
regnum Angliae opprimebatur, inde aufero.*[12] He committed the said Ranulph

7. [*Ed.:* In every thing there arises something which exterminates the thing itself.]
8. [*Ed.:* (of) trained genius,]
9. [*Ed.:* profound wickedness,]
10. [*Ed.:* by delivery of a ring and a rod,]
11. See this charter at large in Mat. Par. See libr. rubeū in principio.
12. [*Ed.:* Because the kingdom was oppressed by unjust exactions, I, out of respect for God and the

then Bishop of Durham to prison for his intolerable misdeeds, and injuries to the Church, where he lived without love, and died without pity, saving of those, that thought it pity, he lived so long.

"Shall not be sold."

Fleta, *ubi supra,* saith,[13] *vendi non debent nec legari:*[14] Yet the King may commit the temporalties of them during the vacation, as by the statute of 14. Ed. 3. appeareth.

Chapter 6

Heirs shall be married without Disparagement.

This is an ancient maxime of the Common Law: see more hereof in the first part of the Institutes sect. 107. 108. 109.

Chapter 7

| A Widow, after the Death of her Husband, incontinent, and without any [16] difficulty, shall have her Marriage and her Inheritance; and shall give nothing for her Dower, her Marriage or her Inheritance, which her Husband or she held the day of the death of her Husband; and she shall tarry in the chief house of her Husband by forty days after the death of her Husband, within which days her Dower shall be assigned her, if it were not assigned her before, or that the house be a Castle. And if she depart from the Castle, then a competent house shall be forthwith provided for her, in the which she may honestly dwell, until her Dower be to her assigned, as aforesaid; and she shall have in the mean time her reasonable Estovers of the Common. And for her Dower shall be assigned unto her the third part of all the Lands of her Husband, which were his during Coverture, except she were endowed of less at the Church-door. No Widow

---

love which I have for you all, make the holy Church of God free, so that I shall not sell or put to farm, nor on the death of an archbishop, bishop, or abbot, accept anything from the property of the Church or its men until the successor enters it, and I do away with all the bad customs with which the kingdom of England was oppressed.]

13. Flet. *ubi supra.* 14 E. 3. ca. 4. 5. F. N. B. 59. b.

14. [*Ed.:* ought not to be sold or bequeathed:]

shall be distrained to marry herself: Nevertheless she shall find Surety that she shall not marry without our Licence and Assent, if she hold of Us, nor without the Assent of the Lord, if she hold of another.

It appeareth by Bracton of ancient time,[1] that a woman being *Heire, sine Dominorum dispositione & assensu, haereditatem habens, maritari non potest, nec etiam in vita antecessorum de jure sine assensu Domini capitalis, quod si olim fecissent, haereditatem amitterent sine spe recuperandi, nisi solum per gratiam: hodie tamen aliam poenam incurrunt, sicut inferius dicetur, & hoc ideo ne cogatur Dominus homagium capere de capitali inimico, vel de alio minime idoneo.*[2]

Also it appeareth by the same Author,[3] *quod si mulier dotem habens pro voluntate sua alicui nuberet, praeter assensum Warranti sui de dote, olim ex tali causa dotem amitteret, nunc tamen non amittet.*[4]

Item cum semel legitime maritatae fuerint, & postea viduae, iterum non cus-todientur sub custodia Dominorum, licet teneantur assensum eorum requirere maritandi se, &c.[5] And herewith agreeth Glanvile, who wrote before this stat-ute.[6]

Hereby you may see what had beene used of ancient time in these cases: But at this day widowes are presently after the decease of their husbands with-out any difficulty to have their marriage (that is, to marrie where they will without any licence, or assent of their Lords) and their inheritance, without any thing to be given to them; but in this branch the King is not included, as hereafter in the end of this Chapter shall appeare.

---

1. Bracton li. 2. fol. 88. Fleta li. 5. cap. 23. 35. H. 6. 52. Mat. Par. 407.

2. [*Ed.:* Heir, without the approval and consent of [her lord], a woman who has an inheritance may not be married (not even, as of right, in the lifetime of her ancestor) without the consent of the chief lord. If women did so in former times, they lost the inheritance beyond hope of recovery, except by grace; today, however, they incur another penalty, as will be explained below. This is lest the lord be forced to take the homage of his chief enemy or some other unsuitable person.]

3. Mirrour. cap. 1. §. 3. See the 1. part of the Institutes sect. 36.

4. [*Ed.:* that if a woman who has dower marries someone at her will, without the consent of her warrantor of the dower, she would at one time have lost the dower for that reason; but now she does not.]

5. [*Ed.:* If they were once lawfully married, and then widowed, they shall not be kept in the wardship of their lords, though they are bound to seek their consent to marry, etc.]

6. Glanvil. lib. 7. cap. 12. Fleta. lib. 3. cap. 23.

"And she shall tarry in the chief house of her Husband by forty days after the death of her Husband."[7]

And this is called her Quarentine, and if the Widow be witholden from her Quarentine, she shall have her Writ, *De quarentena habenda*[8] to the Sherife, which reciting this Statute, is in nature of a Commission to him, *Quod vocatis coram vobis partibus praedictis, & auditis inde earum rationibus, eidem B.C. Viduae plenam & celerem justitiam inde fieri faciatis juxta tenorē cartae prae-dictae, ne pro defectu justitiae querela ad nos perveniat iterata.*[9,10] | By force of [17] which Writ, the Sherife may make processe against the defendant, retournable within two or three dayes &c. and may, and ought (if no just cause may be shewed against it) speedily to put her in possession; and the reason why such speed is made, is for that her Quarentine is but for forty dayes.

"A Widow, &c. shall tarry &c."

Therefore if she marry within the forty dayes, she loseth her Quarentine, for then her Widowhood is past, and she hath provided for her selfe, and the Quarentine is appropriate to her Widowes estate.[11]

"within which days her Dower shall be assigned her."[12]

Here it appeareth how speedily Dower ought to be assigned, to the end the Widow might not be without livelihood.

"after the death of her Husband."

The day wherein the husband dieth, shall be accounted the first day, so as she shall have but thirty nine after.[13]

---

7. Bract. li. 2. c. 40. Britton. c. 103. Fleta. li. 5. c. 23.

8. [*Ed.*: for having quarantine.]

9. [*Ed.*: That, calling before you the aforesaid parties, and hearing their arguments therein, you cause full and speedy justice to be done therein to the same B. C., widow, according to the tenor of the aforesaid charter, so that the suit should not come before us again for want of justice.]

10. Register. 175. F. N. B. 161.

11. 1 Mar. Br. Dower 101.

12. Britton ca. 103.

13. Dier 7 E. 6. fo. 76. 4. & 5. Phil. & Mar. fol. 161.

"or that the house be a Castle."[14]

This is intended of a Castle, that is warlike, and maintained for the necessary defence of the Realm, and not for a Castle in name maintained for habitation of the owner, but hereof see more in the first part of the Institutes, Sect. 36. & 242. *De aedibus kernelatis.*[15] *Kernellare,* or *cernellare,*[16] by some is derived from the French word *kerner,* or *cerner,*[17] to fortifie, inviron, or inclose round about: And by others, from *karnean,* or *carnean,*[18] a battlement of a wall; or from *karnele,* or *carnele,*[19] imbatteled, or having imbattlements; and the truth is, it beareth all these significations in the Lawes of England, and the use of it in Castles and forts was to defend himselfe by the higher place, and to offend the assailants at the lower.

Brittons words be,[20] *Si le chief mees foit chief del Countee, ou del Barony, ou Castle, &c.*[21] So as it appeareth by him that she is not to have her Quarentine of that, which is *Caput Comitatus, seu Baroniae,*[22] and with him, agreeth Fleta,[23] but Bracton only speaketh *de Castro.*[24] The ancient Law of England had great regard of honour and order.

"then a competent house shall be forthwith provided for her, in the which she may honestly dwell,"[25]

But this must be of a house, whereof she is Dowable, for she must have her Quarentine of that; whereof she may be endowed.

---

14. Bract. li. 2. fol. 46. Britton ca. 103. Fleta lib. 5. ca. 23. 30. E. 3. Dow. 81. 30 E. 1. vouch. 298 8 H. 3. Dower 196 8 H. 3. Dower 194 17. H. 3. ibid. 192. Rot. pat. part. 1. nu. 17. Escheat 4. E. 1. m. 88.

15. [*Ed.:* On crenellated buildings.]

16. [*Ed.:* to crenellate.]

17. [*Ed.:* fortress.]

18. [*Ed.:* battlement.]

19. [*Ed.:* having battlements.]

20. Britton *ubi supra.*

21. [*Ed.:* If the chief house is the chief of the earldom, or of the barony, or castle, etc.]

22. [*Ed.:* Chief of the earldom or barony.]

23. *Ubi supra.*

24. [*Ed.:* of a castle.]

25. Britton *ubi supra.*

"and she shall have in the mean time her reasonable Estovers of the Common:"

Britton saith,[26] *Que eux eient des issues del intier de les terres lour covenable sustenance, &c.*[27]

Fleta saith,[28] *Ubi inveniantur ei necessaria honeste de haereditate communi, donec rationabilis dos fuerit ei assignata.*[29]

So as *estoverium*[30] here is taken for sustenance: There is an opinion in our Books,[31] that the Widow cannot kill any of the Oxen of the husbands, whiles she remain in the house; But the register saith,[32] *Quod interim habeant rationabilia estoveria de bonis eorundem maritorum,*[33] which seemeth to be an exposition of this Branch.

In the Statute intituled, *De catallis felonum,*[34] it is said, *Cum ibidem captus coram Justiciariis nostris fuerit convictus de felonia, tunc resid' catallorum ultra estoverium suum secundum Regni consuetudinem nobis remaneant;*[35,36] where estovetium signifieth sustenance, or aliment, or nourishment. This word estoverium commeth of the French verb *estover, id est, alere,* to sustain, or nourish, and this agreeth with the said old Books, and in this sense it is taken in the Statute of Gloc.[37] *Trover estovers in viver & vesture,*[38] that is, things that concern the nourishment, or maintenance of man *in victu & vestitu,*[39] wherein is contained meat, | drink, garments, and habitation. *Alimentorum appellatione* [18] *venit victus, vestitus & habitatio.*[40]

---

26. Britton *ubi supra.*

27. [*Ed.:* That they should have their suitable maintenance from the issues of the whole of the lands, etc.]

28. Fleta *ubi supra.*

29. [*Ed.:* Where necessaries shall be decently found for her, from the common inheritance, until reasonable dower is assigned to her.]

30. [*Ed.:* The estover would otherwise be the right to take wood from wastes and commons.]

31. 19 H. 6. 14. b.

32. Registr. 175.

33. [*Ed.:* That in the meantime they shall have reasonable estovers of the property of said husbands.]

34. [*Ed.:* Concerning the chattels of felons.]

35. [*Ed.:* when someone taken there shall be convicted of felony before our justices, then the rest of the chattels shall remain to us besides his estover (sustenance) according to the custom of the realm.]

36. Vid. Mag. Chart. 2. pt fol. 66. Bract. li. 3. fo. 137.

37. Gloc. ca. 4.

38. [*Ed.:* To find estovers in food and clothing.]

39. [*Ed.:* in food and clothing.]

40. [*Ed.:* Under the description of *alimenta* (alimentary necessaries) come food, clothing, and habitation.]

When estovers are restrained to woods, it signifieth housebote, hedgebote, and ploughbote.

"And for her Dower shall be assigned unto her the third part of all the Lands of her Husband, &c."

See for this in the first part of the Institutes, Sect. 37.

"No Widow shall be distrained to marry herself, &c.[41]"

This is to be understood of Widowes Tenants in Dower of Lands holden of the King by Knights service in chiefe, and thereupon she is called the Kings Widow, and if the Kings Widow marry without license, she shall pay a fine of the value of her Dower by one year.

And the reason of this Law is yeelded wherefore they should not marry without the Kings license,[42] *Ne forte capitalibus inimicis Domini Regis maritentur.*[43]

And old Readers have yeelded this reason, lest they should marry unto strangers, and so the treasure of the Realme might be carried out, and others say that the reason is for that upon the assignement of her Dower she is sworn in the Chancery,[44] *Que el ne marier sans license, & pur ceo si el fait encont son serement el ferra fine.*[45]

Others say that it is a contempt to marry without the Kings license, and against this Statute, and therefore for this contempt she shall make a fine.

If the Kings Tenant in *Capite*[46] dye seised, his heire female of full age, if she marry without the Kings license, she shall pay no fine, for she is no Widow, and the Words be *nulla vidua distringatur, &c.*[47,48]

---

41. Prer. Regis. cap. 4. Stamford. prer. 17. F. N. B. 265. c. Britton fol. 28. a. & 19. b.

42. Rot pat. 4. E. I. m. 31. Bract. *ubi supra.* Fleta lib. I. ca. 12.

43. [*Ed.:* Lest indeed they should marry the lord king's chief enemies.]

44. 35 H. 6. 52. Fortes.

45. [*Ed.:* That she should not marry without licence, and therefore if she acts against her oath she shall be fined.]

46. [*Ed.:* in chief.]

47. 35 H. 6. 52. 15 E. 4. 13.

48. [*Ed.:* no widow shall be distrained, etc.]

If the Queen being the Widow of a King be endowed, and marry without the Kings license, because she is endowed of the seison of the King himselfe, she is out of this Statute: But at the Parliament holden in anno 6.H.6.[49] it is enacted by the King, the Lords temporall, and the Commons, that no man should contract with, or marry himselfe to any Queen of England, without the special license or assent of the King, on pain to lose all his goods, and lands; to which Act the Bishops, and other Lords Spirituall gave their consent, as farre forth, as the same swerved not from the Law of God, and of the Church, and so as the same imported no deadly sin.

"If she hold of another.[50]"

This is to be understood, where such a license of marriage in case of a common person, was due by custome, prescription, or speciall tenure, the words being *si de alio tenuerit;*[51] and this exposition is approved by constant and continuall use and experience, *Et optimus interpres legum consuetudo.*[52]

Chapter 8

We, or our Bailiffs, shall not seize any Land or Rent for any Debt, as long as the present Goods and Chattels of the Debtor do suffice to pay the Debt, and the Debtor himself be ready to satisfy therefore. Neither shall the Pledges of the Debtor be distrained, as long as the principal Debtor is sufficient for the payment of the Debt; and if the principal Debtor fail in payment of the Debt, having nothing wherewith to pay, or will not pay where he is able, the Pledges shall answer for the Debt; and if they will, they shall have the Lands and Rents of the Debtor, until they be satisfied of that which they before paid for him, except that the Debtor can shew himself to be acquitted against the said Sureties.[1]

| "We." [19]

These words being spoken in the politique capacity doe extend to the successors, for in judgement of Law the King in his politique capacity dieth not.

---

49. Rot. parl. anno 6 H. 6. nu. 41.
50. See the first part of the institutes. sect. 174.
51. [*Ed.:* if she hold of another;]
52. [*Ed.:* Custom is the best interpreter of laws.]
1. Pl. Com. 457. in Sir Thos. Wrothes case. Pl. Com. in the Lord Berklies Case, &c.

"or our Bailiffs."[2]

In this place the Sheriffe and his underbailiffes are intended and meant, and
to this day the Sheriffe useth this in his Returns, *Infra balivam meam,*[3] for
Infra comitatum, &c.[4]

"shall not seize any Land or Rent for any Debt, as long as the present Goods
and Chattels of the Debtor, do suffice to pay the Debt,"[5]

By order of the Common Law, the King for his debt had execution of the
body, lands, and goods of the debtor: This is an act of grace, and restraineth
the power that the King before had.

"Rent."

For the severall kinde of rents, see the first part of the Institutes; Lit. lib. 2.
cap. 12. whereunto you may adde, 1. *Redditus assisus,* or *redditus assisae:* vulgarly
rents of Assise are the certain rents of the Freeholders, and ancient Copiholders,
because they be assised, and certain, and doth distinguish the same from *redditus mobiles,* farm rents for life, years, or at will, which are variable and incertain. 2. *Redditus albi,* White rents, blanch Farmes, or rents, vulgarly and
commonly called quitrents; they are called white rents, because they were paid
in silver, to distinguish them from work-dayes, rent cummin, rent corn, &c.
And again these are called, 3. *Redditus nigri,* black maile, that is, black rents,
to distinguish them from white rents; see Rot. claus. 12. Hen. 3. m. 12. *Rex
concessit hominibus de Andevor maneria de M.F.A. &c. Reddendo per annum
ad Scaccaȓ Regis Lxxx. li. blanc, de Antiqua firma.*[6] 4. *Redditus resoluti* be rents

---

2. See the first part of the Institutes, And hereafter cap. 28.

3. [*Ed.:* Within my bailiwick.]

4. [*Ed.:* Within the county, etc.]

5. See Artic. super Cart. cap. 12. li. 3. fol. 12. b. Sir William Herberts case. 5. Eliz. Dier 224. Walter de
Chirtons case. 24 E. 3. Pl. Com. 31. *Debet semper principalis excut antequa perveniatur ad sidei jussores.* An
act of grace, see W. 2. ca. 10. & 29. 18 E. 1. Stat. de quo warranto optime. Art. super Cart. ca. 12. & 14.
Custumier de Norm. cap. 60. Vide 43. El. c. 13.

6. [*Ed.:* The king has granted to the men of Andover the manors of M., F., A., etc., rendering at the
king's Exchequer eighty pounds a year of the old white rent.]

issuing out of the mannors, &c. to other Lords, &c. *Feodi firma,* see Farm, for this kinde of rent, *vide infra* Gloc. cap. 8.

After the Statute of 33. Hen. 8. cap. 39. was made for levying of the Kings debts the usuall processe to the Sheriffe at this day, is, *Quod diligenter per sacramentum proborum & legalium hominum de baliva tua, &c. inquiras quae & cujusmodi bona & catalla, & cujus precii idem (debitor) habuit in dicta baliva tua,&c. Et ea omnia capias in manus nostras, ad valentiam debiti praedict', & inde fieri fac'debitum praedict', &c. Et si forte bona & catalla praedict' (debitoris) ad solutionem debiti praedict' non sufficerent, tunc non omittas propter aliquam libertatem, quin eam ingrediaris, & per sacramentum praefaꝶ proborum, & legalium hominum diligenter inquiras, quas terras, & quae tenementa, & cujus annui valoris, idem (debitor) habuit, seu seisitus fuit in dicta baliva tua, &c. Et ea omnia & singula in quorumcunque manibus jam existunt, extendi fac', & in manus nostras capias, &c. Et capias praedict' debitorem, ita quod habeas corpus praedict' (debitoris) ad satisfac' nobis de debito praedict'.*[7]

Whereby it appeareth, that if the goods and chattels of the Kings Debtor be sufficient, and so can be made to appeare to the Sheriffe, whereupon he may levy the Kings debt, then ought not the Sheriffe to extend the Lands, and Tenements of the Debtor, or of his heire, or of any Purchaser, or terre-Tenant.[8] To conclude this point with the Authority of old and Auncient Ockham.

| *Terrae & tenementa debitoris regis, ad quascunq; manus quocunq; titulo devenerunt, post debitum Regis inceptum Regi tenentur, si non aliunde satisfacere possit.*[9,10]   [20]

---

7. [*Ed.:* That you diligently enquire, by the oath of good and lawful men of your bailiwick etc., what and what manner of goods and chattels, and of what price, the same (debtor) had in your said bailiwick etc.; and take them all into our hands to the value of the aforesaid debt, and cause the aforesaid debt to be made up therefrom, etc.; and if the goods and chattels of the aforesaid (debtor) should not suffice to pay the aforesaid debt, then do not omit on account of any liberty to enter it, and by the oath of the said good and lawful men diligently enquire what lands and tenements, and of what annual value, the same (debtor) had or was seised of in your said bailiwick, etc., and cause all and singular of them to be valued, in whose hands soever they now are, and take them into our hands, etc. And take the aforesaid (debtor), so that you have the body of the aforesaid (debtor) to satisfy us of the aforesaid debt.]

8. See cap. 18. Glanv. li. 10 ca 3. Britton cap. 28. Fleta lib. 2. ca. 62. F. N. B. a 37. f, Pl. Com. 440. Pepys Case. lib. 3 fol. 13. Sir William Herberts case. lib. 7. fol. 17. 18, 12. 50. ass. p 5. 21 E. 4. 21.

9. Ockham, cap. quod vicecomes a fundis ejus, &c.

10. [*Ed.:* The lands and tenements of the king's debtor, into whose hands soever and by whatsoever

"Neither shall the Pledges of the Debtor."

As pledges, or sureties to keepe the peace, pledges for a fine to the King upon a contempt, &c. are within this branch, but otherwise it is of mainperners, and this appeareth by Glanvile, to be the Common Law before the making of this act.[11]

And the author of the Mirror saith, *ceux sont pleges queux plevisher aut' chose que corps de home, car ceux ne sont propment pledges, mes sont main-perners pur ceo queils supposont plevishables sont liver a ceux per baille Corps pur Corps.*[12]

"and if the principal Debtor fail in the payment, &c. or will not pay where he is able."

Some have thought that this branch hath taken away the next precedent, concerning pledges, but both doe stand well together, for *reddere noluerit cum possit*[13] must be understood, when the principall is able, and yet his ability cannot bee made to appeare, being in money, treasure or the like, or in debts owing to him, which he conceales, and will not *reddere*[14] so *as de non apparentibus, & non existentibus eadem est lex,*[15] and in that case *plegii de debito respondeant,*[16] and yet the former branch concerning pledges doth stand, where the pledges can make it appeare to the Sheriffe, that he may levie the Kings debt: see in the statute of *articuli super cartas.*[17] cap. 11.

---

title they come, after the king's debt has become due, shall be held to the king unless he can be satisfied from elsewhere.]

11. Custumier de Nor. cap. 60. fol. 73. &c. 76. Glanvil. lib. 12. cap. 3.

12. [*Ed.:* pledges are those who stand surety for something other than a man's body, for those are not properly pledges but mainpernors, because those for whom they are surety are delivered to them in bail, body for body.]

13. [*Ed.:* will not pay though he is able.]

14. [*Ed.:* repay.]

15. [*Ed.:* the law is the same concerning things not appearing or not existing.]

16. [*Ed.:* the pledges shall answer for the debt.]

17. [*Ed.:* Statute of 28. Edward 1 (1300) in which Edward confirmed Magna Charta and the Charter of the Forest, without the savings clause he had used in 1297.]

"and if they will they shall have the Lands and Rents of the Debtor, &c."

[a18] Upon these words some have said that the writ *de plegiis acquietandis*[19] is grounded, and seeing no mention is made in this Statute of any deed, the pledges shall have that Writ without any deed. And if the pledges have any deed, covenant, or other assurance for their indemnitie, then may they take their remedie at the Common Law; [b20] but it appeareth by Glanvile that this was the Common Law, for he saith, *Soluto vero eo quod debetur ab ipsis plegiis, recuperare inde poterint ad principalem debitorem, si postea habuerit unde eis satisfacere possit per principale placitum*,[21] and set downe the [c22] Writ *de plegiis acquietandis*.

Note here is a Chapter omitted, viz. *nullum scutagium, vel auxilium ponam in regno nostro nisi p commune conciliũ regni nostri*,[23] which clause was in the Charter, anno 17. *Regis Johannis*, and was omitted in the exemplification of this great Charter, by Ed. I. vide Cap. 30.

Chapter 9

The City of London shall have all the old Liberties and Customs which it hath been used to have. Moreover, We will and grant, that all other Cities, Boroughs, Towns, and the Barons of the Five Ports, and all other Ports, shall have all their Liberties and free Customs.

[d1] This Chapter is excellently interpreted by an ancient Author, who saith, *In pointe que demaunde, que le Citie de Londres eit ſes auncient franchises, & ſes frank Customes, est interpretable in cest maner, que les Citizens eient lour fraun-*

---

18. *a* Britton. cap. 28 Fleta lib. 2. c. 56 F. N. B. 137. Reg. 158. 43. E. 3. 11. 2. 44. E. 3. 21. 48. E. 3. 28. 32. E. 3. m̄rans des faitz. 179. 1. E. 46. Dyer. 22. Eliz. 170.

19. [*Ed.:* for acquitting pledges.]

20. *b* Glanvil. lib. 10. cap. 4. 5.

21. [*Ed.:* When that which is owed has been paid by the same pledges, they may have recourse to the principal debtor for its recovery, if he should afterwards have assets with which to satisfy them, by means of the principal plea.]

22. *c* Regist. 158. Mat. Paris 247. a. Wendov. Wals. 40 Vide postea Stat. de Tallagio concedendo. 34. E. 1.

23. [*Ed.:* I shall impose no scutage or aid in our realm except by the common council of our realm.]

1. *d* Mirror. ca. 5. §. 2. Fleta lib. 2. cap. 48. Pl. Com. fol. 400. 5. H. 7. 10, 19. 8. H. 7. 4. 11. H. 7. 21. 28. Assis. 24. 45 E. 3. 26. See acts of Parliament Art. super chartas c. 7. W. 3. cap. 9. 7. R. 2. nient im primee. 9 H. 4. cap. 1. 2 H. 6. cap. 1. &c. See the first of the Instit. sect. 7. 31. c

*chises, dont ils font inherit per loyall title, de dones, & confirmements des royes, & les queux ilz ne ont forsfeits per nul abusion, & que ilz eient lour franchises, & customes, que sont sufferable per droit, & nient repugnant al Ley: Et le interpretation que est dit de Londres soit intendu de les cinque ports, & des autres lieus;*² And this interpretation agreeth with divers of our later Books.³

[21]

It is a maxime in Law, that a man cannot claim any thing by custome or pre-|-scription against a Statute, unlesse the custome, or prescription be saved by another Statute; For example: They of London claim by custome, to give lands without license to mortmain, because this custome is saved, and preserved, not onely by this Chapter of Magna Charta, but by divers other Statutes, *& sic de caeteris.*⁴ See more in particular concerning London, in the fourth part of the Institutes, Cap. of the Courts of the City of London.

Chapter 10

No Man shall be distrained to do more Service for a Knight's Fee, nor any Frehold, than therefore is due.¹

That this was the auncient Law of England, appeareth by Glanvill,² and also that the Writ of *Ne injuste vexes*³ was not grounded upon this Act appeareth also by him, for he saith, *Et alia quaedam placita, veluti, si quis conqueratur se curiae de Domino suo, quod consuetudines, & indebita servitia, vel plus servitii exigit ab eo, quā inde facere debeat:*⁴ And setteth down the form of the writ

---

2. [*Ed.:* The point in question, that the city of London shall have its old liberties and free customs, is interpretable in this way, that the citizens should have their liberties which they have inherited by lawful title, by the gifts and confirmations of the kings, and which they have not forfeited for any abuse, and that they should have their liberties and customs which are allowable by right and not repugnant to the law. And the interpretation which is made for London is to be understood also for the cinque ports and other places.]

3. 8 H 7. 4. b.

4. [*Ed.:* likewise concerning similar things.]

1. Custumier de Norm. cap. 114. fol. 132. b.

2. Glanv. li. 12. ca. 9. 10. Reg fol. 4. & 59. b. Bracton fo. 329. Fleta li. 5. cap. 38. lib. 2. c. 60. Brit. c. 27. fo. 60. b.

3. [*Ed.:* Prohibition against a lord who distrains his tenant by demanding more services than the tenant owes.]

4. [*Ed.:* And certain other pleas, for example, when anyone complains in court that this lord is demanding customs and services which are not due, or more service than he ought to do.]

of *Ne injuste vexes; Rex N. salutem. Prohibeo tibi ne injuste vexes, vel vexari permittas H. de libero tenemento suo, quod tenet de te in tali villa, nec inde ab eo exigas, aut exigi permittas consuetudines vel servitia, quae tibi inde facere non debet, &c.*[5]

And another ancient Author which wrote of the ancient Laws long before this Statute, maketh mention of the Writ of *Ne injuste vexes*.[6]

Hereby it appeareth how they are deceived, that hold that this Writ is grounded upon this Act, and how necessary the reading of ancient Authors is, to give the ancient Common Law his right, as hereby it appeareth.[7]

The words of the Statute be, *nullus distringatur*,[8] therefore if the Lord incroach more Rent of the same nature, by the voluntary payment of the Tenant, be shall not avoid this incroachment in an avowry but in an assise *cessavit*,[9] or *ne injuste vexes*, the Tenant shall avoyd the incroachment; This rule holdeth not in case of a successor, or of the issue in taile, for they shall avoyd it in an avowry, but if the service incroached be of another nature, the Tenant shall avoyd that season in an avowry, for *majus servitium*[10] implieth a greater exaction of the same nature: if the incroachment of the same nature be gotten by cohertion of distresse, there the Tenant shall avoyd that season in an avowry, for *nullus distringatur ad faciendum majus servitium*.[11] But if an incroachment be made upon a Tenant in tail, or Tenant for life, or any other, who cannot maintain a Writ of *ne injuste vexes*, nor a *contra formam collationis*,[12] nor other remedy, he shall have an action upon this Statute;[13] for this Statute intendeth to relieve those, which had no remedy by the Common Law.

---

5. [*Ed.:* The king to N., greeting. I prohibit you from unjustly vexing H., or permitting him to be vexed, in respect of his free tenement which he holds of you in such and such a vill, or from demanding from him, or allowing to be demanded, customs and services which he ought not to do for you, etc.]

6. Mirror ca. 2. § 19. & cap. 5. § 1.

7. F. N. B. 10. c. Pl. Com. 243. b.

8. [*Ed.:* no one shall be distrained,]

9. [*Ed.:* Writ to recover lands from one who has not performed services or paid rents for 2 years.]

10. [*Ed.:* more service.]

11. [*Ed.:* no one shall be distrained to do more service.]

12. [*Ed.:* Writ against an abbot to return lands given for charitable purposes that have been used otherwise.]

13. Pl. Com. 94. 243. 10. H. 7. 11. b. 30 H. 6. 5. b. 22. ass. 68. 28. ass. 33. 12. E. 4. 7. b. 8. E. 4 28. b. 4. E. 2. Avow. 202. 18. E. 2. ibidem. a 17. 20. E. 3. ibid. 131. 5. E. 4. 2. 16E. 4. 11. 20. E. 4. 11. 12. H. 423. F. N. B. 10. h. See the first part of the Inst. sect.

Chapter 11

Common Pleas shall not follow our Court, but shall be holden in some place certain.[1]

Before this Statute, Common pleas might have been holden in the Kings Bench, and all originall Writs retournable into the same Bench: And because the Court was holden *Coram Rege,*[2] and followed the Kings Court, and removable at the Kings will, the Retourns were *Ubicunque fuerimus, &c.*[3] whereupon I many discontinuances ensued, and great trouble of jurors, charges of parties, and delay of Justice, for these causes this Statute was made.

[22]

"Common Pleas."

Here it is to be understood, a division of Pleas, for *Placita*[4] are divided in *Placita Coronae,*[5] and *Communia placita:*[6] *Placita Coronae* are otherwise, and aptly called *criminalia,*[7] or *mortalia,*[8] and *placita communia* are aptly called *civilia:*[9] *Placita Coronae* are divided into high Treason, misprision of Treason, petit Treason, Felony, &c. and to their accessories,[10] so called, because they are *contra coronam & dignitatem;*[11] and of these the Court of Common pleas cannot hold plea; of these you may reade at large in the third part of the Institutes. Common or civill pleas are divided into reall, personall, and mixt.

They are not called *Placita Coronae,* as some have said, because the King *jure Coronae*[12] shall have the suite,[13] and Common pleas, because they be held by common persons. For a plea of the Crown may be holden between common

---

1. Mirror cap. 5. §2.
2. [*Ed.:* Before the king,]
3. [*Ed.:* Wheresoever we shall be, etc.]
4. [*Ed.:* Pleas.]
5. [*Ed.:* Pleas of the crown,]
6. [*Ed.:* Common pleas:]
7. [*Ed.:* Criminal pleas before the crown.]
8. [*Ed.:* mortal.]
9. [*Ed.:* civil:]
10. Mirror ca. 1. §4. Stamf. Pl. cor. fo. 1. Vide cap. 17.
11. [*Ed.:* against the [king's] crown and dignity;]
12. [*Ed.:* crown prerogative.]
13. Vide cap. 17.

persons, as an appeale of murder, robbery, rape, felony, mayhem, &c. and the King may be party to a common plea, as to a *Quare impedit*,[14] and the like.

Now as out of the old fields must come the new corne, so our old books do excellently expound, and expresse this matter, as the Law is holden at this day, therefore Glanvill saith,[15] *Placitorum aliud est criminale, aliud civile;*[16] where *Placitum criminale,* is *Placitum Coronae;* and *Placitum civile,*[17] *placitum commune,* named in this Statute.

And Bracton that lived when this Statute was made, saith,[18] *Sciendum quod omnium actionum sive placitorum, (ut inde utatur aequivoce) haec est prima divisio, quod quaedam sunt in rem, quaedam in personam, & quaedam mixtae; Item earū quae sunt in personam, alia criminalia, & alia civilia, secundum quod descendunt ex maleficiis vel contractibus; Item criminalium, alia major, alia minor, alia maxima, secundum criminum quantitatem.*[19]

Fleta saith,[20] *Personalium injuriarum quaedam sunt criminales, & quaedam civiles; criminalium quaedam sententialiter mortem inducunt, quaedam vero minime.*[21]

Britton calleth them pleas *de la Corone,*[22] & Common pleas, and the Court taketh his name of the Common pleas.[23]

To treat of the jurisdiction of this Court, doth belong to another part of the Institutes, but a word or two of the Antiquity of the Court of Common pleas, which is the lock and the key of the Common Law.

Glanvill saith,[24] *Placita in superioribus, &c. sicut & alia quaelibet placita*

14. [*Ed.:* Writ of re-election to recover presentation.]
15. Glanv. li. 1. cap. 1.
16. [*Ed.:* Of pleas, some are criminal and others civil.]
17. [*Ed.:* Civil plea.]
18. Bracton lib. 3. fol. 101. b. Fleta li. 2. cap. 58.
19. [*Ed.:* It is to be known that the first classification of all actions or pleas (to use these terms synonymously) is that some are real, some personal, and some mixed. Of those which are personal, some are criminal and some civil, according to whether they derive from misdeeds or contracts. Of those which are criminal, some are major, others minor, and others are of the most serious kind, according to the magnitude of the crime.]
20. Fleta li. 1. cap. 15.
21. [*Ed.:* Of personal wrongs, some are criminal and some civil; and of criminal some lead to sentence of death and some not.]
22. [*Ed.:* of the crown.]
23. Britton fol. 3. &c.
24. Glanv. lib. 11. c. 1. & lib. 2. cap. 6.

civilia, &c. solet autem id fieri corā Justiciariis Domini Regis in Banco residentibus, &c.[25] And in another place, *Coram Justic' in Banco sedentibus.*[26]

Bracton in divers places cals the Justices of the Court of Common pleas,[27] as Glanvill did, *Justiciarii in Banco residentes,*[28] so called for that the Retourns in the Kings Bench, are *Coram Rege ubicunque fuerimus in Anglia,*[29] as hath been said, because in ancient time it was, as hath been said, removable, and followed the Kings Court.

And therefore all Writs retournable, *Coram Justiciariis nostris apud Westm.*[30] are retournable before the Judges of the Common Pleas, and all Write retournable, *Coram nobis ubicunque tunc fuerimus in Anglia,*[31] are retournable into the Kings Bench.[32]

Britton speaking of the Court of Common Pleas, saith,[33] *Ouster ceo voilloms que Justices demurgent continualment à Westm. ou ailours, ou nous voudrous ordinaire a pleader Common pleas &c.*[34]

Fleta saith,[35] *Habet & (Rex) curiam suam & justiciarios suos residentes, qui recordum habent in hiis, quae coram eis fuer'placitata, & qui potestatem habent de omnibus placitis, & actionibus realibus, personalibus, & mixtis &c.*[36]

It is manifest that this Court began not after the making of this Act, as some have thought, for in the next Chapter,[37] and divers others of this very great Charter mention is made *De Justiciariis nostris de Banco,*[38] which all men know to be the Justices of the Court of Common pleas, commonly called the

25. [*Ed.:* The above pleas, etc., and all other civil pleas, etc., are accustomed to be made before the king's justices sitting on the bench, etc.]

26. [*Ed.:* Before the justices sitting on the bench.]

27. Bract. li. 3. fol. 105. b. & 108. b.

28. [*Ed.:* Justices sitting on the bench.]

29. [*Ed.:* The king's court held throughout England.]

30. [*Ed.:* Before our justices at Westminster.]

31. [*Ed.:* Before us, wheresoever we shall then be in England.]

32. Artic. super. Cart. cap. 5. Fleta lib. 2. cap. 2. F. N. B. 69. m.

33. Britton.

34. [*Ed.:* Moreover we will that justices stay continuously at Westminster, or wherever we ordain common pleas to be pleaded, etc.]

35. Fleta li. c. 28. et. 54

36. [*Ed.:* And the king has his court and his resident justices, who make a record of those things that are pleaded before them, and who have power concerning all pleas and actions, real, personal, and mixed.]

37. [Fleta li] & cap. 13. 7. E. 4. 53. D. & St. 12. b.

38. [*Ed.:* Of our judges of the bench.]

Common | Bench, or the Bench, and Doct. and Stud. saith, that it is a Court   [23]
created by Custome.

The Abbot of B. claimed conusans of plea in Writs of assise, &c.[39] in the
times of King Etheldred, and Edward the Confessor, and before that time,
time out of minde, and pleaded a Charter of confirmation of King Henry the
first to his predecessor, and a graunt, &c. so that the Justices of the one Bench,
or of the other should not intermeddle.

It appeareth by our Books that the Court of Common pleas was in the
reign of Henry the first.[40]

That there was a Court of Common pleas in anno. 1. H. 3.[41] which was
before this Act; *Martinus de Pateshull,*[42] was by Letters Patents constituted
chiefe Justice of the Court of Common pleas in the first yeare of H. 3.

It is resolved by all the Judges in the Exchequer Chamber,[42] that all the
Courts, viz. the Kings Bench, the Common Place, the Exchequer, and the
Chancery, are the Kings Courts, and have been time out of memory, *Issint
que home ne poet scaver que est plus auncient.*[43]

"shall not follow our Court."

Divers speciall cases are out of this Statute.

1. The King may sue any action for any Common plea in the Kings Bench,
for this generall act doth not extend to the King.[44]

[45] 2. If any man be in *custodia Mareschalli*[46] of the Kings Bench, any other
may have an action of Debt, Covenant, or the like personall action by Bill
in the Kings Bench, because he that is in *custodia Mareschalli* ought to have
the priviledge of that Court, and this Act taketh not away the priviledge any
Court, because if he should be used in any other Court, he should not in

---

39. 26. Ass. p. 24.
40. 4. E. 3. 49. 39. E. 3. 21.
41. Rot. pat. 1. H. 3.
42. 9. E. 4. 53.
43. [*Ed.:* So that no one can know which is the more ancient.]
44. 21. H. 3. brief. 883. Tr. 26. E. 1. Coram Rege Northhampton. Tr. 18. E. 1. Coram Rege Rot. 62. 31.
E. 3. prer. 28. 17. E. 3. 50.
45. 31 H. 6: fo. 10,11 Artic. super cart. cap. 4. Pl. Com. 208. b. 38. ass. p. 20. sumis.
46. [*Ed.:* in the custody of the marshal.]

respect of his priviledge answer there, and so it is of any officers, or ministers of that Court: The like Law is of the Court of Chancery, and Exchequer.

3. Any action that is *Quare vi & armis*,[47] where the King is to have a fine, many be purchased out of the Chancery, retournable into the Kings Bench, as *ejectione firmae trñs, vi & armis*,[48] forcible entry, and the like.

4. And a *replevin*[49] may be removed into the Kings Bench, because the King is to have a fine, and so it is in an assise brought in the County where the Kings Bench is.[50]

5. Albeit originally the Kings Bench be restrained by this Act to hold plea of any real action, &c. yet by a mean they may. As if a writ in a real action be by judgment abated in the Court of Common pleas, if this judgement in a Writ of Error be reversed in the Kings Bench, and the Writ adjudged good, they shall proceed upon that Writ in the Kings Bench, as the Judges of the Court of Common pleas should have done, which they doe in the default of others, for necessity, lest any party that hath right should be without remedy, or that there should be a failer of Justice, and therefore Statutes are alwayes so to be expounded, that there should be no failer of Justice, but rather than that should fall out, that case (by construction) should be excepted out of the Statute, whether the Statute be in the negative, or affirmative.[51]

6. In a redisseisin[52] or the like.

"our Court."

Are words collective, and not onley extend to the Kings Bench, but into the Court of Eschequer, Vide Artic. super Cart. Cap. 4.[53]

When judgement is given before the Sheriffe, and the Tenant hath no goods, &c. in that County, he may have a *Certiorare*[54] to remove the Record into the Kings Bench, and there have execution, for that is not *Placitum*.[55] See

---

47. [*Ed.*: Why with force and arms; the pleading form for trespasses.]
48. [*Ed.*: ejection from the land by force & arms.]
49. [*Ed.*: an action to recover possession of goods.]
50. 9 H. 7. 10. 19 E. 3. assise 84. 1. H. 7. 12. Reg. F. N. B. 177. 14. H. 7. 14. 16. E. 3. bre. 661.
51. Stat. de Mirton, cap. 10.
52. [*Ed.*: A second action to recover seisin; the redeseisor is liable to imprisonment.]
53. F. N. B. 1907 224. 246.
54. [*Ed.*: Writ to review a record on appeal.]
55. [*Ed.*: Plea.]

more hereof in the fourth part of the Institutes, Cap. Of the Court of Eschequer.

Chapter 12

I Assises of *Novel Disseisin* and of *Mortdauncestor* shall not be taken but in the   [24]
Shires, and after this manner: If We be out of this Realm, our Chief Justicers
shall send our Justicers through every County once in the year; which with the
Knights of the Shires shall take the said Assises in those Counties; and those
things that at the coming of our foresaid Justicers being sent to take those Assises
in the Counties, cannot be determined, shall be ended by them in some other
place in their Circuit; and those things, which for difficulty of some Articles
cannot be determined by them, shall be referred to our Justices of the Bench,
and there shall be ended.

Before the making of this Statute, the Writs of assise of *Novel disseisin,*[1] and
Mordanc'[2] were retournable, either *coram Rege,*[3] or into the Court of Common
Pleas, and to be taken there, and this appeareth by Glanvill,[4] *Coram me, vel
coram Justiciariis meis.*[5] But since this Statute, these Writs are retournable,
Coram Justiciariis nostris ad assisas, cum in partes illas venerint;[6] by force of
these words, *Mittent Justiciarios nostros per unumquemque comitat̄ nostrum semel in anno, qui cum militibus eorundem comitatuum capiant in comitat̄ illis
assisas prædict'.*[7]

"but in the Shires."[8]

This tendes greatly to the ease of the Jurors, and for saving of charges of the
parties, and of time, so as they might follow their vocations, and proper businesse, and the rather, for that the Assise of *Novel disseisin,* was *frequens &*

1. [*Ed.:* Real action to recover recently deseised lands.]
2. [*Ed.:* Assize to reclaim lands lost at the death of an ancestor.]
3. [*Ed.:* before the king.]
4. Glanv. li. 13. ca. 3. & 33. F. N. B. 177. f. Registrum.
5. [*Ed.:* Before my justices.]
6. [*Ed.:* Before our justices of assize when they come into those parts.]
7. [*Ed.:* Shall send our justices through every of our counties once a year, who with the knights of the
same counties shall take the aforesaid assizes in those counties.]
8. Mirror ca. 5. § 2. See W. 2. ca. 30.

festinum remedium[9] in those dayes, and so was the assise of *Mordanc'* also: It is a great benefit to the subject to have justice administred onto him at home in his owne Country.

For an assise of *Novel disseisin,* and assise of *Mordanc'* see the first part of the *Institutes.*[10]

And where Bracton saith,[11] *Succurritur ei, (i. disseisito) per recognitionem assisæ novæ disseisinæ multis vigiliis excogitatam, & inventam recuperandæ possessionis gratia, quam disseisitus injuste amisit, & sine judicio, ut per summariam cognitionem absq; magna juris solemnitate quasi per compendium, negotium terminetur.*[12] See the *Custumier de Normand',* (composed, as hath been said, in 14.H.3.) sect. 91. & 93. of the Assise of *Novel disseisin,* which being invented and framed in England, as Bracton and others have testfied, must of necessity be transported into Normandy.[13]

But where we yeeld to Bracton, that the Assise of *Novel disseisin* was so invented, so he must yeeld to us, that it was a very auncient invention, for Glanvill maketh mention thereof, and of the Assise of *Mordaunc',* as hath been said, and by the Mirror also the antiquity of Assise *De novel desseisin* doth appeare, who saith, that this writ of Assise of *Novel disseisin,* was ordained in the time of Ranulph de Glanvill.[14]

But the case of 26. *Assise* before touched, doth prove that the Writs of *Assise* are of farre greater antiquity, for there it appeareth that in an *Assise of Novel disseisin,* claimed to have Conusans of Plea, and Writs of *Assise,* and other originall Writs out of the Kings Courts by prescription time out of minde of man, I in the times of S. Edmond, and S. Edward the Confessor, Kings of this Realme before the Conquest, and shewed divers allowances thereof: but true it is, as the ancient Authors affirme, that a new forme of Writs of Assise, for the more speedy recovery of possession, which were called *Festina remedia,*[15]

[25]

---

9. [*Ed.:* a frequent and speedy remedy.]

10. See the first part of the Institutes. sect. 234.

11. Bract. 1. 4. fo. 164.

12. [*Ed.:* The disseised person is aided by a recognition of the assize of novel disseisin, which was thought up and contrived after many wakeful nights for recovering the possession of that which he has unjustly lost, so that the matter is determined by a summary recognition without great formality of law, as it were, by a short cut.]

13. See the Preface of the 2. pt of the Institutes.

14. Glanv. lib. 13. ca. 3. & 33. Custumier de Norm. *ubi supra.* Mir. ca. 2. § 15. 26. Ass. p. 24.

15. [*Ed.:* A speedy remedy,]

was invented in England since the Conquest, & were called *Brevia de assisa nova disseisina;*[16] which Writs so altered continue so untill this day, and according to the alteration is cited in the *Custumier cap.* 93. fol. 107. b.

If an assise be taken *in proprio comitatu,*[17] and the tenant pleade, and after the assise is discontinued by the *non venu*[18] of the Justices, this Act extends to the Assise, but not to a reattachment thereupon, for that the Assise was first arrained and examined in the proper County, neither doth this Act extend to a Writ of attaint, brought upon the verdict of the recognitors of the Assise:[19] And herewith agreeth Britton,[20] who saith, *Et tout conteine la grand Chie des franchises, que ascuns assises soient prises in Counties, pur ceo ne intent nul que certifications, & attaints auter foitz estre pledes, &c.*[21]

And Bracton saith,[22] *Et si ad hoc se habeat communis libertas, quod assisæ extra comitatum capi non debeant, non sequitur quod propter hoc remaneant juratæ in com capiendæ; aliud enim habet privilegium assisa, & aliud jurata.*[23]

An assise is brought in the Kings bench,[24] then being in the County of Suff. (as it may be, as hath been said) of lands lying in that County, the tenant plead in barre, the pl' reply and pray the Assise, the Kings bench is removed to Westm. and there the pl' prayed the Assise, this Statute is, that the Asisse shall not be taken but in the County, and now the Kings bench is in another County, and the originall cannot goe out of this place, for when a Record is once in this Court, here it must remaine, wherefore by th' advise of all the Judges, the Assise was awarded at large, *quia nihil dicit,*[25] and a *Nisi prius*[26] granted in the County of Suff. that there might the Assise be taken. A case

---

16. [*Ed.:* Writs of assize of novel disseisin;]

17. [*Ed.:* in the proper county,]

18. [*Ed.:* non-arrival.]

19. 24. E. 3. 23. 2. E. 3. 23. 1. 1. E. 4. 1.

20. 6. E. 3. 55. 56. Britton cap. 97. fol. 240. F. N. B. 181.

21. [*Ed.:* Whereas it is contained in the great charter of liberties that some assizes shall be taken in the counties, this does not mean that no certificates or attaints be pleaded at other times, etc.]

22. Bracton. lib. 4. fol. 291.

23. [*Ed.:* If someone has a common liberty, that assizes ought not to be taken outside the county, it does not follow from this that juries should remain to be taken in the county; for the assize has one privilege and the jury another.]

24. 6. E. 3. 55. 56. 19. E. 3. ass. 84.

25. [*Ed.:* because he says nothing.]

26. [*Ed.:* a court sitting with a jury.]

worthy of observation, how by this exposition both the parties sute was preserved, and the purvien of this statute observed.

Yet in some case notwithstanding this negative Statute, the asisse should
not have been taken in his proper County.[27] And therefore if a man be disseised
of a Commote or Lordship Marcher in Wales, holden of the King in *Capite*,[28]
as for example of *Gowre*, the Writ of assise should have been directed to the
Sherife of Gloc. within the Realme of England, and albeit the land of Gowre
was out of the power of the Sherife of Gloc. being out of his County within
the dominion of Wales, and this Statute saith that the assise shall not be taken
but in his proper County, yet was the assise taken in the County of Gloc. and
Judgement thereupon given and affirmed in a Writ of error: and the reason
is notable, for the Lord Marcher though he had *jura Regalia*,[29] yet could not
he doe justice in his owne case, and if he should not have remedy in this case
by the Kings writ out of the Chauncery in England, he should not have right
and no remedy by Law given for the wrong done unto him, which the Law
will not suffer, and therefore this case of necessity is by construction excepted
out of the Statute. And it was well said in an old booke,[30] *Quamvis prohibetur
quod communia placita non sequantur curiam nostram, non sequitur propter hoc,
quin aliqua placita singularia sequantur Dominum Regem*,[31] and the like in this
negative Statute.

Hereby it appeareth (that I may observe it once for all) that the best ex-
positors of this and all other Statutes are our bookes and use or experience.

More shall be said hereof in the exposition of the Statute of W. 2.

"of *Mortdauncestor*."

See the first part of the Institutes, sect. 234. Custumier de Norm. cap. 98.
fol. 115.

27. 18. E. 2. assise 382. 13. E. 3. Jurisd. 23. Rot. Parliam. de anno 18. E. 1. inter petitiones. 28. E. 3.
cap. 2.

28. [*Ed.:* in chief.]

29. [*Ed.:* royal (or regalian) rights.]

30. 20. H. 3. tit. brev. 881.

31. [*Ed.:* Although it is prohibited that common pleas should follow our court, it does not follow from
this that other kinds of pleas should follow the lord king.]

"If We be out of this Realm, our Chief Justicers."

This *Capitalis Justitiarius*[32] (when the King is *extra Regnum,* out of the Realme)
is well described by Ockham, *Rege extra Regnum agente, br̄ia dirigebantur sub
nomine præsidentis Justitiarii & testimonio ejusdem.*[33] This is he that I is con- [26]
stituted by letters patents when the King is out of the Kingdome, to be *custos
sive gardianus Regni,*[34] keeper of the Kingdome, and *locum tenens Regis,*[35] and
for his time is *Prorex,*[36] such as was Edward Duke of Cornewall 13. E. 3. Lionell
Duke of Clarence 21. E. 3. And the *teste* to all originall Writs, were *teste Lionello
filio nostro charissimo custode Angliae &c.*[37] John Duke of Bedford 5. H. 5.
Richard Duke of Warwick 3. E. 4. and many others:[38] before whom as keepers
of the Kingdome, Parliaments have been holden, and as hath been said, the
teste[39] of originall Writs are under the name of the Keeper, which no officer
can doe, when the King is within the Realme. In 8. H. 5. a great question
arose whether if the Kings Lieutenant, or Keeper of his Kingdome under his
teste, doth summon a Parliament, the King being beyond sea, and in the meane
time the King returne into England, whether the Parliament so summoned
might proceed: it was doubted that *in praesentia majoris cessaret potestas minoris,*[40] and therefore it was enacted that the Parliament should proceed, and
not be dissolved by the Kings returne.[41] Now that this Statute is to be intended
of such a Lieutenant or keeper of the Kingdome, it is proved by this Act it
selfe, *Capitales Justitiarii nostri mittent Justitiarios nostros.*[42] that is, they shall
name and send Justices by authority under the great seale under their owne
teste; which none can doe but the King himselfe if he be present, or his Lieutenant, or the keeper or guardian of his Kingdome, if he be, as this Act

32. [*Ed.:* Chief justiciars.]
33. [*Ed.:* When the king was doing business outside the realm, writs were directed under the name of
the presiding justice and witnessed by the same.]
34. [*Ed.:* keeper or guardian of the realm,]
35. [*Ed.:* the king's lieutenant,]
36. [*Ed.:* viceroy,]
37. [*Ed.:* witness our beloved son Lionel keeper of England, etc.]
38. Rot. Parliament 13. E. 3. nu. 11. 5. H. 5. nu. 1. 3. E. 4. nu. 14. 21. E. 3. fol. 37.
39. [*Ed.:* a witness.]
40. [*Ed.:* in the presence of a greater man, the power of a lesser ceases,]
41. 8. H. 5. cap. 1.
42. [*Ed.:* Our chief justiciars shall send our justices.]

speaketh, *extra Regnum:*[43] and this exposition is made *ex verbis & visceribus Actus.*[44] But then it is demanded, whether this *locum tenens Regis, seu custos Regni,*[45] was called *capitalis Justitiarius* before the making of this act, and this very name you shall read in Glanvile, who saith *Praeterea sciendum, quod secundum consuetudines Regni, nemo tenetur respondere in Curia Domini sui de aliquo libero tenemento suo sine praecepto domini Regis, vel ejus Capitalis Justitiarii,*[46] where *Capitalis Justitiarius* is taken for *Custos Regni.*[47]

It is to be observed, that before the raigne of King Ed. 1. the Kings Chiefe Justice was some time called *summus Justitiarius,*[48] sometime *praesidens Justitiarius,*[49] and sometimes *Capitalis Justitiarius.* In *anno primo* E. 1. his chiefe Justice was called *Capitalis Justitiarius ad placita coram Rege tenenda,*[50] and so ever since; and this chiefe Justice is created by Writ, and all the rest of the Justices of either bench, by letters patents.[51]

In Glanviles time,[52] and before, the Kings Justices were called *Justiciae,* the returnes of Writs being *coram Justiciis meis,*[53] so as the Kings Justices were antiently called *Justitiae,* for that they ought not to be only *Justi* in the *concrete,* but *ipsa Justitia,*[54] in the abstract. Since that time, as by this great Charter in many places it appeareth, they are called *Justitiarii à Justitia.*[55] The honourable manner of the creation of these Justices you may read in Fortescue.[56]

---

43. [*Ed.:* outside the realm.]

44. [*Ed.:* from the words and innermost parts of the act.]

45. [*Ed.:* King's lieutenant, or keeper of the realm.]

46. [*Ed.:* It is further to be known that, according to the customs of the realm, no one is bound to answer in his lord's court for any freehold of his without a command from the lord king or his chief justiciar.]

47. [*Ed.:* keeper of the kingdom.]

48. [*Ed.:* principal Justice.]

49. [*Ed.:* presiding Justice.]

50. [*Ed.:* chief justice for holding pleas before the king.]

51. Glanvil. lib. 12. cap. 25. Rot. Pat. an. 1. E. 1. Hereof you may reade more in the 4. part of the Institut. cap of the Court of Kings bench.

52. Glanvil. lib. 2. c. 6. Hovend. fol. 413.

53. [*Ed.:* before my Justices.]

54. [*Ed.:* Justice itself.]

55. [*Ed.:* [called] justices from justice.]

56. Fortescu. cap. 51.

"in some other place in their Circuit."

This is taken largely and beneficially, for they may not only make adjour-nement before the same Justices in their Circuite, but also to Westm. or to Serjeants Inne, or any other place out of their Circuite, by the equity of this Statute, and according as it had been alwayes used:[57] for constant allowance in many cases doth make Law.

a The Statute speaking only of an adjournment in Assise of *novell disseisin, &c.*[58] and yet a certificate of an Assise is within this Statute.

b *Sed rerum progressus ostendunt multa, quae initio praevideri non possunt.*[59]   *b Regula.*

c[60] Time found out, that because the justices of Assise came not but once in the yeare, and that any adjournment could not have beene made by this Act, unles the jurors had given a verdict, for this Act saith *propter difficultatem aliquorum articulorum,*[61] and not upon demurrer, doubtfull plea, *Estoppel, &c.*[62] or for preservation of the Kings peace, and no provision was made by this Act, if the ten in the assise of *Mordaunc.* had made a foreine vowcher, or pleaded a foreine plea: all these are holden by the Statute of W. 2. cap. 30 as shall appeare when we come thereunto.

Chapter 13

| Assises of *Darrein Presentment*[1] shall be alway taken before our Justices of the   [27]
Bench, and there shall be determined.

It appeareth by Glanvil,[2] that before this Statute the Writ of Darrein pre-sentment was retornable *coram me vel Justic. meis.*[3] And the reason of this Act was for expedition, for doubt of the laps.

---

57. 12. H. 4. 20. 29. Ass. 1. 27. Ass. 5. 60. 4. E. 3. 41.
58. *a* 12. H. 4. 9.
59. [*Ed.:* The course of events shows up many things which were not provided for at the outset.]
60. *c* 48. E. 3. 7. 47. ass. 1. 39. E. 3. 6. 32 ass. 9. 21. E. 3. 3. 42. E. 3. 11.
61. [*Ed.:* on account of the difficulty of any articles,]
62. *7. H. 6. 9. 3. E. 3. 16. 8. ass. 15 15. E. 3. ass. 96. 17. E. 3. 28. 14. E. 3. ass. 110. 20. E. 3. ass. 123. 22. E. 3. 5. 29. ass. 7 34. ass. 3. 43. ass. 1. 3. H. 4. 18. 22. H. 6. 19.
1. [*Ed.:* Assize to recover an advowson by descent from one's ancestors.]
2. Glanvil. lib. 13. cap. 16. 18. 19. Bracton. lib. 4. fol. 238. &c. Britton cap. 90. fol. 222. Fleta lib. 5. c. 11. Regist. fol. 30. F. N. B. fol. 30. W. 2. cap. 30. 5. Mar. Dier. 135. 9. Eliz. Dier. 260.
3. [*Ed.:* before me or my justices.]

By the Statute of W. 2. it is provided, that justices of *Nisi prius*[4] may give judgement in an assise of *Darrein presentment*,[5] and *Quare impedit*.[6]

Chapter 14

A Freeman shall not be amerced for a small Fault, but after the manner of the Fault, and for a great Fault, after the greatness thereof, saving to him his Contenement; and a Merchant likewise, saving to him his Merchandise; and any other's Villein than ours shall be likewise amerced, saving his Wainage, if he fall into our mercy. And none of the said Amercements shall be assessed but by the oath of honest and lawful Men of the Vicinage. Earls and Barons shall not be amerced but by their Peers, and after the manner of their Offence. No Man of the Church shall be amerced after the quantity of his Spiritual Benefice, but after his Lay Tenement, and after the quantity of his Offence.

"A Freeman."

A free man hath here a speciall understanding, and is taken for him, *qui tenet libere*,[1] for a free-holder, as it is taken in the *venire fac*.[2] Where *duodecim liberos, &c*.[3] *homines* are taken for free-holders, and this appeareth by this Act which saith, *salvo contenemento suo*,[4] whereof more shall be said in this Chapter. The words of this Act being *liber homo*, it extendeth as well to sole Corporations, as Bishops &c. as to lay men, but not to Corporations aggregate of many, as Major and Commonalty, and the like, for they cannot be comprehended under these words *liber homo, &c*.[5]

"shall not be amerced."

This Act extends to amerciaments and not to fines imposed by any Court of Justice: what amerciaments be, and whereof this word Amerciament cometh,

---

4. [*Ed.*: court sitting with a jury.]
5. [*Ed.*: reelection to recover presentation.]
6. [*Ed.*: Actions to recover an advowson (and) a presentation.]
1. [*Ed.*: who holds freely,]
2. [*Ed.*: Writ for summoning a jury.]
3. [*Ed.*: twelve free men, etc.]
4. [*Ed.*: saving his contenement,]
5. [*Ed.*: free man, etc.]

see the 8. book of my Reports, see also there, that this Statute is in some cases of amerciaments, to be intended of private men, and not of amerciaments of officers, or ministers of Justice, so as *liber homo,* is not intended of officers, or ministers of Justice.[6] And how, and in what cases the afferment shall be, you shall also read there, together also with the ancient Authors, and many other authorities of Law, concerning these matters.[7]

It appeareth by Glanvile[8] that this Act was made in affirmance of the common Law, as hereafter shall appeare, but yet the Writ *de moderata misericordia,*[9]   [28]
is grounded upon this Statute, for it reciteth the Statute and giveth remedy to the partie that is excessively americied,

"saving to him his Contenement."

First for the word, you shall read it in Glanvile,[10] *Est autem misericordia Domini Regis, qua quis per juramentum legalium hominum de viceneto eatenus amerciandus est, ne quid de suo honorabili contenemento amittet.*[11]

And Bracton. *Salvo contenemento suo.*[12,13]

Fleta, *continentia.*[14,15]

2. For the signification, Contenement signifieth his countenance, which he hath, together with, and by reason of his free-hold, and therefore is called contenement, or continence and in this sense doth the Statute of 1. E. 3.[16] and old Nat. Brev. use it, where countenance is used for contenement: the armor of a Souldior is his countenance, the books of a Scholler his countenance, and the like.

6. Vide W. 1. cap. 6.

7. W. 1. cap. 18. 11. H. 4. 5. Lib. 8. fol. 39. 40. Greyslies case.

8. Glanvil. lib. 9. cap. 11. Fleta lib. 2. c. 60. 10. E. 2. action sur le statut. 84. Regist. 86. 184. 187.

9. [*Ed.:* Writ based on Magna Carta for one emersed in a court not of record for an offense more serious than his actions.]

10. Glanvil. *ubi sup.*

11. [*Ed.:* The mercy of the lord king means that someone is to be amerced by the oath of lawful men of the neighbourhood, but not so as to lose his decent contenement. ("Contenement" is the land held by estate.)]

12. [*Ed.:* saving his contenement.]

13. Bracton lib. 3. fol. 116.

14. Fleta. lib. 1. c. 43. W. 1. cap. 6.

15. [*Ed.:* contenement.]

16. 1. E. 3. cap. 4. Stat. 2. Vet. N. B. fol. 11.

"and a Merchant likewise, saving to him his Merchandise;"

For trade and traffique is the livelihood of a Merchant, and the life of the Commonwealth, wherein the King and every subject hath interest, for the Merchant is the good bayliffe of the Realme to export and vent the native commodities of the Realme, and to import and bring in the necessary commodities for the defence and benefit of the Realme.

"and any other's Villein than ours shall be in likewise amerced, saving his Wainage."[17]

Here Villanus[18] is taken for one that is a bondman, *nativus de sanguine*[19] or *servus*.[20]

A Villein is free to sue, and to be sued, by and against all men, saving his Lord.

"saving his Wainage."

Wainagium, is the contenement or countenance of the Villen, and cometh of the Saxon word *Wagna,* which signifieth a Cart or Waine, wherewith he was to doe Villein service, as to carry the dung of the Lord out of the scite of the Mannor unto the Lords land, and casting it upon the same, and the like, and it was great reason to save his wainage, for otherwise the miserable creature, was to carry it on his back, it is said here *Wainagio suo,*[21] but yet the Lord may take it at his pleasure.[22]

But hereby it appeareth, that albeit the Law of England, is a Law of mercy, yet is it a Law, which is now turned into a shadow, for where by the wisdome of the Law, these amerciaments were instituted to deterre both demaundants and plaintiffs from unjust suits, and tenants, and defendants from unjust defences, which was the cause in ancient times of fewer suits, but now we have

---

17. See the first part of the Institutes sect. 172. 189.
18. [*Ed.:* serfs.]
19. [*Ed.:* nief, or serf, by blood.]
20. [*Ed.:* serf.]
21. [*Ed.:* The tenament of a villein.]
22. See the first part of the Instituts sect. 172.

but a shadow of it. *Habemus quidem fenatus-consultum, sed in tabulis recon-ditum, & tanquam gladium in vagina repositum.*[23,24]

"Earls and Barons shall not be amerced but by their peers, &c."[25]

Although, this statute be in the negative, yet long usage hath prevailed against it, for the amerciament of the Nobility is reduced to a certainty, *viz.* a Duke 10 l. an Earle 5 l. a Bishop, who hath a Baronie 5 l. &c. in the Mirror it is said that the amerciament of an Earle was an C l., and of a Baron an C. marks.

It is said that a Bishop shall be amercied for an escape 100 l. A Bayler shall be amercied for a negligent escape of a Felon attaint 100 l. and of a Felon indited only 5 l.

If a Noble man and a Common person joyne in an action, and become non-sute, they shall be severally amercied: viz. the Noble man at C s. and the Common person according to the Statute, therefore when a Noble man is plaintiffe, it is pollicy rather to discontinue the action, then to be non-suite.

"by their Peers."

By his peeres, that is, by his equalls.

| The generall division of persons by the law of England, is either one that   [29]
is noble, and in respect of his nobility of the Lords house of Parliament, or one of the Commons of the Realme, and in respect thereof, of the house of Commons in Parliament,[26] and as there be diverse degrees of Nobility, as Dukes, Marquesses, Earles, Viscounts and Barons, and yet all of them are comprehended within this word, Pares, so of the Commons of the Realme, there be Knights, Esquires, Gentlemen, Citizens, Yeomen, and Burgesses of severall degrees, and yet all of them of the Commons of the Realme, and as every of the Nobles is one a Peer to another, though he be of a severall degree, so is it of the Commons, and as it hath been said of Men, so doth it hold of Noble Women, either by birth, or by mariage, but see hereof Cap. 29.

---

23. [*Ed.:* We have a certain *senatusconsultum* (enactment), but it lies buried in the tablets like a sword in its sheath.]

24. Cecero.

25. Mirror cap. 1. Sect. 3. 38. E. 3. 31. 4. H. 6. 7. 9. H. 6. 2. 19. E. 4. 9. 21. E. 4. 77. b. Mirror. cap. 4. de amerciam. 3. E. 3. Coron. 370 Stanf. pl. cor. fol. 35. b. Mirror. *ubi sup.* Britton fol. 17. b. & 34. b.

26. Britton cap. 2. fol. 36.

Bracton saith,[27] *Comites vero vel Barones, non sunt amerciandi, nisi per Pares suos, & secundum modum delicti, & hoc per Barones de Scaccario, vel coram ipso Rege. Nulla Ecclesiastica persona amercietur secundum quantitatem beneficii sui Ecclesiastici, sed secundum Laicum tenent-suum.*[28]

"Man of the Church."

For Ecclesiasticall persons, and their diversities, and degrees, see the first part of the Institutes, *ubi sup.*

"Benefice."

Benefice. *Beneficium* is a large word, and is taken for any Ecclesiasticall promotion or Spirituall living whatsoever.

Here appeareth a priviledge of the Church, that if an Ecclesiasticall person be amercied (though amerciaments belong to the King) yet he shall not be amercied in respect of his Ecclesiasticall promotion, or benefice, but in respect of his lay fee, and according to the quantity of his fault, which is to be afferred: and Bracton setteth downe the oath of the afferers of amerciaments, *& ad hoc fideliter faciend. affidabunt amerciatores, quod neminem gravabunt per odium, nec alicui deferent propter amorem, & quod celabunt ea quae audierunt.*[29]

Chapter 15

No Town nor Freeman shall be distrained to make Bridges nor Banks, but such as of old time and of right have been accustomed to make them in the time of King Henry our Grandfather.

Here it is to be observed, that in the raigne of King John, and of his elder brother King Richard, which were troublesome and irregular times, diverse

27. Bracton. lib. 3. fol. 116. b. Brit. fol. 2. b. Fleta. lib. 1. cap. 43. & lib. 2c. 60. Vide lib. nigr. Scaccarii parte 1. cap. 4. Of Ancient time the Barons of the Exchequer were Barons and Peers of the Realme. See the first part of the Institutes Sect. 133. Bracton lib. 3. fol. 116. Fleta lib. 1. c. 43.

28. [*Ed.:* Earls or barons are not to be amerced except by their peers, and according to the manner of the offence, and this is by the barons of the Exchequer or before the king himself. No ecclesiastical person shall be amerced according to the size of his ecclesiastical benefice, but according to his lay tenement.]

29. [*Ed.:* and the amercers shall be sworn faithfully to this, that they should not vex anyone through hatred, nor favour anyone through affection, and that they should conceal what they hear.]

oppressions, exactions, and injuries, were incroached upon the Subject in these Kings names, for making of Bulwarks, Fortresses, Bridges, and Bankes, contrary to Law and right.

But the raigne of King Henry the second is commended for three things, first, that his privy Counsell were wise, and expert in the Lawes of the Realme. Secondly, that he was a great defender and maintainer of the rights of his Crowne, and of the Lawes of his Realme. Thirdly, that he had learned and upright Judges, who executed Justice according to his Lawes. Therefore for his great and never dying honour, this and many other Acts made in the raigne of Hen. 3. doe referre to his raigne, that matters should be put in use, as they were of right accustomed in his time, so as this Chapter is a declaration of the common Law, and so in the raignes of Hen. 4. and Hen. 5. the Parliaments referre to the raigne of King Edw. 1. who was a Prince of great fortitude, wisedome and justice.[1]

And diverse Statutes referre to King Edward the third who was a noble, wise, and warlike King, in whose raigne, the Lawes did principally flourish.

| "Banks."   [30]

Is here taken for *Ripa*, which is *extrema & eminentior terrae ora, quam fluvius utrinque alluit.*[2]

But the making of bulwarks, fortresses, and other things of like kinde, were not prohibited by this Act, because they could not be erected, but either by the King himself, or by Act of Parliament.[3]

Chapter 16

No Banks shall be defended from henceforth, but such as were in defence in the time of King Henry our Grandfather, by the same Places and the same Bounds, as they were wont to be in his time.

---

1. See cap. 35. 37. See chart. de Foresta cap. 1. & 3. Rot. Parliam. nu. 82. 13. R. 2. c. 5. 4. H. 4. cap. 2. 3. H. 5. cap. 8. 27. H. 6. cap. 2.

2. [*Ed.:* the utmost and more prominent line of the land which a river flows against on both sides.]

3. 4. H. 8. cap. 1. 2. & 3. Phil. & Mar. cap. 1.

That is, that no owner of the Banks of rivers shall so appropriate, or keep the rivers severall to him, to defend or barre others, either to have passage, or fish there, otherwise, then they were used in the raigne of King H. 2.

This Statute, saith the Mirror,[1] is out of use, *Car plusors riverssont ore appropries & engarnies, & mise in defence, que soilount estre commons a pisher & user en temps le Roy Henry 2.*[2]

Chapter 17

No Sheriff, Constable, Escheator, Coroner, nor any other our Bailiffs, shall hold Pleas of our Crown.

One of the mischiefes before this Statute was, That none of them here named, could command the Bishop of the Diocesse to give the delinquent his Clergy, where he ought to have it, for as Bracton saith,[1] *Nullus alius, praeter regem, possit Episcopo demandare, &c.*[2] And therewith agreeth our other old, and later Books,[3] that the Bishop is not to attend upon any inferiour Court, nor that any inferiour Court can write unto, or command the Bishop, but the King, (that is) the Kings great Courts of Record, and such, as since that time have authority by Act of Parliament.

Another cause was, that the life of man, which of all things in this world, is the most precious, ought to be tried before Judges of learning, and experience in the Laws of the Realme: For *ignorantia Judicis est saepenumero calamitas innocentis. Et cum ex quo Magna charta de libertatibus Angliae alias concessa, (quam quidem chartam Dominus Rex in Parliamento suo apud Westm. an. Regni sui 28. ad requisitionem omnium praelatorum, Comitum, Baronum, & communitatis totius Regni, de novo concessit, renovavit, & confirmavit) placita coronae ipsi Domino Regi specialiter reservantur, per quod nullus de Regno hujusmodi placita tenere potest, seu habere, sine speciali concessione, post confirmationem*

Regula.

1. Mirror ca. 5. § 2.
2. [*Ed.:* For many rivers are now appropriated, and stocked, and put in defence, which used to be common for fishing and using in the time of King Henry II.]
1. Bract. li. 3. fo. 106.
2. [*Ed.:* No one other than the king may send for a bishop, etc.]
3. Brit. c. 104. fo. 248. Fleta li. 5. ca. 24. 8 E. 3. 59. 40 E. 3. 2. 14. H. 4. 27. 15. E. 3. conusans 41. 14. H. 7. 26. 21. H. 7. 34. 35.

chartae praedictae factae.[4,5] In the same yeare, and terme, *Coram Rege,*[6] a complaint by the Abbot of Feversham, both cases adjudged in the Kings Bench,
whereunto they were referred by the Parliament. See Michael.17. Edw. 1. in
Banco. Rotulo. 33. Southampton.

The Chapter of Magna charta here intended, and in both the said Records
I expressed, is this 17. Chapter of Magna charta now in hand. By these Records   [31]
two things are to be observed. 1. That this is a generall Law, by reason of these
words, *Vel alii balivi nostri,*[7] under which words are comprehended all Judges
or Justices of any Courts of Justice. 2. Albeit it be provided by the ninth
Chapter of Magna Charta, *Quod Barones de quinque portubus, & omnes alii
portus habeant omnes libertates, & liberas consuetudines suas;*[8] That these ge-
nereall words must be understood of such liberties, and customes onely, as
are not afterwards in the same Charter by expresse words taken away, and
resumed to the Crown.[9] And therefore if the Maior and Barons of the Cinque
Ports had power before this Act to hold pleas of the Crown, yet by this Act
of the seventeenth Chapter, they are abrogated, and resumed: a notable and
a leading judgement. Both these Records being within two years after the
confirmation of King E. 1. of Magna Charta, are worthy to be read and observed.

"Sheriff,"

See for his name, office, and antiquity in the first part of the Institutes. sect.
234.[10]

---

4. [*Ed.:* ignorance in the judge is oftentimes a disaster for the innocent. And since the great charter
of the liberties of England—which charter the lord king (Edward I), at Westminster in the twenty-eighth
year of his reign, at the request of all the prelates, earls, barons, and commonalty of the whole realm, has
newly granted, renewed, and confirmed—it was granted that pleas of the crown of the selfsame lord king
should be specially reserved, so that no one of the realm can hold or have such pleas without a special
grant, after the confirmation made of the aforesaid charter.]

5. Pasch. 30. E. 1. Coram Rege Kane. The Mayor and Barons of the 5. Ports. compl. in Parliament.

6. [*Ed.:* Before the king (i.e. in the King's Bench).]

7. [*Ed.:* Or our other bailiffs.]

8. [*Ed.:* That the barons of the cinque ports, and all other ports, should have all their liberties and free
customs.]

9. See Pasch. 33. E. 1. Coram Rege. The Prior of Tinemouths case, Northumberl.

10. I. pt. Institutes sect. 234, 248.

"Constable."

Is here taken for *Castellanus,* a *Castellein,* or Constable of a Castle, for so doth the Mirror interpret it.[11] And *Castellanus est qui custodit castellum, aut est Dominus castelli;*[12] And so doth Bracton; *Debet, &c. ostendere castellano, sicut constabulario turris, &c.*[13] And therewith agreeth Fleta,[14] *Item nullae prisae capiantur de aliquo per aliquem constabularium, castellanum, praeterquam de villa, in qua situm est castrum.*[15]

And the Statute of W. 1.[16] agreeth herewith, *Des prises, des constables, ou castelleins, faits des autres, &c.*[17]

And *Castellani* were men in those dayes of account, and authority, and for pleas of the Crown, &c. had the like authority within their precincts, as the Sheriffe had within his Bailiwick before this Act, and they commonly sealed (which I have often seen in many, and have cause to know, that some of the auncient family of de Sperham in Norff. did) with their portraiture on horse-back.

Now for the number of Castles, in ancient time, within this Realme, *Certum est Regis Henrici secundi temporibus Castella 1115. in Anglia extitisse.*[18]

And it is to be observed, That regularly every Castle containeth a Mannor, so as every Constable of a Castle is Constable of a Mannor, and by the name of the Castle the Mannor shall passe, and by the name of the Mannor the Castle shall passe.[19]

For this word, *Constabularius,* his office, and antiquity, see the first part of the Institutes. sect. 379.

And albeit the franchises of Infangthiefe, and Outfangthiefe, to be heard and determined within Court Barons belonging to Mannors, were within the said mischiefe, yet we finde, but not without great inconvenience, that the

---

11. Mirror cap 5. § 2. Bracton lib. 5. fo. 363. li 2. fo. 69. Vide cap. 19.

12. [*Ed.:* A castellain is he who keeps a castle, or is lord of the castle.]

13. [*Ed.:* Ought, etc. to show the castellain or constable of the tower, etc.]

14. Fleta lib. 2. ca. 43.

15. [*Ed.:* Also, no prises shall be taken from anyone by any constable or castellain, except of the vill in which the castle is situated.]

16. W. 1. ca. 7. & 31.

17. [*Ed.:* Of prises taken by constables, or castellains, from others, etc.]

18. [*Ed.:* It was certified in the time of King Henry II that there were 1,115 castles in England.]

19. See the first part of the Institutes, fol. 5. Verbo Holme.

same had some continuance after this Act. But either by this Act, or *per desuetudinem*,[20] for inconvenience, these franchises within Mannors are antiquated and gone.[21]

"Coroner,"

His name is derived *à Corona,* so called, because he is an Officer of the Crown, and hath Conusance of some pleas, which are called *Placita coronae.*[22]

For his antiquity, see the Mirror,[23] who (treating of Articles established by the ancient Kings, Alfred, &c.) saith, *Auxi ordains suer Coronours in chescun County, & Viscounts a garder le peace, quant les Countees soy demisterent del gard, & Bayliffes in lieu de centeners,*[24] (that is) Coroners in every County, and Sheriffes were ordained to keep the peace, when the Earles dismist themselves of the custody of the Counties, and Bayliffes in place of Hundreders.

For his dignity and authority, Britton saith in the person of the King,[25] *Purceo que nous volons, que Coroners sont in chescun Country principals gardens de | nostre peace, a porter Record des pleas de nostre Corone, & de lour views, & abjurations, & de utlagaries, volons que ilz sont eslieus solonque ceo, que est contein in nous Statutes de lour election, &c.*[26]   [32]

And a Common Merchant being chosen a Coroner, was removed, for that he was *Communis Mercator.*[27],[28]

*[29] By the auncient Law, he ought to be a Knight, honest, loyall, and sage, *Et qui melius sciat, & possit officio illi intendere.*[30] For this was the policy of

---

20. [*Ed.:* by disuse.]

21. Lamb. leg. Ed. c. 26 Bract. li. 3. fo. 154. Brit. ca. 15. fo. 90. Fleta li. 1. ca. 47. Hovend. pte posterior. fol. 345. Mat. Par. Anno 1259. 44. H. 3. pl. Parl. 18. E. 1. Rot. 11. 2 R. 3. 10.

22. [*Ed.:* Pleas of the crown.]

23. Mirror cap. 1. § 3.

24. [*Ed.:* There were also ordained coroners in every county, and sheriffs to keep the peace, when the earls gave up the custody, and bailiffs instead of the hundreders.]

25. Brit. ca. 3. fol. 3. Stam. Pl. Cor. 48. c.

26. [*Ed.:* [Therefore] we will that the coroners in every county shall be keepers of our peace, and bear record of the pleas of our crown, and of their views, abjurations, and outlawries; and we will that they be elected according to that which is contained in our statutes concerning their election, etc.]

27. [*Ed.:* A common merchant.]

28. Rot. brevium. 5. E. 3. nu. 38. Registr. 177. W. 1. cap. 10.

29. *Registr. 177.

30. [*Ed.:* And, who knows best and is best able to hold that office.]

prudent antiquity, that Officers did ever give a grace to the place, and not the place only to grace the Officer.

But what authority had the Sheriffe in pleas of the Crown before this Statute?[31] This appeareth by Glanvill, that the Sheriffe in the Tourn, (for that is to be intended) held plea of theft, for he saith; *Excipitur crimen furti, quod ad Vice-comitem pertinet, & in Comitatibus placitatur;*[32] But he may enquire of all felonies by the Common Law, except the death of man.

And what authority had the Coroner? the same authority he now hath, in case when any man come to violent, or untimely death, *super visum corporis, &c.*[33] Abjurations, and out-lawries, &c. appeales of deaths by bill, &c. This authority of the Coroner, viz. the Coroner solely to take an indictment, *super visum corporis;* and to take an appeale, and to enter the appeale, and the Count remaineth to this day. But he can proceed no further, either upon the indictment, or appeale, but to deliver them over to the Justices. And this is saved to them by the Statute of W. 1. cap. 10. And this appeareth by all our old Books, Book cases, and continuall experience.[34]

And for the further authority of the Coroner in case of high treason, see the Book of 19. Hen. 6. fol. 47.[35] and consider well thereof.

But the authority of the Sheriffe to heare and determine theft, or other felonies by the Common Law, (except the death of man) in the Tourn, is wholly taken away by this Statute, howbeit his power to take indictments of felonies, and other mis-deeds within his jurisdiction, is not taken away by this Act.[36]

Chapter 18

If any that holdeth of Us Lay-Fee do die, and our Sheriff or Bailiff do shew our Letters Patents of our Summon for Debt, which the dead man did owe to Us, it shall be lawful to our Sheriff or Bailiff to attach and inroll all the Goods and

---

31. Vide postea c. 35. Glanv. li. 1. cap. 2. & lib. 14. cap. 8. W. 2. cap. 13. 22. E. 4. fol. 22.

32. [*Ed.:* The crime of theft is excepted, for it belongs to the sheriff and is pleaded in the counties;]

33. [*Ed.:* upon the view of the body, etc.]

34. Mirror cap. 1. § Coroners. & cap. 5. § 2. Bracton lib. 3. fol. 121. Brit. c. 1. fol. 3. Fleta li. 1. cap. 18. 25. 22. Ass. 97. 98, &c. 3. H. 7. cap. 3. Stamf. Pl. co. 64. 116, 117.

35. 19. H. 6. fol. 47.

36. W. 2. c. 13. 1. E. 3. Stat. 2. ca. 17. 1. E. 4. 3. 1. R. 3. cap. 4.

Chattels of the Dead being found in the said Fee, to the value of the same Debt, by the sight and testimony of lawful men: So that nothing thereof shall be taken away, until we be clearly paid off the Debt; and the Residue shall remain to the Executors, to perform the Testament of the Dead; and if nothing be owing unto Us, all the Chattels shall go to the use of the Dead; saving to his Wife, and Children, their reasonable parts.[1]

By this Chapter three things are to be observed; First, that the King by his prerogative shall be preferred in satisfaction of his debt by the Executors, before any other; Secondly, that if the Executors have sufficient to pay the Kings debt, I the heire that is to beare the countenance, and sit in the seate of his [33] ancester, or any purchaser of his lands shall not be charged. Thirdly, if nothing be owing to the King, or any other, all the Chattells shall goe to the use of the dead, that is, to his Executors, or Administrators, saving to his Wife and Children their reasonable parts, which is *consilium*,[2] and not *praeceptum;*[3] and the nature of a saving regularly is, to save a former right, and not to give, or create a new, and therefore, where such a Custome is, that the Wife and Children shall have the Writ *de rationabili parte bonorum*,[4] this Statute saveth it. And this Writ doth not lye without a particular Custome, for that the Writ in the Register is grounded upon a Custome, which (as hath been said) is saved by this Act.

*[5] But that it was never the Common law (though there be great variety in books) heare what Bracton saith, who wrote soone after this Act. *Neq; uxorem, neq; liberos amplius capere de bonis defuncti patris vel viri mobilibus, quam fuerit eis specialiter relictum, nisi hoc sit de speciali gratia testatoris, utpote si bene meriti in ejus vita fuerint, &c. vix enim inveniretur aliquis civis, qui in vita magnum quaestum faceret, si in morte sua cogeretur invitus bona sua relinquere pueris indoctis, vel luxuriosis, & uxoribus male meritisi & ideo necessarium est valde, quod illis in hac parte libera facultas tribuatur. Per hoc enim tollet maleficium,*

---

1. Ockham Regist 281. b. 17. E. 3. 73. 27. E. 3. 88. 29. E. 3. 13. 41. E. 3. 15. 41. E. 3. execut. 38. 4. E. 4. 16. F. N. B. 28. b. 33. H. 8. c. 39. See before cap. 8.

2. [*Ed.:* advice,]

3. [*Ed.:* command,]

4. [*Ed.:* for a reasonable share of the goods,]

5. Mirror cap. 5. § 2. Glanv. lib. 12. c. 20. Bracton. 1. 2. fol. 60. b. Fleta. l. 2. cap. 50. Regist. 142. 34. E. 1. detinew 60. 1. E. 2. ib. 56. 17. E. 2. ib. 58. 30. E. 3. 2. 26. 31. E. 3. rn'der 6. 39. E. 3. 6. 10. 17. E. 3. 17. 40. E. 3. 38. 3. E. 3. det. 156. 1. E. 4. 6 7. E. 4. 21. 13. H. 4 Sever. 30. 31. H. 8. Rationab. parte Bro. 6. Bract. 1. 2. fol. 61.

animabit ad virtutem & tam uxoribus, quam liberis bene faciendi dabit occa-
sionem, quod quidem non fieret, si se scirent indubitanter certam partem obtinere
etiam sine testatoris voluntate.[6]

Note the reason hereof maketh against perpetui-ties.

But the administrators of a man, that die intestate, or executor of any, that make no disposition of his whole personall estate, goods, debts, and chattells, the administrators, or executors after the debts paid and Will performed, ought not to take any thing to his or their owne use, but ought, though there be no particular Custome, to divide them, according to this Statute: and the said ancient, and latter authorities (then which there can be no better direction) may guide them therein: and this right doth this Statute of Magna Charta save by these words, *salvis uxori, & liberis suis, rationabilibus partibus suis.*[7] So as though the Statute doth give no Action, yet their parts are saved hereby, which by Glanvile, and other ancient Authors appeare to belong to them; and the executor, or administrator shall be allowed of this distribution, according to this Statute, upon his account before the Ordinary.

Chapter 19

No Constable, nor his Bailiff, shall take Corn or other Chattels of any man, if the man be not of the town where the Castle is, but he shall forthwith pay for the same, unless that the will of the seller was to respite the Payment: And if he be of the same town, the Price shall be paid unto him within forty days.

Here also it appeareth, that in this Chapter *Constabularius*[1] is taken for *Castellanus:*[2,3] and this taking by *Castelleins,* though the Castell was kept for the defence of the Realme, was an unjust oppression of the Subject, and this

---

6. [*Ed.:* Neither the wife nor the children shall take more of the movable goods of the deceased father or husband than was specially left to them, except by the special favour of the testator, for instance if they have deserved well of him in their lifetime, etc. For there would scarcely be found any citizen who would undertake a great enterprise in his lifetime if, on his death, he was compelled against his will to leave his goods to ignorant or extravagant children, and undeserving wives; and therefore it is highly necessary that he should have freedom of action in this respect, for thereby he will curb misconduct, encourage virtue, and give occasion both to wives and children to do well, which some might not do if they knew without doubt that they would obtain a certain share irrespective of the testator's wishes.]

7. [*Ed.:* saving to his wife and children their reasonable shares.]

1. [*Ed.:* Constable.]

2. [*Ed.:* Castellain.]

3. See W. 1. cap. 7. & 31.

expresly appeareth by the Mirror,[4] *Ceo que est defendu a Constables a prender le autre, defend droit a touts gents de cy que nul difference parenter prise dautrui maugre soen, et robbery, lequel cel prise soit de chivalls, de vitaille, de merchandise, de carriage, de ostiels, ou des autres manners de biens.*[5] And this appeareth also by Fleta, l. 2. cap.43. *Quia multa gravamina multis inferuntur per diversas districtiones, quae quidem sub colore prisarum advocantur, &c. inhibetur in Magna charta de liberta-l-tibus* &c.[6] no purveyance shall be taken, but only [34] for the houses of the King, and Queene, and for no other person: so as the grievance before this, and other like Acts, is wholly taken away.[7]

Chapter 20

No Constable shall distrain any Knight for to give Money for keeping of his Castle, if he himself will do it in his proper person, or cause it to be done by another sufficient man, if he may not do it himself, for a reasonable cause. And if we do lead or send him in an army, he shall be free from Castle Guard for the time that he shall be with us in fee in our host, for the which he hath done service in our wars.

Here *Constabularius*[1] is taken in the former sense: see the first parte of the Institutes Sect. 96.

See this Act in Fleta:[2] And note, this Act (consisting upon two branches) is declaratory of the Common Law, for first, that he, that held by Castle gard, that is, to keepe a tower, or a gate, or such like of a Castle in time of warre might doe if, either by himself, or by any other sufficient person for him, and in his place.[3] And some hold by such service, as cannot doe it in person, as Major, and Comminalty Deane, and Chapter, Bishops, Abbots, etc. Infants being purchasers, women, and the like, and therefore they might make a dep-

---

4. Mirror. cap. 5. §. x.

5. [*Ed.:* That which is forbidden to constables to take from others should be forbidden to all men, inasmuch as there is no distinction between something taken from another against his will and robbery, whether the taking is of horses, victuals, merchandise, carriage, lodging, or other manner of goods.]

6. [*Ed.:* Because many grievances are suffered by many people through various distresses, which are avowed under pretext of prises, etc., it is forbidden in the great charter of liberties, etc.]

7. 36. E. 3. cap. 2. 23. H. 6. cap. 2.

1. [*Ed.:* Constable.]

2. Fleta lib. 2. ca. 43.

3. See the 1. part of the Instit. 96.

uty by order of the Common Law. If two joyn-tenants hold by such service, if one of them performe, it is sufficient.

For the second; if such a tenant be by the King led, or sent to his host, in time of warre, the tenant is excused and quit of his service for keeping of the Castle, either by himself, or by another during the time, that he so serve the King in his host, for that when the King commandeth his service in his host, he dispenceth with his service, by reason of his tenure, for that one man cannot serve in person in two places, and when he serves the King in person in one place, he is not bound to finde a deputy in the other, for he is not bound to make a deputy, but at his pleasure, and this is also declaratory of the ancient Common Law. See the first part of the Institutes III. 121.

Chapter 21

No Sheriff nor Bailiff of ours, or any other, shall take the Horses or Carts of any man to make carriage, except he pay the old price limited; that is to say, for carriage with two horse, x d. a day, for three horse, xiv d. a day. No Demesne Cart of any Spiritual Person or Knight, or any Lord, shall be taken by our Bailiffs. Nor We, nor our Bailiffs, nor any other, shall take any man's Wood for our Castles, or other our necessaries to be done, but by the Licence of him whose the Wood is.[1]

[35] | This Chapter consisteth of three branches, the first setteth down the auncient hire or allowance for the carriage for the King; the second setteth down, who are exempted from that carriage; the third, concerning purveyance of wood.

For the first, the carriage must be taken for the King, and Queen only, and for no other, implied in these words, *Nullus Vicecomes vel balivus noster,*[2] and this is explained by divers other Statutes, and by our Books.[3]

The hire or allowance is certainly expressed, as aunciently due, *Reddat liberationem antiquitus statutam;*[4] So as this also is declaratory of the auncient Law, and the hire or allowance ought to be paid in hand, for the Statute saith, *Nullus capiat, &c. nisi reddat, &c.*[5]

---

1. W. 1. c. 1. verb. & que nul sace &c. Artic. super cart. cap. 2. Regist. fol. 98. Bracton lib. 3. fol. 177. Britton fol. 33. 36. 38. Fleta lib. 1. c. 20. see cap. Itineris.

2. [*Ed.:* No sherriff or bailiff of ours.]

3. W. 1. cap. 1. & 32. 36. E. 3. cap. 2. 38. H. 6. cap. 2. Fleta lib. 2. ca. 1. & 24. 32. E. 3. Barre 259. 7. H. 3. tit. Waste.

4. [*Ed.:* Pay old livery as laid down in olden times;]

5. [*Ed.:* No one shall take, etc. unless he pays, etc.]

And this *liberatio antiquitus statuta*,[6] is, (as it appeareth by this Act) *per diem*, by the day.

Aver-penny,[7] and *averagium*,[8] are words common in auncient Charters, and signifie to be free from the Kings carriages, *cum averiis*,[9] and this is meant where it is said, *Aver-penny, hoc est, quietum esse de diversis denariis pro* * *averagiis Domini Regis*.[10]

For the second branch: No demean, or proper Cart for the necessary use of any Ecclesiasticall person, or of any Knight, or of any Lord, for or about the demean Lands of any of them, ought to be taken for the Kings carriage, but they are exempted by the auncient Law of England from any such carriage.[11]

This Statute extendeth not to any person Ecclesiasticall, of what estate, order, or degree soever: and this was an auncient priviledge belonging to holy Church.

Also it extendeth to all degrees, and orders of the lesser, and greater Nobility, or dignity, as of Knighthood, Dukes, Marquesses, Earles, Viscounts, and Barons, for albeit there were no Dukes, Marquesses, or Viscounts within England at the making of the Statute, yet this Statute doth extend to them, for they are all *Domini*,[12] Lords of Parliament, and of the Barony of England; and this also was an ancient priviledge belonging to these orders and dignities: And all this concerning the Ecclesiasticall and temporall State was (amongst other things for the advancement and maintenance of that great peace-maker, and love-holder, hospitality) one of the auncient ornaments, and commendations of the Kingdome of England.

The third branch is, That neither the King, nor any of his Baylies, or Ministers, shall take the wood of any other, for the Kings Castles, or other necessaties to be done, but by the license of him whose wood it is.[13] And all

---

6. [*Ed.:* livery as laid down in olden times,]

7. [*Ed.:* Annual rents paid in lieu of a tenant's service to a lord.]

8. [*Ed.:* Service with horse and carriage due a lord; also arriage.]

9. [*Ed.:* with cattle.]

10. Rastall * i. carragiis cum averiis. [*Ed.:* Aver-penny is to be quit of all money for the carriages of the lord king.]

11. W. 1. cap. 1. 14. E. 3. cap. 1. 1. R. 2. cap. 3. 10. E. 2. Vet. Mag. Chart. pt. 2. fo. 46. Fleta lib. 3. cap. 5.

12. [*Ed.:* Lords.]

13. W. 1. cap. 1. & 32. See 25. E. 3. ca. 6. 35. H. 8. cap. 17. 5. Eliz. cap. 8. 7. H. 3. tit. Wa. 141 11. H. 4. 28. Pl. Com 322.

Statutes made against this branch (amongst others) before the Parliament of 42 E. 3. are repealed: And this branch, amongst others, hath (as hath been said) béen confirmed, and commanded to bee put in execution at 32. Sessions of Parliament. And so it was resolved by all the Judges of England, and Barons of the Exchequer, Mich. 2. Jac. Reg. upon mature deliberation; and that the Kings Purveyor could take no Timber, growing upon the inheritance of the Subject, because it was parcell of the inheritance, no more then the inheritance it selfe.[14] Whereof the King, and Counsell being informed, the King by his Proclamation, by advice of his Counsell, under the great Seale, 23. *Aprilis, anno* 4. declared the Law to be in these words: First, when We were informed, that some inferiour Ministers had presumed to goe so farre beyond their commission, as they have adventured, not onely to take timber trees growing,

[36]   which being | parcell of Our Subjects inheritance, was never intended by Us to be taken without the good will, and full consent of the owners, but have accustomed also to take greater quantities of provisions for Our house, and Stable, then ever came, or were needfull, to Our use, &c. As by the said proclamation bearing date 23. Aprilis anno 4. Jac. Reg. appeareth. And divers Purveyors were according to the said resolution of the Judges punished in the Starchamber, for purveying of Timber growing, without the consent of the Dooners.

Boscus is an ancient word used in the Law of England, for all manner of wood, and the Italian useth the word *bosco* in the same sense, and the French, *boys,* accordingly. *Boscus* is divided into two sorts, viz. high-wood, *haut-boys,* or timber, and Coppice wood (so called, because it is usually cut) or underwood. High-wood is properly called *Saltus, Quia arbores ibi exiliunt in altum.*[15] It is called in Fleta,[16] *maeremium.*

The Common Law hath so admeasured the Prerogative of the King, as he cannot take, nor prejudice the inheritance of any, and (as hath been said) a man hath an inheritance in his woods.[17]

And see the Statute of Marlebridge.[18] Anno 52. H. 3. Magna Charta *in*

---

14. 42. E. 3. cap. 1. Mic. 2 Ja. resolved 11. H. 4. fo. 28. No purveyance of gravell, because it is part of the inheritance. See 47. E. 3. fo. 18 Issue taken upon the sale of timber for reparation of Calais.

15. [*Ed.: Saltus,* because the trees leap up (*ex-* + *salio*) to a great height.]

16. Fleta *ubi supra.*

17. Pl. Com. 236.

18. Marlebr. cap. 5.

singulis teneatur, tam in hiis, quae ad regem pertinent, quam ad alios,[19] and 31 other Statutes. So as all pretence of prerogative against Magna Charta is taken away.

See hereafter the exposition of the Statute *De tallagio. Anno* 34. E. 1. & *de prisis, Anno* 18 E. 2. *vet. Magna Charta.* fol. 125. 1 part.[20]

Chapter 22

We will not hold the Lands of them that be convict of Felony but one year and one day, and then those Lands shall be delivered to the Lords of the Fee.

This appeareth by Glanvill,[1] to be due to the King by his auncient Prerogative, for he saith, *Sin autem de alio, quam de Rege tenuerit is, qui utlagatus est, vel de felonia convict. tunc quoque omnes res suae mobiles Regis erunt, terra quoq; per unum annum remanebit in manu Domini Regis, elapso autem anno, terra eadem ad rectum Dominum, scilicet ad ipsum, de cujus feod. est, revertetur, veruntamen cum domorum subversione, & arborum extirpatione.*[2]

This Chapter of Magna Charta doth express that, which doth belong to the King, viz. the yeare, and the day, and omit the Waste, as not belonging to him, and this is notably explained by our auncient Books with an uniforme consent: Bracton treating of the yeare, and the day in this case due to the King, saith,[3] *Sed quae sit causa, quare terra remanebit in manibus Domini Regis? Videtur quod talis est, quia revera, cum quis convictus fuerit de aliqua felonia, in potestate Domini Regis erit, prosternendi aedificia, extirpandi gardina, & arandi prata, & quoniam hujusmodi verterentur in grave damnum dominorum, pro communi utilitate provisum fuit,*[4] *quod hujusmodi aedificia, gardina, & prata remanerent, & quod Dominus Rex propter hoc haberet commoditatem totius terrae*

---

19. [*Ed.:* The Magna Carta shall be binding in all its particulars, those pertaining to the King no less than the others.]

20. 34. E. 1. Vet. Magna Charta. fol. 37. 2. Part.

1. Glanv. li. 7. ca. 17. fol. 59.

2. [*Ed.:* But if the outlaw or convicted felon held of someone other than the king, then all his movable goods shall go to the king, and his land also shall remain in the hand of the lord king until one year has elapsed, and then the same land shall revert to the chief lord, that is, to him of whose fee it is, subject to [the king's right to] pull down houses and root up trees.]

3. Bracton lib. 3. fol. 129. & 137.

4. Nota. Provisum fuit. [*Ed.:* Note, it was provided.]

illius per unum annum, & unum diem, & sic omnia cum integritate reverterentur in manus Dominorum capitalium, nunc autem petitur utrumque, s. finis pro termino, & similiter pro vasto, & non video rationem quare, &c.[5]

And Britton treating of this very matter, saith,[6] *Lour biens mobles sont les nous, et lour heires disherit et voilons aver lour tenements de qui que unques sont tenus, le an, et le jour, issint que lour heritages, demourgent un an & un jour in* [37]   *nostre maine, | si que nous ne saisons estre perie les tenements, ne gaster les boys, ne arer les prees, sicome lensoloit saire in remembrance des selons attaints, &c.*[7]

Fleta saith,[8] *Si autem utlagati, vel alii convicti terram liberam habuerint, illa statim capienda est in manus Regis, & per unum annum, & unum diem tenend', ad capitales Dominos post illum terminum reversura, & hoc habetur ex Statuto Magnae Chartae, quod tale est, nos non tenebimus terras illorum, qui convicti fuerint de felonia, nisi per unū annū, & unum diem, & tunc reddantur terrae illae Dominis feodorū, causa verò talis termini Regis, quia in signum feloniae olim provisum fuit, quod aedificia talium prosternentur in terram, extirpentur gardina, ararentur prata, truncarentur bosci, & quoniam hujusmodi verterentur in grave damnum dominorum feodorum, pro communi utilitae provisum fuit, quod hujusmodi dura, & gravia cessarent & quod Rex propterea per annum & diem totius terrae commoditatem perciperet, secus autem, si terra non esset eschaeta Dominorum, post quem terminum Dominis proprietariis integre absque vasto vel destructione reverterentur.*[9]

---

5. [*Ed.:* But what is the reason why the land shall remain in the lord king's hands? It seems to be this, because when someone has been convicted of some felony it will be in the king's power to pull down his buildings, root up his gardens, and plough up his meadows; and since such things used to result in great damage to lords, it was provided for the common weal that the buildings, gardens and meadows should remain, and that the lord king for that reason should have the profit of the whole of that land for a year and a day, so that everything should revert in its entirety into the hands of the chief lords. Now, however, both are sought: that is, a fine for the term, and likewise for the waste. I do not know the reason why, etc.]

6. Britton cap. 5. fol. 14.

7. [*Ed.:* Their movable goods are ours, and their heirs disinherited, and we will have their tenements (from whomever they are held) for a year and a day, so that their inheritances shall remain in our hands for a year and a day, provided that we do not cause the tenements to be destroyed, or the woods wasted, or the meadows ploughed, as used to be done with them in remembrance of the attained felons, etc.]

8. Fleta li. 1. cap. 28.

9. [*Ed.:* If outlaws or other convicts have free land, it is at once to be seized into the king's hand and kept for a year and a day, reverting after the end of that period to the chief lords; and this is from the statute of Magna Carta, which is as follows: We shall not hold the lands of those who are convicted of felony except for a year and a day, and then they shall return to the lords of the fees; and the cause of the

The Mirror speaking of this Chapter saith,[10] *Le joint des terres aux selons tener per un an, est desusie, car p la ou le Roy ne duist aver que le gast de droit, ou sine, pur salver le sief de lestripment, preignont les Ministers le roy ambideux.*[11] Upon all which it appeareth, that the King originally was to have no benefit in this case, upon the attainder of felony, where the frée-land was holden of a Subject, but onely in detestation of the crime, *Ut poena ad paucos, metus ad omnes perveniat,*[12] to prostrate the houses, to extirpe the gardens, to eradicate his woods, and to plow up the medows of the felon, for saving whereof, *et pro bono publico,*[13] the Lords, of whom the Lands were holden, were contented to yeeld the lands to the King for a year, and a day, and therefore not only the Wast was justly omitted out of this Chapter of Magna Charta, but thereby it is enacted, that after the year and day, the land shall be rendred to the Lord of the fee, after which no Waste can be done.

And where the treatise of *Prerogativa Regis,* made in 17. Edw. 2. saith *Et postquam Dominus Rex habuerit annum, diem, & vastum, tunc reddatur tenementum illud capitali Domino feodi illius, Nisi prius faciat finem pro anno, die, et vasto.*[14] Which is so to be expounded, that forasmuch, as it appeareth in the said old books, that the Officers, and Ministers, did demaund both for the Waste, and for the year, and day, that came in lieu thereof, therefore this Treatise names both, not that both were due, but that a reasonable fine might be paid for all that, which the King might lawfully claim. But if this act of 17. Edw. 2. be against this branch of Magna Charta, then is it repealed by the said Act of 42. Edw. 3. cap. 1.

Hereby it also appeareth, how necessary the reading of auncient Authors

---

king's term is that it was once laid down as a mark of felony that the buildings of felons should be knocked to the ground, their gardens rooted up, their meadows ploughed up, and their woods cut down, and because such things caused great damage to the lords of the fees, it was enacted for the common weal that such harsh and grave measures should cease and that the king should instead take the profit for a year and a day of the whole land, though it is otherwise if the land does not escheat to the lords, after which term it should return to the proper lords in its entirety and without waste or destruction.]

10. Mirror cap. 5. § 2.

11. [*Ed.:* The point concerning felons' lands to be held for a year and a day is disused, for whereas the king ought not have nothing but the waste by right, or the year in the name of a fine to save the fee from being stripped bare, the king's ministers take both.]

12. [*Ed.:* That a penalty imposed on a few should be a warning to many,]

13. [*Ed.:* and for the public good.]

14. [*Ed.:* And after the lord king has had the year, day, and waste, the tenement shall then be yielded up to the chief lord of that fee, unless he has previously made fine for the year, day, and waste.]

is for understanding of auncient Statutes. And out of these old Books, you may observe, that when any thing is given to the King in lieu, or satisfaction of an auncient right of his Crown, when once he is in possession of the new recompence, and the same in charge, his Officers and Ministers will many times demand the old also, which may turn to great prejudice, if it be not duly, and discreetly prevented.[15]

"We will not hold the Lands."

If there be Lord, Mesne, and Tenant, and the Mesne is attainted of felony, the Lord Paramount shall have the Mesnalty presently. For this prerogative belonging to the King extend onely to the Land, which might be wasted, in lieu whereof the yeare and day was granted.

And this is to be understood when a Tenant in fee-simple is attainted, for when Tenant in taile, or Tenant for life is attainted, there the King shall have the profits of the Lands, during the life of Tenant in taile, or of the Tenant for life.

"be convict."

Here *Convicti* in a large sense is taken for *Attincti*,[16] for the nature, and true sense of both these words, see the first part of the Institutes, and likewise for this word *felony* there.[17]

[38]

| "of Felony."

Must be understood of all manner of Felonies punished by death, and not of petit larceny, which notwithstanding is felony.

Chapter 23

All Wears from henceforth shall be utterly put down by Thames and Medway, and through all England, but only by the Sea-coasts.[1]

---

15. Vide Stamford. Pl. Cor. 190. 191. Vide 3. E. 3. coron. 3. 27. 3. E. 3. ibid. 58. 3. E. 3. ibid. 310. Pasc. 31. E. 1. Cor. Rege Norff. Wil. de Ormesby.

16. [*Ed.*: Persons attainted.]

17. See the first part of the Institutes sect. 745.

1. 25. E. 3. cap. 4. 1. H. 4. cap. 12. 12. E. 4. cap. 7.

Rex, &c.[2] *Noveritis nos pro communi utilitate Civitatis nostrae London' & totius Regni nostri concessisse, & firmiter praecepisse, ut omnes Kidelli qui sunt in Tamisia, vel Medeweia, ubicunque fuerint in Tamisia, vel in Medeweia amoveant', & non de caetero Kidelli alicubi ponant' in Tamisia, vel in Medeweya, super forisfactur' decem libr' sterlingorum: quietum etiam clamavimus omne id, quod custodes Turr' nostrae London' annuatim percipere solebant de praedictis Kidellis: Quare volumus & firmiter praecipimus, ne aliquis custos praefat' turr' aliquo tempore post hoc, aliquid exigat ab aliquo, nec aliquam demandam, aut gravamen, sive molestiam alicui inferat occasione praedictorum Kidellorum, satis enim nobis constat, & per fideles nostros sufficienter nobis datum est intelligi, quod maximum detrimentum, & incommodum praedictae Civitati London', nec non & toto Regno nostro occasione praedictorum Kidellorum perveniebat; quod ut firmum, & stabile perseveret imperpetuum, praesentis paginae inscriptione & sigilli nostri appositione communimus, sicut carta Domini Regis Johannis Patris nostri quam Barones nostri London' inde habent rationabilit' testat'.*[3]

"Wears"

Kidels is a proper word for open weares whereby fish are caught.[4]

It was specially given in charge by the Justices in Eire, that all Juries should enquire, *De hiis qui piscantur cum Kidellis & Skarkellis.*[5,6]

And it appeareth by Glanvill,[7] that this *pourpresture* was forbidden by the

---

2. Rot. cart. 18. Feb. Anno 11. H. 3.

3. [*Ed.:* The king, etc. Know ye that we, for the common utility of our city of London, and the whole of our realm, have granted and firmly commanded that all kiddles (fishing-weirs) which are in the Thames or Medway, wherever they are in the Thames or in the Medway, should be removed, and from thenceforth no kiddles shall be placed anywhere in the Thames or in the Medway, upon forfeiture of ten pounds sterling. We have also quitclaimed all that which the keeper of our tower of London used to receive annually from the aforesaid kiddles. And therefore we will and firmly command that no keeper of our tower of London at any time hereafter should exact anything from anyone or impose any demand, vexation, or molestation upon anyone, by reason of the aforesaid kiddles, for it sufficiently appears to us, and by our faithful subjects has been given to us sufficiently to understand, that the greatest detriment and trouble has come to the aforesaid city of London and the whole of our realm by reason of the aforesaid kiddles. And we communicate this, so that it should be preserved as firm and established for ever, by the writing on this present page and by the affixing of our seal, just like the charter of the lord King John, our father, whereof our barons of London have reasonably testified.]

4. Lib. 10. fo. 138. in the case of Chester Mill. Keylw. 15. H. 7. 15

5. [*Ed.:* of those who fish with kiddles (fishing-weirs) and fish-traps.]

6. Cap. Itineris. nu. 5 Tr. 5. E. 2. Coram Rege. Rot. 18.

7. Glanv. li. 9. ca. 11.

Common Law, for he saith, *Dicitur autem purprestura, vel porprestura proprie, quando aliquid super Dominum Regem injuste occupatur, ut in dominicis Regis, vel in viis publicis obstructis, vel in aquis publicis transversis à recto cursu, vel quando aliquis in Civitate super Regiam plateam aliquid aedificando occupaverit, & generaliter quoties aliquid sit ad nocumentum Regii tenementi, vel Regiae viae, vel Civitatis,*[8] and every publique River or streame, is *alta Regia via,*[9] the Kings high-way.

Pourpresture commeth of the French word *pourprise,* which signifieth a close, or inclosure, that is, when one encroacheth, or makes that severall to himselfe, which ought to be common to many.

Chapter 24

[39] | The Writ that is called Praecipe [in capite] shall be from henceforth granted to no person of any Freehold, whereby any Freeman may lose his Court.[1]

This is for reformation of an abuse, and wrong offered to the Lord, of whom the land was holden, and yet upon this Statute, the tenant cannot pleade, that the lands are not holden of the King in chiefe, for two causes, first for that this Act was made for the benefit of the Lord, of whom this land is holden, and he cannot pleade it, because he is an estrang', and if one claiming to be Lord should be admitted, another might come in and pretend the like, and so infinite. Secondly, this Act extends to the Chancery, for the words be *Breve &c. non fiat,*[2] so in that Court the Writ is made: and therefore when the Writ is granted in the Chancery, and returned into the Court of Common pleas, that which is by this Act prohibited in the Chancery, extendeth not to the Court of Common pleas; and therefore they cannot admit of such a plea; now the tenant, least he be concluded, must take the tenure by protestation, and

8. [*Ed.:* It is called a purpresture, or more properly *porprestura,* when something unjustifiably encroaches upon the lord king, as in the king's demesnes, or by obstructing public ways, or in diverting public watercourses from their right course, or when someone has encroached on royal land in a city by building something, and generally whenever anything is done to the nuisance of a royal tenement or a royal way or city.]

9. [*Ed.:* a royal highway.]

1. Mirror cap. 5. § 2 Bracton lib. 5. fol. 328 & 414. b. Registr 4. 3. E. 3. 23. 6. E. 3. 15. 38. E. 3. 13. 39. E. 3. 26. F. N. B. 5. c.

2. [*Ed.:* The writ, etc. shall not be made,]

the King, though he be not party to the Record, yet shall he take advantage of the Estoppel, for he is ever present in Court.[3]

And since this Statute no man ought to have this Writ out of the Chancery upon a suggestion, but oath must be made, before the granting thereof, that the land is holden of the King in *Capite.*[4]

See Mich. 4. E. 1. *de banco* Rot. 114. Norff. Barth. de Redhams case, *pro terris in curia comitis warren apud Castleacre, notabile recordum super hoc Statutum. Per breve praecipitur Justiciariis quod inquirant, si terrae tenentur de Rege in Capite.*[5,6] See the Writ in the Register. 4. b. by which Writ power is given to the Justices, that if it may appeare to them, that the land is not holden in *Capite,* then that the plea be holden in the Lords Court, according to this Statute. And for that the demandant Peter Grellye, confessed that the lands were not holden of the King in Capite, but of Edmond brother of the King, thereupon the entrie was, *Ideo Petrus perquirat sibi per breve de recto pat' in curia ipsius Ed. versus R. si voluerit.*[7] Mich. 14. E. 1. Rot. 48. Som. acc. Regist. fo. 4.b. & 6.a.

And the Lord, of whom the land is holden, shall upon this Statute, have his Writ of disceit against the Demandant, which have recovered by default, and recover his damages, but the Record of the judgement shall stand in force;[8] and concerning the conclusion of the tenure, the Lord shall have remedy against the King by petitions of right. But if the recovery be given upon triall against the tenant, then the tenant hath concluded himself for the tenure, because his protestation cannot availe him, when his plea is found against him: But the Lord may have in that case; his action against the tenant, and his petition of right to the King, to be restored to his Seigniorie, and by that meanes the tenant himselfe may be relieved.[9]

---

3. 20. E. 3. estoppel. 187. 22. E. 3. 17. 40. E. 3. 30.

4. [*Ed.:* in chief.]

5. [*Ed.:* for lands in the court of Earl Warenne at Castleacre, a notable record upon this statute. The justices are commanded by writ that they should inquire whether lands are held of the king in chief.]

6. Mic. 7. E. 1. in banco rot. 65. Lanc'. acc. Peter Grellyes case.

7. [*Ed.:* Therefore let Peter obtain for himself a writ of right patent in the court of the said Edward, if he will.]

8. 8. E. 4. 6. 6. E. 3. 15 Vet. N. B. 13. a. F. N. B. 98. n.

9. See the first part of the Institutes sect. 192. 17. E. 3. 31. 36. 37. 59. 32. E. 3. Avowry 113. 45. E. 3. petition 9.

"Writ."

Dicitur ideo breve, quia rem de qua agitur, & intentionem petentis paucis verbis breviter enarrat, sicut facit regula Juris, quae rem, quae est, breviter enarrat.[10,11]

    Breve quidem cum sit formatum ad similitudinem regulae juris, quia breviter & paucis verbis intentionem proferent is exponit & explanat, sicut regula juris rem quae est breviter enarrat.[12]

    And Fleta defines a Writ,[13] *totidem verbis,*[14] as Bracton hath done.

[40]   There is a great diversity betweene a Writ, and an Action, (although by some they are often confounded) which will best appeare by their severall definitions.

    Actio nihil aliud est, quam jus prosequendi in judicio quod alicui debetur.[15]
And with Bracton agreeth Fleta.[16]

    Actio nihil aliud est, quam jus prosequendi in judicio quod alicui debetur, & quod nascitur ex maleficio, vel quod provenit ex delicto, vel injuria.[17]

    And the Mirror saith,[18] *Action nest aut' chose que loiall demand de son droit. Actors sont queux suont lour droit per pleint, &c.*[19]

    So as the first diversity between an Action, and a Writ is, that an Action is the right of a suite, and the Writ is grounded thereupon, and the meane to bring the demandant or pl' to his right.

    The second diversity, a Writ grounded upon right of Action is ever *in soro contentioso,*[20] but so are not all Writs, for that Writs are much more large, then Actions are, as shall appeare by the division of Writs.

---

10. Bract. lib. 3. f. 112. cap. 12. nu. 2. & lib. 5. fol. 413. c. 17. nu. 2.

11. [*Ed.:* It is therefore called *breve* (a writ), because it sets out *breviter* (briefly) and in few words the matter in dispute, and the intention of the plaintiff, as does a rule of law, which briefly sets out the matter which it concerns.]

12. [*Ed.:* Some writs are formed like a rule of law, because they briefly and in few words expound and explain the intention of the plaintiff, just as a rule of law briefly sets out the matter which it concerns.]

13. Fleta. lib. 2. c. 12.§ dicuntur etiam brevia.

14. [*Ed.:* in exactly the same words,]

15. [*Ed.:* An action is nothing other than pursuing to judgment the right which is owed to anyone.]

16. Bracton. lib. 3. fol. 98. b. cap. 1. Fleta lib. 1. cap 16. § actio & § 3. Actors.

17. [*Ed.:* An action is nothing other than pursuing to judgment the right which is owed to anyone, or which arises from wrongdoing, or comes from wrong or injury.]

18. Mirror. cap. 2 § 1. nest.

19. [*Ed.:* An action is nothing other than a lawful demand of one's right. Actors (plaintiffs) are those who pursue their right by plaint, etc.]

20. [*Ed.:* in a contentious forum,]

Of Writs grounded upon rights of Action, some be criminall, and some be civill or common.[21]

Of Criminall, some be *in personam*,[22] to have judgement of death, as Writs of appeale, of death, robberie, rape, &c. and some to have judgement of dammage to the partie, fine to the King, and imprisonment, as Writs of Appeale of *Mayhem &c.*

Of Writs Civill or Common, some be reall, some personall, and some mixt. And of these, some be originall, and all they goe out of the Chancery, and some judiciall, and they issue out of the Court, where the plea depended. Some Conditionall, as Writs of *Error, redisseisin, &c.*[23] some without Condition, some retornable, and some not retornable. And all these are warranted, either by the Common Law, or grounded upon some Act of Parliament. Which are so well knowne, as this little touch shall suffice.[24]

Of Originall Writs, some be *brevia formata*,[25] and some *ex cursu*,[26] some *magistralia, & saepius variantur.*[27,28]

Regularly the Kings Writs are, *ex debito Justitiae*,[29] to be granted to the subject, which cannot be denied, and some be *ex gratia*,[30] as superseded[a31] speciall liberties, and [b32]Writs of Protections for the safegard of the Subject, being in the Kings warre out of the Realme.

In nature of Commissions; as Writs of *Error*, of *Oier*, and *Terminer*, of election of Knights and Burgesses of the Parliament, of election of a Coroner, or of discharging of him, of selection of Verderers, [33]*De ventre inspiciendo.*[34] [d35]*De viis & venellis mundandis*,[36] Regist. 267. Of the surety of the good be-

---

21. Bracton. lib. 3. fol. 101. cap. 3. nu. 1. Fleta lib. 1. cap. 16.

22. [*Ed.:* in the person (personal).]

23. [*Ed.:* Writ to correct an error in an earlier matter, or to recover land a second time, etc.]

24. Glanvil. lib. 1. c. 1. Bracton *ubi sup.* Fleta *ubi sup.* Mirror *ubi sup.* Plowd. Com. 73. &c. Regist. 187.

25. [*Ed.:* [specially] formed writs.]

26. [*Ed.:* of [common] course.]

27. [*Ed.:* magistral, and they are more often varied.]

28. Bract. l. 5. 413. b. Fleta. lib. 2. cap. 12

29. [*Ed.:* by the duty of Justice,]

30. [*Ed.:* of grace,]

31. *a* Dier. 23. Fitz. 377. a.

32. *b* F. N. B. 28. 29.

33. *c* Regist. 227.

34. [*Ed.:* Writ for inspecting the belly (of a woman alleged to be pregnant).]

35. *d* Ibid. 267.

36. [*Ed.:* For cleaning out ways and lanes.]

haviour, or of the peace. ^{e37} *De odio & atia.*³⁸ Association, of *de admittendo in socium,*³⁹ of *Si non omnes,*⁴⁰ and the like. Writs of *Justicies.*

Of Writs of *Praecipe,*⁴¹ some be, *quod reddat,*⁴² as Writs of right &c. debt, &c. Some be *quod permittat,*⁴³ as Writs *De quod permittat.* Some be *quod faciat,*⁴⁴ as *de consuetudinibus & servitiis. De domo reparanda.*⁴⁵ And of Writs of *Praecipe,* some containe severall precepts, and some joynt, and some are sole.

Writs Mandatory, and extrajudiciall, whereof some be affirmative, and some negative. Affirmative, as calling of men to the upper house of Parliament to be Peers of the Realme. *De Comitat' commissis.*⁴⁶ Regist. 295. Of *Conge de eslier,*⁴⁷ licence to choose a Bishop. Regist. 294. b.*De regio assensu.*⁴⁸ Regist. ibid. To call one to be Chiefe Justice of England. To call apprentices of Law to be servants. *De brevibus & Rot. deliberandis.*⁴⁹ Regist. 295.⁵⁰ *De restitutione spiritualium.*⁵¹ Regist. 294. b.⁵² Negative, as *De non ponendis in assisis, & juratis. De securitate invenienda, quod se non divertat ad partes exteras sine licentia. De non residentia clerici Regis. De clerico infra sacros ordines constituto non eligendo in officium. Ne fines capias pro non pulchre placitando.*⁵³

Of Writs, some are for furtherance of Justice, and for outting of delayes, and to proceed. As the Writ *De procedendo ad judicium,*⁵⁴ that the Justices

---

37. *e* Regist. 133. b. Fitz. N. B. 185. Regist. 206. F. N. B. ib.
38. [*Ed.:* Of hatred and spite.]
39. [*Ed.:* for admitting in association.]
40. [*Ed.:* a command to act or show cause not to act, particularly to allow a common recovery.]
41. [*Ed.:* a command, the general form of such writs.]
42. [*Ed.:* for recovery.]
43. [*Ed.:* that he permit.]
44. [*Ed.:* that he do.]
45. [*Ed.:* For [performing] customs and services; for repairing a house.]
46. [*Ed.:* For committing counties.]
47. [*Ed.:* licence to elect [a bishop].]
48. [*Ed.:* Of the royal assent.]
49. [*Ed.:* For delivering writs and rolls.]
50. Regist. 295. F. N. B. 170.
51. [*Ed.:* For restoring spiritualties.]
52. Regist. 294. F. N. B. 165. a. F. N. B. 85. a. Regist. 58. b. Artic. sup. cart. c. 6. Regist. 187. b. ibid. 179. a. F. N. B. 240. d.
53. [*Ed.:* For not being put on assizes and juries; for finding surety; that he should not go away to foreign parts without licence; for non-residency of the king's cleric; for not electing a clerk in Holy Orders to an office; for not taking fines for beaupleader.]
54. [*Ed.:* For proceeding to judgment.]

shall not surcease to doe common right, for no commandement under the great Seale, | petit Seale, or message from the King. Or [a55] if the Judges of themselves delay judgement, there lyeth also a *procedendo ad judicium.*[56] Againe, there is a *procedendo in loquela, & ad judicium*[57] after Aid of the King. A Writ *de executione judicii.*[58]

[59] Some for advancement of Justice not to proceed.

[c60] Regularly Writs are directed to the Sherifes, or Coroners, or but in speciall cases to the partie, or others. To the partie, as Writs of prohibitions, *Ne exeat regnum.*[61] To others, as to Judges Temporall, Ecclesiasticall, and Civill. To Serjeants at Armes. To the [d62] party that hath the custody of an idiot. To the [e63] Major, and Bayliffes, *&c. ad amovendum eos ab officio, quousq; inquisitio foret de eorum gestu.*[64,f65] *Liberate thesaurario, & camerariis, thesaurario & baronibus.*[66]

Note of Writs of right (whereof the *praecipe* in *Capite*[67] is one) some be close, and some be patent.

Writs of right retornable into the Court of Common pleas be patent, and Writs directed into auncient Demesne, are close; and the reason wherefore in other Courts of the Lords, the Writs shall be patent, is, because there is a clause in those Writs, *& nisi feceris, Vicecomes N. hoc faciat ne amplius clamorem audiamus pro defectu recti:*[68] which clause is not in the other Writs, and necessary it is that such Writs should be patent, that the Sherife might take notice thereof.

[41]

---

55. *a* F. N. B. 153. b 2. E. 3. ca. 8. 5. E. 3. ca. 9. 14. E. 3. cap. 14. Regist. fo. 186. F. N. B. 153. Regist. 18. F. N. B 20.

56. [*Ed.:* Writ for proceeding to judgment.]

57. [*Ed.:* For proceeding in a suit, and to judgment.]

58. [*Ed.:* For executing a judgment.]

59. *b* Regist. 124. 125 revocat brevis de audiendo &c. All Writs of supersedeas.

60. *c* Pl. Com. fol. 73. &c. See 12. H. 4. 24. in debt not cited in that case. Regist. 114. 115. Writs of Audita querela &c. prohibitions ad jura regal.

61. [*Ed.:* He shall not leave the realm.]

62. *d* Regist. 267. 2.

63. *e* ib. 126. b.

64. [*Ed.:* to remove them from office until there has been an enquiry into their behaviour.]

65. *f* Ib. 192. b. 193. a. b.

66. [*Ed.:* Deliver to the treasurer and chamberlains, treasurer and barons.]

67. [*Ed.:* in Chief.]

68. [*Ed.:* and unless you will do this, let the sheriff of N. do it, that we hear no more complaints for want of right.]

Chapter 25

One Measure of Wine shall be through our Realm, and one Measure of Ale, and one Measure of Corn, that is to say, the Quarter of London; and one Breadth of dyed Cloth, Russets, and Haberjects, that is to say, Two Yards within the Lists. And it shall be of Weights as it is of Measures.

This Act concerning measures and weights, that there should be one measure and one weight through England, is grounded upon the Law of God.[1] *Non habebis in sacculo diversa pondera, majus, & minus, non erit in domo tua modius major & minor, pondus habebis justum & verum, & modius aequalis erit tibi, ut multo vivas tempore super terram &c.*[2] And this hath often by authority of parliament been enacted, but never could be effected, so forcible is custome concerning multitudes, when it hath gotten an head, therefore good Lawes are timely to be executed, and not in the beginning to be neglected.

For Weights and Measures, there are good Lawes made before the Conquest:[3] *In dimensione, & pondere nihil esto iniquum ab iniquitate vero deinceps quisq; temperet: Per commune concilium regni statuimus, quod habeant per univerum Regnum mensuras fidelissimas, & signata, & pondera fidelissima & signata, sicut boni praedecessores statuerunt.*[4]

"one Breadth of dyed Cloth, &c."

True it is that broade cloathes were made, though in small number, at the time, and long before this Statute, but in the beginning of the raigne of Edward 3.[5] the same came to so great perfection, as in the 11. yeare of his raigne, all men were prohibited to bring in privillie, or apertly by himself, or any other, any clothes made in any other places, &c And this is the worthiest and richest

---

1. Stat. de 31. E. 1. 14. E. 3. cap. 12. 27. E. 3. cap. 10. See the Custum. de Norm. cap. 16. Deut. 25. v. 13. 14.

2. [*Ed.:* You shall not have in your bag various weights, greater and less, nor shall there be in your house greater and lesser measures, but you shall have a just and true weight; and equal measure will be given to you, so that you will live upon the earth for a long time, etc. Deuteronomy 25: 13–14.]

3. Int' leges Canut. cap. 9. Int' leges Will. Regis conq.

4. [*Ed.:* So that henceforth there should be nothing unequal in measures and weights, by reason of iniquity, we have enacted by the common council of the realm that the most trustworthy and marked measures should be used throughout the realm, and the most trustworthy and marked weights, as our good predecessors have enacted.]

5. Mirror. cap. 5. § 2. Vet. Mag. Cart. cap. Itin. f. 151. 11. E. 3. cap. 30.

commoditie of this Kingdome, for divide our native commodities exported into tenne parts, and that which comes from the sheepes back, is nine parts in value of the tenne, and setteth | great numbers of people on worke. For the breadth, and length of Clothes, see many Statutes made after this Act.

[42]

Chapter 26

Nothing from henceforth shall be given for a Writ of Inquisition, nor taken of him that prayeth Inquisition of Life or of Member, but it shall be granted freely, and not denied.

"a Writ of Inquisition."

That is the Writ *de odio & atia*,[1] anciently called *Breve de bono & malo*,[2] and here, of life, and member, which the Common Law gave to a man, that was imprisoned, though it were for the most odious cause, for the death of a man, for the which, without the Kings Writ he could not be bayled, yet the Law favouring the liberty, and freedome of a man from imprisonment, and that he should not be detained in prison, untill the Justices in Eire should come, at what time he was to be tried, he might sue out this writ of inquisition directed to the Sherife,[3] *quod assumptis tecum custodibus placitorum Coronae in pleno comitatu per sacramentum proborum, & legalium hominum de &c. inquiras (inde appellatur Breve inquisitionis) utrum A. captus, & detentus in prisona &c. pro morte W. unde rettatus (1. accusatus existit) rettatus sit odio, & atia &c. nisi indictatus vel appellatus appelatus suerit, coram Iustitiariis nostris ultimo itinerantibus in partibus illis, & pro hoc captus, & imprisonatus,*[4] For by the Common Law, *in omnibus autem placitis de felonia, solet accusatus per plegios*

---

1. [*Ed.*: of hatred and spite.]

2. [*Ed.*: Writ of good and ill.]

3. Mirror. cap. 5. §. 2. Regist. fol. 133. Glanv. lib. 14. c. 3. Bract. 1. 3. f. 121. Fleta. lib. 1. c. 23. 25. W. 1. cap. 11 Gloc. c. 9. W. 2. cap. 29. Hill. 32. E. 1. coram Rege Rott. 71. & 79. 5. H. 7. 5.

4. [*Ed.*: that, taking with you the keepers of the pleas of the crown, in full county, by the oath of good and lawful men of, etc., you enquire (whence it is called a writ of enquiry) whether A. who was taken, etc. and detained in prison, etc. for the death of W., whereof he has been accused, was accused out of hatred and spite, etc., if he has not been indicted or appealed before our last justices in eyre in those parts, and for that reason taken and imprisoned.]

dimitti, praeterquam de placito de homicidio, ubi ad terrorem aliter statutum est.[5,6] In this Writ, fower things are to be observed.

First, though the offence, whereof he was accused, were such, as he was not bayleable by Law, yet the Law did so highly hate the long imprisonment of any man, though accused of an odious, and heynous crime, that it gave him this Writ for his reliefe.

Secondly, If he were indited, or appealed thereof, before the Justices in Eyre, he could not have this Writ, because this Writ was grounded upon a surmise which could not be received against a matter of record.

Thirdly, Upon this Writ, though it were found, that he was accused *de odio & atia,* and that he was not guilty, or that he did this Act *se defendendo, vel per infortunium,*[7] yet the Sherife by this Writ had no authority to bayle him, but then the party was to sue a Writ *de ponendo in ballium,*[8] directed to the Sherife, whereby he was commanded,[9] *quod si praedictus A. invenerit tibi 12. probos, & legales homines de comitatu tuo &c. qui eum manucapiant habere coram Justiciariis nostris ad primam assisam. &c. Standum, &c. tunc ipsum A. &c. praedictis duodecim tradas in ballium.*[10]

Lastly, that there was a meane by the Common Law, before inditement, or appeale, to protect the innocent against false accusation, and to deliver him out of prison.

Odium, signifieth, hatred, and *atin* or *acia* in this Writ signifieth malice, because that malice is *acida,* that is, eager, sharpe and cruell.

And this branch, for further benefit, and in favour of the prisoner, doth enact,[11] that he shall have it gratis, without fee, and without delay, or deniall, of which the Mirror saith thus,[12] *Le defence que se fait del breife de odio, & atia, que le Roy ne son Chancelor ne preignont pur le breife granter se doit extend*

---

5. [*Ed.:* in all pleas of felony the accused ought to be released by pledges, except in a plea of homicide, whereof it is enacted otherwise to cause dread, etc.]

6. Glanv. lib. 14. c. 1.

7. [*Ed.:* in self-defence or by misfortune,]

8. [*Ed.:* for putting in bail,]

9. Hill. 32. E. 1. *ubi. sup.*

10. [*Ed.:* that if the aforesaid A. shall find you twelve good and lawful men of your county, etc., who mainprise to have him before our justices at the first assize, etc., to stand [to right], etc., then deliver him the said A., etc. to the aforesaid twelve men in bail.]

11. Regist. f. 133. 134.

12. Mirror c. 5. § 2.

a touts breifs remedials, & le dit breife ne doit solement extender a felonies de homicide, mes a touts felonies, & ne solem̄t in Appeles, mes en inditements.[13]

 I But this writ was taken away by a later Statute, viz.in 28. Edw. 3.[14] because as some pretended, it became unnecessary, for that Justices of Assise, Justices of Oyer Termimer, Justices of Gaole delivery came at the least into every County twice every year; but within 12. years after this Statute, it was it enacted, as often hath been said, that all Statutes made against Magna Charta (as the said act of 28. Edw. 3. was) should be voyd, whereby the Writs of *Odio & atia, & De ponendo in balium*[15] are revived, and so in like cases upon all the branches of Magna Charta. And therefore the Justices of Assise, Justices of *Oyer & Terminer,* and of Gaole delivery have not suffered the Prisoner to be long detained, but at their next comming have given the Prisoner full and speedy Justice by due triall, without detaining him long in Prison:[16] Nay, they have been so farre from allowance of his detaining in Prison without due triall, that it was resolved in the case of the Abbot of S. Albon by the whole Court, that where the King had graunted to the Abbot of S. Albon, to have a Gaole, and so have a Gaole delivery, and divers persons were committed to that Gaole for felony, and because the Abbot would not be at cost to make deliverance, he detained them in prison long time without making lawfull deliverance, that the Abbot had for that cause forfeited his franchise, and that the same might bee feifed into the Kings hand.[17]

For his committing to prison is onely to this end, that he may be forth coming, to be duly tried, according to the Law and custome of the Realme.[18] The Abbot of Crowland had a gaole, wherein divers men were imprisoned, and because he detained some that were acquited of felony after their fees paid, the King seised the goale for ever.

And it is provided by the Statute of 5. H. 4.[19] that none be imprisoned by

[43]

---

13. [*Ed.:* The prohibition which is made with respect to the writ *de odio et atia,* that neither the king nor his chancellor should take anything for granting the writ, ought to extend to all remedial writs; and the said writ ought not to extend only to felonies of homicide, but to all felonies, and not only in appeals but in indictments.]

14. 28. E. 3. ca. 9. Stamf. Pl. Cor. 77. F. N. B. 92. 42. E. 3. ca. 1.

15. [*Ed.:* putting in bail.]

16. See the Statute of Gloc. ca. 9.

17. 8. H. 4. 18. 20. E. 4. 6. Bro. tit. forfeiture.

18. 20. E. 4. 6.

19. 5. H. 4. cap. 10. Lib. 9. fol. 119. Seignior Zanchars Case. See the statute of Gloc. cap. 9.

any Justice of Peace, but in the Common gaole, to the end they might have their triall at the next Gaole delivery, or Sessions of the peace. Vide cap. 29.

And some say, that this Statute extendeth to all other Judges, and Justices for two reasons. 1. They say, that this Act is but declaratory of the Common Law. 2. *Ubi lex est specialis, & ratio ejus generalis, generaliter accipienda est.*[20]

Breve Regis De bono & malo[21] is so called of the words, *De bono & malo,* contained in the Writ. This Writ lay when A. B. was committed to prison for the death of a man, the King did write to the Justices of Gaole delivery;[22] *Quod si A. B. captus, & detentus in gaola praedicta pro morte C.D. de bono & malo super patriam inde ponere voluerit, & ea occasione (& non per aliquod speciale mandatum nostrum) detentus sit in eadem, tunc eandem gaolam de praedicto A. B. secundum legem, & consuetudinem Angliae, deliberetis.*[23] So as without question the Writ *De bono & malo,* is not the Writ *De odio & atia,* as some have imagined.

Note, in those dayes the Justices of Gaole delivery would not proceed in case of the death of a man, without the Kings Writ: For in the same Record it appeareth, that R. W. *Indictatus de morte W.E. non tulit breve Regis de bono, & malo, ideo retornatur gaolae, & sic de aliis.*[24]

Chapter 27

If any do hold of Us by Fee-ferm, or by Socage or Burgage, and he holdeth Lands of another by Knights Service, We will not have the Custody of his Heir, nor of his Land, which is holden of the Fee of another, by reason of that Fee

[44]   ferm, Socage, or Burgage; neither will We have the | Custody of such Fee-ferm, or Socage, or Burgage, except Knights Service be due unto Us out of the same

---

20. [*Ed.:* Where a law is in special terms, but the reason for it is general, it is to be taken generally.]

21. [*Ed.:* the king's writ *de bono et malo* (of good and ill).]

22. Hil. 32. E. 1. Coram Rege Eború. Roger le Wildes Case. See the forme of this Writ at large in this Record.

23. [*Ed.:* That if A. B., who has been arrested and detained in the aforesaid prison for the death of C. D., wishes to put himself for good and ill upon the country, and is detained therein for that reason (and not by any special command of ours), then deliver that gaol of the aforesaid A. B. according to the law and custom of England.]

24. [*Ed.:* R. W., indicted for the death of W. E., had not proffered the lord king's writ of good and ill, therefore he is returned to gaol. And likewise in similar cases.]

Fee-ferm. We will not have the Custody of the Heir, or of any Land by occasion of any Petit Serjeanty, that any man holdeth of Us by Service to pay a knife, an arrow, or the like.

"by Fee-ferm."[1]

Fée farme properly taken is, when the Lord upon the creation of the Tenancy reserve to himselfe, and his heires, either the rent, for the which it was before letten to farme, or at least a fourth part of that farme rent.

But Britton saith,[2] *Fee farmes font terrestenus in fee, a rendre pur eux per annle veray value. ou plus, ou meins,*[3] and is called a fee farme, because a farme rent is reserved upon a graunt in fee. And regularly, as it appeareth by this act, lands granted in fee farme are holden in socage, unlesse an expresse tenure by Knights service be reserved, as it appeareth hereafter in this Chapter.

"or by Socage."[4]

[5] Tenere per firmam Albam est tenere libere in socagio. Vide in libro nigro Scaccarii, capite De officio clericorum de firma blanca.[6] It is commonly called blanch Farme. *Lucubrat̄ Ockham, firma blanca, & vide ibi antiquum verbum [dealbari.]*[7]

"Burgage."[8]

See the *Custumier de Normandie* cap.32. and the Commentaries upon the same.

---

1. See the Statute of Gloc. cap. 4 F. N. B. 210. 45. E. 3. 15.

2. Brit. fol. 164. b. Bract. li. 2. fo. 35. Fleta lib. 1. ca. 10. Mirror ca. 2 § 17.

3. [*Ed.:* Fee farms are lands held in fee, paying rent for them to the true value by the year, or more, or less.]

4. See the first part of the Institutes sect. 117.

5. * Rot. claus. 12. H. 3. m. 12.

6. [*Ed.:* To hold by blanch-farm (white rent) is to hold freely in socage: see the Black Book of the Exchequer, in the chapter concerning the office of the clerks of the blanch-rent.]

7. [*Ed.:* It is called by Ockham 'blanch-farm'; and see the old word *dealbari* (lit. to be whitewashed).]

8. Litt. sect. 162.

"by Knights Service,"[9]

See *le Custumier de Norman. cap. 33. De gard de Orphelines,*[10] fol. 49. and the Comment upon the same.

This Act, as well concerning tenures in fee farme, socage, and burgage, as by little serjanty, is declaratory of the Common Law,[11] and constantly in use to this day, and needeth no further explanation.

Chapter 28

No Bailiff from henceforth shall put any man to his open Law, nor to an Oath, upon his own bare saying, without faithful Witnesses brought in for the same.

The Mirror treating of this Chapter saith,[1] *Le point que defend, que nul Bayliffe met frank home a serement sans sute present, est interpretable en cest manner, Que nul Justice, nul Minister le Roy, ne auter seneschall, ne bailif ne eit power a mitter frank home a serement faire, sans le Commaundement le Roy, ne puit resceive aucun testmoignes, que testmoignent le monstrance estre veray.*[2]

By this it appeareth, that under this word *balivus,* in this Act is comprehended every Justice, Minister of the King, Steward and Bayliffe.[3]

"his own bare saying,"

For as Bracton saith, *Vox simplex nec probationem facit, nec praesumptionem* [45] *inducit; Item non per sectam, quae fieri | potest per domesticos, & familiares, secta*

9. Ibid. sect. 103.

10. [*Ed.:* concerning the wardship of young orphans.]

11. Glanv. li. 7. ca. 9.

1. Mirror cap. 5. § 2. Fleta li. 2. cap. 56. W. 2. ca. 35. des hauts homes.

2. [*Ed.:* The clause which forbids a bailiff to put a free man on oath without present suit, is interpretable in this way: that no justice or minister of the king, nor any other steward or bailiff, should have power to force a free man to make an oath without the king's command, or to receive any witnesses to give evidence that the showing is true.]

3. Fleta ubi supra. Vide Vet. Magna Charta. pt 2. in stat. Hibern. 68. b. See the first part of the Institutes. Sect. 248. Brac. l. 5 fo. 400. b.

enim probationem non facit, sed levem inducit praesumptionem, & vincitur per probationem in contrarium, & per defensionem per legem.[4]

It appeareth by Glanvill,[5] that the defendant ought to make his Law, *12. manu*. And so it appeareth by a judgement in the same yeare, and term, that this great Charter was made, for there, in debt the defendant waged his Law,[6] *Ideo consideratum est per Curiam, quod defendens se duodecima manu venit cum lege.*[7]

Every wager of Law doth counterbaile a Jury,[8] for the defendant shall make his Law, *de duodecima manu,*[9] viz. an eleven, and himselfe. And it should seeme, that this making of Law was very auncient, for one writing of the auncient Law of England saith, *Hujus purgationis non omnis evanuit vetustate memoria, nam per haec tempora de pecunia postulatus, debitum nonnunquam duodecima, quod aiunt, manu dissolvit.*[10]

How much, and for what cause the Law respecteth the number of 12. see the first part of the Institutes.[11]

The party himselfe, when he maketh his Law, shall be sworne *de fidelitate,*[12] that is, directly or absolutely, and the others *de credulitate,*[13] that is, that they beleeve that he saith true.

To make his Law, is as much as to say, as to take his oath, &c. and it is so called, because the Law giveth him that meane by his owne oath, to free himselfe.

And the reason, wherefore in an action of Debt upon a simple contract, the Defendent may wage his Law, is, for that the Defendant may satisfie the party in secret, or before witnesse, and all the witnesses may die, so the Law

---

4. [*Ed.:* A simple voice does not amount to proof, or raise a presumption. Nor can proof be made by suit which is made up of servants and friends, although it raises a light presumption, and may be overcome by proof on the contrary side and by a denial by wager of law.]

5. Glanv. li. 1. ca. 9.

6. Mich. 9. H. 3. tit. Ley 78.

7. [*Ed.:* Therefore it is decided by the court that the defendant, with himself as the twelfth hand, should come with his law.]

8. 33. H. 6. 8.

9. [*Ed.:* with the twelfth hand.]

10. [*Ed.:* The memory of this ancient form of purgation has not wholly vanished, for in these days one sued for money has sometimes dissolved the debt with the twelfth hand (as they say).]

11. See the first part of the Institutes. Sect. 234.

12. [*Ed.:* on his faith,]

13. [*Ed.:* concerning their belief,]

doth allow him to wage his Law for his discharge: and this, for ought I could ever reade, is paculiar to the Law of England, and no mischiefe insueth hereupon, for the Plaintiffe may take a Bill or Bond for his money, or if it be a simple contract, he may bring his action upon his case upon his agreement or promise, which every contract executory implieth, and then the Defendant cannot wage his Law.

Chapter 29

No Freeman shall be taken or imprisoned, or be disseised of his Freehold, or Liberties, or free Customs, or be outlawed, or exiled, or any other wise destroyed; nor will We not pass upon him, nor condemn him, but by lawful judgment of his Peers, or by the Law of the Land. We will sell to no man, we will not deny or defer to any man either Justice or Right.[1]

"No Free, &c."

This extends to Villeins, saving against their Lord, for they are free against all men, saving against their Lord. See the first part of the Institutes, sect. 189.

"No Freeman."

Albeit *homo* doth extend to both sexes, men and women, yet by Act of Parliament it is enacted, and declared, that this Chapter should extend to Duchesses, Countesses, and Baronesses, but Marchionesses, and Vicountesses are omitted, but not withstanding they are also comprehended within this Chapter.[2]

[46] | Upon this Chapter, as out of a roote, many fruitfull branches of the Law of England have sprung.

And therefore first the genuine sense hereof is to be seene, and after how the same hath been declared, and interpreted. For the first, for more perspicuity, it is necessary to divide this Chapter into severall branches, according to the true construction and reference of the words.

---

1. See the Statute anno 34. E. 1. de tallagio, &c. an excellent Law.
2. 20 H. 6. cap. 9. Stamf. Pl. Cor. 152. b. 25. E. 3. 43. b. li. 6. fol. 52. The Countesse of Rutlands case.
11. H. 4. 1 5. 3. H. 6. 58. 48. E. 3. 30. 35. H. 6. 46.

This Chapter containeth nine severall branches.

1. That no man be taken or imprisoned, but *per legem terrae,*[3] that is, by the Common Law, Statute Law, or Custome of England;[4] for these words, *Per legem terrae,* being towards the end of this Chapter, doe referre to all the precedent matters in this Chapter, and this hath the first place, because the liberty of a mans person is more precious to him, then all the rest that follow, and therefore it is great reason, that he should by Law be relieved therein, if he be wronged, as hereafter shall be shewed.

2. No man shall be disseised, that is, put out of seison, or dispossessed of his free-hold (that is) lands, or livelihood, or of his liberties, or free customes, that is, of such franchises, and freedomes, and free customes, as belong to him by his free birth-right, unlesse it be by the lawfull judgement, that is, verdict of his equals (that is, of men of his own condition) or by the Law of the Land (that is, to speak it once for all) by the due course, and processe of Law.

3. No man shall be out-lawed, made an *exlex,*[5] put out of the Law, that is, deprived of the benefit of the Law, unlesse he be out-lawed according to the Law of the Land.

4. No man shall be exiled, or banished out of his Country, that is, *Nemo perdet patriam,* no man shall lose his Country, unlesse he be exiled according to the Law of the Land.

5. No man shall be in any sort destroyed (*Destruere. i. quod prius structum, & factum fuit, penitus evertere & diruere*)[6] unlesse it be by the verdict of his equals, or according to the Law of the Land.

6. No man shall be condemned at the Kings suite, either before the King in his Bench, where the Pleas are *Coram Rege,*[7] (and so are the words, *Nec super eum ibimus,*[8] to be understood) nor before any other Commissioner, or Judge whatsoever, and so are the words, *Nec super eum mittemus,*[9] to be understood, but by the judgement of his Peers, that is, equalls, or according to the Law of the Land.

3. [*Ed.:* by the law of the land,]
4. See W. 1. ca. 15.
5. [*Ed.:* outlaw,]
6. [*Ed.:* To destroy, in other words that something which was previously constructed and made should be utterly overthrown and undone.]
7. [*Ed.:* Before the king.]
8. [*Ed.:* Nor shall we go upon him.]
9. [*Ed.:* Nor shall we put upon him.]

7. We shall sell to no man Justice or Right.

8. We shall deny to no man Justice or Right.

9. We shall defer to no man Justice or Right.

The genuine sense being distinctly understood, we shall proceed in order to unfold how the same have been declared, and interpreted. 1. By authority of Parliament. 2. By our books. 3. By precedent.

"No Freeman shall be taken, or imprisoned."

Attached and arrested are comprehended herein.

1. No man shall be taken, (that is) restrained of liberty, by petition, or suggestion to the King, or to his Councell,*[10] unlesse it be by indictment, or presentment of good, and lawfull men, where such deeds be done. This branch, and divers other parts of this Act have been notably explained by divers superseded[a.11] Acts of Parliament, &c. quoted in the margent.

2. No man shall be desseised, &c.

b.[12] Hereby is intended, that lands, tenements, goods, and chattells shall not be seised into the Kings hands, contrary to this great Charter, and the Law of the Land; Nor any man shall be disseised of his lands, or tenements, or dispossessed of his goods, or Chattels, contrary to the Law of the Land.

c.[13] A custome was alledged in the town of C. that if the Tenant cease by two years, that the Lord should enter into the freehold of the Tenant, and hold the same untill he were satisfied of the arrerages, and it was adjudged a [47] custome | against the Law of the Land, to enter into a mans freehold in that case without action or answer.

King H. 6. graunted to the Corporation of Diers within London, power to search, &c., and if they found any cloth died with Logwood,[14] that the cloth should be forfeit:[15] and it was adjudged, that this Charter concerning

---

10. *See W. 1. ca. 15.

11. *a* 5. E. 3. cap. 9. a 5. E. 3. ca. 4. 37. E. 3. ca. 8. 38. E. 3. ca. 9. 42. E. 3. ca. 3. 17. R. 2. cap. 6. Rot. Parl. 43. E. 3. Sir Jo. a Lees case. nu. 21, 22, 23, &c. lib. 10. fol. 74. in case del Marshalsea.

12. *b* Sec 43. Ass. p. 21 where this branch of Magna Charta, and other Statutes are cited, *nota bone*, the usurpation to an advowson is within this Act. 5. E. 3. cap. 9. 25. E. 3. cap. 4.

13. *c* 43. E. 3. 32.

14. [*Ed.:* Diers (people who dye cloth) . . . Logwood (an expensive American tree yielding black dye.).]

15. Lib. 8. Tr. 41. l. fol. 125. Case dé Londres.

the forfeiture, was against the Law of the Land, and this Statute: For no forfeiture can grow by Letters Patents.

No man ought to be put from his livelihood without answer.

3. No man outlawed, that is, barred to have the benefit of the Law. Vide
for the word, the first part of the Institutes.[16]

Note to this word *utlagetur,*[17] these words, *Nisi per legem terrae,*[18] do refer.

"of his . . . Liberties."

This word, *libertates,* liberties, hath three significations:

1. First, as it hath been said, it signifieth the Laws of the Realme, in which
respect this Charter is called, *Charta libertatum.*

2. It signifieth the freedomes, that the Subjects of England have;[19] for example, the Company of the Merchant Tailors of England, having power by
their Charter to make ordinances, made an ordinance, that every brother of
the same Society should put the one half of his clothes to be dressed by some
Clothworker free of the same Company, upon pain to forfeit r. s. &c. and it
was adjudged that this ordinance was against Law, because it was against the
Liberty of the Subject, for every Subject hath freedome to put his clothes to
be dressed by whom he will, *& sic de similibus:*[20] And so it is, if such or the
like graunt had been made by his Letters Patents.

3. Liberties signifieth the franchises, and priviledges, which the Subjects
have of the gift of the King, as the goods, and Chattels of felons, outlawes,
and the like, or which the Subject claim by prescription, as wreck, waife, straie,
and the like.

So likewise, and for the same reason, if a graunt be made to any man, to
have the sole making of Cards, or the sole dealing with any other trade, that
graunt is against the liberty, and freedome of the Subject, that before did, or
lawfully might have used that trade, and consequently against this great Charter.[21]

---

16. 2. & 3. Ph. et Mar. Dier. 114, 115.
17. [*Ed.:* be outlawed.]
18. [*Ed.:* Unless by the law of the land.]
19. Tr. 41. Eliz. Coram Rege. Rot. 91. in trñs int. Davenant & Hurdes.
20. [*Ed.:* and likewise of similar cases:]
21. Tr. 44. Eliz. Coram Regé. lib. 11. fol. 84. 85. &c. Edw. Darcies case.

Generally all monopolies are against this great Charter, because they are against the liberty and freedome of the Subject, and against the Law of the Land.

"free Customs."

Of Customes of the Realme, some be generall, and some particular, of these reade in the first part of the Institutes. And liberties added, for that the Customes of England bring a freedome with them.

4. No man exiled.

By the Law of the Land no man can be exiled, or banished out of his native Countrey, but either by authority of Parliament, or in case of abjuration for felony by the Common Law:[22] and so when our books, or any Record speak of exile, or banishment, other then in case of abjuration; it is to be intended to be done by authority of Parliament:*[23] as Belknap and other Judges, &c, banished into Ireland.

This is a beneficially Law, and is construed benignly and therefore the King cannot send any Subject of England against his will to serve him out of this Realme, for that should be an exile, and he should *perdere patriam:*[24] no, he cannot be sent against his will into Ireland, to serve the King as his Deputy there, because it is out of the Realme of England: for if the King might send him out of this Realme to any place, then under pretence of service, as Ambassadour, or the like, he might send him into the furthest part of the world, which being an exile, is prohibited by this Act. And albeit it was accorded in the Upper house of Parliament, Anno 6. Edw. 3. nu. 6. that such learned men [48] in the Law, as should I bee sent, as Justices, or otherwise, to serve in Ireland, should have no excuse yet that being no Act of Parliament, it did not binde the Subject. And this notably appeared by a Record, in 44. Edw. 3.[25] Sir Richard Pembrughs Case, who was Warden of the Cinque Posts, and had divers offices, annuities, and lands graunted to him for life, or in fee by the King under the

---

22. Rot. Parliam. 19. E. 1. Rot. 12. Boilands case. 31. E. 1. Cui in vita 131. 18. E. 3. 54. Matravers case. Parliam. 15. E. 2. Exilium Hugonis.

23. *Rot. Parliam. 13. R. 2. nu. 28. Stam. Pl. Cor. 116. 117. 35. E. 1. cap. 1.

24. [*Ed.:* lose his country:]

25. Rot. claus. Anno 44. E. 3. Sir Richard Pembrughs Case.

great Seale, *Pro servitio impenso, & impendendo,*[26] The King commanded Sir Richard to serve him in Ireland, as his Deputy there, which he absolutely refused, whereupon the King by advice of his Councell, seised all things graunted to him, *pro servitio impendendo,* (in respect of that clause) but he was not upon that resolution committed to prison, as by that Record it appeareth: And the reason was because his refusall was lawfull, and if the refusall was lawfull to serve in Ireland parcell of the Kings Dominions, *à fortiori,*[27] a refusall is lawfull to serve in any forein Country. And it seemeth to me, that the said seisure was unlawfull, for *pro servitio impenso & impendendo,* must be intended lawfull service within the Realme.

5. No man destroyed, &c.

That is, fore-judged of life, or limbe, disherited, or put to torture, or death.[28]

The Mirror writing of the auncient Laws of England, saith,[29] *Soloient les Roys faire droit a touts, pereux, ou per lour Chiefe Justices, et ore les faits les Royes per lour Justices Comissaries errants assignes a touts pleas: En aid de tiels eires font Tornes de Viscounts necessaries, & views de frankpl. & quant que bones gents a tiels inquesls inditerent de peche mortel, soloient les Royes destruere sans respons, &c. Accord est, que nul appelee, ne enditee soit destroy sans respons.*[30]

Thomas Earle of Lancaster was destroyed, that is, adjudged to die, as a Traitor, and put to death in 14. Edw. 2. and a Record thereof made: And Henry Earle of Lancaster his brother, and heire was restored for two principall errors in the proceeding against the said Thomas Earle,[31] 1. *Quod non fuit araniatus, & ad responsionem positus tempore pacis eo quod cancellaria, & aliae curiae Regis fuer' apertae, in quibus lex fiebat unicuique, prout fieri consuevit. 2. Quod contra cartam de libertatibus, cum dictus Thomas fuit unus parium, & magnatum Regni, in qua continetur.*[32] (and reciteth this Chapter of Magna Charta, and specially,

26. [*Ed.:* for service performed and to be performed.]

27. [*Ed.:* so much the more so.]

28. 5. E. 3. cap. 9. 28. E. 3. cap. 3. Fortescue cap. 22.

29. Mirror cap. 2. § 3.

30. [*Ed.:* The kings used to do right to all by themselves, or by their chief justices, and now the kings do it by their itinerant commissary justices assigned for all pleas; in aid of which eyres the sheriffs' tourns are necessary, and views of frankpledge; and whenever good men at such inquests indict of mortal sin, the kings used to destroy [the accused] without answer, etc., [but now] it is agreed that no one appealed or indicted of felony should be destroyed without answer.]

31. Pasc. 39. E. 3. Coram Rege, John of Gaunts case. Rot. Parl. 4 E. 3. nu. 13. Countee de A und. case. Rot. Parl. 42. E. 3. nu. 23. Sir Jo. of Lees case.

32. [*Ed.:* That he was not arraigned and put to answer, [although it was] in time of peace, inasmuch

quod Dominus Rex non super eum ibit, nec mitter, nisi per legale judicium parium suorum, tamen per recordum praedictum, tempore pacis absq; aranamento, seu responsione, seu legali judicio parium suorum, contra legem, & contra tenorem Magnae Chartae).[33] he was put to death: More examples of this kinde might be shewed.

Regula.   Every oppression against Law, by colour of any usurped authority, is a kinde of destruction, for, *Quando aliquid prohibetur, prohibetur & omne, per quod devenitur ad illud:*[34] And it is the worst oppression, that is done by colour of Justice.[35]

It is to be noted, that to this Verb *destruatur,*[36] are added *aliquo modo,*[37] and to no other Verb in this Chapter, and therefore all things, by any manner of meanes tending to destruction, are prohibited: As if a man be accused, or indicted of treason, or felony, his lands, or goods cannot be graunted to any, no not so much as by promise, nor any of his lands, or goods seised into the Kings hands, before attainder: For when a Subject obtaineth a promise of the forfeiture, many times undue meanes and more violent prosecution is used for private lucre, tending to destruction, then the quiet and just proceeding of Law would permit, and the party ought to live of his own untill attainder.[38]

"by . . . judgement of his Peers."[39]

By judgement of his Peers, Onely a Lord of Parliament of England shall be tried by his Peers being Lords of Parliament: and neither Noblemen of any other Country, nor others that are called Lords, and are no Lords of Parliament

---

as the Chancery and other king's courts were open, in which law was done to everyone in the usual way; secondly, that against the charter of liberties, whereas the said Thomas was one of the peers and great men of the realm, in which it is contained.]

33. [*Ed.:* that the lord king will not go upon him, or put upon him, except by the lawful judgment of his peers, nevertheless by the aforesaid record, in time of peace, without any arraignment or answer, or lawful judgment of his peers, against the law, and against the tenor of Magna Carta.]

34. Lib. 10. fol. 74. In the case of the Marshalsea.

35. [*Ed.:* When something is prohibited, everything is prohibited whereby it may be arrived at.]

36. [*Ed.:* be destroyed.]

37. [*Ed.:* in any way.]

38. Rot. Parl. 15. E. 3. nu. 6. &c.

39. 11. E. 3. breve. 173. 6. R. 2. proces. Pl. ultimo. 20. E. 4. 6. 20. Eliz. Dier 360. Lib. 9. fol. 117. Seignior Zanchars case.

are accounted *Pares,* Peers within this Statute. Who shall be said *Pares,* Peeres, or Equalls, see before Cap. 14. § per Pares.

Here note, as is before said, that this is to be understood of the Kings sute I for the words be, *nec super eum ibimus, nec super eum mittemus, nisi per legale* [49] *judicium parium suorum.*[40,41] Therefore, for example, if a Noble man be indicted for murder, he shall be tried by his Peeres, but if an appeale be brought against him, which is the suite of the party, there he shall not be tried by his Peeres, but by an ordinary jury of twelve men: and that for two reasons. First, for that the appeale cannot be brought before the Lord high Steward of England, who is the only Judge of Noblemen, in case of Treason, or Felony. Secondly, this Statute extendeth only to the Kings suite.

And it extendeth to the Kings suite in case of treason, or felony, or of misprision of treason, or felony, or being accessary to felony before, or after, and not to any other inferior offence. Also it extendeth to the triall it selfe, whereby he is to be convicted: but a Nobleman is to be indicted of treason, or felony, or of misprision, or being accessary to, in case of felony, by an inquest under the degree of Nobility: the number of the Noble men that are to be triers are, 12. or more.

And a Peer of the Realme may be indicted of treason, or felony, before commissioners of *Oier & Terminer,* or in the Kings bench, if the treason or felony be committed in the county where the Kings bench sit: he also may be indicted of murder, or manslaughter, before the Coroner, &c. But if he be indicted in the Kings bench, or the indictment removed thither, the Noble man may plead his pardon there before the Judges of the Kings bench, and they have power to allow it, but he cannot confesse the indictment, or plead not guilty before the Judges of the Kings bench, but before the Lord Steward;[42] and the reason of this diversity, that the triall or judgement must be before or by the Lord Steward, but the allowance of the pardon may be by the Kings bench, is because that is not within this Statute.

If a Noble man be indicted, and cannot be found, process of Outlawrie shall be awarded against him *per legem terrae,*[43] and he shall be Outlawed *per*

---

40. [*Ed.:* nor shall we go upon, or put upon him, except by lawful judgment of his peers.]

41. 1. H. 4. 1. 13. H. 8. 1. 10. E. 4. 6.

42. 19. H. 7. Edm. de la Pole Earle of Suff. case. Hil. 13. Jacob. the Lord Norrice case coram Rege.

43. [*Ed.:* by the law of the land.]

judicium Coronatorum,[44] but he shall be tried *per judicium parium suorum,*[45] when he appeares and pleads to issue.[46]

"by lawful judgement"

By this word legale, amongst others, three things are implied, 1. That this manner of triall was by Law, before this Statute. 2. That their verdict must be legally given, wherein principally it is to be observed. 1. That the Lords ought to heare no evidence, but in the presence, and hearing of the prisoner. 2. After the Lords be gone together to consider of the evidence, they cannot send to the high Steward to aske the Judges any question of Law, but in the hearing of the prisoner, that he may heare, whether the case be rightly put, for *de facto jus oritur;*[47] neither can the Lords, when they are gone together, send for the Judges to know any opinion in Law, but the high Steward ought to demand it in Court in the hearing of the prisoner. 3. When all the evidence is given by the Kings learned Councell, the high Steward cannot collect the evidence against the prisoner, or in any sort conferre with the Lords touching their evidence, in the absence of the prisoner, but he ought to be called to it; and all this is implied in this word, legale. And therefore it shall be necessary for all such prisoners, after evidence given against him, and before he depart from the Barre, to require Justice of the Lord Steward, and of the other Lords, that no question be demanded by the Lords, or speech or conference had by any with the Lords, but in open Court in his presence, and hearing, or else he shall not take any advantage thereof after verdict, and judgement given: but the handling thereof at large and of other things concerning this matter, belongs to another treatise, as before I have shewed, only this may suffice for the exposition of this Statute. See the 3. part of the Institutes, cap. Treason.[48]

And it is here called *Judicium parium,*[49] and not *veredictum,*[50] because the

---

44. [*Ed.:* by judgment of the coroners.]

45. [*Ed.:* by judgment of his peers.]

46. Stamf. pl. cor. 130.

47. [*Ed.:* the law arises out of the facts.]

48. Pasch. 26. H. 8. in the case of the L. Dacres of the north, resolved by all the Judges of England as Justice Spelman report. See the 3. part of the Institutes cap. treason.

49. [*Ed.:* judgment of peers.]

50. [*Ed.:* verdict.]

Noble men returned, and charged, are not sworne, but give their judgement upon their Honour, and ligeance to the King, for so are all the entries of record, separately beginning at the *puisne*[51] Lord, and so ascending upward.

| And though of ancient time the Lords, and Peeres of the Realme used in Parliament to give judgement,[52] in case of treason and felony, against those, that were no Lords of Parliament, yet at the suite of the Lords it was enacted, that albeit the Lords and Peeres of the Realme, as judges of the Parliament, in the presence of the King, had taken upon them to give judgement, in case of treason and felony, of such as were no Peeres of the Realme, that hereafter no Peeres shall be driven to give judgement on any others, then on their Peeres according to the law. [50]

This triall by Peeres was very auncient, for I reade, that William the Conqueror, in the beginning of his raigne,[53] created William Fitzosberne (who was Earle of Bretevil in Normandy) Earle of Hereford in England, his sonne Roger succeeded him, and was Earle of Hereford, who under colour of his sisters mariage at Erninge, neare Newmarket in Cambridge shire, whereat many of the Nobility, and others were assembled, conspired with them to receive the Danes into England, and to depose William the Conqueror, (who then was in Normandy) from his Kingdome of England: and to bring the same to effect, he with others rose. This treason was revealed by one of the conspirators, viz. Walter Earle of Huntingdon an English man, sonne of that great Syward Earle of Northumberland: for which treason this Roger Earle of Hereford was apprehended, by Urse Tiptost then Sheriffe of Worcester shire, and after was tried by his Peeres, and found guilty of the treason *per judicium Parium suorum*,[54] but he lived in prison all the daies of his life.[55] You have heard in the exposition of the 14. Chapter, who are to be said Peeres, somewhat is necessary to be added thereunto, It is provided by the Statute of 20. H. 6.[56] That Dutchesses, Countesses, and Baronesses, shall be tried by such Peeres as a Noble man, being a Peere of the Realme ought to be; which Act was made in declaration, and affirmance of the Common law: for Mar-

---

51. [*Ed.:* most recently created.]
52. Rot. Parliam. 4. E. 3. nu. 6.
53. Anno 8. Will. conq.
54. [*Ed.:* by judgment of his peers.]
55. Anno 8. W. 1.
56. 20. H. 6. cap 9.

quesses, and Vicountesses not named in the Act shall be also tried by their Peeres, and the Queene being the Kings consort, or dowager, shall also be tried, in case of treason, *per Pares,*[57] as Queene Anne, the Wife of King Henry the eight was *Termino Pasch. anno* 28. Hen. 8.[58] in the Towre of London before the Duke of Norff. then high Steward.

If a Woman that is Noble by birth, doth marry under the degree of Nobility, yet shee shall be tried by her Peeres, but if shee be noble by marriage, and marry under the degree of Nobility shee loseth her Dignity, for as by marriage it was gained, so by marriage it is lost, and shee shall not be tried by her Peers. If a Dutchesse by marriage doe marry a Baron, shee loseth not her dignity, for all degrees of Nobility, as hath been said, are *Pares.*[59] If a Queene Dowager marry any of the Nobility, or under that degree, yet loseth shee not her Dignity, as Katherine Queene Dowager of England, married Owen ap Meredith ap Theodore Esquire, and yet shee by the name of Katherine Queene of England, maintained an Action of Detinew, against the Bishop of Carlile.

And the Queene of Navarra marrying with Edmund the brother of Edw. 1. sued for her Dower by the name of Queene of Navarra and recovered.[60]

"or by the Law of the Land."

But by the Law of the Land. For the true sense and exposition of these words, see the Statute of 37. Edw. 3. cap. 8. where the words, by the law of the Land, are rendred, without due process of Law, for there it is said, though it be contained in the great Charter, that no man be taken, imprisoned, or put out of his free-hold without proces of the Law;[61] that is, by indictment of presentment of good and lawfull men, where such deeds be done in due manner, or by writ originall of the Common law.

Without being brought in to answere but by due Proces of the Common law.

No man be put to answer without presentment before Justices, or thing of

57. [*Ed.:* by peers.]
58. Pasch. 28. H. 8. Spelmans report.
59. 22. H. 6. 47. 11. H. 6. 51.
60. Rot. Parliam. 26. E. 1. Rot. 1.
61. 25. E. 3. cap. 4.

record, or by due proces, or by writ originall, according to the old law of the land.[62]

Wherein it is to be observed, that this Chapter is but declaratory of the old law of England. Rot. Parliament. 42. E. 3. nu. 22. 23. the case of Sir John a Lee, the Steward of the Kings house.

| "by the Law of the Land." [51]

i. Per legem Angliae,[63] and hereupon all Commissions are grounded, wherein is this clause, *facturi quod ad justitiam pertinet secundum legem, & consuetudinem Angliae, &c.*[64] And it is not said, *legem & consuetudinem Regis Angliae,*[65] lest it might be thought to bind the King only, nor *populi Angliae,*[66] lest it might be thought to bind them only, but that the law might extend to all, it is said *per legem terrae, i. Angliae.*[67]

And aptly it is said in this Act, *per legem terrae,* that is, by the Law of England:[68] For into those places, where the law of England runneth not, other lawes are allowed in many cases, and not prohibited by this Act. For example: If any injury, robbery, felony, or other offence be done upon the high sea, *Lex terrae*[69] extendeth not to it, therefore the Admirall hath conusance thereof, and may proceed, according to the marine law, by imprisonment of the body, and other proceedings, as have been allowed by the lawes of the Realme.

And so if two English men doe goe into a foreine Kingdome, and fight there, and the one murder the other, *lex terrae* extendeth not hereunto, but this offence shall be heard, and determined before the Constable, and Marshall, and such proceedings shall be there, by attaching of the body, and otherwise, as the Law, and custome of that court have beene allowed by the lawes of the Realme.[70]

---

62. 28. E. 3. cap. 3. 37. E. 3. cap. 8. 42. E. 3. cap. 3.
63. [*Ed.:* By the law of England,]
64. [*Ed.:* to do what belongs to justice according to the law and custom of England, etc.]
65. [*Ed.:* law and custom of the king of England,]
66. [*Ed.:* of the people of England,]
67. [*Ed.:* by the law of the land, that is, England.]
68. 19. H. 6. 7.
69. [*Ed.:* law of the land.]
70. 13. H. 4. 5.

Against this ancient, and fundamentall Law, and in the face thereof, I finde an Act of Parliament made,[71] that as well Justices of Assise, as Justices of peace (without any finding or presentment by the verdict of twelve men) upon a bare information for the King tofore them made, should have full power, and authority by their discretions to heare, and determine all offences, and contempts committed, or done by any person, or persons against the forme, ordinance, and effect of any Statute made, and not repealed &c. By colour of which Act, making this fundamentall Law, it is not credible what horrible oppressions, and exactions, to the undoing of infinite numbers of people, were committed by Sir Richard Empson Knight, and Edm. Dudley being Justices of peace, throughout England; and upon this unjust and injurious Act (as commonly in like cases it falleth out) a new office was erected, and they made Matters of the Kings forfeitures.

But at the Parliament, holden in the first yeare of Hen. 8.[72] this Act of 11. Hen. 7. is recited, and made voide, and repealed, and the reason thereof is yeelded, for that by force of the said Act, it was manifestly known, that many sinister, and crafty, feigned, and forged informations, had been pursued against divers of the Kings subjects, to their great dammage, and wrongfull vexation: And the ill successe hereof, and the fearefull ends of these two oppressors, should deterre others from committing the like, and should admonish Parliaments, that in stead of this ordinary, and pretious triall *Per legem terrae,* they bring not in absolute, and partiall trialls by discretion.

If one be suspected for any crime, be it treason, felony &c. And the party is to be examined upon certaine interrogatories, he may heare the interrogatories, and take a reasonable time to answer the same with deliberation (as there the time of deliberation was tenne houres) and the examinate, if he will, may put his answere in writing, and keepe a Copie thereof:[73] and so it was resolved in Parliament by the Lords Spirituall, and Temporall in the case of Justice Riehill. See the Record at large.

And the Lord Carew being examined, for being privy to the plot, for the escape of Sir Walter Rawleigh attainted of treason, desired to have a copy of his examination, and had it, as *Per legem terrae* he ought.[74]

71. 11. H. 7. cap. 3.
72. 11. H. 8. cap. 6.
73. Rot. pl. 1. H. 4. memb. 2. nu. 1.
74. Anno 16. Jacobi Regis.

Now here it is to be knowne, in what cases a man by the Law of the land, may be taken, arrested, attached, or imprisoned in case of treason or felony, before presentment, indictment, &c. Wherein it is to be understood, that Process of law is two fold, viz. By the Kings Writ, or by due proceeding, and warrant, either in deed, or in law without Writ.

As first, where there is any witnesse against the offendor, he may be taken and arrested by lawfull warrant, and committed to prison.

| When treason and felony is committed, and the common same and voice   [52] is, that A. is guilty, it is lawfull for any man, that suspects him, to apprehend him.[75]

[a76] This same Bracton describeth well, *Fama quae suspicionem inducit, oriri debet apud bonos, & graves, non quidem malevolos, & maledicos, sid providas & fide dignas personas, non semel, sed saepius, quia clamor minuit, & defamatio manifestat.*[77]

[b78] So it is of Hue and Cry, and that is by the Statute of Winchester, which is but an affirmance of the Common Law: Likewise if A. be suspected, and be fleeth, or hideth himselfe, it is a good cause to arrest him.

[c79] If treason or felony be done, and one hath just cause of suspition, this is a good cause, and warrant in Law, for him to arrest any man, but he must shew in certainty the cause of his suspition: and whether the suspition be just, or lawfull, shall be determined by the Justices in an action of false imprisonment brought by the party grieved, or upon a *Habeas corpus, &c.*[80]

A felony is done, and one is pursued upon Hue and Cry, that is not of ill fame, suspicious, unknown, nor indicted;[81] he may be by a warrant in Law, attached and imprisoned by the Law of the Land.

A Watchman may arrest a night-walker by a warrant in Law.[82]

If a man woundeth another dangerously, any man may arrest him by a

---

75. 7. E. 4. 20. 8. E. 4. 3. 9. E. 4. 27. 11. E. 4. 2. 2. H. 7. 15. b. 4. 4. H. 7. 18. 5. H. 7. 5. a. 26. H. 8. 9. 27. H. 8. 23.

76. *a* Bracton. fo. 143.

77. [*Ed.:* The rumour which begets a suspicion ought to arise from good and serious men, not men of ill will and slanderers, but careful and trustworthy persons, and it must not be only on one occasion, but frequently, that complaint arises and the bad reputation is manifested.]

78. *b* 29. E. 3. 9. 39. E. 3. 39. 26. E. 3. 71. W. 1. cap. 9.

79. *c* 11. H. 4. 4. b. 20. E. 4. 6. b. 14. H. 8. 16. 27. H. 8. 23.

80. [*Ed.:* Writ to challenge the lawfulness of an incarceration.]

81. 29. E. 3. 39.

82. 4. H. 7. 2. 5. H. 7. 5.

warrant in Law, untill it may be known, whether the party wounded shall die thereof, or no.[83]

If a man keep the company of a notorious thiefe, whereby he is suspected, &c. It is a good cause, and a warrant in Law to arrest him.[84]

If an affray be made to the breach of the Kings peace, any man may by a warrant in Law restrain any of the offenders, to the end the Kings peace may be kept, but after the affray ended, they cannot be arrested without an expresse warrant.[85]

See now the Statutes of 1. & 2. Phil. & Mar. cap. 13. & 2. & 3. Phil. & Mar. cap. 10.

Now seeing that no man can be taken, arrested, attached, or imprisoned but by due processe of Law, and according to the Law of the Land, these conclusions hereupon doe follow.

First, that a commitment by lawfull warrant, either in deed or in Law, is accounted in Law due processe or proceeding of Law, and by the Law of the Land, as well as by processe by force of the Kings Writ.

2. That he or they, which doe commit them, have lawfull authority.

3. That his warrant, or *Mittimus*[86] be lawfull, and that must be in writing under his hand and seale.

4. The cause must be contained in the warrant, as for treason, felony, &c. or for suspition of treason or felony, &c. otherwise if the *Mittimus* contain no cause at all, if the Prisoner escape, it is no offence at all, whereas if the *Mittimus* contained the cause, the escape were treason, or felony, though he were not guilty of the offence; and therefore for the Kings benefit, and that the Prisoner may be the more safely kept, the *Mittimus* ought to contain the cause.

5. The Warrant or *Mittimus* containing a lawfull cause, ought to have a lawfull conclusion, viz. and him safely to keep, untill he be delivered by Law, &c. and not untill the party committing doth further order. And this doth

83. 10. H. 7. 20.
84. 26. E. 3. 7. a.
85. 38. H. 8. faux imprisonment. Br. 6.
86. [*Ed.:* We commit, an order committing a person to custody of a gaoler.]

evidently appeare by the Writs of *Habeas corpus*, both in the Kings Bench, and Common Pleas, Eschequer, and Chancery.[87]

Rex Vicecom̃ Londoñ salutem. Praecipimus vobis, quod corpus A.B. in custodia vestra detent̃, ut dicitur, una cum causa dertentionis suae, quocunq; nomine praed. A.B. censeatur in eisdem, habeatis coram nobis apud Westm̃ die Jovis prox' post Octabis S. Martini, ad subjiciend', & recipiend' ea, quae curia nostra de eo adtunc, & ibidem ordinar̃ contigerit in hac parte, & hoc nullatenus omittatis, periculo incumbente, & habeatis ibi hoc breve, Teste Edw. Coke 20. Nov. anno Regni nostri 10.[88]

This is the usuall forme of the Writ of *Habeas corpus* in the Kings Bench, | Vide Mich. 5. Edw. 4. Rot. 143. Coram Rege, Kefars Case, under the Teste of Sir John Markham. [53]

Rex Vicecom̃ Londoñ salutem. Praecipimus vobis, quod habeatis coram Justiciariis nostris, apud Westm̃ die Jovis prox' post quinque septiman. Pasche, corpus A. B. quocunque nomine censeatur, in prisona vestra, sub custodia vestra detent̃, ut dicitur, una cum die, & causa captionis & detentionis ejusdem, ut iidem Justiciar̃ nostri, visa causa illa, ulterius fieri fac', quod de jure, & secundum legem, & consuetudinem Regni nostri Angliae foret faciend', & habeatis ibi hoc breve, Teste, & c.[89,90]

The like Writ is to be graunted out of the Chancery, either in the time of the Terme, (as in the Kings Bench) or in the Vacation; for the Court of Chancery is *officina justitiae*,[91] and is ever open, and never adjourned, so as the

---

87. 13. H. 7. Kelway 34. b. See more before hereof in the Exposition upon the Statute of 1. E. 2. De frangentibus prisonam. Out of the Kings Bench, though there be not any priviledge, &c.

88. [*Ed.:* The king to the sheriffs of London, greeting. We command you that you have the body of A. B., which is said to be detained in your keeping, together with the cause of his detention, by whatever name the aforesaid A. B. is known in the same, before us at Westminster on the Thursday next after the octaves of St Martin, to undergo and receive those things which our court shall happen then and there to order for him, and this in no way omit under the incumbent danger, and have there this writ. Witness Edward Coke on the twentieth day of November in the tenth year of our reign.]

89. [*Ed.:* The king to the sheriffs of London, greeting. We command you that you have the body of A. B., by whatever name he is known, who is said to be detained in your keeping, together with the day and the cause of his detention, before our justices at Westminster on the Thursday next after five weeks from Easter, that our same justices, having seen that cause, may further cause to be done what ought rightfully to be done according to the law and custom of our realm of England; and have there this writ. Witness, etc.]

90. In the Common Pleas, for any man priviledged in that Court, and the like in the Eschequer.

91. [*Ed.:* the workshop of justice.]

Subject being wrongfully imprisoned, may have justice for the liberty of his person as well in the Vacation time, as in the Terme.[92]

By these Writs it manifestly appeareth, that no man ought to be imprisoned, but for some certain cause: and these words, *Ad subjiciend', & recipiend', &c.*[93] prove that cause must be shewed: for otherwise how can the Court take order therein according to Law.

And this doth agree with that which is said in the holy History,[94] *Sine ratione mihi videtur, mittere vinctum in carcerem, & causas ejus non significare.*[95] But since we wrote there things, and passed over to many other Acts of Parliament; see now the Petition of Right, *Anno Tertio Caroli Regis,*[96] resolved in full Parliament by the King, the Lords Spirituall, and Temporall, and the Commons, which hath made an end of this question, if any were.

Imprisonment doth not onely exrtend to false imprisonment, and unjust, but for detaining of the Prisoner longer then he ought, where he was at the first law, fully imprisoned.

If the Kings Writ come to the Sheriffe, to deliver the Prisoner, if he detain him, this detaining is an imprisonment against the Law of the Land:[97] If a man be in Prison, a warrant cannot be made to the Gaoler to deliver the Prisoner to the custody of any person unknown to the Gaoler, for two causes; first, for that thereby the Kings Writ of *Habeas corpus,* or delivery, might be prevented.[98] 2. The *Mittimus* ought to bee, as hath beene said, till hee bee delivered by Law.

If the Sheriffe, or Gaoler detain a Prisoner in the Gaole after his acquitall, unlesse it be for his fees, this is false imprisonment.

In many cases a man may be by the Law of the Land taken, and imprisoned, by force of the Kings Writ upon a suggestion made.

Against those that attempt to subvert, and enervate the Kings Lawes, there lieth a Writ to the Sheriffe in nature of a commission, *Ad capiendum impug-*

---

92. Out of the Chancery generally, though there be not any priviledge, &c. 4. E. 4.

93. [*Ed.:* to undergo and receive, etc.]

94. Act. Apost. ca. 25. ver. ult.

95. [*Ed.:* It seems to me without reason to put a convicted person in prison and not to signify the causes thereof.]

96. [*Ed.:* in the third year of King Charles.]

97. Hil. 32. E. 1. Coram Rege. Rot. 71 & 79.

98. So it was holden Pasch 34 Eliz. by all the Justices. 8. H. 4. 18 20. E. 4. 6.

natores juris Regis, & ad ducendum eos ad Gaolam de Newgate;[99,100] which you may reade in the Register at large. *Ubi supra.* And this is *lex terrae,*[101] by Processe of Law, to take a man without answer, or summons in this case: and the reason is, *Merito beneficium legis amittit, qui legem ipsam subvertere intendit.*[102]

If a Souldier after wages received, or prest money taken, both absent himself, or depart from the Kings service;[103] upon the certificate thereof of the Captain into the Chancery, there lieth a Writ to the Kings serjeants at Armes, if the party be vagrant, and hideth himself, *Ad capiendum conductos prosiciscend' in obsequium nostrum, &c. qui ad dictum obsequium nostrum venire non curaverint.*[104] And this is *lex terrae,* by processe of Law, *pro defensione Regis, & Regni,*[105] or for the same cause, a Writ may be directed to the Sheriffe, *De arrestando ipsum, qui pecuniam recepit ad proficiscendum in obsequium Regis, & non est profectus.*[106]

If a man had entred into Religion, and was professed, and after he departed from his house, and became vagrant in the Country against the rules of his Religion, upon the Certificate of the Abbot, or Prior thereof into the Chancery, a Writ should be directed to the Sheriffe, *De apostata capiendo,*[107,108] whereby he was | commanded in these words; *Praecipimus tibi quod praefatum, &c.* [54] *Sine dilatione arrestes, & praefat̄ Abbat̄, &c. liberes secundum regulam ordinis sui castigand';*[109] And this was *Lex terrae,* by Processe of Law, *in honerem religionis.*[110]

If any lay men with force and strong hand, doe enter upon, or keep the possession either of the Church, or of any of the houses, or glebe, &c. belonging thereunto, the Incumbent upon certificate thereof of the Bishop, or

99. [*Ed.:* to take the offenders against the king's laws and lead them to Newgate gaol.]

100. Regist. 64. Rot. Pat. 21. E. 3. pt. 1. impugnatores jurium Regis.

101. [*Ed.:* law of the land.]

102. [*Ed.:* He deservedly loses the benefit of the law who intends to subvert the law itself.]

103. Regist. 24. & 191.

104. [*Ed.:* To arrest those who have been hired to set out in our service, etc. but have not cared to come to our said service.]

105. [*Ed.:* for defence of the king and the realm,]

106. [*Ed.:* To arrest him, who received money to set out in the king's service and has not turned up.]

107. [*Ed.:* for taking an apostate.]

108. Regist fol. 267. F. N. B. 233, 234. 20 E. 2. Cor. 233. 6. E. 3. 17. 22. E. 3. 2.

109. [*Ed.:* We command you that you arrest the said, etc. without delay, and deliver him to the aforesaid abbot, etc. to be chastised according to the rule of his order.]

110. [*Ed.:* in honour of religion.]

without certificate upon his own surmise may have a Writ to the Sheriffe,[111] *De vi laica amovenda*,[112] by which the Sheriffe is commanded in these words;[113] *Pracipimus tibi quod omnem vim laicam seu armatam, quae se tenet in dicta Ecclesia, seu domibus eidem annexis, ad pacem nostram in Cõm tuo perturband', fine dilatione amoveas, & si quos in hac parte resistentes inveneris, eos per corpora sua attachias, & in prisona nostra salvo custodias, &c.*[114] and this is *lex terrae*, by Processe of Law, *pro pace Ecclesiae*.[115]

Also a Writ of *Ne exeas Regnum*[116] may be awarded to the Sheriffe, or Justices of Peace, or to both, that a man of the Church shall not depart the Realme; the effect whereof is;[117] *Quia datum est nobis intelligere, quod A.B. clericus versus partes exteras, ad quamplurima nobis, & quamplurima de populo nostro prae-judicialia, & damnosa, ibidem prosequend', transire proponit, &c. tibi praeci-pimus, quod praedict' A.B. coram te corporaliter venire facias, & ipsum ad suf-ficientes manucaptores, inveniend', &c. Et si hoc coram te facere recusaverit, tunc ipsum A.B. proximae gaolae committas salvo custodiend', quousque hoc gratis facere voluerit.*[118] And there is another Writ in the Register directed to the party, either of the Clergy or Laity. And this is *lex terrae*, by Processe of Law, *Pro bono publico Regis et Regni;*[119] Whereof you may reade more at large in the third part of the Institutes, Cap. Fugitives.

Upon a surmise that a man is a Leper, one that hath *morbum elephantia-cum*,[120] so called, because he hath a skin like to an Elephant, there may be a

---

111. Registr. 59, 60. F. N. B. 54. 15. R. 2. ca. 2.

112. [*Ed.:* For removing lay force.]

113. [*Ed.:* We command you that without delay you remove all lay or armed force which holds itself in the said church or the houses thereto annexed, to the disturbance of our peace in your county, and if you find anyone resisting you in this behalf attach them by their bodies, and keep them safely in our prison, etc.]

114. Vide Regist. 284. 289, 290. for the arresting of Purveyors, which make purveyance of the men of the Church.

115. [*Ed.:* for the peace of the Church.]

116. [*Ed.:* That you do not leave the realm.]

117. Registr. 89. F. N. B. 85. 31. H. 8. Dier 43. 1. Mar. 92. 1. Eliz. 165.

118. [*Ed.:* Because it has been given us to understand that A. B., clerk, proposes to go into foreign parts, there to pursue many things prejudicial and damaging to us and our people, etc., we command you that you cause the aforesaid A. B. to come personally before you and find sufficient mainprise, etc.; and if he refuses to come before you, then commit the selfsame A. B. safely to the next gaol until he shall have done this willingly.]

119. [*Ed.:* for the public benefit of King and realm.]

120. [*Ed.:* elephant-disease.]

Writ directed to the Sheriffe,[121] *Quia accepimus quod J. de N. leprosus existit, & inter homines Comitatus tui communiter conversatur, &c. ad grave damnum homin' praed', & propter contagionem morbi praed' periculum manifestum, &c. tibi praecipimus quod assumptis tecum aliquibus discretis & legalibus hominibus de Comitaƚ praed' non suspect', &c. ad ipsum J. accedas, &c. & examines, &c. & si ipsum leprosum inveneris, ut praedict est, tunc ipsum honestiori modo, quo poteris a communione hominum praedict' amoveri, & se ad locum solitarium ad habitand' ibidem, prout moris est, transferre facias indilate, &c.*[122] And this is *lex terrae,* by Processe of Law, for saving of the people from contagion and infection.

But if any man by colour of any authority, where he hath not any in that particular case, arrest, or imprison any man, or cause him to be arrested, or imprisoned, this is against this Act, and it is most hatefull, when it is done by countenance of Justice.[123]

King Edw. 6. did incorporate the Town of S. Albons, and granted to them to make ordinances, &c.[124] they made an ordinance upon paine of imprisonment, and it was adjudged to be against this Statute of Magna Charta; So it is, if such an ordinance had been contained in the patent it selfe.

All Commissions that are consonant to this Act, are, as hath been said, *Secundum legem, & consuetudinem Angliae.*[125,126]

A Commission was made under the great Seale to take J. N. (a notorious felon) and to seise his lands, and goods: This was resolved to be against the Law of the Land, unlesse he had been endicted, or appealed by the party, or by other due Processe of Law.[127]

121. Regist. 2697. F. N. B. 234. Bract. li. 5. fo. 421. Brit. fo. 39. 88. Fleta li. 6. ca. 39. Hil. 7. H. 5. coram Rege. Rot. 7. Rot. claus. 22. E. 3 in dos. 20. pte. m. 14.

122. [*Ed.:* Because we understand that J. de N. is a leper, and commonly mixes with men of your county, etc. to the grave damage of the aforesaid men, and because of the manifest danger of contagion from the aforesaid disease, etc., we command you that, taking with you some discerning and lawful men of the aforesaid county, not suspected, etc., you go to the selfsame J., etc. and examine him, etc. and if you find him to be a leper, as is aforesaid, then without delay cause him to be removed in the most decent way you can from the company of the aforesaid men, and to be transferred to a solitary place to live in, as is customary, etc.]

123. Lib. 10. fo. 74. in the case of the Marshalsea. Rot. Parl. 42. E. 3. nu. 23. Sir John a Lees Case.

124. Lib. 5. fol. 64. Clarks case.

125. [*Ed.:* According to the law and custom of England.]

126. 42. Ass. pl. 5. Rot. parliam. 17. R. 2. nu. 37.

127. Rot. Parliam. 2. H. 4. nu. 60.

It is enacted, if any man be arrested, or imprisoned against the forme of this great Charter, that he bee brought to his answer, and have right.

No man to be arrested, or imprisoned contrary to the forme of the great Charter.

See more of the severall Lawes allowed within this Land, in the first part of the Institutes Sect. 3.

[55]   The Philosophicall Poet doth notably describe the damnable, and dam-l-ned procedings of the Judge of hell,

> *Gnosius hic Radamanthus habet durissima regna,*
> *Castigatque auditque dolos, subigitque fateri.*[128,129]

And in another place,

> —— *leges fixit precio atque refixit.*[130]

First he punisheth, and then he heareth: and lastly, compelleth to confesse, and make and marre lawes at his pleasure; like as the Centurion in the holy history,[131] did to S. Paul: For the text saith, *Centurio apprehendi Paulum jussit, & se catenis ligari & tunc interrogabat, quis fuisset, & quid fecisset:*[132] but good Judges and Justices abhorre these courses.

Now it may be demanded, if a man be taken, or committed to prison *contra legem terrae*[133] against the law of the land, what remedy hath the party grieved? To this it is answered: First, that every Act of Parliament made against any injury, mischiefe, or grievance doth either expresly, or impliedly give a remedy to the party wronged, or grieved, as in many of the Chapters of this great Charter appeareth; and therefore he may have an action grounded upon this great Charter. As taking one example for many, and that in a powerfull, and a late time. Pasch. 2. Hen. 8. *coram Rege rot.* 538. against the Prior of S. Oswin in Northumberland. And it is provided, and declared by the Statute of

---

128. [*Ed.:* Gnosian Rhadamanthus keeps here his iron rule; he chastises and hears charges of wrongdoing and forces confession [Virgil, *Aeneid,* 6. 567.].]

129. Virgil.

130. [*Ed.:* he made laws, and remade them, for a price.]

131. Act. Apost. c. 22. v. 24. 27.

132. [*Ed.:* The centurion commanded Paul to be apprehended and bound in chains, and then he asked him who he was and what he did.]

133. [*Ed.:* against the law of the land.]

36. Edw. 3.[134] that any man feeleth himself grieved, contrary to any article in any Statute, he shall have present remedy in Chancery (that is, by originall Writ) by force of the said Articles and Statutes.

2. He may cause him to be indicted upon this Statute at the Kings suite, whereof you may see a Precedent Pasch. 3. Hen. 8. Rott. 71. *coram Rege.* Rob. Sheffields case.

3. [a][135] He may have an *habeas corpus*[136] out of the Kings Bench or Chancery, though there be no priviledge &c. or in the Court of Common pleas, or Eschequer, for any officer or priviledged person there; upon which Writ the goaler must retourne, by whom he was committed, and the cause of his imprisonment, and if it appeareth that his imprisonment be just, and lawfull, he shall be remaunded to the former Gaoler, but if it shall appeare to the Court, that he was imprisoned against the law of the land, they ought by force of this Statute to deliver him: if it be doubtfull and under consideration, he may be bailed.

In 5. Edw. 4. *coram Rege* Rot. 143. John Keasars case, a notable record and too long here to be recited.

10. Eliz. Rot. Leas case.

In 1. & 2. Eliz. Dier. 175. Scrogs case.

In 18. Eliz. Dier. 175. Roland Hynds case in margine.

4. He may have an Action of false imprisonment 10. Hen. 7. fol. 17. but it is entered in the Court of Common pleas Mich. 11. Hen. 7. Rot. 327. Hilarie Warners case, and it appeareth by the Record, that Judgement was given for the plaintife: a Record worthy of observation.

5. [b][137] He may have a Writ *de homine replegiando.*[138]

Vide Marlebridge Cap. 8.

6. [c][139] He might by the Common law have had a Writ *De odio, & atia,*[140]

---

134. 36. E. 3. cap. 9.

135. *a* See the resolution of all the Judges of Englád in the answere to the articles of the Clergy hereafter at large in the exposition of the statute of artic. Cler. to the 21. and 22. artic. Of the Writ of *Habeas corpus* see more in the exposition upon the stat. of W. 1. cap. 15.

136. [*Ed.:* Writ to determine the legality of any person's detention.]

137. *b* Regist 77. F. N. B. 66. Bract. l. 3. f. 185.

138. [*Ed.:* Writ for replevying a man.]

139. *c* Regist. 83. 268. F. N. B. 249. 258. Bract. l. 3. f. 154.

140. [*Ed.:* Writ of malice and spite.]

as you may see before. Cap. 26 but that was taken away by Statute, but now is revived againe by the Statute of 42. Edw. 3. cap. 1. as there it also appeareth. It is said in [d141] W. 2. *Sed ne hujusmodi appellati, vel indictati diu detineantur in prisona, habeat breve De odio & atia, sicut in Magna Charta, & aliis Statutis dict' est:* [142] and by the said Act of 42. Edw. 3. all Statutes made against Magna Charta are repealed.

"We will sell to no man, &c."

[e143] This is spoken in the person of the King, who in judgement of Law, in all his Courts of Justice is present, and repeating these words, *Nulli vendemus &c.* [144]

And therefore, every Subject of this Realme, for injury done to him *in bonis, terris, vel persona,* [145] by any other Subject, be he Ecclesiasticall, or Temporall, [56] | Free, or Bond, Man, or Woman, Old, or Young, or be he outlawed, excommunicated, or any other without exception, may take his remedy by the course of the Law, and have justice, and right for the injury done to him, freely without sale, fully without any deniall, and speedily without delay.

Hereby it appeareth, that Justice must have three qualities, it must be *Libera, quia nihil iniquius venali Justitia; Plena, quia Justitia non debet claudicare; & Celeris, quia dilatio est quaedam negatio;* [146] and then it is both Justice and Right.

---

141. *d* W. 2. c. 29. Gloc. cap. 9.

142. [*Ed.:* However, lest such appellees or indicted persons be detained too long in prison, one shall have a writ *de odio et atia* (of hate and spite), as is mentioned in Magna Carta and other statutes.]

143. *e* Mirror. c. 1. §. 5. cap. 2. § 13. cap. 5. § 1. 2. Fleta. l. 2. c. 12. Ocham cap. quid sponte offerentibus F. N. B. 96. Rot. Parliam. 8. E. 3. nu. 7. 38. E. 3. n. 23 45. E. 3. n. 19 51. E. 3. n. 58 5. H. 4. nu. 32 20. R. 2. fines 134 34. H. 6. 38. 2. E. 3. c. 10. 1. E. 4. cap. 1. 26. H. 8. cap. 3. 27. H. 8. cap. 11.

144. [*Ed.:* to no one shall we sell, etc.]

145. [*Ed.:* in goods, in lands, or in person,]

146. [*Ed.:* Free, because nothing is more iniquitous than saleable justice; full, because justice ought not to limp; and speedy, because delay is in effect a denial.]

"We will not deny or defer, &c."[147]

These words have beene excellently expounded by latter Acts of Parliament,[147] that by no meanes common right, or Common law should be disturbed, or delayed, no, though it be commanded under the Great seale, or Privie seale, order, writ, letters, message, or commandement whatsoever, either from the King, or any other, and that the Justices shall proceede, as if no such Writs, letters, order, message, or other commandement were come to them.[148] *Judicium redditum per defaltum affirmatur, non obstante breve Regis de progatione judicii.*[149]

That the Common lawes of the Realme should by no meanes be delayed for the law is the surest sanctuary, that a man can take, and the strongest fortresse to protect the weakest of all; *lex est tutissima cassis,*[150] and *sub clypeo legis nemo decipitur:*[151] but the King may stay his owne suite, as a *capias pro fine,*[152] for the King may respit his fine and the like.[153]

All protections that are not legall, which appeare not in the Register,[154] nor warranted by our books, are expresly against this branch, *nulli differemus:*[155] As a Protection under the Great seale granted to any man, directed to the Sherifes, &c. and commanding them, that they shall not arrest him, during a certaine time at any other mans suite, which hath words in it[156] *per praerogativam nostram, quam nolumus esse arguendam;*[157] yet such protections have beene argued by the Judges, according to their oath and duty, and adjudged to be void: As Mich. 11. Hen. 7. Rot. 124.[158] a Protection graunted to Holmes a Vinter of London, his factors, servants and deputies, &c. resolved to be

147. 2. E. 3. c. 8. 14. E. 3 c. 14. 20. E. 3. 1. 2 11. R. 2. cap. 11. Rot. Parl. 2. R. 2. nu. 51. Rot. Parl. 2. H. 4. nu. 64. Regist. 186.

148. 1. E. 3. f. 25. 2. E. 3. 3. 14. H. 3. tit. Jour. 24. 18. E. 3. 47. 39. E. 3. 7. L. 5. E. 4. 132.

149. [*Ed.:* A judgment rendered by default is affirmed notwithstanding the king's writ for prorogation of the judgment.]

150. [*Ed.:* the law is the safest helmet (Coke's own motto).]

151. [*Ed.:* under the shield of law no one is deceived:]

152. [*Ed.:* Writ of arrest for imprisonment until a fine is paid.]

153. Pasch 3. H. 4. coram Rege.

154. Rot. 16. Warwik. Rot. Parl. 5. H. 4. nu. 33. 22. ass. pl. 9. 9. H. 6. 50. b. Fortesc. cap. 51

155. [*Ed.:* to no one shall we delay:]

156. F. N. B. 237. 240. 11. H. 4. 76. 31. E. 3. quare Imp. 161.

157. [*Ed.:* by our prerogative, which we do not wish to be disputed.]

158. Mich. 11. H. 7. Rot. 124. in com. banc.

against Law. Pasch. 7. H. 8. Rot. 66.[159] such a Protection disallowed, and the Sherife amerced for not executing the Writ. Mich. 13. & 14. Eliz. in Hitchcocks case,[160] and many other of latter time: and there is a notable*[161] Record of aucient time in 22. Edw. 1. John de Mershalls case, *non pertinet ad vicecomitem de protectione Regis judicare, imo ad curiam*.[162]

"Justice or Right."

Wee shall not sell deny, or delay Justice and right. *Justitiam vel rectum,* neither the end, which is Justice, nor the meane, whereby we may attaine to the end, and that is the law.[163]

Rectum, right, is taken here for law, in the same sense that jus, often is so called. 1. Because it is the right line, whereby Justice distributative is guided, and directed, and therefore all the Commissions of *Oier,* and *Terminer,*[164] of goale delivery, of the peace &c. have this clause, *Facturi quod ad justitiam pertinet, secundum legem,* and *consuetudenem Angliae,*[165] that is, to doe Justice and Right, according to the rule of the law and custome of England; and that which is called common right in 2. Edw. 3. is called Common law, in 14. Edw. 3. &c. in this sense it is taken, where it is said, *ita quod stet recto in curia, i. legi in curia.*[166] The law is called *rectum,*[167] because it discovereth, that which is tort, crooked, or wrong, for as right signifieth law, so tort, crooked or wrong, signifieth injurie, and *injuria est contra jus*[168] against right: *recta linea est index sui, & obliqui,*[169] hereby the crooked cord of that, which is called discretion, appeareth to be unlawfull, unlesse you take it, as it ought to be, *Discretio est discernere per legem, quid sit justum.*[170] 3. It is called Right, because it is the

---

159. Pasch. 7. H. 8. Rot. 66. in com. banc.

160. Mich. 13. & 14. Eliz. in com. banc. Hitchcock case.

161. 11. H. 4. 57. 39. H. 6. 38.

162. *Pas. 22. E. 1. Rot. 39. coram Rege Essex.

163. W. 1. cap. 1. 1. E. 3. cap. 14. 2. E. 3. cap. 8. 7. H. 4. cap. 14. 1. H. 4. cap. 1. 2. H. 4. cap. 1. 4. H. 4. cap. 1. 7. H. 4. cap. 1.

164. [*Ed.:* "To Hear and Determine," an occasional criminal court, with a jury.]

165. [*Ed.:* to do what belongs to justice according to the law (and) custom of England,]

166. [*Ed.:* so that he stand to right in court, that is, to the law in court.]

167. [*Ed.:* right,]

168. Injuria est in, seu contra jus.

169. [*Ed.:* a straight line is a guide to itself and to the crooked,]

170. [*Ed.:* Discretion is to discern by law what is just.]

best birth-right the Subject hath, for thereby his goods, lands, wife, children, his body, life, honor, and estimation are protected from injury, and wrong: *major haereditas venit unicuiq; nostrum à jure, & legibus, quam à parentibus.*[171],[172]

4. Lastly, *rectum* is sometime taken for the right it selfe, that a man hath by I law to land: As when in so by there lieth *Breve de recto,*[173] in so much that some old readers have supposed, that *rectum* in this Chapter, would be understood of a writ of right, for which at this day no fine in the hamper is paid. As the goldfiner will not out of the dust, threds, or shreds of gold, let passe the least crum, in respect of the excellency of the metall: so ought not the learned reader to let passe any syllable of this Law, in respect of the excellency of the matter. [57]

Chapter 30

All Merchants, if they were not openly prohibited before, shall have their safe and sure Conduct to depart out of England, to come into England, to tarry in, and go through England, as well by land as by water, to buy and sell without any manner of evil tolls by the old and rightful Customs, except in time of War; and if they be of a Land making War against Us, and be found in our Realm at the beginning of the Wars, they shall be attached without harm of body or goods, until it be known unto Us, or our Chief Justice, how our Merchants be entreated there in the Land making war against Us; and if our Merchants be well intreated there, theirs shall be likewise with Us.

"All Merchants."

This Chapter concerneth Merchant strangers.

First it is to be considered, what the ancient Lawes, before this Statute, were concerning this matter.

By the auncient Kings (amongst whom King Alfred was one)[1] *defendu fuit que nul merchant Alien ne hantast Angleterre forsque aux 4 foires, ne que nul*

---

171. [*Ed.:* a greater inheritance comes to each of us from the law and statutes than from our parents.]
172. Cicero.
173. [*Ed.:* Writ of right,]
1. Mirror. cap. 1. § 3.

demurrast in a terre ouster 40. jours.[2] *Mercatorū navigia, vel inimicorum quidem, quaecunq; ex alto (nullis jactata tempestatibus) in portum aliquem invehentur, tranquilla pace fruantor; quin etiam si maris acta fluctibus ad domicilium aliquod illustre, ac pacis beneficio donatum navis appulerit inimica, atq; istuc nautae confugerint, ipsi & res illorum omnes augusta pace potiuntor.*[3,4]

2. It is to be seene what this Statute hath provided.

1. That before this statute, merchant strangers might be publiquely prohibited, *Publice prohibeantur.*[5] And this prohibition is intendable of Merchant strangers in amitie, for this Act provideth afterward for Merchant strangers enemies; and therefore the prohibition intended by this Act, must be by the common or publique Councell of the Realme, that is, by Act of Parliament, for that it concerneth the whole Realme, and is implyed by this word (*publice.*)

2. That all Merchant strangers in amity (except such as be so publiquely prohibited) shall have safe and sure conduct in 7. things. 1. To depart out of England. 2. To come into England. 3. To tarry here. 4. To goe in and through England, as well by land as by water. 5. To buy and to sell. 6. Without any manner of evill tolles. 7. By the old and rightfull customes.

Now touching Merchant strangers, whose Soveraigne is in warre with the King of England.

[58] I There is an exception, and provision for such, as be found in the Realme at the beginning of the warre, they shall be attached with a priviledge, and limitation, viz. without harme of body, or goods, with this limitation, Untill it be knowne to us, or our chiefe Justice, (that is our guardien, or keeper of the Realme in our absence) how our Merchants there in the land in warre with us shall be intreated, and if our Merchants be well intreated there, theirs shall be likewise with us, and this is *jus belli. Et in republica maxime conservanda sunt jura belli.*[6,7]

---

2. [*Ed.:* forbidden that any alien merchant should live in England except for four fairs, and that none should live in the land beyond forty days.]

3. [*Ed.:* All ships whatsoever of merchants, or of enemies, that are brought into any port, not being wrecked by any storms, shall enjoy peaceable protection; but also, if by the action of the sea an enemy ship should land at any abode which is at peace, and the sailors take refuge there, they and all their property shall be in sacred protection.]

4. Int. leges Ethel. cap. 2.

5. [*Ed.:* Publicly prohibited.]

6. [*Ed.:* And it is important to a state to preserve the laws of war.]

7. Regist. 129. de arest. fact. super bonis mercator. alienig. Rot. Parliam. Mich. 18. E. 1. coram Rege

But for such Merchant strangers as come into the Realme after the warre beginne, they may be dealt withall as open enemies; and yet of auncient time three men had priviledge granted them in time of warre. *Clericus, Agricola, & Mercator, tempore belli, Ut oretq; colat, commutet, pace fruuntur.*[8]

a[9] The end of this Chapter was for advancement of trade, and traffique; the meanes for the well using, and intreating of Merchant strangers in all the particulars aforesaid, is a matter of great moment, as appeareth by many other Acts of Parliament, for as they be used here, so our Merchants shall be dealt withall in other Countries.

"evil tolls."

b[10] Evill tolles.

This word *tolnetum,* and *telonium,* and *theolonoium* are all one, and doe signify in a generall sense, any manner of Custome, Subsidie, prestation Imposition, or summe of mony demanded for exporting, or importing of any wares, or merchandizes, to be taken of the buyer. In both these senses it is here taken of severall kinds of tolles: More shall be said hereof, in the exposition of the Statutes of W. 1. and W. 2. In the meane time see John Webbes case lib. 8. fol. 46.

c[11] They are called *mala tolneta,*[12] when the thing demanded for wares or merchandizes, doe so burden the commodity, as the merchant cannot have a convenient gain by trading therewith, and thereby the trade it selfe is lost or hindered. And in divers Statutes *maletout* for *maletot,* or *maletout* is a French word, and signifieth an unjust exaction.

Now this Act after it hath dealt privatively, *sine omnibus malis tolnetis,*[13] it goeth on for more surety affirmatively.

---

fol. 7 reprisel. Tr. 33. E. 1. corā Rege rot. 127. 27. E. 3. Stat. 2. cap. 2. lawe of marke Rot. Parl. 11. H. 4. nu 66. 4. H. 7. c. 7. 14. H. 6. c. 7. 13. H. 6. c. 9. Mat. Par. 96.

8. [*Ed.:* In time of war the cleric and farmer and trader can pray and till and trade in peace.]

9. *a* 2. E. 3. c. 5. 9. E. 3. c. 1. 14. E. 3. c. 2. 25. E. 3. cap. 2. 11. R. 2. c. 7. 14 R. 2. cap. 9. 16. R. 2. cap. 1.

10. *b* Lib 8. fol. 46. John Webbs case. See the exposition of W. 1. c. 31. 46. E. 3. barre 215 39 E. 3. 13. b. F. N. B. 227. d. West. 1. c. 30. W. 2. cap. 25.

11. *c* See Rot. Parl. 17. E. 3. nu. 27. 28 and 21. H. 3. nu. 29. Maletot taken in good part. See the exposition of W. 1. cap. 31.

12. [*Ed.:* male-tolts (evil tolls).]

13. [*Ed.:* without any male-tolts,]

"by the old and rightful Customs."

That is, by auncient and right duties, due by auncient and lawfull custome, which hath been the auncient policy of the Realme to encourage merchant strangers, they have a speedy recovery for their debts and other duties, &c. *Per legem Mercator;*[14] which is a part of the Common law.

This word *consuetudo,* hath in Law divers significations. 1. For the Common law, as *consuetudo Angliae.*[15] 2. For Statute law, as *contra consuetudinem communi consilio regni edit.*[16] 3. For particular customes, as Gavelkind, Borough English, and the like. 4. For rents services, &c. due to the Lord, as *consuetudines & servitia.*[17] 5. For customes, tributes, or impositions, as *de novis consuetudinibus levatis in regno, sive in terra, sive in aqua.*[18] 6. Subsidies, or customes graunted by common consent, that is, by authority of Parliament, *pro bono publico,*[19] and these be antiquae, & *rectae consuetudines,*[20] intended by this Act, this agreeth with that, which hath been said before in the end of the exposition upon the eight Chapter.[21]

Hereby it appeareth that the King cannot set any new impost upon the Merchant, and therefore this Act provideth not only affirmatively, viz. *per antiquas, & rectas consuetudines,*[22] but privatively also, *sine omnibus malis tolnetis,*[23] within which words new impositions are included, and are here called *mala tol neta,* as opposite to ancient and rightfull customes, or subsidies graunted by authority of Parliament.[24]

And where some have supposed, that there was a custome due to the King by the Common Law, as well of the Stranger, as of the English, called *Antiqua*

---

14. [*Ed.:* By the law merchant;]

15. [*Ed.:* the custom of England.]

16. [*Ed.:* against the custom established by the common council of the realm.]

17. [*Ed.:* customs and services.]

18. [*Ed.:* concerning new customs raised in the realm, whether on the land or on the water.]

19. [*Ed.:* for the public good,]

20. [*Ed.:* the old and rightful customs,]

21. Glanvil. lib. 9. c. 7. lib. 12. cap. 9. 10. Regist. 4. 159. F. N. B. 10. 151. cap. Itineris. cap. Escheatre. See before c. 4. Cap. Itnecris.

22. [*Ed.:* that is to say, by the old and rightful customs,]

23. [*Ed.:* without all male-tolts,]

24. See the Statute of Carlile 35. E. 1. for this word Imposition, and from whom it came. Dier. 31. H. 8. 43. 1 Mar. 92. 1. Eliz. Dier., 165.

custuma,[25] viz. for wools wooll-fells and leather, that is to say, for every sack of wooll containing 26. stone, and every stone 14. pound, vi viii d. and for a last | of leather, xiii s. iiii. d. Certain it is, that those customes had their be-   [59] ginning by common consent by Act of Parliament, for King Edward the first by his Letters Patents reciteth,[26] *Cum Praelati, Magnates, & tota communitas quandam novam consuetudinem nobis & haeredibus nostris de lanis, pellibus, & coriis, viz. de sacco lanae dimid' Marc', de 300. pellibus dimid' Marc', & de lasto corii xiii. s. iiii. d.&c.*[27] Herein foure things are to be observed. 1. That these customes had their creation by authority of Parliament, and were not by the Common Law, appearing by these words, *Quandam novam consuetudinem,*[28] so as it was new, and not old. 2. That this new custome was graunted to King Edward the first proved by this word *nobis*.[29] 3. That it was graunted at the Parliament holden, Edw. 1. commonly called W. 1. (though the Record thereof cannot be found) for the said Patent bears date 10. Nov. Anno 3 Edw. 1. which was neare the ending of that yeare, and the Parliament was holden in *Clauso Pasch.* before. 4. That here *consuetudo* signifieth a custome, or Subsidie graunted by common consent by Parliament, and in that sense it is here taken, and likewise in the Statute of 51 Hen. 3. *Statutum de Scaccario*,[30] for in 48 Hen. 3.[31] Proclamation was made, *Contra suggerentes, &c. Regem velle exigere tallagia inconsueta, & introducere extraneos.*[32]

And herewith agreeth the Act of Parliament commonly called *confirmationes cartarum*,[33,34] (which is but an explanation of this branch of Magna Charta) wherein it is enacted, that for no occasion any aide, tasks, or takings shall be

25. [*Ed.:* the old customs,]

26. Rot. Pat. 3. E. 1. m. 1. Rot. finium. 3. E. 1. m. 24. Mich. 26. E. 1. Int retorn. brevium. Ex pte. Remem. Thesaur. in Scac.

27. [*Ed.:* Whereas the prelates, great men, and whole commonalty, [have granted] a certain new custom for us and our heirs of wool, fells and leather, that is to say, half a mark for a sack of wool, half a mark for three hundred fells, and thirteen shillings and fourpence for a last of leather, etc.]

28. [*Ed.:* A certain new custom.]

29. [*Ed.:* us.]

30. [*Ed.:* Statute of the Exchequer.]

31. Rot. Pat. anno 48 H. 3. à tergo.

32. [*Ed.:* Against those suggesting, etc. that the king wanted to exact unaccustomed tolls and introduce strange ones.]

33. [*Ed.:* confirmations of the charters.]

34. Anno 25 E. 1. See more in the Exposition of that Statute.

taken by the King, or his heires, but by the common assent of the Realme, saving the auncient aides, and takings due and accustomed.

And whereas the most of the whole Comminalty of the Realme finde themselves hardly grieved of the maletont (or ill toll) of woolls, that is to say, of every, sack of wooll 40. s. and prayed the said King to release the same, thereupon the said King did release the same, and graunted further for him and his heires, that no such thing should be taken without their common assent, and their good will:[35] and in that Act there is a saving, *Sauve a nous, & nous heires la custume de laynes, pealx, & quiures avant grante per la Comminaltie avandit;*[36] So as this Act of Parliament proveth that the said custome of vi. s. viii. d. for wooll, and xiii. s. iiii. d. for leather was grannted by Parliament.

By the Statute *De tallagio non concedendo,*[37,38] (which is but an explanation of this branch of the Statute of Magna Charta) it is provided: *Nullum tallagium vel auxilium per nos vel haeredes nostros in Regno nostro ponatur, seu levetur sine voluntate & assensu Archiepiscoporum, Episcoporum, Comitum, Baronum, militum, burgensium, & aliorum liberorum Comit' de Regno nostro;*[39] So as Edw.1. in conclusion added the effect of the clause concerning this matter, which in his exemplification he had omitted out of Magna Charta.

See Cap. *itineris de novis consuetudinibus levatis in regno, sive in terra, sive in aqua, &c.*[40] where *consuetudines* are taken for customes.[41]

Upon grant to Merchant Strangers of divers priviledges, liberties, and immunities they graunted to the King and his heires,[42] *De quoliber sacco lanae 40. d. de incremento ultra custumam antiquam dimid' Marc', quae prius fuerit persoluta & sic pro lasto coriorum dimid' Marc', & de trescentis pellibus lanatis*

---

35. Rot. Parliam. 13 H. 4. nu. 18. A new Office graunted with a fee in charge of the Subject, is against this Act of 25. E. 1. and of 34. E. 1. hereafter following.

36. [*Ed.:* Saving to us and our heirs the custom of wool, fells and leather, before granted by the commonalty aforesaid;]

37. [*Ed.:* for not granting tallage.]

38. Anno 34. E. 1. See more in the exposition of this Statute.

39. [*Ed.:* No tallage or aid shall be imposed or levied by us or our heirs in our realm without the will and consent of the archbishops, bishops, earls, barons, knights, burgesses, and other free men of the [commonalty] of our realm;]

40. [*Ed.:* the chapters of the eyre concerning new customs raised in the realm, whether on land or water, etc.]

41. Cap. itineris.

42. Rot. Chartarum. 31 E. 1. nu. 44. Charta Mercatoria.

40. d. ultra certum illud, quod & antiqua custuma fuerit prius datum.[43] Note here the Custome which was graunted 3 Edw. 1. is here called *antiqua Custuma,* and this new Custome to called *nova Custuma,* and sometime the one is called *magna Custuma,* and the other *parva Custuma.*[44]

2. Here it appeareth that Merchants Strangers paid the former Custome.

Moreover by that Charter, poundage of three pence upon the pound was graunted to the King, and his heires by the Merchant Strangers, *Et de quolibet vini nomine Custumae duos solidos, &c.*[45] And this at this day is called Butlerage, and is paid onely by Merchant Strangers; but prisage is paid by the English onely, except the Citizens of London, and this is an auncient duty: for I finde it accounted for in the raigne of H. 3.[46] by the Kings Butler, and is | called [60] *Certa prisa,*[47] which at the first was granted in lieu and satisfaction of purveyance for wines. And lastly, by that Charter it is graunted, *Quod nulla exactio, prisa, vel praestatio, aut aliquod aliud onus super personas Mercatorum alienorum praedict', seu bona eorundem aliquatenus imponatur contra formam expressam superius concessam:*[48,49] So as no imposition can be set without assent of Parliament upon any stranger.

It was ordered and resolved by divers Prelates, Earles, and Barons, by force of the Kings Commission, that no new customes could be levied, nor auncient increased, without authority of Parliament, for that should be against the great Charter.[50] Anno 6. Edw. 2. Rot. Parliament, nu.4. that no tallage shall be assessed but in such manner as it hath been in time of his auncestors, and as it ought to be, and disannull all others.

In Anno 11. Edw. 3.[51] it was made felony to carry wooll out of the Realme, the end whereof was, that our wool should bee draped into cloth. But the

43. [*Ed.:* For every sack of wool forty pence by way of increment, above the old custom of half a mark which has previously been paid, and similarly for a last of leather half a mark, and for three hundred woolfells forty pence beyond that certain sum and old custom which was previously given.]

44. [*Ed.:* great customs, [and the other] petty customs.]

45. [*Ed.:* and for every [*blank*] of wine, two shillings in the name of custom, etc.]

46. Rot. Pat. Anno 40. H. 3.

47. [*Ed.:* Certain prises.]

48. [*Ed.:* That no exaction, prise, or loan, or any other burden shall in any way be imposed upon the persons of the aforesaid alien merchants or their goods contrary to the expressed form granted above.]

49. Fleta lib. 2. ca. 21.

50. Rot. ordinationem. Anno 5 E. 2. in Scaccario.

51. 11 E. 3. cap. 1.

King wanting made this use of this Act: In the 12. and 13. years of his raigne he made dispensations of that Statute in consideration of money paid:[52] but that Statute lived not long. In 13. Edw. 3. a great imposition was set upon woolls, and it is called a great wrong, *Cum populus Regni nostri variis oneribus, tallagiis & impositionibus hactenus praegravetur, quod dolentes referimus,*[53] and there doth excuse himselfe.[54]

Note here is the word *impositiones,*[55] first used, imposed by any King, in any Record that I have observed, and doe remember.

Anno 14. Edw. 3. cap. 21.[56] A Subsidie graunted to the King of wooll, wool-fells, and leather &c. by Parliament, for a certain time in respect of the warres, for which the King graunteth, that after that time, be nor his heires would take more then the old custome.

After this time ended, the King entred into a new device to get money, viz. that by agreement and consent of the Merchants, the King was to have 40.s. of a sack of wooll, &c. but hereof the Commons (that in troth were to beare the burden, for the Merchant will not be the loser) complained in Parliament, for that the graunt of the Merchants did not binde the Commons, and that the Custome might be taken according to the old order, which in the end was graunted, and that no graunt should be made but by Parliament.[57]

No charge shall be levied of the people, if it mere not graunted in Parliament.[58]

In 21. Edw. 3. by authority of Parliament, a Custome was graunted of cloth, for that the wooll was for the most part converted into cloth, which you may see in Orig. Scaccar. 24. Edw. 3. Rot. 13.[59]

By the Statute of 27. Edw. 3. cap. 4. in print,[60] a Subsidie of every cloth to take of the seller (over the Customes thereof due, that is, such as then

---

52. Rot. Parl. 13 E. 3. nu. 12. licence, &c. & 14 E. 3. nu. 3. licence.

53. [*Ed.:* Whereas the people of our realm have before now been aggrieved by various burdens, tallages, and impositions, which we relate with sadness.]

54. Rot. alinance. 12 E. 3. memb. 22 in dors.

55. [*Ed.:* impositions.]

56. 14 E. 3. cap. 21.

57. Rot. Parliam. 17 E. 3. nu. 28. 25 E. 3. nu. 22. 36 E. 3. nu. 26.

58. Rot. Parliam. 21 E. 3. nu. 16.

59. Rot. Parliam. 21 E. 3. Dier 1 Eliz. 165. Int' origin. Scac. 24 E. 3. Rot. 13.

60. 27 E. 3. cap. 4.

endured for a time, and were graunted by Parliament) that is to say, of every cloth of assise, wherein there is no grain, 4. d. &c.

And here it is worthy of observation, that there were two causes of the making of this Statute. 1. For that for cloth no custome was due other then by the Act of 21. Edw. 3. 2. For that wooll being converted to a manufacture, and made into cloth, the ancient custome of *Dimid.*[61] mark for a sack of wool was not by Law payable, because the wooll was turned into another kinde, albeit the cloth was made of the wooll; And this doth notably appeare by the Records of the Exchequer, one of them in the same yeare that the Act of 27. Edw. 3. was made.

Ac jam magna pars lanae dicti Regni nostri eodem regno pannificetur, de qua custuma aliqua nobis non est soluta;[62] And there it appeareth that that was the cause of giving to the King a Subside for cloth by the said Act of Parliament, of 27. Edw. 3.[63] And yet if in any case the King by his prerogative might have set any imposition, hee might have set in that case, because, as it appeareth by the Record, by making of cloth hee lost the custome of wooll.[64]

| Rot. Parliam 45. Edw. 3.[65] No imposition or charge, &c shall be set without   [61] assent of Parliament.

50. Edw. 3.[66] Richard Lions, a Merchant of London punished for procuring new impositions, and so was the Lord Latimer, the kings Chamberlaine. And in the same Parliament, nu. 163.[67] upon complaint that new impositions were set, the King in Parliament assented that the ancient custome should be holden, and no new imposition set.

In the raigne of Edward the first[68] the black Prince of Wales having *Aquitaine* granted to him, did lay an imposition of fuage or focage, *à foco,*[69] upon the Subjects of that Dukedome, viz. a shilling for every fire called harth silver,

---

61. [*Ed.:* Half.]

62. [*Ed.:* And now the great part of the wool of our said realm is made into cloth in the same realm, for which no custom is paid to us.]

63. Int. original. de Scaccar. anno 24 E. 3. Rot. 4. Vide simile. ibid. 24 E. 3. Rot. 13.

64. See the first part of the Institutes, fol. 49. b.

65. Rot. Parliam. 45 E. 3. nu. 42.

66. Rot. parliam. 50 E. 3. nu. 17, 28.

67. Nu. 163. & vide ibidem 191.

68. Rot. Pat. anno 25 E. 3. Created Duke of Aquitaine.

69. [*Ed.:* Fuage (a tax on chimneys) or focage (household fuel, or its tax), "from the fire."]

which was of so great discontentment, and odious to them, as it made them to revolt.

And no King since this time imposed by pretext of any prerogative, any charge upon Marchandises imported into, or exported out of this Realme, until Queen Maries time. See the Statute of 11. Ric. 2. cap. 9. & Rot. Parliament. 8. Hen. 6. num. 29.[70]

And in 3. Hen. 5.[71] the Subsidie of Tunnage and Poundage was graunted to King Hen. 5. during his life, in respect of the recovery of his right in France, (which was the first graunt for life of that kinde) yet therein was a *proviso* that the King should not make a graunt thereof of any person, nor that it should be any precedent for the like to be done to other Kings afterwards; but yet all the Kings after him have had it for life, so forcible is once a precedent fixed in the Crown, adde what *proviso* you will.

And this graunt by Parliament of the Subsidy of Tunnage and Poundage to the King is an argument, that the King taking it of the gift of the Subject, had no power to impose it himselfe.

The Lords and Commons cannot be charged with any thing for the defence of the Realme, for the safeguard of the Sea, &c. unlesse it be by their will in Parliament, that is, in the graunt of a Subsidy, whereunto the King assented.[72]

Non potest Rex subditum renitentem onerare impositionibus.[73,74]

King Philip and Queen Mary, graunted by Letters Patents to the Major Bayliffes, and Burgesses of Southampton, and their Successors, that no Wines called Malmeseyes to be imported into this Realme by any Denizen, or Alien, should be discharged or landed at any other place within this Realme, but onely at the said town and Port of Southampton, with a prohibition, that none should doe to the contrary upon pain to pay treble Custome to the King and Queen, &c. And for that Anthony Donate, Thomas Frederico, and other Merchant Strangers bought divers Buts of Malmesey, &c. and landed them at Goore, and in Kent, Gilbert Gerard the Attourney Generall, informed in the Exchequer against the said Merchant Strangers for the said treble custome,

---

70. Rot. Parl. 8. H. 6. nu. 29. & Rot. Par. 28. H. 6. nu 35.

71. Rot. Parl. 3. H. 5. nu. 50. Stat 2. See in the fourth part of the Institutes. Cap. of the high Court of Parliament. more of the Subsidy of Tunnage. [*Ed.:* Tunnage and Poundage are import tariffs.]

72. Rot. Parliam. 13 H. 4. nu 10.

73. [*Ed.:* The king cannot burden an unwilling subject with impositions.]

74. Fortesc. c. 9. & 18.

&c.[75] Upon which information, as to the said treble Custome, the said Anthony Donat demurred in Law &c. And this case was argued in the Exchequer Chamber by Counsell learned on both sides, and upon conference had two points were resolved by all the Judges. 1. That the graunt made in restraint of landing of the said Wines was a restraint of the Liberty of the Subject, against the Lawes and Statutes of the Realme. 2. That the assessment of treble custome was meerly void, and against the Law. As it appeareth by the report of the Lord Dier under his hand (which I have in my custody.) But after by Act of Parliament, in Anno 5 Eliz. the said Charter is established as to Merchant Strangers onely, but not against Subjects.[76]

And where imposts, or impositions, be generally named in divers Acts of Parliament,[77] the same are to be intended of lawfull impositions, as of Tunnage, and Poundage, or other Subsidies imposed by Parliament, but none of those Acts or any other doe give the King power at his pleasure to impose. Sée the first part of the Institutes, Sect 97.

It is then demaunded, by what Law Custome is paid for Kerseyes, whites, plaine straits, and other new draperies, made of wooll; for it appeareth by Acts of Parliament, and common experience, that all these pay Custome to the [62] King. To this it is answered, That a proportionable Subsidy, or Custome is paid for them within the equity of the said Statute of 27 Edw. 3. cap. 4. and likewise a proportionable Alnage is also due for them by that Act.

Hil. & Pasch. anno 2 Jacobi Regis, great questions were moved, Whether Frisadoes Bayes, Northern Cottons, Northern Dozens, Cloth-rash, Durances, Perpetuanoes, Juft-mocadoes, Sackcloth, Fustians, Worsteds, Stuffes made of Worsted yarn &c. were within the said Act of 27 Edw. 3. as concerning the Subsidy, and Alnage: and if they were not, whether the King by his prerogative might not impose a reasonable Subsidy, or Custome upon them proportionably to the cloth mentioned in the Statute of 27 Edw. 3. And this being questioned before the Lords of the Councell, they wrote to the Judges to be certified what the Law was in these cases, who upon mature deliberation, the 24 of June 1605. resolved, and so certified the Lords by their Letters under all their

75. Int' communia de Termino S. Trin. anno 1 Eliz. Rot. 73.
76. Mag. Chart. ca. 30 9. E. 3 c. 1. 14 E. 3 25. E. 3. cap. 2. 27 & 28 E. 3. of the Staple. 2 R. 2. cap. 1.
77. 23. H. 6. cap. 18. 14. H. 8. ca. 4. 13. El. c. 4 1. Jac. ca. 13 3. Jac. ca. 6. Int'decreta in camera Scac. Mich. 3 & 4 Eliz. Mich. 32 & 33. Eliz. Mic. 39. & 40 Eliz.

hands, That all Frisadoes Bayes, Northern Dozens, Northern Cottons, Cloth-rash, and other new Drapery made wholly of wooll, of what new name soever made, as new Drapery for the use of mans body, are to yeeld Subsidy, and Alnage according to the Statute of 27. E. 3. and within the office of the auncient Alnager,[78] as may appeare by severall Decrees in that behalfe in the Exchequer, in the time of the late Queen: but as touching fustians, canvas and such like made meerly of other stuffe then wooll, or being but mixed with wooll, it

Note this.
was resolved by all the Judges, that no charge could be imposed for the search or measuring thereof, but that all such Letters Patents so made are voyd, as may appeare by a Record of 1. Hen. 4, wherein the reason of the judgement is particularly recited, which the Judges thought good in their Letters to set downe as followeth.

King Henry the fourth graunted the measuring of woollen cloth, and canvas, that should be brought to London, to be sold by any Stranger, or Denizen (except he were free of London) taking an ob. of every whole peece of cloth so measured of the seller, and one other ob. of the buyer, and so after that rate for a greater or lesser quantity, and one penny for the measuring of an C. ells of canvas of the seller, and so much more of the buyer; and though it were averred that two other had enjoyed the same office before with the like fees, viz. one Shearing by the same Kings graunt, and one Clithew, before by the graunt of Ric. 2. (and the truth was, Robert Pooley, in 5. Edw. 3. and John Mareis, in 25. Edw. 3. had likewise enjoyed the same) yet amongst other reasons of the said judgement, it was set downe and adjudged that the former pos-session was by extortion, cohertion, and without right, and that the said Letters Patents were in *onerationem, oppressionem, & depauperationem subditorum Domini Regis. &c. & non in emendationem ejusdem populi;*[79] and therefore the said Letters Patents were voyd. And as touching the narrow new stuffe made in Norwich, and other places of Worsted yarn, it was resolved that it was not grauntable, nor fit to be graunted, for there was never any Alnage of Norwich Worsteds, and for these stuffes, if after they be made, and tucked up for sale by the makers thereof, they should be again opened to be viewed, and mea-sured, they will not well fall into their old plights, &c. as by the said Letters

---

78. [*Ed.:* "Alnage" was a duty paid initially on each ell (42 inches) of wool, collected by the "alnager."]

79. [*Ed.:* the burdening, oppression, and impoverishment, of the lord king's subjects, etc., and not for the improvement of the same people;]

it more at large appeareth.[80] These Letters were openly read at the Councell Table, and well approved by the whole Councell, and the Lords commanded the same to be kept in the Councell Chest to be a direction for them to answer suitors in these cases.

But these judgements in the Exchequer have beene cited for proofe that the King hath power to set impositions upon Merchandizes exported, and imported.

1. A judgement given in the Exchequer in an information against Germane Cioll for 40.s. set by Queen Mary upon every Tun of wine, of the growth of France, to be brought into the Realme.[81] But the case there was this, the Attourney generall informed, that where King Philip, and Queen Mary by their Proclamation, 30 Martii, in the 4. and 5. yeares of their raigne, did will and straitly command, that no wines of the growth of France, should be brought into this | Realme, without speciall licence of the said King and Queene, under paine of forfeiture of such Wine to the King & Queene, *Cumq; etiã dict' nuper Rex & Regina de advisamento Concilii sui ad tunc ordinaver' & decreverunt, quod quaelibet persona, quae in hoc Regnum Angliae induceret hujusmodi vina contra formam proclamationis praedict', solveret pro quolibet dolio hujusmodi vini 40 s. vocat. impost. & c.*[82] and that German Ciol, against the forme and effect of the said Proclamation, had brought into the Realme 338. tunnes of Wines of the growth of France, and had not paid 40 s. for each and every tunne: the Defendant pleaded a licence from the said King and Queene, dated the 9. of Decemb. anno 1. & 2. to bring into the Realme 1500. tunnes of wine, of the growth of Fraunce, in strangers bottoms, with a *non obstante*[83] of any Law, Statute, or Proclamation made or to be made to the contrary, whereupon the demurrer was joyned.

In this Record these things are to be observed, first that a Proclamation prohibiting importation of wines upon paine of forfeiture, was against Law:

[63]

---

80. 13. E. 3. ex. pte Remem. Thesaurar. Rot. Parliam. 25 E. 3. Enacted according to this resolution. 30 E. 3. Compot. Forinseco. in Scaccar. compot. Joh: Mareis.

81. Pasch. 1 Eliz. in Scacc. ex pte Remem. Regis.

82. [*Ed.*: And whereas also the said late king and queen, by the advice of their council, then and there ordained and decreed that whatever person should bring such wine into this realm of England, contrary to the form of the aforesaid proclamation, should pay forty shillings, called an impost, for every tun of such wine, etc.]

83. [*Ed.*: notwithstanding, an order relieving the recipient of an obligation at law.]

for it appeareth not, that any warre was between the Realmes. 2. The Proclamation was made of purpose to set an imposition, for the 40.s is imposed
upon them only, and upon such as should bring in Wines against the said
Proclamation, so as the Proclamation was the ground of this information. 3.
The King and Queene by advice of their Councell, did order, and decree &c.
and sheweth not how, or by what meanes this order and decree was made:
the pleading of such a former licence so insufficiently sheweth, that it was by
agreement and consent.

2. The executors of Customer Smith, were charged in a speciall information
for receiving an imposition of iii.s. iiii.d. set by Queene Elizabeth, under her
privy signet upon every hundred weight of allome made within the dominions
of the Pope, and judgement in the Exchequer was given against them:[84] the
reason of this judgement was, for that Customer Smith received the same as
due to the Queene, and the issue was joyned, *quod praedicti executores non
tenebantur ad computum, &c.*[85] and the validity of the imposition was never
questioned.

3. A judgement was given in the Exchequer, for an imposition set upon
Currants, but the common opinion was, that that judgement was against Law,
and divers expresse acts of Parliament; and so by that which hath been said,
it doth manifestly appeare.[86]

To conclude this point, with two of the *maximes* of the Common law. 1.
*Le common ley ad tielment admeasure les prerogatives le Roy, que ilz ne tolleront,
ne prejudiceront le inheritance dascun,*[87] the Common law hath so admeasured
the prerogatives of the King, that they should not take away, nor prejudice
the inheritance of any: and the best inheritance that the Subject hath, is the
Law of the Realme. 2. *Nihil tam proprium est imperii, quam legibus vivere.*[88]

Upon this Chapter, as by the said particulars may appeare, this conclusion
is necessarily gathered, that all Monopolies concerning trade and traffique are
against the liberty and freedome, declared and graunted by this great Charter,

84. Mich. 38. 39. Eliz. in Scaccari, Rot. 319.

85. [*Ed.:* that the aforesaid executors were not bound to account, etc.]

86. In mem. Scaccar. int. com Pasc. 4. Jacob. Rot. 32. in inform. vers. John Bate de London mercat.
Pl. Com. 236. in the B. Barkleys case. Fortesc sepe.

87. [*Ed.:* The common law has so measured the king's prerogatives that they shall not take away or
prejudice anyone's inheritance,]

88. [*Ed.:* Nothing is more appropriate for a ruler than to live by the laws.]

and against divers other Acts of Parliament, which are good commentaries upon this Chapter.[89]

Lè point del conge del demurrer des merchants aliens est issint interpretable, que ceo ne soit in prejudice des villes, ne des merchants dangleterre, & il soient seremements al Roy & plevyes silz demurront pluis que 40 jours.[90,91]

For the well intreating and ordering of Merchant strangers and denizens, and for *[92] due imployment of their mony upon the native commodities of this Realme, many Statutes have beene made since this great Charter, and have been excellently expounded in the raigne of Queene Elizabeth, but that matter belongs not to this place.

Chapter 31

| If any man hold of any Escheat, as of the Honour of Wallingford, Nottingham, [64] Boloin, or of any other Escheats which be in our hands, and are Baronies, and die, his Heir shall give none other Relief, nor do none other Service to Us, than he should to the Baron, if it were in the Baron's hand; and We in the same wise shall hold it as the Baron held it. Neither shall We have, by occasion of any Barony or Escheat, any Escheat or keeping of any of our men, unless he that held the Barony or Escheat otherwise held of Us in Chief.

By this Chapter it is declared, and enacted, that if any man hold of any escheate as of any honour, or of other escheats, which are Baronies, and were in the Kings hands; First, if he die, his heire being of full age, his heire shall give no other reliefe to the King then he did to the Baron. 2. Nor doe none other service to the King, then he should have done to the Baron. 3. That the King shall hold the honour or Baronie as the Baron held it, that is, of such estate, and in such manner and forme, as the Baron held it. 4. The King shall not have by occasion of any Barony, or escheate, any escheate but of lands holden of such Baronie. 5. Nor any wardship of any other lands then are holden by

---

89. 2. E. 3. c. 9. 9. E. 3. c. 1 25. E. 3. c. 2. 2. R. 2. c. 1. 11. R. 2. cap. 7. 6. R. 2. cap. 1. 12. H. 7. cap. 6.

90. [*Ed.:* The article concerning permission for alien merchants to remain is to be interpreted so that it should not prejudice the towns or the merchants of England; and they shall be sworn to the king and put in pledge if they stay for more than forty days.]

91. Mirror c. 5. §. 5 4. E. 4. c. 15. 5. H. 4. c. 9. 27. H. 6. cap. 3. 17. E. 4. cap. 1. 3. H. 7. cap. 8.

92. *See hereafter the exposition upon the Statutes of imployments.

Knights service of such Baronie, unlesse he, which held of the Baronie, held also of the King by Knights service *in capite*.[1]

All this is meerely declaratory of the Common Law, and here it appeareth that he that holdeth of the King, must hold of the person of the King, and not of any honor, Barony, Mannor or seigniory: and it appeareth farther in our books, that he that holdeth of the King in cheife, must not only hold of the person of the King, but the tenure must be created by the King, or some one of the progenitors, or predecessors Kings of this Realme, to defend his person and Crowne, otherwise he shall have no prerogative by reason of it, for no prerogative can be annexed to a tenure created by a Subject.[2] Note here is not named the honour of Lanc. which was an auncient honor ever since the conquest, which Edw. 3. raised to a Court Palatine, as in the 4. part of the Institutes, cap. Duch. of Lancastre appeareth. see 28. Hen. 6. 11. *per touts les justices.* 1. Edw. 6. Bro. trav. 53. Stamford Prerog. 29 b.

"of any other Escheats."[3]

Some question hath been made of these words, for some have said that these words are to be understood of common escheats, as where the Lord dieth without heire, or where he is attainted of felony: But where the Lord is attainted of high Treason, there the King hath the land by forfeiture of whomsoever the land is held, and not in respect of any escheate by reason of any seigniorie: and therefore where William Riparave a Norman, held lands in fee of the King, as of the honour of Peverell, and Riparave forfeited his said land for Treason, and the King seised it as his escheate of Normandy, in this case the land so forfeited was no part of the honour, as it should have been, if it had come to the King, as a common escheate, for it cometh to the King by reason of his Person, and Crowne, and therefore if he graunt it over &c. the | Patentee shall hold it of the King in chiefe, and not of the honour. And all this is to be agreed, but yet the tenants that held before of the honour by knights service, cannot hold of the King in chiefe. 1. For that they hold not of the person of the King, but of the Honour. 2. Because the tenure was not created by the King, or any of his progenitors, as hath been said.

[65]

---

1. [*Ed.:* in chief.]
2. See the first part of the Institutes sect. 103. 47. E. 3. 21. F. N. B. 5.
3. 47. E. 3. 21. Riparaves case.

And so doth Bracton, who wrote soone after the Statute, expound this great Charter to extend to forfeiture of Baronies for treason, as of the Normans.[4]

And yet to make an end of all ambiguities and questions, the Statute of 1. Edw. 6. was made, which is, as the words be, a plain declaration and resolution of the Common Law. Likewise the Statute of 1. Edw. 3. which provideth, that where the land, that is holden of the King, as of an honour, is aliened without licence, no man shall be thereby grieved, is also a declaration of the Common law.[5]

By this Chapter it appeareth, that a subject may have an honour.

Chapter 32

No Freeman from henceforth shall give or sell any more of his Land, but so that of the Residue of the Lands, the Lord of the Fee may have the Service due to him which belongeth to the Fee.[1]

1 First it is to be seene, what the Common law was before this Statute.

2 What is wrought by this Statute, where the lands are holden of the King.

3 What this Statute hath provided in case where lands are holden of a Subject.[2]

Before this Statute, in case where the tenure was of a common person, the tenant might have made a feofment of a parcell of his tenancy to hold of him, for the seigniory remained intire as it was, and the Lord might distreine in the tenancy parabaile for his rent, and service, but at the Common law, he could not have given a part of his tenancy to be holden of the Lord, for the tenant by this Act could not divide the seigniory of the Lord which was intire, for at the beginning the Lord reserved his seigniory out of the whole tenancy, and might distreine in every part thereof for his seigniory, but if the tenant might have made a feofment of part to hold of the Lord, then had he socluded the Lord of his liberty to distreine for the whole seigniory in every part thereof.

At the Common law the tenant might have made a feofment of the whole tenancy to be holden of the Lord, for that was no prejudice at all to the Lord.

---

4. Bracton 2. fol 87. b. 30. H. 8 tenures Br. 44. 29. H. 8 livery. 28. Br. 3. H. 8 Dier 58.

5. 1. E. 6 cap. 1. E. 3. cap 3. See the 1. part of the Institutes sect. 1.

1. Tr. 1. E. 1 coram. Rege. Not. & Derb. a declaration made of Act. Bract. L 1. Ba. fol. 88 Flet. cap. 3. Mirror. § 2. Custumier Norm. cap. 116.

2. 10. H. 7. 11.

[a3] But in the Kings case it was doubted, whether his tenant might have given part of the tenancy to hold of himselfe, because the Land, and the profit that might come to the King thereby, was removed farther off from him, and the mesnalty was ever of lesse value, then the land, and for that cause the tenancy was called paravaile: [b4] and in 18. Edw. 1. the King answered to a petition in Parliament, *Rex non vult aliquem medium, &c.*[5] and this question remained after this Statute, about the space of 133. years, viz. till the [c6] Statute of 34. Edw. 3. was made, whereby it is provided, that alienations of Lands made by tenants, which held of Henry the third or of other Kings before him, to hold of themselves, that the alienations should stand in force, saving to the King his prerogative of the time of his great Grandfather, his Father, and his own, whereby it appeareth that this pereogative to have a fine for alienation, [d7] began in the raign of Hen. 3. which was by this Act, and therefore he beginneth with Henry the third his great Grandfather.

[e8] To the second point by this Act, where lands are holden of the King, as King, in Capite, be it by Knights service, or in socage in *Capite,* & aliened [66] without licence, | there groweth, as hath been said; to the King a fine: For by the Common law it was against the nature and purity of a fee simple; for the tenant to be resrained from alienation.

But some did hold, that upon this Act the land so aliened without licence was forfeite to the King, by reason of these words, *nullus liber homo det, &c.*[9] and others did hold the contrary, that upon these words, the land was not forfeited, but that it should be seised in the name of a distresse, and a fine to be paid, for the trespasse, which I take to be the better opinion; and the reason why our books speake, that no fine was due before 20. Hen. 3. is, for that about that yeare Henry the third being of full age (as hath been said) did establish and confirme this great Charter, but in truth it was in 21. Hen. 3. as by the Charter it selfe appeareth.

---

3. *a* 29. Ass. p. 19. 20. Ass. p. 17. 26. Ass. p. 37. 20. E. 3. avowry. Rot. Parl. 29. E. 3. nu. 18.

4. *b* Rot. Par. 18. E. 1.

5. [*Ed.:* The king does not wish any mesne, etc.]

6. *c* 34 E. 3. c. 15. the Stat. of W. 1 de quia emptores terr. an. 18. E. 1. F. N. B. 143b. & 235c.

7. *d* Rot. pat. an. 21. H. 3. nu. 4. H. 3. confirmed this chart. made 9. H. 3.

8. *e* 20. Ass. p. 17. 26. Ass. p. 37. 14. H. 4. 2. 3. 15. E. 4. 13. Stamf. prer, cap. 6. fo. 27, 28. 9. E. 3. 36. Hil. 13. E. 3. coram rege. Norff. in turri.

9. [*Ed.:* no free man shall give, etc.]

But this question depended about the space of 100. years &c And was not determined untill the Statute made in 1. Edw. 3. whereby it is enacted, that the king shall not hold them as forfeite in such case, but that of lands so aliened there shall be from thenceforth, a reasonable fine taken in the Channcery, by due proces, which Act was but an exposition of this Chapter of Magna Charta as to lands holden of the King in *Capite* aliened without licence, and extendeth to lands holden of the King by grand Serjantie[10] aliened without licence.[11]

To the 3. the great doubt upon this Act was, that in as much as this Act was a prohibition generall, and imposed no paine or penalty, what paine the tenant, or his feofee should incurre, if he did the contrary; and by the common opinion this Act was thus interpreted: that when a tenant of a common person did alien parcell contrary to this Act, the feoffor himselfe during his life should not avoide it, *quia nemo contra factum suum proprium venire potest,*[12] but that his heire after his decease might avoid it by the intendment of this Act, to the end that men should not purchase such parcell, for feare of losing the same after the death of the feoffor: but if the heire apparent had joyned with his auncester in the feoffment, or after had confirmed it, and thereby had given his assent thereunto, he or his heires should never have avoided it, whether he survived his Father or no; and if the heire entred upon this Statute, the alienee of part might plead that the service, whereby the land was holden, might be sufficiently done of the residue, and thereuppon issue might be taken. And I have seene divers such Precedents betweene this Act of Magna Charta, and 18. Edw. 1.

Then came the Statute of 18. Edw. 1.[13] which enacteth *quod de caetero liceat unicuiq; libero homini terras suas, seu tenemēta sua, seu partē inde ad voluntatem suam vendere, ita tamen quod feoffatus teneat terram illam, seu tenementum illud de capitali Domino per eadem servitia, & consuetudines, per quae feoffator suus illa prius de eo tenuit, & si partem aliquam earundem terrarum, seu tenementorum alicui vendiderit, feoffatus ille partem illam immediate teneat de Domino.*[14]

---

10. [*Ed.:* Tenure by personal military service to the Sovereign, later honorary service.]

11. 1 E. 3. c. 12 See the Statute of quia emptores terrarum. ubi sup. Hil. 2 E. 3. coram Rege Wiltes. Prerog. Regis c. 6. F. N. B. 175. 14. E. 3. quare Imp. 54. Br Alienation sans licence 34. Hill. 43 Eliz. 1. 2. fo 80. 81. Seign. Cromwels case.

12. [*Ed.:* because no one can properly come against his own deed,]

13. E. 1. de quia emptores terra.

14. [*Ed.:* that from henceforth it should be permissible for any free man to sell his lands or tenements, or part thereof, in such a way nevertheless that the feoffee shall hold that land or tenement of the chief

Many excellent things are enacted by this Statute, and all the doubts upon this Chapter of Magna Charta were cleered, both Statutes having both one end, (that is to say) for the upholding and preservation of the tenures, whereby the lands were holden; this Act of 18. Edw. 1. being enacted *ad instantiam magnatum Regni.*[15]

1 First this Statute of 18. Edw. 1. doth begin with a *de caetero liceat*[16] which proveth that before it was not lawfull to alien part, unless sufficient were left, and this approveth the aforesaid common opinion, that in that case, the heire might enter, otherwise this Chapter of Magna Charta, had been in vaine and this *de caetero liceat* had not needed.

2 That by this Statute of 18. Edw. 1. the prohibition and penalty by this Chapter of Magna Charta, to avoide the state of the feoffee is taken away; *de caetero liceat, &c.*

3 The point aforesaid of the Common law, that the tenant could not alien parcell to hold of the Lord, is by this Act of 18. Edw. 1. altered.

4 Another point of the Common law is by this Act altered, that where by the Common Law, he hath aliened parcell to hold of himselfe, this is taken away, and the alienee shall hold of the Lord *pro particula.*[17]

[67] | 5. Where the Tenant had liberty, and election by the common Law to make a feoffement of the whole, to hold either of himselfe, or of the Lord, now this liberty and election is taken away, for by this Act the Land must be immediately holden of the Lord.

6. That the King is bound by this Act, and this appeareth by the Register,[18] that the King cannot charge the feoffee of part with the entire Rent, but there lieth a Writ *De onerando pro rata portione;*[19] But the King may graunt Lands to hold of himselfe, for he is not restrained by this Act, for hereby no man is restrained, but he which holds over of some Lord, and the King holdeth of none.

---

lord by the same services and customs as those by which his feoffor previously held of him, and if he should sell any part of the same lands or tenements to another, the feoffee shall hold that part immediately of the lord.]

15. [*Ed.:* at the instance of the great men of the realm.]
16. [*Ed.:* it should from henceforth be permissible.]
17. [*Ed.:* for his portion.]
18. Registr. 268. F. N. B. 234.
19. [*Ed.:* for charging in proportion;]

But then here riseth a question, If by this Chapter of Magna Charta, a fine for alienation accrued to the King upon an alienation of the Kings Tenant in Capite, and now this restraint (as hath been said) being taken away; how can that prerogative stand when the foundation, whereupon it is built faileth?

But hereunto it is answered. 1. The restraint of Magna Charta, *secundum quid*,[20] as to the avoydance of the state of the feoffee by the heire, is taken away, as hath been said, but not *simpliciter*,[21] for in respect of the King, the fine for alienation remains due, and herewith agreeth constant and continuall usage. 2. The Statute of 1. Edw. 3. enacteth,[22] *Que deformes de tielz terres & tenements alien soit reasonable fine prise in le Chauncery*,[23] and though it saith (*desormes*)[24] from henceforth, that was not, that any fine was due before, but, as hath been said, to take away the question of the forfeiture.

After this Act out of the Office of the *Remembrancer* of the Exchequer, Writs of *Quo titulo ingressus est*,[25] to help the King to his reasonable fine, issued out of the Exchequer, to know how the feoffee came to the whole, or part of the Land, and of what estate, whereupon the feoffee was driven to plead to his great charge and trouble, and therefore upon conference had with the Kings Officers, and the Judges, it was ordained, that seeing the Kings Tenant could not alien without licence, for if he did, he should pay a fine, that for a licence to be obtained, the King should have the third part of the value of the Land, which was holden reasonable, and the feoffee should pay the same because his Land was otherwise to be charged, and he rid of the trouble and charge by the Writ of *Quo titulo ingressus est;* and if the alienation was without licence, then a reasonable fine by the Statute, was to be paid by the alienee, which they resolved to be one yeares value, which ever since constantly and continually hath beene observed and paid.

This fine was to be paid by the alienee, as hath been said, or by those that claimed by or under him, and if the fine be not paid, the Land shall be seised into the Kings hands; and the intent of a Parliament is always intended just,

20. [*Ed.:* in a certain respect,]

21. [*Ed.:* simply,]

22. 17 E. 2 ca. 7. 1 E. 3. ubi supra.

23. [*Ed.:* That from henceforth a reasonable fine shall be taken in the Chancery for such lands and tenements aliened,]

24. [*Ed.:* from henceforth.]

25. [*Ed.:* Writ: by which title he has entered.]

and reasonable; and therefore if a disseisor of Lands in *Capite* make an alienation without licence, and the dissesee enter, the Land shall not be seised for the fine, for the dissesee is in by a title before the alienation, and so in other like cases. If he in the reversion levy a fine of Lands holden in *Capite* without licence, the lessee for life shall not bee charged with the fine, because that estate was before the alienation,[26] but yet in a *Quid juris clamat*,[27] the lessee shall not be compelled to attorne, because the Court will not suffer a prejudice to the King in like manner, as if the reversion had been aliened in *Mortmain* without the Kings licence.

I have been the longer in explaining this Chapter, because it seemed so obscure to some Readers in former times, that they passed it over without any explanation.

Chapter 33

[68] | All Patrons of Abbies which have the King's Charters of England of Advowson, or have old tenure or possession in the same, shall have the Custody of them when they fall void, as it hath been accustomed, and as it is afore declared.

This Statute is intended where the Patron, or Founder of Abbeyes, or Priories by speciall reservation, tenure or custome, ought to have the custody of the Temporalties of the same, during the vacation, as many Patrons and Founders in times past had.[1] But if the King be Founder, he ought to have the Temporalties during the Vacation, of common Right by his Prerogative.

If the King and a common person joyn in a foundation, the King is the Founder, because it is an entire thing.[2]

If a common person found an Abbey, or Priory, with possessions of small value, and the King after endow it with great possessions, yet the common person is Founder. If a common person found a Chauncery, and after the King translate it, and make it a Monastery, and endow it with possessions, yet the common person is in Law the Founder, because he gave the first living so if the translation be from regular to secular, *vel è contra*.[3]

---

26. 45. E. 3. ca. 6. 17. E. 3. 6.

27. [*Ed.:* Writ for reversioner or remainderman to compel a life tenant to attorn to him.]

1. Mirror ca. 5. § 2. F. N. B. 34. 44 E. 3. 24. 38 Ass. 22. 50 Ass. p. 6.

2. 44. E. 3. 24.

3. [*Ed.:* or conversely.]

Chapter 34

No Man shall be taken or imprisoned upon the Appeal of a Woman, for the death of any other than of her Husband.

For this word, Appeale, see the first of the *Institutes*.[1] At the Common Law before this Statute, a woman, as well as a man might have had an appeale of death of any of her auncestors, and therefore the son of a woman shall at this day have an appeale, if he be heire at the death of the auncestor, for the son is not disabled, but the mother onely,[2] for the Statute saith, *Propter appellum foeminae.*[3] Vide more of this in the first part of the Institutes.

*[4] Fleta saith, *Foemina autem de morte viri sui inter brachia sua interfecti, & non aliter poterit appellare;*[5] And therewith agreeth the Mirror, Britton, and Bracton.

By *inter brachia*[6] in these auncient Authors, is understood the wife, which the dead had lawfully in possession at his death, for she must be his wife both of right and in possession, for in an appeale, *Unques accouple in loiall Matrimony,*[7] is a good plea.

A woman at this day may have an appeale of robbery, &c. for she is not restrained thereof.

This Writ of appeale of the death of her husband, is annexed to her Widowhood, as her Quarentine is.

If the wife of the dead marry again, her appeale is gone, albeit the second husband die within the yeare; for shee must before any appeale brought, conti-l-nue *foemina viri sui,*[8] upon whose death she brings the appeale.   [69]

So if she bring the appeale during her Widow-hood and take husband, the appeale shall abate, and is gone for ever.[9]

So likewise if in her appeale she hath judgement of death against the De-

---

1. See the first part of the Institutes. Sect. 500.

2. Glanv. lib. 14. c. 3. 15. E. 2. Coro. 385. 17. E. 4. 1. 20 H. 6. 43. Stamf. Pl. Cor. 58; 59. Bract. li. 4. fol. 148. Brit. fo. 55. Flet. 1 c2. 33. See the first part of the institutes, sect. 24.

3. [*Ed.:* on account of the appeal of a woman.]

4. *Fleta ubi supra. Mirror ca. 5 § 2. & ca. 2. §7. 50. E. 3. 14. 28. E. 3. 9. 1. 3 E. 3. Coron. 357 20. H. 6. 46.

5. [*Ed.:* A woman may appeal for the death of her husband slain between her arms, but not otherwise;]

6. [*Ed.:* between her arms.]

7. [*Ed.:* never joined in lawful matrimony,]

8. [*Ed.:* the wife of her husband,]

9. 11 H. 4. 46.

fendant, if after she take husband, she can never have execution of death against him.

Albeit the husband be attainted of high Treason, or felony, yet if he be slain, his wife shall have an appeale,[10] for not withstanding the attainder he was *vir suus*,[11] but the heire cannot have an appeale, for the blood is corrupted betweene them.

"the Appeal of a Woman."

A hermophrodite, if the male sex be predominant, shall have an appeale of death as heire, but if the female sexe doth exceed the other, no appeale doth lie for her as heire.

Chapter 35

No County Court from henceforth shall be holden but from month to month; and where greater Time hath been used, there shall be greater: Nor any Sheriff or his Bailiff shall keep his Turn in the Hundred but twice in the Year, and no where but in due place and accustomed; that is to say, once after Easter, and again after the Feast of Saint Michael. And the View of Frankpledge shall be likewise at the Feast of Saint Michael, without occasion: So that every man may have his Liberties which he had or used to have in the time of King Henry our Grandfather, or which he hath purchased since. The View of Frankpledge shall be so done, that our Peace may be kept; and that the Tything be wholly kept, as it hath been accustomed; and that the Sheriff seek no occasions; and that he be content with so much as the Sheriff was wont to have for his View-making, in the time of King Henry our Grandfather.

"County Court.[1]"

Quod modo vocatur Comitatus, olim apud Britones temporibus Romanorum in Regno isto Britanniae vocabatur Consulatus; & qui modo vocantur Vicecomites,

---

10. 35. H. 6. 63.

11. [*Ed.:* her husband.]

1. Inter leges R. Ed. Lamb. 129. a. b. Idem verbo Conventus.

tunc temporis Vice-consules vocabantur; ille vero dicebatur Vice-consul, qui Consule absente ipsius vices supplebat in Juris foro.[2]

Curia Comitatus,[3] in Saxon, ᚦᚳᚤᛈᚓᚷᚓᛗᚩᛏᚓ, i. *Comitatus conventus.*[4] *Ejus duo sunt genera, quorum alterum hodie le Countie Court, alterum le Tourne del Viscount, olim Folkmote, vulgo nuncupatur;*[5,6] So as many times *Turn' Vicecomitis*[7] is expressed under the name of *Curia Comitatus,* because it extended through the whole County: and therefore in the red Book of the Exchequer, amongst the Laws of King Hen. 1 cap. 8.[8] *De generalibus placitis Comitatus*[9] it is thus contained, viz.

Sicut antiqua fuerat institutione formatum, salutari Regis imperio vera est recor-|-datione firmatum, generalia*[10] *Comitatuum placita certis locis, & vicibus,*   [70] *& definito tempore per singulas anni provincias convenire debere, nec ullis ultra fatigationibus agitari, nisi propria Regis necessitas, vel commune Regni commodum saepius adjiciant. Intersint autem Episcopi, Comites, Vicedomini, Vicarii, Centenarii, Aldermanni, Praefecti, Praepositi, Barones, Vavassores, Tingrevii, & caeteri terrarum Domini diligenter intendentes, ne malorum impunitas, aut gravionum pravitas, vel judicum subversio solita miseros laceratione confiniant: Agantur itaque primo, debita verae Christianitatis jura, secundo, Regis placita, postremo, causae singulorum, &c. debet enim Shcrysmote,* (i. the Sheriffes Tourne) *bis; Hundreda, & Wapentachia,* (i. the County Courts) *duodecies in anno congregari.*[11,12]

2. [*Ed.:* What is now called a county was called *consulatus* (consulate) by the Britons, in the times when the Romans were in this kingdom of Britain; and those who are now called *vicecomites* (sheriffs) were in those times called *vice-consules* (vice-consuls); and he was called a vice-consul who supplied the place of a consul in his absence in a court of law.]

3. [*Ed.:* County Court.]

4. [*Ed.:* shire-moot, that is, meeting of the county.]

5. [*Ed.:* Of this there are two kinds, one of which is now the county court, and the other is the sheriff's tourn, which was once commonly called the folk-moot.]

6. 12 H. 7. 18. Lamb. 135. Britton ca. 27. Flet. 2. ca. 36, 37.

7. [*Ed.:* the sheriff's tourn.]

8. In libro rubro, in Scaccario. ca. 80.

9. [*Ed.:* concerning the general pleas of the counties.]

10. * i. Turnorum placita.

11. Regis placita. i. The Pleas of the Crown holden in the Sheriffes Tourn also.

12. [*Ed.:* As it was formed by ancient institution, and confirmed of record by the king's authority, the general pleas of the county ought to be convened in certain places, and on certain occasions, and at a definite time of the year, so that no one should be made to litigate too often beyond the point of exhaustion,

And truly did Hen. 1. say, *Sicut antiqua fuerat institutione formatum:*[13] For these Courts of the Tourn, and of the County, and of the Leete or view of frankpledge mentioned hereafter in this Chapter were vary auncient: for of the Tourn you shall reade amongst the Lawes of King Edw.[14] *Statutum est quod ibi (scilicet apud le folkmote) debent populi omnes, &c. convenire, & se fide & sacramento non fracto ibi in unum & simul confederare, &c. ad defedendum Regnum, &c. una cum Domino suo Rege, & terras suas, & honores illius omni fidelitate cum eo servare, & quod illi, ut Domino suo Regi intra & extra Regnum universum Britanniae fideles esse velint, &c. Hanc legem invenit Arthurus (qui quondam fuit inclytissimus Rex Britonum) & ita consolidavit & confederavit Regnum Britanniae universum semper in unum, hujus legis authoritate expulit Arthurus praedictus Saracenos, & inimicos a Regno, lex enim ista diu sopita fuit, donec Edgarus Rex Anglorum, qui fuit avus Edwardi Regis, illam excitavit, & erexit in lucem & per totum Regnum firmiter observari praecepit: & hujus legis authoritate Rex Etheldred subito uno & eodem die per universum Regnum Danos occidit.*[15]

By the Lawes of King Edward, before the Conquest the first, which succeeded King Alured, it is thus enacted:[16]

---

unless for the necessity of the king himself or the benefit of the realm. And there should be present the bishops, earls, vicelords (*vicedomini*), deputies, hundredmen, ealdormen, prefects, provosts, barons, vasours, trithing-reeves (*tingrevii*), and others diligently attending on the lord's lands, lest the impunity of the wicked, or the depravity of the reeves, or the corruption of judges, should subject the wretched to customary oppression. They deal firstly with the due rights of true Christianity, secondly with pleas of the king, and lastly the causes of individuals, etc. The shire-moot ought to meet twice a year, and hundreds and wapentakes twelve times a year.]

    13. [*Ed.:* As it was formed by ancient institution.]

    14. Lamb. fol 135. The oath of Allegeance in the Tourn or Leet.

    15. [*Ed.:* It was enacted that here (that is to say, at the folk-moot) ought all the people, etc. to come and at one and the same time contract together by faith and unbroken oath, etc. to defend the realm, etc., together with their lord king, and with all faithfulness to preserve with him his lands and honours, and that they shall be faithful subjects to him as their lord king within and without the whole realm of Britain, etc. This law was introduced by Arthur, who was at one time the most distinguished king of the Britons, and thus he consolidated and joined together the whole realm of Britain to be always as one, and by authority of this law the aforesaid Arthur expelled the Saracens and enemies from the kingdom. However, this law was long in abeyance until Edward, king of the English, who was grandfather of King Edward, revived it and brought it to light and ordered it to be firmly observed throughout the realm; and by authority of this law King Æthelred suddenly on one and the same day put to death all the Danes throughout the realm.]

    16. Inter leges Edw. Regis. ante conq. 1 cap. 11. fol. 51.

Praepositus quisque. i. Vicecomes, Saxonice Geresa, Anglice Sheriffe, ad quar-
tam circiter septimanam frequentem populi concionem celebrato, cuique jus dicito
aequabile, litesque singulas cum dies condicti adveniant dirimito.[17]

Hereby it appeareth that Common Pleas between party and party were holden in the County Court every month, which agreeth with Magna Charta, and other Statutes and continuall usage to this day.

And amongst the Laws of King Edgar it is thus concerning the Sheriffes Tourn provided.[18]

Celeberrimus ex omni Satrapia bis quotannis conventus agitor, cui quidem illius
Dioecesis Episcopus, & Senator intersunto, quorum alter jura Divina, alter hu-
mana populum edoceto;[19] which also agreeth with Magna Charta, and other Statutes and continuall usage.

By that which hath been said, it appeareth that the Law made by King Henry the first was (after the great heat of the Conquest was past) but a restitution of the auncient Law of England: And forasmuch as the Bishop with the Sheriffe did goe in Circuit twice every yeare, by every hundred within the County (which also appeareth by this Chapter of Magna Charta in these words, *Turnum suum per hundreda, &c.*)[20] it was called *Tour,* or Tourn, which signifieth a circuit, or perambulation.[21]

Now let us peruse the severall branches of this Chapter.

"No County Court from henceforth shall be holden but from month to month, and where greater Time hath been used, there shall be greater:"

This (as hath been said) is an affirmance of the Common Law, and Custome of the Realme.

---

17. [*Ed.:* The provost—that is, *vicecomes,* or (in Saxon) reeve, or (in English) sheriff—around every fourth week shall proclaim a regular assembly of the people, so that right can be done to everyone with equity and all disputes settled when the appointed days arrive.]

18. Inter leges Edgari Regis. ca. 5. fo. 80.

19. [*Ed.:* The satrap shall twice a year convene the most distinguished assembly of everyone, to which the bishop of the diocese and the senator (i.e. ealdorman) shall be present, each of whom shall teach the people the divine laws and the human.]

20. [*Ed.:* his tour through the hundreds, etc.]

21. Britton cap. 29. Fleta lib. 2. ca. 45 Marlebr. cap. 10. 31 H. 6. Leet 11. F. N. B 169. a.

"County Court."

Here *Comitatus* is taken in the common sense for the County Court.

[71]   I That the Realme was divided into counties, long before the raigne of King Alured, viz. in the time of the auncient Britons. See the first part of the Institutes, Sect. 248.

"and where greater Time hath been used."

This is altered by the Statute of 2. E. 6.[22] whereby it is provided that no County Court shall be longer deferred, but one month from Court to Court, and so the said Court shall be kept every month, and none otherwise.

By which Act every County of England, concerning the time of the keeping of the County Court is governed by one and the same Law.

And there is to be accounted 28. dayes to the legall month in this case, and not according to the month of the Kalender.

"Nor any Sheriff or his Bailiff shall keep his Turn in the Hundred, but twice in the Year; and no where but in due and accustomed; that is to say, once after Easter; and again, after the Feast of Saint Michael."

Where this branch saith, *Semel post Pasch. &c.*[23] The Statute of 31. Edw. 3.[24] explaineth it, viz. one time within the month after Easter, and another time within the month after S. Michael, and if they hold them in any other manner, then they should lose their Tourn for that time, which is as much to say, as the Court so holden for that time, shall be utterly void, and the Sheriffe shall lose the profits thereof.[25]

"but in due place . . . accustomed."

This remaineth to this day.[26]

22. 2. E. 6. cap. 25.
23. [*Ed.:* Once after Easter, etc.]
24. 31. E. 3. ca. 15.
25. 38. H. 6. fol. 7. 6 H. 7. 2. Stamf. pl. Cor. 84.
26. 42. E. 3. 4. & 5. Dier 4. & 5. Phil. & Mar. 151.

"in the Hundred."

How Hundreds, and the Courts of the Hundreds first came, see hereafter in this Chapter.

"And the View of Frankpledge, shall be likewise at the Feast of Saint Michael, &c."

It hath appeared before, that of auncient time the Sheriffe had two great Courts, viz. The Tourne, and the County Court: Afterwards for the ease of the people, and specially of the Husbandman that each of them might the better follow their business in their severall degrees, this Court here spoken of, viz. views of frankpledge, or Leet was by the King divided, and derived from the Tourn, and graunted to the Lords to have the view of the Tenants, and Resiants[27] within their Mannors &c. So as the Tenants, and Resiants should have the same Justice, that they had before in the Tourn, done unto them at their own doors without any charge or losse of time, and for that cause come the duty in many. Leets to the Lord *De certo Lete*,[28] towards the charge of obtaining the graunt of the said Leet.[29]

So likewise, and for the same reason were Hundreds, and Hundred Courts, divided and derived from the County Courts, and this the King might doe, for the Tourn and Leet both are the Kings Courts of Record: And as the King may grant a man to have power *Tenere placita*[30] within a certain precinct, &c. before certain Judges, and in a manner exempt it from the jurisdiction of his higher Courts of Justice, so might be due in case of the Tourne, and Hundred Courts: so as the Courts and Judges, may be changed, but the Lawes and Customes, whereby the Courts proceed, cannot be altered. And as the County Court, and Hundred Court are of one Jurisdiction, so the Tourne, and Leet be also of one and the same jurisdiction; for *Derivativa potestas est ejusdem jursdictionis cum primitiva.*[31]   *Regula.*

The style of the Tourn is *Curia franc. plegii Domini Regis tenť apud L. coram*

---

27. [*Ed.:* a resident of a manor, not holding a specified tenency.]
28. 11 H. 4. 89. 13 H. 4.9. lib. 11. fo. 45. Godfreyes case.
29. [*Ed.:* of a certain leet.]
30. [*Ed.:* to hold pleas.]
31. [*Ed.:* Derivative power is of the same jurisdiction as primitive power.]

Vicecomite in Turno suo tali die &c.[32,33] And therefore in some Books it is called the Leete of the Tourn. And therefore where the Sheriffe styled his Court, *Turñ Vicocom teñ tali die apud L. &c.*[34,35] it was received that it was insufficient

[72]   for | that this word Tourn is but the perambulation of the Sheriffe, but by the right style of the Tourn, it appeareth that the Tourn and Leet have but one style, and the same jurisdiction.[36]

But for want of the knowledge of antiquity it was *obiter*,[37] in 18 Hen. 6.[38] denied that the Tourn, and the Leet were of one jurisdiction, and two instances are there put, viz. that the Leet hath conusance of bread and ale, that is, of the assise of bread and ale, and the Tourn hath not conusance thereof; and the other is, that in the Leet they have authority *de presenter ceux, queux no sont lies,*[39] abridged by Fitzh. *a presenter ceux, que ne sont mises in le decennarie.*[40]

To the first it is cleare, That the breach of the assise of bread and Ale is presentable in the Tourn, as a common nusance, and therewith agreeth constant and continuall experience, and reason proveth, that the derivative cannot have conusance of that which the primitive had not, unlesse it be given by some Act of Parliament; and herewith agreeth the style of the Tourn, and the authority of later Books.[41]

As to the second, it is ill reported in the Book it selfe; but if it be intended as Fitzh. abridgeth it, then it is cleare that in the Tourn they that be not put into the decennary may be inquired of, for, as hath been often said, the style of the Tourn is, *Curia visus frank pleg';*[42] and the derivative cannot of common right have more than the primitive.

But both of the Tourn and the Leete, this may be truly said,

32. [*Ed.:* The court of frankpledge of the lord king held at L. before the sheriff in his tourn on such and such a day, etc.]

  33. 31 H. 6. Leet 11. 8 H. 7. 11.

  34. [*Ed.:* the sheriff's tourn held on such and such a day at L., etc.]

  35. 6 H. 7. 2. 8 H. 7. 1.

  36. Mirror ca. 1. §. 16.

  37. [*Ed.:* by the way.]

  38. 18 H. 6. abbr. by F. Leet. 1.

  39. [*Ed.:* to present those who are not bound,]

  40. [*Ed.:* to present those who are not put into the tithing.]

  41. 4 E. 4. 31. 22 E. 4. 22. 12 H. 7. 18. 28 H. 8. Dier 13. b.

  42. [*Ed.:* Court of the view of frankpledge;]

[43] *Tempora mutantur, & nos mutamur in illis;*[44]

Quodque vera institutio istius curiae evanuit, & velut umbra ejusdem ad huc remanet; habemus quidem Senatus consultum, sed in tabulis repositum, & tanquam gladium in vagina reconditum.[45,46]
But now let us return to our *Magna Charta.*

"And the View of Frankpledge shall be likewise at the Feast of Saint Michael, &c."[47]

It is to be observed that the precedent branch is, That *Vicecomes non faciat Turnum per Hundredum nisi bis in anno,*[48] as hath been said, *viz. Semel post Pasch' & iterum post festum Sancti Michaelis;*[49,50] This clause extendeth to the enquiry of felonies, common nusances and other misdeeds, the view of frankpledges, and to all things inquirable in the Tourn. Now by this clause it is provided that the Article of the Tourn concerning the view of frankpledge, being here understood in a particular sense, shall be dealt withall by the Sheriffe in his Tourn but once in the year, viz. at the Tourn holden after Easter, and so it hath been formerly expounded; and therefore it was well resolved is 24 H. 8 that this clause of the Statute of Magna Charta, is to be understood of the Leet of the Tourn, and not of other Leets, and so without question is the Law holden at this day, That he that claimes a Leet by Charter, must hold it at the same dayes which are contained in the Charter, and he that claimes it by prescription may claime to hold it once or twice every yeare, at any such dayes as shall upon reasonable warning be appointed, if the usage hath been so, so that it hath been kept at uncertain times, or else it ought to be kept at

---

43. Pasch. 5. Jac. lib. fo. 78. Bulleins case.
44. [*Ed.:* Times change, and we change with them.]
45. [*Ed.:* The true institution of this court has vanished, and but a shadow thereof remains to this day: we have a certain *senatusconsultum* (statute), but it rests in the records and is like a sword hidden in its sheath.]
46. Cicero.
47. Mirror ca. 1. § 117. & ca. 5. § 2.
48. [*Ed.:* The sheriff shall not make his tour through the hundred except twice a year,]
49. [*Ed.:* that is to say, Once after Easter and again after Michaelmas;]
50. 6 H. 7. 2. & 3.

such certain dayes and times, as by prescription hath been certainly used;[51] and the next words to this clause bee, *Ita scilicet quod quilibet habeat libertates suas, quas habuit, &c.*[52] doe explaine the meaning of this Chapter, that is extended not to the Leets of the Subjects, that they should have their liberties, as before they had; and this also appeareth by the conclusion of this Chapter. *Et quod Vicecomes, &c. contentus sit de eo quod Vicecomes habere consuevit de Visu suo faciendo;*[53] So as it must be *Visus suus,*[54] the Sheriffes View, which of necessity must be parcell of the Tourn; and it is said in the Mirror, that this view of frankpledge (parcell of the Tourn) should be made once every yeare.

"the View of Frankpledge shall be so done, &c."

Here it appeareth that the view of frankpledge should have two ends. 1, *Quod*
[73] *pax* | *nostra teneatur.* 2. *Quod Trithinga teneatur integra.*[55]

For the first, that the Kings peace might be kept; the right institution of the view of *Franke pledge,*[56] and whereon the name came is to be considered, which is as followeth.

Franci plegii. i. Liberi fidejussores, free suretics or pledges; and here it is said *fiat visus de Francis plegiis, ita scilicet quod pax nostra teneatur,*[57] that is, let the view of pledges or sureties for free-men be made, so that our peace may be holden: Now the institution hereof, for the keeping of the Kings peace, was, that every free-man, at his age of 12. years, should in the Leet (if he were in any) or in the Tourne, (if he were not in any Leet) take the oath of alleageance to the King, and that pledges or sureties should be found in manner hereafter expressed for his truth to the King, and to all his people, or else to be kept in prison;[58] This *Franke pledge* consisted most commonly of ten housholds,

---

51. 30 H. 6. Leet 11. 24 H. 8. Br. Leet 23. 22 H. 6. 14. 8 H 74. 12 H. 7. 15. 38 H. 6. 7. Dier 7 Eliz, 233, 234.

52. [*Ed.:* That is to say, so that everyone shall have their liberties which they had, etc.]

53. [*Ed.:* And that [the sheriff should not seek exactions] etc. but be content with what sheriffs are accustomed to have for making their view;]

54. [*Ed.:* his view.]

55. [*Ed.:* Firstly that our peace be kept, and, secondly, That the tithing shall be kept whole.]

56. [*Ed.:* Free sureties.]

57. [*Ed.:* let the view of frankpledge be made, so that our peace shall be kept,]

58. Bract. lib. 3. f. 124. Int. leges Canuti fol. 108. 19. Int. leges Edw. regis fol. 132. cap. de friborgis. Bract. ubi sup. Lamb. verbo centuria & decuria.

which the Saxons called *Theothung*, in the North parts they call them *Tenmentale*, in other places of England *Tithing*, here in this chapter *Trithinga. i. Decemvirale collegium*,[59] whereof the masters of the nine families (who were bound) were of the Saxons called Freoborgh, which in some places is to this day called free Barrowe. i.[60] Free surety, or Franke pledge, and the Master of the tenth houshold was by the Saxon called by divers names, viz. *Theothung-mon*, to this day in the West called *Tythingman*, and *Tihenheofod* and *Freoborher. i. Capitalis plegius*, chiefe pledge: and these ten masters of families, were bound one for anothers family, that each man of their severall families should stand to the Law,[61] or if he were not forth coming, that they should answere for the injury or offence by him committed, *De eo autem qui fugam ceperit, diligenter inquirend' si fuerit in franco plegio, & decenna, tunc erit decenna in misericordia coram Justitiariis nostris, quia non habent ipsum malefactorem ad rectum.*[62,63]

Hereby it appeareth, that the precinct of this *frank pledge* was called *decenna*,[64] because it consisted most commonly, as hath been said, of tenne housholds, and every man of these severall housholds, for whom the pledge or surety was taken were called *decennarii*, because every particular person in the Kingdome was of one *decenna* or other, which names are continued as shadowes of antiquity to this day.[65] *Ordeine suit ancientment, que nul ne demurrast en le realme, sil ne suit en dizein & plevye de frank homes, appenc aux visc' de viewer un sois per an' franke pledges & les plevys, &c.*[66,67]

By the due execution of this Law, such peace (whereof this chapter speaketh) was universally holden within this Realme, as no injuries, homicides, robberies, thefts, riots, tumults, or other offences were committed; so as a man with a

59. [*Ed.:* Tithing, that is, a collection of ten men.]

60. Bract. fol. 19. b.

61. Brit. ubi sup.

62. [*Ed.:* If someone takes flight, it shall be diligently enquired whether he was in frankpledge and tithing, and then the tithing will be in mercy before our justices because they do not have that wrongdoer to do right.]

63. Bract. l. 3. f. 124.

64. [*Ed.:* tithing.]

65. Brit. cap. 12. Fleta lib. 1. cap. 27. acc.

66. [*Ed.:* It was anciently ordained that no one should live in the realm unless he was in a tithing and pledge of free men. It belongs to sheriffs to view the frankpledges and their sureties twice a year, etc.]

67. Mirror. cap. 1. § 17.

white wand might safely have ridden before the Conquest, with much money
about him, without any weapon throughout England; and one saith truely,
conjectura est, eaq; non levis, haud ita multis statuisse prisca tempora sceleribus,
quippe quibus rapinae, furto, caedi, plurimisq; aliis sceleribus mulctae impone-
bantur pecuniariae, cuim hiis hac nostra tempestate, nos omnibus merito capitis
poenam irrogamus, &c.[68,69]

"and that the Tything be wholly kept."

Trithinga or *Tithinga* is expounded for *Theothinga,* which signifieth the
Frankpledge of tenne housholds, as hath been said, and it is notably expounded by Fleta,[70] which there you may read at large, the sense hereof is,
quod Trithinga, sive Theothinga. i. Decemvirale collegium teneatr integrum.[71]
that no man be not within some decenna or other, so as he may be brought
forth to stand to right if he shall offend: *Olim Trithinga significabat tria vel*
quatuor hundreda, quod autem in Trithinga definiri non poterat, ferebatur in
scyram.[72,73]

What persons shall come to the Tourne and Leete &c., and who be exempted, see the Statute of Marlebridge, and the auncient authors.[74]

"the time of King Henry our Grandfather."

Twice repeated in this Chapter: vid. before Cap. 15. 16.

[74] | See the exposition of this Statute Rot. Claus. anno 18. H. 3. nu. 10.

68. [*Ed.:* It is no light conjecture that in early times, when there were far fewer crimes, pecuniary mulcts were imposed for rape, theft, and killing, and many other crimes, whereas in our time we consider all of them worthy of capital punishment, etc.]

69. Lamb. verb. æstimatio capitis.

70. Fleta lib. 2. c. 54. § de Trithingis.

71. [*Ed.:* that the trithing, or theothing, that is, a collection of ten men, shall be kept whole.]

72. Lamb. Int. leges Sanct. Edw. nu. 34. Merton. c. 10.

73. [*Ed.:* At one time the trithing signified three or four hundreds, and what could not be determined in the trithing was carried to the shire.]

74. Marlebridg c. 10. Mirror. c. 1. § 16. Bract. lib. 3. fol. 124. Brit. 19. b. Fleta lib. 1. c. 29. lib. 2. cap. 45.

"and that the Sheriff seek no occasions; and that he be content with . . . the Sheriff was wont to have for his View-making in the time of King Henry our Grandfather."[75]

By the Common law, to avoid all extortion and grievance of the Subject, no Sherife, Coroner, Goaler or other of the Kings Ministers ought to take any reward for doing of his office, but only of the King; and this appeareth by our books, and in so declared and enacted by act of *[76] Parliament in the 3. Edw. 1. And a penalty added to the prohibition of the Common law by that Act: And Fortescue cap. 24. saith, *Vicecomes jurabit super sancta Dei Evangelia, inter articulos alios, quod non aliquid recipiet colore, aut causa officii sui, ab aliquo alio, quam a Rege.*[77]

But after that this rule of the Common law was altered, and that the sherife, Coroner, Goaler, and other the Kings ministers, might in some case take of the subject, it is not credible what extortions, & oppressions have thereupon ensued. So dangerous a thing it is, to make or alter any of the rules or fundamentall points of the Common law, which in truth are the maine pillars, and supporters of the fabrick of the Common-wealth, as elsewhere I have noted more at large, and yet not so largely, as the weight of the matter deserveth.[78]

"and that he be content with . . . the Sheriff was wont to have, &c."[79]

These words are not to be intended of any reward, &c. (for the sherife by Law, as hath been said, could take no reward for doing of his office) but of the profits of the Court of the Tourn, and such only as were accustomed in the raigne of Henry the second. So they must be very auncient, for the which the sherife should (by an auncient law) pay a certaine summe *de proficuis comitatus,*[80] and should be charged in the Exchequer for this certain summe.

75. Mirror. c. 2. §5. Britton. fol. 3. b. 6. a. 18. b. 37. b. Fleta. lib. 1. c. 18. § Item. fi officium. & lib. 2. c. 39. 27. Ass. p. 14. 42. E. 3. 5. 23. H. 6. cap. 10. 17. 1. H. 8. c. 7. 33. H. 8. cap. 22. 21. H. 7. fol. 17.

76. W. 1. cap. 26.

77. [*Ed.:* The sheriff shall swear upon the holy gospels of God, amongst his articles, that he shall not accept anything by reason of his office from anyone other than the king.]

78. See the preface to the 4. part of my reports.

79. 42. E. 3. 5. 38. H. 6. 7. 6. H. 7. 2. 3.

80. [*Ed.:* from the profits of the county,]

And it is to be observed, that if any man be grieved contrary to the purview of this act, he may, as hath been said, for his reliefe therein, have an action up on this Statute, albeit no action be expressly given, which in this, and many other like cases upon the branches of Magna Charta, is worthy of observation.[81]

Chapter 36

It shall not be lawful from henceforth to any to give his Lands to any Religious House, and to take the same Land again, to hold of the same House: Nor shall it be lawful to any House of Religion to take the Lands of any, and to lease the same to him of whom he received it. If any from henceforth give his Lands to any Religious House, and thereupon be convict, the Gift shall be utterly void, and the Land shall accrue to the Lord of the Fee.[1]

This Chapter is excellently abridged, according to the effect thereof, and notably expounded by a Parliament holden by King Edward the first, sonne of Henry the third, the words whereof are these, of late (viz. anno 9. H. 3. cap. 36.) it was provided that religious men should not enter into the fees of any without licence, and will of the chiefe Lords, of whom such fees been holden immediately,[2] whereby it appeareth, that by this Chapter of Magna Charta, a [75]   gift of lands to any reli-l-gious house was prohibited, notwithstanding the Religious house gave not the same back again to hold of the same house, &c. but kept the Lands so given unto themselves in their own hands: and in that case, that the Land should incurre to the Lord of the fee, consider well the words; and the interpretation is worthy of observation for the interpretation of other Statutes in like cases.

For the word *Mortmain*,[3] see the first part of the Institutes.[4]

There were two causes of making of this Statute: one that the services that were due out of such fees, and which in the beginning were created for the defence of the Realme, were unduly withdrawn. 2. The chiefe Lords did lose their Escheats, Wardships, Reliefes, and the like; for which causes, divers prov-

---

81. Regist. 16. 174. 175. F. N. B. 161. d. Marleb. cap. 10.

1. Mirror. c. 5. §. 2. Glanv. 1. 6. c. 7.

2. 3. E. 4. 12. See the 1. part of the Institutes sect. 133. 157. Stat. de 7. E. 1. de religiosis. 23. H. 3. Ass. 436. Britton. fol. 32. b. Fleta. lib. 3. cap. 5.

3. [*Ed.*: inalienable possession, particularly alienation to a corporation.]

4. First part of the Institutes. Cap. Frankalmoigne.

ident Lords at the Creation of the Seigniory had a clause in the deed of feoffment, *Quod licitum sit donatori rem datam dare, vel vendere cui voluerit, exceptis
viris religiosis, & Judaeis.*[5] Vide Bracton, libro 1. fol. 13.[6] Many of these deads
I have seene.

But the Ecclesiasticall persons (who in this were to be commended, that
they had ever the best learned men in the Law, that they could get, of their
Councell)[7] found many wayes to creep out of this Statute, viz. religious men;
as Abbots, Priors, and other Ecclesiasticall persons regular, to purchase Lands
holden of themselves, or take leases for long term for years, and many other
devices they had to escape out of this Statute: and Bishops, Parsons, and other
Ecclesiastical persons secular took themselves to be out of this Statute.

The said Statute of 7. Edw. I. intended to provide against these devices, in
these words, *Quod nullus religiosus, aut alius quicunque*[8] (i. other whatsoever
of like quality of being, a body politique, or corporate, Ecclesiastical, or Lay,
sole, or aggregate of many,)[9] *terras aut tenementa aliqua emere, vel vendere sub
colore donationis aut termini;*[10] And to presvent all other inventions and evasions added these generall words, *Aut ratione alterius tituli cujuscunq; terras
aut tenementa ab aliquo recipere aut alio quovis modo**[11] *arte vel ingenio sibi
appropriare praesumat, sub forisfactura eorundem.*[12]

A man would have thought that this should have prevented all new devices,
but they found also an evasions out of this Statute, for this Statute of 7. Edw.
1. extended but to gifts, alienations, and other conveyances made between
them and others, *Arte vel ingenio, &c.*[13] and therefore they gave over them;
And they pretending a title to the land (that they meant to get) brought a
Praecipe qod reddar,[14] against the Tenant of the land, and he by consent and

---

5. [*Ed.:* That it should be permissible for the donor to give or sell the thing given to anyone he wishes,
except to religious men and Jews.]

6. Bract. li. 1. fol. 13.

7. Fleta lib. 3. cap. 5.

8. [*Ed.:* That no religious person or other whatsoever.]

9. 15 R. 2. cap. 5. 29. Ass. p. 17. Br. 29. H. 8. Mortmain 39.

10. [*Ed.:* shall buy or sell any lands or tenements under colour of a gift or term.]

11. * These words are notably explained. 15 R. 2. ca. 5. 19. H. 6. 56. 41 E. 3. 16. 41 E 3. 21. 29 H. 8. Br.
Mortmain 39. 17. E. 3. 59. 21. E. 3. 46. Rot. Parliam. 5. R. 2. nu. 92. Quant le terre est per covin convey
al Roy.

12. [*Ed.:* Or by reason of any other title whatsoever receive from anyone, or in any other way by craft
or ingenuity presume to appropriate to themselves, lands or tenements, on pain of forfeiture thereof.]

13. [*Ed.:* by craft or ingenuity.]

14. [*Ed.:* Writ requiring the addressee to act or show cause for inaction.]

collusion should make default, and thereupon they should recover the land, and enter by judgement of Law, *Et sic fieret fraus Statuto.*[15]

When this new invention was provided for, and taken away by the Statute of W. 2. yet found they out an evasion out of all these Statutes,[16] for now they would neither get any Land by purchase, gift, lease, or recovery, but they caused the Lands to be conveyed by feoffement, or in other manner to divers persons, and their heires, to the use of them and their successors, by reason whereof they took the profits; but this was enacted by the Statute of 15 R. 2.[17] to be mortmain within the forfeiture of the said Statute of 7. Edw. 1.

But the foundation of all these Statutes, was this Chapter of Magna Charta.

Chapter 37

[76] | Escuage from henceforth shall be taken like as it was wont to be in the time of King Henry our Grandfather.

"Escuage."[1]

Vide for this the first part of the Institutes, lib. 2. Cap. Escuage. sect. 95.

"the time of King Henry our Grandfather."

Here is another reference to the raigne of King Henry the second. See for this before, Cap. 15. &c.

Chapter 38

Reserving to all Archbishops, Bishops, Abbots, Priors, Templars, Hospitallers, Earls, Barons, and all Persons, as well Spiritual as Temporal, all their free Liberties and free Customs, which they have had in time passed. And all these Customs and Liberties aforesaid, which We have granted to be holden within this our Realm, as much as appertaineth to Us and our Heirs, we shall observe; and all

---

15. [*Ed.:* And thus a fraud was made upon the statute.]
16. W. 2. cap. 32. Fleta lib. 3. cap. 5. 45 E. 3. 19.
17. 15 R. 2. cap. 5. 8 H. 4 16.
1. Fleta lib. 2. ca. 60.

Men of this our Realm, as well Spiritual as Temporal, as much as in them is, shall observe the same against all Persons, in like wise. And for this our Gift and Grant of these Liberties, and of other contained in our Charter of Liberties of our Forest, the Archbishops, Bishops, Abbots, Priors, Earls, Barons, Knights, Freeholders, and other our Subjects, have given unto Us the Fifteenth Part of all their Moveables. And We have granted unto them on the other part, that neither We nor our Heirs shall procure or do any thing whereby the Liberties in this Charter contained shall be infringed or broken. And if any thing be procured by any person contrary to the premises, it shall be had of no force nor effect. These being Witnesses; Lord B. Archbishop of Canterbury, E. Bishop of London, J. Bishop of Bathe, P. of Winchester, H. of Lincoln, R. of Salisbury, W. of Rochester, W. of Worcester, J. of Ely, H. of Hereford, R. of Chichester, W. of Exeter, Bishops; the Abbot of St. Edmonds, the Abbot of St. Albans, the Abbot of Bello, the Abbot of St. Augustine's in Canterbury, the Abbot of Evesham, the Abbot of Westminster, the Abbot of Bourgh St. Peter, the Abbot of Reding, the Abbot of Abindon, the Abbot of Malmsbury, the Abbot of Winchcomb, the Abbot of Hyde, the Abbot of Certesey, the Abbot of Sherburn, the Abbot of Cerne, the Abbot of Abbotebir, the Abbot of Middleton, the Abbot of Seleby, the Abbot of Cirencester; H. de Burgh Justice, H. Earl of Chester and Lincoln, W. Earl of Salisbury, W. Earl of Warren, G. de Clare Earl of Gloucester and Hereford, W. de Ferrars Earl of Derby, W. de Mandeville Earl of Essex, H. de Bygod Earl of Norfolk, W. Earl of Albemarle, H. Earl of Hereford, J. Constable of Chester, R. de Ros, R. Fitzwalter, R. de Vyponte, W. de Bruer, R. de Muntefichet, P. Fitzherbert, W. de Aubenie, F. Gresly, F. de Breus, J. de Monemue, J. Fitzallen, H. de Mortimer, W. de Beauchamp, W. de St. John, P. de Mauly, Brian de Lisle, Thomas de Multon, R. de Argenteyn, G. de Nevil, W. de Mauduit, J. de Balun, and others.

This Chapter doth consist of five parts.

First it is enacted, That all the Liberties, and Free Customes, which any | [77] Archbishop, Bishop, Abbot, Prior, Templar, Hospitaller, Earle, Baron, or any person either Ecclestasticall or secular, have had, be safe, that is, whole without prejudice unto them, for the words be *Salvae sint omnibus Archiepiscopis, &c. omnes libertates, &c.*[1] all the liberties, &c. be safe to all Archibishops, &c. so as this is no saving to them, but in effect, an Act that they should enjoy them: for regularly a saving in an Act of Parliament enlargeth not, nor extendeth to

---

1. [*Ed.:* let all liberties, etc. be saved to all archbishops, etc.]

any new thing, but preserveth a right or interest, that is former to things contained in the Act, which by the words of the Act might have been given away. But this clause doth enlarge, and extendeth to all other liberties, and free customes, which any Subject Ecclesiasticall, or Temporall ought to have; and therefore the English Translation, both in this and many other places of this great Charter, is very vicious. But it is principally to be observed, that here is not any saving at all for the King, his heires, or Successors, to the end that the King, his heirs, and Successors, against all pretences of evasions, should be bound by all the branches of both these Charters.

The second is, that all the Customes, and Liberties, which the King had graunted to be holden within his Realme, for him and his heires, the King himselfe and his heires, as much as appertained to him or them, should observe and keepe.

The third is, that all the men of this Realme, as well of the Clergy as of the Laity, the said Customes and Liberties for themselves and their heirs, as much as to them appertained, should observe and keepe.

This is the chiefe felicity of a Kingdome, when good Lawes are reciprocally of Prince and people (as is here undertaken) duly observed.

The fourth is, that for this gift and graunt by the King, of the Liberties contained in this great Charter, and of others contained in the Kings Charter of Liberties of the Forest, the Archbishops, Bishops, Abbots, Priors, Earles, Barons, Knights, Free-holders, and other the Kings Subjects, Citizens, and Burgesses, (assembled in Parliament) gave unto the King one fifteenth;[2] which proveth, that as the fifteenth was graunted by Parliament, so was this great Charter also graunted by authority of the same; But since this time the manner of the fifteenth is altered; for now the fifteenth, which is also called the Task, is not originally set upon the polles, as at this time it was, but now the fifteenth is certainly rated upon every Towne. And this was by vertue of the Kings Commissions into every County of England in 8 Edw. 3. taxations were made of all the Cities, Boroughes, and Towns in England, and recorded in the Exchequer, and that rate was at that time the fifteenth part of the value of every Town, and therefore retaineth the name of the fifteenth still.[3]

And after the fifteenth is graunted by Parliament, then the inhabitants rate

2. Hil. 3. Jacobi. lib. 8. The Princes Case.
3. Rot. pat. 6. E. 3. 2. part. nu. 26.

themselves for payment thereof, and if one towne bee joyned with another in the rate of the totall, and subdivided on each a certain rate in that Commission, and the one is rated too low, and the other too high, there lieth a Writ called, *Ad aequaliter taxand'*[4] to be taken out of the Exchequer to rate the Townes equally. The Subsidie is uncertaine, because it is set upon the person, in respect of his Lands, or goods, which commonly doe ebb and flow.

The fift is, that the King did graunt for him, and his heires, that neither he, nor his heires, shall seeke out any thing, whereby the liberties in this Charter contained may be broken, or weakned: And if by any man against this Charter any thing should be sought out, it should be of no value, and holden for nought. And all these doe evidently appeare in this Chapter.

The sixt and last is *Hiis testibus.*[5]

It is true, that of auncient time nothing passed from the King of Franchises, Liberties, Priviledges, Mannors, Lands, Tenements, and Hereditaments of any estate of inheritance, but it was by the advice of his Councell expressed under *Hiis testibus,* as it was then, and continues to this day in the creation of any to any degree of Nobility, for thereto *Hiis testibus* is still used.

This conclusion of the Kings graunts with *Hiis testibus* was used by King | Henry the third and his Progenitors Kings of this Realme before him, and [78] by his son Edward the first and by Edward the second and Edward the third after him: Afterwards, in the beginning of the raigne of R. 2. I finde the clause of *Hiis testibus* was left out, and in stead thereof came in *Teste me ipso*[6] in this manner, *In cujus rei testimonium has literas nostras fieri fecimus patentes:*[7] *Teste me ipso,* which since by all his Successors Kings, and Queens of this Realme (except in Creations) hath been used.

Those that had *Hiis testibus,* were called Chartae, as this Charter is called Magna Charta, and so is Charta de Foresta, &c. and those other that be *Teste me ipso,* are called Letters Patents, being so named in the clause of *In cujus rei testimonium has literas nostras fieri fecimus patentes.*[8]

And this was the auncient forme also of the Deeds of Subjects, concluding with *Hiis testibus,* which continued untill, and in the raigne of Hen. 8. but

---

4. [*Ed.:* For taxing equally.]
5. [*Ed.:* These being witnesses.]
6. [*Ed.:* Witness myself.]
7. [*Ed.:* In witness whereof we have caused these our letters to be made patent:]
8. [*Ed.:* In witness whereof we have caused these our letters to be made patent.]

now is wholly omitted, and now the witnesses are subscribed under the Deed, or endorsed thereupon.[9]

Now upon this occasion to treat how these clauses, *Datum per manum nostram, per manum Cancellarii nostri, per ipsum Custodem, & Concilium, &c.*[10] entred in, and went out: when these clauses, *De gratia speciali,*[11] and *Ex certa scientia, & mero motu*[12] began, (which continue to this day) and the cause and reason of the inserting of the same; and when and wherefore these clauses were subscribed under the Letters Patents, *Per ipsum Regem, Per breve de privato sigillo, Authoritate Parliamenti, &c.*[13] came in, (which still doe continue) would aske a severall Treastise of it selfe, and not pertinent to our purpose for the understanding of this Charter of Magna Charta, and therefore purposely I speake not of them.

Here be Witnesses to this great Charter, a great number of Reverend, and Honourable personages, in all 63. of which there were of the Clergy 31. whereof there were 12. Bishops, and 19. Abbots, and Hugh de Burgo Chiefe Justice, and 31 Earles and Barons, as hath been said before.

Besides, it was established by Authority of Parliament, which was holden at Westminster, in forme of a Charter, as many others have been, for which, as hath been said likewise, by Parliament the Lords and Commons gave a fifteenth. Of Acts of Parliament in form of a Charter, you may reade at large in the Princess Case, and therefore need not to be recited.[14]

[79]

| Statute of Merton
Editum Anno 20. Hen. 3. (1236)[1]

It is called the Statute of Merton, because the Parliament was holden at the Monastery of the Canons regular of Merton, seaven miles distant from the City of London, which Monastery was founded by Gislebert a noble Norman,

---

9. See the first part of the Institutes. sect. 1.

10. [*Ed.:* Given by our hand; by the hand of our chancellor; by the keeper himself and the council, etc.]

11. [*Ed.:* Of [our] especial grace.]

12. [*Ed.:* Of [our] certain knowledge and mere motion.]

13. [*Ed.:* By the king himself; by writ of privy seal; by authority of parliament, etc.]

14. Hil. 3. Jac. in Cancellaria. The Princes Case. Lib. 8. fol. 19.

1. Bracton li. 2 c. 96. saith it was in anno 18. Hen. 3.

that came in with the Conqueror. And this is that Monastery of Merton, the Prior whereof had a great case in Law, which long depended between him and the Prior of Bingham.[2]

It was Provided in the Court of our Lord the King, holden at Merton on Wednesday the Morrow after the Feast of St. Vincent, the 20th year of the Reign of King Henry the Son of King John, before William Archbishop of Canterbury, and other his Bishops and Suffragans and before the greater part of the Earls and Barons of England there being assembled; for the Coronation of the said King, and Hellianor the Queen, about which they were all called; where it was treated for the Commonwealth of the Realm upon the Articles underwritten; thus it was provided and granted, as well of the foresaid Archbishops, Bishops, Earls and Barons, as of the King himself and others.

"Before William Archbishop of Canterbury, and other his Bishops and Suffragans."

Suffraganeus properly is a vicegerant of a Bishop, instituted to aid and assist him in his spirituall office, and is so called *a suffragiis:* Of these you may read in the Statutes of 26. Hen. 8. 1. & 2. Phil. & Mariae. 1. Eliz.[3] And where some copies have *Coram Cantuar' Archiepiscopo, & Coepiscopis & suffraganeis;*[4] this latter conjunction (&) is more then ought to be; for *suffraganeis suis* must referre to *Coepiscopis,* that is, that the Bishops should aide and assist the Archbishop with their suffrages: for other Suffragans, which were Vicegerents of Bishops, never had Voyce in Parliament, because they held not *per Baroniam,*[5] as all Bishops doe, and many Abbots and Priors, as hath beene said, did, in respect whereof they were Lords of Parliament.[6]

"For the Coronation of the said King."

The king was formerly Crowned at Gloucester on the 18, of October, in the beginning of the first yeare of his raigne, then being about nine yeares old:

---

2. 18 Edw. 4. 22. 19 Edw. 4. 2,7. 20 Edw. 4. 16. 21 Edw. 4. 60.
3. 26 Hen. 8. cap. 14. 1 & 2 Ph. & Mar. ca. 8. 1 Eliz. ca. 1.
4. [*Ed.:* Before the archbishop of Canterbury and [his] co-bishops and suffragans.]
5. [*Ed.:* by a barony,]
6. See the first part of the Institutes. Cap. Frankalmoigne.

And here it appeareth that in the twentieth yeare of his raigne, he was Crowned again, then being about 29. yeares old, twice Crowned, as King Henry the second, and King John before him had been, and as King Richard the second after him was.

"And Hellianor the Queen."

This Elianor was daughter, and one of the heires of Raymond Berengary Earle of Province, she was sister to the Earle of Province, and to Boniface, Archbishop of Canterbury, and she was Crowned at Westminister.

[80] | She survived the King, and of a Crowned Queen became a professed Nun in Ambresbury, and died a Nun there, in the nineteenth yeare of her Widowhood.

The Statutes enacted at this Parliament are divided into eleven Chapters.

Cap. IX.*

[96] | To the King's Writ of Bastardy,[1] whether one being born before Matrimony, may inherit in like Manner as he that is born after Matrimony, all the Bishops answered, That they would not, nor could not answer to it; because it was directly against the common Order of the Church. And all the Bishops instanted the Lords, that they would consent that all such as were born afore Matrimony should be legitimate, as well as they that be born within Matrimony, as to the Succession of Inheritance, forsomuch as the Church accepteth such for legitimate. And all the Earls and Barons with one voice answered, that they would not change the Laws of the Realm, which hitherto have been used and approved.

"Against the common Order of the Church."[2]

For the better understanding of this branch, it is to be known, that in the time of Pope Alexander the third, (who lived Anno Domini 1160, which was Anno 6 Hen. 2.) This constitution was made, that children borne before solemnization of Matrimony, where Matrimony followed, should be as legitimate

---

* [*Ed.:* Note sections 1–8 are here omitted.]

1. See the first part of the Institutes. sect. 399, 400. & 188.

2. Vide Decret. Gregorii 9. fol. 260. col. 1.

to inherit unto their Auncestors, as those that were borne after Matrimony, and thereupon the Statute saith, *Ecclesia tales habet pro legitimis.*[3]

Of this Canon, or constitution Glanvill writeth thus,[4] *Orta est quaestio, si quis antequam pater matrem suam desponsaverat fuerit genitus vel natus, utrum talis filius sit legitimus haeres, cum postea matrem suam desponsaverat: Et quidem licet secundum Canones & leges Romanas talis filius sit legitimus haeres, tamen secundum jus & consuetudinem Regni nullo modo tanquam haeres in haereditate sustinetur, vel haereditatem de jure Regni petere potest.*[5]

And herewith doe agree not onely other auncient Authors,[6] but the constant opinion of the Judges in all succession of ages ever since, of the auncient Law of England. Hereupon these two conclusions doe follow:

1. That any forein Canon or constitution made by authority of the Pope, being (as Glanvill saith) *Contra jus & consuetudinem Regni,*[7] bindeth not untill it be allowed by Act of Parliament, which the Bishops here prayed it might have beene; for no Law, or Custome of England can be taken away, abrogated, or annulled, but by authority of Parliament.[8]

2. That although the Bishops were Spirituall Persons, and in those dayes had a great dependency on the Pope, yet in case of generall bastardy, when the King wrote to them to certifie, who was lawfull heire to any lands, or other inheritance, they ought to certifie according to the Law, and custome of England, and not according to the Romane Canons, and constitutions, which were contrary to the Law, and custome of England, wherein the Bishops sought at this Parliament to be relieved.[9]

See the first part of the Institutes, sect. 399. & 400. and adde thereunto:

Assisa venit, &c. Si Nicholaus de Lewkenor Pat' Thom' de Lewkenor fuit seisitus, &c. de manerio de Southmyms quod Rogerus de Lewkenor tenet, qui dicit

---

3. [*Ed.:* The Church regards them as legitimate.]

4. Glanv. li. 7. c. 15.

5. [*Ed.:* A question has arisen, if someone is begotten or born before his father married his mother, whether such a son is the legitimate heir if the father later marries the mother. Although according to the Canon and Roman laws such a son is the legitimate heir, nevertheless according to the law and custom of the realm he can in no way be maintained in the inheritance as heir nor claim the inheritance by the law of the realm.]

6. Bract. li. 5. fo. 41. 6., 417. Fleta lib. 6. c. 38. Fortescue c. 39. 11 Ass. p. 20.

7. [*Ed.:* Against the law and custom of the realm.]

8. 4 Edw. I. Stat. de Bigamis c. 9. simile.

9. Glanv. ubi supra.

quod ipse est frater ipsius Thomae antenatus de eodem Patre, & eadem Matre,
& est seisitus de pradictis tenementis, & clamat per eundem discensum, et petit
Judiciū.[10] *Thom' dic' quod Rogerus non potest clamare per eundē descensum, quia*
dicit quod idem Rogerus natus fuit extra Sponsalia, &c. Et quia idem Tho' non
potest didicere, quin idem Rogerus sit frater ipsius Tho' antenatus de eodem Patre,
& eadem Matre, & post mortem praedicti Nicholai Patris, &c.[11] *intravit in eisdem*
tenementis ut filius ejus & haeres, Consideratum est quod praedictus Rogerus ind'
Judgement. *sine die. Et Tho. Nich. cap' per Assisam, et sit in misericordia, &c.*

Note by this judgement that the bastard eigne to this intent is accounted
heire, and of the blood with the *Mulier puisne,* as the *Mulier puisne* cannot
have an *Assise of Mortdanc*[12] against him.

We remember not that we have read in any Book of the legitimation, or
adoption of an heire, but onely in Bracton lib. 2. cap. 29. fol. 63. b. and that
to no little purpose; but the surest adoption of an heire, is by learned advice,
to make good assurance of the land, &c.

"And all the Earls and Barons with one voice answered, that they would not
change the Laws of the Realm, which hitherto have been used and approved."[13]

The Nobility of England have ever had the Laws of England in great estimation
and reverence, as their best birth-right, and so have the Kings of England as
their principall royalty and right belonging to their Crown and dignity: This
made King Henry the first that noble King sirnamed *Beauclerk,*[14] to write to
[98]   Pope Pascall, *Notam habeat sanctitas vestra, quod me vivente (auxiliante| Deo)*

---

10. Pasch. 18. Edw. 1. in Banco Rot. 80. Mid. in Ass. de Mordaunc'.
11. Vide Mic. 15 Edw. I. in Banc. Rot. 129. Hertf. Tr. 15. Edw. I. ibid. Rot. 60. Not.
12. [*Ed.:* An assize comes [to make recognition], etc. whether Nicholas de Lewkenor, father of Thomas de Lewkenor, was seised, etc. of the manor of South Mimms, which Roger of Lewkenor holds. Roger says that he is the elder brother of the selfsame Thomas, born of the same father and mother, and is seised of the aforesaid tenements, and claims by the same descent, and he prays judgment. Thomas says that Roger cannot claim by the same descent, because he says that the same Roger was born outside espousals, etc. And because the same Thomas cannot deny that the same Roger is the elder brother of the selfsame Thomas, born of the same father and mother, and that after the death of the aforesaid Nicholas his father, etc. he entered in the same tenements as his son and heir, it is decided that the aforesaid Roger do go therein without day. And let Thomas take nothing by the assize, but be in mercy, etc.]
13. See the first part of the Institutes. sect. 400.
14. Chart. Hen. I.

dignitates & usus regni nostri Angliae non imminuentur, & fi ego (quod absit) in tanta me dejectione ponerem, optimates mei & totus Angliae populus id nullo modo pateretur.[15]

And it is worthy the observation, how dangerous it is (as elsewhere hath been often noted) to change an ancient Maxime of the Common Law.

Some have written,[16] that William the Conquerour being borne out of matrimony, Robert his reputed father did after marry Arlot his mother, and that thereby he had right by the Civil and Cannon Law, but that is *contra legem Angliae*,[17] as here it appeareth. And during this Parliament in the 20. year of Hen. 3. it may be collected by the 23. and 24. Epistles of Robert Grostead then Bishop of Lincoln directed to William Rawleighe (Priest) then one of the Kings Justices, that this matter to bring the *nati ante matrimonium*[18] to be made legitimate was vehemently laboured by the Clergie: And in the 26. Epistle to the Bishop of Canterbury, he findeth fault with the Arch-bishop, for that the King and his Councell had resolved that the Law and Custome, of the Realme in this point should continue still: Whereby it appeareth, that not onely the Nobles, but the King himselfe was against it.

And in the Letters which all the Nobilitie of England by assent of the whole cominalty assembled in Parliament at Lincoln wrote to Pope Boniface, it is this conteyned,[19] *Ad observationem & defensionem libertatum, consuetudinum, & legum paternarum ex debito praestiti sacramenti astringimur, quae manute-nebimus toto posse, totisque viribus cum dei auxilio defendemus, nec etiam per-mittimus aut aliquatenus permittemus, sicut nec possumus nec debemus praemissa tam insolita, indebita, praejudicialia, & alias inaudita dominum nostrum regem, etiam si vellet, facere, seu quomodolibet attemptare:*[20] (and there the inconve-

15. [*Ed.:* May your holiness take note that while I am alive, by the help of God, the dignities and usages of our realm of England will not be diminished, and if (which must not be) I fall down in such matters, my nobles and the whole people of England will in no way allow it.]

16. William Malms. lib. 3. circa initiū Ingulphus lib. 6. cap. 19. See the Custumer de Nor. ca. 27. fo. 42 & 44.

17. [*Ed.:* against the law of England.]

18. [*Ed.:* born before marriage.]

19. Rot. Par. 28. E. 1. apud Lincoln.

20. [*Ed.:* We are constrained by the oath we have taken to observe and defend the liberties, customs and laws of our fatherland, which with the assistance of God we will maintain with all power and defend with all force, and, just as we cannot and ought not, neither shall we permit the foregoing, as unaccustomed, undue, prejudicial and previously unheard of within our realm.]

niences are set down) *praecipae cum praemissa cederent manifeste in exhere-dationem Juris coronae Regis*[21] *Angliae & regiae dignitatis, ac subversionem status ejusdem Regni notoriam, necnon in praejudicium libertatum, consuetudinum & legum paternarum,*[22] sealed by the severall seales of Armes of 104, Earles and Barons, and in the name of all the comminalty of England. And to that effect King Edward the first with also to the Pope.

"The Laws of the Realm."

Here our common lawes are aptly and properly called the lawes of England because they are appropriated to this Kingdome of England as most apt and fit for the government thereof, and have no dependancy upon any forreigne law whatsoever, no not upon the civill or cannon law other then in cafes allowed by the laws of England, as partly hath been touched before: and therefore the Poet spake truly hereof, *Et penitus toto divises orbe Brittannos:*[23] so as the law of England is *proprium quarto modo*[24] to the Kingdome of England; therefore forrein precedents are not to be objected against us, because we are not subject to forrein lawes.

And it is a note worthy of observation, that where at the holding of this Parliament in anno 20 Hen. 3. and before, and some time after, many of the Judges and Justices of this Realme were of the Clergy, as Bishops, Deanes, and Priests, and all the great officers of the Realme, as Lord Chancellor, Trea-suror, Privyseale, President, &c. were for the most part of the Clergy; yet even in those times the Judges of the Realme, both of the Clergy and Laity, did constantly maintaine the lawes of England, so as no incroachment was made upon them or breach unto them by any forreine power as partly hath been shewed in Caudries case:[25] and many more judgements and authorities in law might be produced for the manifestation thereof: See the first part of the

---

21. Jus coronae.

22. [*Ed.:* especially since the foregoing matters would manifestly tend to the disinheritance of the right of our royal crown and royal dignity of England, and to the notorious subversion of the estate of the same realm, and also to the prejudice of the liberties, customs and laws of the fatherland.]

23. [*Ed.:* And the British being utterly divided from the whole world.]

24. [*Ed.:* property in the fourth degree.]

25. Lib. 5. fo. 1. &c. Caudries case. 1 part of the Institutes § 534.

Institutes, many of the Clergy, Judges and Justices of the realme of ancient time.

"And all the Bishops instanted the Lords, that they would consent, &c."

Here was the motion and request, But Bracton saith[26] *Rogarunt Regem & magnates: Et omnes comites & barones una voce responderunt, Nolumus leges Angliae mutare &c;*[27] for so it is in ancient Manuscripts.

| This is the first of this kind, that we remember, that hath been printed, for it is to be understood that by the parliamentary order all motions and petitions made (as this was) though they were denied, and never proceeded to the establishment of a Statute, yet the same were entered into the Parliament roll together with the answers thereunto: but this is the first of this kinde (as hath been said) that hath been printed.[28]   [99]

And yet in our books this is called a Statute, for Sr. Galfred le Scrope chiefe Justice saith, before the statute of Merton the party pleaded not general bastardy, but that he was borne out of espousals; and the Bishop ought to certifie whether he were borne before espousals or not, and according to that certificate to proceed to judgement according to the law of the land: And the prelates answered that they could not to this writ answer, and therefore ever since special bastardy (viz. that the defendant, &c. was borne before espousals) have been tried in the Kings Courts, and generall bastardy in court Christian; and herewith agreeth our old books and the constant opinion of the Judges ever since.[29]

Now for that this point was resolved in Parliament, it is here in a large sense called a Statute.

Cap. X.

It is Provided and granted, that every Freeman, which oweth Suit to the County, Trything, Hundred, and Wapentake, or to the Court of his Lord, may freely make his Attorney to do those Suits for him.

---

26. Bracton lib. 5. fo. 416. 417.
27. [*Ed.:* And all the earls and barons answered with one voice, we will not change the laws of England.]
28. See the last Cha. of Merton the like. 12. Ass. p. 2d.
29. Bract. li. 5. fo. 416. Fleta li. 6. cap. 38. 47. Edw. 3. 14. 21. Edw. 3. 49, 28 ass. 46. 46. Edw. 3. 3.

"Oweth Suit."

Nota, There be two kinds of suits, viz. suit reall, that is, in respect of his reliance to a Leet or Tourne: and suit service, that is, by reason of a tenure of his land of the County, Hundred, Wapentake, or Mannor whereunto a Court Baron is incident: before this Act every one that held by suit service ought to appeare in person, because the suiters were Judges in those Courts,[1] otherwise he should be amercied, which was mischievous, for it might be, that he had lands within divers of those Seigniories, and that the Courts might be kept in one day, and he could be but in one place at one time: But this Statute extends not to suit reall, because he cannot be within two Leets, &c.

"Trything."[2]

Here it signifieth a Court which consisteth on three or foure Hundreds, and doth not here signifie a Leet or view of frankpledge.

"Wapentake."[3]

That, which in some Countries is called a Hundred Court, in some Countries is called a Wapentake. *Quod Angli vocant Hundredum supradicti Comitatus vocant Wapentagium.*[4] Now the reason of the name was this: When any on a certaine day and place took upon him the government of the Hundred, the frée suiters met him with launces, and he descending from his horse, all rose up to him, and he holding his launce upright, all the rest, in signe of obedience, with their launces touched his launce or weapon: for the Saxon word *wapen,* is weapon, and *tac,* is *tactus,* or touching: and thereo this assemblie was called Wapentake, or touching of weapon.[5]

Now albeit he that holdeth by suit service may make an Attorney, yet that

---

1. 41 Edw. 3. Avowry 77. Vid. Glo. c. 8 West. 2. cap. 10.

2. Lamb. int. leges Edw. regis, nu. 34. Magna Cart. c. 35. Temps Edw. I. Attorn. 106. Regist. 172. 23 Edw. 3. cap. 4. F. N. B. 156.

3. Lam. verbo centuria int. leges Edw. regis, nu. 33. Bract. lib. 3.

4. [*Ed.:* What the English call a hundred, those of the above mentioned county call a wapentake.]

5. Mirror, ca. 5. §. 3.

| Attorney cannot sit as Judge, as the free suiter himselfe might doe, for he
cannot depute another in his judiciall place; and the words of the Statute be;
Libere possit facere attornatum ad sectas illas pro eo faciendas.[6]

"Freeman."

This doth extend to Free-holders in ancient demesne but not to Copie-
holders.[7]

"Make his Attorney."

[8] He must make a Letter of Attorney under his seale, which the Steward ought
to allow; and if he doe not, the suiter may have a Writ out of the Chancery
for the allowance of him: or if he doubted that he should not be allowed, he
might have a Writ before-hand to receive him as Attorney:[9] and such a Writ
shall serve during the life of the tenant, &c. for the words of another Writ
be, *Et quia virtus Brevium nostrorum de hujusmodi Attornato faciendo terminum
non capit, nec terminus limitatur durantibus personis, &c.*[10]

What such an Attorney may doe, and who cannot be Attorney, sée the
Statute of West. 1.[11]

"To do those suits for him."

So as by force of this Act he may doe such suit, as the Frée-holder ought to
doe.

See the Register 19. This Act extendeth to Justices in Eire.

---

6. [*Ed.:* May freely make his attorney to do those suits for him.]

7. Temps Edw. 1. Attorny 106.

8. F. N. B. 156. Edw. West. 1. cap. 33.

9. F. N. B. 157.

10. [*Ed.:* And because the force of our writs for making such an attorney has no end, nor is a term limited while the persons last, etc.]

11. West 1. cap. 33. Custumier de Norm. cap. 65.

Cap. XI

Concerning Trespasses in Parks and Ponds it is not yet discussed; for the Lords demanded the proper Imprisonment of such as they should take in their Parks and Ponds, which the king denied; wherefore it was deferred.[1]

"Vivariis."

Is a word of large extent, and *ex vi termini*[2] signifieth a place in land or water, where living things be kept. Most commonly in Law it signifieth Parkes, Warrens, and Pilcharies or Fishings; here it is taken for Warrens and Fishings, for that Parks were named before.

"Proper Imprisonment."

This Petition of the Lords in Parliament stood upon three branches: 1. That they might imprison such as they should take in the Parks and Vivaries, which seemed to be against the 29. Chapter of Magna Charta. 2. That they should have *propriam prisonam*,[3] a prison of their own, which no subject can have; for all prison or gaoles are the Kings prisons or gaoles, but a subject may have the custodie or keeping of them.[4] 3. That they should not be imprisoned in the common gaole. All which *Dominus Rex contradixit.*[5]

Statute of Marlebridge,
Editum 52. Hen. 3. *Anno gratiae* 1267.

"Marlebridge"

[1]Now called Marleborough, a Town in Wiltshire, the greatest fame whereof is the holding of this Parliament there: *Henricus vero, &c. Concilium convocavit*

---

1. [*Ed.:* The Statutes at Large translated *paris & vivariis* as "parks and ponds." Coke here clearly means *vivariis* in its wider meaning.]
2. [*Ed.:* of the word's definition.]
3. [*Ed.:* proper imprisonment.]
4. See the like before, cap. 9.
5. [*Ed.:* The Lord the king denied.]
1. Polyd. Virg. p. 314. 10.

Marlebrigium, quod est pagus celebris comitatus Wilceriae, qui in eo conventu primum leges ab se latas, & praesertim Magnae chartae de concilii sententia approbandas, deinde alias condendas curavit, quae ad statum & commodum regni maxime conducerent.[2]

This Towne in our Books is called a Citie, and the Fréemen thereof Citizens.[3]

"52 Hen. 3."

This king raigned longest of any King since the Conquest, or before, that we remember; for he raigned 56. yeares. But the great and famous Quéene Elizabeth was of greater yeares then any of her progenitors, for she attained néere to 70. yeares. So King Henry the third raigned longest, and Quéen Eliz. lived longest. She raigned the yeares of the Emperour Augustus, and lived the yeares of King David.

> In the Year of Grace, One thousand two hundred sixty-seven, the two-and-fiftieth Year of the Reign of King Henry, Son of King John, in the Utas of Saint Martin, the said King our Lord providing for the better Estate of his Realm of England, and for the more speedy Ministration of Justice, as belongeth to the Office of a King, the more discreet Men of the Realm being called together, as well of the higher as of the lower Estate: It was Provided, agreed, and ordained, that whereas the Realm of England of late had been disquieted with manifold Troubles and Dissensions; for Reformation whereof Statutes and Laws be right necessary, whereby the Peace and Tranquillity of the People must be observed; wherein the King, intending to devise convenient Remedy, hath made these Acts, Ordinances and Statutes underwritten, which he willeth to be observed for ever firmly and inviolably of all his Subjects, as well high as low.

This generall Preamble to all the Statutes of Marlebridge both consist on foure parts.

1. The end wherefore these Statutes were made, for *sapiens incipit a fine,*[4]

---

2. [*Ed.:* Henry [III] called together the council of Marlborough, which is a celebrated region in the county of Wiltshire, and in that meeting he first caused the laws laid down by him, especially Magna Carta, to be approved by the determination of the council, and then caused others to be made which greatly conduced to the estate and benefit of the realm.]

3. 39 Edw. 3. fo. 15.

4. [*Ed.:* the wise man begins with the end,]

and that is twofold; 1. *Ad meliorationem regni Angliae.* 2. *Ad exhibitionem justitiae (prout regalis officii exposcit utilicas) pleniorem.*[5]

Of what members this parliament consisted, *Convocatis discretioribus ejusdem regni, tam majoribus, quàm minoribus.*[6]

3. What was the cause of calling this Parliament, *Cum regni Angliae multis tribulationibus & dissentionum incommodis nuper esset depressum.*[7] The many fearfull and dangerous troubles and dissentions the King and his Barons, which I had rather you should reade in History, then I should relate, grew originally out of this root, that the King sometimes allowed, and sometimes disallowed *Magna Charta,* and *Charta de Foresta.*

4. What should be the remedy that peace and tranquillity might ensue, *Utcum regnum &c. reformatione legum & jurium quibus pax & tranquillirat incolarum conservetur indigeat, ad quod remedium salubre per ipsum regem & suos fideles provisiones, ordinationes, & statuta subscripta, ab omnibus regni suis incolis tam majoribus quàm minoribus firmiter & inviolabiliter temporibus perpetuis statuerit observari.*[8]

This remedy that should for ever in all future times be inviolably observed, consisted upon two parts.

1. For establishing of *Magna Charta,* and *Charta de Foresta,* whereof more shall be said when we come to the first Chapter. In the meane time, this is to be observed, that after this Parliament neither *Magna Charta,* nor *Charta de Foresta,* was ever attempted to be impugned or questioned; whereupon peace and tranquility, whereof this Preamble speaketh, have ever since ensued.

2 For enacting of new Lawes, or declaring of old, with addition of great punishment.*

---

5. [*Ed.:* Firstly, for the betterment of the realm of England, and secondly for the speedier execution of justice, as belongs to the office of a king.]

6. [*Ed.:* Calling together the more discerning persons of the realm, both great and small.]

7. [*Ed.:* Whereas the realm of England has recently been oppressed with many troubles and dissensions.]

8. [*Ed.:* That whereas the realm, etc., for reformation whereof statutes and laws are essential for the preservation of peace and tranquility, the king and his faithful subjects have thereto provided for a convenient remedy the underwritten provisions, ordinances, and statutes, to be firmly and inviolably observed by all people of the realm, both great and small, for ever.]

* [*Ed.:* Chapters 1–30 are here omitted.]

Statutum de Westminster primer.

Editum Anno 3 Edw. 1. (1275)

The Preface of the Statute of W.1.

| These be the Acts of King Edward, Son to King Henry, made at Westminster   [156]
at his first Parliament general after his Coronation, on the Monday of Easter
Utas, the Third Year of his Reign, by his Council and by the assent of Archbishops, Bishops, Abbots, Priors, Earls, Barons, and all the Commonalty of the
Realm, being thither summoned: Because our Lord the King had great zeal and
desire to redress the State of the Realm in such Things as required Amendment
for the common profit of Holy Church, and of the Realm: And because the
State of the Holy Church had been evil kept, and the Prelates and Religious
Persons of the Land grieved many ways, and the People otherwise intreated than
they ought to be, and the Peace less kept, and the Laws less used, and the
Offenders less punished, than they ought to be, by reason whereof the People
of the Land feared the less to offend; the King hath ordained and established
these Acts underwritten; which he intendeth to be necessary and profitable unto
the whole Realm.

"These be the Acts"

Stabilimina, or *stabilimenta,* Establishments, or Assurances comuting of *sta-*
bilis, and that againe *à stando,* of standing; And justly may not onely these
Chapters challenge that name, but all other the Statutes name in the raigne
of this King may be styled by the name of Establishments, because they are
more constant, standing, and durable Laws, then have been made ever since:[1]
so as King Edward the first who (as Sir William Herle Chiefe Justice of the
Court of Common Pleas, that lived in his time, said, *Fuit le pluis sage Roy que*
unques fuit[2]) may well bee called our Justinian.

The Pref-
ace of the
Statute of
West. 1.

"At his first Parliament general."

So called, because all the Laws then made were general, and that great and
honourable Assembly were not entangled with private matters, but with such

---

1. 5 E. 3. 14.
2. [*Ed.:* Was the wisest king that ever was.]

onely, as were for the generall good of the Common-wealth, for the end of this Parliament, is, as hereafter in the Preface is expressed, *Pour le common profit de Saint Esglise, & dei Realm.*[3]

| "after his Coronation,"

He began his raigne the 16. day of November, Anno Dom. 1272. he then being in the land of Palestine; and after his returne into England, was crowned the 19. day of August, in the 2. yeare of his raigne, (and not the 9. day of December, in the 1. yeare of his raigne, as some have mistaken) as evidently appeareth by this Preface, and by ancient Records hereafter remembred.[4]

"on the Monday of Easter Utas,"[5]

That is, *in crastino clausi Paschae,* or *in crastino octabis Paschae,*[6] which is all one: in English, the morrow of the *utas* of Easter. It is called *utas of huit,* which signifieth eight, viz. the eighth day after, including Easter day it selfe for one.

Note, this Parliament was summoned to be holden at London *in quindena* of the Purification after his, Coronation, and prorogued from thence until the morrow after the *utas* of Easter to be holden at Westminster. And the number of eight was much respected in the ancient Lawes, as amongst the Lawes of King Edward the Confessor. *Pax regis die qua coronatus est quae dies tenet octo, indienatali Domini dies octo, in Paschate dies octo, in Pentecoste dies octo, &c.*[7] Now the eighth day, accounting the feast day for one, is *clausum festi*[8] that is the closing up of the feast for many purposes.

"The Third Year of his Reign."[9]

This proveth that he was crowned in Anno 2. for if he had been crowned in Anno 1. of his raigne, then this Parliament should have been holden in the

3. [*Ed.:* For the common profit of Holy Church and of the realm.]
4. Vet. Mag. Chart. fo. 144.
5. Glanv. li. 1. c. 6.
6. [*Ed.:* on the morrow of the close of Easter [or] on the morrow of the octave of Easter,]
7. [*Ed.:* The king's peace is kept on the day he was crowned for eight days, at Christmas for eight days, in Easter time for eight days, at Whitsun for eight days, etc.]
8. [*Ed.:* the close of the feast.]
9. Vide vet. Mag. Char. 1. part, fo. 144. b.

2. yeare: and this is proved by other matter of Record. But the truth is, that the 19. day of December, in Anno 1. of his raigne, he was not returned into England.

Rex venerabili in Christo Patri, Roberto Cant' Archiepiscopo, totius Angliae Primati, salutem.[10] *Quia generale Parliamentum nostrum, quod cum Praelatis & Magnatibus regni proposuimus habere London' ad quindenam Purificationis beatae Mariae proxim' futur', quibusdam certis de causis prorogavimus usque in crastinum clausi Paschae proxim' sequen'; vobis mandamus rogantes quatenus eidem Parliamento ibidem in eodem crastino clausi Paschae intersitis ad trac-tandum & ordinandum una cum Praelatis & magnatibus regni nostri de negotiis ejusdem regni, & hoc nullatenus omittatis. Teste Rege apud Woodstock, 27. die Decembris.*

Rex in primo generali Parliamento suo post coronationem suam in crastino octabis Paschae,[11] *Anno regni sui 3. de voluntate sua, & Consiliarioorm suorum consilio, & communitatis regni sui ibidem convocat' consensu, ad honorem Dei, &c. ordinavit & statuit quod &c.*

Rex Edw. tenuit primum generale parliamentum suum post coronationem suam in crastino octabis Paschae, Anno 3. regni sui.[12,13]

"By his Council."

This proveth that this King and other Kings before him had a Privie Councell, which appeareth by the Writs of Parliament, that Parliaments are ever sum-

---

10. Dors. claus. An. 3. E. 1. m. 21.

11. Rot. pat. An. 4. E. 1. m. 9. 14.

12. [*Ed.:* The king to the venerable father in Christ, Robert, archbishop of Canterbury, primate of all England, greeting. Because for certain causes we have prorogued our general parliament, which we proposed to have with our prelates and great men of the realm at London at the quindene of the Purification of the Blessed Mary next to come, until the morrow of the close of Easter next following, we command you with respect to the same parliament that you be there on the same morrow of the close of Easter to treat and take order concerning the business of our realm together with the prelates and great men of the same realm, and this in no way omit. Witness the King at Woodstock, on the twenty-seventh day of December.

The king in his first general parliament after his coronation, on the morrow of the octave of Easter in the third year of his reign, of his free will and by the consent of the councillors of his council and of the commonalty of his realm, called together there, to the honour of God, etc. ordained and enacted that, etc.

King Edward held his first general parliament after his coronation on the morrow of the octave of Easter in the third year of his reign.

13. Rot. pat. An. 10. E. 1.

moned to be holden *de advisamento consilii nostri*.[14] Of this see more in this
first Chapter.

"By the assent of Archbishops, Bishops, Abbots, Priors, Earls, Barons, and all
the Commonality of the Realm, being thither summoned."

Here is a compleat Parliament for the making or enacting of Lawes, the King,
the Lords Spirituall and Temporall, and the Commons:[15] For if an Act be
made by the king, and the Lords Spirituall and Temporall, or by the King
and the Commons, this bindeth not, for it is no Act of Parliament; for the
Parliament concerning making or enacting of Lawes consisteth of the King,
the Lords Spirituall and Temporall, and the Commons; and it is no Act of
[158]   Parliament, unlesse it be made by the King, | the Lords and Commons. And
where it is said, by all the Commonalty, all the Commons of the Realme are
represented in Parliament by the Knights, Citizens and Burgesses.[16]

The purpose of this Parliament is to redresse the state of the Church and
of the Realme in those things that need amendment. The end is twofold, *Pur
le common profit de saint Esglise, & de son Realme.*[17]

There were five things that needed amendment.

1. For that the State of the Realme and of holy Church (which are ever like
Hipocrates twins) had been ill governed.

2. That the Prelates and other men of the Church many wayes had been
grieved, and the people otherwise entreated then they ought to have been.

3. The Peace had not been well kept, which was against a maine Maxime
of the Law, *Inprimis interest reipublicae, ut pax in regno conservetur, & quaecunq;
paci adversentur, providè declinentur:*[18] Which Maxime hath been repeated and
affirmed by authority of Parliament.[19]

4. That the Lawes had not been put in execution against another principle
of the Common Law, *Nihil infra regnum subditos magis conservat in tran-*

---

14. [*Ed.:* by the advisement of our council.]

15. See the 4. part of the Instit. cap. of the high Court of Parliament.

16. H. 7. 27.

17. [*Ed.:* For the common profit of Holy Church and of his realm.]

18. [*Ed.:* First, it is in the interests of the state that peace should be preserved in the realm, and whatsoever
works against the peace should be assiduously suppressed:]

19. 3 E. 6. cap. 12. 1 Mar. cap. 12.

quilitate et concordia, quam debita legum administratio.[20] Affirmed also in Parliament.[21]

5. Offendors seldome punished, *Et impunitas continuum affectum tribuit delinquendi;*[22] for this Statute saith, By reason whereof the people of the land feare lesse to offend.

The remedy hath two excellent qualities, which ought to be inseparable to every Act of Parliament, viz. to be profitable, and convenient.

Here shall you see the effects of the Writs of Parliament, as they be at this day: First, the Writ is, *Nos de advisamento Concilii nostri;*[23] and this Act saith, *Le roy per son councel.*[24]

2. The Writ is, *Pro quibusdam arduis & urgentibus negotiis nos, statum & defensionem regaeni nostri Angli concernentibus:*[25] and it is expressed in this Act, *Que nostre Seigniour le Roy ad graund volunt, & desire del estate de son Realme redresser, en les choses ou mestier est damendement, & ceo pur le common profit de saint Esglise & de son Realme, & pur ceo que lestate de son realme & de saint Esglise ad estre malement gard, &c.*[26]

And here it is to be observed, that this noble and wise King Edward the first was contented in a free and generall Parliament to heare of the misgoverment of the State of the Realme and of the Church, and never sought to cover those irregular proceedings, either in his fathers time, or his owne; and thought it should be greater honour for him to rip up these grievous ulcers both in the Church and Common-wealth, and to cure them by wholsome rules and lawes, then to cover them, lest it should be vainly feared they should reflect upon his fathers, or his owne misgovernment, where in truth all the salt fault should rest upon great Counsellors, and Officers, and Ministers of Justice, and other the Kings Officers and Ministers[27] and so it hath falne out

20. [*Ed.:* Nothing in the kingdom better preserves the subjects in tranquility and peace than the due administration of the laws.]

21. 32 H. 8. cap. 9.

22. [*Ed.:* And continuous impunity encourages men to offend.]

23. [*Ed.:* We, by the advice of our council.]

24. [*Ed.:* The king by his council.]

25. [*Ed.:* For certain arduous and urgent business concerning us and the defence of our realm of England.]

26. [*Ed.:* That our lord the king has a great wish and desire to reform the condition of his realm, in those things which are in need of amendment, and that for the common profit of Holy Church and his realm, and because the estate of his realm and of Holy Church has been badly kept, etc.]

27. Rot. Parl. 50 E. 3 nu. 10. 15, 16, 17, 18, &c. Rot. Parl. 5 H. 4. nu. 8. 7 H. 4. nu. 30, 41. 9 H. 4. indemnitie des Seigniors, &c. 1. H. 5. nu. 8. &c.

in divers other Kings times. This Preamble to all the Statutes is worthy of due and deliberate consideration.

Of this worthy King we have spoken in other places; This we will adde out of an approved Author, *Nemo in consiliis illo argutior, in eloquio torrentior, in periculis securior, in prosperis cautior, in adversis constantior.*[28]

Now this Parliament holden at Westminster, is called Westminster the first for excellencie.*

Statutum de Glocester,
Editum Anno 6 Edw. 1. (1278)

[277] | This Parliament was holden at Glocester bordering upon Wales, for the better preservation of peace in Wales, Lluellin Prince of Wales, and the Welsh-men being a little before this Parliament brought to quietnesse.

> The Year of Grace M.C.C. lxviii, and the Sixth of the Reign of King Edward Son of King Henry, at Gloucester, in the month of August, the King himself providing for the Amendment of his Realm, and for a fuller Administration of Justice, as the good of the Kingly Office requireth, having called unto him the more discreet persons of his Kingdom, as well of the greater as of the less: It is Established and Ordained with one accord, That Whereas the same Kingdom, in many divers Cases, as well of Franchises as of other Things, wherein aforetime the Law hath failed, and to avoid the grievous Damages and innumerable Disherisons which this Default of the Law hath caused to the People of the Realm, hath need of divers Additions to the Law, and of new Provisions, therefore the Statutes, Ordinances, and Provisions under-written should be stedfastly observed by all the People of the Kingdom.
>
> Whereas the Prelates, Earls, Barons, and others of the Kingdom, claim to have divers Franchises, for the Examination and Judgment whereof the King had appointed a day to the said Prelates, Earls, Barons, and others: It is Provided and granted with one accord, that the aforesaid Prelates, Earls, Barons, and others, may use such sort of Franchises, so that nothing accrue to them by Usurpation or Occupation, and that they occupy nothing against the King, until the next coming of the King through the County, or the next coming of the Justices in Eyre for Common Pleas into the same County, or until the King

---

28. [*Ed.:* No one was more impressive in advice, more burning in eloquence, more secure in danger, more cautious in prosperity, more constant in adversity.]

 * [*Ed.:* Chapters 1–51 here omitted.]

shall otherwise order: Saving the King's Right when he shall put the same in Suit, according to what is contained in the King's Writ. And hereof Writs shall be issued to the Sheriffs Bailiffs and others, in Behalf of every Demandant; and the Form of the Writ shall be changed according to the Diversity of the Franchises that each man claimeth.

I And the Sheriffs shall cause it to be commonly proclaimed throughout their   [278]
Bailliwicks, that is to say, in Cities Boroughs Market Towns and elsewhere, that all those who claim to have any Franchises by the Charters of the King's Predecessors, Kings of England, or in other manner, shall come before the King or before the Justices in Eyre, at a certain day and place, to shew what sort of Franchises they claim to have, and by what Warrant. And the Sheriffs themselves shall then be there in their proper persons, with their Bailiffs and Officers, to certify the King upon the aforesaid Franchises and other matters touching the same. And this Proclamation before the King shall contain Warning of three Weeks. And in like manner shall the Sheriffs make Proclamation in the Circuit of the Justices; and in like manner shall come in their proper persons, with their Bailiffs and Officers, to certify the Justices of such sort of Franchises, and other matters touching the same. And this Proclamation shall give warning of forty days, as the common summons containeth; So that if the Party who claimeth the Franchise come before the King, he shall not be put in Default before the Justices in Eyre; forasmuch as the King of his special Grace hath granted that he will save the Party harmless in respect of this adjournment. And if any such Party be impleaded upon such sort of Franchises before two of the aforesaid Justices, the same Justices before whom the Party is in Plea, shall save him harmless before other Justices; and the King likewise before himself, when he shall know from the Justices that the Party was in Plea before them, as it is before said. And if they that claim to have such Franchises come not at the day aforesaid, then the Franchises shall be taken into the King's hand by the Sheriff of the place, in name of Distress; so that they shall not use such sort of Franchises until they come to receive Justice. And when they come upon that Distress, their Franchises shall be replevied, if they demand them; upon which Replevin they shall answer forthwith in the form aforesaid. And if peradventure the parties except, that they ought not to answer thereupon without an original Writ, then if it can be known that they have, by their own act, usurped or occupied any Franchises upon the King or his predecessors, they shall be told forthwith to answer without Writ; and shall thereon receive I such Judgment as the King's   [279]
Court shall award. And if they alledge further that their Ancestor or Ancestors died seised of the same Franchises, they shall be heard, and forthwith Inquiry shall be made of the Truth, and according thereto the Justices shall proceed in the business. And if it be found that their Ancestor died seised thereof, then the King shall have an original Writ out of his Chancery in the form made for

that purpose. "The King to the Sheriff, Greeting: Summon by good summoners such an one, that he be before Us, at such a place, upon our next coming into the County; or before our Justices at the first Assises, when they shall come into those parts; to shew by what Warrant he holds his View of Frank-pledge in his Manor of N. in the same County; and let the Sheriffs have there the Summoners and this Writ: or thus; by what Warrant he holds the hundred of B. in the County aforesaid: or thus; by what Warrant he claims to be quit of Toll, for him or his men, throughout our Realm, by continuance after the death of such an one late his predecessor. And have there the summoners and this Writ." And the Forms of the Writs shall be charged according to the diversity of the Franchises and of the Case, and according to the Discretion of the Chancery, and of the Justices. And if the Parties come at the day, let them answer; whereupon Replication shall be made, and Judgment given. And if they come not, neither essoin themselves before the King, and the King tarry longer in that County, the Sheriff shall be commanded to cause them to appear at the fourth day; at which day if they come not, and the King tarry longer in that County, the proceeding shall be as it is in the Circuit of the Justices. And if the King depart out of that County, the Parties shall be adjourned unto a short day, and shall have reasonable delays according to the discretion of the Justices, as in actions personal. And the Justices in Eyre shall proceed herein, in their Circuits, according to the Ordinance aforesaid and according as such sort of Pleas ought to be proceeded upon in the Eyre.

Concerning Complaints made and to be made of the King's Bailiffs, and of other Bailiffs, it shall be done according to the Ordinance before made thereof, and according to the Inquests before had thereupon. And the Justices in Eyre shall do therein, according to what the King hath enjoined them, and according to the Articles which the King hath given them in charge.

"Year of grace 1267."

This should be 1278. for that was *Anno* 6 Edw. 1. this Parliament being holden in August, *anno* 6 Edw. 1. for 1267. was in 51 Hen. 3.[1]

This Chapter concerning Liberties and Franchises, and the *Quo warranto,*[2] (and intituled *Statutum de quo warranto)* hath been supposed by many to be

---

1. Vet. Mag. Chart. fol. 130.
2. [*Ed.:* Writ used to limit conduct to the extent of a royal license or charter.]

enacted in Latin, *Anno* 30 Edw. 1. and therefore some have omitted to insert it in the 6. yeare; but it is utterly mistaken: for the King in the 30. yeare did publish and proclaime this Act under the great Seale,[3] and doth recite it to be made, *Anno Dom.* 1278. and in the 6. yeare of his raigne. *Vide* 14. Edw. 1. *Inter originals de Anno* 14 Edw. 1. *Breve de libertatibus allocandis,*[4] and there is another Statute made | in 18 Edw.1. called *Statutum de quo warranto novum,*[5] so called, in respect of this former Statute. [280]

And besides; the Statute in French differeth from the recitall thereof in 30 E.1 which, for that it agreeth with the Record, we will follow it when we come to the body of the Act.

"Providing for the Amendment of his Realm, and for a fuller Administration of Justice."

Which by the said Proclamation in 30. E.1. is rendred thus. *Ad Regni sui Angliae meliorationem, & exhibitionem Justiciae pleniorem:*[6] two excellent ends of a Parliament, *Regni melioratio,*[7] that is for the common good of the Kingdome, the Parliament being *Commune concilium,*[8] and *exhibitio Justiciae plenior,*[9] for nothing is more glorious, and necessary, then full execution of Justice.

And it is added, *Prout Regalis officii exposcit utilitas;*[10] and accordingly at this Parliament many profitable and just Laws were made, as one speaking of this Parliament saith truly,[11] *In quo quaedam de Regni statu decreta sunt, quae nunc ut jura, & aequitate plena maxime usurpantur.*[12] And that I may speak once for all, it is worthy of observation that the Statutes made in this noble Kings time are so agreeable to common right and equity, as few or none of them have been abrogated, but being founded upon these two pillars, (the

3. Lib. 9. fol. 28. In the case of Strata Marcella.
4. [*Ed.:* A writ for allowing liberties.]
5. [*Ed.:* New [statute] of quo warranto.]
6. [*Ed.:* For the improvement of his realm of England and the fuller provision of justice:]
7. [*Ed.:* Improvement of the realm.]
8. [*Ed.:* The common council.]
9. [*Ed.:* fuller provision of justice,]
10. [*Ed.:* As belongs to the duty of the royal office;]
11. Pol. Virgil.
12. [*Ed.:* In which certain decrees were made concerning the state of the realm, which are now made the greatest use of as full of right and fairness.]

amendment of the Kingdome, and the due execution of Justice) remaine and continue as just and constant Laws to this day.

"Such manner of Liberties."

For the better understanding of this Act it shall be necessary out of History to shew the cause of the making hereof.

The truth is, that the King wanting money, there were some innovatores those dayes, that perswaded the King, that few or none of the Nobility, Clergy, or Commonalty, that had franchises of the graunts of the Kings predecessors, had right to them for that they had no Charter to shew for the same, for that in troth most of their Charters either by length of time, or injury of wars[13] insurrections, or by casualty were either consumed, or lost: whereupon (as commonly new inventions have new wayes) it was openly proclaimed, that every man, that held those liberties, or other possessions by graunt from any of the Kings Progenitors, should before certain selected persons thereunto appointed shew, *quo jure, quove nomine ill' retinerent, &c.*[14] whereupon many that had long continued in quiet possession, were taken into the Kings hands, *Eo quod nula tabella constarent:*[15] Hereof the Story saith, *Visum est omnibus edictum ejusmodi post homines natos longe acerbissimum: Qui fremitus hominum? quam irati animi? quanto in odio princeps esse repente coepit?*[16]

The good King understanding hereof, and finding himselfe abused by ill counsell, and considering the Statute of Magna Charta,[17] at the Parliament holden in the end of his fourth yeare by Proclamation, and at the petition of the Lords and of the Commons now at this Parliament, by authority of Parliament provideth remedy, as hereafter you shall heare: This is fully agreed upon in all our Histories, only the time in some of them (as oftentimes in other cases it falleth out) is mistaken, which by this Act shall be rectified according to true Chronologie.

---

13. Vide Vet. Magna Charta. fol. 130. Stat. de Quo Warranto. Pol. Virgil.

14. [*Ed.:* by what right or by what name he retained them, etc.]

15. [*Ed.:* So that no records remained.]

16. [*Ed.:* Such an edict seemed to everyone very oppressive, long after the men were born. What grumbling of men, what angry minds, in what sudden odium the prince began to be held.]

17. Mag. Charta. cap. 1, 9, 38.

"And likewise agreed."

It was rightly said *concorditer concessum,* for that the said innovation was like to have been a cause of great discord betweene the King and the better sort of his Subjects.

"That the said Prelates, Earls, Barons, and others shall use such manner of liberties, after the form of the writ here following."

| This forme of a Writ is more satisfactory, then any other forme is, and this was the auncient use.   [281]

"*Cum nuper in Parliamento nostro apud Westm'*"[18]

That is, in the last Parliament holden after Michaelmas, towards the end of the fourth year of his raigne, & therefore the great grievances abovesaid must be before that Parliament, for the cure was after the disease, and the remedy after the grievance.

"*Provisum sit et Proclamatum*"[19]

But this was never (that I can finde) recorded: Now by this Act it is provided that a Writ shall be granted.

"*Quibus hucusque rationabiliter usi sunt*"[20]

See the Register 162, 163. *De libertatibus allocandis,*[21] & F.N.B. 229, 230.

---

18. [*Ed.:* Whereas lately, in our parliament at Westminster (This language and the next three captions are not in the excerpt commencing this chapter; they are from the Writ of summons, which Coke prescribes for use as the summons described in the statute of Gloucester.).]

19. [*Ed.:* It was provided and proclaimed.]

20. [*Ed.:* Which until now they have reasonably used.]

21. [*Ed.:* For allowing liberties.]

"Usque ad adventum nostrum per Comitatum praedictum, vel usque proximum
adventum Justiciariorum Itinerantium, &c."[22]

That is, untill the Court of Kings Bench came thither, or the next comming
of the Justices in Eyre: So all men should quietly enjoy their Franchises, which
they had reasonably used, untill the Court of Kings Bench, or untill the Justices
in Eyre came into that County: Here it is to be observed, that this good King
and his Councell in Parliament referred the party grieved to a legall proceeding,
which implieth, that a contrary course was holden before. But you will demand, What remedy was this for him, that could not produce his Charter,
to be left to the Law: I answer, that this was a full and perfect remedy according
to Justice and right; for the better apprehension whereof these distinctions
are to be observed: First, these Franchises intended by this Act be of two sorts,
The one may be claimed by usage and prescription, as wreck of the Sea, Waste,
Stray, Faires, Markets, and the like, which are gained by usage, and may become due without matter of Record: And Felons goods, outlawes goods, and
the like, which grow not due but by matter of Record, and therefore cannot
be claimed by usage in *paiis,*[23] but by Charter: And yet all these at the first
were derived from the Crowne.[24]

Secondly, *Judicis officium est, ut res, ita tempora rerum Quaerere;*[25] All these
were granted either before the time of memory, or after the time of memory:
if before the time of memory, then for the former sort, such as might be claimed
by prescription, the party grieved might prescribe, and by Law he ought to
be relieven. And for such as lay in point of Charter graunted before time of
memory, the party grieved had two remedies, either by allowance, or confirmation; by allowance in the Kings Bench, or before the Justices in Eyre, and
in some case before the Justices of the Court of Common Pleas, and in the
Exchequer; or by confirmation of the King under the great Seale: and these
were sufficient for him without shewing the Charter, and the equity of the

---

22. [*Ed.:* Until our next coming into the aforesaid county or until the next coming of the justices in
eyre, etc.]

23. [*Ed.:* on oath, not in court.]

24. 8 E. 3. 18. 17 E. 3. 11. 26. Ass. 24 30 Ass. 31. 34. Ass. 14. 38 Ass. 1. 1 H. 4. 3. 12 H. 4. 23. 8 H. 6 8.
2 E. 4 22. 7 H. 6. 33. 9 H. 7. 12. 10 H. 7. 14. 16 H. 7 16 20 H. 7 7. Kelwey 189, 190. 8 H. 8.

25. [*Ed.:* The office of a judge is to seek out the things and also the times of things.]

Law herein was notable, for that no Charter before time of memory was pleadable by Law.

If these Franchises either of the one sort or other were graunted within memory, yet if the same had been allowed, as is aforesaid, the same might also be claimed by force of the Charter and allowance, without shewing the Charter, because it had been adjudged and allowed of Record. And it is to be knowne that all Franchises, which any man had either by prescription or by Charter, ought to be claimed before Justices in Eyre, or else for non-claime the same might bee left, as hereafter shall bee said: So as the remedy provided by this Act was plenary and perfect to give reliefe to them that right had.[26]

| To this for the time may be added, that ancient Charters, whether they [282] be before time of memory, or after, ought to be confirmed, as the Law was taken when the Charter was made, and according to ancient allowance.[27,28] Now what time of memory is, see the first part of the Institutes, sect. 170.

But now by the Statutes of 3 Edw.6. and 13 Eliz. there is further remedy given: for albeit the Charter or Letters Patents be lost, yet the exemplification or constat[29] of the Roll may be shewed forth,[30] &c. And when any claimed before the Justices in Eyre any Franchises by an ancient Charter, though it had expresse words for the Franchises claimed, or if the words were generall, and continuall possession pleaded of the Franchises claimed, or if the claim was by old and obscure words, and the party in pleading, expounding them to the Court, and averring continuall possession according to that exposition; the Entry was ever *Inquiratur super possessionem & usum, &c.*[31] which I have observed in divers Records of those Eyres, agreeable to that old Rule, *Optimus interpres rerum usus.*[32]

26. 18 H. 6. prescript. 45. 2 E. 3. 29. 8 H. 8. Kelwey 189. stat. de 18 E. 1. De quo warranto novum. Lib. 9 fol. 29. in case de Strat Marcella.

27. 34 Ass. pl. 14. 40 Ass. 21. 6 E. 3. 54, 55. 7 E. 3. 40, 41 18 E. 3. Conus. 39 12 H. 4. 12. 14 H. 6. 12. 33 H. 6. 22. 35 H. 6. 54. 9. H. 7 11. 10 H. 6. 13. 16 H. 7. 9.

28. Regist. 158. 5 E. 3. 50, 51. 6 E. 3. 18 20 H. 6. 34. 34 H. 6. 36 Dier. 8 El. 245.

29. [*Ed.:* Certificate stating the question in issue.]

30. *a* 3 E. 6. c. 4. 13 El. ca. 6 lib. 5. fo. 52, 53. Pages case.

31. [*Ed.:* enquire upon the possession and usage, etc.]

32. [*Ed.:* Usage is the best interpreter of things.]

"Habeant praemunitionem per 40 dies."[33]

This was by Writ of the common Summons of the Eyre, by the space of 40. dayes before the sitting of the Justices in Eyre.

Now leaving all that is evident, and needeth no exposition, let us come to the next that is worthy of observation.

"Et si forte exceperint quod non tenentur sine brevi."[34,35]

Here is an ancient maxime in the Law implyed, that regularly no man ought to answer for his Freehold, Franchises, or other thing without originall Writ *secundum legem terrae;*[36] and that the[37] Statutes to that end provided are but declarations of the ancient Common Law, as here it is to be seen in case of Franchises in the Kings own case.

"Et si ulterius dicunt quod antecessores sui inde obierint seisiti, statim, audiantur & *statim veritas inquiratur, &c."*[38]

By this is appeareth that a descent of Franchises doth put the King to his Writ of *Quo warranto,*[39] which Writ is here expressed; and note that the *Quo warranto* is in nature of the Kings Writ of Right for Franchises and Liberties, wherein judgement finall shall be given either against the King for the point adjudged, or for the King; and the *Salvo jure*[40] for the King serveth for any other title then that which was adjudged; and therefore William de Penbrogge the Kings Attorney,[41] for prosecuting of a *Quo warranto* against the Abbot of Fischamp for Franches within the Mannour of *Steynings sine praecepto,*[42] was committed to the Gavle.

---

33. [*Ed.:* Let them have forty days' warning.]

34. [*Ed.:* And if they take exception that they are not bound without writ, etc.]

35. Bract. li. 1. fo. 5. & 171. 6 E. 3. 50 22E. 3. 3. 24 E. 3. 1 23. 43 E. 3. 22. 11 H. 4. 86. 9 H. 6. 58.

36. [*Ed.:* according to the law of the land:]

37. Magna Charta, cap. 29. 25 E. 3. cap. 4. Stat. 5. 28 E. 3. ca. 3. 42 E. 3. ca. 3.

38. [*Ed.:* And if they further say that their ancestors died seised thereof, they shall be heard at once and the truth enquired into at once.]

39. Stat. de 18 E. 1. de quo war' nov. 6 E. 35. 8 E. 3. 10, 11. 16 E. 4. 6 3 H. 7. 15. Stanf. Praerog. 74.

40. [*Ed.:* Saving the right.]

41. Pasch. 9. E. 1. Coram rege Rot. 17. Sussex.

42. [*Ed.:* Without a precept.]

"Et si non venerint, &c. praecipiatur vicecom' quod faciat eos venire, &c. fiat sicut in Itinere Justiciariorum."[43,44]

If before the Justice in Eyre the party come not, the Franchise should be seised into the Kings hands *nomine distruction,*[45] which the party in the same Eyre might replevy; but if he did not replevy them while the Eyre sate in that County, the Franchises were lost and forgotten for ever.

Therefore if the party now upon the *Venire facias,*[46] (which this Act doth give) come not while the Eyre sit in that County, the Franchises be lost for ever.

And so it is in the Kings Bench, if the party come not in upon the *Venire facias* during that term, and replevy his Franchises, they be lost for ever. And therefore we concurre not with that chief Justice that said, that Non-claim of Liberties before Justices in Eyre lost the Liberties, for that (saith he) was but of the Kings Grace to grant a Replevy of them, and not of Right;[47] for this opinion is against the authority of our Books, and the continuall practice before the Justices in Eyre.   [283]

See the Statutes of 18 E.1. *De quo warranto novum,*[48] and *De tallagio non concedendo.*[49]

"De querimoniis factiset faciendis de ballivis regis & aliorum fiat secondum ordinationem prius inde factam."[50]

That is, according to the Articles of the Justices in Eyre called *Capitula Itineris*[51] collected and authorised amongst other things, as here it appeareth, by ordinance of Parliament, and entered into the Parliament Roll, which you may see in old Magna Charta, fol. 150, 151, &c.

---

43. 2 E. 3. 29. 6 E. 3. 5. 15 E. 4. 6, 7.

44. [*Ed.:* And if they do not come, etc., the sheriff shall be commanded to cause them to come, etc., as in the eyre of the justices.]

45. [*Ed.:* in the name of a distress.]

46. [*Ed.:* A writ commanding the sheriff to summon a jury.]

47. Pl. Com. 372. in le Signior Zouches case.

48. [*Ed.:* new [statute] of quo warranto.]

49. [*Ed.:* for not granting tallage.]

50. [*Ed.:* concerning complaints made and to be made of the King's bailiffs, and the bailiffs of others, let it be done according to the ordinance previously made therein.]

51. [*Ed.:* chapters of the eyre.]

"Juxta articulo eisdem Justic' nostris tradit'"[52]

The French saith, *Solonque les articles que le roy lour ad livere.*[53] These Articles were delivered by the King to the Justices in Eyre to be enquired of, heard, and determined by them through all the Counties of England, which afterwards were increased, as by the same may appear.*

Statutum de Westminst Secundo,
Editum Anno 13. Edw. 1. (1285)

The Preface of the Statute of W.2.

[331] | Whereas of late our Lord the King, in the Quinzim of Saint John Baptist, the Sixth Year of his Reign, calling together the Prelates, Earls, Barons, and his Council at Gloucester, and considering that divers of this Realm were disherited, by reason that in many Cases, where Remedy should have been had there was none provided by him nor his Predecessors, ordained certain Statutes right necessary and profitable for his Realm, whereby the People of England and Ireland, being Subjects unto his Power, have obtained more speedy Justice in their Oppressions, than they had before; and certain Cases, wherein the Law failed, did remain undetermined, and some remained to be enacted, that were for the Reformation of the Oppressions of the People: Our Lord the King in his Parliament, after the Feast of Easter, holden the Thirteenth Year of his Reign at Westminster, caused many Oppressions of the People, and Defaults of the Laws, for the Accomplishment of the said Statutes of Gloucester, to be rehearsed, and thereupon did provide certain Acts, as shall appear here following.

It is commonly called Westminster the Second: Westminster, because this Parliament was holden at Westminster; and the Second, in respect of the former Parliament holden at Westminster, called Westminster the first.**

---

52. [*Ed.:* according to the articles delivered to our same justices.]
53. [*Ed.:* according to the articles which the king has delivered to them.]
* [*Ed.:* Chapters 1–15 are here omitted.]
** [*Ed.:* Chapters 1–50 are here omitted.]

Statut. de Westminster 3.

Editum Anno 18 Edw. 1. Ad Parliamentum post
festum Hil. & Paschae.[1] (1290)
In the Parliament Roll it is intituled,
Statutum Regis de terris vendendis & emendis.[2]

I It is called the Statute of Westm. 3. because two notable Parliaments had   [500]
been before holden at Westminster, the one called Westm. 1. and the other
called Westm 2.[3] In respect whereof, and of the excellencie of it, this Parliament
being holden at Westminster, is called Westm. 3.*

1. [*Ed.:* The third statute of Westminster, enacted in the eighteenth year of Edward I at the parliament
after the feasts of Hilary and Easter.]
2. [*Ed.:* The king's statute concerning the selling and buying of lands.]
3. I. part of the Institutes, sect. 140.
* [*Ed.:* Chapters 1–3 are here omitted.]

C. The Third Part of the *Institutes*

> *T*he Third Part of the Institutes of the Laws of England: Concerning High Treason, and other Pleas of the Crown, and Criminal Causes, first published in 1644, inventories the criminal law. It also covers, by way of many of the annotations, many points of criminal procedure. The complete table of offenses is reprinted here to provide a sense of Coke's view of the whole field. — *Ed.*

Epigrams from the Title Page:

ECCLES 8.11.
Quia non profertur cito contra malos sententia,
absque timore ullo filii hominum perpetrant mala.[1]

Inertis est nescire quod sibi liceat.[2]

---

1. [*Ed.:* Because sentences against wrongdoers are not passed quickly, the sons of men commit wrongs with no fear.]
2. [*Ed.:* It is idle not to know one's rights.]

A Table of the Severall
Chapters of the Third part of the Institutes,
of the Pleas of the Crown.

Multi multa, nemo omnia novit.[1]

---

1. [*Ed.:* (There are) a great many, no one knows them all.]

The Epilogue.

Deo, Patriae, Tibi.

A Proeme to the third Part of the *Institutes.*

In the second part of the *Institutes* we have spoken onely of Acts of Parliament, (viz.) of *Magna Carta,* and many ancient and other Acts of Parliament, which we have explained, and therein observed which of them are declaratory of the ancient Lawes of this Realme, which are introductory of new, and which mixt: All of them (excepting a very few) concerning *Common Pleas,* and these two great Pronouns, *Meum* and *Tuum.*[1]

In this Third part of the *Institutes,* we are to treat *De malo,*[2] viz. of *High Treason,*[3] and other *Pleas of the Crowne,* and Criminall Causes,[4] most of them by Act of Parliament, and some by the Common Law: in which Cases the Law of all other is most necessary to be knowne, because it concerneth the safety of his Majestie, the quiet of the Common-wealth, and the life, honour, fame, liberty, blood, wife, and posteritie of the party accused, besides the forfeiture of his lands, goods, and all that the hath: for it is truly said of these Laws, *Reliquae leges privatorum hominum commodis prospiciunt, hae regieae majestati, subditorum vitae, ac publicae tranquillitati consulunt.*[5] And that in these Cases the ancient Maxime of the Law principally holdeth, *Misera servitus est, ubi jus est vagum; aut incognitum.*[6,7] And where some doth object against the lawes of *England,* that they are darke and hard to be understood, we have specially in these and other parts of the *Institutes* opened such windowes, and made them so lightsome, and easie to be understood, as he that hath but the light of nature, (which *Solomon* calleth the candle of Almighty God, *Prov.* 20. 27.) adding industrie and diligence thereunto, may easily discerne the same.

---

1. [*Ed.:* mine (and) thine (i.e. property).]

2. [*Ed.:* This phrase was frequently used to designate several species of essoin such as "de malo lecti," of illness in bed; "de malo veniedi," of illness, (or misfortune) in coming to the place where the court sat; "de malo villae," of illness in the town where the court sat.]

3. See the 1. part of the Institutes Sect. 500.

4. *Malum non habet efficientem, sed deficientem causam.* Evill hath not an efficient, but a deficient cause, by reason of the want of some vertue or notable good.

5. [*Ed.:* The rest of the laws look to the benefit of private individuals, but these have regard to the king's majesty, the life of his subjects, and public tranquility.]

6. [*Ed.:* It is a wretched state of slavery which subsists where the law is vague or uncertain.]

7. Stamford.

And that may be verified of these Lawes, that *Lex est lux,* Prov. 6. 23. the Law it selfe is a light. See *Rom.* 2. 14. And when we consider how many acts of Parliament (published in print) that have made new treasons and other capitall offences, are either repeated by generall or expresse words, or expired: How many Indictments, attainders of treasons, felonies, and other crimes, which are not warrantable by law at this day: And how few Book-cases there have been published of treasons, (though a subject of greatest importance) & those very slenderly reported: We in respect of the places which we have holden, and of our own observation, and by often conferences with the Sages of the law in former times concerning criminall causes or *Pleas of the Crowne,* have thought good to publish this Third part of the *Institutes,* wherein we follow that old and sure rule, *Quod judicandum est legibus, et non exemplis.*[8] A worke ardous, and full of such difficultie, as none can either feele or beleeve, but he onely which maketh tryall of it. And albeit it did often terrifie me, yet could it not in the end make me desist from my purpose; (especially in this worke) so farre hath the love and honour of my country, to passe through all labours, doubts and difficulties, prevailed with me.

This, as other parts of the *Institutes,* wee have set forth in our English tongue, not onely for the reasons in the Preface to the first Part of the *Institutes* alledged, which wee presume may satisfie any indifferent and prudent reader: but specially this Treatise of the *Pleas of the Crowne,* because, as it appeareth by that which hath been said, it concerneth all the subjects of the realme more neerly by many degrees, then any of the other. Hereunto you may adde that which *Robert Holcoth* an English man surnamed *Theologus magnus,*[9,10] upon the second Chapter of the book of *Wisdome,* in or about the 20. yeare of King *E.*3. wrote to this effect. *Narrant historia quod cum* Willielmus *dux* Normannorum *regnum* Angliae *conquisivisset, deliberavit quomodo linguam* Saxonicam *possit destruere, &* Angliam, & Normanniam *in idiomate accordav i., & ideo ordinavit, quod nullus in curia regia placitaret nisi in Gallico, & iterum quod puer quilibet ponendus ad literas addisceret Gallicu, & per Gallicam Latinum, quae duo usque*

8. [*Ed.:* Judgment should be according to laws, not precedents.]
9. [*Ed.:* Great theologian.]
10. Bal. cont. 3. fo. 148.

hodie ob servantur. Haec ille.[11] But the statute of 35 *E.*3. cap.15.[12] made not long after *Holcoth* wrote, hath taken these edicts of a Conqueror away, and given due honour to our English language, which is as copious and significant, and as able to expresse any thing in as few and apt words, as any other native language, that is spoken at this day. And (to speake what we think) we would derive from the Conqueror as little as we could.

When *Henry* the first died, all the issue male of the Conqueror, and of his sonnes were dead without issue male.

The wife of King *H.* 1. was *Mawde* daughter of *Malcolme* King of *Scotland* surnamed *Canmor,* and of *Margaret* his wife, who was the granchild of *Edmond Ironside* King of *England. viz.* The said King *Edmond* had issue *Edward* surnamed the *Outlaw,* because he lived a long time beyond sea with *Salamon* King of *Hungary* out of the extent of the lawes of this Realme. *Edward* had issue the said *Margaret* his eldest daughter, famous for her piety and vertue; she had issue *Mawde* wife of King *H.* 1. who by her had issue *Mawde,* of whose English blood by *Geffery Plantagenet* Earle of *Anjou* all the Kings of England are lineally descended.

We have in this Third part of the *Institutes* cited our ancient Authors, and bookes of Law, *viz. Bracton, Britton,* the *Mirror* of *Justices, Fleta,* and many ancient records, never (that we know) before published, to this end, that seeing the *Pleas of the Crown* are for the most part grounded upon, or declared by statute Lawes, the studious Reader may be instructed what the Common Law was before the making of those statutes, whereby he shall know, whether the statutes were introductory of a new law, declaratory of the old, or mixt, and thereby perceive what was the reason and cause of the making of the same, which will greatly conduce to the true understanding thereof.

We shal first treat of the highest, and most hainous crime of *High Treason, Crimen laesae Majestatis;*[13] and of the rest in order, as they are greater and more odious then others.

---

11. [*Ed.:* The histories tell that when William, duke of Normandy, had conquered the kingdom of England, he deliberated how to do away with the Saxon tongue and make England and Normandy agree in language; and therefore he ordained that no one should plead in the king's court except in French, and also that every boy should be put to school to learn French, and, through French, Latin, which two are observed to this day.]

12. 35 E. 3. ca. 15.

13. [*Ed.:* crime of lèse-majesté (treason).]

Cap. I.
Of High Treason.

By the statute of 25 E.3.[1] *de proditionibus*[2] is declared in certaine particular cases, what offences shall be taken to be treason, with this restriction, that if any other case supposed to be treason should happen before any justices, the justices should tarry without going to judgment of the treason, till the case be shewed before the king and his parliament, whether it ought to be adjudged treason or other felony: therefore we will lay our foundation upon, and begin with that act of parliament, the letter whereof *in proprio idiomate*[3] ensueth.

Also, whereas divers opinions have been before this time, in what case treason shall be said, and in what not; the king at the request of the lords and of the commons, hath made a declaration in the manner as hereafter followeth: that is to say, when a man doth compasse or imagine the death of our lord the king, of my lady his queene, or of their eldest sonne and heire: or if a man doe violate the kings compagnion, or the kings eldest daughter unmarried, or the wife of the kings eldest sonne and heire: or if a man doe levie warre against our lord the king in his realme, or be adherent to the kings enemies in his realme, giving to them aide and comfort in the realme or elsewhere, and thereof be provably attainted of open deed by people of their condition. And if a man counterfeit the kings great or privie seale, or his money: and if a man bring false money into this realme counterfeit to the money of England, as the money called Lusheburgh, or other like to the said money of England, knowing the money to be false, to merchandize or make payment, in deceipt of our said lord the king and of his people. And if a man slay the chancellor, treasurer, or the kings justices of the one bench or the other, justices in eire, or justices of assize, and all other justices assigned to heare and determine, being in their place doing their offices. And it is to be understood, that in the cases above rehearsed, it ought to be judged treason, which extend to our lord the king and his royall majestie; and of such treason the forfeiture of the escheates pertaineth to our lord the king, as well of the lands and tenements holden of others, as of himself.

---

1. 25 E. 3. cap. 2.
2. [*Ed.*: Of treason. This act is in the Statute of Purveyors (stat. 5, 1350).]
3. [*Ed.*: in its proper language.]

And albeit nothing can concerne the king, his crowne, and dignity, more then *crimen laesae majestatis,*[4] high treason: yet at the request of his lords and commons, the blessed king by authority of parliament made the declaration, as is above-said: and therefore, and for other excellent lawes made at this parliament, this was called *benedictum parliamentum,*[5] as it well deserved. For except it be Magna Charta, no other act of parliament hath had more honour given unto it by the king, lords spirituall and temporall, and the commons of the realme for the time being in full parliament, then this act concerning treason hath had. For by the statute of 1 H.4. cap. 10. reciting that where at a parliament holden 21 R.2. divers paynes of treason were ordained by statute, in as much as there was no man did know how to behave himselfe, to doe, speak, or say, for doubt of such paines: It is enacted by the king, the lords and commons, that in no time to come any treason be judged otherwise, then it was ordained by this statute of 25 E.3. The like honour is given to it by the statute of 1 E.6. cap. 12. and by the statute of 1 Ma. cap. 1. sess. 1. different times, but all agreeing in the magnifying and extolling of this blessed act of 25 E.3. Of this act of 1 *Mariae,* we shall speak more hereafter. But to proceed to give a light touch how other acts of parliament have been called. The parliament holden at Oxford, *an.* 42. H.3. was called *insanum parliamentum.*[6] 12 E. 2. the parliament of whitebands, *albarum fibularum* or *metellarum,*[7] 5 E.3. *parliamentum bonum,*[8] 10 R.2. *parliamentum quod fecit mirabile,*[9] that wrought wonders. 21 R.2. *magnū parliamentū.*[10] 6 H.4. *parliamentū indoctū,*[11] lack-learning parliament. 4 H.6. *parliamentū fustiū,* the parliament of bats. The session of parliament in *an.* 14. H.8. called the black parliament. The act of 1 E.6. was called *parliamentū pium,* the pious parliament. And the said act of 1 Mar. *parliamentū propitium,*[12] the merciful parliament. The parliaments

4. [*Ed.:* crime of lèse-majesté (i.e. treason).]
5. [*Ed.:* blessed parliament.]
6. [*Ed.:* unsound (or insane) parliament.]
7. [*Ed.:* of white buckles (or bands, according to Coke).]
8. [*Ed.:* good parliament.]
9. [*Ed.:* the parliament that wrought wonders.]
10. [*Ed.:* the great parliament.]
11. [*Ed.:* the unlearned parliament.]
12. [*Ed.:* the merciful parliament.]

of queen Elizabeth stiled *pia, justa, et provida*.[13] The parliament holden *anno* 21 of king James, called *foelix parliamentum*,[14] the happy parliament. And the parliament holden in the third yeare of our soveraigne lord king Charles, *benedictum parliamentum*,[15] the blessed parliament. The severall reasons of these former appellations appeare of record and in history, and the latter are yet fresh in memory. At the making of the statute of 25 E.3. the high courts of justice were furnished with excellent men, *viz.* Sir William Shardshill knight (shortly written in bookes Shard) lord chiefe justice of the kings bench, and his compagnions justices of that court; Sir John Stonor knight, commonly written in books Stone, lord chief justice of the court of common pleas, and his compagnions justices of that court; and Gervasius de Wilford, lord chiefe baron of the exchequer, men famous in their profession, and excellent in the knowledge of the lawes. At the making of the statute of 1 H.4. were Sir Walter Clopton knight, lord chiefe justice of the kings bench, and his compagnions justices of that court; and Sir William Thirning knight, lord chief justice of the court of common pleas, and his compagnions justices of that court; and Sir John Caffie knight, lord chiefe baron of the exchequer; men equall to any of their predecessors in the knowledge of the lawes. At the making of the statute of 1 E.6. were Sir Richard Lister knight, lord chiefe justice of the kings bench, and his compagnions justices of that court; and Sir Edward Montague knight, lord chiefe justice of the court of common pleas, and his compagnions justices of that court; and Sir Roger Cholmeley knight, lord chiefe baron of the exchequer; men of that excellency, as they were worthy of the name of The worthies of the law, At the making of the statute of 1 Mar. were Sir Thomas Bromley knight, lord chiefe justice of the kings bench, and his compagnions justices of that court; and Sir Richard Morgan, knight, lord chiefe justice of the court of common pleas, and his compagnions justices of that court; and Sir D. Brook knight, lord chiefe baron of the exchequer, men renouned for their great knowledge and judgement in their profession. All these we have named in the honour of them, and of their families and posterities, for that they in their severall times were great furtherers of these excellent lawes concerning treason. *In memoria aeterna erit justus*.[16] And all this was done in

---

13. [*Ed.:* pious, just and provident.]
14. [*Ed.:* the happy parliament.]
15. [*Ed.:* blessed parliament.]
16. [*Ed.:* He will be just in eternal memory. [cf. 1852-22].]

severall ages, that the faire lillies and roses of the crowne might flourish, and not be stained by severe and sanguinary statutes. But let us come to the act it selfe, and for the better understanding thereof, and of the book-cafes, and other records grounded upon the same: let us divide this act concerning high treason into severall classes or heads, and then prosecute the same in order.

The first concerneth death,

By compassing or imagining the death of the — King, Queene, Prince, — and declaring the same by some overt deed.

By killing and murdering of the — Chancellor. Treasurer. Justices of the one Bench or other. Justices in eyre. Justices of assize. Justices of oier and terminer, &c. — In their places doing their offices.

The second concerneth, violation, that is, to violate or carnally to know — the kings consort, or queene. the kings eldest daughter unmarried. the princes wife.

The third is levying war against the king.

The fourth is adhering to the kings enemies within the realme, or without, and declaring the same by some overt act.

The fifth is counterfeiting of — the great seale. the privie seale. the king's coyne.

The sixth and last, by bringing into this realme counterfeit money to the likenesse of the kings coine, &c.

So as treason is *membrum divisum,*[17] and these severall classes or heads are

17. [*Ed.:* a divided limb.]

membra dividentia.[18] And if the offence be not within one of these classes or heads, it is no treason.

(1) [*Treason*] is derived from [*trahir*] which is treacherously to betray. *Trahue,* betrayed, and *trahison, per contractionen,* treason, is the betraying it selfe.

Detegit imbelles animos, nil fortiter audens Proditio.[19]

Inter leges Canuti, fo 1. 118. ca. 61. *Proditiones* (hlaꞃoꝓ ꞃpice) *numerabantur inter scelera jure humano inexpiabilia.*[20] Treason is divided into two parts, *viz.* high treason, *alta proditio,*[21] and into petit treason, *proditio parva.*[22] The Latin word used in law is *proditio (à prodere)*[23] and thereof cometh *proditioniè,* which of necessity must be used in every indictment of treason, and cannot be expressed by any other word, peripharsis, or circumlocution.

(2) [*Ad fait declarisement.*][24] This law is for the most part declaratory of the ancient law, and therefore this word *(declarisement)* is used. But yet the studious reader shall observe, that in divers clauses it addeth to the former law, whereunto this word *(declarisement)* will sufficiently extend.

[When a man][25]

This extendeth to both Sexes, *Homo* including both Man and Woman. This Act is generall, and therefore extendeth to persons which claimed a priviledge to be exempted from Secular Jurisdiction. (For example,)[26] Adam, de Orleton Bishop of Hereford was indicted of High Treason for aiding the Mortimers.

---

18. [*Ed.:* the limbs into which it is divided.]

19. [*Ed.:* He betrays peaceful minds, treachery daring nothing boldly.]

20. [*Ed.:* Treasons are accounted among those offences which are not emendable by the law of man.]

21. [*Ed.:* high treason.]

22. [*Ed.:* petty treason.]

23. [*Ed.: proditio* (treachery) from *prodere* (to reveal).]

24. [*Ed.:* declaration.]

25. [*Ed.:* This English caption is here substituted for a French caption in the original text.]

26. *a* Rot. Romana. 17 E. 2. m. 6. Rot. Claus. 1 E. 3. part. 1. memb. 13. Artic. Cleri. 9 E. 3. cap. 15. & 16. Tr. 21 E. 3. coram Rege Rot. 173. *Privilegium seculare non competit seditioso equitanti cum armus, &c. secundum leges eclesia.* 25 E. 3. stat. 1. cap. 4. which was before this Act. Mich. 31 E. 3. coram Rege Rot. 55. Buck. Abbot de Misseny. See in the Chap. of Clergy in what cases the priviledge of Clergy is taken away.

&c. with Men, and Armour against King E.2, &c. Whereupon he was arraigned, and alledged *Se absque ofsensa Dei, & Sanctxae Ecelesiae, & absque licential Domini summi Pontificis non posse nec debere respondere in hac parte.*[27] And thereupon the Archbishop of Canterbury, York, and Dublin, and their Suffragans came to the Barre, claimed his priviledge, and took him away, and he was so far from punishment, as he was after translated to Worcester, and after to Winchester. But this Statute (to cleare all doubts) extendeth to all persons, *[28]as well Ecclestasticall as Temporall, and so hath it ever since been put in execution, as hereafter in divers Cases it appeareth. See hereafter Cap. Murdre & Larceny.

A Man that is *non compos mentis,*[29] as shall be said more fully hereafter in the next Section, or an Infant within the age of discretion is not *(un home)*[30] within this Statute; for the principall end of punishment is, That others by his example may feare to offend, De poena ad paucòs, metus ad omnes perveniar:[31] But such punishment can be no example to Mad-men, or Infants that are not of the age of Discretion. And God forbid that in Cases so penall, the Law should not be certaine; and if it be certaine in case of Murder and Felony, *à fortiori,*[32] it ought to be certaine in case of Treason.

If a man commit Treason or Felony and confesseth the same, or be thereof otherwise convict, if afterward he become *De non sane memorie (qui patitur exilium mentis)*[33] he shall not be called to answer: Or if after judgement he become *De non sane memorie,*[34] he shall not be executed, for it cannot be an example to others.

27. [*Ed.:* Without offence to God and the Holy Church, and without licence of the lord high pontiff (i.e. the pope), he neither can nor ought to answer in this behalf.]

28. *To persons, Eccesasticall and Temporall. Bract. lib. 3. 120. 121. 134. 135. Britton. 5. 18. Fleta. cap. 23. 30. Mirror. cap. 1. 6. cap. 2. § 11. de appeale de homicide. 3 E. 3 cor. 383. 25. E. 3. 42. cor. 139. 26. ass. 27. 3 H. 7. cap. 1. 3 H. 7. 1. 12. 21 H. 7. 3. 31. 1. Mar. Dier. 104. Tr. 32. E. 1. Coram Rege. 15. 8. E. 2. Corone. 369. 395. Custum. de Norm. cap. 79. fo. 94. 95. 33. H. 8. cap. 20. 1 & 2 Mar. c. 10.

29. [*Ed.:* Sound of mind. Having use and control of one's mental faculties.]

30. [*Ed.:* a man (i.e. person).]

31. [*Ed.:* That the punishment may reach a few, but the fear of it affect all.]

32. [*Ed.:* So much more so, with stronger reason; much more.]

33. [*Ed.:* of unsound mind (one who suffers a loss of mind).]

34. [*Ed.:* of unsound memory or mind; synonymous with "non compos mentis."]

And all Aliens[35] that are within the Realme of England, and whose Sove-
[5] l-raignes are in amity with the King of England, are within the protection of
the King, and doe owe a locall obedience to the King, (are homes within this
Act) and if they commit High Treason against the King, they shall be punished
as Traytors, but otherwise it is of an Enemy, whereof you may reade at large
Lib. 7. Calvins Case. fol. 6. &c 17, &c.

[Doth compasse.][36]

Let us see first what the compassing or imagining the beath of a Subiect was
before, and at the time of the making of this Statute, [a][37]when *Voluntas reputabatur pro facto.*[38] And [b][39]Bracton saith, that *Spectatur voluntas & non exitus,
& nihil interest utrum quis occidat, aut causam mortis praebeat.*[40] So as when
the Law was so holden, he must *causam mortis praebere,*[41] that is, declare the
same by some open deed tending to the execution of his intent, or which
might be cause of death, as Justice [c][42]Spigurnel[43] reporteth a Case adiudged;
That a man's wife went away her Avowterer, and they [d][44]Compassed the Death
of the Husband, & as he was riding towards the Sessions of Oier and Terminer
and Gaole-delivery, they assaulted him and stroke him with weapons, that he
fell downe as dead, whereupon they fled; the Husband recovered and made
Hue and Cry, and came to the Sessions and shewed all this matter to the
Justices, and upon the Warrant of the Justices, they were taken, indicted, and
arraigned; and all this speciall matter was found by Verdict; and it was adjudged
that the man should be hanged, and the woman burnt. And Sir William

---

35. To Aliens.

36. [*Ed.:* This English caption is here substituted for a French caption in the original text.]

37. *a* See hereafter, cap. 73. Where & how *Vuluntas reputabatur pro facto,* by the ancient law, and the change thereof.

38. [*Ed.:* The intention is to be taken for the deed.]

39. *b* Bracton, fol.

40. [*Ed.:* The intention shall be regarded, not the outcome, and therefore whether someone kills or only furnishes the cause of death is of no significance.]

41. [*Ed.:* furnish the cause of death.]

42. *c* 15 E. 2. tit. Cor. 383.

43. [*Ed.:* The Spigurnel is the sealer of the royal writs.]

44. *d* Note this word [*compassed.*]

Beresford Chiefe Justice of the Common Pleas said, That before him and his Companions Justices of Dier and Terminer and Gaole-delivery, a Youth was arraigned, for that he would have stolen the goods of his Master, and came to his Masters bed, where he lay asleepe, and with a knife attempted with all his force to have cut his throat; and thinking that he had indeed cut it, he fled, whereupon the Master cried out, and his Neighbours apprehended the youth; and all this matter being found by speciall Verdict, in the end he was adjudged to be hanged, &c. *Quia* *[45] *voluntas reputabitur pro facto.* So as it was not a bare compassing or plotting of the death of a man, either by word, or writing, but such an overt deed, as is aforesaid, to manifest the same. So as if a man had compassed the death of another, and had uttered the same by words or writing, yet he should not have died for it, for there wanted an overt deed tending to the execution of his compassing. [46e]But if a man had imagined to murder, or rob another, and to that intent had become Insidiator viarum,[47] and assaulted him, though he killed him not, nor took any thing from him, yet was it felony, for there was an overt deed. But in those dayes, in the Case of the King, if a man had compassed, or imagined the death of the King (who is the Head of the Common-wealth) and had declared his compassing, or imagination by words or writing, this had been High Treason, and a sufficient overture by the ancient Law. And herewith agree all our ancient Books. Glanvil saith, *Cum quis de morte Regis, &c. infamatur, &c.*[48]

Bracton in the title *De criminibus laesae majestatis. Ipse accusatus praeloquutus fuit mortem regis.*[49] And Britton. fol. 16. *Grand treason est a compasser nostre mort,* and fo. 39.b. *Cyface lenensor son appeale &c. que il oya mesme céi*

---

45. [*Ed.:* Because intention is taken for the deed.] *Sid haec voluntas non intellecta fuit de voluntate nudis verbis, aut scriptus propalata, sed mundo manifescata fuit per apertum factum, Id est, cum quis dederat operam, quantum in ipse fuit, ad occidendis, & sic de similibus.*

46. *e Insidiator viarū.* See hereafter, ca. 5. De Heresie, 25. H. 3. 42. 27. ass. p. 38. 4 H. 4. ca. 2. 13 H. 4. 7. per Gascoign. But see 9. E. 4. fo. 26. Insidiator viarum without taking of some-what, resolved to be no felony, V. lib. 11. fo. 29. b. Al. Poulters Case. Vid. postea cap. 16. Robbery, in fine. Glanvil. lib. 14. cap. 14. lib. 1. c. 2. Bract. lib. 3. f. 118. Britton fol. 16. & 39. b. Note the word *compasse.* Fleta lib. 1. c. 21. Mirr. cap. 1. §. 5. cap. 2. §. 11. Note this word *Compasse.* Mirror c. 2. §. 11. De lappeale de Majestie. Rot. pat. 25. E. 3. part 1. m. 16. Vide Mic. 4. H. 4. Coram Rege. Rot. 22. See hereof more in the 57 Cha. of Appeales. Bracton, Britton, Fleta, &c.

47. [*Ed.:* Highwaymen, persons who lie in wait in order to commit some felony or other misdmeanor.]

48. [*Ed.:* Whoever is accused, etc. of the king's death, etc.]

49. [*Ed.:* of crimes of lèse-majesté (treason). The accused discussed (or arranged) the death of the king.

John pur parler tiel mort, ou tiel treason &c.[50] And Fleta saith in his title *De crimine laesae majestatis, Si quis mortem regis ausu temerario machinatus fuerit, &c. quamvis voluntatem non perduxit ad effectum.*[51] And the Mirror saith, *Crime de majestic est un peche horrible fait al roy &c. p. ceux q occirent le roy, ou compassant a faire.*[52] And it will delight you (in respect of reverend antiquity) to heare a president of an appeale (which then and after was in use) of high treason, *en pleine pliam &c. en temps roy Edmond en cestes parolx. Rocelyn icy dit vers Waligrot illonq q a tiel iour tiel anne del raigne de tiel roy, en tiel lieu vient celuy Waligrot a céi Rocelyn, et luy trova destre en company, et en aide ensemblement ove Atheling, Thurkild, Ballard, et autres de faire prisoner, ou en tache pur occire nré seignior le roy Edmond, ou en auter manner p. coupe felon-iousment, et a ceo faire fuer' entreinres a ceo counsel celer, et a ceo felony issint fornir solong lour poier.*[53] By all which it is manifest, that compassing, mach-

[6] inating, counselling, &c. I to kill the King, though it hath no other declaration thereof but by words, was High-treason by the Common law. And see hereafter, *verb. per overt fait, et de ceo provablement, &c.*[54]

50. [*Ed.:* High treason is compassing our death.

[And] fo. 39b. The accuser shall make his appeal, etc. that he heard this same John speak about such death, or such treason, etc.]

51. [*Ed.:* of the crime of lèse-majesté (treason). Whoever shall inadvisedly dare to plot the death of the king, etc., even if he does not carry his intention into effect.]

52. [*Ed.:* crime of lèse-majesté (treason) is a horrible sin committed against the king, etc. by those who kill the thing or compass so to do.]

53. [*Ed.:* in full parliament, etc. in the time of King Edmund, in these words: Rocelyn, who is here, speaks against Waligrot, who is there, that on such and such a day, in such and such a year of the reign of such and such king, in such and such a place, there came this Waligrot to this Rocelyn and found him to be in company and in aid together with Atheling, Thurkild, Ballard, and others, to make prisoner or to kill our lord King Edmund, or in another way by felonious deed, and in doing this they were bound to conceal this counsel and to carry out this felony according to their power.]

54. [*Ed.:* by overt act, and thereof probably [attainted], etc.]

[doth compasse or imagine.][55]

So as there must be a comapassing or imagination, for an Act done *per infortunium*,[56] without compassing, intent, or imagination: is not within this Act, as it appeareth by the expresse words thereof. *Et actus non facit reum, nisi mens fit rea.*[58] And if it be not within the words of this Act, then by force of a clause hereafter, viz. *Et pur ceo que plusors auters, &c.*[59] It cannot be adjuged treason, untill it be declared treason by Parliament, which is the remedie in that case, which the makers of the law provided in that case. This compassing, intent, or imagination, though secret, is to be tryed by the peers, and to be discovered by circumstances precedent, concomitant, and subsequent, with all endeavour evermore for the safety of the King. This was the case of Sr. Walter Tirrel a French Knight, who the first day of August Ann. 13 Williel. 2. Ann. dom. 1100 being a hunting with the King in the new forest, was commanded by the King to shoot at a Hart,[60] *Exiit ergo telum volatile, et obstante arbore in obliquum reflexum faciens, per medium cordis regem sauciavit, qui subito mortuus corruit.*[61]

Regula.[57]

It appeareth also by the Custumer of Normandy treating of treason, and the exposition of the same, that this act was not treason.[62] To calculate or seek to know by setting of a figure or witchcraft, how long the King shall raigne or live, is no treason, for it is no compassing, or imagination of the death of the King, within this statute of 25 E.3. And this appeareth by the judgement of the Parliament in 23. Eliz. whereby this offence was made felony during the life of Queen Eliz. which before was punishable by fine and imprisonment.

---

55. [*Ed.:* This English caption is here substituted for a French caption in the original text.]

56. [*Ed.:* By misadventure. Homicide "per infortunium" is committed where a person, doing a lawful act, without any intention of hurt, unfortunately kills another.]

57. [*Ed.:* The Rule.]

58. [*Ed.:* An act does not make [the doer of it] guilty, unless the mind be guilty, that is, unless the intention be criminal. The intent and the act must both concur to constitute the crime.]

59. [*Ed.:* and because many others, etc.]

60. Mat. Par. pa. 51. Holling. pa. 26. b. Mar. Westm. W. Malmesbury.

61. [*Ed.:* Therefore he released a flying dart, and a tree standing in the way caused it to deflect and strike the king in the middle of his heart, who immediately fell dead.]

62. Custum. de Nor. cap. 14. Vide inter Indictamenta de 17 E. 4. de Th. Burdit ar. sed judicandum est legibus, & non exemplis. 23 Eliz. cap. 2.

[63]The ancient law was, that if a mad man had killed or offered to kill the King, it was holden for treason; and so it appeareth by King Alfreds law before the Conquest, and in lib. 4. in Beverlyes case. But now by this statute and by force of these words, *Fait compasser ou imaginer la mort,*[64] he that is *non compos mentis*[65] and totally deprived of all compassings, and imaginations, cannot commit High Treason by compassing or imagining the death of the King: for *furiosus solo ferore punitur:*[66] but it must be an absolute madnesse and a totall deprivation of memorie. And this appeareth by the statute of 39. H. 8.[67] for thereby it is provided that if a man being *Compos mentis* commit High Treason, and after accusation, &c. fall to madnesse, that he might be tryed in his absence, &c. and suffer death, as if he were of perfect memory, for by this statute of 25 E.3. a mad man could not commit High Treason. It was further provided by the said Act of 33 H.8. that if a man attainted of treason became mad, that notwithstanding he should be executed; *[68]which cruell and inhumane law lived not long, but was repealed, for in that point also it was against the common law, because by intendment of law the execution of the offender is for example, *ut poena ad paucos metus ad omnes perveniat,*[69] as before is said: but so it is not when a mad man is executed, but should be a miserable spectacle, both against law, and of extreame inhumanity and cruelty; and can be no example to others.

[Death.][70]

[a71]He that declareth by overt act to depose the King, is a sufficient overt act to prove, that be compasseth and imagineth the death of the King. And so

---

63. *Inter leges Alveredi. cap. 4. Lib. 4. fo. 124. Beverlies case. Ovid. Scilicet in superis etiam fortuna luenda est. Nec veniam laeso numine, casus habet.

64. [*Ed.:* Do causes to compass or imagine the death.]

65. [*Ed.:* not sound of mind; insane.]

66. [*Ed.:* a madman is punished only by his madness.]

67. 33 H. 8. cap. 20.

68. *1 & 2 Ph. & Mar. ca. 10. a Bract. li. 3. fo. 118. Britton. cap. 8. a disheriter. Glanv. lib. 1. cap. 2. Fleta lib. 1. cap. 21. Mirror ca. 1. §. 5. Vers Roy de la re.

69. [*Ed.:* that the punishment may reach a few, but the fear of it affect all.]

70. [*Ed.:* This English caption is here substituted for a French caption in the original text.]

71. *a* 13 Eliz. cap. i. *nota declared.* Brook tit. treason. 24.

it is to [b72]imprison the King, or to take the King into his power, and manifest the same by some overt act, this is also a sufficient overt act for the intent aforesaid.[73] But peruse advisedly the statutes of 13 Eliz: cap. 1. 2. & 14 Eliz. cap. 1.

[Of our Lord the King.][74]

There words extend to all his successors, as it hath been always taken.

[The King.][75]

Is to be understood of a King regnant, and not of one that hath but the name of a King, or a nominative King, as it was resolved in the case | of King Philip, [7] who married Queen Mary, and was but a nominative King, for Queen Mary had the office and dignity of a king, so as she wanted within this Act of 25 E. 3. And hee that had the name, and not the office and dignity of the King was not within it. And therefore an Act was made, that to compasse or imagine the death of King Philip, &c.[76] during his marriage with the Queen, was treason. A Queen regnant is within these words, (*nré seignior le Roy*) for she hath the office of a King.

This Act is to be understood of a King in possession of the Crowne,[76] and Kingdome: for if there be a King regnant in possession, although he be *Rex de facto, et non de jure,* yet is he *seignior le Roy*[77] within the Purview of this statute. And the other that hath right, and is out of possession, is not within this Act.[78] Nay if treason be committed against a King De facto, et non de jure, and after the King *de jure* commeth to the Crowne, he shall punish the treason done to the King *de facto:* And a pardon granted by a King *de jure,* that is not also *de facto,* is voyde.

72. *b* 1 H. 4. 1. 19. H. 6. 47. 13. H. 8. 12. *vide infra verb.* ¶ *Per overt fait.* [*Ed.:* of open deed.]
73. 3 Mar. Dier. 131. pl. 7.
74. [*Ed.:* This English caption is here substituted for a French caption in the original text.]
75. [*Ed.:* This English caption is here substituted for a French caption in the original text.]
76. 1 & 2 Phi. & Mar. cap. 10.
77. [*Ed.:* King in fact but not in law . . . the Lord King.]
78. *Vide* 11 H. 7. c. 1. 4. E. 4. 1. 9. E. 4. 1. 2.

If the Crown descend to the rightfull heire, he is *Rex* before Coronation: for by the Law of England there is no interregnum:[79] and Coronation is but an ornament or solemnity of honour. And so it was resolved by al the Judges Hil. 1. Ja. in the case of Watson and Clarke Seminary priests:[80] for by the law there is alwayes a King, in whose name the lawes are to be maintained, and executed, otherwise Justice should faile. Divers Kings before the Conquest voluntarily renounced their Kingly office: And so did King H.2. in the 16. yeare of his reigne, and Henry his sonne was created and crowned.

It appeareth by Britton, that to compasse the death of the father of the King,[81] is treason, and so was the law holden long after that: for after King E.2. had dismissed himselfe of his kingly office, and duty, and his sonne by the name of E. 3. was crowned, and king regnant, those cursed Caitifs Thomas Gourny, and William Ocle, and others were attainted of High Treason for murthering the Kings father, who had been King by the name of E.2. and had judgement to be drawne, hanged, and quartered.

*[82]The like judgement was given against Sir John Matrevers knight, and others, as being guilty of the death of the Kings uncle, Edmond Earl of Kent, which at that time (being so neer of the bloud royall) was by some holden also treason. But now this Act of 25 E.3. hath restrained High treason in case of death (*al nré seignior le Roy, sa compaigne, et al eigne fitz, et heire le Roy.*[83]

Nicholas de Segrave was charged in open parliament *in praesentia dñi. Reg. comitum, baronum, et aliorum de consilio Regis tunc ibi existent,*[84,85] that the King in the warre of Scotland being amongst his enemies, Nicholas Segrave his liege man, and holding of the King by homage, and fealty, served him for his aid in that warre, did maliciously move contention and discord without cause, with John de Crombewell, charging him with many enormious crimes, and offered to prove it upon his body. To whom the said John answered, that

79. [*Ed.:* An interval between reigns. The period between the death of a sovereign and the election of another.]

80. Hil. 1 Ja. in the case of Watson and Clark seminary priests. 9 F. 4. 1. b.

81. See the preamble, *Auxint pur ces que divers opinions ount estre eius ceux heures, que qen case doit estre dit treason, et in quel case nëi.* Rot. parliam. 4 E. 3. num. 5.

82. *Eodem Rot. num. 3. & 4.

83. [*Ed.:* to our lord the king, his companion, and to the king's son and heir.]

84. Plac. in Parliam. E. 1. *anno regni sui* 33. North. Rot. 17. & 22.

85. [*Ed.:* in the presence of the lord king, the earls, barons, and others of the king's council then being there.]

he would answer him in the Kings Court, as the Court should consider, &c. and thereupon gave him his faith. After Nich. withdrew himselfe from the Kings Host, and from the Kings aid, leaving the King amongst his enemies, *in periculo hostium suorum,*[86] and adjourned the said John to defend himself in the court of the King of France, and prefixed him a certaine day, *Et sic quantum in eo fuit, subjiciens, et submittens dominium regis, et regni subiectioni dñi. regis Franciae, ad hoc faciendum, iter suum arripuit usque Dovoriam, ad transfrerandum, &c.*[87] All which the said Nich. confessed, *et voluntari dñi. regis de alto et basto inde se submisit. Et super hoc dñs Rex volens habere avisamentum Comitum, Baronum, Magnatum, et aliorum de consilio suo, injunxit eisdem in homagio, fidelitate, & ligeantia quibus ei tenentur, quod ipsum fideliter consulerent, qualis poena pro tali facto sic cognito fuerit infligenda: qui omnes, habito super hoc diligenti tractaru, & avisamento, consideratis, & intellectis omnibus in praedicto facto contenus, &c. dicuut quod hujusmodi factum meretur amissionem vitae & membrorum, &c.*[88] So as this offence was then solemnely in parliament adjudged High treason. But this is | taken away by this Act of 25 E.3. being [8] not under any of the classes, or heads specified in this act.

So piracy by any of the Kings subjects upon another, was taken to be treason before this Act,[89] for so is the book to be intended, because a pirat is *Hostis humani generis.*[90] But by this Act it is not now to be judged treason. See hereafter in the chapter of Piracy.

One doth marie a Queen regnant, if the husband compasse the death of the Queene, and declare the same by over act, he is guilty of treason, and punishable by this act, for to this and many other purposes, she is a distinct

86. [*Ed.:* in danger from his enemies.]

87. [*Ed.:* and thus, subjecting and submitting as far as he could the lordship of England to the subjection of the lord king of France, in order to do this he travelled to Dover to obtain a passage, etc.]

88. [*Ed.:* And thereof submitted himself of high and low to the will of the lord king. And thereupon the lord king, wishing to have the advice of the earls, barons, great men, and others of his council, enjoined them upon the homage, faith and allegiance with which they were bound, that they should faithfully advise him what punishment ought to be inflicted for such a deed, having been thus confessed; and, after a diligent discussion thereupon had, everything contained in the same deed having been taken into advisement, considered and understood, etc., all of them say that a deed of this kind deserves loss of life and limbs, etc.]

89. 40. Afs. 25.

90. [*Ed.:* An enemy of mankind.]

person by the common law. And so if a Queene wife of a King regnant, compasse the death of the King, and declare the same by overt act, she is guilty of treason, and punishable by this act. So as (that we may speak it once for all) by these and many others that might be cited,[91] (some whereof shall hereafter be touched) the preamble of this act appeareth to be true, that divers opinions had been before the making of this act, what offences should be adjudged High treason, and what not.

This statute having restrained the compassing, &c. of death to the King, Queene, & Prince, it came to passe after the making of this act, that in 3 R.2.[92] two Citizens of London, John Kerby Mercer, and John Algore Grocer conceiving malice against John Imperiall Janevois of S. Mary in Genoa that came as Ambassador from the state of Genoa to the King (under the Kings Letters of safe conduct, for alliance to be had betweene the King and the Duke and Comminalty of Genoa aforesaid) for that the said John Imperiall had obtained a [93]monopolie to furnish this land (keeping his staple at Southampton of all such wares as came from the Levant, so plentifully as was to be had in all the west parts of Christendome, the said John Imperiall was killed by them,[94] as more at large appears by the record. And albeit the said John Imperiall was an Ambassadour under the Kings safe conduct, and the killing of him was *justi belli causa*,[95] yet the killing of him was no treason, because it was not under any of the said classes or heads,[96] until it was at that time declared by parliament in these words, *Quel case examine & dispute inter les seigniors, & commons, & puis mŕe al Roy en pleine parliament, estoit illonques devant nŕe seignior le Roy declares, determinus & assentus, que tiel fait, & coupe est treason, & crime de royall majestie blemye, en quel case il ne doir allower a nulluy priviledge del clergie*,[97] and accordingly the said Kerby and Algore were attainted of High

---

91. Britton cap. 8. and other ancient Authors *ubi supra*.

92. Rot. parlia. 3 R. 2. num. 18. See Placita coram rege Hill. an. 3 R. 2. (Cavendish) rot. 8. London Holl. cron. 3 R. 2. pa. 422. 60. b. & c.

93. Monopoly.

94. *nota* his end.

95. [*Ed.*: by reason of a just war.]

96. 2 Regum cap. 10. 4. 12. 31. The killing of a foreine Ambassadour. *Honor legati, honor mittentis est, & proregis dedecius redundat in regem.*

97. [*Ed.*: Which case being examined and disputed by the lords and commons, and then shown to the king in full parliament, it was therefore before our lord the king declared, determined and assented that such a deed and offence is treason, and a crime of lèse-majesté, in which case he ought not to be allowed any privilege of the clergy.]

treason in the Kings bench, Hill. 3 R.2. *ubi supra:* but this declaration is taken away by the statute of 1 Mariae, as hereafter shall be said, and yet of this declaration we shall make much use hereafter.

In the 22 yeare of E.3. which was about 3 yeares before the making of this act, one John at Hill had murdered A. de Walton the Kings Ambassadour,[98] *nuncium dñi regis miss. ad mandatum regis exequendum:*[99] this was adjudged High treason, for which he was drawne, hanged, and beheaded, &c. For true it is, *quod legatus ejus vice fungitur, a quo destinatur, & honorandus est sicut ille cujus vicem gerit, & legatos violare contra jus gentium est.*[100] But by this Act of 25 E.3. it is restrained to the death de *nře seignior le Roy,*[101] and therefore, *prorex,*[102] is not within this statute.

[Of my Lady [his queene].][103]

This word compaigne, (which is all one with consort or wife) was used, that compassing, &c. must be during the marriage with the King, for after the Kings death she is not sa compaigne, and therefore it extendeth not to a Queene dowager, and for this cause this word compaigne, was used in this Act.

[Their eldest sonne and heire.][104]

The eldest sonne and heire of a Queen Regnant is within this Law.[105] Before this Statute some did hold, that to compasse the death of any of the Kings children, was Treason. But by this Act it is restrained to the Prince, the Kings Sonne, being heire apparant to the Crowne for the time being: and he need not be the first begotten sonne, for the second after the decease of the first

---

98. 22. Ass. p. 49. *More dun Ambassad. le roy.*

99. [*Ed.:* the lord king's ambassador sent to carry out the king's command:]

100. [*Ed.:* that a legate functions in [the king's] stead, and is to be honoured in the same way as the person whom he represents, and to violate legates is against the law of nations.]

101. [*Ed.:* of our lord the king.]

102. [*Ed.:* a viceroy.]

103. [*Ed.:* This English caption is here substituted for a French caption in the original text.]

104. [*Ed.:* This English caption is here substituted for a French caption in the original text.]

105. Britton *ubi supra.*

[9]   begotten without issue, is *Fitz eigne*[106] within | this statute, & *sic de caeteris.*[107] If the heire apparent to the Crowne be a collaterall heire apparent, he is not within this statute, untill it be declared by Parliament, as it was in the Duke of Yorks case.

Roger Mottimer Earle of March was in *Anno Domini* 1487 (11 R.2.) proclaimed heire apparent. Anno 39 H.6. Richard Duke of York was likewise proclaimed heire apparent. And so was John de la Poole Earle of Lincolne, by R.3. And Henry Marquise of Exeter, by King Henry the eighth. But none of these or of the like, are within the Purvieu of this statute. And now that we have handled compassings and imaginations, let us proceed to the residue which concerne Acts and Deeds.

Heire is here taken for heire apparant, for he cannot be heire in the life of the Father.

[If a man doe violate the kings compagnion.][108]

The Mirror saith,[109] *Crime de Majestie vers le Roy p ceux Avowterors q̄ spergissent la feme le Roy.*[110] Whereby it appeareth that this was High Treason by the common Law.

Violare is here taken for *carnaliter cognoscere;*[111,112] and it is no treason, unlesse it be done during the marriage with the King, and extendeth not to a Queen Dowager, as hath been said. And if the wife of the King doth yeeld and consent to him that committeth this treason, it is treason in her.[113]

---

106. [*Ed.:* firstborn son.]
107. [*Ed.:* and likewise concerning the rest.]
108. [*Ed.:* This English caption is here substituted for a French caption in the original text.]
109. Mirror ca. 1. §. 5. Brit. c. 23. fo. 43. 2.
110. [*Ed.:* Crime of [lèse-]majesté against the king by adulterers who defile the king's wife.]
111. 33 H. 8. cap. 21.
112. [*Ed.:* Violate . . . carnally knew.]
113. Pasch. 28 H. 8. in Spilmans Reports in Case of Queen Anne. 33 H. 8. *ubi supra,* in case of Queen Katherine.

[The wife of the kings eldest sonne and heire.][114]

This also extendeth to the wife of the Prince during the coverture betweene them, and not to a Dowager, and if the wife yeeld and consent to him that commits this treason, it is treason in her.

[Heire.]

Here is taken *ut supra,* for heire apparant.

[or the kings eldest daughter unmarried.][115]

(That is,) eldest Daughter not married at the time of the Violation, albeit there had been an elder daughter then she, who is dead without issue.[116] The Mirror. *Avowterors q̃ spergissent la file le Roy eignes legittime, avant ceo q el soit marie.*[117]

And the reason that the eldest only is here mentioned, is, for that for default of issue Male, she only is inheritable to the Crowne.

[Or if a man doe levie warre against our lord the king.][118]

[a][119]This was High Treason by the Common Law, for no subiect can levie warre within the Realme without authority from the King, for to him it only belongeth. See F.N.B. 113.a. *Le Roy de droit saver & defender son realme vers enemies, &c.*[120]

[b][121]A compassing or conspiracy to levie war, is no Treason, for there must

---

114. [*Ed.:* This English caption is here substituted for a French caption in the original text.]

115. [*Ed.:* This English caption is here substituted for a French caption in the original text.]

116. *Mir. cap. 1. § 5. See Brit. cap. 23. fo. 43. 44. &c. cap. 29. fol. 71. 1 Mat. Parl. 2. c. 1.

117. [*Ed.:* Adulterers who defile the king's eldest lawful daughter, before she is married.]

118. [*Ed.:* This English caption is here substituted for a French caption in the original text.]

119. *a* Glanvil lib. 1. cap. 2. 14. c. 1. Bracton. lib. 3. fol. 118. Britton. f. 16. &c. Fleta. li. 1. ca. 21. Mir. ca. 1. §. 5.

120. [*Ed.:* The king ought of right to preserve and defend his realm against enemies, etc.]

121. *b* 1 Mar. 98. b. Diet. in Sir N. Thregmortons Case. See 21 E. 3. 23. 21 R. 2. cap. Repeale. 1 H. 4. cap. 3. 8 E. 3. 20. See hereafter, cap. 73. against going or riding armed.

be a levying of war in facto. But if many conspire to levie war, and some of them do levie the same according to the conspiracy, this is High Treason in all, for in Treason all be principals, and war is levied.

If any levie war to expulse strangers, to deliver men out of prisons, to remove Counsellors, or against any statute, or to any other end, pretending Reformation of their own heads, without warrant; this is levying of war against the King: because they take upon them Royall Authority, which is against the King. There is a diversity betweene levying of war and committing of a great Riot, a Rout, or an unlawfull assembly. [c122]For example, as if three, or foure, or more, doe rise to burne, or put downe an inclosure in Dale, which the Lord of the Manor of Dale hath made there in that particular place; this or the like is a Riot, a Rout, or an unlawfull Assembly, and no Treason. But if they had risen of purpose to alter Religion established within the Realme, or Laws, or to go from Town to Town generally, and to cast downe Inclosures, this is a levying of war (though there be no great number of the Conspirators) within the Purvien of this Statute because the pretence is publick and generall,

[10] and not | private in particular. And so it was resolved in the Case of Richard Bradshaw Miller, Robert Burton Major, and others of Oxfordshire,[123] whose Case was. That they conspired and agreed to assemble themselves with so many as they could procure at Enslowe-Mill in the said County, and there to rise, and from thence to go from Gentlemans house to Gentlemans house, and to cast downe Inclosures, as well for enlargement of High-wayes as of errable Lands. And they agreed to get Armour and Artillery at the Lord Norrys his house, and to weare them in going from Gentlemans house to Gentlemans house for the purpose aforesaid, and to that purpose they persuaded divers others: and all this was confessed by the offenders. And it was resolved, That this was a compassing and intention to levie war against the Queen, because the pretence was publick within the statute of 13 Eliz. ca.i. (the Letter whereof herein shortly followeth,) and the Offenders were attainted and executed at Enslowe Mill.

And this diversity is proved by a latter Branch of this Act.

Et si per case ascun home de cest realme chimancha arme discovert secretment ove gents armes, contre ascun autre, pur luy tuer, ou disrober, ou pur luy prender,

---

122. *c* Sec Rot. Parl. in Cro. Epiphan. 20 H. 1. Rot. 23. Humfrey de Case. 4 Eliz. 210. b. Dier. See the statute of 1 Mar. ca. a. By Mar. ca. 2. By which, Grand Riots, in some Cases be made felony.

123. Pasch. 39. Eliz. by all the Judges of England, I being Attourney. Generall, and present.

ou retayner tanq il face fine, ou ransome pur sa deliverance, nest lentention le Roy & de son counsell, q en tiel case soit adjudge treason, mes soit adjudge felony, ou trespasse, solonq le ley del tŕe auncienement use.[124] Whereby it appeareth, that bearing of armes in warlike manners, for a private revenge or end, is no levying of war against the king within this statute. So that every gathering of force is not High Treason. And so it was resolved in Parliament in 5 H.4 Rot. Parliam. nu 11. & 12.[125] the Earle of Northumberlands Case.

By the said Statute of 13 Eliz. cap.1.[126] it is enacted, declared, and established. "That during the naturall life of Queene *Elizabeth,* if any within the Realme or without, should compasse, imagine, invent, devise, or intend to levie war against her Majesty, within this Realme, or without, and the same declare by writing or word, &c. that it should be High Treason:" So during the life of the Queen a conspiracy to levie war was High Treason, though no war were levied; and upon that law, Bradshaw, Burton and others, were attainted of High Treason, for conspiracy only to levie war. But it was resolved by all the Justices, that it was no treason within the statute of 25 E.3. as hath been said. The words in this law are [levie guerre][127] An actual Rebellion or Insurrection is a levying of war within this Act, and by the name of levying war is to be expressed in the Indictment. If any with strength and weapons invasive and defensive, doth hold and defend a Castle or Fort against the King and his power, this is levying of war against the King within this Statute of 25 E.3.

[Or be adherent to the kings enemies in his Realme, giving to them aide and comfort in the realme or elsewhere.][128]

It was resolved by all the Judges of England in the reigne of King H.8. that an Insurrection against the Statute of Labourers, for the inhansing of salaries

124. [*Ed.:* And if anyone of this realm happens to ride armed, overtly (or) secretly, with men of arms, against any other, to slay him, or rob him, or take him, or detain him until he has made fine or ransom for his deliverance, it is not the intention of the king and his council that in this case it shall be adjudged treason, but it shall be adjudged felony, or trespass, according to the law of the land anciently used.]

125. Rot. Parl. 5. H. 4. nu. 11,12.

126. 13 Eliz. cap. 1. b. The Indictments and Attainders of treason by force to this statute are not more to be followed, because the statute, which made them good, is expired. Dier, 3. & 4 Ph. & Mar. 144. 10 E. 4. 6. 1 Mar. Treason, Br. 24 Ter. Mic. 8 H. S. Mich. 7 H. 5. Coram Rege. Heref. Rot. 20.

127. [*Ed.:* levying war.]

128. [*Ed.:* This English caption is here substituted for a French captrion in the original text.]

and wages, was a levying of war against the King, because it was generally against the Kings Law, and the offenders took upon them the reformation thereof, which subiects by gathering of power ought not to do. It was specially found, that divers of the Kings subjects did minister and yeeld victuals to Sir John Oldcastle Knight, and others, being in open war against the King, and that they were in company with them in open war; but all this was found to be *pro timore mortis, & quod recefierunt, quam cito procuerunt;*[129] and it was adiudged to be no Treason, because it was for feare of death. *Et actus non facit reum, nisi mens fit rea.*[130] And therefore this in them was no leying of war against the King within this Act.

[Adherent.]

[a][131] This is here explained, viz. in giving aide and comfort to the Kings enemies within the Realme or without: Delivery or surrender of the Kings Castles or Forts by the Kings Captaine thereof to the Kings enemie within the realme or without for reward, &c. is an adhering to the Kings enemy, and consequently treason declared by this Act. 6.[132] A. is out of | the Realme at the time of a Rebellion within England, and one of the Rebels flye out of the Realme, whom A. knowing his treason doth aide or succour, this is no treason in A. by this branch of 25 E.3. because the traytor is no enemy, as hereafter shall be said; and this statute is taken strictly.

[11]

129. [*Ed.:* for fear of death, and that they fell back as far as they could.]

130. [*Ed.:* An act does not make [the doer of it] guilty, unless the mind be guilty; that is unless the intention be criminal.]

131. *a* Rot. Parl. 20 E. 1. nu. 2. *John de Brittaines* case. Rot. Parl. 33 E. 7. Rot. 6. Rob. des Ros *de Werkes* case. 8 E. 3. 20, 38 E. 3. 31. 2. Parl. 4. R. 2. nu 17, 18, &c. 5 R. 2. Triall 54. Hil. 18 E. 3 coram rege. Rot. 145. Eborum. 43. Ass. 28 42. Ass. 29. *Gulbert de M.* was a Scot. Rot. Parl. 7 R. 2. nu. 15 17. 243. 7. H. 4. 47. Cust. de Norm. ca. 73.

132. *b Vid.* 13 Eliz. Dier. 298.

[Enemies.][133]

[134] *Inimicus* in legall understanding is *hostis*,[135] for [c136]the subjects of the King, though they be in open war or rebellion against the King, yet are they are not the Kings enemies, but traytors; for enemies be those that be out of the allegiance of the King. If a Subject jouyne with a foraine Enemy and come into England with him, he shall not be taken prisoner here and ransomed, or proceeded with as an enemy shall, but he shall be taken as a traytor to the King.

[d137]An Enemy comming in open hostility into England, and taken, shall be either executed by Marshall-Law, or ransomed; for he cannot be indicted of treason, for that he never was within the protection or ligeance of the King, and the Indictment of Treason saith, *Contra ligeantiam suam debitam*.[138]

[e139]David Prince of Wales levied war against E.1. This was Treason, for that he was within the homage and ligeance of the King, and had judgement given against him as a Traytor, and not as an enemy. And albeit in many presidents of Indictments, Subiects that be Rebels, and Traytors, &c. be called *proditores & inimici*;[140] yet within this statute they are not *inimici*.

[f141]In the Duke of Northfolks Case the question was, a league being between the Queene of England and the King of Scots, whether the Lord Herise and other Scots *in aperto praelio* burning and wasting divers Townes in England without the assent of the King, were enemies in law within this statute, and resolved that they were. [g142]See more hereafter in this third part of the Institutes. cap.49. of Piracy, &c. upon the statute of 28. H.8. cap.15.

---

133. [*Ed.:* This and the prior English caption are in the original text.]

134. See hereafter. 35 H. 8. cap. 2.

135. [*Ed.:* [*inimicus*] enemy; [*hostis*] enemy.]

136. *c* 43 Ass. 28,29. 33 H. 6. 1. 19 E. 4. 62 & 4 Mar. Treason. Br. 32. 1 Mar. ibid. 24. 21 E. 3. 23. 22 ass. p. 49. 13 El. Dyer 298. Ex libro de Griffin de Perkin Werbeck.

137. *d* Dier 4. Mar. fo. 145. a. Lib. 7. fo. 6. b. Calvins Case.

138. [*Ed.:* against his due allegiance.]

139. *e* Fleta. lib. 1. c. 16.

140. [*Ed.:* traitors and enemies.]

141. *f* Mich. 13 & 14. Eliz. per justice. 19 E. 4. 6. b. 18 H. 6. ca. 4. 10 H. 6. cap. 1.

142. *g* 27 E. 3. cap. 13. 31 H. 6. cap. 4. 7 E. 4. 14. 13 E. 4. 9. 21 E. 3 16, 17. Regist. 129. Fit. N. B. 114.

[Or elsewhere.][143]

That is to say, out of the Realme of England. But then it may be demanded, how should at this time this foraine treason be tried? And some [h][144]of our Books doe answer, that the offender shall be indicted and tried in this Realme where his land lyeth, and so it was adjudged in 2 H.4 But now by the statute of 35 H.8. cap.2. (which yet remains in force) All offences made or declared, or hereafter made or declared treasons, misprisions of treason, and conceale-ments of treason, committed out of the Realme of England, shall be inquired of, heard, and determined, either in the Kings Bench or before commissioners in such Shire as shall be assigned by the King. If it be before Commissioners, it hath been commonly used, that the King doth write his name in the upper part of the Comminssion. But in the Case of *Patrick O Cullen* an Irishman, the Queene did put her Signature to the Warrant to the Lord Keeper, and not to the commission: *[145]and it was holden by the Justices that the one way and the other was a sufficient assignement by the King within the statute of 35 H.8.

[i][146]It was resolved by all the Judges of England, that for a treason done in Ireland the offender may be tryed by the statute of 35 H.8. in England, because the words of the statute be, "All Treasons committed out of the Realme of England, and Ireland is out of the Realme of England." And so it was resolved in Sir John Parrots Case. And our word here [*per ailors* elsewhere] is as much as out of the Realme of England. See Pasch. 2 H.4. *coram Rege Rot. 8. Salop.* Treason in Wales.

[k][147]All treasons done upon the Sea shall be inquired, heard, and determined in such shires and places of the Realme as shall be limited by the Kings Com-mission, in like forme and condition, as if the same had been done upon the

143. [*Ed.:* This English caption is here substituted for a French caption in the original text.]

144. *h* 4 Ass. p. 15. 5 R. 2. *ubi supra.* 19 E. 4. 6. b. Dier. 3 Mar. 18 32. Pasch. 2 H. 4. *coram rege.* Rot. 8 Wallis. 35 H. 8. cap. 2. 3 Mar. *ubi supra.* 13 Eliz. Dier. 198. Stanford Pl. Cor. fo. 90. a. & b. See the first part of the Institutes, 440.

145. *Hil. 36 Eliz. in the Case of Patrick O Cullen, for a Treason at Brussels *in partibus Marinis.*

146. *i* 33 El. in Ornicks case. lib. 7. f. 23. *Calvins* case. *Vid.* Dier. Mich. 19 & 20 Eliz. fo. 360 lib. 11. fo. 63. in *Doct. Fosters* Case.

147. *k* 23 H. 8. ca. 15. This Act concerning Treasons is not taken away by the statute of 35 H. 8. cap. 2. *Vide infra cap.* 49. fo. 181. of Piracy, &c. Vid. 5 Eliz. c. 5.

land, &c. after the common course of the lawes of this land. And by the preamble it appeareth, that it could not be tryed by the Common law, but by the Civill law before the Lord Admirall. See hereafter in the exposition of the statute of 28 H.8. cap. 15. & infra, cap. 49.

| [And thereof be provably attained of open deed by people of their condition.][148]   [12]

In this branch 4 things are to be observed. [g][149]First this word [*provablement*] probably, that is, upon direct and manifest proof, not upon coniectural or presumptions, or inferences, or straines of wit, but upon good and sufficient proofe. And herein the adverb [*provablement*] probably, hath a great force, and signifieth a direct and plain proof, which word the King, the Lords, and Commons in Parliament did use, for that the offence was so hainous, and was so heavily, and severely punished, as none other the like, and therefore the offender must probably be attainted, which words are as forcible, as upon direct and manifest proof. Note, the word is not [probably] for then *commune argumentum*[150] might have served, but the word is [provably,] be attainted.

2 This word [*attaint*] necessarily implyeth that he be proceeded with, and attainted according to the due course, and proceedings of law, and not by absolute power, or by other meanes, *[151]as in former times had been used. [h][152] And therefore if a man doth adhere to the enemies of the King, or be slaine in open warre against the King, or otherwise die before the attainder of treason, he forfeiteth nothing, because (as this Act saith) he is not attainted: wherein this Act hath altered that, which before this Act, in case of treason, was taken for law. And the statute of 34 E.3. cap.12. saves nothing to the King, but that which was *in esse*,[153] and pertaining to the King of the making of that Act. And this appeareth by a judgement in parliament in *Anno* 29 H.6. cap.1. That

---

148. [*Ed.:* This English caption is here substituted for a French caption in the original text.]

149. *g* See 1 E. 6. ca. 12. the last clause. 5 E. 6. ca. 11. 1 & 2 Ph. & Mar. ca. 10. & 11. 1 Eliz. cap. 6. 13 Eliz. cap. 1. Stanf. pl. Cor. 89. & 164. Br. coron. 4. Mar. 220. Dier. 2 Mar. fo. 99.

150. [*Ed.:* common argument.]

151. *Rot. parl. an. 33 E. 1. Rot. 6. Jo. Salvyns case.]

152. *h* 43. Ass. 28. 8. E. 3. 20. 7 H. 4. 27. 34. E. 3. cap. 12. Lib. 4. fo. 57. the Sadlers case.

153. [*Ed.:* in being.]

*[154]Jack Cade being slaine in open rebellion could no way be punished, or forfeit any thing, and therefore was attainted by that act of High treason.

[Of open deed.][155]

per apertum factum,[156,157] This doth also strengthen the former exposition of the word (provablement,)[158] that it must be provably, by an open act, which must be manifestly proved.[159] As if divers doe conspire the death of the King, and the manner how, and thereupon provide weapons, powder, *[160]poison, assay harness, send letters, &c. or the like, for execution of the conspiracy. Also preparation by some overt act, to depose the King, or take the King by force, and strong hand, and to imprison him, untill he hath yeelded to certaine demands, this is a sufficient overt to prove the compassing and imagination of the death of the King: for this upon the matter is to make the King a subiect, and so dispoyle him of his kingly office of royall government. And so it was resolved by all the Judges of England. Hill 1 Jac. *regis,* in the case of the Lo. Cobham,[161] Lord Gray, and Watson and Clarke Seminary priests: And so had it been resolved by the Justices, Hill.43. Eliz. in the case of the Earles of E. and of S. who intended to goe to the court where the Queen was, and to have taken her into their power, and to have removed divers of her Counsell, and for that end did assemble a multitude of people; this being raised to end aforesaid was a sufficient overt act for compassing the death of the Queen. And so by woful experience in former times it hath fallen out, in the cases of King E.2. R.2. H.6. and E.5 that were taken, & imprisoned by their subjects. And this is made more plain by the legall forme of an inditement of treason: For first it is alledged according to this act, *Quod*[162] *proditoriè compassavit,*

154. *29 H. 6. cap. 1.
155. [*Ed.:* This English caption is here substituted for a French caption in the original text.]
156. [*Ed.:* by overt act.]
157. vide supra verbo ¶ *Mort.* fo. 6.
158. [*Ed.:* probably.]
159. Vide 21 R. 2. cap. 3. but it is repealed by 1 H. 4. ca. 3.
160. *Hill. 36. Eliz. Docter Lopes case 13 Eliz. c. 1. Brooks. Treason 24.
161. Hill. a Ja. R. Lo. Cobhams case.
162. *In ancient time *traditiosè, & felonicè* parl. 33 E. 1. rot. 6. Robert de Ros his case, but now *praeditoriè* is necessarily required. vide Britton fo. 16. et 19. 1. Mar. Br. treason. 24.

& imaginatus fuit mortem & destructionem dñi regis, & ipsum dom, regem intersicere, &c.[163] In the second part of the inditement is alledged the overt act, *et ad illam nephandam, & proditoriam comapassationem, imaginationem, & propositum suum perficiend' & perimplend'*[164] and then certainly to set downe the overt fact for preparation to take, and imprison the King, or any other sufficient overt act, which of necessity must be set downe in the Inditement. Hereby it appeareth how insufficeint many inditements were of High treason, wherein it was generally alledged, that *per apertum factum compassavit, & imaginatus fuit mortem dom. regis, &c.*[165] *[166]For example *Termo Mic. anno* 5 E.6. Edward Duke of Somerset was indited before Commissioners of Oyer and terminer in London, *quod ipse deum prae oculis suis non habens, sed instigatione diabo-\-lica seductus, apud Holborne in parochia Sancti Andreae infra civitatem London, viz. 20 die Aprilis anno regni domini Regis Edw. sexti quinto, & diversis diebus & vicibus antea & postea falso, maliciose, & proditorie *[167]per aperium factum circumivit, compassavit, & imaginavit cum diversis aliis personis praedictum dominū Regem de statu suo regali deponere & deprivare, &c.*[168] Which Indictment,[169] and all others of like forme were against law, as hath been said, and of the matter of this Indictment that noble Duke was by his Peers found not guilty. But then it may be demanded, for what offence he had judgement of death, and 2. what law made it an offence. The offence appeareth in his Indictment, for the former part thereof contained High Treason, whereof he was acquited, & the latter part contained one only offence of felony (whereof he was found guilty) in these words, *Et ulterius Juratores praed. praesentant,*

[13]

163. [*Ed.:* that he traitorously compassed and imagined the death and destruction of the lord king, and to kill the selfsame lord king, etc.]

164. [*Ed.:* and in order to carry out and fulfil that his wicked and traitorous compassing, imagining and purpose.]

165. [*Ed.:* by overt act he compassed and imagined the death of the lord king, etc.]

166. *Ter. Mic. 5 E. 6. Lib. Intr. Coke fo. 48a. *Sanguimis maladicta sitis, &c.*

167. *Per. apertum factum.

168. [*Ed.:* that he, not having God before his eyes but being seduced by the instigation of the devil, at Holborn in the parish of St. Andrew within the city of London, that is to say, on the twentieth day of April in the fifth year of the reign of the lord King Edward the sixth, and on various days and in various places before and since, falsely, maliciously and traitorously by overt act went about, compassed and imagined, with various other persons, to depose and deprive the aforesaid lord king of his royal estate, etc.]

169. Vid. hereafter ca. 5. de Heresie, generall Indictments against Lolards, &c.

quod praesatus Edwardus dux Somerset Deū prae oculis suis non habens,[170] *sed instigatione diabolica seductus 20 Maii An. regni dicti Dom. Regis Edwardi sexti quinto supradicto, ac diversis aliis diebus & vicibus antea & postea apud Holborn in praed. paroch. Sancti Andreae in civitate London, & apud diversa alia loca infra civitatem London praed. felonice ut selo dicti Dom. Regis per aperta verba & facta procuravit, movit, & instigavit complurimos subditos ipsius domini Regis ad insurgendum, & apertam rebellionem & insurrectionem infra hoc regnum Angliae movend' contra ipsum dominum Regem, & ad tunc & ibid. felonice ad capiendum & imprisonandum prae nobilem Johannem comitem Warwick de privato consilio domini Regis ad tunc existen', contra pacem dicti domini Regis coronam & dignitatem suam, & contra formam statuti in hujusmodi casu editi & provisi.*[171] The statute whereupon this Indictment was intended to be grounded, was the branch of the statute of 3 & 4 E.6.[172] by which it is provided, [That if any person or persons by ringing of any Bel, &c. or by malicious speaking or uttering of any words, or making any Dutery, &c. or by any other deed or act shall raise or cause to be raised or assembled any persons to the number of 12 or above, to the intent that the same persons should do, commit, and put in use any of the acts or things above mentioned (whereof to take and imprison any of the Kings most honorable Privie Counsell was one) and the persons to the number of 12 or above so raised and assembled after request and commandement (in such sort as in that Act is prescribed) shall make their above and continue together, as is aforesaid, (in the Act) or unlawfully perpetrate, doe, commit, or put in use any of the acts or things abovesaid, that then all and singular persons by whose speaking, deed, act, or any other the meanes above specified any persons to the number of 12 or above, shall be

---

170. The residue of the Indictment of the Duke of Sumerset.

171. [*Ed.:* And moreover the aforesaid jurors present that the said Edward, duke of Somerset, not having God before his eyes but being seduced by the instigation of the devil, on the twentieth day of May in the above-mentioned fifth year of the reign of the said lord King Edward the sixth, and on various other days and in various other places before and since, at Holborn in the aforesaid parish of St. Andrew in the city of London, and at various other places within the city of London aforesaid, feloniously as a felon of the said lord king, by overt words and deeds procured, moved and instigated many subjects of the selfsame lord king to rise up and to move open rebellion and insurrection within this realm against the selfsame lord king, and then and there feloniously to take and imprison the most noble John, earl of Warwick, then being one of the lord king's privy council, against the peace of the said lord king, his crown and dignity, and against the form of the statute published and provided for such case.]

172. To take and imprison one of the Privie Councell. Contra forman. Statut. 3 & 4 E. 6. cap. 5.

raised or assembled for the doing, committing, or putting in use any of the acts or things above mentioned, shall be adiudged for his so speaking or doing a felon, and suffer execution of death as in case of felony, and shall lose his benefit of Sanctuary and Clergy.] Hereby it doth manifestly appeare, that the truth concerning this Noblemans attainder, and execution in divers things, is contrary to the vulgar opinion, and some of our Chronicles, and in some points contrary to law. First, that for the felony made by the said branch of the said Act he could not have had his Clergie, for Clergie in that Case is expressly ousted by the said Act. 2. That he was not indicted for going about, &c. the death of the Earle of Warwick then of the Kings Privie Counsell, but only for his taking or imprisonment, and therefore could not be indicted upon the statute of 3 H.7.[173] as some have imagined. 3. That the Indictment is altogether insufficient, for it pursueth not the words or matter of the said branch of the said Act, as by comparing of them it manifestly appeareth; which (we being desirous that truth may appeare in all things) we have thought good upon this occasion to adde for advancement of truth. 4. That being but attained of felony, he could not by law be beheaded, as elsewhere we have shewed.[174] And this Act that created the felony saith, that such a felon shall suffer execution of death, as in case of felony. 5. Lastly, this whole Act was justly holden to be a doubtfull and dangerous statute, and therefore was deservedly repealed. And after the fall of this Duke, see the preamble of the statute of Subsidie of 7 E.6.[175]

| And now to returne to Cases of High Treason. If a man be arraigned upon [14] an Indictment of High Treason, and stand mute, he shall have such judgement, and incurre such forfeiture, as if he had been convicted by Verdict, or if he had confessed it. For this standeth well with this word provablement, for *fatetur facinus, qui judicium fugit:*[176] but otherwise it is in case of Petit Treason, Murder, or other Felony.[177]

If a subiect conspire with a foraine Prince beyond the seas to invade the Realme by open hostility, and prepare for the same by some overt act, this is a sufficient overt act for the death of the King, for by this Act of Parliament

---

173. 3 H.7. ca. 14.
174. Lib. 9. fo. 114. in Seignior Sanchers case.
175. 1 Mar. cap. 12. 1 Eliz. ca. 16. 7 E. 6. ca. 12.
176. [*Ed.:* he who flees judgement confesses himself to be guilty.]
177. 13 Eliz. Dier 298 13 Eliz. cap. 1. *Nota bene Vide supra verba* Mort.

in that Case there must be an overt act.[178] *Qui capiti, aut saluti Regis persidiose sive solus, sive servis aut sicariis mercede conductis itipatus insidiabitur, vita & fortunis ejus omnibus privator.*[179] So as thereby an overt act was required.

The composition and connexion of the words are to be observed, viz. [thereof be attained by overt deed.] *[180]This relateth to the severall and distinct treasons before expressed, (and specially to the compassing and imagination of the death of the King, &c. for that it is secret in the heart) and therefore one of them cannot be an overt act for another. As for example: a conspiracy is had to levie warre, this (as hath been said, and so resolved) is no treason by this Act untill it be levied, therefore it is no overt act or manifest proofe of the compassing of the death of the King within this Act: for the words be (*de ceo. &c.*[181]) that is, of the compassing of the death. For this were to confound the severall Classes, or *membra dividentia, & sic de caeteris, &c.*[182]

[183]Divers latter Acts of Parliament have ordained, that compassing by bare words or sayings should be High Treason; but all they are either repealed or expired. And it is commonly said, that bare words may make an Heretick, but not a Traytor without an overt act. And the wisdome of the makers of this law would not make words only to be Treason, seeing such variety amongst the witnesses are about the same, as few of them agree together. But if the same be set downe in writing by the Delinquent himselfe, this is a sufficient overt act within this statute.

[184]Cardinall Poole, albeit he was a subject to H.8. and of the Kings blood, (being descended from George Duke of Clarence, Brother to King E.4.) yet he in his Booke of the Supremacy of the Pope, written about 27 H.8. incited Charles the Emperour, then preparing against the Turke, to bend his force against his naturall Sovereigne Lord and Countrey; the writing of which Booke was a sufficient overt act within this statute: and to move the Emperour the

---

178. *Inter leges Alveredi, cap. 4.

179. [*Ed.:* Whoever shall plot treacherously against the life or safety of the king, whether by himself or by servants or hired assassins, shall lose his life and all his possessions.]

180. *So resolved by the Justices Pasc. 35 Eliz. which we heard and observed.

181. [*Ed.:* thereof, etc.]

182. [*Ed.:* the limbs into which it is divided (i.e. constituent parts); and likewise concerning the rest, etc.]

183. *a* 26 H. 8. cap. 13. 1. E. 6. cap. 13. 1 & 2 Ph. & Mar. cap. 9,10. 1 Eliz. cap. 6. 13 Eliz. ca. 1,&c. 14 Eliz. cap. 1.

184. *b* See the fourth part of the Institutes, ca. 26. Brook treason 24 writing of Letters.

rather in that Book, he made H.8. almost as ill as the Turk, in these words, *in Anglia sparsum nune est hoc semen, ut vix a Turcico internosci queat, idque authoritate unius coaluit.*[185]

[186] In the Preamble of the statute of 1 Mar. concerning the repeale of certaine Treasons, &c. It is agreed by the whole Parliament, that lawes justly made for the preservation of the Common-wealth without extreame punishment, are more often obeyed and kept, then lawes and statutes made with great and extreame punishments; and in speciall; such lawes and statutes so made: whereby not only the ignorant and rude unlearned people, but also learned and expert people minding honesty, are oftentimes trapped and snared, yea, many times *for words only, without other fact or deed done or perpetrated: *Nota. therefore this Act of 25 E.3. doth provide, that there must be an overt deed. But words without an overt deed [d187]are to be punished in another degree, as an high misprision.

[By people of their condition.][188]

That is, *per pares,* or their equals, whereof we have spoken before in the ex-position of the [e189]29 Chapter of Magna Carta, *Verb. per judicium parium suorum,*[190] and more shall be and said hereafter. This Branch (*p gents de jour condition*) extendeth only to a conviction by Verdict, whereof the statute particularly speaketh; but yet where the party indicted confesseth the offence or standeth mute, he shall have judgement as in case of High Treason. For this branch being affirmative, is taken *comulativè* | and not *privativè.*[191] And   [15]

185. [*Ed.:* In England this seed is now so widely scattered that it is hardly to be distinguished from Turkey, and by authority of one has coalesced.]

186. *c* 1 Mar. cess. 1. c. 1 See the statute of 3 H. 7. hereafter, cap. 4. directly in the point by the judgment of the Parliament. *Nota,* this Act of 25 E. 3. saith. *per overt sait, per apertum factum,* and not *per apertum dictum,* by word or confession. See 25 H. 8. c. 52. Eliz. Barton, Edw. Locking, and others attained by Parliament for divers words and conspiracies which being not within this Act without an overt act they could not be attainted by the Common law.

187. *d* See in the chapter of Misprision.

188. [*Ed.:* This English caption is here substituted for a French caption in the original text.]

189. *e* Mag. Car. ca. 29.

190. [*Ed.:* by people of their condition.]

191. [*Ed.:* communal (and not) private.]

therefore seeing upon confession, or standing mute, the judgement in case of high treason was given at the common law, this Act being, as it hath been said, affirmative, taketh not away the same: And (to say once for al) the clause hereafter of restraint of like cases, &c. extends onely to offences, and not to tryalls, judgements, or executions.

[And if a man counterfeit the Kings great Seale.][192]

All our ancient Authors agree that this was High treason by the common law; and for this offence his judgement was to be drawn, hanged, and quartered, at the common law, as in other cases of High treason, (the counterfeiting of the Kings mony excepted.) See *The second part of the Institutes, W. 1 cap. 5.*[193]

[194]In ancient time every treason was comprehended under the name of felony, but not *é contra:*[195] And therefore a pardon of all felonies was sometime allowed in case of High treason. But the law is, and of long time hath been otherwise holden:[196] and if the inditement were *felonicè,*[197] and not *proditoriè,*[198] (for the King may lessen the offence, if it please him)[199] then the pardon of felonies is good at this day, for no Inditement can be of High treason without this word (proditoriè:) and *in qualiber prodicione implicatur felonia, quia in quolibt brevi de exigendo super quolibet indictamento de proditione proclamator facit sic, I. B.*[200] An exigent on thy head of treason and felony.

A Compassing, intent, or going about to counterfeit the great seale is no treason, but there must be an actuall counterfeiting, also it must be to the

---

192. [*Ed.:* This English caption is here substituted for a French caption in the original text.]

193. Bract. l. 3. fo,118. Brit. fo. 10. &c. Bract. l. 5. fo. 414. Fleta l. 1. ca. 21. Mirror ca. 1. § 6. de sausonerie. 29 Ass. pa. 49.

194. *1 E. 3. tit. Chfe F. 13. 22 Ass. Pl. 49.

195. [*Ed.:* on the contrary.]

196. 2 R. 3. 9.

197. [*Ed.:* feloniously.]

198. [*Ed.:* treasonably.]

199. 3 H. 7. 10. 2.

200. [*Ed.:* in every treason there is implied felony, because in every writ of exigent upon every indictment for treason the crier says this.]

likenesse of the Kings great seale, the words be, *Counterface le grand seale le Roy.*[201]

Now it is to be seen what shall be said a forging or counterfeiting of the great seale. If the Lord Chancellor, or Lord Keeper put the great seale to a Charter &c. without warrant, this is no treason, because the great seale is not counterfeited. But it seemeth by Briton fo. 10. b. that it was treason at the common law, and of that opinion is Fleta fo. 29.a. but it is not treason now (without question) by the negative clause of this Act.

If a man take wax lawfully imprinted with the great scale from the patent, and fix it to a writing purporting a grant from the King, there have been divers opinions in this case what the offence is, which we will rehearse.

In 40. E.3.[202] which was about 15. years after the making of this Act, it was not holden High treason, but a great misprision, for that it is no counterfeiting of a new, but an abuse of the true great seale.

In 42 E.3.[203] the Abbot of Bruer caused Rob. Rigge his Commsiogne to rase a Charter of R.1. and put out the manner of Fisfetruda, and in place thereof put in Efleghe. And this offence was heard, and sentenced before the King and his Counsell in the Star-Chamber, as a great offence and misprision: for if it had been High treason, it should have had another tryall, and yet this was a great abuse of the great seal.

2 H.4.[204] The taking of Great Seal from one Patent, and fixing it to a Commission to gather mony, &c. was adjudged to be such an offence, as the offender had judgement to be drawne, and hanged. The record of which case we have perused, and the effect thereof is this. The partie is indited generally for counterfeiting of the great seal, whereunto he pleaded not guilty, and the Jury found him not guilty of the counterfeiting of the great seale, as was supposed by the inditement, and found further specially, that he tooke the great seale from one patent, and put it to the commission, and that the party put the same in execution, and there judgement was given, that he should be drawne and hanged: which (whatsoever the offence was) ought not to have been given upon this verdict,[205] the Jury finding him not guilty of the offence

---

201. [*Ed.:* counterfeits the king's great seal.]

202. 40 Ass. p. 33.

203. Rot. Claus. 42 E. 3. nu. 8. in Coro.

204. 2 H. 4. fo. 25.

205. *Errores ad sua principi a referre, est refferre.* To bring errors to their beginning, is to see their last.

alledged in the inditement: And besides the judgement is such, as is given in case of Petit treason, and not of high treason. Hereby it appeareth how dangerous it is for any to report a case by the ear, specially concerning treason, unlesse he had advisedly read the Record: for (as I take it) the misreport of this case hath hatched errors, and he mistooke the judgment, if it had been High treason, for then it should have been drawne, hanged, and quartered.

[16] | 37. H.8. Br. tit. Treason.[206] A Chaplain had fixed such a great Seale to a Patent of dispensation with non-residence, and this was holden a misprision, and not High treason, for it was an abuse of the great seale, and no counterfeiting of it. Stanford saith that it was adjudged in his time according to the book of 2 H.4. *Et sic ex errore sequitor error.*[207,208]

G. Leak a clark of the Chancery joyned two cleane parchments fit for letters patents so close together with mouth glew, as they were taken for one, the uppermost being very thinne, and did put one labell through then both, then upon the uttermost he writ a true patent, and got the great seale put to the labell, so the labell and the seale were annexed to both the parchments, the own written, and the other blanck: he cut off the glewed skirts round about, and tooke off the uppermost thinne parchment (which was written, and was a true and perfect patent) from the labell, which with the great seale did still hang to the parchment, then he wrote another patent on the blancke parchment, and did publish it as a good patent. Hereupon two questions were moved. 1. Whether this offence be High treason or no. 2. If it be High treason, then whether he may be indited generally for the counterfeiting of the great seale, or els the speciall fact must be expressed. And upon conference had between the Judges, upon great advisement and consideration it was in the end, concerning the first point, resolved by the Justices (saving a very few) upon the authorities aforesaid, and for that it was no counterfeiting of the great seale within this statute, that this offence was neither High treason, nor Petit treason, because it is not within either of the branches of this statute,[209] but it is a very great misprision, and the party delinquent liveth at this day. As to the 2. point it was resolved, that if the speciall matter had amounted

206. 37 H. 8 Br. Treason.

207. [*Ed.:* And so from error follows error.]

208. Stanf. Pl. Coron. fo. 3. c. Bracton agreeth with it. *Ubi supra.* Leaks Case. Hil. 4. Ja. R.

209. 40. Ass. 33. 42 E. 3. Rot. Cl. *Ubi supra.* 37 H. 8. Br. dev.

to counterfeiting of the great seale in law within this act, then he might have been generally indited of High treason for counterfeiting the great seale. As if a man in an affray kill a Constable that comes to keep the Kings peace without any expresse malice prepensed, this is murder in law, and yet the delinquent may bee generally indited of murder by malice prepensed.

And [a210]Fleta who wrote before this act telleth us, that *Crimen falsi dicitur, cū quis illicitus (cui non fuerit ad hoc data authoritas) de sigillo regis rapto vel invento, & brevia cartasque consignaverit.*[211] But whatsoever offence it was before the making of this statute, it is after this statute no High treason, because it is no counterfeiture of the great seale, but a misusor thereof.

Qui [b212] *convictus fuerit pro falsatione sigilli dom. regis, quòd tradatur Episcopo Sarum, qui eum petiit ut clericum suum sub poena & in forma qua decet, quia videtor concilio quod in tali casu non admittenda est purgatio, &c.*[213] Hereby it should appeare that in those dayes a man might have had his Clergie for this offence, and therefore as some hold, it was not then holden to be High treason, & herein also is the preamble of this act, concerning divers opinions in case of treason, verified.

This statute naming the great seale and privie seale, the forging and the counterfeiting of the privie signet, or of the signe manuell was not within this statute. But by the [c214]statute of 1 Mar. it is made High treason in both cases. Alteit that in this act there is no mention made of [d215]ayders and consentors to this counterfeiting, yet they are within the purvien of this statute, for there be no accessaries in High treason.

---

210. *a* Fleta l. 1. ca. 22 Britton fo. 10. b. See before. fo. 15.

211. [*Ed.:* The crime of forgery is when anyone illicitly (to whom power has not been given for such purposes) has signed writs or charters with the kings's seal, either stolen or found.]

212. *b* Rot. Parl. Hil. 18 E. 1. fo. 92. nu. 125.

213. [*Ed.:* and he, having been convicted of forging the lord king's seal, is delivered to the bishop of Salisbury, who claimed him as his clerk, under the penalty and in the form which is fitting, because it seems to the council that in such case purgation is not to be admitted, etc.]

214. *c* 1 Mar. cap. 6. 1 & 2 Ph. & Mar. ca. 11.

215. *19 H. 6. 47 3 H. 7. 10. Stanf. Pl. Coron. 3. vide postea ca. 64. *Principall & access.* See Mich. 13 & 14 Eliz. Dier 296. Coniers Case.

[Or his money.][216,217]

[e218] This was treason by the common law, as it appeareth by all the said ancient authors, *ubi supra (verbo, Si home counterface le grand seale)*[219] and therefore the opinion in 3 H.7. is holden for no law, that it was but felony before this act. [f220]The forging of the Kings coine, is High treason, without utterance of it, for by this act the counterfeiting is made High treason. See the second part of the Institutes. W. 1. cap. 15. [g221] See *Thom. Walsingham. Hypodigme Neustrie. An. Dom. 1278. Judei protonsura monetae in magna multitudine ubique per Angliam suspenduntur, &c.*[222]

[h223] *Si ipse qui facit monetam authoritate regis, &c. illam facit minus in pondere vel allaiata, viz. Alcumino vel alio falso metallo contra ordinationem, &c.*[224] This is there holden to be High Treason, and by that Book taken for a counterfeiter of the Kings money within the Purvien of this statute. [a225]And herewith agreeth Britton, who saith, *Des sauceres q. ount nostre monye counterfet ou pluis de allaye mise in nostre monye, q. nuster, ne serroit solonq le forme & usage de nostre Realme.*[226]

[b227] *Ordeine fuit q. nul roy de cest realme ne puit changer sa money, ne impairer, ne amender, ne auter monye faire q̄ de ore & argent, sans lassent de couts les*

[17] (margin)

---

216. *d* See Mar. Par. *Anno* 34 H. 3. pag. 753. *de pecunia approbata & reprobata.* Et Walsingham 28 E. 1. *Anno Dom.* 1300. stat. 31 E. 1. *de weights & measures.* Rast. 7.

217. [*Ed.:* This English caption is here substituted for a French caption in the original text.]

218. *e* Vet. Magna Chart. ca. Itin. fo. 151. a. 22 Ass. p. 49. 3 H. 7. 10. 25 E. 3. 42. b. Coro. 130.

219. [*Ed.:* "If a man counterfeit the great seal."]

220. *f* 6 H. 7. 13. 1 R. 3. 1.

221. *g* Wals. Hyp. Neustrie pa. 69. 1278. 6 E. 1.

222. [*Ed.:* The Jews were hanged in large numbers throughout England for clipping money.]

223. *h* 3 H 7. 10. a. b.

224. [*Ed.:* If someone who makes money by the king's authority makes it of lesser weight, or mixed with alloy, that is to say, with alchemy or other false metal, against the ordinance, etc.]

225. *a* See Inter leges Athelstani, ca 14. Canusi,cap 61. Britton cap. 5. fo. 10. b. See the Mirror, ca. 1. §6. De la mony falsifie acc' with 3 H. 7. and ca. 5. §. 1. and Fleta ca. 22. acc'.

226. [*Ed.:* Of forgers who have counterfeited our money, or put more alloy into our money than there ought to be according to the form and usage of our realm.]

227. *b* Mirr. ca. 1 § 3. inter Artic. perveils royes ordeinus Rot. Par. 17 E. 3. nu. 15. Vide hic postea cap. 31. 45. E. 3. ca. 13. 9 H. 5. cap. 11. Stat. 1. See the second part of the Institutes, ca. 20 Artic. super Cart, and the exposition upon the same.

Counties.[228] It was ordained, that no king of this Realme might not change his money, nor impaire, nor amend the same, nor other money make then of Gold or Silver, without assent of Parliament.

[c229]Clipping, washing, and filing of the money of this Realme, was no counterfeiting of it within this Act. And therefore being a like Case, it was declared by Parliament in *Anno 3 H.5.* cap. 6. to be High Treason; but that Act being repealed by 1 Mariae the statute of 5 Eliz. cap. 11. hath [d230] declared that clipping, washing, rounding, or filing, for wicked lucre and gaine, &c. to be High Treason. And by the statute of [e231]18 Eliz. it is declared, That if any person for wicked lucre or gaines-sake, shall by any art, wayes, or meanes whatsoever, impaire, diminish, falsifie, scale, or lighten the Kings money, &c. it is High Treason, for being a like case, it was to be declared by Parliament.

Forging [f232]or counterfeiting of foraine money, which is not currant within the Realme, is misprision of Treason, and the offender shall forfeit, as for concealement of High Treason.

[His money.][233]

[g234] This extendeth only so the Kings money coyned within this Realme; and therefore after this statute, if a man had counterfeited the money of another kingdome, though it were currant within this Realme, it was no treason, untill it was so declared by Parliament [h235]in *An.* 1 Mariae, and in *An.* 1 & 2 Ph.& M. and the said Acts of 5 Eliz. & 18 Eliz. do extend to forrain coyne currant within this Realme. And it is holden, that at the making of this statute of 25 Edw. 3. there was no money currant within this Realme, but the Kings own coyne. [i236]See the statute called *Statutum de moneta magnum. & statutum*

228. [*Ed.:* It is ordered that no king of this realm could change his money, or worsen or amend it, or make money other than of gold and silver, without the assent of all the counties.]

229. *c* 3 H. 5. ca. 6. 1 E. 6. cap. 12. 5 Eliz. cap. 11.

230. *d Nota,* for wicked lucre and gain.

231. *e* 18 Eliz. cap. 1.

232. *f* 14 Eliz. cap. 3.

233. [*Ed.:* This English caption is here substituted for a French caption in the original text.]

234. *g* See hereafter, cap. Principall & Accessory.

235. *h* 1 Mar. cap. 6. 1 & 2 Ph. & Mar. cap. 11.

236. *i* Ver. Mag. Carta, part. 2. fol. 38, 39, 40.

de moneta parvum.[237] And it is to be knowne, that if any doe counterfeit the Kings coyne contrary to this statute of 25 Edw. 3. [k238]He shall have the punishment of his body, but as in case of Petit Treason, that is, to be drawne and hanged till he be dead, but the forfeiture of his lands is as in other cases of High Treason, for this statute is but a declaration of the Common law, and the reason of his corporall punishment is, for that in this case he was only drawne and hanged at the Common law, but a woman in that case was to be burnt.

[l239]The Abbot of Missenden in the County of Buckingham for counterfeiting and resection of the Kings money, was adjudged to be drawne and hanged, and not quartered. The want of observation of the said distinction hath made some to erre in their judgement. Nota. This Act of 25. E. 3. maketh no expression of the judgement, therefore such judgement as was at the Common law either in case of High Treason or Petit Treason must be given.

But if one be attainted for diminishing of the Kings mony upon any of the statutes made in Queen Maries time, or in the time of Queen Elizabeth, because it is High Treason newly made, the offender shall have judgement as in case of High Treason, which judgement you may see in the first part of the Institutes. Sect. 747.

[m240]And when a woman commits High Treason and is quick with childe, she cannot upon her arraignment plead it, but she must either pleade not guilty, or confesse it: and if upon her plea she be found guilty, or confesse it, the cannot alleage it in arrest of judgement, but judgement shall be given against her: and if it be found by an inquest of Matrons that she is quick with childe, (for *priviment enfent*[241] will not serve) it shall arrest, and respite execution till she be delivered, but she shall have the benefit of that but once, [18]   though she be againe quick | with childe: so as this respite of execution for

---

237. [*Ed.:* The great statute of money, and the little statute of money.]

238. *k* Fleta lib. 1. c. 22 who wrote before this statute which is but a law Declaratory, as it appeareth before. 23 Ass. p. 2. Dier 6 Eliz. Term. Tr. MS. *Pro tonsura monete trabe & pend.* Tr. 24 H. 8. in Justice Spilmans Reports, accord.

239. *l* Mich. 31 E. 3. coram rege. Rot. 55. Buck. within 6 yeares after making of our statute.

240. *m* 25 E. 3. 42. b. Cor. 130. 23 Ass. p. 2. 22 Ass. p. 71. 22 E. 3. Cor. 253. 12. Ass. p. 11. 8 E. 2. Cor. 410.

241. [*Ed.:* secretly pregnant.]

this cause is not to be granted, only in case of felony, whereof Justice Stanford speaketh,[242] but in case of High Treason, and Petit Treason also.[243]

[If a man bring false money into this realme counterfeit to the money of England, knowing the money to be false, etc.][244]

By this branch six things are to be observed. First, that the bringing in of counterfeit money, and not the counterfeiting is expressed in this word [*apport.*][245] Secondly, that it must be brought from a foraine Nation, and not from Ireland, or other place belonging to or being a member of the Crowne of England, and so it hath been resolved,[246] so wary are Judges to expound this statute concerning Treason, and that in most benigne sense: For albeit Ireland be a distinct Kingdome, and out of the Realme of England to some purposes,[247] as to Protections and fines levied, &c, as hath been said: yet to some intent it is accounted as a member of or belonging to the Crowne of this Realme. And therefore a Writ of Error is maintainable here in the Kings Beach of a judgement given in the Kings Bench in Ireland, so as the Judges did construe this statute not to extend to false money brought out of Ireland. Thirdly, it must be to the similitude of the money of England. Fourthly, that the bringer of it into this Realme, must know it to be counterfeit. Fiftly, uttering of false money in England,[248] though he know it to be false and counterfeit to the likenesse of the coyne of England, is no treason within this statute, unlesse he brought it from a foraine Nation, for the words be, *si home apport faux money en cest realme.*[249] But if money false or clipped be found in the hands of any that is suspicious, he may be imprisoned untill he hath found

242. Stanford f. ult. b.
243. *Vid.* Hereafter, cap 30. Rot. Par. 17 E. 3. nu. 15.
244. [*Ed.:* This English caption is here substituted for a French caption in the original text.]
245. [*Ed.:* Import tax or payment.]
246. 7 H. 7. 1 C.
247. Lib. 7. Calvins case, *ubi supra.*
248. 3 H. 7. 10.
249. [*Ed.:* If a man import false money into this realm.]

his warrant, *per statutum de moneta magn' vet. Mag. Cart. fo. 38. 2 parte.*[250] Lastly, he must merchandize therewith, or make payment thereof, expressed in these words, *Pur merchandizer, on paiment faire in deceipt nostre seignior le roy & son people.*[251] See more, *De moneta regis,*[252] and of the derivation thereof in The second part of the Institutes, in *Artic' super cartas,* cap. 10.

[If a man slay the Chancellor, Treasurer, or the Kings Justices of one Bench or the other Justices in Eire, or Justices in Assize, and all other Justices assigned to hear and determine, being in their place doing their offices.][253]

In this case albeit one intend to kill any of these here named in their place, and doing their office, and thereupon strike or wound any of them, this is no treason: For our statute saith, *Si home tuast Chancelor, &c.*[254] If a man kill the Chancellour, &c. For if it be treason, death must ensue. And the reason wherefore it is treason in these cases is, because fitting judicially in their places, (that is, in the Kings Courts) and doing their office in administration of justice, they represent the Kings person, who by his Oath is bound that the same be done. And this Act extends only to the persons here particularly named, and to no other: and therefore extendeth not to the Court of the Lord Steward, or of the Constable and Marshall, nor to the Court of the Admiralty, or any other, nor to any Ecclesiasticall Court. Nay, it extends not to the High Court of Parliament, if any Member of the Lords House, or House of Commons be slaine in his place, and doing his office, because it is *casus omissus,*[255] and not mentioned in this Act. But in all those Cases it is wilfull murder, for the Law implyeth malice.

250. [*Ed.:* by the great statute of money, Old Magna Carta [and *Statuta Vetera*], part 2, fo. 38.]
251. [*Ed.:* to trade with or to make payment, in deceit of our lord the king and his people.]
252. [*Ed.:* concerning the king's money.]
253. [*Ed.:* This English caption is here substituted for a French caption in the original text.]
254. [*Ed.:* If a man kill the chancellor, etc.]
255. [*Ed.:* an omitted case.]

[And it is understood, that in the cases above rehearsed, it ought to be judged Treason, which extend to the Lord our King and his Royall Majestie: And such treason is the forfeiture of the escheates pertaineth to our Lord the King, as well as the lands and tenements holden of others, as of himself.][256]

[257] This is an affirmance of the Common Law, and the reason there of is, for that the offence is committed against the soveraigne Lord the King, who is the light and the life of the Common-wealth: and therefore the Law | doth [19] give to the King in satisfaction of his offence, all the Lands, &c. which the offender hath, and that no subject should be partaker of any part of the forfeiture for this offence.

And where the words be [Lands and Tenements holden, &c.] yet the forfeiture extends to *[258]rents charges, rents seck, Commons, Corrodies, and other hereditaments which are not holden, for in case of High Treason the tenure is not materiall.[259]

This clause hath 7. limitations. First, this Act extends not [b260]to lands in tayle, (saving only for the life of tenant in tayle) but the forfeiture of escheats is to be understood of such Lands and Tenements, as he might lawfully forfeit. And these generall words take not away the statute of *donis conditional'* [261] [c262]but latter statutes give the forfeiture of estates in tail. 2. Nor doth this Act extend to uses, but *[263]latter statutes doe name uses. 3. [d264]For to rights of actions, where the entrie is taken away, and so is the law cleerly holden at this

---

256. [*Ed.:* This English caption is here substituted for a French caption in the original text.]

257. *a* Rot. Parliam. 20 E. 1 nu. 2. John de Britains case. 3 Reg. 21. 15. See *inter leges Alueredi,* cap. 4. *ubi supra. Vita & fortunis omnibus privator.* Cust. de Norm. ca. 14. 22 lib. Ass. pl 49.

258. *Brook Esch 9.

259. See hereafter. *Verbo, Et de tiel manner de treason, &c.* Otherwise it is in case of Petit Treason and felony.

260. *b* 7 H. 4. 27. See hereafter in the title of *Premunir, Verb.* (de tres, &c.) Vid. 26 H. 8. cap. 13.

261. [*Ed.:* conditional gifts (i.e., the Statute of Westminster II, c. 1, *De donis*)]

262. *c* 26 H. 8 ca. 13. in fine. 33. H. 8. ca. 20. 5 & 6 E. 6. ca. 11. Lib. 7. fo. 12,13.

263. *33 H. 8. ca. 20. 5 E. 6. ca 11.

264. *d* Lib. 3 fo. 210. 7 H. 4 6 &c.

day. 4. Nor to any conditions, but by a [e265]latter statute conditions, unless they be inseparably knit to the person, be given to the King. 5. Nor to rights of entry, where any was in the lands [f266]by title before the treason committed, but such a right of entry is since given by latter statutes. 6. For to Lands or Tenements, or Rights [g267]*in auter droit,*[268] as in the right of the Church, nor to lands in the right of a wife, but only during the coverture, and it extendeth to land which the offender hath [h269]for life, for the forfeiture of the profits during his life. 7. It extendeth not to *[270]a foundership of an house of religion in Free almoign, for that is annexed to the bloud of the Founder. Here goods and chattels be not named, but the forfeiture of them is implyed in the judgement.

[i271]*Nota Lector,*[272] the said Acts of 26 H.8. 33 H.8. 33 H.8. 5. and 6 E.6. doe yet remain in force, notwithstanding the said statute of 1 Mar. as it hath been often adjudged and resolved, and namely *Mich. 21. Ja.* in the Exchequer Chamber in a writ of error, upon a judgement given in the Exchequer, between Ratcliffe, and the Lord Sheffeild, by all the Judges of England, and is agreeable to common experience.

See more of High Treason in the next Chapter following, cap. 2. *verbo. Et pur ceo que plusors auters cases, &c.*[273]

Cap. II.
Of Petit Treason.

And[1] moreover there is another manner of Treason, that is to say,[2] when a servant slayeth his Master, or a wife her husband, or when a man secular or religious

---

265. *e* 33 H. 8. c. 20. lib. 7. fo. 11. Englefields case.

266. *f Englefields case. Ubi supra.*

267. *g* 5 E. 6. *ubi supra.* 1 Mar. Dier 123. Dier. 12 El. 289. Temps H. 8. Br. Coron. 5.

268. [*Ed.:* in another's right. An executor, administrator, or trustee sues "in autre droit."]

269. *h* 1 Mar. Dier. 108.

270. *24 E. 3. 33. 72. Corody Br. 5 Temps H. 8. Escheat. 239.

271. *i* 12 El. Dier 289. Lib. 3. fo. 10. 35. Lib. 7. fo. 33. 34. lib. 8. 72. 166. lib 9. fo. 140. Stanf. Pl. Corone. 187. a.

272. [*Ed.:* Note, reader.]

273. [*Ed.:* And because various other cases, etc.]

1. [*Ed.:* The text of this paragraph is an English translation in the First Edition. The text of the original French, which preceded this paragraph in that edition, has been omitted.]

2. Britton ca. 3. & cap. 22.

slayeth his Prelate to whom he oweth | faith and obedience. And of such treason the Escheats ought to pertain to every Lord of his own fee, &c.

It was called High or Grand treason in respect of the royall Majesty against whom it is committed, and comparatively it is called Petit Treason (whereof now this statute speaketh) in respect it is committed against subjects and inferiour persons, whereof this Act doth enumerate three kinds.

[When a servant slayeth his Master.][3]

This was Petit Treason by the Common Law, for so it appeareth by the [a4]book of 12. Ass. that a woman servant killed her Mistris, wherefore she had judgement to be burnt, which is the judgement at this day of a woman for Petit treason. And herewith agreeth 21 E.3. where the reader must know, that in stead of *Mere* in that case you must read *Maister*.

[b5]And upon this Act, if the servant kill the wife of his Master, it is Petit treason, for he is servant both to the husband and wife.

[c6]If the child commit Parricide in killing of his father or mother (which the Law-makers never imagined any childe would doe) this case is out of this statute, unlesse the childe served the father or mother for wages, or meat, drink or apparell, for that it is none of these three kinds specified in this Law. And yet the offence is far more hainous and impious in a child then in a servant, for *Pecata contra naturam sunt gravissima:* but the Judges are restrained by this Act, to interpret this Act, *à simili or à minore ad majus,*[7] as hereafter shall be said. And *[8]some say that Parricide was petit treason by the Common Law.

[d9]A servant of malice intended to kill his Master, and lay in wait to doe it whilest he was his servant, but did it not till a year after he was out of service, and it was adjudged Petit treason within this Act.

---

3. [*Ed.:* This English caption is here substituted for a French caption in the original text.]

4. *a* 52 Ass. p. 30. 21 E. 3. 17. F. coron. 447. Statham tit. cor. 21 E. 3. 22 Ass. p. 49.

5. *b* 19 H. 6. 47. Pl. Com. 86. b. Dier. 3 Mar. 128. 7 El. 235.

6. *c* Exodus, c. 21. v. 15. 17. Lev. 20. v. 9. 1 Mar. per Bromley & Portman of the report of Justice Dalison. vid. 1. R. 3. 4. *In culeo paricide cum simia cane, gallo, & serpent: inclusi mari olim mergebantur: sed nos non habemus talem consuetudenem.*

7. [*Ed.:* Sins against nature are the worst. . . . from like [to like], or from lesser to greater.]

8. *22 E. 1. Math. Par. 874.

9. *d* 33 Ass. p. 7. Li. 1. f. 99. *Shelbys* case. 10 H. 6. 47. Pl Com. 260.

[Or a wife her husband.][10]

[c11]This was petit treason by the Common Law, as it appeareth in our books. If the wife procure one to murder her husband, and he doth it accordingly, in this case the wife being absent is but accessory, and shall be hanged and not burnt, because the accessory cannot be guilty of Petit treason, where the principall is not guilty but of murder: and the *[12]accessory must follow the nature of the principall: but if he that did the murder had been a servant of the husband, it had been treason in them both, and the wife should have been burnt. And so it is in the case before of a servant and in the case hereafter of a Clerk.

If the wife and a stranger kill the husband, it is Petit treason in the wife, and murder in the stranger, and so it is in the case of the servant next before, and of the Clerk next after.

Before this statute it was Petit treason, *si quis falsaverit sigillum domini sui de cujus familia fuit.*[13] Britton agreeth herewith.[14] But these are taken away by this Act, and all other saving these, that are here expressed.

[Or when a man secular or religious slayeth his Prelate to whom he oweth faith and obedience.][15]

[16] This clause is understood only of an Ecclesiasticall person, be he secular, or regular, if he kill his Prelate, or Superiour, to whom he oweth faith, and obedience, it is Petit Treason: and so it was at the Common Law. And Petit Treason both presuppose a trust and obedience in the offender, either Civill, as in the wife and servant, or Ecclesiasticall, as in the Ecclesiasticall person.

---

10. [*Ed.:* This English caption is here substituted for a French caption in the original text.]

11. *e* 15 E. 2. Coron. 383. 19 H. 6. 47. See c. Pr. & Acc' Dier. 34 H. 8. 50. Dier. 16 El. 332. Saunders case. Pasch. 32 E. 3. Rot. 62. coram rege. Ph. Cliftons case.

12. *40 Ass. p. 15.

13. [*Ed.:* if anyone forged the seal of his lord, whose servant he was.]

14. Fleta li 1. ca. 22. Britton fo. 16.

15. [*Ed.:* This English caption is here substituted for a French caption in the original text.]

16. 19 H. 6. 47.

Aidors, abettors, & procurers of any of these Petit Treasons, are within this Law.[17]

If the servant kill his Mistris, viz. his Masters wife, this is treason (as hath been said) not by equity, for that is denied as well in Petit Treason, as High Treason, but it is within the letter of this statute,[18] for she is a Master.

In High Treason there is no accessories, but all be principalls, and there-|-fore whatsoever act or consent will make a man accessory to a felony, before   [21] the act done, the same will make him a principall in case of High Treason. But in case of Petit Treason, there may be accessories, either before, or after the act done, as in case of Murder or Homicide.

Here it appeareth that Acts of Parliament may bind men of the Church, Secular, or Regular, & no benefit of Clergy allowed unto them in case of treason: but *[19]hereof you shall read at large in the Exposition of the 15. chapter of *Articuli cleri*.[20]

[And of such treason the Escheats ought to pertain to every Lord of his own fee, &c.][21]

[22]See hereof hereafter in the chapter of Forfeiture. b[23]If a man seised in fee of a Fair, Market, Common, rent, charge, rent seck, Warren, Corrody, or any other inheritance, that is not holden, and is attainted of felony, the King shall have the profits of them during his life: but after his decease, seeing the blood is corrupted, they cannot descend to the heir, *[24]nor can they escheat because they be not holden, they perish and are extinct by Act in law: For in Escheats for Petit Treason or felony, a tenure is requisite, as well in the case of the King, as of the subject.

---

17. 40 Ass. *ubi supra.* & 16 Fl. *ubi sup.*

18. 19 H. 6. 47. by all the Judges.

19. *a* See the 2. pt of the Institutes. Artic. cleri. ca. 15. Hil. 3 R. 2. *coram rege* Rot. 8. London, Jo. Imperials case.

20. [*Ed.:* Articles of the Clergy, 9 Edw. 2. st. 1 (1315).]

21. [*Ed.:* This English caption is here substituted for a French caption in the original text.]

22. For Escheats see the 1. part of the Institut. Sect. 1. fo. 13. a.

23. *b* See before ca. 1. *verbo, Dèes térres & tenements,* b & c.

24. * See 1. pt of the Institutes fo. 13. verb. *Averala terre per escheat.* Mic. 4 H. 4. *coram rege.* Rot. 22. Anglia.

An Approver in case of felony, refusing the combate with the Appellee, shall have like judgement that is for Petit Treason, *Probator recusans duellum adjudicatur suspendi, & trahi in odium falsae accusationis:*[25] but yet it is not Petit Treason, because it is none of the three specified in this Act.

The case which *Shard* reciteth in 40 Ass.[26] that a Norman being Leader of an English ship, who had English men with him, and robbed divers upon the sea, and were taken and found guilty: and as to the Norman it was but felony (because Normandy was lost by King John, and was out of the ligeance of E.3.) and as to the English it was adjudged treason, and the offenders drawn and hanged, which was the judgement of Petit Treason: but this case must be intended to fall out before this statute of 25 E.3. for it is none of the Petit Treasons mentioned in this Act.

And[27,28] because that many other like cases of treason may happen in time to come, which a man cannot think nor declare at this present time: It is accorded, that if any other case supposed treason, which is not above specified, doth happen before any Justice, the Justice shall tarry without going to judgement of the treason, till the cause be shewed and declared before the King and his Parliament, whether it ought to be judged treason or other felony.

[Like cases of treason.][29]

In this case, the Judges shall not judge *à simili,*[30] or by equity, argument, or inference of any treason, High or Petit, for no like case shall be adjudged treason, &c. And note this branch extendeth (as hath been said) to the offence, viz. treason, and not to tryall, judgement, or execution.

---

25. [*Ed.:* An approver refusing battle is adjudged to be hanged and to attract the odium of a false accusation.]

26. 40 Ass. 25. Vide 2 H. 5. cap. 6.

27. *Rerum progressus ostendunt multa, qua initio previderi non possunt.*

28. [*Ed.:* The text of this paragraph is an English translation in the First Edition. The text of the original French, which preceded this paragraph in that edition, has been omitted.]

29. [*Ed.:* This English caption is here substituted for a French caption in the original text.]

30. [*Ed.:* from like [to like].]

[Any other case supposed treason.][31]

No other case, though of as high or higher nature, &c. shall be adjudged treason High or Petit, as before it appeareth in the case of Paricide, Anno 1 Mariae, *ubi supra.*

[Treason.]

Either High Treason, or Petit Treason, so as this branch extendeth as hath been said to the offence of treason only.

| [Which is not above specified.][32]   [22]

[33]This word [specifie] is to be specially observed, for it is as much to say, as particularized, or set downe particularly: so as nothing is left to the construction of the Judge, if it be not specified and particularized before by this Act. A happy sanctuary or place of refuge for Judges to flye unto, that no mans blood and ruine of his family do lie upon their consciences against law. And if that the construction by arguments *à simili,*[34] or *à minori ad majus*[35] had been left to Judges, the mischiefe before this statute would have remained, viz. diversity of opinions, what ought to be adjudged treason, which this statute hath taken away by expresse words: and the statute of 1 Mar.[36] doth repeate all treasons, &c. but only such as be declared and expressed in this Act of 25 E.3. wherein this word [expressed] is to be observed.

In the Parliament holden *Anno* 5 H.4.[37] the Earle of Northumberland came before the King and Lords in Parliament, and by his Petition to the King, acknowledged to have done against his allegiance: and namely, for gathering

---

31. [*Ed.:* This English caption is here substituted for a French caption in the original text.]

32. See the exposition upon the statute *De frang. prisonam.* 1 H. 6. 5. 9 E. 4. 26, &c. See 1 Mar. of Justice Dalisons Report, *ubi supra.*

33. [*Ed.:* This English caption is here substituted for a French caption in the original text.]

34. [*Ed.:* from like [to like].]

35. [*Ed.:* from lesser to greater.]

36. 1 Mar. cap. 1.

37. Rot. Parl. 5 H. 4. nu. 11, 12. See nu. 15. Ibid.

of Power and giving of Liveries, whereof he prayeth pardon: and the rather, that upon the Kings Letters he yeelded himselfe, and came to the King unto Yorke, where he might have kept himselfe away. The which Petition the King delivered to the Justices by them to be considered. Whereupon the Lords made protestation, that the order thereof belonged to them, as Peers of the Parliament, to whom such judgement belonged in weighing of this statute of 25 E.3, &c. and they judged the same to be no treason, nor felony, but only *trespasse finable* at the Kings will. And the opinion in 27 Ass.[38] is denied, that if one of the Indicters discover the counsell of the King, that it should be treason; because it is not specified before in this Act, and therefore neither High Treason, nor Petit Treason.

[Till the cause be shewed and declared before the King and his Parliament.][39]

By this it is apparent, that any like or other case ought to be declared by the whole Parliament, (and not by the King and Lords of the Upper-House only, or by the King and the Commons, or by the Lords and Commons.) And so was it done by the whole Court of Parliament in 3 R.2. *ubi supra.* 5 Eliz. 18 Eliz. *ubi supra,* and many other Acts of Parliament.

John Duke of Gwyen and of Lancaster, Steward of England, and Thomas Duke of Glocester, Constable of England, the Kings Uncles, complained to the King,[40] that Thomas Talbot Knight, with other his adherents, conspired the death of the said Dukes in divers parts of Cheshire, as the same was confessed and well knowne, and prayed that the Parliament might judge of the fault (which Petition was just, and according to this branch of the statute of 25 E.3.) but the Record saith further: whereupon the King and Lords in the Parliament adjudged the same fact to be open and High Treason: which judgement wanting the assent of the Commons, was no declaration within this Act of 25 E.3. because it was not by the King and his Parliament according to this Act, but by the King and Lords only.

---

38. 27 Ass. p. 63.
39. [*Ed.:* This English caption is here substituted for a French caption in the original text.]
40. Rot. Par. 17. R. 2. nu. 20.

[Whether it ought to be judged treason or other felony.][41]

[42]This Declaration may be absolute, or *sub modo*,[43] for a time.

By this which hath been said it manifestly appeareth,[44] what damnable opinions those were concerning High Treason, of Tresilian Chiefe Justice of the Kings Bench, Sir Robert Belknap Chiefe Justice of the Common Bench, Sir John Holt, Sir Roger Fulthorp, and Sir William Burghe, Knights, fellowes of the said Sir Robert Belknap, and of John Lockton one of the Kings Serjeants, that were given to King R. the 2. at Nottingham, in the Eleventh yeare of his reigne. But more detestable were the opinions of the Justices in 21 R.2. and of Hanckford and Brinchley the Kings Serjeants, (and the rather, because they took no example by the punishment of the former) which affirmed the said opinions to be good and lawfull,[45] saving Sir William Thirning | Chiefe Justice [23] of the Common Bench gave this answer: That declaration of treason not declared belongeth to the Parliament; but to please, he said, that if he had been a Lord or a Peer of Parliament, if it had been demanded of him, he would have made the like answers. These Justices and Serjeants being called in question in the Parliament holden *Anno* 1 H.4.[46] for their said opinions, answered (as divers Lords Spirituall and Temporall did) that they durst no otherwise do, for feare of death. It was thereupon enacted, that the Lords Spirituall and Temporall, or Justices, be not from thenceforth received to say, that they durst not feare of death to say the truth. Which opinions being so manifestly against our said Act of 25 E.3. afterwards in the Parliament holden 1 H.4.[47] it is affirmed by authority of Parliament, that in the said Parliament of 21 R.2. divers Statutes, Judgements, Ordinances, and Stablishments were made, ordained, and given, erroniously and dolefully in great disherison and finall destruction and undoing of many honourable Lords, and other liege

---

41. 13 El. cap. 1, 2. 14 El. ca. 1,2,&c.
42. [*Ed.:* This English caption is here substituted for a French caption in the original text.]
43. [*Ed.:* conditional.]
44. Anno 21 R. 2. in Latin.
45. 11 R. 2. ca. 1., & 4.
46. Rot. Pall. 1 H. 4. nu. 97 *Melius est omnia mala pati quam malo consentive.*
47. 1 H. 4. ca. 3.

people of this Realme, and of their heires forever.[48] And therefore not only that Parliament of 21 R.2. and the circumstances and dependances thereupon, are wholly reversed, revoked, voided, undone, repealed, and annulled for ever, but also the Parliament holden in 11 R.2. by authority of which Parliament: Tresilian, Belknap, and the rest of those false Justices and Serjeants aforesaid were attainted, is confirmed, for that it was (as there the Parliament affirmeth) for the great honour and common profit of the Realme.

[And if percase any man of this Realme ride armed, &c.][49]

For exposition hereof, see the Chapter hereafter against riding or going armed.

For the better instruction of the Reader to discerne what offences be High Treason or Petit Treason at this day, it shall be necessary to adde hereunto the statute of 1 Mar. whereby it is enacted,[50] [That no Act, Deed, or Offence, being by Act of Parliament or Statute made treason, petit treason, or misprision of treason, by words, writing, ciphering, deeds, or otherwise whatsoever, shall be taken, had, deemed, or adiudged to be High Treason, Petit Treason, or misprision of treason, but only such as be declared and expressed to be treason, petit treason, or misprision of treason, in or by the Act of Parliament or Statute made in the 25 yeare of the raigne of the most noble King of famous memory, King Edward the third, touching or concerning treason, or the declaration of treason, and none other, &c. Any Actor Acts of Parliament, Statute, or Statutes, had or made at any time heretofore or after the said 25 year of King E.3. or any other declaration or matter to the contrary in any wise notwithstanding.][51]

Before this Act so many treasons had been made and declared by Act of Parliament since this Act of 25 E.3. some in particular, and some in generall, and in such sort penned, as not only the ignorant and unlearned people, but also learned and expert men were many times trapped and snared: and some-

---

48. See the consequence of erroneous opinions in case of high treason. 1. H. 4. cap. 4.

49. [*Ed.:* This English caption is here substituted for a French caption in the original text.]

50. 1 Mar. ca. 1. *Sessione prima.* The like statute was made, *Anno* 1 E. 6. ca. 12. See the statute of 1 H. 4 ca. 10. to the like effect.

51. Inter leges Canuti cap. 7. *Inprimis justae leges ut efferantur injusitae deprimantur.* Aliter in antiquo 10 MS. *Inprimis ut justae leges erigantur, injustae subvertantur.*

times treasons made or declared in one Kings time, were abrogated in another Kings time, either by speciall or generall words: so as the mischief before 25 E.3. of the uncertainty what was treason, and what not, became to be so frequent and dangerous, as the safest and surest remedy was, by this excellent Act of 1 Mar. to abrogate and repeale all, but only such as are specified and expressed in this statute of 25 E.3. By which law, the safety both of the King and of the subject, and the preservation of the Common-weale is wisely and sufficiently provided for, in such certainty, as *Nihil relictum est arbitrio Judicis.*[52] And certainly the two Rules recited in the Preamble of the said Act of 1 *Mariae,* are assuredly true. The first, [That the state of a King standeth and consisteth more assured by the love and favour of the subject toward their Soveraigne then in the dread and fear of lawes made with rigorous pains and extreme punishment for not obeying their Soveraigne.] And the other, [That lawes justly made for the preservation of the Common-weale without extreme punishment or penalty, are more often, and for the most part better obeyed and kept, then lawes and statutes made | with great and extreme punishment.]   [24] *Mitiùs imperanti melius paretur.*[53,54]

In which Act five notable things are to be observed. First, it extendeth (without exception) to all High Treasons made by any Act of Parliament since the said Act of 25 E.3. Secondly, to all declarations of High Treasons by any Act of Parliament since the said Act of 25 E.3. (as of the said Declaration in 3 R.2. of killing an Ambassadour and the like.) Thirdly, to all Petit Treasons made or declared by any Act of Parliament since the said Act of 25 E.3. Fourthly, albeit misprision of treason is not mentioned in the Act of 25. E.3. yet every misprision of any treason made or declared since that Act by any Act of Parliament, is abrogated. Fifthly, no offence to be treason, petit treason, or misprision of treason, but only such as he declared and expressed to be treason, petit treason, or misprision of treason by the said Act of 25 E.3. Here three things are to be observed: first, that this word [expressed] excludeth all implications or inferences whatsoever, Secondly, here misprision of treason is taken for concealement of high treason or petit treason, and only of high treason or petit treason specified and expressed in the Act of 25 E.3. Thirdly,

52. [*Ed.*: Nothing is left to the whim of the judge.]
53. [*Ed.*: The milder the ruler, the better he is obeyed. [Seneca, *De Clementia,* i. 24, 8.].]
54. *Seneca.*

that no former judgement, attainder, president, resolution, or opinion of Judges or Justices of high treason, petit treason, or misprision of treason, other then such as are specified and expressed in the said Act of 25 E.3. are to be followed or drawne to example: for the words be direct and plaine, [That from henceforth no Act, Deed, or offence, &c. shall be taken, had, deemed, or adiudged to be treason, petit treason, or [a55]misprision of treason, but only such as be declared and expressed in the said Act of 25 E.3. &c. any Act of Parliament or Statute after 25 E.3. or any other declaration or matter to the contrary notwithstanding.] So as there is no high treason, petit treason, or misprision of any treason made or declared by any Act of Parliament or otherwise since the Act of 25 E.3. but only such as have been made since the said Act of 1 Mariae, and of those, only such as were made [b56]perpetuall, and not during the life of Queen Mary or of Queen Elizabeth, whereof there be divers which now are expired, which you may reade being all in print. But there wanted nothing to the perfection of the Statute of 25 E.3. but a limitation of some certaine time wherein the offender should be accused. [c57]*Post intervallum temporis accusator non erit audiendus, nisi docere potest se faisse justis rationibus impeditum.*[58]

[Or the declaration of treason, &c.][59]

[d60]Declarations made during the naturall life of Queen Elizabeth ceased by her death: for Declarations may have limitations as well as Statutes introductory of new lawes.

There is another excellent branch of a Statute made [c61]in 1 & 2 Ph. & Mar. in these words. [And be it further enacted by the authority aforesaid, that all trials hereafter to be had, awarded, or made for any treason, shall be had and used only according to the due order and course of the Common Law.]

---

55. *a* That is, of such treason, high or petit, as is expressed in the Act of 25 E. 3. and of no other treason.

56. *b* 1 Mar. ca. 6. 1 & 2 Ph. & Mar. cap. 11. 5 Eliz. ca. 1. & 11 18 Eliz. cap. 1 13 Eliz. cap. 2 23 Eliz. ca. 1 27 Eliz. ca. 2 3 Jac. cap. 4.

57. *c* Bracton lib. 3. fol. 118. b.

58. [*Ed.:* After a lapse of time an accuser will not be heard, unless he can show that he was hindered for just reasons.]

59. 13 Eliz. cap. 1 14 Eliz. cap. 1 and cap. 2.

60. *d* 13 Eliz. cap. 1 14 Eliz. cap. 1. & cap. 2.

61. *e* 1 & 2 Ph. & M. cap. 10.

All trials.

[f62]Upon these words many things have been observed by others. First, that the Letter of this Act extendeth only to triall of high treasons, or petit treasons, and not to misprision. Secondly, Foraine treasons are to be tried by the statute [g63]of 35 H.8. cap. 2. and so it was resolved by all the Justices of England in *Orurks* Case, and had been so resolved before. But for trials of treasons to be had in Wales, or where the Kings Writ runneth not, in such Shires as the King shall assigne by his Commission by the *[64]statute of 32 H.8. ca. 5. are abrogated by this Act, because they are triable by the law.

[h65]It hath been holden, that upon the triall of misprision of treason there must be two lawfull witnesses, as well upon the triall, as upon the indictment, as it was resolved by the Justices in the Lord Lumleyes Case, Hil. 14. Eliz. reported by the Lord Dier, under his own hand, which we have seen, but left out of the print, which for other purposes is cited hereafter. Thirdly, it hath beene holden, that this Act extendeth not to the Indictment of any treason, but to the triall by Peers, if the offender be noble: or by Freeholders, if the offender be under the degree of nobility: & therefore upon the indictment which is in manner of an | accusation, by the statutes of 1. E.6. and 5 E.6.[66]   [25] two lawfull witnesses are requisite: the words of the statute of 1 E.6. in the last branch be, [That none shall be indicted, arraigned, condemned, or convicted for any treason, Petit Treason, misprision of treason, or for any words before specified to be spoken, after the said first day of February, for which the same offender or speaker that in any wise suffer pains of death, imprisonment, losse or forfeiture of his goods, chatels, lands, or tenements, he be accused by two sufficient and lawfull witnesses, or shall willingly without violence confesse the same.]

Nota that [before specified] doe refer to the words mentioned before in the Act. 1. It is manifest by the connexion of the words, viz. [for any words before

---

62. *f* See the second part of the Institutes, Mag. Charta. cap. 29. Verbo (*per judicium parium.*)

63. *g* 35 H. 8. ca. 2. 3 Mar. Dier 132. lib. 7. fo. 23. in Calvins case. Pasch. 33 Eliz. Orurks case.

64. * 32 H. 8. cap. 4.

65. *h* 1 E. 6. ca. 12. 5 E. 6. ca. 11. Both which are mentioned in the next Section. Hill. 14. Eliz. Dier MS. *Nota.* This is the last resolution of the Judges in this point. At this time *Catlin* and *Dier* were Chiefe Justices, and *Sanders* Chiefe Baron, &c.

66. 1 E. 6. cap. 12. 5 E. 6. ca. 11. See 13 El. cs. 1. See before *Verb.* [*De ceo provablement soit attaint.*]

specified to be spoken, &c.] 2. The treasons in 25 E.3. were mentioned before. 3. The first words be [for any treason, Petit treason, misprision of treason, &c.]

And by 5 E.6. ca.11.[67] it is provided by the last clause save one. [That none shall be indicted, arraigned, condemned, convicted, or attainted for any of the treasons or offencess aforesaid, or for *[68]other treasons that now be, or hereafter shall be, which shall hereafter be perpetrated, committed, or done, unlesse the same offender be thereof accused by two lawfull accusers, &c. unlesse the said party arraigned shall willingly, without violence confesse the same.] Here two things are to be observed. 1. The particular penning of both these Acts, viz. indicted, arraigned, convicted, &c. and the words of 1 & 2 of Ph & Mar. extend to tryals only, & not to the indictment. 2. Two lawfull accusers in the Act of 5 E. 6 are taken for two lawfull witnesses, for by two lawfull accusers, and accused by two lawfull witnesse (as it is said 1 E.6) is all one: which word (accusers) was used, because two witnesses ought directly to accuse, that is, charge the prisoner, for other accusers have we none in the Common Law: and therefore lawfull accusers must be such accusers as Law allow. And so was it resolved in the Lo. Lumleys case by the Justices:[69] for if accusers should not be so taken, then there must be two accusers, by 5 E.6. and two witnesses by 1 E.6. And the strange conceit in 2 Mar. that one may be an accuser by hearsay, was utterly denied by the Justices in the Lo. Lumleys case. And this word [awarded] in the statute of 1 & 2. Ph. & Mar. extendeth to the tryall upon the arraignment, and not to the indictment, for that is not said to be awarded.

And it was resolved by all the Justices in [a70]Rolstons case upon the rebellion in the North, that these words [shall willingly without violence confesse the same] are to be understood where the party accused upon his examination before his arraignment, willingly confessed the same without violence; that is, willingly without any torture: and is not meant of a confession before the Judge, for he is never present at any torture, neither upon his arraignment

---

67. See 1 El. ca. 6. Stanf. pl. Coron, 89. & 164. 4 Mar. Coron. Br. 220. Dier. 2 Mar. 99. & 3 Mar. 132.

68. *Nota* the generality of these words. *Regula Verba generalia generaliter sunt intelligenda.* See hereafter c. 49. of Piracy, &c.

69. Hil. 14. El Lo. Lumleys case. *ubi supra.* 2 Mar. Dier. 99. 100. Thomas Case.

70. *a* Mich. 13 & 14 El. Rolstons case.

was ever any torture offered. And here commeth another [b71]statute made in
1 & 2 Mar. to be considered, by which it is provided, that treason for the
counterfeiting and unpairing of the coin currant in this Realm, &c. the offender therein, &c. shall be indicted, arraigned, tried, convicted, or attainted
by such like evidence, and in such manner and form, as hath been used and
accustomed within this Realm, at any time before the first year of King E.6.
&c. Wherein the speciall penning of this Act is to be observed, which in case
of treason concerning the counterfeiting or impairing of coin, &c. hath by
particular words restored the evidence requisite by the Common Law, before
the statute of 1 E.6. as well upon the indictment as the triall. But the Act of
1 & 2 Ph & Mar.cap. 10.[72] extends to trialls only in other cases of High Treason,
and therefore that Act extendeth not to the indictment of other High treasons.
Also it is most necessary (as many doe hold) that there should be two lawfull
accusers, that is, two lawfull witnesses at the time of the indictment, for that
it is commonly found in the absence of the party accused, and it may be when
the party suspected is beyond sea, or in remote parts, and may be obtained
thereupon; and therefore seeing the indictment is the foundation of all, it is
most necessary to have substantiall proof in a cause so criminall, where *pro-
bationes oportent esse luce clariores.*[73] | Lastly, if the indictment were part of the   [26]
tryall, then ought he that is noble, and a Lord of Parliament be indicted of
High Treason, &c. by his Peers: for the tryall of him (without question) must
be by his Peers: but the indictment of Peers of the Realm is always by Freeholders, and not by their Peers, as hereafter shall appear. We have been the
longer herein in respect of some variety of opinion (for want of due and intire
consideration had of all and every part of that which hath been said) upon
serious study touching this point, without respect of a common wandring
opinion.[74]

And it seemeth that by the ancient Common law one accuser, or witnesse
was not sufficient to convict any person of High Treason: [a75]For in that case,

71. *b* 1 & 2 Ph. & Mar. c. 11. supra.
72. 1 & 2 Ph. & Ma. cap. 10.
73. [*Ed.:* proofs ought to be clearer than light.]
74. See Magna Cart. c. 29. and the exposition thereupon.
75. *a* Pat. 25. E. 3. part. 1. nu. 16. Rot. Parl. 21 R. 2. nu. 19. 21. the D. of Norff. case. Rot. Pat. 3 H.
4. Balleshuls case. Rot. Vascon. 9 H. 4. nu. 14. John Bolemers case. Rot. Parl. 2 H. 6. nu. 9. the Earl of

where is but one accuser, it shall be tried before the Constable and Marshall by Combat, as by many records appeareth. [b76]But the Constable and Marshall have no jurisdiction to hold plea of any thing, which may be determined or discussed by the Common Law. And that two witnesses be required, appeareth by our [c77]books, and I remember no authority in our books to the contrary: and the Common law herein is grounded upon the law of God expressed both in the old and new Testament: [d78]*In ore duorum aut trium testium peribit qui interficietur: Nemo occidatur uno contra se dicente testimonium.*[79]

And this seemeth to be the more clear in the triall by the Peers, or Nobles of the Realm, because they come not *de aliquo vicineto,*[80] whereby they might take notice of the fact in respect of vicinitie, as other Jurors may doe.

Having now rehearsed what others have said and holden, we upon due consideration had of the whole matter will set down our own opinion, and reasons, in these Four points following. First, that the statute of [e81]5 E.6. cap. 11. is a generall law, and extends to all High treasons, as well by the Common Law declared by the statute of 25 E.3. as to any other statute made or to be made, the negative words of which statute be: [No person shall be [f82]indicted, arraigned, convicted, condemned, or attainted for any treason, that now is, or hereafter shall be, &c.] Which words without all question are generall, and so to be taken. The words of that statute be further, [Unlesse the same offender be accused by two lawfull accusers,] These two lawfull accusers are in judgment of law taken for two lawfull witnesses, and that for two causes: First, they must be lawfull, that is, allowed by the Laws of the Realm: and by the law, upon the arraignment of the Prisoner upon the indictment of treason, no

---

Ormonds case. Rot. Pat. 8 H. 6. pt. 2. nu. 7. between Upton and Dowy. Vide the 4. part of the Institutes. cap. the Court of Chivaliry, &c. See Bract. lib. 3. fo. 119. a.

76. *b* 13 R. 2. ca. 2.

77. *c* Mirror ca. 3. §. *ordenance de attaint.* Bract. l. 5. f. 354. 48 E. 3. 30. 35 H. 6. 46. Fort. ca. 32. 15 E. 4. f. 1. Pl. Com. fo. 8.

78. *d* Deu. 17. 6. 19. 15. Mat. 18. 16. John 18. 23. 2 Cor. 13. 1. Heb. 10. 28.

79. [*Ed.:* He who ought to be slain shall perish by the mouths of two or three witnesses; but no one shall be killed when there is only one witness against him.]

80. [*Ed.:* from any venue (i.e. neighbourhood).]

81. *e* And so I hold the statute of 1 E. 6. c. 12. to be a generall Law, and to extend to all high treasons, &c.

82. *f Nota* as well upon the indictment as the arraignment of treason there ought to be two accusers. See Dier 2 & 3. Ph. & Mar. 132.

other accuser can be heard, but witnesses only. Secondly, the words of the statute are [Which said accusers at the time of the arraignment of the party accused, if they be then living, shall be brought in person before the party so accused, and avow, and maintain that which they have to say to prove him guilty of the treason., unlesse the party arraigned shall willingly without violence confesse the same,] as by that Act it appeareth. Now to avow and maintain that which they have to say, to prove him guilty of the treason, is the proper office and duty of witnesses, and so it is said in the statute of ^{g83}1 E.6. c.12. in the last clause (by two lawfull witnesses.) See the statute of 5 El. c.1. where it is said [accused by good and sufficient testmony:] to the same intent, the statute of 1 & 2 Ph.& Mariae ca.11. for the word [accused.]

^{i84}*Puniantor accusatores penes dominum regem, quòd amodò Rex eis de facili non credat: et talis poena fiat eis, qualis debeat fieri illis, qui injuste fideles dn̄i regis exhaeredari & desturi fecerunt, &c.*^{85}

2. That this Act of 5 E.6. extend as well to Petit Treason, as High Treason, for the words be [any treason] and so doth the statute of 1 E.6. ca.12.

3. That the statute of 1 & 2 Ph. & Mar. cap.10. doth not abrogate the said Act of 1 E.6. or of 5 E.6. For that Act of 1 & 2 Ph. & Mar. extends only to trialls by the verdict of twelve men *de vicineto,*^{86} of the place where the offence is alleadged, and ^{k87}the indictment is no part of the triall, but an information or declaration for the King, and the evidence of witnesses to the Jury is no part of the triall, for by law the tryall in that case is not by witnesses, but by the ver-|-dict of twelve men, and so a manifest diversity between the evidence to a Jury, and a tryall by Jury. And the word [awarded] in that statute doth prove that that Act extended only to the *venire facias*^{88} for trial, for neither

[27]

83. *g* 1 E. 6. ca. 12. the last clause. 5 El. ca. 1. 1 & 2 Ph. & Mar. ca. 11. Bract. li. 3. f. 118. *Qui accusat integrae samae fit, & non criminosus.*

84. *i* Star. de Kenelw. *secunda parte* Vet. Mag. Cart. cap. 16.

85. [*Ed.:* The accusers shall be punished by the lord king, so that thereafter the king should not so easily believe them; and such punishment shall be given them as ought to be given them that unjustly cause the faithful subjects of the lord king to be disinherited and destroyed.]

86. [*Ed.:* from the neighborhood, or vicinage.]

87. *k* See the first part of the Institutes. Sect. 194. See Fortescue ca. 26,27. Juries ought to be informed by evidences, and witnesses.

88. [*Ed.:* Writ to the sheriff of the county in which a cause is to be tried, commanding him that he "cause to come" before the court, on a certain day twelve good and lawful men of the body of his county qualified according to law, by whom the truth of the matter may be the better known, and who are in no

the indictment nor the evidence can be said to be awarded: *Veritas quae minime defensator, opprimitur, & qui non improbat, approbat. Et sic liberè animam meam liberavi.*[89]

[a][90]The tryal against an Aliennee, that lived here under the protection of the King, and amity being between both Kings, for High treason, shall by force of this Act of 1 & 2 Ph. & Mar. be tried according to the due course of the Common Law, and therefore in that case he shall not be tried *per medieratem linguae,*[91] as he shall be in case of Petit Treason, murder, and felony, if he prayeth it.

4. [b][92]That a tryall in a forein county upon examination before three of the Councell, &c. by the statute of 33 H.8. ca.23. is abrogated by this Act of 1 & 2 Ph. & Mar. being a tryall contrary to the due course of the Common Law, which is to have it tryed by Jurours of the proper County, [c][93]but the indictment being found in the proper County, it may be by speciall commission heard and determined before Commissioners in any forein county, but the tryall must be by Jurours of the proper county; and this is warranted by the course of the Common Law. And albeit when the Term begins, all Conmisssions of Oier and Terminer in the county where the Kings Bench sit, be suspended during the Term, yet if an Indictment be found before such Commissioners before the tearm, there may be a speciall commission made to commissioners in the same county, sitting the Kings Bench in that county, to hear and determine the same during the tearm: for the Kings Bench hath no power to proceed thereupon, till the indictment be before them. And it is the better, if the speciall commission bear *Teste* after the beginning of the tearm. Note

---

wise of kin either to the plaintiff or to the defendant, to make a jury of the county between the parties in the action, because as well the plaintiff as the defendant, between whom the matter in variance is, have put themselves upon that jury, and that he return the names of the jurors, etc.]

89. [*Ed.:* Truth, when not defended, is oppressed; and he who does not disapprove, approves; and so I have freely delivered my mind.]

90. *a* 27 E. 3. ca. 8. 28. E. 3. ca. 18. 8 H. 6 ca. 29. 1 Mar. fo. 144. Shirleys case, & so it was resolved by all the Judges Hil. 36 El. in the case of Doctor Lopez, Emanuel Loysie, and Stephen Ferreira de Gama.

91. [*Ed.:* by [a jury] half of [a foreign] tongue.]

92. *b* 33 H. 8. c. 23. 3 Mar. Dier 132. Dier 12. El. 286. b. li. 11. fo. 63. a. in Doctor Fosters case.

93. *c* 27 Ass. p. 1. 21 Ass. p. 12. W 1. c. 3. &c. Mic 25 & 26 El. *per les Justices* in Somerviles and Ardens case. Dier 12 El. 286. b. All this was resolved Mic. 1. Ja. in Sir Walter Raleighs case. Pl. Com. 388. Count de Leicesters case.

a diversity between generall commissioners of Oier and Teminer, and such a speciall commission; and the Court of Kings Bench may be adjourned, and in the mean time the Commissioners may sit there.

[d94]And where it is provided by the statute of 33 H.8. cap. 23. that peremptory challenge should not from thenceforth be admitted or allowed in cases of High Treason, or misprision of treason: [e95]This branch is abrogated by the said Act of 1 Mar. For the end of challenge is to have an indifferent tryall, and which is required by law; and to bar the party indicted of his lawfull challenge, is to bar him of a principall matter concerning his tryall: and all Acts of Parliament concerning incidents to tryalls contrary to the course of the Common law, are abrogated by the said words, [and that all trialls hereafter, &c.] but all this is to be understood of persons under the degree of Nobility; For in case of a triall of a Noble man, Lord of Parliament, he cannot challenge at all any of his Peers.

[f 96] Henry Garnet Superiour of the Jesuites in England upon his arraignment for the Powder Treason, did challenge *Burrrell* a Citizen of London peremptorily, and it was allowed unto him by the resolution of all the Judges, [g97]So as in case of High Treason, or misprision of High Treason, a man may challenge 35. peremptorily, which is under three Juries, but more he cannot.

Lastly, all statutes made before the said Act of 1 & 2 Ph. & Mar. for tryall of High Treason, Petit Treason, or misprision of Treason, contrary to the due course of the common law, are abogated by the said Act of 1 & 2 Ph. & Mar. and tryalls by the due course of the common law, with challenges incidents in those cases are restored.

[h98]If a man be indicted of High Treason, he may at this day plead a forein plea, as he might doe by the common law, and shall be tryed in the forein county: but otherwise it is in cases of Petit Treason, murder, or felony, for there it shall be tryed in the county where the indictment is taken.

94. *d* 33 H. 8. c. 23.

95. *e* And so it was resolved. An. 1 Ja. in Sir Walter Raleighs case, by all the Judges and had been resolved so before. Stan. pl. cor. 157.

96. *f* 3 Ja. R. in Garnets case. And so was it resolved M. 25 & 26 El. in Somerviles & Ardens case.

97. *g* Br. tit. Challenge 217.

98. *h* 22 H. 8. c. 14. 32 H. 8. c. 3. See 4. H. 8. c. 2. and 22 H. 8. c. 2. pleading &c. for being taken out of Sanctuary in a forain county in case of murder or felony. See hereafter. ca. Sanctuary, all sanctuaries taken away: & note that the stat. of 22 H. 8. &c. extend only to Indictments and not to Appeals.

And forasmuch as the proceeding against a noble Peer of the Realm, being a Lord of Parliament in some points agrees, and in other points differeth from the proceeding against a subject under the degree of Nobility: It shall be necessary to shew wherein they agree, and wherein they differ.

[28]   ❘ 1. The Noble Peer of the Realme must be indicted before Commissioners of Oier and Teminer or in the Kings Bench,[99] if the treason, misprision of treason, felony or misprision thereof be committed in that County where the Kings Bench sit, as it was resolved in the case of Tho. D. of N. in An. 13. Eliz. And this is common to both degrees to be indicted by Jurors of that County where the offence was committed.

2. When he is indicted,[100] then the King by his Commission under the Great Seale constitutes some Peer of the Realme, to be *hac Vice,*[101] Steward of England: For his stile in the Commission, is, *(Seneschallus Angliae)*[102] who is Judge in this case of the treason or felony, or of the misprision of the same committed by any Peer of the Realm. This commission reciteth the Indictment generally as it is found: and power given to the Lord Steward to receive the Indictment, &c. and to proceed, *Secundum legem & consuetudinem Angliae.*[103] And a commandement is given thereby to the Peers of the Realme, to be attendant and obedient to him: and a commandement to the Lieutenant of the Tower to bring the prisoner before him.

3. A *Certiorari*[104] is awarded out of the Chancery to remove the indictment it selfe before the Steward of England *indialté,*[105] which may either beare date the same day of the Stewards Commission, or any day after.

4. The Steward directs his precept under his seale to the Commissioners, &c. to certifie the indictment such a day and place.

5. Another Writ goeth out of the Chancery directed to the Licutenant of the Tower to bring the body of the prisoner before the Steward at such day and place as he shall appoint.

---

99. 1 H. 4. 1.
100. 1 H. 4. 1. 10 E. 4. 6. b. 13 H. 8. 12.
101. [*Ed.:* for that occasion.]
102. [*Ed.:* Seneschal of England; the Lord Steward's title.]
103. [*Ed.:* According to the law and custom of England.]
104. [*Ed.:* Writ of common law origin issued by a superior to an inferior court requiring the latter to produce a certified record of a particular case trial herein.]
105. [*Ed.:* without delay.]

6. The Lord Steward maketh a precept under his seale to the Lieutenant of the Tower &c. and therein expresseth a day and place when he shall bring the prisoner before him.

7. The Steward maketh another precept under his seale to a Serjeant at Armes, to summon *Tot & tales dominos, magnates, & proceres hujus regni Angliae praedicti R. Comitis E. pares, per quos rei veritas melius sciri poterit, quòd ipsi personaliter compareant coram praedicto Seneschallo apud Westm. tali die & hora, ad faciend, ea quae ex parte domini Regis forent facienda, &c.*[106] Wherein Four things are to be observed. First, that all these precepts most commonly beare date all in one day. Secondly, that no number of Peers are named in the precept, and yet there must be Twelve or above. Thirdly, that the precept is awarded for the returne of the Peers before any arraignment or plea pleaded by the prisoner. Fourthly, that in this case the Lords are not de Vicineto, and therefore the sitting and triall may be in any County of England. And herein are great differences between the case of a Peer of the Realme, and of one under the degree of nobility.

8. At the day, the Steward with six Serjeants at Armes before him takes his place under a Cloth of State, and then the Clerk of the Crown delivereth unto him his Commission, who redelivereth the same unto him.[107] And the Clerk of the Crown causeth a Serjeant at armes to make three Oyes and commandement given in the name of the Lord High Steward of England to keep silence: and then is the Commission read.[108] And then the Usher delivereth to the Steward a white rod, who re-delivereth the same to him againe, who holdeth it before the Steward. Then another Oyes is made, a commandement given in the name of the High Steward of England, to all Justices and Commissioners to certifie all Indictments and Records, &c. Which being delivered into Court, the Clerk of the Crown readeth the return. Another Oyes is made, that the Lieutenant of the Tower, &c. returne his Writ and Precept, and to bring the prisoner to the Bar: which being done, the Clerk reads the retorne. Another Oyes is made, that the Serjeant at armes return his precept with names

---

106. [*Ed.:* Such and so many lords, great men and nobles of this realm of England who are peers of the aforesaid R., earl of E., by whom the truth of the matter may be better known, that they do personally appear before the aforesaid steward at Westminster on such and such a day and hour, to do what should be done on behalf of the lord king, etc.]

107. 1 H. 4. 1.

108. 1 H. 4. 1.

of the Barons and Peers by him summoned, and the return of that is also read. Another Oyes is made, that all Earles, Barons and Peers (which by the commandement of the High Steward be summoned) answer to their names, and then they take their | places and sit down, and their names are recorded: and the entry of the Record is, that they appeare, *Ad faciendum ea quae ex parte Domini Regis eis injungentur.*[109] And when they be all in their places, and the prisoner at the Bar, the High Steward declares to the prisoner the cause of their assembly, and perswades him to answer without feare, that he shall be heard with patience, and that justice should be done.[110] Then the Clerk of the Crown reades the Indictment, and proceeds to the arraignment of the prisoner, and if he plead not guilty, the entry is, *Et de hoc de bono & malo ponit se super Pares suos &c.*[111] Then the High Steward giveth a charge to the Peers, exhorting them to try the prisoner indifferently according to their evidence.

9. The Peers are not sworn, but are charged, *Super fidelitatibus, & ligeantiis Domino Regi debitis:*[112] for so the Record speaketh.

10. Then the Kings learned Councell give evidence, and produce their proofes for the King against the prisoner.

11. But the prisoner, when he pleadeth not guilty, whereby he denieth the fact, he needs have no advice of Councell to that plea. But if he hath any matter of law to plead, as Humfrey Stafford in 1 H.7. had, viz. The priviledge of Sanctuary, he shall have Councell assigned to him to plead the same, or any other matter in law:[113] as to plead the generall pardon, or a particular pardon, or the like. And after the plea of not guilty, the prisoner can have no Councell learned assigned to him to answer the Kings Councell learned, nor to defend him. And the reason thereof is, not because it concerneth matter of fact, for *Ex facto jus oricur:*[114] but the true reasons of the law in this case are: First, that the testimonies and the proofs of the offence ought to be so

---

109. [*Ed.:* To do what they should be enjoined to do on behalf of the lord king.]

110. 1 H. 4. 1.

111. [*Ed.:* And thereof for good and ill he puts himself upon his peers, etc.]

112. [*Ed.:* Upon the faiths and allegiances due to the lord king.]

113. In Scotland in all criminall cases, yea in cases of High Treason, *Pars rea* may have Councell learned. *Vide* hereafter upon the statute of 31 Eliz. concerning witnesses.

114. [*Ed.:* The law arises out of the fact.]

clear and manifest, as there can be no defence of it. *[115]Secondly, the Court ought to be in dread of councell for the prisoner, to see that nothing be urged against him contrary to law and right: nay, any learned man that is present may informe the Court for the benefit of the prisoner, of any thing that may make the proceedings erroneous. And herein there is no diversity between the Peer and another Subject. And to the end that the triall may be the more indifferent, seeing that the safety of the prisoner consisteth in the indifferency of the Court, the Judges ought not to deliver their opinions before-hand of any criminall case, that may come before them judicially. And we reade, that in the case of Humfrey Stafford that arch-traytor,[116] Hussey, Chiefe Justice, besought King Henry the Seventh, that he would not desire to know their opinions before-hand for Humfrey Stafford, for they thought it should come before them in the Kings Bench judicially, and then they would do that which of right they ought: and the King accepted of it. And therefore the Judges ought not to deliver their opinions beforehand upon a case put, and proofs urged of one side in absence of the party accused: especially in cases of high nature; and which deserve so fatall and extreme punishment. For how can they be indifferent, who have delivered their opinions before-hand without hearing of the party, when a small addition, or substraction may alter the case? And how doth it stand with their Oath, who are sworn,[117] That they should well and lawfully serve our Lord the King and his people in the office of a Justice? and they should do equall law, and execution of right to all his subjects, &c. See more of this matter in the 13 Section here following.

12. There be alwayes either all, or some of the Judges ever attendant upon the High Steward, and sit at the feet of the Peers, or about a Table in the middest, or in some other convenient place.

13. After all the evidence given for the King, and the prisoners answers, and proofs at large, and with patience heard: then is the prisoner withdrawn from the Bar to some private place under the custody of the Lieutenant, &c. And after that he is withdrawn, the Lords that are tryers of the prisoner go to some place to consider of their evidence: and if upon debate thereof, they shall doubt of any matter, and thereupon send to the High Steward to have conference

---

115. * See more here of ca. 63. Councell learned in Pleas of the Crown.
116. 1 H. 7. fo. 26.
117. 18 E. 3.

with the Judges, or with the High Steward, they ought to have no conference, either with the Judges or the High Steward, but openly in Court, and in the

[30]   pre-l-sence, and hearing of the Prisoner; as it was resolved by all the Justices of England in the reign of King H.8. in the case of the Lord Dacres of the North.[118] And this was a just resolution: for when the Lords should put a case, and ask advice thereupon, the prisoner ought by law to be present, to see that the case or question be rightly put: and therefore that nothing be done in his absence, untill they be agreed on their verdict. Hereupon it followeth, that if the Peers of the Realm, who are intended to be indifferent, can have no conference with the Judges, or with the High Steward in open Court in the absence of the prisoner: *à fortiori,*[119] the Kings learned Counsell should not in the absence of the party accused, upon any case put, or matter shewed by them, privately participate the opinion of the Judges: and upon so just a resolution the case succeeded well, for the Peers found the Lord Dacres not guilty.

14. A Noble man cannot waive his triall by his Peers, and put himselfe upon the triall of the Country, that is, of twelve Freeholders: for the statute of Magna Carta is,[120] that he must be tried *per Pares.*[121] And so it was resolved in the Lord Dacres case, *Ubi supra.*

15.*[122]The Peers ought to continue together (as Juries in case of other Subjects ought to do) untill they be agreed of their Verdict: & when they are agreed, they all come again into the Court, and take their places, and then the Lord High Steward publickly in open Court, beginning with the puisne Lord, (who in the case of the Lord Dacre was the Lord Mordant,) said unto him: By Lord Mordant, Is William Lord Dacre guilty of the treasons, whereof he hath been indicted or arraigned, or of any of them. And the Lord standing up said, Not guilty: and so upward of all the other Lords *seriatim:*[123] who all gave the same Verdict: In which case the entry is, *Super quo W. Comes E. & caeteri anredicti Pares instanter super fidelitatibus & ligeantiis dicto Domino*

---

118. Pasch. 26 H. 8. in the case of the Lord Dacres of the North reported by Justice Spilman which we have seen.

119. [*Ed.:* with stronger reason.]

120. Mag. Cart. ca. 29.

121. [*Ed.:* by peers.]

122. * Resolved by all the Judges. Mich. 13 & 14 El. in the case of Tho. Duke of Norff. 1 H. 4. fo. 1. 10 E. 4. 6. b. 13 H. 8. fo. 12. Tr. 26 H. 8. Spilmans Report.

123. [*Ed.:* one by one.]

Regi dibitis, per praefatum Senescallum ab inferiori Pare usq; ad supremum se-
paratim publice examinati dicunt, quòd W. Dominus Dacre non est culp. &c.[124]

16. The Peers give their Verdict in the absence of the prisoner, and then is the prisoner brought to the Bar again: and then doth the Lord Steward acquaint the prisoner with the verdict of his Peers, and give judgement accordingly, either of condemnation or acquitall. But it is not so in the case of another subject: for there the verdict is given in his presence.

17. Every Lord of Parliament, and that hath voice in Parliament, and called thereunto by the Kings Writ, shall not be tried by his Peers,[125] but only such as sit there *Ratione Nobilitatis,*[126] as Dukes, Marquisses, Countes, Viscounts or Barons, and not such as are Lords of Parliament, *ratione Baroniarum, quas tenent in jure Ecclesiae,*[127] by reason of their Baronies which they hold in the right of the Church, as Arch-Bishops, and Bishops, and in time past some Abbots and Priors, but they shall be tried by the country, that is, by Freeholders, for that they are not of the degree of Nobility.

18. [a128]No Noble man shall be tried by his Peers, but only at the suit of the King upon an indictment of high treason, or misprision of the same, petit treason, murder, or other felony, or misprision of the same. But in case of a Premunire or the like, though it be at the suit of the King, he shall not be tried by his Peers, but by Freeholders. And so in an Appeale at the suit of the party for petit treason, murder, robbery, or other felony, he shall be tryed by Freeholders. See more hereof in the second part of the Institutes, Magna Carta, cap. 29.

19. [b129]And albeit a man be Noble, and yet no Lord of the Parliament of this Realm, (as if he be a Nobleman of Scotland, or of Ireland, of France, &c.) he shall be tried by Knights, Esquires, or others of the Commons. And

---

124. [*Ed.:* Whereupon W., earl of E., and the other aforementioned peers, upon the faiths and allegiances due to the said lord king, being forthwith publicly and severally examined by the said steward, from the lowest peer to the highest, say that W., Lord Dacre, is not guilty, etc.]

125. Rot. Roman 17 E. 2. m. 6. Adam Orleton B. of Hereford. 2 H. 4. Marks B. of Carlisle. Stanf. Pl. Coron. li. 3. ca. 62. fo. 153. in Temps H. 8.

126. [*Ed.:* by reason of nobility.]

127. [*Ed.:* baronies which they hold in right of the church.]

128. *a* 10 E. 4. 6. b. Mag. Cart. c. 29.

129. *b* 11 E. 3. bre. 473. 8 R. 2. proces. pl. ultimo 20 E. 4. 6. 20 El Dier 360. 38 H. 8. Br. treason. Seignior Sancars case. Lib. 9. fo. 117.

so it is of the sonne of a Duke, Marquise, Earle, &c. he is Noble, and called Lord: and yet because he is no Lord of Parliament, he shall be tried as one under the degree of a Peer, and Lord of Parliament.

20. No Peer of the Realme, or any other subject shall be convicted by Verdict but the said offences must be found by above Four & twenty, viz. by twelve, or above, at his indictment, or by twelve Peers, or above, if he be Noble, and by | twelve, and not above, if he be under the degree of Nobility.

[31]

21. A Peer of the Realme being indicted of treason, or felony, or of misprision, as is aforesaid,[130] and duly transmitted to the Lords, may be arraigned thereof in the upper House of Parliament, as frequently in Parliament Rolls it doth appeare: but then there must be appointed a Steward of England, who shall put him to answer: and if he plead not guilty, he shall be tried *per Pares suos*,[131] and then the Lords Spirituall must withdraw, and make their proxies: but no Appeal of treason can be in Parliament, [a][132]but is ousted by the statute of 1 H.4. cap. 14.

22. [b][133]And as the beginning (viz. the finding of the indictment by Freeholders) is equall to them both: so the most extreme and heavie judgement, if they be found guilty, is equall to both, &c. which you may reade in the first part of the Institutes, Sect. 147.

23. [c][134]And though the Commission of the Lord Steward be only in these latter times *hac vice,* yet may the same be adjourned, as other Commissions *hac vice* may. And so it was holden in the Lord Dacres case. And so it was done by the Steward of England in the case of R. Earle of S. and of F. his wife, who adjourned his Commission until the next day.

24. If execution be not done according to the judgement, then the High Steward in the case of a Peer of the Realm, or the Court of Commissioners in case of another subject, may by their precepts under their seales command execution to be done according to the judgement: but in case of High Treason, if all the rest of the judgement (saving the beheading, which is part of the judgement) be pardoned, this ought to be under the Great Seale of England.

---

130. 10 E. 4. 6. Rot. Par. 21 R. 2 Countee de Arundels case. Rot. Parliam. 5 H. 4. nu. 11,12. 31 H. 6. nu. 49. Countee de Devons case. 28 H. 6. nu. 19. Duke of Suff.

131. [*Ed.:* by his peers.]

132. *a* 1 H. 4. cap. 14.

133. *b* 1 H. 4. 1. Stanf. Pl. Coron. 182. E. K. See hereafter cap. judgement and execution.

134. *c* Pasch. 26 H. 8 *ubi supra.* 1. 5 E. 4. 33. 12 H. 4. 20.

25. And when the service is performed, then is an Oyes made for the dissolving of the Commission; and then is the White Rod, which hath been borne and holden before the Steward, by him taken in both his hands, and broken over his head.

Lastly, the Indictments together with the Record of the arraignment, triall, and judgement, shall be delivered into the Kings Bench, there to be kept and inrolled.

Hitherto we have spoken when a Noble man doth appear, and plead not guilty, and put himself upon his Peers: Now let us see what shall be had against him when he is indicted, and appears not, and cannot be taken: and generally he shall be outlawed, *per judicium Coronatorum.*[135] But how doth that stand with Magna Charta,[136] *Nec super eum ibimus, nec. super eum mitremus, nisi per legale judicium parium suorum?*[137] That is to be intended, when he appears and pleads not guilty, and puts himself upon his Peers: but when he absents himself, and will not yeild himself to the due tryall of his Peers, then he shall be outlained *per judicium Coronatorum,* or else be should take advantage of his own contumacy, and flying from judgement. [d138]For process to be awarded upon the indictment or appeal of treason, felony or trespas either against a Nobleman or any other, see the statute of 6 H.6. and 8 H.6. and if the process & order prescribedly those statutes be not pursued, the outlawry may be reversed by writ of error, which writ ought to be granted to him *ex merito Justitiae,*[139] as it was adjudged in Ninian Menvils case: and those statutes doe extend as well to the Kings Bench, as to other courts having by commission power to hear and determine the same, and very few outlawries of treason or felony, are of force and validity in law, for that these Acts are not pursued.

And these Acts are well expounded by our *[140]books, and therefore they shall not need to be recited at large. This is necessary to be added, that the

---

135. [*Ed.:* by judgment of the coroners.]

136. Mag. Cart. ca. 29.

137. [*Ed.:* Nor shall we go upon him, nor send upon him, except by the lawful judgment of his peers.]

138. *d* See hereafter in the chapter of judgement & execution concerning reversing of Outlawries. 6 H. 6. c. 1. 8 H. 6. ca. 10. Mich. 26 & 27 Eliz. in br̄e de error coram Rege in Ninian Menvills case Utlary de haut treason reverse in Bank le Roy.

139. [*Ed.:* out of favour to justice.]

140. * 19 H. 6. fo. 1. 2. 11 H. 6. 54. 1 E. 4. 1. 30 H. 6. proces. 192. 31 H. 6. 11. Vide F. N. B. 115. l Li. Intr. R. f. 122. Stanf. Pl. cor. 68. 69. 182. l.

opinion of Stanf. Pl. Cor. 182. l. upon the statute of 33 H.8. c.10 is, where the attainder is not erroneous, but lawfull by the course of the law: and so it was resolved, Tr. 28 Eliz. and thereupon [141]the statute of 28 Eliz. ca.2. was made, that no attainder that then was for any High Treason should be reversed for error where the party was executed. But that Act extendeth only to attainders before that Act, and where the party attainted suffered pains of death, as hath been said.

[32] | But admitting the proces be awarded according to these statutes, & the truth is; that the party indicted of High Treasons (be he noble or other) at the time of the outlawry pronounced, is out of the realm, &c. whether may he avoid the same by writ of error? The answer is, that he might have avoided the same by writ of error at the common law: but now in case of High Treason he is barred of his writ of error by the statutes of 26 H.8. and 5 E.6.[142] which statutes are expounded to extend generally to all treasons, but those statutes extend not to any other offence then high treason only, and therefore all other offences remain as they did at the common law for that point.

Now for that all indictments for any offence whatsoever, as well of Noblemen, as of any under the degree of Nobility, ought by the common law of the Realm to be by persons duly returned, and by *[143]lawfull liege people, indifferent as they stand unsworn and without any denomination of any: a good and profitable law *[144]was made in that behalf at the Parliament holden in 11 H.4. in these words. Item because that now of late a[145]Inquests were taken at Westm' of persons named to the b[146]Justices, without due return of the Sherif, of which persons some were coutlawed before the said Justices of record, and some fled to Sanctuary for treason, and some for felony, there to have refuge; by whom as well many offenders were indicted, as other lawfull liege people of our Lord the King, not guilty by conspiracy, abetment, and false imagination of other persons for their speciall advantage and singular lucre, against the course of the common law used and accustomed before this time. Our said Lord the King for the greater ease and quietnesse of his people, will

141. *e* 28 El. ca. 2.
142. See the first part of the Insti. Sect. 26 H. 8. cap. 13. 5 E. 6. cap. 11. 12 El. Dier 287.
143. * Artic. sup. cart. cap. 9. 28 E. 1. 20 E. 3. cap. 6. 34 E. 3. c. 4. 42 E. 3 c. 11. Regist. 172. Rast. pl. 117.
144. * 11 H. 4. ca. 9.
145. *a* Stanf. pl. cor. 87. c.
146. *b* Rot. Parl. 11, H. 4. nu. 15. in the kings bench.

and granteth, that the same indictment so made, with all the dependance thereof be [d][147] revoked, adnulled, void, and holden for none for ever. And that from henceforth no indictment be made by any such persons, but by enquests of the Kings lawfull [e][148] liege people, in the manner, as was used in the time of his Noble Progenitors, returned by the Sherifs, or baylifs of franchises, without any [f][149] denomination to the Sherifs, or baylifs of franchises before made by any person of the names, which by him should be impanelled, except it be by the officers of the said Sherifs or baylifs of franchises sworn and known to make the same, [g][150] and other officers to whom it pertaineth to make the same according to the law of England. And if any indictment be made hereafter in any point to the contrary, that the same indictment be also void, revoked, and for ever holden for none.

The body of this Act consisteth upon two distinct Purviens or Branches, the one to remedy a mischief past, the other to provide for the time to come. The first branch consisteth of a preamble, and a purvien: and the preamble containeth these eight parts. First, it sheweth divers inquests had been taken at Westminster by persons named to the Justices. Secondly, without due return of the Sherif. Thirdly, of which some were outlined before the said Justices of record. Fourthly, some fled to Sanctuary for treason, and some for felony. Fifthly, by whom many offenders were indicted. Sixthly, some not guilty, Seventhly, by conspiracy, &c. Eighthly, that all this was against the course of the common law. By the body of the Act, it is enacted that the same indictment, with all the dependence thereof, be revoked, and made void. Then followeth the second branch or purvien for the time to come, and this purvien consisteth of divers parts: First, in describing by what persons indictments ought to be found, and therein 1. *privatè*,[151] that is, not by any such persons, having reference to the preamble, which persons we have before particularly distinguished. 2. *Positivè*,[152] that all indictments must be found by persons of these

---

147. *d* Vid. 11 H. 4. fo. 41. 21 H. 6. 30. 9 E. 4. 16. 3 H. 6. 55. 26 Ass. 28. *d* 11 H. 4. 41.

148. *e* 14 H. 4. 19.

149. *f* 21 E. 3. 5. 15 E. 3. chal. 113, 27 Ass. pa. 65. 28 Ass. 24. 22 49 E. 3. 1. 49 Ass. 1. 28. 43 E. 3. chall. 94. 6 R. 2. chall. 102. 7 H. 4 10. 21 E. 4. 74. 19 H. 6. 9. 21 H. 6. 12. 14 H. 7. 1.

150. *g* Nota.

151. [*Ed.:* taking away (i.e., negatively).]

152. [*Ed.:* Positively.]

qualities. 1. They must be the Kings lawfull liege people. 2. Returned by the sherifs, or baylifs of franchises, and other officers to whom it pertaineth. 3. Without any denomination to the sherifs, baylifs, or other officers: and this purvien is in affirmance, and declaratory of the Common law.

The second part of the purvien is introductory of a new law, viz. that if any Indictment be made hereafter in any point to the contrary, that the same indictment be void, revoked, and holden for none. Wherein these two things [33]   are to | be observed: 1. That this is a generall law, and extendeth to all indictments for any crime, default, of offence whatsoever: for the words be [if any indictment] generally without naming of any Court, or before whom. 2. If the indictment be found by any persons that are outlawed or not the Kings lawfully liege people, or not lawfully returned, or denominated by any, viz. by all are any of these, that then the indictment is void, for the words be, [if any indictment be made hereafter in any point to the contrary, &c.] Upon this statute in the case of Robert Scarlet before the Justices of Assise at Bury in the County of Suffolk, in Sommer Vacation, 10 Ja. R. these points were resolved and adjudged: First, where at the Sections of the Peace holden at Woodbridge in the said County of Suffolk, Robert Scarlet by confederacy between him and the Clerk, that was to read the pannell of the grand Jury returned by the Shirif, (whereof he was none, albeit he laboured the Sherif to have returned him) that the Clerk should read him as one of the pannell, which was done accordingly, and he sworn. It was resolved and adjudged that this case was within this statute, for that he was not returned by the Sherif. Secondly, that where the rest of the great inquest giving faith to him indicted seventeen honest and good men upon divers penall statutes, which was done by the said Robert Scarlet maliciously: It was resolved and adjudged, that albeit he *[153]alone was sworn without the return of the Sherif, and all the rest duly returned, yet that this case was within this statute, and all the indictments found by him and the rest were void by this statute: for hereby it appeared what mischief such a one might doe. Thirdly, that Robert Scarlet upon this case had offended against the said Act, and might be indicted thereupon: and accordingly he was upon sufficient proof of the fact, as is aforesaid, indicted upon the said Act, and pleaded not guilty, and was found guilty. Fourthly, that this Act extended not only to indictments of treason and felony, but of

153. *47 E. 3. 1. 7 H. 4. 10. 21 E. 4. 74.

all other offences and defaults whatsoever, according to the generality of the words. Fifthly, consideration was had of the Act of 3 H.8. cap.12.[154] and resolved clearly that this statute had not altered the Act of 11 H.4 in. any thing concerning the offence of Scarlet, as upon that, which shall be said of the Act of 3 H.8. shall appear. And upon hearing of Councell learned what they could say in arrest of judgement, at last judgement was given, that he should be fined and imprisoned, and ordered by the Court that no process should goe out upon the said indictments found by the said great inquest, whereof Scarlet was one.

But not withstanding this good law, through the subtilty, & untrue demeanor of Sherifs, and their Ministers, great extortions and oppressions be and have been committed and done to many of the Kings subjects by means of returning at Sections holden within counties and shires for the body of the shire, the names of such persons as for the singular advantage, &c. of the said Sherifs and their Ministers, will be wilfully forsworn and perjured by the sinister labour of the said Sherifs and their Ministers, by reason whereof many substantiall persons, the Kings true subjects have been wrongfully indicted of murders, felonies, and misdemeanors: and sometime by labour of the said Sherifs and their Ministers, divers great felonies and murders have been concealed, &c. For remedy of which mischiefs it is enacted by the said statute of 3 H.8. cap.12. That the Justices of Gaol Delivery, or Justices of Peace, whereof one to be of the Quorum, in their open Sessions may reform the panell returned by the Sherif to inquire for the King, by putting to and taking out the names of the persons so impanelled by the discretion of the said Justices, &c. and that the Sherif shall return the panells so reformed. This Act extends only to Justices of Gaol Delivery, and of the Peace: The body of the Act for offences is generall and evident. Vide 11 H.7. cap.24.[155]

Nota Lector,[156] that the aforesaid Parliament of 11 H.4. begun in *Quindena Hilarii, Anno 11 H.4.* and the same tearm, viz. Hill 11 H.4. fo.41.[157] it was according to the said Act of 11 H.4. resolved by Gascoign Chief Justice, and all the rest of the Justices, that an indictment of felony found by an inquest

---

154. 3 H. 8. ca. 12]
155. Vid. 11 H. 7. c. 24.
156. [*Ed.:* Note, reader.]
157. Hil. 11 H. 4. f. 41.

before 3 H.9. whereof one was outlawed of felony, and another was acquited
[34]   by the | general pardon, so as they were not *probi et legales homines*[158] to
enquire as the law willeth, and after the party had pleaded not guilty to the
felony, it was awarded, that all the indictments by them found, were adnulled
and made void. Herewith agreeth Stanford in his Pleas of the Crown, fo. 87.
& 88. Vide F. tit. Indictment 25. & Coron. 89. and Brook tit. indictment.
2.[159] Note the Act saith, that they were outlawed before themselves, so as the
Court may take knowledge thereof of themselves, or of any other, as *amicus
curiae:*[160] but the safest way for the party indicted is to plead, upon his arraignment, the speciall matter given unto him by the statute of 11 H.4. for
the overthrow of the indictment, with such averments, as by law are required,
(agreeable to the opinion of the Lord Brook. *Ubi supra.*) and to plead over
to the felony, and to require councell learned for the pleading thereof, which
ought to be granted,[161] and also to require a copy of so much of the indictment,
as shall be necessary for the framing of his plea, which also ought to be granted.
And these Laws made for indifferency of Indicters, ought to be construed
favourably, for that the indictment is commonly found in the absence of the
party, and yet it is the foundation of all the rest of the proceeding.

To draw to an end concerning Tryals: It is regularly true, that by the Common law the tryall shall be in the County, where the indictment is taken: and
by the aforesaid Act of 35 H.8.[162] treasons and misprisions of treasons committed or done out of the Realm, &c. shall be enquired of, heard, and determined before the Justices of the Kings Bench, &c. Now the case fel out
upon this statute to be thus: *[163]One was indicted before the Justices of the
Kings Bench, at the Tearm holden at Hertford, by a Jury of the County Hertford, for divers high treasons committed out of this Realm and after the tearm

158. [*Ed.:* fit and lawful men.]

159. Stanf. Pl. cor. 87,88. F. tit. Indictment 25. & Coron. 89. Br. tit. indict. 2.

160. [*Ed.:* friend of the court, a third party appearing to argue a point by grace of the court.]

161. Vid. lestatutes de 1 R. 3. ca. 4. 33 H. 6. c. 2. W. 2. ca. 13. 1 E. 3. stat. 2. ca. 17 All tending that
indictments may be duly had.

162. Dier 3 Mar. 131, 132. Stanf. pl. cor. 90. 35 H. 8. ca. 2.

163. * Mich. 35 & 36 El. in the case of Francis Dacres.

was adjourned to Westm. in the County of Midd. The question was, by which of the Counties the party indicted should be tried: And it was resolved, that he should be tried by men of that County where the indictment was taken. But otherwise it is upon the statute of 5 El. ca.1.[164] the case being, that Horn Bishop of Winch. tendred to Edmond Bonner late Bishop of London,[165] in the County of Surrey, within his Dioces the oath of Supremacy according to the Act of 1 Eliz. which Bonner refused, and this was certified by the Bishop of Winch. into the Kings Bench, then sitting at Westminister in the County of Midd. Now by the statute of 5 El. he that refuseth the oath is to be indicted of a Premunire[166] by a Jury of Midd. as a Jury of that County might doe for any offence done in that County, and extendeth only to the indictment, where the words of the Act of 35. H.8. be, [shal be enquired of, heard, and determined,] the question upon the statute of 5 Eliz. was, if Bonner should appear and plead not guilty, by what County he should be tried, whether by a Jury of Midd. where the indictment was, or by a Jury of Surrey, where the offence was committed; and resolved that he should be tried by a Jury of Surrey: for the statute of 5 El. extendeth to the indictment only, and leaveth the triall to the Common law, which appointeth tryall to be, where the offence is committed, and so a manifest diversity between the two cases: for regularly by the Common Law in all Pleas of the Crown, *Debet quis juri sabjacere, ubi deliquit.*[167,168]

It is now necessary to be known, how Prisoners (to speak once for all) committed for treason, or any other offence ought to be demeaned in prison. Bracton saith, *Solent praesides in carcere continendos damnare, ut in vincalis contineantur, sed hujusmodi interdicta sunt à lege, quia carcer ad continendos, non ad puniendos haberi debeat:*[169] And in another place he saith, *Cum autem*

---

164. 5 El. cap. 1.

165. Mich. 6 & 7 El. Dier fo. 234. Bonners case.

166. [*Ed.:* The offense of introducing foreign influence into the kingdom, used to regulate Catholics.]

167. [*Ed.:* One [everyone] ought to be subject to the law [of the place] where he offends.]

168. Bract. lib. 3. fo. 154. b. *Vincula qui sensit, didicit succurrere vinctis.* Bract. lib. 3. fo. 105. a. Stanford 78. Bract. li. 3. f. 137. Note Shackells about the feet ought not to be, but for fear of escape. Mirror c. 2. §. 9.

169. [*Ed.:* Gaolers are accustomed to inflict harm upon prisoners, as by keeping them in shackles, but such things are forbidden by law, because a gaol ought to be for containment and not for punishment.]

*taliter captus coram Justic. est producendus, produci non debet ligatis manibus,
(quamvis interdum gestans compedes proptere vasionis pericu'um,) et hoc ideo, ne
videatur coactus ad aliquam purgationem suscipiendam.*[170]

[a171]If felons come in judgement to answer, &c. they shall be out of Irons,
and all manner of bonds, so that their pain shall not take away any manner
of reason, nor them constrain to answer, but at their free will. [b172]And in
another place he saith, and of prisoners we will that none shall be put in Irons,
but those | which shall be taken for felony, or trespas in Parks or Vivaries or
which be found in arerages upon account,[173] and we defend that otherwise
they shall not be punished nor tormented. [c174]*Omnes autem attachiabiles licet
vicocomiti in prisona custodire, &c. nos tamen ad puniend', sed ad custioniend'
&c.*[175] [d176]It is an abuse that prisoners be charged with Irons, or put to any
pain before they be attainted.

[35]

[e177]*Quidam facerdos arraniatus de felonia posuit se super patriam, &c stetit ad
barram in ferris, sed per praeceptum Justic. liberator à ferris.*[178] And there is no
difference in law, as to a Priest and a Lay man, as to Irons.

[f179]*Presentat quod ubi quidam Roberrus Bayhons de Tanesby captus fuit, &c
in prisona castri Lincoln detentus pro quodam debito Statut. mercatorii in custodia
Tho. Boteler Constabularii castri de Lincoln ibi praed. Tho. le Botelet posuit ipsum
Robertum in profundo Gaole inter lenones in vili prisona contra* *[180]*formam Statut.&c. & eodem profoundo detinuit, quousque idem Robertus fecit finem cum
eo de 40 s. quos ei solvit per extorsionem.*[181]

---

170. [*Ed.:* When such a person is arrested in order to be produced before a justice, he ought not to be
produced with his hands tied (except occasionally handcuffs to prevent escape) and this is because it ought
not to appear that he has been brought to undergo any expiation.]

171. *a* Brit. c. 5. fo. 14.

172. *b* Cap. 11. fo. 17.

173. W. 2. c. 1. after judgement. Lib. 3. fo. 44. Lib. 8. fo. 100. 24 H. 8. Dier 249. Pl. Com. 360. a.

174. *c* Fleta li. 1, ca. 26.

175. [*Ed.:* All other attachable persons the sheriffs may keep in prison, etc.—not, however, to punish
them, but to keep them, etc.]

176. *d* Mirror c. 5. §:l.

177. *e* § E. 2. cor. 432.

178. [*Ed.:* A certain priest, being arraigned of felony, put himself upon the country, and stood at the
bar in irons, but by command of the justices he was freed from the irons.]

179. *f* Tr. 7 E. 3. coram rege Rot. 44.

180. * 1 E. 3. c. 7.

181. [*Ed.:* [It is presented] that, whereas a certain Robert Bayhens of Tanesby was arrested and detained

So as hereby it appeareth, that where the law requireth that a prisoner should be kept in *salva & arcta custodia,*[182] yet that that must be without pain or torment to the prisoner.

Hereupon two questions do arise, when and by whom and Rack or Brake in the Tower was brought in.[183]

To the first, John Holland Earle of Huntingdon, was by King H.6 created Duke of Exeter, and *Anno 26 H.6.*[184] the King granted to him the office of the Constableship of the Tower: He and William De la Poole Duke of Suffolk, and others, intended to have brought in the Civill Lawes.[185] For a beginning whereof, the Duke of Exeter being Constable of the Tower first brought into the Tower the Rack or Brake allowed in many cases by the Civill Law;[186] and thereupon the Rack is called the Duke of Exeters Daughter, because he first brought it thither.

To the second upon this occasion, Sir John Fortescue Chiefe Justice of England, wrote his Book in commendation of the lawes of England; and therein preferreth the same for the government of this countrey before the Civill Law; and particularly that all tortures and torments of parties accused were directly against the Common Lawes of England, and showeth the inconvenience thereof by fearfull example, to whom I refer you being worthy your reading. So as there is no law to warrant tortures in this land, nor can they be justified by any prescription being so lately brought in.

And the Poet in describing the iniquity of Radamanthus, that cruell Judge of Hell, saith,[187]

Castigatque, auditque dolos, subigitque fateri.[188]

---

in prison in Lincoln Castle for a certain debt of statute merchant, in the custody of Thomas Boteler, constable of Lincoln Castle aforesaid, there the aforesaid Thomas le Boteler put the selfsame Robert in a deep gaol amongs the pimps (*lenones*) in a vile prison, contrary to the form of the statute, etc., and detained him in the same deep place until the same Robert made fine with him for forty shillings, which he paid him by extortion.]

182. [*Ed.:* in safe and strict custody.]

183. Tortures, the rack, &c.

184. Rot. Pat. 26 H. 6.

185. Rot. Parl. 28 H. 6. nu. 30.

186. Hollenshed. pa. 670. &c. Innocentem cogit mentiri dolor. Fortescue. ca. 22. fo. 24.

187. Virgil.

188. [*Ed.:* He chastises and hears charges of wrongdoing and forces confession. (Virgil, *Aeneid,* 6. 567.)]

First, he punished before he heard, and when he had heard his deniall, he compelled the party accused by torture to confesse it. But far otherwise doth Almighty God proceed *postquá reus diffamatus est. 1. Vocat. 2. Interrogat. 3. Judicat.*[189,190] To conclude this point, it is against Magna Carta, cap. 29. *Nullus liber homo, &c. aliquo modo destruatur, nec super cum ibimus, nec super eum mittemus, nisi per legale judicium parium suorum, aut per legem terrae.*[191] And accordingly all the said ancient Authors are against any paine, or torment to be put or inflicted upon the prisoner before attainder, nor after attainder, but according to the judgement. And there is no one opinion in our Books, or judiciall Record (that we have seen and remember) for the maintenance of tortures or torments, &c.

And now, to conclude this Chapter of Treason.[192] It appeareth in the holy Scripture, that traytors never prospered, what good soever they pretended, but were most severely and exemplarily punished: As [a][193]Corah, Dathan and Abiram, by miracle: *Dirupta est terra sub pedibas eorum, & aperiens os suum de voravit illos, &c.*[194] [b][195]Athalia the daughter of Amri, *interfecta est gladio.*[196] [c][197]Bagatha and Thara against Assuerus, *Apponsus est uterq; corum in patibula.*[198] [d][199]Absolon against David. *Suspensus in arbore, & Joab infixit tres Lanceas in corde ejus.*[200] [e][201]Achitophel with Absolon against David. *Suspendio interiit,*[202] he hanged I himselfe. [f][203]Abiathar the traiterous High Priest against Solomon. *Abiathar Sacerdoti dixit Rex, &c. Et quidem vir mortis es, sed hodiè*

[36]

---

189. [*Ed.:* after the accused person has been charged, firstly to summon, secondly to interrogate, thirdly to adjudge.]

190. Luke 16. 1., 2. &c. John 7. 51. Nunquid lex nostra judicat hominem nisi prius audierit ab ipso?

191. [*Ed.:* No free man, etc. shall be in any way destroyed, nor shall we go upon him, nor send upon him, except by the lawful judgment of his peers, or by the law of the land.]

192. Proditor illudit verbis, dum verbera cudit.

193. *a* Numb. 16. 31, 32. & 27. 3.

194. [*Ed.:* The earth broke up beneath their feet, and its opening mouth devoured them, etc.]

195. *b* 2 Regum 11. 16.

196. [*Ed.:* is killed by the sword.]

197. *c* Esth. 12. 2,3.

198. [*Ed.:* each of them was hanged on a gibbet.]

199. *d* 2 Sam. 18. 9. 14.

200. [*Ed.:* hanged in a tree, and Joab thrust three darts into his heart.]

201. *e* 2 Sam. 17. 23.

202. [*Ed.:* died by hanging [himself].]

203. *f* 1 Reg. 2. 26, 27.

te non interficiam, &c. Ejecit ergo Solomon Abiathar, ut non esset Sacerdos.[204] [g205]Shimei against David, *gladio interfectus,*[206] [h207]Zimri against Ela, who burnt himselfe. [i208]*Theudas (qui occisus est, & circiter 400 qui credebant ei, dispersi sunt & redacti ad nihilum)*[209] and Judas Galilaeus, *ipse periit, & omnes quotquot consenserunt ei, dispersi sunt.*[210] Lastly, [k211]Judas Iscariot, *secundum nomen ejus vir occisionis,*[212] the traytor of traytors. *Et hic quidem possedit agrum de mercede iniquitatis suae, & suspensus crepuit medius, & diffusa sunt omnia viscera ejus.*[213]

Peruse over all our Books, Records, and Histories, and you shall finde a principle in law, a rule in reason, and a trial in experience, That treason doth ever produce fatall & finall destruction to the offender, and never attaineth to the desired end, (two incidents inseparable thereunto.) *[214]And therefore let all men abandon it, as the most poisonous bait of the Devill of hell, and follow the precept in holy Scripture, Feare God, honour the King, and have no company with the Sedicious.

See more of Treason in the next Chapter of Misprision, &c. and in Principall and Accessory, in the title of Judgement and Execution: and in the Chapter of Monomachia, single combate, &c. the residus of this Act of 25 E.3.

204. [*Ed.:* The king said to Abiathar the priest, etc., 'You are a man worthy of death, but today I will not kill you, etc.' Therefore Solomon thrust out Abiathar from being a priest.]

205. *g* 2 Sam. 16. 5, 6 1 Reg. 2. 8. &c. 46.

206. [*Ed.:* killed by the sword.]

207. *h* 1 Regum 16. 9. &c. 18.

208. *i* Act. Apost. 5. 36,37.

209. [*Ed.:* who was slain, and around four hundred who believed in him were scattered and reduced to nothing.]

210. [*Ed.:* Judas of Galilee . . . perished, and all those who agreed with him were dispersed.]

211. *k* Act. Apost. 1. 18. Math. 27. 5. laqueo se suspendit *Qui molitur insidias in patriam, id facit quod insanus nauta perforans navem in qua ipse illeg.*

212. [*Ed.:* Judas Iscariot, in accordance with his name a man of slaughter.]

213. [*Ed.:* And this man purchased a field with the gains of his iniquity, and fell headlong in the middle of it, and all his bowels gushed out.]

214. **Felix quem faciunt aliena periculi cautum.* Prov. 24. 21.

Cap. III.
Of Misprision of Treason.

Misprisio commeth of the French word *Mespris*,[1] which properly signifieth neglect or contempt: for [*mes*] in composition in the French signifieth *mal*, as *mis* doth in the English tongue: as mischance, for an ill-chance, and so mesprise is ill apprehended or known. In legall understanding it signifieth, when one knoweth of any treason or felony, and concealeth it, this is misprision, so called, because the knowledge of it is an ill knowledge to him, in respect of the severe punishment for not revealing of it: For in case of misprision of High Treason,[2] he is to be imprisoned during his life, to forfeit all his goods, debts, and duties for ever, and the profits of his lands during his life: and in case of felony, to be fined and imprisoned. And in this sense both the said statute of 1 & 2 Ph. & Mar. speak, when it saith, Be it declared, and enacted, by the Authority aforesaid, that concealement or keeping secret of any High Treason be deemed and taken only misprison of treason, and the offenders therein to forfeit and suffer, as in cases of misprision of treason, and the offenders therein to forfeit and suffer, as in cases of misprision of treason hath heretofore been used. *[3]But by the Common law concealement of High Treason was treason, as it appeareth in the case of the Lord Scrope, *An. 3 H.5.* and by Bracton, lib.3. fo.118.b. & 119a.

[a4]It is Misprision of High Treason, for forging of money, which neither is the money of this Realme of England, nor currant within the same.

[b5]Misprision of High Treason in concealing of a Bull, &c. See the statute.

[c6] It is said in 2 R.3. that every treason or felony includeth in it a misprision of treason or felony. Therefore if any man knoweth of any High Treason, he ought with as much speed as conveniently he may to reveale the same to the King, or some of his Privie Councell, or any other Magistrate. And misprision in a large sense is taken for many great offences which are neither treason nor

---

1. *Misprisio proditionis.* See Bract. lib. 3. fo. 118. b. & 119. 2a.

2. See hereafter ca. 65. of misprisions, &c. See hereafter in Theftbote. ca. 61. 1 & 2 Ph. & Mar. *Ubi supra.* See 1 E. 6. c. 12. and 1 El. ca. 6. 25 H. 8. ca. 12.

3. *Hil. 14 El. cited by the Lo. Dier in the Lo. Lumleys case. MS.

4. *a* 14 El. ca. 3.

5. *b* 13 El. ca. 2.

6. *c* 2 R. 3. fo. 9. Stanf. 57. c

felony, whereof we shall speak more hereafter, being in this place restrained to misprision of treason.

See John Coniers Case Dier 296. That the receiving of one that hath counterfeited the Kings Coine, and comforting of him knowing him to have counterfeited the Kings coine, is but misprision.

See more of misprision of treason in the Chapters of High Treason, and of Principall and Accessory.

| Cap. IV.

[37]

Felony by compassing or conspiring to kill the King, or any Lord or other, of the Kings Counsell.

Next hereunto we have thought good to speak of the Statute of 3 H.7.[1] the letter of which law ensueth.

Item,[2] Forasmuch as by quarrels made to such as have been in great authority, office, and of counsell with Kings of this Realme, hath ensued the destruction of Kings, and the undoing of this Realme; so as it hath appeared evidently, when compassing of the death of such as were of the Kings true subjects was had, the destruction of the Prince was imagined thereby: and for the most part it hath growne, and been occasioned by envie, and malice of the Kings own housholdservants; as now of late such a thing was likely to have ensued: *And for so much as by the law of this land, if actuall deeds be not had, there is no remedy for such false compassings, imaginations, and confederacies had against any Lord, or any of the Kings Counsell, or any of the Kings great Officers in his Houshold, as Steward, Treasurer, & Comptroller: and so great inconveniencies might ensue, if such ungodly demeaning should not be straitly punished before that actuall deed were done. Therefore it is ordained by the King, the Lords Spirituall and Temporall, and the Commons of the said Parliament assembled, and by authority of the same, That from hence forward, the Steward, Treasurer, and Comptroller of the Kings house for the time being, or one of them, have full authority and power to enquire by Twelve sad men, and discreet persons of the Chequer Roll of the Kings honourable houshold, if any servant admitted

*Nota.

1. 3. H. 7. cap. 14.
2. [*Ed.:* Also.]

to be his servant sworne, and his name put into the Chequer Roll of his houshold, whatsoever he be, serving in any manner, office, or roome, reputed, had and taken, under the state of a Lord, make any confederacies, compassings, conspiracies, or imaginations with any person or persons, to destroy or murder the King, or any Lord of this Realme, or any other person sworne to the Kings Counsell, Steward, Treasurer, or Comptroller of the Kings house; that if it be found before the said Steward for the time being, by the said twelve sad men, that any such of the Kings servants as is abovesaid, hath confederated, compassed, conspired, or imagined, as is abovesaid, that he so found by that Inquiry, be put thereupon to answer. And the Steward, Treasurer, and Comptroller, or two of them have power to determine the same matter according to the Law. And if he put him in triall, that then it be tried by other twelve sad men of the same houshold: and that such misdoers have no challenge, but for malice. And if such misdoers be found guilty by confession, or otherwise, that the said offence be judged felony, and they to have judgement and execution as felons attainted ought to have by the Common Law.

[38] | This Act divideth it self into Two generall parts, viz. the Preamble, And the body of the Act. In the preamble Three things are to be observed.

1. That by quarrels made to such, as are in great Authority, office, and of Counsell with the Kings of the Realm, have ensued the destruction of the Kings, and the undoing of the Realm, as in the Records of Parliament, and Histories of King E.2. R.2. King H.6. &c. you may read. And as King William Rufus was slain in the new Forest by the glance of an arrow, so the overthrow of the king, &c. hath followed by glances, and consequents, when the bow of destruction hath been aimed at the overthrow of those, who were in great Authority neer about, and dear to the King, not daring in direct manner to aim at the King himself. Therefore, the first conclusion is, that when the compassing of the death of such, as were of the Kings true subjects was had, the destruction of the Prince was imagined thereby.

2. That for the most part, it hath grown by envy and malice by the Kings own houshold servants: and the reason thereof is, for that they being of the Kings houshold, have greater and readier means either by night, or by day to destroy such as be of great Authority, and neer about the King: and such an attempt and conspiracy was before this Parliament made by some of this Kings houshold servants, and great mischief was like thereupon to have ensued, which was the cause of the making of this Act.

3. The conclusion of the Preamble is, [3]that by the law of the land, if actuall deeds be not had, there is no remedy for such false compassings, &c. This is a true declaration: For the bare conspiracy of the death of any Lord or other of the Kings Councell, or of the Steward, Treasurer, or Comptroller, unlesse they had been slain indeed, was no felony before this Act, and so resolved upon the contempt and conspiracy aforesaid.

In the body of this Act, Six things are enacted. First, that the offender must have three qualities. 1. He must be the Kings servant sworn. 2. His name must be put in the Cheque Roll of the Kings houshold. 3. He must be under the state of a Lord: and if he conspire with any other, that is not of the Kings, houshold, yet is the conspiracy within this Act, but he of the Kings houshold is only the felon within the purvien of this statute, as it appeareth by the words of the statute.

Secondly, Against what persons the offence made felony by this Act is to be committed: and in number they be Four. 1. To destroy or murder the King. By this Act it expresly appeareth by the judgement of the whole Parliament,[4] that besides the confederacy, compassing, conspiracy, or imagination, there must be some other overt act or deed tending thereunto, to make it treason within the statute of 25 E.3. And therefore the bare confederacy, compassing, conspiracy, or imaginations by words only, is made felony by this Act. But if the Conspirators doe provide any weapon, or other thing, to accomplish their devilish intent, this and the like is an overt act to make it treason. 2. Any Lord of this Realme being sworn of the Kings Councell: for by the Purvien of this Act, he must be also of the Kings Councell: this is understood of the Kings Privy Councell, and so throughout the Act. 3. Any other of the Kings Councell (that is, the Kings Privy Councell) being under the degree of a Lord. 4. The Steward, Treasurer, and Comptroller of the Kings houshold, being great officers, though they be not of the Kings Councell.

Thirdly, The third generall part expresseth the persons to whom power is given to enquire & determine this felony. The Steward, Treasurer, and Comptroller, or any one of them may enquire. And they or two of them have power

---

3. See before in the chapt. of High treason. Verb. Overt Act.
4. See before in the chapt. of High treason. *Ubi sup.*

by this Act to hear and determine the same:[5] and though the words be for
the Inquiry, that they three, or any of them, &c. yet an Indictment taken
before two of them is good, because it is for advancement of Justice. And this
Act is in nature of a Commission to them, for other Commission they need
not to have: and this you may see in divers other Acts of Parliament of like
nature. If any the houshold servants conspire the death of the Steward, Treasurer, and Comptroller, yet by force of this Act they are Judges of the cause,
and none other can be, and in that case, I they will assist themselves for their
direction, with some grave and learned men in the laws. But if the death of
any one of them be compassed, then it is more convenient that it be heard
and determined before the other two.

[39]

Fourthly, the fourth part setteth forth, first, how the Inquiry, & after the
triall shall be made, that is, that the Inquiry must be made by twelve sad men
and discreet persons of the Cheque Roll of the Kings houshold: and when
the offender hath pleaded not guilty, the tryall shall be by the like persons.
And here though this Act limiteth the inquiry to be by twelve, yet if it be
Inquired of by more then twelve, the presentment is good, but the tryall must
be by twelve only.

Fifthly, no challenge shall be made, but for malice.

Sixthly, by the consert of the whole Act, the conspiracy, that is to be heard
and determined by this Act, must be plotted to be done within the Kings
houshold.[6]

The offender against this statute shall have the benefit of his Clergy: for
whensoever Felony is made by any statute, and the benefit of Clergy is not
expresly taken away, the offender shall have his Clergy.

See the statute of 3 & 4 E.6.[7] whereby amongst other things in some case
it was High treason, and in some case felony, to intend, or goe about to kill,
or imprison any of the Kings Privy Councell, &c. from which felony, the
benefit of Sanctuary, and Clergy was taken away: but these treasons and felonies
are repealed by the statute of 1 Mar.

5. 18 E. 3. 1. 23 Ass. 17. 27 H. 6. 8. 27 H. 8. 13.
6. *Vide.* lib. Plac. Coke fo. 482.
7. 3 & 4 E. 6. ca. 5.

Cap. V.
Of Heresie.

Concerning Heresie five things fall into consideration. First, who be the Judges of Heresie. Secondly, what shall be adjudged Heresie. Thirdly, what is the judgement upon a man convicted of Heresie. Fourthly, what the law alloweth him to save his life. Fifthly, what he shall forfeit by judgement against him.

Touching the First, an Heretique may be convicted [a1]before the Archbishop and other Bishops, and other the Clergy at a generall Synod, or Convocation, as it appeareth both by our books, and by history. See the statute of 25 H.8. cap.19. revived by 1. El.cap.I.

[b2]And the Bishop of every Dioces may convict any for Heresie, and so might he have done before the statute of 2 H.4. ca.15. as it appeareth by the Preamble of that Act in these words.

Whereas the Diocesans of the said Realme cannot by their jurisdiction spirituall, without aid of the said royall Majesty, sufficiently correct the said false and perverse people, (i. Heretiques, named before) because the said false and perverse people doe goe from Dioces to Dioces, and will not appear before the said Diocesans, but the same Diocesans and their Iurisdiction spirituall, and the keys of the Church with the censures of the same, doe utterly contemn and despise.

Now that statute doth provide, that the Diocesan of the same place, such person or persons, &c. may cause to be arrested, and under safe custody in his prisons to be detained. From this Act and other Acts and Authorities quoted in the margent, these Two conclusions are to be gathered. First, that the Dio-l-cesan hath jurisdiction of Heresy, and so it hath been put in use in all Queen   [40] Elizabeths reign:[3] and accordingly it was resolved by Flemming Chief Justice, Tanfield chief Baron, Williams, and Crook Justices, Hil. 9. Ja. R. in the case of Legate the Heretique, and that upon a conviction before the Ordinary of Heresy, the writ of *De haeretico comburenedo*[4] doth lie. Secondly, that without

---

1. *a* Bract. 1. 3. fo. 123. & 124. in Conc' Oxon. Newburg. li. 2. ca. 13. 6 H. 3. Stow. Holl. 203. 2 H. 4. Rot. Parl. nu. 29 Sautries case. Fitz. N. B. 269. a. 1 El. ca. 1.

2. *b* Vid. 23 H. 8. ca. 9. F. N. B. *ubi supra.* 5 El. ca. 23. 10 H. 7. 17. b. Doct. & Stud. lib. 2. ca. 29. Br. 2. Mar. tit. Heresy 1.

3. Mat. Hammond Anno 21 El. Holl. 1579. Stowe. 1161. Hil. 9. Ja. Regis. Legates case.

4. [*Ed.:* Writ for burning a heretic.]

the aid of that Act of 2 H.4. the Diocesan could imprison no person accused of Heresy, but was to proceed against him by the censures of the Church. And now seeing, that not only the said Act of 2 H.4. but 25 H.8. c.14. are repealed,[5] the Diocesan cannot imprison any person accused of Heresy, but must proceed against him, as he might have done before those statutes, by the censures of the Church, as it appeareth by the said Act of 2 H.4. c.15. Likewise the supposed statute of 5 R.2. c.5. and the statutes of 2 H.5. c.7. 25 H.8. c.14. 1 & 2 Ph. & Mar. c.6. are all repealed, so as no statute made against Heretiques standeth now in force: and at this day no person can be indicted, or impeached for Heresy before any temporall Judge, or other, that hath temporall jurisdiction, as upon perusall of the said statutes appeareth.

Every Archbishop of this Realm may cite any person dwelling in any Bishops Dioces within his province for causes of Heresy,[6] if the Bishop, or other Ordinary immediate thereunto consent, or if that the same Bishop, or other immediate Ordinary, or Judge doe not his duty in punishment of the same.

2. Touching the second point, if any person be charged with Heresy before the High Commissioners, they have no authority to adjudge any matter or cause to be heresy, but only such, as hath been so adjudged by the authority of the Canonicall, Scripture, or by the first four generall Councells, or by any other generall Councell, wherein the same was declared heresie by the expresse and plain words of the Canonicall, Scripture, or such as shall hereafter he determined to be heresy by Parliament, with the assent of the Convocation: for so it is expresly provided by the said Act of 1 El. And albeit this Proviso extendeth only to the said high Commissioners, yet seeing in the high Commission, there be so many Bishops, and other Divines, and Learned men, it may serve for a good direction to others, especially to the Diocesan, being a sole Judge in so weighty a cause.

No manner of Order, Act, or Determination for any matter of Religion, or cause Ecclesiasticall, had or made by the Authority of the Parliament in *Anno 1 El.*[7] shall be accepted, deamed, interpreted, or adjudged Heresy, Schism, or Schismaticall opinion, any order, decree, sentence, constitution, or law (whatsoever the same be) notwithstanding.

---

5. *Vide* 1 E. 6. c. 12. 1 El. c. 1.
6. 23 H. 8. ca. 9.
7. 1 El. ca. 1.

There was a statute supposed to be made in 5 R.2.[8] that Commissions should be by the Lord Chancellor made, & directed to Sherifs, and others, to arrest such as should be certified into the Chancery by the Bishops, and Prelates, *[9]Masters of Divinity, to be preachers of heresies, and notorious errors, their fautors, maintainers, and abetters, and to hold them in strong prison, until they will justifie themselves to the law of holy Church. By colour of this supposed Act, a[10]certain persons, that held, that images were not to be worshipped, &c. were holden in strong prison, until they (to redeem their vexation) miserably yeelded before these Masters of Divinity to take an oath, and did swear to worship images, b[11]which was against the morall and eternall law of Almighty God. We have said (by colour of the said supposed statute, &c.) not only in respect of the said opinion, but in respect also, that the said supposed Act, was in truth never any Act of Parliament, though it was entred in the Rolls of the Parliament, for that the Commons never gave their consent thereunto. And therefore in the c[12]next Parliament, the Commons preferred a bill reciting the said supposed Act, and constantly affirmed, that they never assented thereunto, and therefore desired that the said supposed statute might be aniented, and declared to be void: for they protested, that it was never their intent to be justified, and to bind themselves and their successors to the Prelates, more then their Ancestors had done in times past: and hereunto the King gave his royall assent in these words, *y pleist au | Roy.*[13] And mark well the [41] manner of the penning the Act: for seeing the Commons did not assent thereunto, the words of the Act be, It is ordained and astented in this present Parliament, that, &c. And so it was, being but by the King and the Lords.

It is to be known, that of ancient time, when any Acts of Parliament were made, to the end the same might be published, and understood, especially before the use of printing came into England, the Acts of Parliament were ingrossed into parchment, and bundled up together with a writ in the Kings name, under the great seal to the Sherif of every County, sometime in Latin,

---

8. 5 R. 2. Stat. 2. cap. 5. repealed by 1 E. 6. c. 12. & 1 Eliz. ca. 1.

9. *In diebus iliis* Masters of Divinity (and Batchelors of Divinity) now Doctors of Divinity and Batchelors.

10. *a* Rot. claus. 19 R. 2. m. 17. in Dors.

11. *b* Exod. 20. 4. Levit. 26. 1. Deut. 5. 8. & 16. 22. Psal. 97. 7. I John 5. 21.

12. *c* Rot. Parl. 6 R. 2. nu. 62. Vide 7 H. 4. nu. 62. Rot. Parl.

13. [*Ed.:* it pleases the king.]

and sometime in French, to command the Sherif to proclaim the said statutes within his bayliwick, as well within liberties, as without. And this was the course of Parliamentary procedings, before printing came in use in England, and yet it continued after we had the print, till the reign of H.7.

Now at the Parliament holden in 5 R.2. John Braibrook Bishop of London being Lord Chancellor of England, caused the said Ordinance of the King and Lords to be inserted into the Parliamentary writ of Proclamation to be proclaimed amongst the Acts of Parliament: which writ I have seen, the purclose of which writ, after the recitall of the Acts directed to the Sherif of N. is in these words. *Nos volentes dictas concordias, sive ordinationes in omnibus et singulis suis Articulis inviolabiliter observari, tibi praecipimus quòd praedictas concordias, sive ordinationes in locis infra balivam tuam, ubi melius expedire volueris, tam infra libertates, quam extra, publicé proclamari, et teneri facias juxta formam praenotatam. Teste Rege apud Westm. 26 May, Anno regni Regis R.2.5.*[14] But in the Parliamentary proclamation of the Acts passed in *Anno 6 R.2.* the said Act of 6 R.2. whereby the said supposed Act of 5 R.2. was declared to be void, is omitted: and afterwards the said supposed Act of 5. R.2. was continually printed, and the said Act of 6 R.2. hath by the Prelates been ever from time to time kept from the print.

Certain men called *Lollards* were indicted for heresy,[15] upon the said statute of 2 H.4. for these opinions, viz. *Quod non est meritorium ad Sanctum Thomam, nec ad Sanctam Mariam de Walsingham peregrinari. 2. Nec imagines Crucifixi et aliorum sanctorum adorare. 3. Nulli sacerdoti confiteri nisi soli deo, &c.*[16] Which opinions were so far from heresy, as the makers of the statute of 1 Eliz. had great cause to limit what heresy was.

And afterwards they thought not good to contain these opinions in any indictment, but indicted them in general words, one of which indictments as to Lollardy and heresy followeth.[17] *Jurati dicunt super eorum Sacramentum,*

14. [*Ed.:* We, wishing the said agreements or ordinances to be inviolably observed in each and every point, command you that you cause the aforesaid agreements or ordinances to be publicly proclaimed and kept in those places in your bailiwick where you shall think it most expedient, both within liberties and without, according to the above mentioned form. Witness the king at Westminster, the twenty-sixth day of May in the fifth year of the reign of King Richard the second.]

15. Coram Rege Hil. 1 H. 5. Rot. 4. & 5.

16. [*Ed.:* [1] That it is not meritorious to make pilgrimages to St. Thomas, nor to St. Mary of Walsingham. 2. Nor to adore images of the crucifix and of other saints. 3. No priests are made except by God alone, etc.]

17. Indictment generall. *Vide supra* ca. 1. *Verbo, Per overt fait.* Lollardi & *falsi haeretici.*

quod A. R. E. D. Lollardi & falsi haeretici die Jovis post hebdornadam Paschae, Anno regni Regis H.6. post conquestum Nono, apud Abendon in Com' Berks infra virg. falso et proditiorie ut communes proditores, et insurrectores conspiraverunt, imaginati fuerut, et ad invicero consoederaverunt cum quamplurimis proditoribus illis associatis, & felonibus de eorum comitiva, et eorum falsa malitia praecogitata, ut communes Infidiatores altaram viaram,[18] ad fidem catholicam destruendam et ibidem falso et proditorie ut communes proditores, et felones dictidñi Regis secerunt, et scripserunt diversas falsas billas, & scripturas seditiosas, & nonnulla fidei & doctrinae Christianae contraria continentes, & eas populo domini regis publicandas & credendas falsò, damnabiliter in diversis locis, viz. in civitatibus London, Sarum, & villis de Coventria & Marleburgh, nequiter posuerunt, fixerunt, & projecerunt, ae indies sic scribere, affigere & projicere & ponere non cessant, nec formidant, in gravissimam majestatis, & coronae dignitatis Regis nostri offensam, & Christianae fidei ludibrium, & pacis dicti domini regis perturbationem & omnium Christi fidelium injuriam & contemptum,[19] Which generall indictment, and all other of like form were utterly insufficient in law: For albeit the words of the statute be generall, yet the indictment must contain certainty, whereunto the party indicted may have an answer. Also where the parties are indicted, *ut communes inidiatores viaram,*[20] that also is insufficient, as it appeareth by the statute of 4 H.4. ca.2.

I John Keyser was excommunicated by the greater excommunication before [42] Thomas Archbishop of Canterbury, and Legate of the Apostolique See, at the suit of another, for a reasonable part of goods,[21] and so remained eight months:

---

18. *Communes insidiatores viarum. Vide sup.* c. 1. f. 5. *Ad fidem Catholicam destruendá. Diversas falsas billas & scripturas, &c.*

19. [*Ed.:* The jurors say upon their oath that A. R., E. D., Lollards and false heretics, on the Thursday after Easter week in the ninth year of the reign of King Henry the sixth after the conquest, at Abingdon in the county of Berkshire, within the virge, falsely and traitorously as common traitors and insurgents conspired, plotted and combined together with many other traitors associated with them, and felons of their company, and by their false malice aforethought, as common besetters of highways to destroy the catholic faith, and there falsely and traitorously, as common traitors and felons of the said lord king, made and wrote various false bills and seditious writings containing many things contrary to Christian faith and doctrine, and falsely, damnably and wickedly set, fixed and cast them forth in various places, that is to say, in the cities of London and Salisbury and the towns of Coventry and Marlborough, in order to publish them to the lord king's people and that they might be believed by the same people, and from day to day did not cease or fear so to write, fix and cast them forth, to the gravest offence of the majesty and crown of our kingly dignity and in mockery of the Christian faith, and disturbance of the said lord king's peace, and the injury and contempt of all faithful in Christ.]

20. [*Ed.:* as common besetters of highways.]

21. Mich. 5. E. 4. Rot. 143. *Coram Rege. In rationabili parte bonorum.*

The said Keyser openly affirmed that the said sentence was not to be feared; neither did he fear it. And albeit the Archbishop, or his Commissary hath excommunicated me, yet before God I am not excommunicated: and he said that he speak nothing but the truth, and it so appeared; for that he the last harvest standing so excommunicate, had as great plenty of wheat, and other grain, as any of his neighbours, saying to them in scorn (as was urged against him) that a man excommunicate should not have such plenty of wheat. The Archbishop denying these words to be within the said Act of 2 H.4. did by his warrant in writing comprehending the said cause, by pretext of the said Act commit the body of the said Keyser to the Gaol at Maidstone, for that (saith he) in respect of the publishing of the said words, *dictum Johannem non immerito habemus de haeresi suspectum.*[22] By reason whereof the said John Keyser was imprisoned in Maidstone Gaol and in prison detained under the custody of the Keeper there, untill by his counsell he moved Sir John Markham then Chief Justice of England, and other the Judges of the Kings Bench, to have an Habeas corpus, and thereupon (as it ought) an Habeas corpus was granted: Upon which writ the Gaoler returned the said cause, and speciall matter, and withall, according to the writ, had his body there. The Court upon mature deliberation perusing the said statute, (and upon conference with Divines) resolved, that upon the said words Keyser was not to be suspect of Heresy within the said statute, as the Archbishop took it. And therefore the Court first bayled him, and after he was delivered: for that the Archbishop had no power by the said Act for those words to commit him to prison.

Hillary Warner being an Inhabitant within the parish of S. Dunstans in the West, held opinion,[23] published there, & in divers other places, *quòd non tenebatur solvere aliquas decimàs Curatori, sive Ecclesiae parochiali ubi inhabitabat.*[24] Whereupon Richard Bishop of London commanded Edward Vaughan and others to arrest the said Hillary Warner: by force whereof they did arrest him, and detained him in prison a day and a night, and then he escaped. Hillary Warner brought his Action of false imprisonment against Edward Vaughan and others: In bar whereof the Defendants pleaded the statute of 2 H.4. and that the Plaintif held and published the opinion aforesaid; which opinion was, *Contra fidem Catholicam, seu Determinationem Sanctae*

---

22. [*Ed.:* we had some reason to suspect the said John of heresy.]
23. Mich. 11 H. 7. Rot. 327. *In communi banco.*
24. [*Ed.:* that he was not bound to pay any tithes to the curate or parochial church where he lived.]

Ecclisiae,[25] and that the Defendants, as servants to the said Bishop, and by his commandment did arrest the Plaintiff, and justified the imprisonment; whereupon Hillary Warner the Plaintif demanded in law, and after long and mature delieration it was by Brian Chief Justice, and the whole Court of Common Pleas adjudged, that the said opinion was not within the said statute of 2 H.4. for that it was an error, but no Heresy. Which I have the rather reported,[26] for that the Reporter of this case did not only misreport the time of the bringing of the Action, but the statute, which was the ground of the matter in law, and leaveth out the judgement. The record it self is worthy the reading.

Upon that which hath been said touching the said statute of 2 H.4. Four conclusions doe necessary follow. First, that seeing, that many opinions were by the Bishops taken to be heresy, which in troth had no shadow of heresy, and so mistaken, and unjustly extended by the Bishops further then the Purvien,[27] and true intention thereof, as by that which hath been, and might be said, appeared, the makers of the said Act of Parliament of 1 El. had great reason to limit (as hath been said) what opinions should be judged Heresy by authority of that commission grounded upon that Act. Secondly, that if any Ecclesiasticall Judge or Commissioner shall by pretext of any statute, or other cause, commit any man to prison, upon motion in Court on the behalf of the party imprisoned, the Judges of the Common Law ought to grant an *Habeas corpus* for him: upon the reforn of which writ, if it shall appear to the Judges, that the imprisonment is well | warranted by law, the party shall be [43] remanded: and if the imprisonment be without warrant of law, then the party ought to be delivered. Thirdly, if the imprisonment be not warranted by law, the party imprisoned may have his action of false imprisonment, and recover his damages. Fourthly, that when an Act of Parliament is made concerning matter meerly sprituall, as Heresie, &c. yet that Act being part of the lawes of the Realm, the same shall be construed and interpreted by the Judges of the Common Lawes, who usually confer with those that are learned in that profession. But let us now descend to the third point.

25. [*Ed.*: Against the catholic faith or the determination of Holy Church,]

26. Hil. 10. H. 7. f. 17.

27. See in the second part of the Institutes, the exposition upon the statute of *Artic. Cleri*, the resolution of all the Judges of England to the 21 and 22 articles, or objections.

3. To the third. [a28]It appeareth by Bracton, Britton, Fleta, Stanford, and all our Books, that he that is duly convict of Heresie, shall be burnt to death.

4. To the fourth, [b29]The Ecclesiasticall Judge at this day cannot commit the person that is convict of heresie to the Sheriffe, albeit he be present, to be burnt; but must have the Kings Writ *De haeretico comburendo*,[30] according to the Common Law: for now all Acts of Parliament (as hath been said before) against Hereticks are repealed. And the reason wherefore Heresie is so extremely and fearfully punished, is, for that *Gravius est aternam, quam temporalem laedere majestatem: and Haeresis est lepra animae.*[c31] [32]The party duly convicted of Heresie, may recall, and abjure his opinion, and thereby save his life, but a Relapse is fatall: For as in case of a disease of the body, after recovery, recidivation is extremely dangerous: So in case of Heresie (a disease of the soule) a relapse is irrecoverable. And as he that is a Leper of his body, is to be removed from the society of men, lest he should infect them, by the kings Writ *De leproso amovendo:*[33] So he that hath *lepram animae,* that is, to be convicted of Heresie, shall be cut off, lest he should poyson others, by the Kings Writ *De haeretico comburendo.* But if the Heretick will not after comviction abjure, he may by force of the said Writ [d34]*De haeretico comburendo* be burnt without abjuration.

5. As to the fifth. [e35]The statute made in the 2 year of H.5. cap.7. whereby the forfeiture of lands in fee-simple, and goods, and chattels was given in case of Heresie, standeth repealed by the Act of 1 Eliz. cap.1. The Books that speak of this forfeiture are grounded upon the said Act of 2. H.5. which then stood in force, saving 5 R.2. which was before that statute: for there, though Belknap swore, *Per ma foy si home soit miscreant, sa terre est forfeitable, & le seigniour avera ceo p. voy descheate;*[36] yet was his opinion never holden for law: for neither

---

28. *a* Mir. cap. 4. *de Majestie.* Bracton, *ubi supra.* Britton cap 9. Fleta lib. 1. ca. 35. Register. F. N. B. 269.

29. *b* F. N. B. 269. Rot. Par. 2. H. 4. nu. 29. Sautryes case. *Bre de haeretic. comburendo per regem & concilium in Parliamento.*

30. [*Ed.:* Writ for burning a heretic.]

31. [*Ed.:* It is more serious to hurt the eternal majesty than an earthly majesty, [and] heresy is leprosy of the soul.]

32. *c* 2 Mir. tit. Heresie. Br. 7.

33. [*Ed.:* for removing a leper.]

34. *d* 2 Mar. *ubi supra.*

35. *e* Vid. Doct. & Stud. lib. 2. ca. 29. Br. tit. Forfeiture 112. Stan. pl. cor. 35. I. 2. Mar. Br. tit. Heresie.

36. [*Ed.:* By my faith, if someone is an unbeliever his land is forfeitable, and the lord shall have it by way of escheat.]

lands, nor goods [f37]before the making of that statute of 2 H.5. were forfeited by the conviction of heresie, because the proceeding therein is meerely spitituall, *pro salute animae*,[38] and in a Court that is no Court of Record. And therefore the conviction of heresie worketh no forfeiture of any thing that is temporall, viz. of lands or goods. [g39]For what cause the said hereticks were called Lollards you may reade in Caudries case, and Linwood thereto agreeth. *[40]And it is to be observed, that in proceeding against Lollards, the Prelates, besides their opinions, did charge them with hainous offences: As conspiracy with multitudes of people, insurrection, rebellion, or some other treason, or great crimes.

We have spoken thus much of this argument, because there be divers wandring opinions concerning some of these points, that are not agreeable to the law, as it standeth at this day. See the fourth part of the Institutes, cap. Chancery, in the Articles against Cardinall Woolsey. Artic. 44.

| Cap. VI.

[44]

Of Felony by Conjuration, Witchcraft, Sorcery, or Inchantment.

The first Act of Parliament that made any of these offences felony, was the statute [a1]of 33 H.8. which was repealed by the statutes of 1 E.6. cap.12. and 1 Mariae. But [b2]before the Conquest it was severely punished: sometimes by death, sometimes by exile, &c. [c3]And after, it was made felony by the statute of 5 Eliz. and againe by 1 Jac. which repealeth 5 Eliz.

A Conjurer is he that by the holy and powerfull names of Almighty God invokes and conjures the Devill to consult with him, or to do some act.

A Witch[4] is a person that hath conference with the Devill, to consult with him or to do some act.

---

37. *f Vid.* hereafter in case of Piracy.

38. [*Ed.:* For the good of his soul. All prosecutions in the ecclesiastical courts are pro salute animae.]

39. *g* Lib. 5. Caudries case. fol. 25. b.

40. *[1 H. 5. fo. 6. a. Rot. Parl. 5. H. 5. nu. 11. in the case of Sir John *Oldcastle.* Pasch. 9. H. 6. *John Sharps case,* &c. Rot. Parl. 7. H. 4. nu. 67. 11 H. 4. nu. 29. 3 H. 5. nu. 39. 1 H. 6. nu. 20.

1. *a* 33 H. 8. ca. 8. 1 E. 6. cap. 12.

2. *b Inter leges Alveredi* fo. 23. Edwardi & Guthruni, cap. 11. Ethelstani, ca. 6. Canuti. 4,5.

3. *c* 5 Eliz. ca. 16. 1 Jac. cap. 12. A Conjurer deseribed.

4. A Witch described.

An Inchanter,[5] Incantator, is he, or she *qui carminibus, aut cantiunculis Daemonem adjurat.*[6] They were of ancient time called *Carmina,* because in those dayes their Charmes were in verse,

> *Carminibus Circe socios mutavit Ulyssis,*[7]
> By Charmes in Rhyme (O cruell Fates!)
> Circe transform'd Ulysses mates.

And again.

> *Carmina de Coelo possunt detrudere Lunam,*[8]
> By Rhymes they can pul down full soon,
> From lofty sky the wandring Moon.

[9]*A sorcerer, *sortilegus, quia utitur fortibus in cantationibus daemonis.*[10] Thou shalt not suffer a witch to live.[11] *Non est augurium in Jacob, nec divinatio in Israel.*[12] And the Holy Ghost hath compared the great offence of rebellion to the sinne of witchcraft.

And here it justly may be demanded, what punishment was against these devilish and wicked offenders before these statutes, which were made of very late time.

And it appeareth by our ancient [d13]books that these horrible and devilish offenders, which left the everliving God, and sacrificed to the devill, and thereby committed idolatry, in seeking advice and aide of him, were punished by death. *[14]The Mirror saith, *Que sorcery et devinal sont members de heresie.*[15] And there he describeth heresie. *Heresie est un maeuvase et faux creance surdant de error en la droit foy Christien:*[16] and after saith, *Le judgment de heresie est de arse in cendre.*[17] And herewith agreeth Britton: *Sorcerers, sorceresses, &c. et*

---

5. An Inchanter described.
6. [*Ed.:* who calls up an evil spirit with incantations or chants.]
7. [*Ed.:* Circe transformed Ulysses' companions by incantations.]
8. [*Ed.:* By incantation they can pull down the moon from the sky.]
9. *A sorcerer described.
10. [*Ed.:* a fortune teller that uses the power of incantations to demons.]
11. Exod. cap. 22. 17. Deut. ca. 18. 10, 11, 12. Num. ca. 23. 23. 1 Reg. ca. 15. 23.
12. [*Ed.:* There is no enchantment against Jacob, nor divination against Israel.]
13. *d* Linewood de officio arch-presb. § Ignorantia.
14. *Mir. cap. 1. §. 5. & cap. 2. § 12. & cap. 4. § *De majestie.* Brit. fo. 16 b. & 71. F. N. B. 269. b.
15. [*Ed.:* That sorcery and divination are species of heresy.]
16. [*Ed.:* Heresy is a wicked and false belief arising from error in the true Christian faith.]
17. [*Ed.:* The judgment for heresie is burning to cinders.]

miscreants soient arses.[18] And Fleta: *Christiani autem apostatae, fortilegi, et hu-jusmodi detractari debent, et comburi.*[19] And burning then was, and yet is the punishment for hereticks. So as the conusance of these offences, if they be branches of heresie, (as the law was then taken) belonged (as to this day heresie doth) to ecclesiasticall judges. In which case when they have given sentence, there lieth a writ *de haeretico comburendo.*[20]

I have seen a report of a case in an ancient Register, that in October *anno* 20 H.6. Margery Gurdeman of Eye, in the county of Suffolk, was for witchcraft and consultation with the devill, after sentence and a relapse, burnt by the king's writ *de haeretico comburendo.* e[21]And this agreeth with antiquity, for witches, &c. by the laws before the conquest were burnt to death.

A man was taken in Southwark with a head and a face of a dead man, and with a book of sorcery in his male, and was brought into the king's bench before Sir John Knevett then chief justice: but seeing no indictment was against him, the clerks did swear him, that from thenceforth *[22]he should not be a sorcerer, and was delivered out of prison, and the head of the dead man and the book of sorcery were burnt at Tuthill at the costs of the prisoner.[23] So as the head and his book of sorcery had the same punishment, that the sorcerer should have had by the ancient law, if he had by his sorcery praied in aid of the devill.

The holy history hath a most remarkable place concerning the reprobation and death of king Saul.[24] *Mortuus est ergo Saul propter iniquitates suas, eò quòd praevaricatus sit mandatum Domini, et non custodierit illud,*[25] *sed insuper Py-thonissam consuluerit, nec speraverit in Domino, propter quod interfecit eum, et transtulit regnum ejus ad David filium Isai.*[26] So Saul died for his transgression which he committed against the Lord, even against the word of the Lord which

---

18. [*Ed.:* Sorcerers, sorceresses, and heathens are to be burnt.]

19. [*Ed.:* Christians who are still non-believers are to be tortured, and giving the proper recanting, are burnt.]

20. [*Ed.:* [writ] for burning heretics.]

21. *e Int. leges* Edw. ca. 11. fo. 55. & Ethelstani ca. 6. fo. 60. & Canuti cap. 5. fo. 5. 45 E. 3. 17. b.

22. *Some think that this should be the oath of allegiance, *Que il serra foiall et loiall, &c. Vid.* 25 E. 3. 42. B. Coron. 131.

23. See hereafter ca. 74. of perjury, verb. That as well the judge, &c.

24. 1 Chron. chap. 10. v. 13, 14. 1 Reg 15. 23.

25. *Nota.* 1 Reg. 28. 8.

26. [*Ed.:* So Saul died for his transgression, which he committed against the word of the Lord, which he kept not, and also for asking the counsel of one that had a familiar spirit, to inquire of it. And inquired not of the Lord; therefore he slew him and turned the Kingdom unto David the son of Jesse.]

he kept not: And also for asking counsell of one that had a familiar spirit, to enquire of it, and enquired not of the Lord; therefore he flew him, and turned the kingdome unto David the sonne of Isai.

Therefore it had been a great defect in government, if so great an abomination had passed with impunity. And this is the cause, that we have proved how and in what manner conjuration, witchcraft, &c. were punished by death, &c. before the making of the said late statutes.

[27]But now let us peruse the statute made in the first year of king James, which only standeth in force, and divideth itself into five severall branches.

¶ 1. If any person or persons shall use, practice, or exercise any Invocation or Conjuration of any evill and wicked Spirit.

Here the Devill by the holy, and powerfull names of Almighty God is invoked (as hath been said): and this invocation, or conjuration, of a wicked Spirit is felony without any other act or thing, save only the apparition of the spirit. See W.1. cap 1. in the Oath of the Champion, &c.

¶ 2. Or shall consult, covenant with, entertaine, employ, feed, or reward, any evill or wicked Spirit, to, or for any intent or purpose.

By this branch, if any consult, &c. (howsoever the wicked spirit appeareth and commeth) these actions (here mentioned) with or to that wicked spirit, to or for any intent or purpose, is felony without any other act or thing.

¶ 3. Or take up any dead man, woman, or childe, out of his, her, or their grave, or any other place where the dead body resteth, or the skin, bone, or any part of a dead person, to be imployed or used in any manner of Witchcraft, Sorcery, Charme, or Inchantment.

Albeit the offender that commits these barbarous, and inhumane dealings with the bodies of the dead, do not actually imploy or use them in witchcraft, sorcery, charme, or inchantment: yet if he did them of purpose to use therein, it is felony, for the words of this branch be, [to be imployed or used in any matter of witchcraft, &c.]

---

27. 1 Jac. cap. 12.

¶ 4. Or shall use, practice, or exercise any Witchcraft, Inchantment, Charme or Sorcery, whereby any person shall be killed, destroyed, wasted, consumed, pined, or lamed, in his, or her bodie, or any part thereof.

By this branch, no other witchcraft, inchantment, charme, or sorcery (then is before specified) is felony, unlesse by means thereof some person be killed, destroied, wasted, consumed, pined, or lamed, &c. Which words have reference only to this last generall clause.

¶ 5. That then every such offender or offenders, their aiders, abetters, and counsellors, being of any the said offences duly and lawfully convicted, and attainted, shall suffer paines of death, as a felon, or felons, and shall lose the priviledge, and benefit of Clergie and sanctuary.

Albeit accessories before be here specially named, yet accessories after may be of this felony, as afterwards is said upon the statute of 3 H.7. for taking away of women, and upon the statute of 8 H.6 for stealing of Records.

The second part of this Act concerneth Felony in a second degree; and the branches thereof are also in number Five.

| ¶ 1. If any person, or persons take upon him or them by Witchcraft   [46]
Inchantment, Charme, or Sorcery, to tell or declare, in what place any treasure of gold or silver should or might be found, or had in the earth, or other secret places.

The mischiefs before this part of this Act was: That divers Impostors, Men and Women would take upon them to tell, or do, these Five things here specified, in great deceipt of the people, and cheating and cousening them of their money, or other goods. Therefore was this part of the Act made, wherein these words [take upon him or them] are very remarkable. For if they take upon them, &c. though in truth they do it not, nor can do it, yet are they in danger of this first branch.

¶ 2. Or where goods, or other things lost, or stolen should be found or become.

Herein they become offenders, if they take upon them as aforesaid. And note, the taking upon them, to tell and declare, governe both these branches.

¶ 3. Or to the intent to provoke any person to unlawfull love.

Herein also they become offenders, by taking upon them, as is aforesaid. Here is the change of a new Verbe, viz. [to provoke] So as the sense is, If any person or persons shall take upon him or them by witchcraft, inchantment, charms or sorcery, to the intent, to provoke any person to unlawfull love.

¶ 4. Or whereby any cattell or goods of any person shall be destroyed.

The Letter of this branch is this: If any person shall take upon him by witchcraft, inchantment, charm, or sorcery, whereby any cattell or goods of any person should be destroyed. Although this be not sententious, yet the meaning thereof is to be taken, by supplying these words after sorcery [any thing] and not to turn [destroyed] into the Infinitive Mood, as the rest be, for then it satisfieth not the meaning of the makers: for a taking upon them to destroy cattell, &c. if they be not destroyed, is not within the danger of this Act, and therefore must be supplyed as is aforesaid.

¶ 5. Or to hurt or destroy any person in his or her body, although the same be not effected or done.

As in the case of cattell or goods, the destruction must be (as is aforesaid) effected and done: so in case of the person of man, woman, or childe, though the hurt be not effected, or done; yet is the taking upon him, &c. to hurt or destroy any person. &c. within this branch.

¶ Being therefore lawfully convicted.

Here [convicted] is taken in a large sense for attainted, and the rather, for that after in this Act the words be [Lawfully convicted and attainted, as is aforesaid.]

¶ Shall for the said offence, &c.

Here are expressed the punishments inflicted upon these Impostors, Mountebanks, and cheating Quacksalvers, viz. 1. To suffer imprisonment by the space of a whole year without bail or mainprize. 2. Once every quarter of the year these Mountebanks are to mount the Pillory, and to stand thereupon in some Market Towne six houres, and there to confesse his or her error, and offence.

¶ And if any person being once convicted of the same offences, &c.

Here is also [convicted] taken for attainted, for he shall not be drawn in question for the second offence, to make it felony, till judgement be given against him for the first; for the Indictment of felony recites the former attainder, and the second offence must be committed after the judgement. And so it is in the case of Forgery upon the statute of 5 Eliz. and in case of conveighing of Sheep alive out of this Realme, and some others.[28]

¶ Saving to the wife of such person as shall offend in any thing contrary to this
    Act, her title of dower, and also to the heire and suc-|-cessor of every person,   [47]
his or their titles of inheritance, succession, and other rights, as though no such
    attainder of the Ancestor or Predecessor had been made.

The judgement against a felon is, that he be hanged by the neck untill he be dead:[29] and albeit nothing else is expressed in the judgement, yet by the Common law many things are therein implied; as the losse of his wives Dower, the losse of his inheritance, corruption of his blood, forfeiture of his goods, &c. Now a saving will serve for any thing, that is implied in the judgement, as in this case for the wives Dower, and also for the heirs inheritance, and for all the rest of the things implied in the judgement.[30] But a saving will not serve against the expresse judgement in case of felony, for that should be repugnant; as saving the life of the offender should be void, because it is repugnant to the expresse judgement, viz. that he be hanged by the neck untill he be dead. Also where the saving is to the heir, it is well saved by the name of the heir, because notwithstanding the forfeiture implied in the judgement, his inheritance is saved, and by consequent the blood not corrupted, for if the blood were corrupted, he could not inherit as heir, but notwithstanding this saving the lands are forfeited during his life.

The statute at 5 Eliz.[31] for preservation of the wives Dower, and the heirs inheritance, in case of forgery, is penned in this form. Provided alway, that

---

28. 5 Eliz. cap. 14. 3 Eliz. cap. 3.
29. See the 1. part of the Institutes. Sect. 747.
30. Vide lib. 1. in the case of Alton Woods. fo.
31. 5 El. cap. 14.

such attainder of felony shall not in any wise extend to take away the Dower of the wife of any such person attaint: nor to the corruption of blood, or disherison of any heir or heirs of any such person attaint.

The words of the statute of 8 Eliz.[32] be, Provided always that this Act shall not extend to corruption of blood, or be prejudiciall or hurtfull to any woman claiming Dower by or from any such offender, &c. Wherein it is to be observed, that by the avoidance of corruption of blood, the inheritance is impliedly saved. See the manner of the penning of the Act of 31 Eliz.[33] concerning this matter and divers others.

And surely it is very convenient that when new felonies be made by Act of Parliament,[34] that such savings or provisions be made both for the wives Dower, and the heirs inheritance, as were had and made in these presidents.

[134]

| Cap. LXII.
Of Indictments.

Concerning Indictments we have spoken somewhat in the First part of the Institutes. Sect. 194. 208.[1] And you may read in my Reports many resolutions concerning Indictments, viz. Lib. 4. fo. 40, 41, 42. &c. lib. 5. fo. 120, 121, 122, 123. li.7. fo. 5. 6. 10. li.8. fo. 57. 36. 37. li.9. fo. 62, 63. 116. 118.

We will add one point adjudged in the case between Burgh and Holcroft before mentioned in the Chapter of Appeals,[2] which was, that where it is provided by the statute *de Artic. super Cartas cap.3. En case de mort del home (deins le verge) on office del Coroner appent as views, & enquests de ceo faire, soit maunde al Coroner del pais que emsemblement ove le Coroner del hostel Roy face loffice que appent, &c.*[3] And in that case one man was Coroner both of the Kings house, and of the County, & the Indictment of manslaughter was taken before him as Coroner both of the Kings house, and of the County. And it

---

32. 8 El. ca. 3.

33. 31 El. ca. 4.

34. See the Statute of 3 Ja. ca. 4.

1. See the 1. pt of the Institutes. sect. 194,195.

2. Holcrosts case. *Artic. super* Cart. ca. 10. The same was again resolved in Wrots case, *ubi supra.*

3. [*Ed.:* In case of homicide within the virge, when it belongs to the office of coroner to make inspections and inquiries thereof, let the coroner of the place be ordered that he, together with the coroner of the king's household, should perform the office which belongs, etc.]

was adjudged that the Indictment was good, because the mischief expressed in the statute was remedied, as well when both offices was in one person, as when they were in divers: and therefore in this case the rule did hold, *Quando duo jura concurrunt in una persona, aequum est, ac si esset in diversis.*[4]

| Richard Weston Yeoman, late servant of Sir Gervase Elwys, Lieutenant of the Tower, and under the Lieutenant, Keeper of Sir Thomas Overbury then prisoner in the Tower, was indicted:[5] For that he the said Richard the 9 day of May An. 11 Ja. Regis, in the Tower of London, gave to the said Sir Tho. Overbury poyson called Roseacre in broth, which he the said Sir Thomas received. *Et ut idé Rich. Weston praesatum Tho. Overbury magis celeriter interficeret & murdraret, 1 Junii Anno 11 Ja. Regis supradict,*[6] gave to him another poyson called White Arsenick, &c. & that 10 Julii An. 11. suprad. gave to him a poyson called Mercury Sublimat' in Tarts, *ut praedict' Tho. Overbury magis celeriter interficeret & murdraret:*[7] and that a person unknown in the presence of the said Richard Welson, and by his commandment and procurement, the 14 of *Septemb. anno 11. supradict.* gave to the said Sir Thomas a glyster mixt with poyson called Mercury sublimat, *ut praedictum Thomam magis celeriter interficeret & murdraret. Et praedictus Thomas Overbury de seperalibus venenis praedictis et operationibus. inde, à praedictis separalibus temporibus, &c. graviter languebat usque ad 15 diem Septemb. Anno 11. supradicto, quo die dictus Thomas de praedictis seperalibus venenis obiit venenatus, &c.*[8] And albeit it did not appear of which of the said poysons he died, yet it was resolved by all the Judges of the Kings Bench, that the indictment was good; for the substance of the indictment was, whether he was poysoned or no. And upon the evidence it appeared, that Weston within the time aforesaid had given unto Sir Thomas Overbury divers other poysons, as namely the powder of Diamonds, Cantharides, *Lapis Causticus,* and powder of Spiders, and *Aqua fortis* in a glyster.[9]

---

4. [*Ed.:* when two rights concur in one person, it is the same as if they were in two separate persons.]

5. Sir Tho. Overburies case. Mich. 13. Jac. See before ca 7. Of murder more of this case.

6. [*Ed.:* And so that the same Richard Weston might more speedily kill and murder the said Thomas Overbury, on the first [day] of June in the eleventh year of King James mentioned above.]

7. [*Ed.:* so that he might more speedily kill and murder the aforesaid Thomas Overbury.]

8. [*Ed.:* so that he might more speedily kill and murder the aforesaid Thomas. And the aforesaid Thomas Overbury was seriously ill from the several poisons aforesaid, and from the working thereof, from the several aforesaid times until the fifteenth day of September in the above-mentioned eleventh year, on which day the aforesaid Thomas died poisoned by the several poisons aforesaid.]

9. [*Ed.:* [*lapis causticus:*] caustic stone [perhaps a compound of lime] [*aqua fortis:*] nitric acid.]

And it was resolved by all the said Judges, that albeit these said poysons were not contained in the Indictment, yet the evidence of giving of them was sufficient to maintain the Indictment: for the substance of the Indictment was (as before is said) whether he were poysoned or no. But when the cause of the murder is laid in the Indictment to be by poyson, no evidence can be given of another cause, as by weapon, burning, drowning, or other cause, because they be distinct & several causes: but if the murder be laid by one kind of weapon, as by a Sword; either Dagger, Styletto, or other like weapon is sufficient evidence, because they be al under one Classis or cause.[10] And afterwards, Ann Turner, Sir Gervase Helwys, and Richard Franklyn a Physitian, (purveyor of the poysons) were indicted as accessories before the fact done: And it was resolved by all the said Judges, that either the proofs of the poysons contained in the Indictment, or of any other poyson were sufficient to prove them accessories: for the substance of the Indictment of them as accessories was, whether they did procure Weston to poyson Sir Thomas Overbury: and because that not only Anne Turner, and Richard Franklyn, but some of the degree of Nobility were indicted as accessories in another County, viz. in the County of Midd. divers notable points were resolved upon the statute of 2 E.6.[11] First, if the Accessory be in the County of Midd. where the Kings Bench is, and the principall did the felony, &c. in another County, that the Court of the Kings Bench is within the words of that Act, viz. (and that the Justices of Gaol Delivery, or Oier and Terminer, or two of them, &c.) for the causes and reasons given in the Lord Zanchers case Lib.9. fo.117, 118, &c. Secondly, if the Indictment be taken in the Kings Bench, then the Justices shall not write in their own names, *quia placita sunt coram rege.*[12] Thirdly, divers presidents were shewed where the Accessory was in the County of Midd. where the Kings Bench sat, and the principall was attainted in another County, that the Justices of the Kings Bench have removed the Record of the attainder of the principall before them by *Certiorari,*[13] & so it was done in the Lord Zanchers case, *ubi supra.* The like president was shewed in a case where the

---

10. Vide li. 9. fo. 67. Mackallies case Acc.

11. 2 E. 6. cap. 24.

12. [*Ed.:* because the pleas are before the king.]

13. [*Ed.:* A writ of common law issued by a superior to an inferior court requiring the latter to produce a certified record of a particular case tried therein. The writ is issued in order that the court issuing the writ may inspect the proceedings and determine whether there have been any irregularities.]

principall was attainted in the County of Dorn. and the Accessory was in Midd. and the Kings Bench sitting there, the Justices of the same Court removed the attainder before them by *Certiorari*. Fourthly, it was resolved, that the Lord Steward of England, who is a Judge in case of High Treason, or felony committed by any of the Peers of the Realm, is within these words, Justices of Gaol-de-l-livery, or Oier and Terminer, because he is a Justice of [136] Oier and Terminer, for his authority is by Commission, and the words of his Commission be after divers recitals, *Et superinde, audiend, examinand, & respondere compellend, & sine debit' terminand:*[14] so as he hath power to heare and determine. And where the words be [or any two of them] that is to be intended, where there be two or more Justices,[15] And yet where there is but one, it extendeth to him. As the Statute of Merton cap. 3. power being given to the Sheriffe in case of Redisseisin, the words be, *Assumptis recum Coronatoribus placitorum Coronae, &c.*[16] in the Plurall number. And yet where there is but one Coroner in the County the Statute extends thereunto, and the Sheriffe shall take that one. Also the words of the statute are further, That then the Justices of Gaole delivery or of Oier and Terminer, or other there authorized: within which words, [or other there authorized] the Lord Steward is included. Fifthly, if the Record of the attainder were by Writ of Certiorari removed out of London into the Kings Bench, then there arose another doubt upon the said Statute, if afterward any proceeding should be had against any Peer, for that the words, of the Statute be, The Justices, &c. shall write to the *Custos Rotulorum* or Keeper of the Record where such principall shall hereafter be attainted; and the attainder in this case was in London, and the Kings Bench was in Middlesex: so as if the Record should be removed into the Kings Bench in Middlesex, the Record should not be where the attainder was had; and consequently the Lord Steward could not write to the Kings Bench. And therefore to prevent all questions, it was resolved, That in this case of the Lord Steward, no *Certiorari* should be granted, but a speciall Writ should be directed according to the words of the said Act to the Commissioners of Oier and Terminer in London, to certifie whether the principall was convict or acquitted: and they made a particular Certificat accordingly, so as the Record of the attainder of the principall, did notwithstanding that Certificat, remain with the Commissioners of Oier and Terminer in London: so as if any further

14. [*Ed.:* And thereupon to hear, examine, compel to answer, and without [delay] to determine.]
15. 39 H. 6. 42. 23 Ass. p. 7.
16. [*Ed.:* Taking with you the coroners of the pleas of the crown, etc.]

proceeding should be had, the Lord Steward might write to them, as after he did in the case of R. Earl of S. and F. his Wife.

And it is to be observed, that the ancient wall of London (a mention whereof doth yet remain) extendeth through the Tower of London; and all that which is on the West part of the Wall, is within the City of London, viz. in the Parish of All-Saints Barking, in the Ward of the Tower of London: and all that is on the East part of the Wall is in the County of Middlesex; and the Chamber of Sir Thomas Overbury was within the Tower on the West part of the said Wall, and therefore Weston was tried within the City of London.

And where it is often said in many [17a]Acts of Parliament, [18b]Records, and [19c]Book cases, that the King cannot put any man to answer, but he must be apprised by Indictment, Presentment, or other matter of Record. True it is, in Pleas of the Crown or other common offences, Nusances, &c. principally concerning others, or the publick, there the King by law must be apprised by Indictment, Presentment, or other matter of Record; but the King may have an Action for such wrong as is done to himselfe, and whereof none other can have any Action but the King, without being apprised by Indictment, Presentment, or other matter of Record, as a [20d]*Quare impedit.*[21] [22e]*Quare incumbravit,*[23] a Writ of [24f]Attaint, [25g]of Debt, [26h]Detinue of Ward, [27i]Escheat, [28k]*Scire fac. pur repealer patent, &c.*[29]

---

17. *a* Mag. cart. ca. 29 5 E. 3. cap. 9. 25 E. 3. c. 4. stat. 5. 28 E. 3. ca. 3. 37 E. 3. cap. 18. 38 E. 3. cap. 9. 42 E. 3. cap. 3.

18. *b* Rot. claus. 18 H. 3. m. Rot. Parl. 15 E. 3. nu. 9,10. & 15. 42 E. 3. nu. 29. Sir John A Lees case 17 R. 2. nu. 37. 2 H. 4. nu. 60.

19. *c* 7 E. 3. fo. 26. 50. *Vide* 6 E. 3. fo. 33. & 8 E. 3. 30 26 E. 3. 74. tit. rescous 21. 43. E. 3. 32. per Knivet 2. E. 3. fo. 7. John de Britains case. 3 E. 3. 19. 45. E. 3. Decies tantum 12.

20. *d* 5 1. 2. *Quar. Imp.* 167. 33. E. 3. Bie 916.

21. [*Ed.:* *Quare:* A real action to recover a presentation, the right to appoint a benefit or advowson, or other interest in church lands.]

22. *e* 17. E. 3. 50. 74. F. N. B. 48. f. 13. E. 3. Jurid. 23.

23. [*Ed.:* Writ against a bishop who confers a benefice on a clerk during a dispute between others having a claim to it.]

24. *f* 42. E. 3. 26. F. N. B. 107. D.

25. *g* 19. H. 6. 47. 34. H. 6. 3. &c.

26. *h* 39. H. 6. 26. 1. H. 4. 1. 15 E. 3. Corody 4.

27. *i* Regist. fo. 165. a. F. N. B. fo. 7. b. 21. H. 3. Bre 882. Britton fo. 28. b. cap. 18.

28. *k* 16 E. 3. Bre 651.

29. [*Ed.:* Writ summoning a person to show cause why a privilege under letters patent should not be revoked.]

D. The Fourth Part of the *Institutes*

The Fourth Part of the *Institutes* of the Laws of England, Concerning the Jurisdiction of the Courts, first published in 1644, inventories the courts, their various jurisdictions and powers, and some of the particular forms of procedure before them. In some ways, this part is the work in which Coke's authority was the strongest. He had served as chief justice of the Common Pleas and the King's Bench, sat in the Star Chamber and in the Treasurer's Court. He had been member and speaker of Parliament, a member of the Council Board, a Recorder for two different cities, a sheriff, an officer of Cambridge, and a member of many special commissions. That said, his continuing struggle to assert the privileges of the common law courts suggests that his views of the local courts and the court of privilege were not universally shared, although later many of those courts were abolished or reformed more along Coke's lines of thought.—*Ed.*

Epigrams from the Title Page:

PROVERBS 22.28.

Ne transgrediaris antiquos terminos quos posuerunt patres tui.[1]

Terminos propriae potestatis egressus in aliam messem
perperam mittit falcem suam.[2]

---

1. [*Ed.:* Do not pass the ancient boundaries which your fathers have set.]

2. [*Ed.:* He who wanders outside the boundaries of his own ability wrongly puts his sickle into another's harvest.]

A Table of the Severall
Courts in this Fourth part of the Institutes, Treated of.

The Epilogue.

Deo, Patriae, Tibi.
Proaemium.[1]

In the two former parts of the *Institutes* we have principally treated *De communibus placitis*,[2] and of those two great Pronouns [*Meum & Tuum*.][3] In the Third we have handled *Placita Coronae*[4] and Criminall causes. But because *Rerum ordo confunditur, si unicuique jurisdictio non servetur,*[6] We in this Fourth and last part of the *Institutes* are to speak of the Jurisdiction of the Courts of Justice within this Realm.

Regula.[5]

Jurisdictio est authoritas judicandi sive jus dicendi int' partes de actionibus personarum et rerum secundum quod deductae fuerunt in judicium per authoritatem ordinariam seu delegatam:[7,8] And again, [b9] *Jurisdictio est potestas de publico introducta cum necessitate juris dicendi.*[10] It is derived of *Jus,* and *ditio,* i. *potestas juris.*[11]

Curia
quid?[12]

Curia hath two severall significations, and accordingly it is severally derived. It signifieth the Kings Court, where his royall person, and his honourable houshold doe reside, and is all one with *Palatium Regium*[13] and is derived ἀπὸ τοῦ κυρίου,[14] of the Lord, because the Sovereign Lord resideth there. It also signifieth a Tribunall, or Court of Justice, as here it doth, and then it is

Festus.

derived *à cura, quia est locus, ubi publicas curas gerebant.*[15]

Of Jurisdictions some be Ecclesiasticall, and some Civill, or Temporall: of

1. [*Ed.:* To God, To the Country, To you. Preface.]

2. [*Ed.:* Of common pleas.]

3. [*Ed.:* Mine and Thine.]

4. [*Ed.:* Pleas of the crown. All trials for crimes and misdemeanors wherein the king is plaintiff on behalf of the people.]

5. Rule.

6. [*Ed.:* The order of things is confounded if every one preserves not his jurisdiction.]

7. *Jurisdictio quid?* Bract. 1. 2. fo. 400, 401. Brit. fo. 1. & 32. Fleta Hen. 6. ca. 36. unde, &c.

8. [*Ed.:* Jurisdiction is the authority of adjudicating or stating the law between parties concerning actions of persons and matters, according as they are brought to judgment, by ordinary or delegated authority.]

9. Lib. 10. f. 73. 2. *En le case del Marshalsea.*

10. [*Ed.:* Jurisdiction is a power introduced for the public good, on account of the necessity of dispensing justice.]

11. [*Ed.:* [*Jurisdictio* is derived from] *jus* (law) and *dicio* (authority), that is, authority of law.]

12. [*Ed.:* What is a court?]

13. [*Ed.:* royal palace.]

14. [*Ed.:* from the Lord.]

15. [*Ed.:* from *cura* (care, charge) because it is a place where public affairs are transacted.]

both these some be primitive, or ordinary without commission; some derivative, or delegate by Commission. Of all these, some be of record, and some
not of record; some to enquire, hear, and determine, some to enquire only;
some guided by one law, some by another; the bounds of all and every severall
Courts being most necessary to be known. For as the body of man is best
ordered, when every particular member exerciseth his proper duty: so the body
of the Common wealth is best governed, when every severall Court of Justice
executeth his proper jurisdiction. But if the eie, whose duty is to see, the hand,
to work, the feet, to goe, shall usurp, and incroach one upon anothers work:
As for example, the hands or feet, the office of the eie to see, and the like;
these should assuredly produce disorder, and darknesse, and bring the whole
body out of order, and in the end to distruction: So in the Common wealth
(Justice being the main preserver thereof) if one Court should usurp, or incroach upon another, it would introduce incertainty, subvert Justice, and bring
all things in the end to confusion.

Now when I considered how much it would tend to the honour of the
Kings Majesty, and of his Laws, to the advancement of justice, the quiet of
the subject, and generally to the good of the whole Common wealth (no King
in the Christian world having such Tribunals, and Seats of justice, as his Majesty hath, which, God willing, in this Treatise we shall make to appear) that
all the high, honourable, venerable, and necessary Tribunals, and Courts of
Justice within his Majesties Realms and Dominions, as well Civill as Ecclesiasticall, might be drawn together, as it were, in one map, or table, (which
hitherto was never yet done) that the admirable benefit, beauty, & delectable
variety thereof might be, as it were, *uno intuitu*[16] beholden, and that the
manifold jurisdictions of the same might be distinctly understood and observed. We having (as else where we have said)[17] collected some materials
towards the raising of this great and honourable building, and fearing that
they should be of little use after my decease, being very short, and not easily
of others to be understood, if I should have left them as they were;

Out of the duty that I owe to his most excellent Majesty, and my zeal, and
affection to the whole Common wealth, I have adventured to break the ice
herein, and to publish more at large those things which in our reading we

16. [*Ed.:* with one glance.]
17. In the preface to the First part of the *Institutes.*

had observed concerning Jurisdiction of Courts. I confesse it is a labour of as great pains, as difficulty: for as in an high and large building, he that beholds the same after it is finished, and furnished, seeth not the carriages, scaffolding, and other invisible works of labour, industry and skill in Architecture: so he that looketh on a book full of variety of important matter, especially concerning sacred Laws, after it is printed and fairly bound and polished, cannot see therein the carriage of the materials, the searching, finding out, perusing, and digesting of authorities in law, Rols of Parliament, judiciall Records, Warrants in law, and other invisible works, *tam laboris, quam* *[18] *ingenii:* [19] yet I was the rather incouraged thereunto, both because I have published nothing herein, but that which is grounded upon the authorities and reason of our books, Rols of Parliament, and other judiciall Records, and especially upon the resolution of the Judges of latter times upon mature deliberation in many cases never published before; wherewith I was well acquainted, and which I observed and set down in writing, while it was fresh in memory.

There be amongst the Kings Records divers and many Rols, where of you shall find little or no mention (that we remember) in our books, viz. *Rot. Parliament. Rot. Placitorum Coronae, Rot. Placitorum Parliament. Rot. Claus. Rot. Brevium, Finium, Inquisitionum, Liberationum, Rot. Cartarum, Eschaetriae, Pat. Rot. Ordinationum, Rot. Franciae, Scotiae, Vasconiae, & Almaniae, Rot. Romana, Rot. Judaeorum, Rot. Ragman, Brangwin, Rot. Contrariensium*[20] (And the reason of the naming of this Roll thus, was for that *Thomas* Earl of Lancaster (a man singularly beloved) taking part with the Barons against King Edward the second in hatred of the *Spencers,* it was not thought safe for the King, in respect of their power and greatnesse, to name them Rebels or Traitors, but *Contrarients*) and some others. In this and other parts of our Institutes we cite divers Records out of many of these Rols: Herein, as in the rest of our works, you shall observe, that in the course of our reading we took all in our

18. *Minerva quasi nervos minuens.*

19. [*Ed.:* both of labour and of skill.]

20. [*Ed.:* rolls of parliament, rolls of pleas of the crown, rolls of the pleas of parliament, close rolls, rolls of writs, rolls of fines, of inquisitions, of liveries, charter rolls, [rolls] of escheatery, patent rolls of ordinances, rolls of France, Scotland, Gascony and Germany, Roman rolls, rolls of the Jews, ragman rolls, Brangwin rolls, contrariant rolls.]

way, and omitted little or nothing, forthere is no knowledge (seemeth it at the first of never so little moment) but it will stand the diligent observer in stead at one time or other.

And thus for all our pains, wishing the benevolent reader all the profit, we (*favente Deo, & auspice Christo*)[21] begin with the High, and most Honourable Court of Parliament.

---

21. [*Ed.:* with God's favour, and with the assistance of Christ.]

Of the High and Most Honourable
Court of Parliament

Cap. I.
Of What Persons this Court consisteth.

[1] | This Court consisteth of the Kings Majesty sitting there as in his Royall politick capacity,[1] and of the three Estates of the Realm: viz. On the Lords Spirituall, Archbishops and Bishops, being in number 24, who sit there by succession in respect of their Counties, or*[2] Baronies parcell of their Bishopricks, which they hold also in their politick capacity; And every one of these when any Parliament is to be holden, ought, *ex debito justitiae*[3] to have a Writ of Summons. The Lords Temporall, Dukes, Marquisses, Earls, Viscounts, and Barons, who sit there by reason of their dignities which they hold by descent or creation, in number at this time 106: and likewise every one of these being of full age ought to have a Writ of Summons *ex debito justitiae.* The third estate is the Commons of the Realme whereof there be [4a] Knights of Shires or Counties, Citizens of Cities, and Burgesses of Burghes. All which are respectively elected by the Shires or Counties, Cities and Burghes, by force of the Kings Writ *ex debito justitiae,* and none of them ought to be omitted: and

---

1. See the first part of the Institutes, Sect. 164. for the ancient and latter names of Parliament, and the antiquity thereof. *Modus tenendi, Parl. cap.* 2.

2. *All the Bishopricks of England be of the Kings Progenitors incorporation, to have succession and foundation, *Tenendum per comitatū seu baroniam* and were of ancient time donative, and these Bishops are called by Writ to the Parliament as other Lords of Parliament be Rot. Claus. 9. Hen. 4. m. 1. Glanvil. lib. 7. ca. 1. vers finem, Bract. lib. 5. fo. 412. 427. a. 10 Hen. 4. 6. 21. Edw. 3. 60. 17. Edw. 3. 40. 48. 73. *Dicetus* Deane of London.

3. [*Ed.:* As a debt of justice; as a matter of right.]

4. *a* 5 Ric. 2. cap. 4. stat. ult. fo are they ranked. Prov. 11. 14. *Salus ubi multa consilia.* Rot. Parl. 7. Hen. 4. nu. 2. *Multorum consilia requiruntur in magnis.*

these represent all the Commons of the whole Realme, and trusted for them, and are in number at this time 493.

Of what number.

In the beginning Romulus ordained an hundred Senators for the good government of the Common Wealth: afterwards they grew to 300, and so many were of the House of Commons in Fortescues time; who treating with what gravity Statutes are made, saith; *Dum non unius, aut centum solum consultorum virorum prudentia, sed plus quam trecentorum electorum hominum, quali numero olim senatus Romanorum regebatur, ipsa statuta edita sunt.*[5,6] Festus.

Erant autem Senatores majorum gentium, & Senatores minorum gentium, ex patriciis & nobilibus electi, hii ex populo.[7,8]

And it is observed that when there is best appearance, there is the best success in Parliament. At the Parliament holden in the Seventh year of the raign of Henry the fifth[9] holden before the Duke of Bedford, Gardian of England, of the Lords Spirituall and Temporall, there appeared but thirty in all: at which Parlia-|-ment there was but one Act of Parliament passed, and that of no great weight. In *Anno* 50 Edw.3.[10] all the Lords appeared in person, and not one by Proxie. At which Parliament, as it appeareth in the Parliament Roll, so many excellent things were sped and done, as it was called *bonum Parliamentum.*[11] [2]

And the King and these three Estates[12] are the great Corporation or Body politick of the Kingdome: and do sit in two houses, viz. the King and Lords in one house, called the Lords House, and the Knights, Citizens and Burgesses in another house, called the House of Commons.

---

5. Fortescue cap. 18. fo. 40.

6. [*Ed.:* Because the statutes are made by the wisdom not of one experienced man, nor of a hundred only, but of more than three hundred elected men, the same sort of number as once ruled the Roman Senate.]

7. Cicero lib. 1. Epist. famil.

8. [*Ed.:* There were senators of the greater people, and senators of the lesser people, chosen from the patricians and nobles and from the people.]

9. Rot. Parl. 7 Hen. 5.

10. Rot. Parl. 50 Edw. 3. *Bonum Parliamentum.*

11. [*Ed.:* the good parliament.]

12. 14 Hen. 8. 3. per Fineux Hollens. Chron. 34 Hen. 8. 956, 957. Dier 38 Hen. 8. 60, 61. 2 & 3 Edw. 6. ca. 36.

[a13] For this word [Commons] see the statute of 28 Edw.3. whereby it is provided that the Coroners of Counties shall be chosen in full County *per les Commons de mesme les Counties.*[14] Commons are in legall understanding taken for the frank Tenants or Freeholders of the Counties.[15] And whosoever is not a Lord of Parliament and of the Lords House, is of the house of the Commons either in person, or by representation, partly coagmentative, and partly representative.

But of ancient time both Houses sat together. In 8 Hen.4. an Act of Parliament concerning the succession of the Crown intailed to Henry the fourth whereunto all the Lords severally sealed, and Sir John Tebetot the Speaker in the name of the Commons, put to his seale.

Note, that in the Letters to the Pope by all the Nobility of England at the Parliament holden in 28 Edw.1. the conclusion is this, *In cujus rei testimonium sigilia nostra tam pro nobis quam pro tota Communitate praed. Regni Angliae praesentib' sunt appensa.*[16] Thereby I gather, that at this time the Commons had no Speaker, but both Houses sat together, for if the Commons had then had a Speaker, they would have appointed him to have put to his seale for them, as in 8 Hen.4. they did. Certain it is, that at the first both Houses sat together, as it appeareth in the Treatise *De modo tenendi Parliamentum.*[17] Vide Rot. Parl. 5 Edw.3. nu.3. and in other places in the same Roll, and in 6 Edw.3. in divers places it appeareth that the Lords and Commons sat together, and that the Commons had then no continuall Speaker, but after consultation had, they agreed upon some one or more of them that had greatest aptitude for the present businesse to deliver their resolution, which wrought great delaies of proceeding, and thereupon the Houses were divided, and the surest mark of the time of the division of them is, when the House of Commons at the first had a continuall Speaker, as at this day it hath.

Of ancient Time both houses sat together.

After the division the Commons sat in the Chapter house of the Abbot of Westminster.[18]

---

13. *a* 28 Edw. 3. ca. 6. Regist. 177. F. N. B. 164. k. PL. R. 212. Stanf Pl. Cor. 49.

14. [*Ed.:* by the common people of the same counties.]

15. *b* For this distinction, see the second part of the *Institutes,* Mag. Cart. *Verb.* [*per pares.*] fo. 29. a.

16. [*Ed.:* In witness whereof our seals are appended to these presents, both for ourself and for the whole commonalty of the aforesaid realm of England.]

17. [*Ed.:* Of the manner of holding parliament.]

18. Rot. Parl. 50 Edw. 3. nu. 8.

And this Court is aptly resembled to a Clock which hath within it many wheels, and many motions, all as well the lesser as the greater must move: but after their proper manner, place, and motion; if the motion of the lesser be hindered, it will hinder the motion of the greater.

The Names.

This Court is called by severall names, as anciently [*Witenage Mote*] *Conventus sapientum; Parliamentum,*[19] of which we have spoken in another place;[20] *Comitia, a coeundo, quia coeunt ibi deliberaturi de* [a21] *arduis & urgentibus negotiis regni, & statum, & defensionem regni, & Ecclesiae Anglicanae concernentibus.* [b22] *Commune concilium regni,* [c23] *Generale concilium regni, &* [d24] *Concilium regni,*[25] and *Assisa generalis,* and *Assisa ab assidendo,* as *Assisa de Clarendon* 22 Hen. 1.[26]

Upon some of the Records and Rols of the Parliament it is written,

> *Perlege quae regni clarissima Conciliorum*
> *Sunt monumenta, aliter nil praeter somnia cernis.*[27]

[e28] And *Virgil* writing of the Parliament of the Gods useth the same word of *Concilium*[29] in the same sense.

> *Panditur interea domus omnipotentis Olympi,*
> *Conciliumq; vocat divûm pater, atq; hominum Rex, &c.*[30]

---

19. [*Ed.:* meeting of wise men, parliament.]

20. See the first part of the *Institutes,* Sect. 164. ubi supra.

21. *a Breve Parliam.*

22. *b Brevia originalia de vasto, &c.*

23. *c* W. 1. *in exordio.*

24. *d* Glanvil lib. 8. cap. 10. & lib. 13. cap. 32. Lib. 9. cap. 10. Bracton lib. 3. tract. 2. cap. 2.

25. [*Ed.: Comitia* (assembly), from *coeundo* (going together), because they go together there to deliberate concerning the hard and urgent business of the realm, and the defense of the realm, and matters concerning the English Church; common council of the realm; general council of the realm; council of the realm.]

26. [*Ed.:* general assize, [the word 'assize' coming from] *assidendo* (sitting down), as in the Assize of Clarendon, 22 Hen. i.]

27. [*Ed.:* Read through these [rolls], which are the clearest monuments of the councils of the realm, or else you will discover nothing but nonsense.]

28. *e* Aeneidos 10. *conciliū Deorū.*

29. [*Ed.:* Council.]

30. [*Ed.:* Meanwhile there is thrown open the house of the almighty Olympus, and the father of the gods and king of men calls a council, etc. [Virgil, *Aeneid,* x. 1.]

Tacitus in vita Agricolae[31] in the time of the Britons calleth it *Conventus, à conveniendo.*[32]

[3] | *Ingulphus,* who died before 1109. saith[33] *Rex Eldredus convocavit magnates, Episcopos, proceres, & optimates ad tractandum de publicis negotiis regni.*[34] *Tully* calleth it, *Consessum senatorum, à considendo.*[35]

Parliaments in Scripture.

And the like Parliaments have been holden in Israel,[36] as it appeareth in the holy History. *Convocavit David omnes principes Israel, duces, tribunos, & praepositos turmarum, tribunos, centuriones, & qui praeerant substantiis & possessionibus regis, filiosque suos, cum eunuchis, & potentes, & robustissimos quosque in exercitu Jerusalem.*[37] And when they were all assembled, the King himself shewed the cause of calling that Parliament. *Audite me fratres mei & populus meus, cogitavi ut aedificarem domum in qua requisceret arca foederis Domini,*
Prepara- *& ad scabellum pedum Dei nostri, & ad aedificandum omnia praeparavi,* &c[38],[39]
tion.   [b40] And the like Parliament did King Solomon son of King David hold. *Congregavit Solomon majores natu Israel, & cunctos principes, tribunos, & capita familiarum de filiis Israel in Jerusalem, &c.*[41] [c42] There was also a Parliament holden in the time of the Judges. *Convenit universus Israel ad civitatem quasi*

31. [*Ed.:* in the life of Agricola.]
32. [*Ed.: Conventus* (meeting), from *conveniendo* (coming together).]
33. 34 Hen. 6. 40. 2. Prisot.
34. [*Ed.:* King Eldred convoked the great men, bishops, peers, and nobles, to treat concerning the public business of the realm.]
35. [*Ed.: Consessus* (assembly) of senators, from *considendo* (sitting down together).]
36. 1 Chron. ca. 28.
37. [*Ed.:* David called together all the princes of Israel, leaders, tribal chiefs, divisional commanders, centurions, and those who controlled the king's property and possessions, and their sons, with eunuchs, and the mighty and most powerful men, in a great multitude, to Jerusalem.]
38. *Actus activorum sunt in patiente disposito,* saith the Philosopher.
39. [*Ed.:* Hear me, my brethren and my people, I have had it in mind to build a house in which might repose the ark of the covenant of the Lord, and for the footstool of our God, and I have made everything ready for the building, etc.]
40. *b* 2 Chron ca. 5. 2.
41. [*Ed.:* David assembled the greater men of Israel, and all the princes, tribal chiefs, and heads of the families of the children of Israel, in Jerusalem.]
42. *c* Judges 20. 11. *Conventus.*

homo unus eadem mente, & uno consilio, &c.[43] And that Parliament builded on such unity, had blessed successe.

In this Court of Parliament the King is *Caput, principium & finis.*[44] And as in the naturall body when all the sinews being joyned in the head do join their forces together for the strengthning of the body, there is *ultimum Potentiae:*[46] so in the politique body when the King and the Lords Spirituall and Temporall, Knights, Citizens, and Burgesses, are all by the Kings command assembled and joyned together under the head in consultation for the common good of the whole Realm, there is *ultimum Sapientiae.*[47]

Modus te-
nend.
Parl.[45]

What Properties a Parliament Man Should have.

It appeareth in a Parliament Roll,[48] that the Parliament being, as hath been said, called *Commune concilium,*[49] every member of the House being a Counseller, should have three properties of the Elephant: First, that he hath no gall: Secondly, that he is inflexible and cannot bow: Thirdly, that he is of a most ripe and perfect memory: which properties, as there it is said, ought to be in every member of the Great Councell of Parliament. First, to be without gall, that is, without malice, rancor, heat, and envy, *In Elephante melancholia transit in nutrimentum corporis.*[50] Every gallish inclination (if any were) should tend to the good of the whole body, the Common wealth. Secondly, that he be constant, inflexible, and not to be bowed, or turned from the right, either for fear, reward, or favour, not in judgement respect any person.[51] Thirdly, of a ripe memory, that they remembring perils past, might prevent dangers to come, as in that Roll of Parliament it appeareth. Whereunto we will adde two other properties of the Elephant, the one, that though they be *Maximae virtutis, & maximi intellectus,*[52] of greatest strength, and understanding, *tamen*

---

43. [*Ed.:* The whole of Israel gathered at the city as if they were one man, and of one mind, and of one counsel, etc.]

44. [*Ed.:* The head, beginning, and end. (referring to the king, as head of parliament).]

45. [*Ed.:* Mode of holding parliaments.]

46. [*Ed.:* the utmost of power.]

47. [*Ed.:* the utmost of wisdom.]

48. Rot. Parl. *anno* 3 Hen. 6. nu. 3.

49. [*Ed.:* common council.]

50. [*Ed.:* In the elephant, melancholy tends to the nourishment of the body.]

51. Virg. Georg. *Illum non populi fasces, non purpura regum Flexit.*

52. [*Ed.:* of the greatest strength and understanding.]

gregatim semper incedunt,[53,54] yet they are sociable, and goe in companies: for *animalia gregalia non sunt nociva, sed animalia solivaga sunt nociva.*[55] Sociable creatures that goe in flocks or heards are not hurtfull, as Deer, Sheep, &c. but Beasts that walk solely, or singularly, as Bears, Foxes, &c. are dangerous and hurtfull. The other that the Elephant is *Philanthropos, homini erranti viam ostendit,*[56] and these properties ought every Parliament man to have.

Of Records of Parliament.

The reason wherefore the Records of Parliament have been so highly extolled, is, for that therein is set down in cases of difficulty, not only the judgment, or resolution, but the reasons, and causes of the same by so great advice.[a57] It [4] is | true that of ancient time in judgements at the Common law, in cases of difficulties either criminall, or civill, the reasons and causes of the judgement were set down in the Record, and so it continued in the reigns of Edw.1. and most part of Edw.2. and then there was no need of Reports: but in the reign of Edw.3. (when the law was in his height) the causes and reasons of judgments, in respect of the multitude of them are not set down in the Record, but then the great Casuists and Reporters of cases (certain grave and sad men) published the cases, and the reasons and causes of the judgments or resolutions, which from the beginning of the reign of Edw.3. and since we have in print.[58] But these also, though of great credit, and excellent use in their kind, yet far underneath the Authority of the Parliament Rols, reporting the Acts, Judgements, and resolutions of that highest Court.

---

53. [*Ed.:* nevertheless they always go about in herds.]

54. Aristotle, Bartholomaeus.

55. [*Ed.:* animals which go in herds (or flocks) are not harmful, whereas animals which go alone are harmful.]

56. [*Ed.:* philanthropist, showing the way to the lost man.]

57. *a* Mich. 5 Edw. 1. *in comuni banco.* Rot. 100. Linc. Pasch. 19 Edw. 1. Rot. 145. Abbot de Selby. Pasch. 28 Edw. 1. Coram Rege Rot. between the King and Venables in *Quare Impedit.* Mich. 3 Edw. 2. Coram Rege Rot 6 and many others where the causes and reasons, pro & contra, have been set down, &c. 6 Edw. 3. fo. 5. per Herle. 3 Edw. 4. 2. b. 7. a. 19 Hen. 6. 63. a. Per Fray.

58. 22 Edw. 4. 18 per Hussey. Rot. Par. 19 Edw. 1. Rot. 12. Margery Weylands case. *Nota quia optime, &c.*

The Summons of Parliament.

The King *de advisamento concilii*[59] (for so be the words of the Writ of Parliament) resolving to have a Parliament, doth out of the Court of Chancery send out writs of Summons at the least forty days before the Parliament begin:[60] Every Lord of Parliament either Spirituall, as Archbishops, and Bishops, or Temporall, as Dukes, Marquisses, Earls, Viscounts and Barons; Peers of the Realm, and Lords of Parliament ought to have severall writs of Summons.

Temporall Assistants.

And all the Judges of the Realm, Barons of the Exchequer of the Coif, the Kings learned Councell,*[61] and the Civilians Masters of the Chancery are called to give their assistance and attendance in the upper house of Parliament, but they have no voices in Parliament; and their writs differ from the writs to the Barons: for their writs be, *Quòd intersitis nobiscum & cum caeteris de consilio nostro* (and sometimes *nobiscum* only) *super praemissis tractaturi, vestrumque consilium impensuri;*[62] but the writ to the Barons is, *Quod intersitis cum praelatis, magnatibus & proceribus super dictis negotiis tractaturi, vestrumque consilium impensuri.*[63]

Spirituall Assistants *Procuratores Cleri.*[64]

And in every writ of Summons to the Bishops, there is a clause requiring them to summon these persons to appear personally at the Parliament,[65] which is

---

59. [*Ed.:* by the advice of the council.]

60. Prov. 13 16. *Sapiens omnia agit cum consilio. Vide infra.* These writs of Summons you shall find in former times in the close Rol, for they are not in the Register, and in that Rol and the writs *De expensis militum, civium & burgensium, & procuratorum cleri,* and these are in the Register also.

61. Regist. 261. F. N. B. 229. a. ib. called Attendants.

62. [*Ed.:* that you be present with us and with others of our council (and sometimes 'with us' only) to treat upon the foregoing and give your counsel.]

63. [*Ed.:* that you be present with the prelates, magnates and peers to treat upon the said business and to give your counsel.]

64. [*Ed.:* Proctors of the clergy.]

65. Mod. Tenend. parl. ca. 2. Rot. Claus. 8 Edw. 2. m. 15. Dors. Ib. 5 Edw. 2 m. 15. Ib. 1 I Edw. 3 part I. m. 1. Ib. 22 Edw. 3. part 2. m. 3. Ib. 36 Edw. 3. m. 16. Rot. Par. 18 Edw. 3. nu. 1. 3 Ric. 2. 11 Ric. 2. 21

in these words, *Praemonientes Decanum & capitulum Ecclesiae vestrae Nor-wicensis, ac Archidiaconos totumque clerum vestrae Dioces. quod iidem Decani & Archdiaconi in propriis personis suis, ac dictum capitulum per unum, idemque clerus per duos procuratores idoneos plenam & sufficientem potestatem ab ipsis capitulo & clero divisim habentes praedict' die & loco personaliter intersint ad consentiendum hiis quae tunc ibidem de communi consilio dicti regni nostri divina favente clementia contigerit ordinari:*[66] and the Bishop under his seal make Certificate accordingly. And these are called *Procuratores cleri,* and many times have appeared in Parliament as Spirituall Assistants, to consider, consult and consent, *ut supra,*[67] but had never voices there, because they were no Lords of Parliament. Some have thought, that because the Clergy were not party to the election of the Knights, Citizens, and Burgesses, that these *Procuratores Cleri* were appointed to give their consent for them, but then they should have had voices, which questionlesse they never had. And by the words of the writ it was to consent to those things which by the Common Councell of the Realm should happen to be ordained, so as their consent was only to such things as were ordained de *communi concilio Regni,*[68] and that there might be an Act of Parliament without them: and in many cases multitudes are bound by Acts of Parliament which are not parties to the elections of Knights, Cit-izens, and Burgesses, as all they that have no | freehold, or have freehold in Auncient demesne, and all women having freehold or no freehold, and men within the age of one and twenty years, &c. And it appeareth by the treatise *De modo tenendi Parliament',* &c.[69] that the Proctors of the Clergy should appear, *cum praesentia eorum sit necessaria*[70] (which proveth that they were voicelesse Assistants only) and having no voices, and so many learned Bishops having voices, their presence is not now holden necessary.

[5]

Ric. 2. Procuratores Cleri. Reg. 261a. F. N. B. 229. a. Procuratores de Clero. In fascicul. literarum procurat. &c. 13 Hen. 4. & 5. Hen. 5. See hereafter tit. Proxies.

66. [*Ed.:* Warning the dean and chapter of your church of Norwich, and the archdeacons and all the clergy of your diocese, that they the same dean and archdeacons in their own persons, and the said chapter by one suitable proctor, and the same clergy by two, having severally full and sufficient power from them the said chapter and clergy, that they be personally present at the aforesaid day and place to give assent to those things which shall then and there happen to be ordained by the common council of the said realm by the favour of God's clemency:]

67. [*Ed.:* as above.]

68. [*Ed.:* by the common council of the realm.]

69. [*Ed.:* Of the manner of holding Parliament.]

70. [*Ed.:* when their presence is necessary.]

It is to be observed that in the writs of Parliaments to the Bishops (being Lords Ecclesiasticall secular)[71] they are named by their Christian names and name of their office; as, *Rex, &c. Reverendissimo in Christo patri Johanni eadem gratia Archiepiscopo Cantuar'.*[72] or *Rex,* &c. *Reverendo in Christo Patri Johanni Episcopo Norwicens.* &c.[73] But if the Sirname be added it makes not the writ vicious.

But the Abbots and Priors being Lords of Parliament, religious and secular, might be named by the name of their office only, as *Rex dilecto sibi in Christo Abbati Sancti Edmondi de Bury. &c.*[74]

A Duke, a Marquisse, an Earl, and Viscount are regularly named by their Christian names, and the names of their dignities, and rarely (yet sometimes) by their Sirnames; nor are they named by their knighthood, if they have any, but rarely. If a Baron be a knight, he is regularly named by his Christian name, Sirname, and by Miles or Chivalier, and his Barony. If he be no knight, then he is named by his Christian name, and the name of his Barony; but if the Sirname be added, it maketh not the writ vicious. And this, holdeth as well where the Baron taketh his dignity of a place, as where he taketh it of his Sirname; but where the Sirname is dignified, there to make a formall writ, it is good to add the place of his Barony.

Of ancient time the Temporall Lords of Parliament were commanded by the Kings writ to appear, *In fide & homagio, quibus nobis tenemini,*[75] and in the reign of Edw.3. *in fide & ligeancia,*[76] and sometime, *in fide & homagio*[77] but at this day constantly *in fide & ligeancia,* because at this day there are no feudall Baronies in respect whereof homage is to be done, which in 21 Edw.3 was the true cause of this alteration.

The Ecclesiasticall Barons secular or regular were commanded by the Kings

---

71. 12 Edw. 3. bre 4. fo. 31 Edw. 3. bre 342. 32 Edw. 3. bre 291. 7 Hen. 6. 27. 21 Edw. 4. 15. For these regular Lords of Parliament, and when they ceased, see hereafter. pa. 7 Edw. 4. bre 163. 7 Hen. 6. 29. 11 Edw. 3. bre 473.

72. [*Ed.:* The king, etc., to the most reverend father in Christ, John, by the same grace archbishop of Canterbury.]

73. [*Ed.:* The king, etc., to the reverend father in Christ, John, bishop of Norwich, etc.]

74. [*Ed.:* The king to his beloved in Christ the abbot of St. Edmund's of Bury, etc.]

75. [*Ed.:* in the faith and homage which you bear unto us.]

76. [*Ed.:* in the faith and allegiance.]

77. [*Ed.:* in the faith and homage.]

writ to be present, *in fide & dilectione, quibus nobis tenemini;*[78] as the Bishops are at this day.

We find in the Rols of Parliament a writ in *Anno* 23 Ric.2. and successively in every Parliament untill and in the fift year of Hen.6 amongst the Barons that came to the Parliament, it is said *Magistro Thomae de la Warre,* and some say that the addition of *Magister,* was to distinguish him from them that were knights: as in the Roll of 1 Edw.4. amongst the Barons it is said, *Johanni de Audeley armigero,*[79] for that the rest of the Barons (saving himself) and the Lord Clynton were Chivaliers. And others doe hold that he was of the Clergy before the dignity descended to him, and in that respect he was called Magister.

In the Roll of 5 Hen.5 and in many succeeding Rols we find Baron applied to the Lord of Greystock, as *Radulpho Baroni de Greistock, and Johanni Baroni de Greistock,* and to few other.

In many Rols we find the Barons that were Knights, named Chivaliers, wherein we observed,[80] that they liked to be called Chivaliers rather that *milites* after the legall word (for *Eques auratus?* is not used in Law.) For example, In *anno* 1 Edw.4. Edmundo Grey de Ruthin Chivalier, &c. and under subscribed thus, *Milites omnes, exceptis Johanne de Audeley armigero, & Johanne domino de Clynton.*[81] And in 3 Edw.4. all the Barons (saving the Lord Scales) have the additions of Chivaliers, and subscribed thus, *Equites aurati omnes, praeter dominum, Scales.*[82] And in 7 Edw.4. all the Barons have the addition of Chivaliers and therefore subscribed thus. *Equites aurati omnes.*[83] Hereby and by many others it appeareth that the Barons, if they were Knights, were so named; and that they were not named Chivaliers unlesse they were Knights. But in the reign of Hen.8. and I since, Barons are named Chivaliers in the writ of Summons, though they be no Knights.

[6]

Baner legally *Banerium,*[84] *vexillum, Banerher, unde Banerherius or Banerius,* i. *Baro, vexillarius major, & Banerettus* a diminutive of *Banerius, vexillarius*

78. [*Ed.:* in the faith and love which you bear unto us.]
79. [*Ed.:* Master to John de Audeley, esquire.]
80. 11 E. 3. tit. Bre 473.
81. [*Ed.:* all knights except John de Audeley, esquire, and John, Lord de Clynton.]
82. [*Ed.:* all knights except the Lord Scales.]
83. [*Ed.:* all knights.]
84. *De Baneretto, & unde.*

minor.[85] A Baron is called *Banerherius* or *Banerius* of the Banner, (being the Ensigne of his honour) serveth for a guide and direction: so the Baron observing the end of his Nobility should be an example and guide to others, as well in war as in peace, in all notable habilities and vertues, and so of the Baneret: both the Baron and the Baneret hath one kinde of Baner: for the Baneret is created in the field in the Kings Host, and (amongst other things) by cutting the sharp point of his Pennon, and making it a Banner i. *Vexillum Baronis:*[86] so as the Baneret hath the Baner, but not the dignity of the Baron. And this doth notably appear by the case in 22 Edw.3.[87] the very words of which resolution I will first set downe, and then the effect. *Un suit challenge pur ceo que il suit a Baner, & non allocatur: car sil soit a baner, & ne tient per barony,* il serra in Assise[88] That is, one was challenged because he had the Banner and was a Baneret & *non allocatur* by the rule of the Court, because albeit he had the Banner, yet *ne tient per Barony,* that is, he was no Baron of Parliament.

Nota seriem temporis,[89] John Coupland a valiant Leader in *Anno* 20 Edw.3. neer Durham, at Nevils Castle, took in *aperto praelio,*[90] David the second, King of Scots; for which King Edw.3. created him Knight Baneret, and gave him lands and livings, and in 22 Edw.3. the case in law fell out.

For this order of Knighthood see Camdens Britannia 124, and for this case of Sir John Coupland, Camden in Linc. pag. 618. See 35 Hen.6. fo.46. There the challenge was that he was a Baneret a Lord of Parliament. See 48 Edw.3. 30. 48 Ass. pl. *ultimo.* Lib. 6. fo. 55. But Sir John Coupland was not the first Baneret that England had, as[91] some have thought, and was with us before the reign of Edw.3. for in *Pelle exitus*[92] anno 8 Edw.2. *in Scaccario Johannes de Cromlewele Banerettus.* And *ex compoto Garderobae*[93] Anno 9 Edw.2. *Nicholaus*

---

85. [*Ed.: Baneriun* (banner), whence *banerius* (banner-bearer), that is to say, a baron, or greater banner-bearer, and a banneret (a diminutive of *banerius*), a lesser banner-bearer.]

86. [*Ed.:* that is, the banner of a baron.]

87. 22 Edw. 3. 18. tit. Challenge, 119.

88. [*Ed.:* Someone was challenged because he was a banneret, and it was not allowed; for if he is a banneret, and does not hold by a barony, he may serve on an assize.]

89. [*Ed.:* Note the sequence of time.]

90. [*Ed.:* in the open field of battle.]

91. Speed. See hereafter.

92. [*Ed.:* Statute dealing with the exacting of revenues.]

93. [*Ed.:* of the wardrobe accounts.]

de Gray was declared by Writ of Edward the Second to be *de familia regis tanquam Banerettus,*[94] both for his precedency and sallery.

For summoning of the Commons a Writ goeth out to the Lord Warden of the Cinque Ports for the election of the Barons of the same, who in law are Burgesses, and to every Sheriffe of 52 Counties in England and Wales for the choise and election of Knights, Citizens, and Burgesses, within every of their Counties respectively.

The beginning of the Parliament.

At the retorne of the Writs the Parliament cannot begin but by the Royall presence of the King either in person or by representation. By representation two wayes,[95] either by a Gardian of England by Letters Patents under the Great Seale when the King is *in remotis*[96] out of the Realme: or by Commission under the Great Seale of England to certain Lords of Parliament representing the person of the King, he being within the Realme in respect of some infirmity.

The Royall Person represented two wayes.

[a][97] The patent of the Office of a Gardien of England reciteth his speedy going beyond sea, or *in remotis,* or urgent occasions and the cause thereof. *Nos quòd pax nostra tam in nostra absentia quam praesentia inviolabiliter observetur, & quòd fiat communis justitia singulis conquerentibus in suis actionibus & querelis, de fidelitate dilecti & fidelis nostri Edwardi ducis Cornubiae, & comitis Cestriae filii nostri primogeniti plenarie confidentes, constituimus ipsum custodem dicti regni nostri ac locum nostrum tenent' in eodem regno quam diu in dictis transmarinis partibus moram fecerimus, vel donec inde aliud duxerimus.*[98] (And

94. [*Ed.:* In the issue of the pell, in the Exchequer, in 8 Edw. II. John of Cromwell, banneret. And in the wardrobe account, 9 Edw. II, Nicholas de Gray [was declared to be] of the king's household as a banneret.]

95. Rot. Parl. 3. Hen. 6. nu. 1. Hen. 6. sat in Parliament when he was 3 or 4 years old, and so did he in the 6 and 8 yeare of his reign.

96. [*Ed.:* in distant parts.]

97. *a* Rot. pat. An. 24. Edw. 3. m. 18. The Patent of the Gardianship.

98. [*Ed.:* We, [wishing] that our peace be inviolably preserved as well in our absence as when we are present, and that common justice should be done to all plaintiffs in their actions and plaints, and being fully confident of the faithfulness of our beloved and faithful Edward, duke of Cornwall, and earl of Chester, our firstborn son, have constituted him guardian of our said realm and our lieutenant in the same realm so long as we remain in parts beyond the seas, or until we provide otherwise.]

this is that *capitalis Justiciarius,*[99] mentioned in Mag. Carta cap. 11. when the King is *extra regnum*[100]) with a clause of assistance. But yet if any Parliament is to be holden,[101] there must be a speciall Commission to the Gardien, to begin the Parliament, and to proceed therein: but the *Teste* of the Writ of Summons shall be in the Gardiens name.

| A Parliament was holden in *quinti quinto,*[102] viz. *Anno 5 Hen.5.*[103] before   [7]
John Duke of Bedford, brother and Lieutenant to the King, and Gardien of England, and was summoned under the *Teste,*[104] of the Gardien or Lieutenant. [[105] It is enacted, that if the King being beyond the seas, cause to summon a Parliament in this Realme, by his Writ under the Teste of his Lieutenant: and after such summons of Parliament gone out of the Chancery, the King arriveth in this Realm: that for such arrivall of the same King such Parliament shall not be dissolved, but the Parliament shall proceed without new summons.]

[a][106] In 3. Edw.4. a Parliament was begun in the presence of the King and prorogued untill a further day: and then William Archbishop of York the Kings Commisary by Letters Patents held the same Parliament and adjourned the same, &c. The cause of the said prorogation was, for that the King was enforced to go in person to Glocerstershire to represse a rebellion there.

As hath been said, the Kings person may be represented by Commission under the Great Seale to certain Lords of Parliament authorizing them to begin the Parliament, and both the Gardien and such Commissioners do sit on a forme placed neer to the degrees that go up to the Cloth of Estate.

And in 28 Eliz. the Queen by her Commission under the Great Seale bearing date the 28 of October *Anno* 28,[107] reciting that she for urgent occasions could

---

99. [*Ed.:* The chief justiciary; the principal minister of state and guardian of the realm in the King's absence.]

100. [*Ed.:* out of the realm.]

101. See Rot. Parl. 25 Edw. 3. nu. 10.

102. [*Ed.:* in the fifth of the fifth (i.e. the fifth [year] of [King Henry] the fifth).]

103. Rot. parl 5. Hen. 5. nu. 1.

104. [*Ed.:* to bear witness formally.]

105. 8 Hen. 5. cap. 1. in. print. *Nota, Quia in praesentia majoris cessat stas potestas minoris.* And the Letters Patents of this office is with 2 *quamdiu in partibus transmarinis moram fecerimus, &c. ut sup.* Rot. Parl. 3. Edw. 4.

106. *a* Rot. 1. 13, 14. Like Letters Patents to the Earl of Warw. in the same Parliament. nu. 15.

107. Parl. 28 Eliz. See an excellent president hereof, Rot. claus. Anno 8 Edw. 2. 7. Sept. m. 26. & 1 pars pat. An 8. Edw. 2. m. 26. with a commandement of attendance. Simile 10 Edw. 2. a part pat. m. 20. 13 Edw. 3. nu. 1. stat. 2. in absentia gardiani Angliae.

not be present in her Royall Person, did authorize John Whitguift Archbishop of Canterbury, William Baron of Burghley Lord Treasurer of England, and Henry Earle of Derby Lord Steward of the Houshold then being, *Ad inchoandum, &c. tenendum, &c. & ad procedendum, &c. & ad faciend' omnia & singula, &c. nec non ad Parliamentum adjornandum & prorogandum*, &c.[108] which Commission is entred *in haec verba*[109] in the Journall Book in the Lords house, and in the upper part of the page above the beginning of the Commission is written, *Domina Regina repraesentatur per Commissionarios*, viz. &c.[110] The 29 day of October, the said Commissioners sitting on a forme before the Cloth of Estate, after the Commission read, adjourned the Parliament untill the 15 of February following, &c. And this Parliament began the 29 of October, and not the 15 of February, wherein the Printed Book is mistaken, for then the Parliament begun, and was prorogued.

Thus much shall suffice, when the Kings person shall be represented.

But when the Parliament shall not begin at the day of the returne, but for certaine urgent causes then to be prorogued untill another day, and then to be holden before the King, there is a ready way for the effecting thereof, and

Prorogued by Writ Patent.

that is by Writ Patent under the whole Great Seale reciting the Writ of Summons, and to bear Teste before the retorne thereof, and signed above with the Kings signe Manuell, and directed *Praelatis, magnatibus, proceribus hujus regni, ac militibus, civibus, & burgensibus convocatis & electis ad hoc Parliamentum pro quibusdam causis & considerationibus, &c.*[111] to prorogue the Parliament to a certaine day, and at the retorne of the Summons, this Writ being read in the Upper House before certaine of the Lords of Parliament, and of the Commons there assembled, and prorogation made accordingly, the Parliament is prorogued: And this was so done in *Anno* 1 Eliz. the retorne of the Summons of Parliament being the 9 of October,[112] and by such a Writ it was prorogued

---

108. [*Ed.:* to begin, etc. to hold, etc. and to proceed, etc. and to do all and singular the things, etc. and not adjourn and prorogue the parliament, etc.]

109. [*Ed.:* word for word]

110. [*Ed.:* the lady queen is represented by the commissioners, namely, etc.]

111. [*Ed.:* To the prelates, magnates [and] peers of this realm, and to the knights, citizens and burgesses convoked and chosen to this parliament for various causes and considerations, etc.]

112. Dier. 3 Eliz. 203. a And herein the printed book of statutes erreth, for here the Parliament begun not.

untill the 25 of February following, at what time in judgement of law the Parliament did begin, and was holden, and not on the 9 of October, as it was adjudged. A like prorogation was made by the Queens like Writ of the Parliament holden *Anno* 5 Eliz. at both which dayes of prorogation, the Parliament did hold before the Queen her selfe, untill the dissolution of the same, which Writs are entred *in haec verba* in the Journall book.

What is to be done the first day of the Parliament.

On the first day of the Parliament, the King or most commonly the Lord Chancellor or Keeper of the Great Seale in the presence of the Lords and Commons, do shew the causes of the calling of his High Court of Parliament, but the | King may appoint any other: as many times,[113] the Chiefe Justice of England, and sometime,[114] some other, as may appear in the Parliament Rols, only one I will transcribe.

   [b115] At this day Sir Henry Green the Kings Chiefe Justice (although the Lord Chancellor were present) in the presence of the King, the Lords and Commons, declared the causes of the Parliament[116] in English, viz. For redresse of matters touching the Church, for observation of the peace, for the affairs of Scotland, for the inhauncing of the price of Wooll, &c, [d117] But at the next meeting Simon Langham Bishop of Ely shewed the causes of Parliament, and in the end, he did in the Kings name require the Commons to make choice of a learned and discreet man to be their Speaker: and when a Bishop was Lord Chancellor, he took a text of Scripture which he repeated in Latin, and discoursed upon the same. But when a Judge was Lord Chancellor, he took no text, but in manner of an Oration shewed summarily the causes of the Parliament.

[8]

And, so it was done ever after.

---

113. 22 Edw. 3. Sir William Thorpe chiefe Justice.

114. *a* 17 Edw. 3. nu. 7,8, Sir Bart de Burgherst 25 Edw. 3 nu. 1. 6. 27 Edw. 3. nu. 2. 28. Edw. 3. nu. 1. 29 Edw. 3. nu. 1. Sir William Sharshull Chiefe Just. 45 Edw. 3. nu. 8. Sir Robert Thorpe Chiefe Justice 47 Edw. 3. nu. 2. Sir Jo. Knivet Chief Justice. 50 Edw. 3. nu. 2. Sir Jo. Knivet chiefe Justice, 51. Edw. 3. nu. 13. by Sir Robert Ashton the Kings Chamberlain.

115. *b* Parl. 36 Edw. 3. nu. 1. Simon Langham b. of Ely chancellor.

116. The causes of Parliament were in ancient time shewed in the Chamber De peint, or St. Edwards Chamber.

117. *d* Parlia. 27. Edw. 3. nu. 1.

The Election of the Speaker.

It is true the Commons are to chuse their Speaker: but seeing that after their choice the King may refuse him, for avoiding of expence of time and contestation, the use is (as in the *Conge de ellier*,[118] of a Bishop) that the King doth name a discreet and learned man whom the Commons elect: but without their election no Speaker can be appointed for them, because he is their mouth, and trusted by them, and so necessary, as the House of Commons cannot sit without him: and therefore a grievous sicknesse is a good cause to remove him,[119] as in 1 H.4. John Chenye Speaker chosen and allowed, was for sicknesse, so as he could not serve, discharged, and Sir John Doreward chosen in his place: and so was William Stutton, after he was chosen and allowed Speaker, removed for grievous sicknesse, and Sir John Doreward chosen in his place. At the Parliament holden in 15 Hen.6. Sir John Tirrell Knight was chosen and allowed Speaker, and for grevious sicknesse removed, and William Beerly Esq; chosen in his place, &c.

But sicknesse is no cause to remove any Knight, Citizen or Burgesse of the House of Commons:[120] So note a diversity between the Speaker, and any other of the House of Commons, and this diversity being not observed begat an error by some opinion in 38 Hen.8. tit. Parliament Brook 7. for continuall experience is to the contrary.

The presentment of the Speaker.

What the speaker shall do when he is chosen.

When the Commons have chosen their Speaker, the person elected standing in his place disabling himselfe to undergoe so weighty a charge, as in his discretion he thinks fit, desires them to proceed to a new choise: which being denied, and he set in the Chaire, then he prayeth them to give him leave, that he may disable himselfe to the King:[121] after this they present him to the King in the Lords House; where after he hath disabled himselfe to speak before the

---

118. [*Ed.:* permission to elect [a bishop].]

119. Sicknesse cause to remove the Speaker. 1 Hen. 4. nu. 62. 63. Rot. Parl. 1 Hen. 5. nu. 9,10,11. Rot. Parl. 15 Hen. 6 nu. 10. & 27.

120. Sickness no cause to remove a Member of the Commons. 38 Hen. 8. Parl. Br. 7.

121. The King may allow of his excuse, and disallow him, as Sir John Pophan was. 28 Hen. 6. nu. 6.

King, and for the whole body of the Realme, and made humble suit to the King, left by his insufficiency the businesse of the Realme may be hindred, to be discharged, and a more sufficient man to be chosen: if he be allowed by his Majestie, then he maketh a Protestation consisting on three parts: First, that the Commons in this Parliament may have free speech, as of right and by custome they have used and all their ancient and just priviledges and liberties allowed to them. Secondly, that in any thing he shall deliver in the name of the Commons (if he shall commit any error) no fault may be arrected to the Commons, and that he may resort again to the Commons for declaration of their true intent, and that his error may be pardoned. The third is; that as often as necessity for his Majesties service, and the good of the Common wealth shall require, he may by the direction of the House of Commons have accesse to his Royall Person.

The protestation of the Speaker.

I This is in the Parliament Rols called a Protestation in respect of the first part,[122] the nature whereof is to be an exclusion of a conclusion, and herein that the House of Commons be not concluded to speak only of those things which the King or Lord Chancelor, &c. hath delivered to them to be the causes of the calling of this Court of Parliament, but in a Parliamentary course of all other arduous and urgent businesse which principally consist in these five branches as it appeareth in the Writs of Summons to the Lord Spirituall and Temporall, viz.

[9]

The matters of Parliament.

1. Touching the King. 2. The state of the Kingdome of England.[123] 3. The defence of the Kingdome. 4.[124] The state of the Church of England: and 5. The defence of the same Church. And this appeareth by expresse words in the Parliament Writ in these words: *Pro quibusdam arduis urgentibus negotiis, nos, statum, & defensionem regni nostri Angliae, & Ecclesiae Anglicanae con-*

---

122. Rot. Par. 1. Ric. 1. nu. 15. &c. Rot. Parl. 2. Hen. 4. nu. 8. Sir Arnold Savage Speaker. 5 Hen. 4. nu. 8. 7 Hen. 4. nu. 11. Sir Jo. Tibetost speaker. & ibid. nu. 30. 1 Hen. 5. nu. 7. 2 Hen. 5. nu. 10. And so in succeeding times called a Protestation.

123. Rot. Parl 9 Hen. 4. An Act intituled *Indemnitie des Seigniors, et Commons,* not printed.

124. See West 1. Anno 3 Edw. 1. in the preamble, the state of the Realme & of holy Church. And the 2 part of the Institutes, West 1. cap. 1. and in the preamble.

cernentibus quoddam Parliamentum nostrum, &c. teneri ordinavimus, &c.[125] And these words the state and defence of the Kingdome are large Words, and include the rest. And though the state and defence of the Church of England be last named in the Writ, yet is it first in intention, as if appeareth by the title of every Parliament: As for example,[126] To the honour of God and of holy Church, and quietness of the people, &c.

Now for as much as divers lawes and statutes have been enacted and provided for these ends aforesaid, and that divers mischiefs in particular, and divers grievances in generall concerning the honour and safety of the King; the state and defence of the Kingdome and of the Church of England might be prevented, an excellent law was made *Anno* 36 Edw.3.[127] which being applyed to the said Writs of Parliament doth in few and effectuall words set downe the true subject of a Parliament in these words. For the maintenance of the said Articles and Statutes, and redresse of divers mischiefs and grievances which daily happen, a Parliament shall be holden every year, as another time was ordained by[128] a Statute.

Before the Conquest Parliaments were to be holden twice every year, *Celeberrimus autem ex omni satrapia bis quotannis Conventus agitur.*[129] King Edward the First kept a Parliament once every two year for the most part, and now it is enacted, that a Parliament shall be holden once every year.

The Roman vanquished our Ancestors the ancient Britains, for that they assembled not, they consulted not in common with them, not Common Councels, as *Tacitus* in *vita Agricolae* saith.[130] *Nec aliud adversus validissimas gentes pro nobis utilius, quam quod in*[131] *commune non consulunt. Rarus ad propulsandum commune periculum conventus: Ita dum singuli pugnant, universi vincuntur.*[132] But to return to the matters of Parliament.

Nota,
Commune
concilium
Conventus.

---

125. [*Ed.:* for certain hard and urgent business concerning us, the state and defence of our kingdom, and the English Church, we have ordered our parliament, etc. to be held, etc.]

126. *a* 36 Edw. 3. 50 Edw. 3. &c.

127. 36 Edw. 3. cap. 10. Parliaments ought to be holden once in a year.

128. 4 Edw. 3. cap. 14. Inter leg. Edgar cap. 5.

129. [*Ed.:* The most celebrated [king] twice every year convened a meeting of every satrap.]

130. Tacitus in *vita Agricolae,* pag. 306.

131. [*Ed.:* Note, the common council, the assembly.]

132. [*Ed.:* Nor indeed have we anything more useful against the strongest peoples than that they do not collaborate with each other. Rarely will they meet to repulse a common danger; and therefore, when they fight separately, they are all conquered. Tacitus, *Agricola,* xii. 2.].

And it is enacted and declared by Authority of Parliament in *Anno* 4 Hen.8.[133] That all suits, accusements, condemnations, executions, fines, americiaments, punishments, corrections, charges, and impositions at any time from thenceforth to be put, or had upon any member, either of that present Parliament, or at any Parliament at any time after that Act to be holden, for any Bill, speaking, reasoning, or declaring of any matter or matters concerning the Parliament, to be communed, or treated of, be utterly void and of none effect. Which latter branch is generall. Now what matter or matters concern the Parliament appear before. And this clause of the Act of 4 Hen. 8. is declaratory of the ancient law and custome of the Parliament.

Neq; timida probitas, neque improba fortitudo Rei publicae est utilis.[134]

And this doth not only appear by the Writs directed to the Lords of Parliament, but by the Writs for election of the Commons.[135] For example. the Writ to the Sheriffe of Norfolk for election of the Knights Citizens, and Burgesses within that County is *Rex Vicecomiti Norff. Salutem. Quia nos de avisamento & assensu concilii nostri pro quibusdam arduis & urgentibus negotiis, nos, statum, & Defensionem regni nostri Angliae & Ecclesiae Anglicanae concernentibus quod-\-dam. Parliamentum nostrum apud, &c. teneri ordinaverimus, & ibidem cum Praelatis, magnatibus, & proceribus dicti regni nostri colloquium habere & tractatū: ipsi Vicecom. Norff. praecipimus firmiter injungend', quod facta proclamatione in proximo comitatu tuo post receptionem ejusdem brevis, duos milites gladiis cinctos, &c. elegi faceret, &c.[136] ad faciendum & consentiendum hiis quae tunc ibidem de communi concilio nostro Angliae (favente Deo) contingerent ordinari[137] super negotiis antedictis, ita quòd pro defectu potestatis hujusmodi, seu propter improvidam electionem Militum, Civium & Burgensium praedict' dicta negotia nostra infecta non remanerent quovismodo.[138]* And this power extendeth equally to all Knights, Citizens and Burgesses of Parliament.

[10]

Nota ad Faciendum & consentiendum.

Nota, super negotiis antedictis.

---

133. 4 Hen. 8. c. 8.

134. [*Ed.:* Neither weak wisdom nor abuse of power—public matters are (to) benefit.]

135. The like Writ to all the other Counties, saving in Wales they have but one Knight and one Burgesse.

136. And every City two Citizens, and out of every Burgh two Burgesses.

137. [*Ed.:* Note, concerning the aforementioned matters.]

138. [*Ed.:* The king to the sheriff of Norfolk, greeting. Because we, by the advice and assent of our council, for certain arduous and urgent causes concerning us, the state and defence of our realm of England, and the English Church, have ordered a certain parliament to be held at, etc., there to discuss and treat with the prelates, magnates and peers of our said realm, we command you the said sheriff of Norfolk, with firm injunction, that, having made proclamation in your next county meeting after the receipt of the same writ, you cause to be elected, etc. two knights girt with swords, etc., to do and to consent to those things

What the Speaker shall doe after his allowance.

After the Commons with their Speaker are come from the Lords house, and that the Speaker is set in the Chair, then he desireth the Commons, that seeing they have chosen him for their mouth, that they would favourably assist him in their arduous and important affairs, and that he will doe them the best service he can with all diligence and faithfull readinesse, or to the like effect.

The Writs of Summons of Parliament, which are to be found in the close Roll from time to time.

Seeing the summons of Parliament (as hath been said) is by the Kings Writs, which tend to the beginning of the Parliament, it shall be necessary to speak somewhat of those writs. And it is to be observed, that the substance of those writs ought to continue in their originall essence without any alteration, or addition, unlesse it be by Act of Parliament. For[139] if originall writs at the Common law can receive no alteration or addition but by Act of Parliament, *à multo fortiori,*[140] the writs for the Summons of the highest Court of Parliament can receive no alteration, or addition, but by Act of Parliament. Where[c141] the writs of Summons issued out of the Chancery, and were returnable in the Court of Parliament, the return thereof could not be altered, and returnable into the Chancery, but by Act of Parliament. And because the words of the writ for election of Knights, &c. were,[d142] *duos milites gladiis cinctos,* &c.[143] it required an Act of Parliament, that notable Esquires might be eligible.

Walsingham saith, that in *Anno Domini* 1404., which was *anno* 6 Hen.4.[144]

---

that with God's favour should then and there happen to be ordained by our common council of England upon the aforementioned business, so that our said business should in no way remain undone for want of such power or because of the careless election of the knights, citizens and burgesses aforesaid.

139. Bract. l. 5. f. 413. Britton 122. 227. Fleta li. 2. ca. 12. West 2. ca. 25. 1. pt of the Inst. Sect. 101. *Epist. ad librum.*

140. [*Ed.:* by far the stronger reason.]

141. *c* 7 Hen. 4. ca. 15. Rot. par. 5. Ric. 2. nu 1. 2. &c. they be now returned in to the Chancery, and kept in the office of the Clerk of the Crown there.

142. *d* 23 Hen. 6. ca. 15.

143. [*Ed.:* two knights girt with swords, etc.]

144. Parl. 6 Hen. 4. This was called *Indoctum Parliamentum,* lack-learning Parliament.

in the writs of the summons of Parliament, there was added by the King a commandment in the writ, that no Lawyer should be returned Knight or Burgesse, (but the historian is deceived, for there is no such clause in those writs, but it was wrought by the Kings Letters by pretext of an Ordinance in the Lords House, in 46 Edw.3) But at the next Parliament in 7 Hen.4.[145] at the grievous complaint of the Commons, being interrupted of their free election by those letters (which were letters of Justice and right) it is amongst other things, enacted, That elections[146] should be freely, and indifferently made notwithstanding any prayer, or commandment to the contrary, i. *sine prece*,[147] by any prayer or gift, & *sine precepto*,[148] without commandment of the King by writ, or otherwise, or of any other; which was a close, and prudent salve, not only for that fore, but for all other in like case, and is but an Act declaratory of the ancient law and custome of Parliament.

Petitions in Parliament.

On the first day of the Parliament, after the Commons be departed to choose their Speaker, then are certain Justices Assistants, and Civilians Masters of the Chancery Attendants, viz. four Justices, and two Attendants | appointed to be receivers of the Petitions of England, Ireland, Wales, and Scotland, and that those that will deliver their petitions, are to deliver them within six days following. At that time there are other Justices and Civilians attendants, viz. three Justices, and two Attendants appointed to be reveivers of petitions for Gascoign and other[149] places beyond the Seas, and of the Isles, and that they deliver their petitions within six days, &c.

[11]

Receivers of Petitions of England, Ireland, Wales, Scotland.

    Then are appointed of the Nobility Lords of Parliament and Bishops, viz. Six of the Nobility, and two Bishops to be triers of the said Petitions for England, Ireland, Wales, and Scotland, they together, or four of the Prelates and Lords aforesaid, calling to them the Kings learned Councell, attendants in Parliament when need should be, and to sit in the Chamber of the Treasury.

Triers of petitions.

---

145. Rot. Parl. 46 Edw. 3. nu. 13. 5 Ric. 2. c. 4. 7 Hen. 4. ca. 15. See hereafter more of this matter, in this chapt. pa. and who be eligible, &c.
146. Nota. West 1. ca. 5. 3 Edw. 1.
147. [*Ed.:* that is, without prayer.]
148. [*Ed.:* and without command.]
149. *Gascoign, Guyan, Poiters, Normandy, Anjou, &c.

The like appointment of the Nobility and Bishops to be triers of the Petitions for Gascoign, and other places beyond the Seas, and of the Isles, and a place appointed for their sitting, calling to them the Kings learned Councell when need should be. For Petitions to be preferred into the Lords House in Parliament for the Countries and places aforesaid, this was the ancient constant law, and custome of the Parliament continued untill this day. Wherein these three things are to be observed. First, the extent of the Jurisdiction of the Parliament of England. Secondly, that for expediting of causes, there should be receivers of all Petitions, both of Judges of the Realm for their knowledge in the laws of the Realm, and of Civilians attendants, who might prepare and inform the triers, being Lords of Parliament, of the quality of those Petitions. Thirdly, that there should be of the Lords Spirituall and Temporall triers of those Petitions to try out whether they were reasonable, and good and necessary to be offered and propounded to the Lords.

Of Petitions in Parliament some be of Right, some of Grace, and some mixt of both: some preferred by the Lords Spirituall, some by the Lords Temporall, some by the Commons, some by the Lords and Commons. *Extra Parliamentum nulla petitio est grata, licet necessaria; In Parliamento nulla petitio est ingrata, si necessaria.*[150,151] All Petitions ought to contain convenient certainty and particularity, so as a direct answer may be given to them.

[b152] Petitions being timely preferred (though very many) have been answered by the law and custome of Parliament before the end of the Parliament. This appeareth by the ancient Treatise, *De modo tenendi Parliamentum*, &c.[153] in these words faithfully translated in a fair and ancient Manuscript, for Bils and Petitions. The Parliament ought not to be ended while any Petition dependeth undiscussed or at the least, to which a determinate answer is not made.

And in the Parliament Rols, there is a Title towards the end of the Parliament. The Petition of the Commons, &c. with their answer entred and re-

---

150. [*Ed.:* Outside parliament no petition is acceptable, even if it is necessary; in parliament no petition is unacceptable if it is necessary.]

151. *a* Ro. Par. 18. Edw. I. fo. 3. & 16. 50 Edw. 3. nu. 125. 66. 81. 17 Edw. 3. nu. 55,56. 36 Edw. 3. nu. 25. 43 E. 3. nu. 19. 45 Edw. 3. nu. 33. 47 Edw. 3. nu. 16. 1 Ric. 2. nu. 132. &c.

152. *b* Ro. Par. 17 Edw. 3. nu. 60. 25 Edw. 3. nu. 60. 50 Edw. 3. 212. 1 Ric. 2. 134. &c. 2 Ric. 2. nu. 38. 1 Hen. 4. 132. 2. Hen. 4. 3. 25. 3 Hen. 4. 113. 23 Edw. 3. nu. 42. 25 Edw. 3. nu. 12. 36 Edw. 3. nu. 31. 50 Edw. 3. nu. 52.

153. [*Ed.:* Of the manner of holding parliament, etc.]

corded in the Roll of Parliament.[c154] And one of the principall ends of calling of Parliaments is for the redresse of the mischiefs and grievances that daily happen.* Innovations and Novelties (sometimes tearmed in Rols of Parliament Novelries) in Parliamentary proceedings are most dangerous, and to be refused.[d155] And sometime the King doth answer the Petition of the Commons by the assent of the Prelats, Counts, Barons, and Commons themselves, such unity hath been for the common good in Parliaments in former times.

*Innova-
tions &
Novelties.*

Appointment of Committees of Grievances, &c.

The Commons being the generall Inquisitors of the Realm, have principall care in the beginning of the Parliament to appoint days of Committees, viz. of grievances (both in the[e156] Church and Common-wealth) of | Courts of Justice, of priviledges, and of advancement of trade. These Committees when they meet, they elect one of them to sit in the Chair in likenesse of the Speaker: the Committee may examine and vote the questions handled by them, and by one, whom they appoint, report their resolution to the House, and the House, sitting the Speaker, to determine the same by question.

[12]

Absents, Proxies.

Any Lord of the Parliament by licence of the King upon just cause to be absent,[157] may make a Proxy: and in the bundle of Proxies *Anno. 5* Hen.5. it appeareth, that in those days a Spirituall Lord of Parliament might have made his Proxie to the Procurators of the Clergy, or to any other Clerk, but at this day he cannot make it but to a Lord of Parliament; but a Knight, Citizen, or Burgesse of the house of Commons cannot by any means make any Proxy, because he is elected and trusted by multitudes of people.

154. *c* 36 Edw. 3. ca. 10. 18 Edw. 3. ca. 1. 4. 50 Edw. 3. nu. 17. Lions case. Rot. Par. 1 Hen. 5. nu. 17. 13 Hen. 4. nu. 9. 11 Hen. 4. c. 9.

155. *d* 36 Edw. 3. Rot. 19. &c.

156. *e* Bracton. *Gravius est aeternam quam temporalem laedere majestatem.* And it appeareth by the statute of 36 Edw. 3. cap. 10. That it is one of the principall ends of the Parliament to redresse grievances. And the words of the Writ of Parliament be, *De arduis & urgentibus negotiis statum & defensionem Ecclesiae Anglicanae concernentibus.*

157. 21 Edw. 4. 50. The ancient Record, *De modo tenend' Parl. &c. vers. finem, optime.*

Of the ancient Treatise called *Modus tenendi Parliamentum.*

Now for Antiquity and Authority of the ancient Treatise, called *Modus tenendi Parliamentum, &c.* whereof we make often use in this part of the Institutes;[158] certain it is, that this Modus was rehearsed and declared before the Conquerour at the time of his Conquest, and by him approved for England, and accordingly the Conquerour according to Modus held a Parliament for England, as it appeareth in 21 Edw.3.fo. 60.

After King Henry the second had conquered Ireland, he fitted and tran-scribed this *Modus* into Ireland in a parchment Roll, for the holding of Par-liaments there, which no doubt Henry the second did by advice of his Judges, being a matter of so great weight and legall. This *Modus* in the parchment Roll transcribed as aforesaid, by Henry the second remained in Ireland, and in *anno* 6 Hen.4. was in the custody of Sir Christopher Preston Knight, a man of great wisdome and learning, which Roll King Henry the fourth in the same year, *De assensu Johannis Talbot Chivalier,*[159] his Lieutenant there, and of his Councell of Ireland, exemplified for the better holding of the Par-liaments there; and in the exemplification it expressly appeareth that Henry the second did transcribe this *Modus,* as is abovesaid.

This *Modus* was seen by the makers of the statute of Magna Carta, *Anno* 9 Hen.3. ca.2. concerning the reducing of the[160] ancient reliefs of entire Earl-domes, Baronies, and Knights fees according to such proportions as is con-tained in the *Modus,* which they could not have done so punctually, if they had not seen the same, whereof you may read more at large in the First part of the Institutes, Sect. 103. fo.76. *Verbo Relief.* And some part of this *Modus* is cited in the Parliament Roll, *Anno* 11 Ric.2. and other Records of Parliament, and upon diligent search we can find nothing against it. But many very ancient copies you may find of this *Modus,* one whereof we have seen in the reign

---

158. See the Second part of the Inst. Mag. Carta ca. 2. pag. 7,8. See the first part of the Institutes Sect. 164. fo. 110. See the 2. part Inst. pa. 8. the Charter of King Hen. 1. at his Coronation having relation to *Modus tenendi Parl.* See also the Charter of King John anno 17. Math. Par. 246. *per antiquum relevium, viz. haeres comitis pro comite integro 100 l. haeres Baronis pro Baronia integra 100 mart. & haeres militis de feodo militis integro. 5. l.* See Mag. Cart. cap. 2.

159. [*Ed.:* Concerning the assent of John Talbot, knight.]

160. It is justly called *antiquum relevium,* because it is according to the proportion of this ancient Modus.

of Hen.2. which containeth the manner, form, and usage of Gilbert de Scrogel Marshall of England, in what manner he occupied and used the said room and office in all his time, and how he was admitted, &c. at the Coronation of Henry the second and of his Knight marshall, and other inferiour officers, &c. and adjoyned thereunto, and of the same hand is this Modus, as fit for him to know.

But less it might be said to me, as it was once said to an Oratour who having spoken much in commendation of Hercules: It was demanded of one that stood by, *Quis vituperavit? Ad quod non fuit responsum.*[161] But now let us return to Proxies.

A Lord of Parliament by licence obtained of the Queen to be absent,[162] made a Proxy to three Lords of Parliament, *Conjunctim & divisim dans eis-potestatem tractandi, tractatibusque auxilium & consilium impendendi, atque statutis & ordinationibus, quae inactitat' contigerint, consentiendi, ita quod non sit melior conditio occupantis.*[163] And one of the Procurators gave consent to a bill, and I the two others said, not content. And first it was by order of the Lords debated amongst the Judges and Civilians attendants, and conceived by them that this was no voice, and the opinion was affirmed by all the Lords of Parliament *seriatim.*[164] Another question was moved at that time, that if a Lord of Parliament make a Proxy, and after come into the Lords house of Parliament, and sit there without arguing, consenting or speaking any thing: and it was conceived by the Judges and Civilians, that his sitting there without saying any thing was a revocation in law of his proxy, *a Fortiori,*[165] if he moved, or spake to any matter there propounded, and their opinion was resolved by the Lords seriatim. And these were the proxies of the Bishop of Bathe, the Lord Howard Chamberlain, and of the Lord Windesor.

King John in the 13 year of his reign being in extreant fear of both the Pope

[13]

---

161. [*Ed.:* Who has disparaged him? To which no answer was made.]

162. At the Parliament holden An. I Eliz.

163. [*Ed.:* Giving them jointly and severally power to treat, and to give assistance and counsel to the discussions, and to consent to the statutes and ordinances which happen to be enacted, provided that they should not be in a better position than the occupant.]

164. [*Ed.:* one by one.]

165. [*Ed.:* with strong reason,]

and the French King, and especially of his own subjects (and what is fear, saith Solomon, but a betraying of the succours that reason offereth)[166] sent Ambassadours to Admiralius Murmelinus great Emperour of Turky Sir Thomas Hertington and Sir Ralph Nicholson Knights, and Sir Robert of London Clerk, *nuntios suos secretissimos,*[167] to offer to be of his Religion, and to make his Kingdome Tributary to him, and he and his subjects to be his vassals, and to hold his Kingdome of him. But that Infidell great Prince, as a thing unworthy of a King, to deny his religion, and betray his kingdome, utterly refused to accept. King John in the 14 year (the next year) of his reign by his Charter 15 May, by the threats and perswasion of the Popes Commissary Pandulphus surrendred his kingdomes of England and Ireland to Pope Innocent the Third, *cum communi consilio Baronum*[168] (as he inserted therein) and that thence forward he would hold his Crown as feodary to the Pope, paying for both the said kingdomes 1000. marks. Whereupon doing homage and fealty to the Pope by the hand of Pandulphus and taking off the Crown from his head surrendred it to the Pope by Pandulphus, at whose feet he laid also the royall Ensignes, his Scepter, Sword and Ring; all which was afterward accepted, approved and ratified by the Pope, by his Bull which was called *Bulla aurea.*[169]

    Gregorius papa petiit à Rege Edw.1.[170] *per literas annum censum 1000 merc. Rex respondet se sine praelatis & proceribus regni non posse respondere, & quod Jurejurando in Coronatione sua fuit astrictus, quod jura regni sui servaret illibata, nec aliquid quod Diadema tangat regni ejusdem absque ipsorum requisit' consilio faceret.*[171]

    In *anno* 40 Edw.3,[172] the Pope by his Ambassador demanded of the King Homage for the kingdome of England and land of Ireland, and the averages of 1000. marks by the year, granted by King John to Pope Innocent the third

---

166. Lib. Sap 17. 13. Mat. Par. pa. 233.

167. [*Ed.:* his most secret messengers.]

168. [*Ed.:* with the common counsel of the barons.]

169. [*Ed.:* the golden bull.]

170. Rot. Cl. An. 3. Edw. 1. m. 9. in *Schedula.*

171. [*Ed.:* Pope Gregory by a letter asked King Edward I for an annual payment of one thousand marks. The king answered that he could not answer without the prelates and peers of the realm, and that he was constrained by his coronation oath that he would preserve the rights of his kingdom intact, and that he would not do anything which touched the crown of the same realm without seeking their counsel.]

172. Rot. Par. 40 E. 3. nu. 8. An Act never yet printed.

and his successors, and threatned that if it were not paid, the Pope was resolved to proceed against the King. Whereupon the King in the same year calleth his Court of Parliament, and in the beginning of that Parliament (saith the Record),[173] *Fuit monstre a les Prelates, Dukes, Countes, Barons, les Chivaliers des Counties, Citizens & Burgesses en le presence le Roy per le Chancelor, coment' ils avoient entendue les causes del summons del Parliament en generall, mes la volunte le Roy fuist que les causes feussent monstres a eux en especiall: lour disoit coment le Roy avoit entendue que le Pape per force dun fait quel il dit que le Roy Johan fesoit au Pape de luy faire homage pur le realme D'engleterre & la terre D'irland,& que percause du dit homage qil luy deveroit paierchescun an perpetuelment mille marcs, est en volunte de faire proces deversle Roy & son roialm pur le dit service & cens recoverir; de qoi le Roi pria as dits Prelats, Dukes, Countes & Barons lour avys & bon conseil, & ce qil enferrior, en case que le Pape vorroit proceder devers luy, ou son dit roialme per celle cause: & les Prelats requeroient an roy quils se purroient per eux soul aviser & respondre lendemain, queux Prelatz le dit lendemain adeprimes per eux mesmes, & puis les autres Dukes, Countes, Barons & Gentz respondirent & disoient, que le dit Roy Johan ne nul autre purra mettre lui, ne son roialme, ne son people| en tiele subjection sanz assent & accorde deux: & les communes sur ce demandez & avisez respondirent en mesme le manere; sur qui feust ordeine, & assentu per commune assent en manere quensuyt.*[174] *En se present Parlement tenuz a Westm' Lundy proschein apres la invention de la Seinte Croice lan du reign le Roy Edward quarantisme, tant sur lestat de Seinte Eglise, come des droits de son roialm & de sa Corone maintenir, entre autres choses estoient monstrez coment ad este parlee, & dit que le Pape per force dun fait que le il dit que le Roi Johan, iadis Roy d'engleterre fesoit au Pape au perpetuite de luy faire homage pur le Roialme Dengleterre & la terre de Irland, & per canse dudite homage de luy rendre un Annuel rent: ad este en volunte de faire processe devers le Roi pur les ditz services & ceus recoverir; la quele chose monstree as Prelats, Ducs, Countes, Barons, & la commun' pur ent avoir lour avys & bon conseil, &* [14]

---

173. I have thought good to transcribe it *in proprio Idiomate.*

174. No King can put himself nor his Realm, nor his people, in such subjection without assent of the Lords and Commons in Parliament, and therefore if K. John had done it by the Common Councell of his Barons as his Charter purported, yet it bound not, for that it was not done in Parliament by the King, the Lords and Commons: and albeit it might (as here it appeareth, it cannot be done without Authority of Parliament) yet it is *contra legem & consuetudinem Parliamenti,* to doe such a thing as by the next Record in 42 Edw. 3. appeareth.

demandee de eux ce qe le Roi enferra en case que le Pape vorroit proceder ou rien attempter devers lui ou son roialme per celle cause? Queux Prelats, Ducs, Countes, Barons & Communes en sur ce plein deliberacion responderont & disoient dune accorde, que le dit Roy Johan ne nul autre purra mettre luy ne son roialme ne son people en tiel subjection sanz assent de eux, & come piert per pluseurs evidences, que si ce feust fait, ce feust fait sanz leur assent, & encontre son serement en sa Coronacion, Et outre ce le Ducs, Countes, Barons, Gents & Communes accorderent & granterent que en case que le Pape se afforceroit ou rien attempteroit per proces, ou en auter manere de fait de constreindre le Roi ou ses subjects de per fair ce quest dit q'il voet clamer telle partie qils resistront & contreesterront ove toute leur puissance.[175]

175. [*Ed.:* It was shown to the prelates, dukes, earls, barons, knights of the shires, citizens, and burgesses, in the king's presence, by the chancellor, that they had heard the causes of the summons of the parliament in general, but it was the king's wish that the causes should be shown to them in detail; and he told them that the king had understood that the pope, by virtue of a deed which the said King John had made to the pope to do him homage for the kingdom of England and the land of Ireland, and by reason of the said homage to pay him a thousand marks every year for ever, is about to proceed against the king and his realm to recover the said service; and concerning this the king asked the said prelates, dukes, earls and barons their advice and good counsel, and what he should do in case the pope should proceed against him or his said realm for this cause; and the prelates requested the king that they might discuss it among themselves and answer the next day; and the next day the same prelates by themselves, and later the others, dukes, earls, barons, and people, answered and said that neither the said King John nor any other could put himself, or his realm, or his people, in such subjection without their consent and agreement; and the commons, being thereupon asked and advised, answered in the same way; whereupon it was ordained and assented by the common assent in the following manner. In this present parliament held at Westminster on the Monday next after the Invention of the Holy Cross in the fortieth year of the reign of King Edward, both upon the estate of Holy Church and to maintain the rights of his realm and of his crown, amongst other things it was shown that it had been spoken and stated that the pope was minded, by virtue of a deed which he said that King John, late king of England, made to the pope to do him homage in perpetuity for the kingdom of England and the land of Ireland, and by reason of the said homage to render unto him an annual rent, to proceed against the king to recover the said services, and this having been shown to the prelates, dukes, earls, barons, and the commons, to have their advice and good counsel therein, and it being asked of them what the king should do in case the pope would proceed or attempt anything against him or his realm for that cause, the same prelates, dukes, earls, barons and commons, having had full deliberation thereof, answered and said with one accord that neither the said King John nor any other could put himself, or his realm, or his people, in such subjection without their consent and agreement, and it appeared by various evidences that if this had been done it had been done without their consent, and against his coronation oath. Moreover the dukes, earls, barons, people and commons agreed and granted that in case the pope would enforce this or attempt anything by process or in any other way to cause the king or his subjects to do what he said he would claim in that behalf, they would resist and withstand it with all their power.]

This Noble and prudent King took the fairest and surest way to give satisfaction, whereof the Pope being certified, the matter ever since hath rested in quiet.

*176 It is declared by the Lords and Commons in full Parliament, upon demand made of them on the behalf of the King, that they could not assent to any thing in Parliament, that tended to the disherison of the King and his Crown, whereunto they were sworn. See hereafter in the case of Ireland.

Lex &
consuetudo
Parlia-
menti.

Lex & consuetudo Parliamenti.[177]

By the ancient law,[178] and custome of the Parliament a proclamation ought to be made in Westminster in the beginning of the Parliament, that no man upon pain to lose all that he hath, should during the Parliament in London, Westminster, or the suburbs, &c. wear any privy coat of plate, or goe armed, or that games or other playes of men, women, or children, or any other pastimes or strange shews should be there used during the Parliament: and the reason hereof was, that the High Court of Parliament should not thereby be disturbed, nor the members thereof (which are to attend the arduous and urgent businesse of the Church and Common wealth) should not be withdrawn.

[179]* It is also the law, and custome of the Parliament, that when any new device is moved on the Kings behalf, in Parliament for his aid, or the like, the Commons may answer, that they tendred the Kings estate, and are ready to aid the same, only in this new device they dare not agree without conference with their Countries; whereby it appeareth, that such conference is warrantable by the law and custome of Parliament.

And it is to be observed, though one be chosen for one particular County, or Borough, yet when he is returned, and sit in Parliaments, he serveth for the whole Realm, for the end of his comming thither, as in the writ of his

---

176. *Ro Par. 42. Edw. 3. nu. 7.

177. [*Ed.:* The law and custom (or usage) of parliament.]

178. 7 Edw. 2. Stat. *De defensione port and arma.* 2 Edw. 3. ca. 3. Rot. Par 6. Edw. 3. nu. 1. 13 Edw. 3. nu. 2. 14 Edw. 3. nu 2. 15 Edw. 3. nu 2. 17 Edw. 3. nu. 3. 18 Edw. 3. nu. 2. 20 Edw. 3. nu. 1. 25 Edw. 3. slat. 1. nu. 58. 25 Edw. 3. stat 2 nu. 5. &c. Privy coat or Armour. Games or plays. Rot. Par. Ann. 13 Edw. 3. nu. 5. & 8.

179. *See hereafter.

election appeareth, is generall, *ad faciendum & consentiendum hiis quae tunc & ibidem de communi consilio dicti regni nostri (favente deo) contigerint ordinari super negotiis praedictis, i. pro quibusdam arduis & urgentibus negotiis nos, statum, & defensionem regni nostri Angliae & Ecclesiae Anglicanae concernentibus,*[180] which are rehearsed before in the writ.

Lex &
consuetudo
Parlia-
menti.

[15]

And as every Court of Justice hath laws and customes for its direction, some I by the Common law, some by the Civill and Canon law, some by peculiar lawes and customes, &c.[181] So the High Court of Parliament *Suis propiis legibus & consuetudinibus subsistit.*[182] It is[183] *lex & consuetudo Parliamenti,* that all weighty matters in any Parliament moved concerning the Peers of the Realm, or Commons in Parliament assembled, ought to be determined, adjudged, and discussed by the course of the Parliament, and not by the Civill law, nor yet by the Common laws of this Realm used in more inferiour Courts; which was so declared to be *secundum legem & consuetudinem Parliamenti,*[184] concerning the Peers of the Realm, by the King and all the Lords Spirituall and Temporall; and the like *pari ratione*[185] is for the Commons for any thing moved or done in the House of Commons: and the rather, for that by another law and custome of Parliament, the King cannot take notice of any thing said or done in the House of Commons, but by the report of the House of Commons: and every member of the Parliament hath a judiciall place, and can be no witnesse. And this is the reason that Judges ought not to give any opinion of a matter of Parliament, because it is not to be decided by the common laws, but *secundum legem ad consuetudinem Parliamenti:* and so the Judges in divers Parliaments have confessed.[186] And some hold, that every offence committed in any Court punishable by that Court, must be punished (proceeding crim-

---

180. [*Ed.:* to do and to consent to those things that with God's favour should then and there happen to be ordained by our common council of England upon the aforementioned business (that is, for certain arduous and urgent causes concerning us, the state and defence of our realm of England, and the English Church).]

181. *Ista lex ab omnibus est quaerenda, a multis ignorata, a paucis cognita.* Fleta lib. 2 cap. 2.

182. [*Ed.:* subsists according to its own laws and customs.]

183. Rot. Par. 11 Ric. 2. nu. 7. See the first part of the *Institutes.* Sect. 3. Verb. *En la ley.* Rot. Parl. 2 Hen. 4. nu. 11.

184. [*Ed.:* according to the law and custom of parliament.]

185. [*Ed.:* For the like reason; by like mode of reasoning.]

186. Rot. Parl. 3. Hen. 6. In le Countee de Marshalls case. Rot. Par. 27 Hen. 6. nu. 18. the Earle of Arundels case.

inally) in the same Court, or in some higher, and not in any inferiour Court, and the Court of Parliament hath no higher.[187]

Upon his petition exhibited to the King,[188] wherein the question was, whether the power which he had raised was High Treason, &c. which petition (saith the King) let be delivered to the Justices by them to be considered. Whereupon the Lords made protestation, that the order thereof belonged to them, which was to them allowed, and they resolved it to be no treason.

And because we have a case in 3 Edw. 3. 19. concerning the law and custome of Parliament, we have thought good to set down the Record of that case *De verbo in verbum*,[189] and then to examine the report of the said case, and the opinion there delivered, wherein we shall desire the learned to consider well the statute of 5 Ric. 2. stat.2. cap.4. and thereupon to consider what (as that statute speaketh) hath been done of old times, &c. And how that Act saith done, and not said.

Johannes Episcopus Winton in misericordia pro pluribus defaltis. Idē Iohannes Episcopus attachiat' fuit ad respond' Domino Regi,[190] *de eo quare cum in Parliamento Regis apud novā Sarū nuper tent' per ipsum Dominū Regem inhibitum fuisset, ne quis ad dictum Parliamentum summonitus ab eodem recederet sine licenc' Regis: Idem Episcopus durante Parliamento praedict. ab eodem sine licentia Regis recessit in Regis contemptum manifestum, & contra inhibitionem Regis supradictam. Et unde idem Dominus Rex per Adam de Fincham, qui sequitur pro eo, dicit, quod praedictus Iohannes Episcopus fecit ei transgress. & contemptum praedict. &c. in contempt. Regis mille librarum. Et hoc offert verificare pro Domino Rege, &c.*

Et praedictus Episcopus in propria persona sua venit,[191] *& defendit omnem contemption & transgress. & quicquid, &c. & dicit, quod ipse est unus de paribus regni, & Praelatus sacros. Ecclesiae, & eis in est venire ad Parliamentum Domini Regis per summonitionē & pro voluntate ipsius Domini Regis cum sibi placuerit, Et dicit, quòd si quis | eorum deliquerit erga Dominum Regem in Parliamento aliquo, in Parliamento debet corrigi & emendari, & non alibi in minor' cur' quàm in Parliamento: per quod non intendit, quod Dominus Rex velit in cur' hic de hujusmodi*

Note, that this was by writ originall.

The Declaration.

Nota hoc.
[16]

187. Rot. Parl. 31 Hen. 6 nu 26,27,28. Baron Thorps case.

188. 5 Hen. 4. nu. 22. The Earl of Northumberlands case. Vid. Rot. Parl. 9 Hen. 4. *Indemnity des Seigniors & Commons.*

189. [*Ed.:* word for word. Literally, from word to word.]

190. Pasch. 3. Edw. 3 *coram Rege* Rot. 9. in Dors. Southr.

191. The Plea of the Bishop to the jurisdiction of the Court.

transgr. & contempt. factis is Parliamento responderi, &c. Et super hoc datus est eis dies coram Rege à die Sancti Trin. in quindecem dies ubicunq; &c. salvis rationibus. Ad quem diem praed. Episcopus venit in propria persona sua, & datus est ei dies coram domino Rege à die Sancti Mich. in 15 dies ubicunq; &c. in eodem statu quo nunc &c. salvis rationibus suis, &c. Ad quem diem venit praedict. Adam qui sequitur, &c. Et similiter praedictus Episcopus in propria persona sua. Et praedictus Adam pro praedicto Domino Rege dicit, quòd cum placeat ei Parliamentum suum tenere pro utilitate regni sui de regali potestate sua facit illud summoneri ubi & quando, &c. pro voluntate sua, & etiam facit prohiberi existentibus tunc ad Parliamentum, ne quis eorum abinde recedat contra prohibitionem suam, &c. absque licentia, &c.

This is the allegation of the Kings Attorny.

Et si quis eorum abinde recedat contra prohibitionem, &c. in contempt. regis, &c. bene liceat ipsi Domino Regi sumere sectam erga hujusmodi delinquentes in qua curia placeat sibi, &c. Et ex quo Dominus Rex pro voluntate sua Parliamenta sua tenet, &c. petit judicium pro ipso domino rege, si idem Dominus Rex duci debeat, seu compelli ad prosequend' in hac parte alibi contra voluntatem suam, &c.

 Et praedictus Episcopus dicit ut prius, quòd cum aliquis deliquerit in Parliamento,

The B. maintains his former plea to the jurisdic-tion.

ibidem debet corrigi & emendari, &c. & licet aliquis summonitus esset veniendi ad Parliamentum, & non venisset ibidem, debet puniri, per quod non intendit, quòd dominus rex velit alibi responderi quam in Parliamento, &c. Et super hoc datus est eis dies usque, in Crō. Animarum ubicunque, &c. in eodem statu quo nunc, &c. Ad quem diem venit tam praedict. Adam, qui sequitur pro domino rege, quam praedict. Episcopus in propria persona sua. Et datus est eis dies coram domino rege in Octab. Sancti Hilarii ubicunque, &c. salvis rationibus suis, &c. Ad quem diem praedict. Episcopus venit, & datus est ei dies ulterius coram domino rege in Octab. Pur. beatae Mariae ubicunque, &c. Ad quem diem venit tam praedictus Episcopus, quam Iohannes de Lincoln' qui sequitur pro domino rege, & datus est eis dies ulterius coram domino rege à die Paschae in quinque septimanas ubicunque, &c. Salvis rationibus, &c. Ad quem diem venit tam praed. Episcopus in propria persona sua, quàm praedict. Iohannes de Lincoln, qui sequitur pro dicto domino rege, &c. Et datus est eis dies ulterius a die Sancti Michaelis in 15 dies ubicunq; &c. salvis sibi rationibus suis hinc in dicend' &c.[192]

---

192. [*Ed.:* John, bishop of Winchester, in mercy for various defaults. The same Bishop John was attached to answer the lord king for that, whereas in the king's parliament lately held at New Sarum it was ordered by the selfsame lord king that no one summoned to the said parliament should leave the same without the king's licence: the same bishop, during the aforesaid parliament, left the same without the king's licence, in manifest contempt of the king, and against the above-mentioned prohibition by the king. And thereupon the same lord king, by Adam de Fincham, who sues for him, says that the aforesaid Bishop John committed

| And this is all that is in the Record, whereby it appeareth that the plea [17] of the Bishop to the Jurisdiction of the Court after divers dayes given did stand, and was never over ruled agreeably to the said resolutions in former times, that Judges were not to determine matters concerning the Parliament, as is aforesaid. Touching the report of the said case, thus far forth it agreeth, that this contempt cannot be punished in any other Court then in the Kings

---

the aforesaid trespass and contempt against him, etc. in contempt of the king [to the extent of] one thousand pounds. And this he offers to aver for the lord king, etc.

And the aforesaid bishop comes in his own person, and denies all the contempt and trespass, and whatever, etc., and says that he is one of the peers of the realm and a prelate of Holy Church, and it behooves him to come to the lord king's parliament by summons and at the will of the lord king whenever he pleases. And he says that if any of them offends against the lord king in any way in parliament, it ought to be corrected and amended in parliament and not elsewhere in a lesser court than parliament; and so he does not think that the lord king will be answered in this court for such trespass and contempt made in parliament, etc. Thereupon a day is given to them before the king in fifteen days from the day of the Holy Trinity, wheresoever (he should then be in England), etc., saving their arguments. At which day the aforesaid bishop comes in his own person, and he is given a day before the lord king in fifteen days from Michaelmas, wheresoever (he should then be in England), etc., in the same condition as now, etc., saving his arguments, etc. At which day come the aforesaid Adam, who sues (for the lord king), etc., and likewise the aforesaid bishop in his own person. And the aforesaid Adam, for the lord king, says that when it pleases him to hold his parliament for the utility of the realm, he causes it by his royal power to be summoned where and when, etc. at his will, and also causes it to be prohibited to those then at the parliament that none of them should leave contrary to his prohibition, etc., without licence, etc., and if any of them leave contrary to the prohibition, etc. in contempt of the king, etc. it is perfectly permissible for the lord king to commence suit against such offenders in whatever court he pleases, etc. And since the lord king holds his parliaments at his will, etc., he prays judgment for him the said lord king, whether the same lord king ought to be led or compelled to sue in this behalf elsewhere, against his will, etc.

And the aforesaid bishop says, as before, that when anyone offends in parliament, it ought to be corrected and amended there, etc., and even if someone is summoned to come to parliament and does not come there, he ought to be punished, and so he does not think that the lord king will be answered anywhere other than in parliament, etc. Thereupon a day is given them until the morrow of All Souls wheresoever (the king should then be in England), etc., in the same condition as now, etc. At which day come both the aforesaid Adam, who sues for the lord king, and the aforesaid bishop in his own person. And they are given a day before the lord king in the octaves of St. Hilary, wheresoever (he should then be in England), etc., saving their arguments, etc. At which day the aforesaid bishop comes, and he is given a further day before the lord king in the octaves of the Purification of the Blessed Mary, wheresoever (he should then be in England), etc. At which day come both the aforesaid bishop and John of Lincoln, who sues for the lord king, and they are given a further day before the lord king in five weeks from Easter day, wheresoever (the king should then be in England), etc., saving their arguments, etc. At which day come both the aforesaid bishop and John of Lincoln, who sues for the lord king, and they are given a further day before the lord king in fifteen days from Michaelmas day, wheresoever (the king should then be in England), etc., saving to themselves their arguments to be published, etc.]

Bench: so as the question is only for that Court. It appeareth that the reporter never saw the said Record, only took it by the care of that which was spoken in Court (a dangerous kind of reporting, and subject to many mistrakings, for seldome or never the right case is put) as in this case it fell out. For first, where the Record saith, that the Parliament was holden at *Sarum;*[193] the report is of a Parliament holden at *Salop.*[194] 2. The Report saith, that John B. of Winchester was arraigned, which implieth that he was indicted, &c. where he was sued by originall Writ. 3. The Inhibition made by the King alledged in the Record, is not in the Report. 4. Concerning the sudden opinion of *Scrope* in this Report: By his opinion the Parliament it selfe could not have punished this contempt; for he saith, *Ceux'q sont Judges de Parliament, sont judges de lour Piers, mes le Roy nad my pier in son terre demesn, pur q̃ il ne poet p eux estre judge, donques ailors cue cy ne poet estre judge,*[195] whereas without question the Parliament might have punished this contempt: and concludeth with a rule at the Common law, that the King may sue in what Court it pleaseth him. But matters of Parliament (as hath been often said) are not to be ruled by the Common law: and it seemeth that the rest of the Judges were against Scrope, for the plea was never over-ruled, as by the Record it appeareth.

Vide per Indictamenta Termino Paschae 1 & 2 Ph. & Mar. coram Rege Rot. 48. Informations preferred by the Attorney Generall against 39 of the House of Commons for departing without license contrary to the Kings Inhibition in the beginning of the Parliament; whereof 6 being timorous Burgesses *ad redimendam vexationem*[196] submitted themselves to their Fines, but whether they paid any, or very small, we have not yet found. And[197] Edmond Plowden the learned Lawyer pleaded, that he remained continually from the beginning to the end of the Parliament, and took a Travers full of pregnancy: and after his plea was *sine die per demise le Roign.*[198]

---

193. [*Ed.:* Salisbury.]

194. [*Ed.:* Shrewsbury.]

195. [*Ed.:* Those who are judges of parliament are judges of their peers, but the king has no peer in his own land, and therefore he cannot be adjudged by them, and therefore he cannot be adjudged anywhere else but here.]

196. [*Ed.:* for vexing redemption.]

197. Mich. 3. & 4 Ph. & Mar. Rot. 36. *inter Plac. Regis & Reginae.*

198. [*Ed.:* without day by the demise of the queen, in other words, without a fixed day of termination specified in the royal grant.]

If offences done in Parliament might have been punished elsewhere, it shall be intended that at some time it would have been put in use. *Vid.* the first part of the Institutes. Sect. 108.

Now the said Informations *Anno* 1 & 2 Ph. & Mar. against 39 of the House of Commons follow in these words.

Pasch. 1 & 2 Ph. & Mar. Regis & Reginae. Midd. ss. Memorand' quod Edwardus Griffyn ar' Attornat' domin.[199] *regis & reginae generalis, qui pro eisdem domino rege & domina regina sequitur, venit hic in Cur' dictorum dñorum regis & reginae coram ipsis rege et regina apud Westm' die Sabbathi proxim' post quind' Pasch. isto eodem Termino, & dat Cur' hic intelligi & informari. Quòd cum ad parliamentũ dominorũ regis & reginae nunc tent' apud West' Annis regnorum suorum primo & secundo inhibitum fuit per ipsos dominum regem et dominam reginam in eodem parliamento, quod nullus ad idem parliament' summonitus, & ibidem interessens, ab eodem parliamento absque speciali licentia dictorũ dominorũ regis et reginae, et Cur' parliament' praedict' recederet, seu seipsum aliquo modo absentaret. Quidam tamen Thomas Denton de   in com' Oxon' ar' Henricus Cary de   in com' gent' Richardus Warde de   in com'   ar' Edmund. Plowden | de Tybmershe in com. Berks armiger, Henricus Chiverton de   in com.   ar. Robertus Browne de   in com.   Johannes Courke de   in com.   Johannes Pethebrige de in com.   Johannes Melhewes de   in com.   Johan. Courtney de   in com. Radulphus Michel de   in com.   Thomas Mathew de   in com.   Richardus Brasey de   in com.   Thomas Massye de   in com.   armig'. Petrus Frechwell de   in com.   miles. Henricus Vernon de Sydbery in com. Derby armig. Willielmus Moore de villa Derb. in com. Derb. gen. Willielmus Banibrigge de   in com. Johannes Eveleigh de   in com.   gen. Nich. Adamps de Dartmouth, alias Clifton Harnys in com. Devon gen. Richardus Phelipps de   in com. ar. Anthonius Dylvington de   in com.   Andreas Hoorde de   in com. Christopherus Hoell de   in com. Dors. gen. Johannes Mannocke de in com. gen. Thomas Phelipps de   in com.   Johannes Hamond de in com.   Johannes Phelipps de   in com.   Willielmus Randall junior, de   in com.   Johannes Moyne de   in com.   Hugo Smyth de   in com.   gen. Rogerus Gerrard de   in com.   gen. Radulphus Scroope de   in com.   gen. Thomas Moore de Hambled. in com. Buck. gen. Willielmus Reade de   in com.   ar. Henricus Mannock de   in com.   ar. Joh. Maynard de Villa Sancti Albani, in com.*

Inihibitum suit.[200]

[18]

---

199. Edw. Griffin.
200. It was Forbidden.

Hertf. ar Nich. Debden de   in com.   gen. & Philippus Tirwhyt de   in com.   ar' qui summoniti fuerunt ad dictum Parliamentum, & in eodem Parliamento comparuerunt, ac ibidem interfuerunt mandat' et inhibitionem dominorum regis et reginae supradict' parvi pendentes, ac statum reipublicae hujus regni Angliae minime curantes aut ponderantes postea scil. 12 die Januarii Annis regnorŭ dictorŭ dominorŭ regis et reginae nunc primo et secundo supradictis, et durante parliamento praedicto ab eodem parliamento sine licentia dictorum dominorum regis et reginae et cur' suae praedict' contemptuose recesserunt in ipsorum dominorum regis et reginae ac mandat' et inhibitionis suorum praedict' ok curiaeque, praedict. contempt' manifestum, ac in magnum reipublicae statum hujus regni Angliae detriment', nec non in perniciosum exemplum omnium aliorum, &c. Unde idem Attornatus dominorum regis et reginae petit advisamentum cur' in praemis. et debit' legis process. vers. eosdem Thomam Denton, Henricum Cary, Richardum Warde, Edm. Plowden, Henricum Chiverton, Robertum Browne, Joh. Courk, Joh. Pethybridge, Joh. Melhewes, Joh. Courtney, Radulph. Michell, Thomam Mathewe, Richardum Brasey, Thomam Massye, Petrum Frechwell, Henricum Vernon, Will. Moore, Will. Banibrigge, Joh. Eveleigh, Nich. Adamps, Richardum Phelipps, Anthonium Dilvington, Andream Hoorde, Christopherum Hoell, Johannem | Mannock, Thomans Phelipps, Johan. Hamond, Joh. Phelipps, Willelman Randall, Joh. Moyne, Hugonem Smith, Rogerum Gerrard, Radulphum Scroope, Tho. Moore, Will. Read, Henricum Mannock, Johan. Maynard, Nicholaum Debden, & Phil. Tyrwhyt fieri ad respondend. domino regi, & dominae reginae de contempt' praedict. &c.

Et modo scil. die Veneris prox' post Crast' animarum isto eodem Termino coram domin. rege et dña regina apud West' ven' praedict' Edm. Plowden per Andream Tusser Attornatū suum:[202] *& habit' audit' Informationis praedictae dic', quod ipse non intendit quod dominus rex & domina regina nunc ipsum Edmun' pro premissis vel aliquo premissorŭ impetere seu occasionare velint aut debent: Quia dicit quod ipse ad dict' Parliament' in informatione praedict' specificat' interfuit & praesens fuit, ac in eodem Parliamento continue remansit, viz. à principio ipsius Parliamenti usque ad finem ejusdem. Absque hoc quod ipse idem Edmund. Plowden dicto 12 die Januarii, An. primo & secundo supradict durant' Parliament' praedict' ab eodĕ Parliament' sine licentia dictorum dominorum regis & reginae, & cur' suae praedict' contemptuose recessit in ipsorum dominorum regis & regine ac mandat' & inhibitionis suorŭ praedict' curiaque praed' contempt' manifest', ac in magnum rei-*

Mandatum & Inhibitionem.[201]

[19]

201. Command and injunction
202. Mic. 3 & 4 Ph. & Mar. Ro. 36. inter plac. regis & reginae.

publicae stat' hujus regni Angliae detriment', nec non in perniciosum exemplum omnium aliorŭ modo & forma prout per informac' praedict' vers. cum supponitur. Et hoc paratus est verificare prout cur. &c. unde pet' judicium: & quod ipse de praemiss. per cur' hic dimittatur, &c.

Midd. *Ve. fac' Thomam Constable de Grimbsbye in com. Lincoln. Ar. Hen. Leigh, de in com. Francis. Farnham de Querne in com. Leic. ar.* Li. lo. Mic. 2 & 3 Ph Regis & Mar. Reginae.[204] *Joh. Holcroft Sen. de in com. milit. Will. Bromley de in com. ar. Tho. Somerset de in com. ar. Georg. Ferrers de Markyat' in com. Hertf. gen Nich. Powtrell de Exincton in com. Nott' ar.* F. Hill. 3 & 4 Ph. & Mar. *Tho. Moyle de in com. Kanc' milit. Tho Waters de in com. ar. Will. Tylcock de civit' Oxon' gen* Li. lo. Hil. 2 & 3 Ph. & Mar. *Tho. Balkden de Wechyngleigh in com. Sur. milit.* Li. lo. Mic, 2 & 3 Ph. et Mar. *Math. Cradock de villa Staff. gen.* Li. lo. Hil. 2 & 3 Ph. & Mar. *Georgium Lye de villa Salop. gen.* Cess. process. per mandat' Attornat' dominorum regis & reginae, quia ulterius prosequi non vult vers. ipsum Geo., Lye. *Joh. Hoord de Bridgenorth in com. Salop. gen.* F. Mic. 5 & 6 Ph. & Mar. *Joh. Alsop de villa de Ludlowe in com. Salop. gen. Wil. Laurence de Civ. Winton. gen.* Li. lo. Mich. 2 & 3 Ph. & Mar. *Robert. Hudson de Civ. Winton. gen.* Li. lo. ut antea. *Edm. Rowse de Donwich in com' Suff. mil. Rob. Coppinge de Donwich in com' Suff. ar. Joh. Harman de Hospicio dom. regis & dom. reginae gen. Will. Crowch de Wellowe in com' Somers. ar. Tho. Lewes de villa de Wels in | com' Somers. gen.* Li. lo. Hil. 2 & 3 Ph. & Mar., *Wil. Godwyn de Wels praed' in com' Somers. gen.* F. Mich. 3 & 4 Ph. & Mar. *Joh. Ashburnham de Ashburnham in com' Suss. ar.* Li. lo. Mic. 2 & 3 Ph. & Mar. *Walt. Reyncum de Civ' Cicest' in com' Suss. gen.* Li. lo. Tr. 2 & 3 Ph. & Mar. *Wil. Moodyere de Slindon in com' Suss. gen.* F. Tr. 4 & 5 Ph. & Mar. *Joh. Roberts de in com' Suss. gen. utlegat. &c. Wil. Pellet de Steininge in com' Suss. gen.* F. Pasch. 2 & 3 Ph. & Mar. *Rich. Bowyer de Arundell in com' Suss. gen.* Li. lo. Mic. 3 & 4 P. & M. *Will. Danby de in com. Westmerl. gen. Rob. Griffyth de Civ' Novae Sarum in com Wilts, Draper.* Li. lo. ut supra. *Joh. Hooper de Civ. Novae Sarŭ in com' Wilts, gen,* Li. lo. Mic. 2. & 3 Ph. & Mar. *Wil. Clark de in com. Grif. Curtys de Bradstock in com' Wilts gen.* Li. lo. ut supra, &c. *Tho. Hil. de Denyses in com. Wilts gen.* F. Hil. 2 & 3 Ph. & Mar. *Edw. Umpton de London gen.* Li. lo. Mic. 2 & 3 Ph. & Mar. *Tho. Parker de in com. Joh. Reade de London gen.* F. Hil. 2 & 3 Ph. & Mar. *Arth. Allen de civ' Bristol Merch. Egid. Payne de civ' Bristol. gen. Wil. Hampshire de London gen.* Li. lo. Mic. 3 & 4 Ph. & Mar. *& Pet. Tayler de Marlborow in com' Wilts, Taylor.*

Nota, the pregnancy of this travers. Sine die per demise le Royne.[203]

[20]

203. Without a day, according to the demise of the King.
204. Per de annis 1 & 2 Ph. & Mar. Rot. 48.

Li. lo. Mic. 3 & 4 Ph. & Mar. *Resp. Regi de quibusdam transgress. & contempt. unde impetit' sunt.*[205]

Mid. *Ve. fac' cr' Trin. Edw. Braxden de civ' Wigorn. gen. Georg. Newport de Droitwich in com' Wigorn. gen. Wil. Wigstone de Wolstone in com' War. mil.* Li. lo. Mic. 2 & 3 Ph. & Mar.[206] *Radulph. Browne de Woodlowes in com' War. gen.* Li. lo. Mic. 3 et 4. Ph. et Mar. *Johan. Harforde de civ' Covent. gen.* Cess. process. &c. *Nich. Fryshe de   in com.   Rich. Rayleton de   in com.   Marc. Wyrley de civ. Lichfield. gen. Walt. Iobson de villa de Kingston super Hull. Jac. Brenne de   in com.   gen. Joh. Payton de   in com. Kanc. ar. Joh. Cheney de   in com. Kanc. armigerum.* Willielmum Oxenden de   in com. Kanc. Armigerum. *Tho. Keys de "in com. Kanc. gen. wil. Hannington de" in com. Kanc. Joh. Tyssars de   in com.   Nich. Crypse de   in com. Kanc. ar. Edw. Herbert de Stawley in com. Salop ar. F. Hil. 4 et 5 praed. Ph. et Mar. &c. Rich. Lloyde de   in com. Kanc. gen. Joh. de Knylle de   in com. ar. Hen. Jones de   in com.   mil. Meredith Gaines de   in com.   gen. & Rich. Bulkeley de   in com.   mil.   Resp. regi de quibusdũ transgr' & contempt. unde impetit' sunt. Et postea, scil. Termino sanct. Trin. Annis 4 & 5 Ph. et Mar. pro eo quod sufficienter hic in cur' testatũ est quod praedict. Joh. Harford habuit licentiam recedere à Parliamento &c. Ideo Edw. Griffyn ar. Attornat. dominorũ regis & reginae generalis qui pro ipsis rege & regina in hac parte sequitur, dicit quod ipse ulterius in hac parte vers. praefatum Joh. Harford prosequi non vult. Ideo cess. hic process. vers. eum omnino, &c.*[207]

Non prof. vers. Harford tantum.

Sine die per demise le Royne.

---

205. Cess. process. vers. Georgium Lye. Sine die per demise le Royne.

206. Per cont' rott' de Annis 1 & 2 Ph. & Mar. Rot. 48.

207. [*Ed.:* Middlesex. Be it remembered that Edward Griffin, esquire, attorney-general of the lord king and [lady] queen, who sues for the same lord king and lady queen, comes here in the court of the said king and lady queen before them the said king and queen at Westminster on the Saturday next after the quindene of Easter this same term, and gives the court here to understand and to be informed that, whereas at the parliament of the lord king and lady queen held at Westminster in the first and second years of their reign it was commanded by them the said lord king and lady queen in the same parliament that no one who had been summoned to the same parliament and was there present should leave the same parliament without the special licence of the said lord king and lady queen and of the court of parliament aforesaid, or absent himself in any other way: nevertheless a certain Thomas Denton of [*blank*] in the county of Oxford, esquire, . . . [*thirty-nine other members listed, including Edmund Plowden*], who were summoned to the said parliament, and appeared in the same parliament, and were there present, little regarding the above-mentioned command and prohibition of the lord king and lady queen, and little caring for or weighing the state of the commonwealth of this realm of England, afterwards, namely on the twelfth day of January in the first and second year of the reigns of the said lord king and lady queen, and during the aforesaid parliament, contemptuously left the same parliament without the licence of the said lord king and lady queen and of their aforesaid court, in manifest contempt of them the said lord king and lady

| And to deal clearly, this is all that we can find concerning this matter. Thus you may observe, that the poor Commons, Members of the Parliament, in *diebus illis*,[208] had no great joy to continue in Parliament, but departed. But now to proceed. [21]

Of Writs of Error in Parliament.

If a Judgement be given in the Kings Bench either upon a writ of Error, or otherwise, the party grieved may upon a petition of Right made to the King in English; or in French (which is not *ex debito Justitiae*,[209] but for decency, for that the former judgement was given *Coram Rege*)[210] and his answer there-

The House of Lords is a distinct Court for many purposes.

---

queen and of their aforesaid command and prohibition and of the aforesaid court, and to the great detriment of the state of the commonwealth of this realm of England, and to the pernicious example of others, etc. And thereupon the same attorney of the lord king and lady queen prayed the advice of the court in the foregoing and due process of law to be made out against the same Thomas Denton . . . [*and other members*], to answer the lord king and lady queen in respect of the aforesaid contempt, etc.

And now, namely on the Friday next after the morrow of All Souls this same term, before the lord king and lady queen at Westminster, comes the aforesaid Edmund Plowden, by Andrew Tusser his attorney; and, having had a hearing of the aforesaid information, he says that he does not think that the present lord king and lady queen will wish or ought to impeach or charge him the said Edmund for the foregoing matters or any of them; because he says that he was present at the said parliament specified in the aforesaid information, and remained continuously in the same parliament, that is to say, from the beginning of the selfsame parliament until the end of the same, without this that he the said Edmund Plowden on the said twelfth day of January in the above-mentioned first and second year, during the aforesaid parliament, contemptuously left the same parliament without the licence of the said lord king and lady queen and of their aforesaid court in manifest contempt of them the said lord king and lady queen and of their aforesaid command and prohibition and of the aforesaid court, and to the great detriment of the state of the commonwealth of this realm of England, nor to the pernicious example of others, etc., in the manner and form as is supposed against him by the aforesaid information. And this he is ready to aver as the court, etc. And so he prays judgment, and that he may be dismissed from the foregoing by the court here, etc. . . . [*process against the other members, some of which is stopped by order of the attorney-general*] . . .

And afterwards, namely in Trinity term in the fourth and fifth years of Philip and Mary, forasmuch as it is sufficiently attested here in court that the aforesaid John Harford had licence to leave the parliament, etc., therefore Edward Griffin, esquire, attorney-general of the lord king and lady queen, who sues for them the said king and queen in this behalf, says that he does not wish to sue further in this behalf against the said John Harford. Therefore let the process here utterly cease against him, etc.]

208. [*Ed.:* in those days,]

209. [*Ed.:* From or as a debt of justice; as a matter of right. The opposite of *ex gratia*.]

210. [*Ed.:* Before the king.]

unto, *fiat Justitia*,[211] have a writ of Error directed to the Chief Justice of the Kings Bench for removing of the Record *in praesens Parliamentum*[212] and thereupon the Roll it self, and a transcript in parchment is to be brought by the Chief Justice of the Kings Bench into the Lords House in Parliament:[213] and after the transcript is examined by the Court with the Record, the Chief Justice carrieth back the Record it self into the Kings Bench, and then the Plaintiffe is to assign the errors, and thereupon to have a Scire fac'[214] against the adverse party, returnable either in that Parliament, or the next; and the proceeding thereupon shall be super tenorem recordi, & non super recordum.[215] All this, and many more excellent matters of learning are contained in the Records following; whereof a light touch is hereafter given, the Records at large being too long here to be rehearsed. And the proceeding upon the writ of Error is only before the Lords in the Upper House, *secundum legem & consuetudinem Parliamenti.*[216]

Queritur Guilielmus de Valencia contra Concilium regis, i. Justic' Coram Rege, pro injusto judicio tangen' allocationem Dionisiae filiae Guilielmi de monte Caniso ut haered': sed dominus Rex ratum habet eorum factum, & judicium redditum est contra Guilielmum de Valencia.[217,218]

If a Nobleman had been erroneously attainted of Treason, &c, he might have had his writ of Error in Parliament,[219] notwithstanding the statute of 33 Hen. 8, ca. 20. for that must be intended of lawfull records of Attainder: but if the Attainder be established by Authority of Parliament, then he must ex-

---

211. [*Ed.:* let justice be done. On a petition to the king for his warrant to bring a writ of error in parliament, he writes on the top of the petition, "Fiat justitia," and then the writ of error is made out, etc. . . .]

212. [*Ed.:* in the present parliament.]

213. 22 Edw. 3 fo. 3. Regist. 17. Lib. Intr. Rast. 284.

214. [*Ed.:* Writ to enforce a judgment or other manner of record.]

215. [*Ed.:* upon the tenor of the record, and not upon the record.]

216. [*Ed.:* according to the law and custom of parliament.]

217. Rot. Par. *Post festum Sancti Hil.* Anno 18 Edw. I. Rot. 8.

218. [*Ed.:* William de Valence complains against the king's council, that is, the justices before the king, for an unjust judgment touching the allowance of Denise, daughter of William de Montchensy, as heir; but the lord king confirms what they have done, and judgment is given against William de Valence.]

219. Rot. Par. 4. E. 3. nu. 13. Rich. Earl of Arundels case. Ib. 28 E. 3. nu. 11, 12. Mortimer Earl of Marches case. See Pasc. 28 Edw. 3. Coram Rege Rot. 37 Wigorn, the same case. 33 Hen. 8. ca. 20. 29 Eliz. ca. 2. Rot. Par. 7 Ric. 2. nu. 20. 8 Ric. 2. nu. 14.

hibite his petition in Parliament to be restored of grace. But now by the statute of 29 Eliz. ca. 2. it is obtained, that no record of Attainder of High Treason that then was, for the which the party attainted had been executed for the same treason should be reversed for error: but this extendeth only to Attainders of High Treason, and not to any Attainder of High treason after that Act, nor to any High treason before, for the which the party was not executed.

The House of the Lords is a distinct Court for many purposes.

The Prior and Covent of Montague by their petition declare, that Richard Seimour had obtained an erroneous judgement against the said Prior in the Kings Bench, upon a judgement given in the Common place upon a fine for the Mannor of Titenhull in the County of Somerset, &c. And the principall error was for denying of aid of the King where it was grantable, and that hanging a writ of Right, the said Richard sued a *Scire fac.* And commandment was given to the Chancelor of England, that he should make a writ of possession and seison to be had, and other processe upon that judgment to be made: In this Record you shall observe excellent pleading.

Error in Parliament upon a judgment in an Appeal of death upon an acquitall of the Defendant, and inquiry of the Abettors, &c.[220]

And (that we may observe it once for all) when one sueth in Parliament to reverse a judgement in the Kings Bench, he sheweth in his bill which he exhibiteth to the Parliament some error or errors, whereupon he prayeth a *Scire facias.*

The Bishop of Norwich sheweth that an erroneous judgment was given against him in the Common place for the Archdeaconry of Norwich belonging to his presentation[221] and prayed that those errors might be heard, and redressed | there: whereunto answer was made that errors, by the law, in the [22]
Common place are to be corrected in the Kings Bench, and of the Kings Bench in the Parliament and not otherwise.

1. Ric. 2. nu. 28, 29, 2 Ric. 2. nu. 31. A writ of Error in Parliament between William Mountacute Earl of Sarum, and Roger of Mortimer Earl of March of a judgment in the Kings Bench.

[a222] The Dean and Chapter of Lichfield recovered in the Common place

220. Rot Par. 13. Ric. 2. nu. 15. Sir Thomas Methams case.

221. Rot. Par. 10 Edw. 3. nu. 48.

222. *a* Ro. Par. 15 Ric. 2. nu. 2.; & 18 Ric. 2. nu. 2; & 18 Ric. 2. nu. 11, 12, 13, 14, 15. This Parliam. of 18 Ric. 2. is not mentioned in the printed book, because no Act passed at this Parliament. See 2 Hen. 4. nu. 40.

against the Prior of Newport Pannel: the Prior by writ of Error reverseth the judgment in the Kings Bench: the Dean and Chapter by writ of Error in Parliament reverseth the judgment in the Kings Bench, and affirmeth the judgment in the Common place, and a commandment given to the Chancelor, that the judgment in the Common place be executed by processe by him to be made.

[b]223 John Sheppy complains of a judgement in the Kings Bench in a writ of Error.

[c]224 Error in Parliament between William Mountacute Earl of Salisbury, and Roger de Mortimer Earl of March, for the Castle, Town, and honour of Denbeigh, &c. upon a judgment given in the Kings Bench, and had a *Scire fac'* returnable the next Parliament.

[d]225 William Seward alias Cheddre complaineth, that where he by that name was presented and inducted to the Parsonage of Wotton Under Egge in the County of Glouc', and thereof continued the possession by the space of four years, untill the King by untrue suggestion presented Sir John Dawtry in the Parsonage of Underhegge in that County, where there was no such parsonage calied Underhegge, as the said William pleaded in a *Quare Impedit*[226] brought by the King in the Kings Bench; upon which writ the King recovered by the Default the Parsonage of Underhegge, and not Under Egge, whereby upon a writ sent to the Bishop of Worcester, the said William was put from his Parsonage of Under Egge; for which mistaking and error, the judgment for the said John in full Parliament was reversed, and a writ awarded to the said Bishop for the restitution of the said William.

The Record and judgment given in the Kings Bench for the King against Edmond Basset for certain lands, &c.[227] was for divers errors reversed in Parliament, and restitution of the premisses with the mean profits restored to the said Edmond.

In error in Parliament between Roger Deyncourt, and Ralph de Adderlye for a judgement given in the Kings Bench for the Mannor of Anslye in Com'

---

223. *b* Ro. Part. 15 Ric. 2. nu. 22.

224. *c* 21 R. 2. nu. 25. 2 Hen. 4. nu. 13.

225. *d* Rot. Par. 1. Hen. 4. nu 91.

226. [*Ed.:* A real action to recover a presentation, a patron's right to an advowson or benefice.]

227. Rot. Par. 15 Ric. 2. nu. 24. & 2 Hen. 4. nu. 38.

Warr'.[228] Sir William Gascoign Chief Justice delivered a copy of the Record and processe, word for word, under his hand, &c. to the Clerk of the Parliament, &c.

In error in Parliament between Richard Quatermayns and William Hore, &c,[229] upon an erroneous judgment given in the Kings Bench in an action of trespasse, and the Plaintif entred his Atturny of Record to proceed therein.

John Beauchamp Lord Abergaveny complained in Parliament upon an erroneous judgment given upon a verdict in the Kings Bench in a *Scire fac'* upon a recognisance in the Chancery for keeping the peace.[230] In the Record whereof are excellent points of learning, as well touching the recognisance, as the processe, and issue.

Error in Parliament, Pasch. 31 Hen. 6.[231] upon a judgment given in an Assize in the Kings Bench, & *intratur super marginem, Rot. mittitur in Parliamentum per Johannem Fortescue Termino Paschae anno* 31 Hen. 6.[232]

And to omit many others, to descend to some of latter times, Richard Whalley recovered in Assize by veredict against divers tenants,[233] who brought a writ of Error in the Kings Bench, where the judgment in the Assize was affirmed, the tenant complained in Parliament for error in the Kings Bench.

Error in Parliament upon complaint of Sir Christopher Heydon Knight of a judgment in a writ of Error in the Kings bench,[234] between the said Sir Christopher Plaintif, and Roger Godsalve and others Defendants, upon a judg-l-ment given for the said Roger, &c. against the said Sir Christopher in an   [23] Assize before Justices of Assize, wherein the judgment in the Assise was affirmed in the Kings bench, whereof the complaint was made, *sed non praevaluit.*[235]

A Peer of the Realm being indicted of treason, or felony, or misprision of

---

228. 5 Hen. 4. nu. 40.

229. Rot. Par. 3. Hen. 5. nu 19.

230. Rot. Par. 10 Hen. 6. nu. 51. & 11 Hen. 6. nu. 40.

231. Rot. Par. 31 Hen. 6.

232. [*Ed.:* and it is entered in the margin, [This] roll is sent into parliament by John Fortescue [chief justice], in Easter term in the thirty-first year of Henry VI.]

233. Rot. Par. 23 El. Dier 23 El. f. 373.

234. Rot. Par. 12 Jac.

235. [*Ed.:* but he did not prevail.]

In case of treason, &c. the Lords Spiritual make their Proctors. The Peers are Judges of treason, &c. during the Parliaments, &c.

treason, may be arraigned thereof in Parliament,[236] a Lord Steward being appointed, and then the Lords Spirituall shall make a Procurator for them; and the Lords, as Peers of the Realm, during the Parliament are Judges, whether the offence be treason, &c. that is supposed to be committed by any Peer of the Realm, and not the Justices, as it appeareth in the Earl of Northumberlands case, Rot. Parl. 5 Hen. 4.nu. 11,12. See in the Parliament holden 21 Ric. 2. sub *titulo Pl. Coronae,* in a Roll annexed, &c. before the Steward of England and other Lords Temporall, Richard Earl of Arundels case. Rot. Parl. 31 Hen. 6. nu.49. Thomas Earl of Debon was arraigned of High Treason before Humphry Duke of Buck' Steward of England *hac vice,* and was acquited by his peers, 10 Edw. 4. fo.6.b. Stanf. Pl. Coron. 153.b.

Of Judicature.

Now order doth require to treat of other matters of Judicature in the Lords house, and of matters of Judicature in the house of Commons. And it is to be known; that the Lords in their House have power of Judicature, and the Commons in their House have power of Judicature, and[237] both Houses together have power of Judicature: but the handling hereof according to the worth and weight of the matter would require a whole Treatise of it self; and to say the truth, it is best understood by reading the Judgments and Records of Parliament at large, and the Journals of the House of the Lords, and the book of the Clerk of the House of Commons, which is a Record, as it is affirmed by Act of Parliament in anno 6 Hen. 8. ca.16.

See Rot. Claus. I Ric. 2. m.5. 8. 38, 39. *A tresage Councell le Roy, les Seigniors & Commons, &c.*[238] Rot. Parl. 1 Hen. 4.nu.79, it is no Act of Parliament, but an Ordinance, and therefore bindeth not in succession. Rot. Par.2 Hen. 5.

236. Rot. Par. 5. Hen. 4. nu. 11, 12. Rot. Par. 21 Ric. 2. sub tit. Plac. Coronae, &c. Rot. Par. 31 Hen. 6. nu. 49.

237. *Vide Placita in Parliam. Anno 33 Edw. 1. Rot. 33. Nicholaus Segrave adjudge praelatos, Comites, Barones & alios de concilio.* At the Parliament at York *anno* 12 Edw. 2. *Consideratum est per Praelatos, Comites, Barones, & Communitatem Angliae* the Lord Awdeleys case. At the Parl. at Westm' 15 Edw. 2. Hugh *le pier adjudge per les seignours &* Commons. Rot. Parl. 42 Edw. 3. nu. 20. Sir John at Lee adjudged by the Lords and Commons. Rot. Pat. 50 Edw. 3. 2. parte, A Pardon to the Lord Latimer of a Judgment in Parliament. Rot. Parl. 50 Edw. 3. nu. 34. Lo. Nevils case.

238. [*Ed.:* To the most wise king's council, the lord and commons, etc.]

nu.13. Error assigned that the Lords gave Judgement without petition or assent of the Commons. Rot. Par. 28 Hen. 6. nu.19. & many others in the reign of King Hen. 6. King Edw. 4.

And of latter times, see divers notable judgements, at the prosecution of the Commons, by the Lords at the Parliaments holden 18 and 21 Jac. Regis. against Sir Giles Mompesson, Sir John Michel, Viscount S. Albone Lord Chancelor of England, the Earl of M. Lord Treasurer of England, whereby the due proceeding of Judicature in such cases doth appear.

Thomas Long, gave the Mayor of Westbury four pound to be elected Burgesse, who thereupon was elected. This matter was examined and adjudged in the House of Commons,[239] *Secundum legem & consuetudinem Parliamenti,*[240] and the Maior fined and imprisoned, and Long removed: for this corrupt dealing was to poyson the very fountain it self.

Arthur Hall a Member of the House of Commons for publishing and discovering the conferences of the House,[241] and writing a book to the dishonor of the House, was upon due examination, *secundum legem & consuetudinem Parliamenti,* adjudged by the House of Commons to be committed to the Tower for six months, fined at five hundred marks, and expelled the House.

Muncton stroke William Johnson a Burgesse of B, returned, into the Chancery of Record, for which upon due examination in the House of Commons,[242] it was resolved that *secundum legem & consuetudinem Parliamenti,* every man must take notice of all the Members of the House returned of Record at his | perill: but otherwise it is of the servant of any of the Members of the House; for there he that striketh, &c. must have notice. And the House adjudged Muncton to the Tower, &c.[243] [24]

If any Lord of Parliament, Spirituall or Temporall, have committed any oppression, bribery, extortion, or the like of the House of Commons, being the generall inquisitors of the Realm (comming out of all the parts thereof) may examine the same, and if they find by the vote of the House, the charge to be true, then they transmit the same to the Lords with the witnesses and proofs.

239. In the book of the house of Comons at the Parliament holden 8 Eliz. Ownsloe Speker. fo. 19.
240. [*Ed.:* According to the law and custom of parliament.]
241. 23 Eliz. ib. fo. 14. Popham Attorney generall Speaker.
242. Ib. 2 Aprilis. 1 Mariae. Vid. 11 Hen. 6 c. 11 5 Hen. 4. ca. 6.
243. See Rot. Parl. 8 Hen. 6. nu. 57.

Priviledge of Parliament.

And now after Judicature, let us speak somewhat of priviledge of Parliament:[244]
Experience hath made the priviledges of Parliaments well known to Parliament
men, yet will we speak somewhat thereof.

Magister militiae Templi petit quòd distringat (catalla unius de concilio) tem-
pore Parliamenti pro redditu unius domus in London: Rex respondet, non videtur
honestum, quod illi de concilio suo distringantur tempore Parliamenti, sed alio
tempore, &c.[245,246] Whereby it appeareth that a Member of the Parliament that
have priviledge of Parliament, not only for his servants, as is aforesaid, but
for his horses, &c. or other goods distreinable.

Querela Comitis Cornubiae, versus Bogonem de Clare & Priorem Sanctae Trin-
itatis London, quòd ipsi tempore Parliamenti ipsum comitem in medio aulae
Westm' ad procurationem ipsius Bogonis citaverunt, quòd compareret coram Arch-
iepiscopo Cantuar' &c. Ipse prior venit & Bogo similiter, & ponunt se in gratiam,
misericordiam, & voluntatem Regis de alto & basso, ob quod mandantur turri
London: Postea venit dictus Bogo & finem fecit domino regi pro praedicta trans-
gressione per duas mille marcas, &c. & quoad praedict' Comitem respondeat Com-
iti 1000. li. pro transgressione sibi fact', &c. & praedictus Prior mittitur ibidem
ad faciend' secundū quod thesaurius ei dicet ex parte dñi Regis.[247,248]

And yet the serving of the said citation did not arrest, or restrain his body

---

244. *Vide Inter leges* Edw. Confess C. 3.

245. *Petitiones coram domino rege ad Parliament' post festum Sancti Mich. Anno* 18 Edw. 1. fo. 7.

246. [*Ed.:* The master of the knights of the Temple prays that he may distrain the chattels of one of
council, in time of parliament, for the rent of a house in London. The king answers that it does not seem
appropriate that those of his council should be distrained in time of parliament, but at some other time,
etc.]

247. *Plac' coram rege & ejus concilio ad Parliam. suum post Festum Sancti Hil. Anno* 18 Edw. 1. fol. 1.
Vide Inf. 10 Edw. 3. more hereof concerning serving of a Citation.

248. [*Ed.:* The complaint of the earl of Cornwall against Bogo de Clare and the prior of the Holy
Trinity, London, that they in time of parliament cited him the said earl in the middle of Westminster Hall,
by the procurement of the said Bogo, to appear before the archbishop of Canterbury, etc. The prior comes,
and Bogo likewise, and they put themselves in the grace, mercy and will of the king, of high and low; and
by reason thereof they were sent to the Tower of London. Later the said Bogo comes and makes fine with
the lord king for the aforesaid trespass, at two thousand marks, etc., and, with respect to the aforesaid earl,
let him answer the earl in one thousand pounds of the trespass done to him, etc. And the aforesaid prior
is sent there to do whatever the treasurer tells him to do on behalf of the lord king.]

and the same priviledge holdeth in case of *Sub poena* or other processe out of any Court of equity.

Rex mandavit Justiciariis suis ad Assisas, Jurat', &c. capiend' assignat' quòd supersedeant captioni eorundem ubi Comites, Barones & alii summoniti ad Parliamentum Regis sunt partes, quamdiu dictum Parliam, duraverit.[249,250]

De non procedendo ad capiend' Assisas versus illos, qui ad Parliamentum Regis apud Eborum venerunt.[251,252]

Rex omnibus balivis & fidelibus suis ad quos, &c. Salutem. Sciatis,[253] *quòd cum curiae nostrae in quibus*[254] *negotia regni nostri dedecantur ubiq; adeo liberae sint & exemptae, & à tempore quo non extat memoria liberae & exemptae fuerunt, quod nec aliqua forum ecclesiasticum concernentia in eisdem curiis nostris fieri seu exequi, nec aliqui easdem curias nostras ad aliqua forum ecclesiasticum contingentia faciendum vel exequendum ingredi debeant, vel consueverunt aliquibus temporibus retroactis, ac Magister Henricus de Harewedon clericus, Edmundus de Lukenore & Johannes de Wedlingburgh de eo quòd ipsi nuper in Cancellaria nostra in praesentia venerabilis Patris I. Cantuariensis Archiepiscopi Cancellarii nostri quasdam citationes sive monitiones dilecto clerico nostro Johanni de Thoresby*[255] *nec non provocationes, appellationes & instrumenta publica super citationibus seu monitionibus praedictis in nostri contemptum & Coronae nostrae ac Regiae dignitatis nostrae praejudicium, & contra libertatem & exemptionem praedict' fecerunt per inquisitionem in quam se inde in curia nostra coram dilecto Cancellario nostro & aliis de concilio nostro posuerunt convicti fuissent & ea occasione prisonae nostrae mancipati in eadem ad voluntatem nostram moraturi. Nos de gratia nostra speciali ad requisitionem Philippae Reginae Angliae consortis nostrae charissimae perdonavimus eisdem Henrico, Edmundo & Johanni impri-*

---

249. Rot. Parliam. *Anno* 8 Edw. 2. in Dors. cl. 8 Edw. 2.

250. [*Ed.:* The king has commanded his justices assigned to take assizes, juries, etc., that they should stay the taking of the same where the earls, barons, and others summoned to the king's parliament are parties, so long as the said parliament shall last.]

251. Ibid. m. 33 & 22.

252. [*Ed.:* Concerning the not proceeding to take assizes against those who come to the king's parliament at York.]

253. *In Scacc' ex Originali de Anno* 10 Edw. 3. Ro. 27. No.

254. That is, in Court of Parliament.

255. Citationes. This John de Thoresby was the Clerk of the Parliament.

sonamentum praedictum; amentum praedictum; Ita tamen quod nobis satisfaciant de redemptione sua occasione praemissorum, & quod super citationibus, moni-

[25] *tionibus, provocationi-|-bus, appellationibus seu instrumentis praedictis in dicta cancellaria, nostra sic factis processum aliquem non faciant, nec quicquam quod in nostri vel juris coronae nostrae praejudicium cedere possit attemptent vel attemptare faciant de caetero quovis modo. In Cujus, &c. Teste Rege apud Turrim London 15 die Aprilis, ex originali de Anno 10 E.3. Rot.27. Not.*[256]

[257] Priviledge of Parliament in informations for the King, generally the priviledge of Parliament do hold, unlesse it be in three cases, viz. Treason, Felony, and the the peace.

Of Statutes, or Acts of Parliament.

There is no Act of Parliament but must have the consent of the Lords, the Commons, and the Royall assent of the King, and as it appeareth by [a258]

256. [*Ed.:* The king to all his bailiffs and faithful subjects to whom (these presents shall come), etc., greeting. Know ye that, whereas our courts in which the business of our realm is transacted, wherever they are, are free and exempt, and since time immemorial have been free and exempt, so that neither matters concerning the ecclesiastical jurisdiction should be done or executed in our same courts nor ought anyone to enter the same courts in order to do or execute anything concerning the ecclesiastical jurisdiction, nor have they been accustomed to do so in times past; and whereas Master Henry de Harwedon, clerk, Edmund de Lukenore, and John de Wedlingburgh, have been convicted by the inquest on which they put themselves in our court before our beloved chancellor and others of our council, for that they lately in our Chancery, in the presence of the venerable father John, archbishop of Canterbury, our chancellor, made out certain citations or monitions to our beloved clerk John de Thoresby, and also provocations, appeals and public instruments upon the aforesaid citations and monitions, in contempt of us and our crown and in prejudice of our royal dignity, and against the liberty and exemption aforesaid, and for that reason have been committed to our prison therein to await our pleasure: We, of our especial grace, at the request of Philippa, queen of England, our most beloved consort, have pardoned the same Henry, Edmund, and John the aforesaid imprisonment; provided nevertheless that they satisfy us of their ransom by reason of the foregoing, and that they make no other process upon the citations, monitions, provocations, appeals or instruments aforesaid, so made in our said Chancery, nor henceforth in any way attempt or cause to be attempted anything which might tend to the prejudice of us or the right of our crown. In witness, etc. Witness the king at the Tower of London on the fifteenth day of April. From the original of the tenth year of Edward III, roll 27.]

257. Rot. Parl. *Anno* 17 Edw. 4. nu. 36. Vid. 21 Edw. 4. fol. 38, 39. Rot. Parl. *Anno* 8. Hen. 6. nu. 57. Vide infra. pa.

258. *a* Vid. 14 Ric. 2 nu. 15. & 13 Hen. 4. nu. 25.

Records and our [b259] Books whatsoever passeth in Parliament by this threefold consent, hath the force of an Act of Parliament.

The difference between and Act of Parliament, and an Ordinance in Parliament, is, for that the [c260] Ordinance wanteth the threefhold consent, and is ordained by one or two of them.

[d261] I have read of a restitution in blood, and of lands of one William de Lasenby by the King, by the assent of the Lords Spirituall, and Commons, (omitting the Lords Temporall) this we hold is an Ordinance, and no Act of Parliament. And when the Clergy is omitted and the Act made by the King, the Lords Temporall, and Commons. See the Rols of Parliament and authorities following, viz. Rot. Parl. Pasch. [e262] 15 E.2. the case of the Spencers.3. Ric. 2. cap.3. in print. Our Soveraigne Lord by the common consent of all the Lords Temporall, and at the petition of the Commons, &c. 7 Ric. 2. cap. 12. accord. 11 Ric. 2. nu.9, 10, 11. See Hen.5. c.7 [f263] 21 Ric. 2. nu.9. & 10. 6. Hen. 6. nu.27. 7 Hen. 8. Kelw. 184. the opinion of the Justices agreeable with the said Acts of Parliament. And note the mutability in this particular case of the Spencers, of this High Court of Parliament. The judgment by Parliament in 15 Edw. 2. against the Spencers, was in the same year by Act of Parliament repealed: that repeale was repealed by authority of Parliament in 1 Edw. 3. that repeal of 1 Edw. 3. was repealed by Act of Parliament in 21 Ric. 2. and that of 21 Ric. 2. was repealed by authority of Parliament in 1 Hen. 4. And so the judgment against the Spencers standeth in force.

The division of Acts of Parliament.

Of Acts of Parliament some be introductory of a new law, and some be declaratory of the ancient law, and some be of both kinds by addition of greater

---

259. *b* 4 Hen. 7. 18. b. p *tours les Justices.* 7 Hen. 7. 14 & 16. 11 Hen. 7. 27. 2. Brook prerogative 134. Fortescue fo. 20. cap. 18. Dier 1 Mar. 92.

260. *c* Rot. Parl. 25 Edw. 3. nu. 16, &c. 39 Edw. 3. 12. 22 Edw. 3. 3. 8 Hen. 6. cap. 29. Dier 4 Mar. 144. 39 Edw. 3. 7. Thorp *male erravit.* Rot. Parl. 37 Edw. 3. nu. 39. 1 Ric. 2. nu. 56. diversity between Acts of Parliament and Ordinance. 2 R 2. stat. 2. nu 28.

261. *d* 13 Hen. 4. nu. 20.

262. *e* Repeal 1 Edw. 3. cap. 2. stat. 1. 15 Edw. 3. tit. petition. Edw. 2. See Rot. Pat. An. 1 H. 4. part 5. m. 36. the Isle of Man given to the king by the Lords Temporall and Commons.

263. *f* Repeal. 1 H. 4. cap. 3.

penalties or the like. Againe, of Acts of Parliament, some be generall, and some be private and particular. All Acts of Parliament relate to the first day of Parliament, if it be not otherwise provided by the Act.[264]

The severall formes of Acts of Parliament.

In ancient time all Acts of Parliament were in form of Petitions. And for the severall forms of Acts of Parliament, see the Princes case in the 8 Book of Reports.[265] Now for the reading, committing, amending, ingrossing, voting, and passing of Bils in either House, and touching conferences with the Lords, and for the priviledge of any Member of either Houses, and of their servants more then hath been said, they be so ordinary and well known, and in such continual practice, as it were but expence of time to treat any more of them. And for that many times the Rols of the Parliament have not been truly in-

[26]   grossed, at I the request of the Commons certain of them are to be appointed, who should be at the ingrossing of the Rols of Parliament.

In former times Acts of Parliament were proclaimed by the Sheriffes.

When I read the case of Premunire in 39 Edw. 3. upon the statute of 27 Edw. 3. at provisors against the Bishop of Chichester, and observing that Sergeant Cavendish of councel with the Bishop objected two things: first, that the Act whereupon the Writ was grounded, was no statute. Secondly, that if it were a statute, it was never published in the County: whom Sir Robert Thorpe Chief Justice answered. Although proclamation be not made in the County, every one is bound to take notice of that which is done in Parliament: for as soon as the Parliament hath concluded any things, the law intends, that every person hath notice thereof, for the Parliament represents the Body of the whole Realm: and therefore it is not requisite that any Proclamation be made, seeing the Statute took effect before. This gave me to understand, that albeit it was not required by law that statutes should be published in the County; yet seeing in those dayes and long after, the use of printing came not into this

---

264. 33 H. 6. fol 17.
265. Dier. 3 Mar. 131. lib. 8. fo. 1. the Princes case. Concerning the ingrossing in Rols of Acts of parliament. Rot. Parl. 7 Hen. 4. nu. 65.

Realm:[266] the use was (as it appeareth by Cavendishes speech) that they should be published in the County, to the end that the Subjects might have expresse notice thereof, and not to be overtaken by an intendment in law, which gave me occasion to search and inquire how this usage was, and how long it continued. And in the end I found, that at every Parliament the Acts that passed were transcribed into Parchment, and by the Kings Writ directed of the Sheriffe of every County of England, and commandement given to him, that all the said statutes in all places through his whole Bayliwick, as well within Franchise as without, where he should finde most fit, that he not only should proclaime them, but to see that they should be firmely observed and kept. And the usage was to proclaim them at his County Court, &c. and there to keep the transcript of the Acts, that who so would, might reade or take copies thereof. And this Writ was sometime in Latine and sometime in French, as in those dayes the statutes were enacted in Latin or in French. But an example of the one, and of the other will more illustrate this matter.

Edwardus Dei grat' Rex Angliae & Franciae,[267] *& Dominus Hiberniae Vic' Norff. Salut. Quaedam statuta p. nos, Praelatos, Comites, Barones, & alios magnates ad Parliamentum nostrum tentum apud Eborum in Crō. Ascensionis ultim' praeterit' ordinavimus & stabilivimus, prout sequitur,*[268] and recite the severall statutes *verbatim.* And then the Writ concludeth. *Et ideo tibi praecipimus, quod statuta illa & omnes articulos in eisdem contentos in singulis locis in baliva tua, tam infra libertates, quam extra, ubi expedire videris, publice proclamari & firmiter teneri & observari facias. Teste, &c.*[269]

Richard p. la grace de Dieu Roy Dengliterre & de France, & Seigniour d'Ireland a nostre Viscount de Norff. Salut. Sachés que al honeur de Dieu, & reverence de

Nota that the Sheriffe that hath Custodiam comitatus, should see the statutes within his County to be kept. At the Parliament An. I Ric. 2.

---

266. *John Moore.* Printing was invented in Meath in Germany, *Anno Domini* 1441. and came to us in the raign of Hen. 6. See Bodin *De Methodo historiae.* li. 7. *Una typographia cum omnibus omnium veterum inventis certare facile potest. Polydor Virgil de invent. rerum lib. 2. cap. 7. Cardan. de varietate rerum lib. 3. cap. 64.*

267. At the Parliament in *Anno* 10 Edw. 3.

268. [*Ed.:* Edward, by the grace of God, king of England and France, and lord of Ireland, to the sheriff of Norfolk, greeting. We have ordained and established certain statues, as follows, [made] by us, the prelates, earls, barons and other great men at our parliament held at York on the morrow of the Ascension last past . . .]

269. [*Ed.:* And therefore we command you that you cause those statutes, and all the articles contained in the same, to be publicly proclaimed in every place within your bailiwick, both within liberties and without, where you shall think fit, and to be firmly held and kept. Witness, etc.]

Saint Esglise & pur nurrer peace, unitie, & concord in touts parts deins nostre
realme, le quel nolus desirons mult entirement, del assent des Prelats, Dukes, Counts
& Barons de mesme nostre realme, al instance & speciall request des Commons
de nostre Realme assembles a nostre Parliament tenus a Westm, a la quinzim de
S. Michaell an de nostre reigne primier avons fait ordeiner & stablier certaine
statuts en amendment & relievement de mesme nostre Realme, & en la forme que
sensuist. Primerment est assentus & establie, que saint Eglise eit & enjoy se touts
les droitures, &c.[270] rehearsing all the statutes that passed at that Parliament.
And the Writ concludeth thus. *Et pur ceo vous mandons que touts les statuts*
faces crier & publier, & firmament tener p. my vostre Baillie solonq; la forme &
tenor de icel, & ceo ne lesses en ascun manner. Donc p testmoignants de nostre
grand seale al Westm. le primier jour de Feverer lan de nostre reigne primier.[271]
And the like Writs continued untill the beginning of the reign of Hen. 7. long
time after printing within the reign of Hen. 6. (as hath bin said) came unto
us.

[27] | Prorogation, Adjournment, Continuance,
                              and what maketh a Session of Parliament.

The passing of any Bill or Bils by giving the Royall assent thereunto, or the
giving and judgement in Parliament doth not make a Session, but the Session
doth continue untill that Session be prorogued or dissolved: and this is evident
by many presidents in Parliament ancient and late.

The Parliament of 14 Edw. 3.[272] began at Westminster the Wednesday after
Mid Lent: the first monday of the Parliament, the ninth part of their Grain,

---

270. [*Ed.:* Richard, by the grace of God king of England and of France, and lord of Ireland, to our
sheriff of Norfolk, greeting. Know ye that to the honour of God and reverence of Holy Church, and to
nurture peace, unity and concord in all parts within our realm, which we very earnestly desire, with the
assent of the prelates, dukes, earls and barons of our realm assembled at our parliament held at Westminster
in the quindene of Michaelmas in the first year of our reign, we have caused to be ordained and established
certain statutes in amendment and relief of our same realm, in the following form. Firstly it is assented
and established that Holy Church shall have and enjoy all her rights, etc.]

271. [*Ed.:* And therefore we command you to cause all the statutes to be proclaimed and published,
and firmly kept, throughout your bailiwick, according to the form and tenor thereof; and do not in any
way fail to do this. Given by witness of our great seal at Westminster on the first day of February in the
first year of our reign.]

272. Rot. Parl. 14 Edw. 3. Stat. primo. nu 7, 8, 9, &c.

Wooll, and Lambe, &c. was granted to the King, on condition that the King would grant their petitions in a Schedule beginning. These be the petitions which by the Commons and Lords was drawne into a forme of a Statute, and passed both Houses, and the Royall assent thereunto, and the same exemplified under the Great Seal. After this the Parliament continued, and divers Acts made, and petitions granted, and in the end that Parliament was dissolved.

In the Parliament holden *Anno* 3 Ric. 2.[273] it is declared by Act of Parliament that the killing of John Imperiall Ambassadour of Jenoa, was High Treason, *crimen laesae majestatis*,[274] and yet the Parliament continued long after, and divers Act of Parliament afterwards made, and petitions granted: and in the end the Parliament dissolved.

In the Parliament begun the first day of March, *Anno* 7 Hen.4.[275] on Saturday the 8 day of May it was enacted by the King, the Lords Spirituall and Temporall, and the Commons, that certain strangers by name, who seemed to be Officers to the Queen, should by a day depart the Realm, and proclamation thereof in kinde made by Writ, by authority of Parliament, which Parliament continued, and divers other Acts of Parliament made, and petitions answered: and on the 22 day of December 8 Hen.4. dissolved.

The Parliament begun 7 November,[276] and on the first day of the Parliament it was resolved by all the Judges, that those that were attainted of treason, and returned Knights, Citizens, or Burgesses of Parliament, that the attainders here to be reversed by authority of Parliament before they could sit in the House of Commons: and that after the attainders reversed, both the Lords, and those of the House of Commons might take their places, for such as were attainted could not be lawfull Judges, so long as their attainders stood in force: and thereupon the attainders were reversed by Act of Parliament, and then they took their places in Parliament, and the Parliament continued, and divers Acts made.

[277]The Bill of Queen Katherine Howards attainder passed both Houses

---

273. Rot. Parl. 3 Ric. 2. nu. 8. &c.

274. [*Ed.:* the crime of lese-majesty, or injuring majesty or royalty; high treason.]

275. Rot. Parl. 7 Hen. 4. nu. 29. &c.

276. Rot. Parl. 2 Hen. 7. nu. 1 Hen. 7. fo. 4. b.

277. *Rot. Par. 33 Hen. 8 begun the 16 day of January, and continued till the first of April following. On the 12 of February the Queen was beheaded in the Tower, sitting the Parliament. *Prorogo, à porro & rogo, unde prorogatio. Adjourner, unde adjournare, & adjournamentum, est ad diem dicere, or diem dare.*

about the beginning of the Parliament, whereunto the King sitting the Parliament by his Letters Patents gave his Royall assent, and yet the Parliament continued untill the first day of Aprill, and divers Acts of Parliament passed after the said Royall assent given. Divers more might be produced, but these shall suffice. So as albeit Bils passe both Houses, and the Royall assent given thereunto, there is no Session untill a prorogation or a dissolution.

The diversity between a prorogation and an adjournment, or continuance of the Parliament, is, that by the prorogation in open Court there is a Session, and then such Bils as passed in either House, or by both Houses, and had no Royall assent to them, must at the next assembly begin again, &c. for every severall Session of Parliament is in law a severall Parliament: but if it be but adjourned or continued, then is there no Session: and consequently, all things continue still in the same state they were in before the adjournment or continuance.

And the title of divers Acts of Parliament be, At the Session holden by prorogation, or by adjournment and prorogation, but never by continuance or adjournment *tantum*. And the usuall form of pleading is; *ad Sessionem tentam, &c. per prorogationem.*[278]

[28]   I We have been the longer and more curious for the clearing of this point for two reasons, 1. For that the adjournment or continuance (as before it appeareth) is much more beneficiall for the Common-wealth for expediting of causes, then a prorogation. 2. In respect of a clause in the Act of Subsidie in the Parliament holden in Anno 18 Jac. Regis, which is but declaratory of the former law, as by that which hath been said appeareth.

When a Parliament is called and both sit, and is dissolved without any Act of Parliament passed, or judgement given, it is no Session of Parliament, but a Convention.

In the 18 year of Ric.2.[279] at a Parliament holden before the Duke of York

---

Rot. Parl. 23 Hen. 8. 24 Hen. 8. nu. 1. 25 Hen 8. nu. 1. 26 Hen. 8. nu. 1. 27 Hen. 8. nu. 1 &c. 2 & 3 E. 6. nu 1. 3 & 4 Edw. 6. nu. 1. &c. 1 Mariae Sess. 2. 28. Eliz. nu. 1. &c. And in every of them it is said [and there continued until such a day;] and yet in them divers adjournments were. See the Journall Book in the Lords House. *Ultimo Junii 14 Eliz. Custos Magni Sigilli ex mandato Dominae Reginae adjournavit praesens Parliament' usq; in festum omnium. Sanctorum.* And in the Parliament in *Anno* 39 Eliz. *Custos magni Sigilli ex mandato Dominae Reginae* (the Queen being absent.)

    278. [*Ed.:* at the session held, etc. by prorogation.]
    279. Rot. Parl. 18. Ric. 2. which began 15 Hilarii.

(the King being in his passage to Ireland) the Petitions of the Commons were answered: and a Judgement given in the Kings Bench for the Prior of Newport; pannell, against the Dean and Chapter of Lichfield was reversed, but no Act of Parliament passed, and therefore this Parliament is omitted in the print; but it is no question but it was a Session of Parliament, for otherwise the Judgment should not be of force: and many times Judgements given in Parliament have been executed, the Parliament continuing before any Bill passed.

The House of Commons is a distinct Court.

Nota, the House of Commons is to many purposes a distinct Court, and therefore is not prorogued, or adjourned by the prorogation or adjournment of the Lords House: but the Speaker upon signification of the Kings pleasure by the assent of the House of Commons, both say: This Court doth prorogue or adjourne it self; and then it is prorogued or adjourned, and not before. But when it is dissolved, the House of Commons are sent for up to the higher House, and there the Lord Keeper by the Kings commandement dissolveth the Parliament; and then it is dissolved, and not before. And the King at the time of the dissolution ought to be there in person, or by representation: for as it cannot begin without the presence of the King either in person or by representation (as before it hath been said) so it cannot end or be dissolved without his presence either in person or by representation.[280] *Nihil enim tam conveniens est naturali aequitati, unumquodq; dissolvi eo ligamine quo ligatum est.*[281]

It is declared by Act of Parliament,[282] that the Kings Letters Patents under his Great Seale, and signed with his hand, and declared and notified in his absence to the Lords Spritiuall and Temporall and Commons assembled in the Higher House of Parliament, is, and ever was of as good strength and force, as if the Kings person had been there personally present, and had assented openly and publickly to the same.

---

280. Bracton.

281. [*Ed.:* For nothing is so consonant with natural equity as that everything should be untied with the same bond by which it has been tied.]

282. 33 Hen. 8. ca. 21. Royall assent by Letters Patents. Dier. 1 Mar. 93. *Commission au 4 seigniors, &c. a doner royall assent & indorcement sait. Soit sait come est desire.*

Of Subsidies and Aides granted by Parliament.

Subsidie is derived of the Verb *Subsidiari,* which signifieth to be ready to help at need, *unde subsidium,* which signifieth aide and help at need, so properly called, when Souldiers were ready to help the foreward of the battell: and aptly was the word so derived, as well because that which we call now *subsidia,* Subsidies, were anciently called *auxilia,* Aides, granted by Act of parliament upon need and necessity: as also, for that originally and principally they were granted for the defence of the Realm, and the safe keeping of the seas, &c. *Communia pericula requirunt communia auxilia.*[283]

This word [Subsidie] is common, as well to the English, as to the French, Concerning Subsidies hear what a stranger truly writeth. *Reges Angliae nihil tale, nisi convocatis primis ordinibus, & assentiente populo, suscipiunt.*[284] *Quae consuetudo valde mihi laudanda videtur; interveniente enim populi voluntate & assensu crescit robur, & potentia regum, & major est ipsorum authoritas, & feliciores progressus.*[285]

Subsidies taken in their generall sense for Parliamentary Aides are divided into perpetuall and temporary: perpetuall into three parts, viz. into *Custuma*

[29] | *antiqua, sive magna,*[286] *custuma nova sive parva,*[287] *and into custome* of Broad cloth. Temporary, whereof there are three kindes, viz. 1. of Tonnage and Poundage of ancient time granted for a year or years incertainly, and of latter times for life. 2. A Subsidie after the rate of 4s. in the pound for lands, and 2 s. 8 d. for goods. And 3 for an Aide called a Fifteenth, And of these in order.

Custuma antiqua sive magna.

Custuma antiqua sive magna was by Act of Parliament granted to King Edward the First his heirs and successors for transportation of three things, viz.[288]

---

283. [*Ed.:* Common dangers require common aids.]

284. Ph. Cominaeus, Lib. 5. fo. 233.

285. [*Ed.:* The kings of England take nothing of this kind except after calling together those of the first rank, and with the assent of the people. This custom seems to me very praiseworthy; for with the will and assent of the people the authority and power of the king grow strong, and his authority is the greater, and his progresses more happy.]

286. [*Ed.:* Reports of Ancient or great customs duties on wool, sheepskin, or wool pelts, and leather.]

287. [*Ed.:* (literally, "small and new customs"). Imports of 3. d in the pound due formerly in England from merchant strangers only, for all commodities imported and exported.]

288. See hereafter, c. 11. Verb. de nous Customes, &c. Rot. sinium Au. 3 Edw. 1. Rot. Pa. 3 Edw. 1. m.

Wools, Woolsels, and Leather, viz. for every sack of wool containing thirty six stone, and every stone fourteen pound, half a mark; and for three hundred woolsels half a mark, and for a last of Leather thirteen shillings four pence, to be paid as well by Strangers as by English. *Praelati, magnates, & tota communitas concesserunt quandam novam consuetudinem nobis de lanis, pellibus & coriis dimid' marc', de 300. pellibus dimid' marc', & de lasta coriorum unam marcam.*[289] In the statute called *confirmationes cartarum Anno* 25 Edw.1.[290] there is a saving in these words, *Save a nous, & nous heires la custome des leynes, pealx & quires grant' perle Comminalty du realm.*[291] See also the like in the preamble:[292] *Salva tamen nobis & haeredibus nostris custuma lanarum, pellium & coriorum per Communitatem dicti regni nobis prim' concess.*[293]

[294] Note it is said in divers Records, *per Communitatem Angliae nobis concess,* '[295] because all grants of Subsidies or Aids by Parliament doe begin in the House of Commons, and first granted by them: also because in effect the whole profit which the King reapeth doth come from the Commons.

Custuma parva & nova.[296,297]

In the 31 year of Edw.1. the Merchant strangers in consideration of certain liberties and priviledges granted to them, and a release to them of all prizes and takings, gave to the King and his heirs, three shillings four pence, *ultra*

Custome is derived of the French word *custom*.

---

1. dat. 10 Novemb, which was in the end of the year, for he began his reign 17 Nov. *Confirmat. Cartarum Vet. Mag. Cart.* 2. parte fo. 36. a.

289. [*Ed.:* The prelates, magnates, and whole community, have granted us a certain new custom of wools, fells and leather, [. . .] half a mark, of three hundred fells half a mark, and of a last of leather one mark.]

290. [*Ed.:* Confirmations of the charters in the year 25 Edw. I.]

291. [*Ed.:* Saving to us, and our heirs, the custom of wools, fells and leather granted by the commonalty of the realm.]

292. *Int. brevia de* Term Mich. 26 Edw. 1. *In offiremem. regis.*

293. [*Ed.:* Saving nevertheless to us and our heirs the customs of wool, fells, and leather first granted to us by the commnalty of our said realm.]

294. *a* 12 Hen. 4. nu. 45. 6 Hen. 6. nu. 11. 12 and. 4. ca. 3. 7. Edw. 4. nu. 30. 1 Edw. 6. ca. 13. 1 Marr. cap. 18. 1 Eliz. ca. 19. & 3 Jac. *Regis accord.*

295. [*Ed.:* granted to us by the commonalty of England.]

296. [*Ed.:* The small and new custom.]

297. i. *Tributum seu vestigal.* Rot. Cart. 31 Edw. 1. nu. 44. called *Carta mercatoria.* This was questioned Rot. ordinat. *Anno* 5 Edw. 2. but allowed of in Parliament, *Anno* 1 Edw. 3. 9 ca. 1. 27. Edw. 3. Stat. Stap. ca. 26. F. N. B. 227. d. 259. a.

antiquam custumam ut prius concess.[298] So as where the Subject paid a Noble, the Stranger paid ten shillings, &c. See the statutes of 1 Hen.7. ca.2. 11 Hen.7. cap.14. 22 Hen.8. cap.8.

Custome of what things, ex antiquo.[299]

And it is to be observed, that of ancient time no Custome was by English or Stranger, but for Wools, Woolfels, and Leather.[300] Hereby it appeareth how necessary the knowledge of ancient Records and of the true originall of every thing is.

In the reign of Edw.3. a great part of the Wools for the which such Custome was granted, and paid, as is aforesaid, was draped into broad Cloth: whereupon question grew, whether upon the transportation of the Cloth, into which the Wool was draped, Custome should be proportionably paid, having regard to the quantity of the Wool so converted into Cloth: and it was resolved, that no Custome should in that case be paid, because the Wool by the labour and industry of man was changed into another kind of merchandise: wherewith the King held himself satisfied, and so it appeareth in the Kings own Writs and Records enrolled in the Exchequer.

Of Wools draped into Cloth no Custome was due.

The first Act of Parliament that gave any Subsidy of Cloth was in *Anno* 21 Edw.3. (not printed) viz. fourteen pence of Lieges and one and twenty pence of Strangers, for every Cloth of Assise, and two shillings four pence of Lieges, and three shillings six pence of Strangers for every Cloth of Scarlet, &c. *Vide inter Original' de Scaccario,*[301] 24 Edw.3. Rot. 13.[302] And the reason of granting the said Subsidies of broad Cloth was, *Quia jam magna pars lanae regni nostri in eodem regno pannificitur, de qua Custuma aliqua non est soluta, per quod proficuum quod de Custumis & Subsidiis lanarum, si extra dictum regnum ducerentur, percipere debemus, in multo diminuuntur, &c.*[303] And yet if in any case

[30]

---

298. [*Ed.:* above the ancient custom as first granted.]

299. [*Ed.:* anciently.]

300. 1 El. Dier 165.

301. [*Ed.:* See among the *Originalia* rolls of the Exchequer.]

302. Int. Orig. de Scaccario. 10. 24 Edw. 3. Rot 13. ib. 27 Edw. 3. Rot 4. See the Second part of the *Institutes, Mag. Cart.* cap. 30. p. 60. By 27 Edw. 3. stat. 1. & ca. 4 Custome of Cloth.

303. [*Ed.:* Because now the great part of the wool of our realm is made into cloth within the same realm, whereof no custom is now paid, so that the profit that we ought to receive from the customs and subsidies of wool, if it was taken out of the realm, is greatly lessened, etc.]

the King might by his Prerogative have set any imposition, he might have set one in that case, for that, as it appeareth by that Record, by making of Cloth the King lost his Customes of Wool: and therefore for further satisfaction of the King for the Custome of Wool; at the Parliament holden in *Anno 27 Edw.3.* a Subsidy was granted to the King his heirs and successors, ([304] over the Customes thereof due) viz. of every whole Cloth of Assise not ingrained, four pence, and for the half of such a Cloth, two pence, and of every Cloth ingrained five pence, and of the halfe two pence half penny, and of every Cloth of Scarlet six pence, and of the half three pence; and the Alnegers fee is granted to him by Act of Parliament. viz. for the measuring of every Cloth of Assise of the Seller a halfpenny, and of half a cloth a farthing for his office, and no more, nor shall they take anything for a cloth that is lesse; and that he take nothing of the Alnage of any cloth but only of such cloth as is to be sold. And both in this Act, and in some Acts in the reign of Hen.3. *consuetudines & custumae,*[305] which are englished, Customes, are taken for the Subsidies that were granted by Parliament, for verily those were ancient and right Customes or Subsidies. And in the statute of 11 Hen.4. Customes and Subsidies are used as *Synonymaes.*[306]

Butlerage.

Butlerage is a Custome due to the King of two shillings of every Tun of Wine brought into this Realm by Strangers: but Englishmen payeth it not.

In libro Rubeo in Scaccario in custodia Rememoratoris Regis,[307] fol. 265.[308] the grant of King John to the Merchants of Aquitain trading for wines thence into England of divers liberties, viz. *De libertatibus concessis mercatoribus vinetariis de Ducatu Aquitaniae, reddendo regi & haeredibus suis 2.S.: de quolibet dolio vini ducti per eosdem infra regnum Angliae vel potestate regis.*[309]

---

304. Viz. the Subsidies granted in *Anno* 21 Edw. 3. The Alnagers fee of the subject granted by Parliament. Mag. Cart. ca. 30. Consuetudines. Stat. de Scaccario. 51 Hen. 3. Custum des Leynes. 11 Hen. 4. ca. 7.

305. [*Ed.:* [both words mean 'customs'].]

306. [*Ed.:* synonyms.]

307. [*Ed.:* In the Red Book of the Exchequer, in the keeping of the king's remembrancer.]

308. Lib. rubeus in Scacc. fo. 265. Vid. 6 Edw. 3. fo. 5. & 6. the Archb. of Yorks case.

309. [*Ed.:* Concerning liberties granted to the wine merchants of the duchy of Aquitaine, paying to the king and his heirs two shillings for every tun of wine brought by the same within the realm of England or the king's jurisdiction.]

All Merchant Strangers in consideration of the grant to them by the King of divers liberties and freedoms, *concesserunt quod de quolibet dolio vini quod adducent vel adduci facerent infra regnum, &c. solvent nobis & haeredibus nostris nomine Custumae duos solidos, &c.*[310,311]

Prisage.

Prisage is a Custome due to the King of the wines brought in by the Merchants of England of every Ship having twenty Tuns or more,[312] two Tuns, viz. one before the Mast, and the other behind, paying twenty shillings for each Tun; and this is called *certa prisa,*[313] and *recta prisa,*[314] and *regia prisa,*[315] as in the Record ensuing appeareth, and hereof Merchant Strangers are discharged, per *cartam mercatoriam,*[316] 31 Edw.1. *Ubi supra.*

Memorandum quod rex habet ex antiqua consuetudine de qualibet nave mercatoris vini 6. carcat' applican' infra aliquem portum Angliae de viginti doliis duo dolia, & de decem doliis unum de prisa regia pro quodam certo ab antiquo constitut' solvend'.[317,318]

Hereby it appeareth that Prisage is due by prescription, and that it was a certainty of ancient time ordained to be paid.

It is called Butlerage because the Kings chief Butler doth receive it, and Prisage, because it is a certain taking or purveyance for wine to the Kings use.[319]

Concerning the Alonging of new Draperies.

In Hilary Tearm, *Anno 2 Jac. Regis,* upon a suit made to the King by the Duke of Lenox, question was moved concerning new Draperies, as Friza-

---

310. Rot. *Cartarum Anno* 31 Edw. 1 nu. 44. called *Carta mercatoria.*

311. [*Ed.:* granted that for every tun of wine which they should bring or caused to be brought within the realm, etc. they would pay to us and our heirs two shillings in the name of custom, etc.]

312. Fleta li. 2. ca. 21. Rot. Pat. 40 Hen. 3. Rot. Pa. 28. E. 1. *pro Math. de Columbar'.*

313. [*Ed.:* certain prise.]

314. [*Ed.:* right prise.]

315. [*Ed.:* royal prise.]

316. [*Ed.:* by the merchant charter.]

317. P. Rec. 20 Ric. 2. Vid. Tr. 33. Edw. 1. Rot. 124. *Prisae Vinorum in Hibernia.*

318. [*Ed.:* Be it remembered that the king has by ancient custom from every merchant-ship laden with wine, landing within any port of England, for twenty tuns of wine, two tuns, and for ten tuns, one, to be paid for the royal prise as established since ancient times.]

319. 43 Edw. 3. ca. 3. & 1 Hen. 8. ca. 5.

l-does, Bayes, Northern Cottons, Northern Dozens, Clothrash, Durances, [31] perpetuanoes, Fustians, Canvas, Sackcloth, Worsteads, and Stuffs made of Worstead yarn, whether the King might grant the Alnaging of them with a reasonable fee, or whether they were within the said statute of 27 Edw.3. And these questions were by the Kings commandment in this Hilary Term referred to all the Judges of England to certifie their opinions concerning the suit to the Lords of his Privy Councell; who upon often hearing of the cause, and mature deliberation, and conference amongst themselves, in the end in Trinity Term following with one unanimous consent, certified in writing in these words following, viz. To the Lords and others of his Majestics most Honourable Privy Councell. Our duties to your Lordships remembred. May it please the same to be advertised, that according to your Letters in that behalf, we have heard the matter touching the tearm of the Alnage, and measurage, that is sought to be granted by his Majesty of sundry kindes, as well of new made Drapery, as of other Stuffs made within this Realm. And upon hearing as well of some of the part of the Master of Orkney, as of others, both of the behalf of the Duke of Lenox and Master Shaw, have informed our selves touching the same. And for our opinions we are resolved,[320] that all new made Drapery made wholly of wool, as Frizadoes, Bayes, Northern Dozens, Northern Cottons, Cloth rash, and other like Drapery, of what new name soever, for the use of mans body, are to yeeld Subsidy and Alnage according to the statute of 27 Edw.3. and within the office of the ancient Alnage, as may appear by severall decrees in that behalf made in the Exchequer in the time of the late Queen. But as touching Fustians, Canvas, Sackcloth and such like made meerly of other stuff then wool, or being but mixed with wool, we are of opinion, that no charge can be imposed for the search or measurage thereof, but that all such Patents so made are void, as may appear by a Record of the 11. year of H.4. wherein the reason of the judgment is particularly mentioned, which we held not amisse to set down to your Lordships, which is thus, The same King Henry the Fourth granted the measurage of all woollen Cloth and Canvas that should be brought to London to be sold by any stranger or denizen (except he were free of London) taking one half penny for every piece of Cloth so measured of the seller, and one other half penny of the buyer, and so after

320. See Rot. Parl. fo Edw. 3. nu. 142 Cogware Kerseys. See hereafter, cap. 67. See Rot. Parl. 9 Hen. 4. nu. 34. Kendall Clothes, &c. 11 Hen. 4. c. 2. enact. 11 Hen. 4. nu. 26. for remants of Cloth, &c. 11 Hen. 4. c. 7. Stat. 2.

the rate for a greater or lesser quantity, and one penny for the measuring of 100. els of Canvas of the seller, and so much more of the buyer. And although it were averrred that two other had enjoyed the same office before with the like fees, *viz.* one Shering by the same Kings grant, and one Clytheroe before by the grant of King Richard the Second yet, amongst other reasons of the Judgment, it was set down and adjudged, that the former possession was by extortion, and coertion, & without right, and that those Patents were *in onerationem, oppressionem & depauperationem populi domini regis, & non in emendationē ejusdem populi, &c.*[321] and no benefit to the King, and therefore the Patents void. And as touching the narrow new stuffe made in Norwich and other places with Worstead yarn, we are of opinion that it is not grantable, not fit to be granted, for we cannot find, that there was ever any Alnage upon Norwich Worsteads. And for these stuffs, if after they be made and tacked up for sale by the makers thereof, they should be again opened to be viewed and measured, they will not well fall into their old plaits to be tacked up as before, which will be (as is affirmed) a great hinderance to the sales thereof in grosse, for that they will not then appear to be so merchandizable, as they were upon the first making of them up: And even so we humbly take our leaves. Serjeants Inn, the 24. of June. 1605. Which Certificate being read by the Lords of the Privy Councell (I being then Atturny generall and present) was well approved by them all, and commandment given, that it should be kept in the Councell Chest to be a direction for them to give answer to all suits of that kind.

And it is to be observed,[322] that Acts of Parliament that are made against the freedome of trade, merchandizing, handycrafts, and mysteries, never live long.

[32] | Good Bils or motions in Parliament seldome die.

Bils, motions.

It is an observation proved by a great number of presidents,[323] that never any good bill was preferred, or good motion made in Parliament, whereof any

---

321. [*Ed.:* to the burdening, oppression and impoverishment of the lord king's people, and not for the improvement of the same people, etc.]

322. 37 Edw. 3. ca. 5, 6. 38 Edw. 3. ca. 2. Lib. 11. fo. 54. de Taylers de Ipswich.

323. 8 Edw. 2. nu. 17 Edw. 3. nu. 49 1 Ric. 2. nu. 82. 4 Ric. 2. nu. 36. 9 Ric. 2. nu. 44. 1 Hen. 4. nu. 121. 2 Hen. 4. nu. 83. 2 Hen. 4. nu. 70. 11 Hen. 4. nu. 47. 1 Hen. 5. 5. nu. 23. 7 Hen. 5. nu. 18. 1 Hen. 6

memoriall was made in the Journall book, or otherwise, though sometime it succeeded not at the first, yet hath it never died, but at one time or other hath taken effect; which may be a great encouragement to worthy and industrious attempts, as taking some few examples for many, which I have quoted in the margent.

The Subsidy of Tunnage and Poundage.

By the subsequent Records you shall observe 13. things 1. The grant of Poundage only. 2. Of Tunnage and Poundage. 3. Severall rates, sometimes 6.d. 8.d.11.d. for Poundage. 4. Sometimes 2, s. 18. d. 3. s. 5. *Hac vice,* 1,2,3,4. years, for life. 6. To Merchants, &c. 7. To have intermission and to vary lest the King should claim it as a duty, 8. Expressed upon free gift. 9. Upon condition to keep the Seas, and for commerce. 10. That is over the consideration and cause of the grant. 11. Granted without retrospect. 12. Sometimes double of Strangers. 13. Cloth excepted, that it be not subject to Tunnage and Poundage. 31 Hen.6.

[a]324 Of poundage only, and 6. d. inthe pound, for two years upon condition, if,

[b]325 6. d. for Poundage, and 2 s. for Tunnage of wine, *hac vice.*

[c]326 6. d. of every pound of merchandize, and 2.s. of every tun of wine, upon condition, &c. *hac vice.*[327]

[d]328 Sometime to have intermission, and to vary, lest the King should claim as duties.

[e]329 For Tunnage of wine 3.s. and 6.d. for Poundage for one year.

[f]330 3.s. for Tunnage of wine, 12 d. for Poundage, *hac vice.*

[g]331 6 d. for Poundage, and 18.d. for Tunnage of wine for three years.

The records.

nu. 41. 7 Edw. 4. nu. 20. *Acts of Parliament.* 2 Edw. 3. cap. 2. 25 Edw. 3. ca 5. 4 Hen. 4. ca. 22. 1 Hen. 5. cap. 1. 15 Hen. 6. ca. 14. 1 Ric. 3. ca. 3. 21 Hen. 8. cap. 5. 23 Hen. 8. cap. 4. 26 Hen. 8. cap. 3. 31 Hen. 8. ca. 1. 32 Hen. 8. cap. 32. 2 Hen. 6. cap. 8. &c 13. 1 & 2 Ph. & Mar. cap. 13. *Vide Infra,* cap. 8. pa.

324. *a* 47 Edw. 3. nu. 12.

325. *b* 6 Ric. 2. nu. 13.

326. *c* 7 Ric. 2 stat. 1.

327. [*Ed.:* on this occasion.]

328. *d* 5 Ric. 2 nu. 40. 9 Ric. 2. nu. 11. 10 Ric. 2. nu. 18. 11 Ric. 2. nu. 12.

329. *e* 13 Ric. 2. nu. 20.

330. *f* 14 Ric. 2. nu. 12.

331. *g* 17 Ric. 2. nu. 12.

[h332] 8. d. for Poundage and 2.s. for Tunnage of wine.

[i333] 2. d. for Poundage, and 3.s. for Tunnage of wine for three years.

[k334] 12. d. for Poundage, and 3.s. for Tunnage of wine for severall times upon condition, sometime for one year. In these and most of the former granted upon condition for due employment [1335] of their own good will, and so entred, and the King to have a certain sum [m336] more expresly.

[n337] 12. d. for Poundage, and 3.s. for Tunnage of wine for four years.

[o338] The like Subsidy is granted to the King for his life upon conditions &c. which was the first grant of Tunnage and Poundage for life, which was a leading grant, as hereafter appeareth.

[p339] The Subsidy of Poundage only for two years.

[q340] Tunnage of wine and Poundage granted for severall years.

[r341] Tunnage and Poundage, *ut prius* of Denizens, double of Strangers.

Note.

[s342] Tunnage of wine and Poundage granted to Henry the Sixth for life with an exception of all woollen Cloth: and here Cloth was first excepted, and was a leading exception in all subsequent acts.

[t343] Tunnage of wine and Poundage granted to Edward the Fourth for life with no retrospect, but for the time to come.

Not printed, for he had many subsidies, but printed none.

[u344] At the Parliament holden *Anno* 1 Hen.7. a like Act was made for the grant of the Subsidies of Tunnage and Poundage to him for his life.

[x345] And the like Subsidy was granted to King Henry the Eighth at the Parliament holden *Anno* 1. of his reign for his life.

[33]

I The like grant was made to Edward the Sixth. Queen Mary, Queen Eliz-

332. *h* 2 H. 4. nu. 9.
333. *i* 4 H. 4. nu. 28.
334. *k* 6 Hen. 4. nu. 9. 8 Hen. 4. nu. 9. 9 Hen. 4. nu. 27.
335. *l* 11 Hen. 4. nu. 45.
336. *m* 13 Hen. 4. nu. 10.
337. *n* 1 H. 5. nu. 17.
338. *o* 3 H. 5. nu. 50.
339. *p* 2 Hen. 6. nu. 14.
340. *q* 3 Hen. 6. nu. 17. 9 Hen. 6. nu. 14.
341. *r* 23 Hen. 6. nu. 16.
342. *s* 31 Hen. 6. nu. 8. & cap. 8.
343. *t* 4 Edw. 4. & 12 Edw. 4. ca. 3. in print.
344. *u* Rot. Par. 1. Hen. 7.
345. *x* Rot. Parl. 1 Hen. 8. not printed. Vid. 6 Hen. 8. ca. 14. in print.

abeth and King James[346] for their severall lives, and in all these it is affirmed, that the like grants were made by Act of Parliament to King Henry the Seventh and King Henry the Eighth.

The consideration of the grant of these Subsidies of Tunnage and Poundage is ever, as is aforesaid, expressed in the grant, for the keeping and safeguard of the Seas, and for intercourse of merchandize safely to come into this Realm, and safely to passe out of the same. And this pertaineth properly to the office of the Lord Admirall to see the consideration of the Act to be performed.[347] They are granted of the free good will of the subjects, and so expressly set down in the Parliament Roll.

In King James his reign, when I was a Commissioner of the Treasury, these Subsidies granted for life amounted to One hundred and threescore thousand pounds *per annum*[348] and so letten to farm. The values of the merchandize for the which the Subsidy of Poundage is paid, do appear in a book of rates in print whereby the Merchant knows what he is to pay. The Subsidy of Tunnage of wine is certain in these Acts by the contents of the Vessels: and none of these Acts doe extend to any other liquid merchandize imported or exported, but unto wines only: and seeing nothing is more incertain then the continuance of the values of merchangdizes wherefore the Subsidy of Poundage is paid, it were good at every grant of them to set down the rates in a schedule annexed to the bill.

A book of rates or values.

Subsidies temporary and usuall at this day.

Subsidies temporary and usuall at this day. And this is when the Commons in Parliament freely grant to the King an aid to be levied of every Subject of his lands or goods after the rate of 4 s. in the pound for lands, and 2 s. 8 d. for goods, and for Aliens for goods double, to such ends and for such considerations, and to be paid at such times, as by the Acts thereof (which are usuall and frequent) doe appear. And in former times in this kind of Subsidy, this order was obserbed, that over and above the Subsidy of Tunnage and Poundage, the Commons never gave above one Subsidy of this kind, and two

346. 1 Edw. 6. ca. 13. 1 Mar. cap. 18. 1 Eliz. cap. 19. 1 Jac. ca. 33.
347. *Rot. Par. 11 Hen. 4. nu 45. 13 Hen. 4. nu. 10.
348. [*Ed.:* yearly.]

Fifteens, (and sometime lesse) one Subsidy amounting to Seventy thousand pounds, and each fifteen at Twenty nine thousand pounds, or near thereabouts; nor above one Subsidy, which did rise to Twenty thousand pounds, the Clergy gave not.

At the Parliament holden in 31 Eliz. the Commons gave two Subsidies, and four Fifteens, which first brake the circle.

In 35 Eliz. three Subsidies and six Fifteens.

In 39 Eliz. three Subsidies and six fifteens.

In 43 Eliz. four Subsidies and eight Fifteens, &c.

In 31 Jac. Regis, three Subsidies and five Fifteens in shorter times then had been before.

In 3 Car. Regis, five Subsidies in shortest time of all.

And it is worthy of observation how quietly Subsidies granted in forms usuall and accustomable (though heavy) are borne; such a power hath use and custome: On the other side, what descontments and disturbances Subsidies framed in new molds doe raise, (such an inbred hatred novelty doth hatch) is evident by examples of former times:

As that of 4 Ric.2.[349] a new invention of Subsidies of the Kings Subjects of either sex by the poll, &c. for the furnishing of the Earl of Buckingham for his going into France, whereupon a strong and a strange Rebellion ensued, wherein three great and worthy Officers were by the rascall Rebels barbarously and wickedly murdred, viz. Simon Sudbury Archbishop of Canterbury, Chancelour of England, the Prior of S. Johns of Jerusalem, Treasurer of England, and Sir John Cavendish Chief Justice of England.

In 4 Hen.7.[350] another like new found Subsidy was granted, which raised a rebellion in the North, in which the noble Earl of Northumberland a Commissioner in that Subsidy, was by the Rebels cruelly and causelesly slain.

[34]　　　I In *Anno* 16 Hen.8.[351] to furnish the King for his going in his royall person into France, a new device for getting of mony was set on foot, which made the headlesse and heedlesse multitude to rise in rebellion, untill Charles Brandon the noble Duke of Suff' quieted, and dispersed them.

At the Parliament holden in 9 Edw.3.[352] when a motion was made for a

---

349. Rot. Part. 4 Ric. 3. nu. 15. 5 Ric. 2. nu. 32.
350. Hollensh. Chron. 769.
351. Hollensh. Chron. 891.
352. Rot. Par. 9 Edw. 3. nu. 5.

Subsidy to be granted of a new kind, the Commons answered, that they would have conference with those of their severall Countries and places, who had put them in trust, before they treated of any such matter.

Vide 9 Hen.6. nu. 15.[353] Every Knights fee to pay 20 s. and so according to the value under or over, and so of the Clergy for lands purchased since 20 Edw.I. And all other having 20 l. lands not holden as is aforesaid, 20 s. &c. This whole Subsidy for certain doubts the King utterly released, so as there is no mention made of the same: But hereof thus much shall suffice.

Saepe viatorem nova, non vetus orbita fallit.[354]

Of Fifteens, Quinzims, &c.

A Fifteen is a temporary Aid granted to the King by Parliament, which without further inquiry is certain, and therein differeth from the Subsidy, which is ever uncertain, untill it be assessed.

Fifteens, Quinzim or Task or Quinta decima.

The Fifteen of ancient time was the fifteenth part of goods moveable, but in 8 Edw.3. all the Cities, Boroughs, and towns in England were rated certainly at the fifteenth part of the value at that time generally upon the whole town, whereof you shall read more at large in the Second part of the Institutes, in the last Chapter of Magna Carta[355] *Verb, Quintam decimam partem bonorum mobilium.*[356]

Of Tenths.

There is *decima pars*[357] of the Laity, and for the most part of Cities and Boroughs by their goods (Vid.1 R.2. nu.26.) which proportionably is, *secundum decimam quintam partem*[358] That which we call Tar, Tallage, Tenth, and Fifteen, the Saxons called *Geldinn,*[359] we use the word changing g to y, for *gelding, yeelding,* &c.

---

353. 9 Hen. 6. nu. 15. 10 Hen. 6. nu. 50.
354. [*Ed.:* A new path often fails the traveller, but not the old.]
355. Second part Inst. Mag. Carta cap. ultimo.
356. [*Ed.:* Fifteenth part of the movable goods.]
357. [*Ed.:* tenth part.]
358. [*Ed.:* according to the fifteenth part.]
359. Doomsday. Norff. in Wanelunt, i. Wayland, & ibid. in Frebringe in Massingham, &c.

No*[360] Subsidy before the end of the Parliament, because it is to accompany the pardon.

Of Acts of Parliament of confirmation of Letters Patents.

We have read of particular Acts of confirmation of Letters Patents; but the first of lands, &c. that was the more generall, was the statute of 31 Hen.8. ca.13,[361] of Monasteries (to make those lands the more passable) but after that, generall Acts of confirmation of Letters Patents have been very frequent.

How the Lords give their voices.

In the Lords House, the Lords give their voices from the puisne Lord *seriatim*[362] by the word of [content,]or [not content.]

A bill was preferred at the Parliament holden in *Anno* 6 Hen.6 that no man should contract or marry himself to any Queen Dowager of England without speciall licence and assent of the King, on pain to lose all his goods and lands.[363] The Bishops and Clergy assented to this bill, by the word of [content,] as far forth as the same swerved not from the law of God and of the Church, and so as the same imported no deadly sin. At this time there were besides the Arch-|-Bishops and Bishops, 27 Abbots and 2 Priors, (albeit in troth the number was many times uncertain, as in the close Roll it appeareth) which severally held *per Baroniam,*[364] and were Lords of Parliament, and so continued untill they were dissolved in the reign of Henry the Eight. The entry of the said Act of 6 Hen.6. in the Roll is: It is enacted by the King, Lords Temporall and Commons, that no man should contract or marry himself to any Queen of England, without the speciall license and assent of the King, on pain to lose all his goods and lands. The Bishops and Clergy assented to this Bill, as far forth as the same Swerved not from the law of God; and of the Church, and so as the same imported no deadly sinne.

(margin:) How many Lords Spirituall in Former times.

[35]

---

360. *Rot. Par. 11 Ric. 2. nu. 11. This is contained in the Act of Subsidy, and so an Act of Parliament; and accordingly Subsidies, &c. have been granted, as in the book of statutes appeareth.

361. Rot. Par. 2. H. 5. nu. 20. 1 H. 6. nu. 46. 3 H. 7. 106, the Queen. 6 H. 8. to the Duke of Suff.

362. [*Ed.:* one by one.]

363. Rot. Par. 6 Hen. 6. nu. 27.

364. [*Ed.:* by a barony.]

This is holden to be an Act of Parliament: First, for that the assent of the Clergie could not be conditionall. Secondly, it was not against the law of God nor of the Church, nor imported any deadly sinne to make this law by authority of Parliament, as it appeareth by Magna Carta, cap.7. which had by 32 Acts of Parliament been confirmed, and many others.

This Law was made after the mariage of Queen Katherine Dowager of Henry the Fifth with Owen ap Meredith ap Grono (descended of the Princes of Wales) by whom she had issue Edmond of Hadham aforesaid, Earle of Richmond, and Jasper of Hatfeild, after Earle of Pembroke, and Duke of Bedford.

How the Commons give their voices.

The Commons give their voices upon the question, by Yea or No, and if it be doubtfull, and neither party yeild, two are appointed to number them;[365] one for the Yea. another for the No: the Yea going out, and the No sitting: and thereof report is made to the House. At a Committee, though it be of the whole House, the Yeas go of one side of the House, and the Noes on the other, whereby it will easily appear which is the greatest number.

How Parliaments succeed not well in five Cases.

It is observed by ancient Parliament men out of Record, that Parliaments have not succeeded well in five Cases. First, when the King hath been in displeasure with his Lords, or with his Commons. 2. When any of the Great Lords were at variance between themselves. 3. When there was no good correspondence between the Lords and the Commons. 4. When there was no unity between the Commons themselves. 5. When there was no preparation for the Parliament before it began.

[a366] For the 1: So essentiall is the Kings good will towards his Commons that it was one of the petitions of the Commons to the King, that he would require the Archbish. & all others of the Clergy to pray for his estate, for the

---

365. Pl. Com. 12 & mistaketh it, and that the Clerk number them.

366. *a* Rot. Parl. 37 Edw. 3. nu. 2. and the Writ to the Clergie, *De orgando pro rege & regno*, which was usuall in those dayes.

peace & good government of the land, for the continuance of the Kings good will towards his Commons: Whereunto the thrice noble King assented with these effectuall words, The same prayeth the King: & many times the like petitions for the Lords. [b367] How the King in all his weighty affairs had used the advice of his Lords & Commons, (so great a trust & confidence he had in them.) Alwaies provided, that both Lords & Commons keep them within the circle of the Law & custome of the Parliament.

[c368] For the second: at the Parliament holden in 4 Hen.6. what variance was there between the Duke of Gloc. and the B. of Winchester, and their friends on either side: the successe was, that little was done in any Parliamentary course at that Parliament, and that little was of no moment.

[d369] At the Parliament holden in the third year of Hen.6. the great controversie was between John Earl Marshall, and Richard Earl of Warwick with like successe.

[e370] The like controversie between William Earle of Arundell and Thomas Earl of Devon, for superiority of place, with like event. And many more might be cited. [f371] And always in the beginning amity was made between the Grandees of the Realm by shaking of hands and kissing, and sometime by submission.[372]

For the third, when it was demanded by the Lords and Commons what might be a principall motive for them to have good successe in Parliament, it was answered, *Eritis insuperabiles, si fueritis inseparabiles. Explosum est illud diverbium: Divide, & impera, cum radix & vertex imperii in obedientium consensu rata sunt.*[373]

[36] | For the fourth, unity between the Commons themselves.[374] It is most necessary in both these, and agreeable to the Parliament in the Book of Judges. *Quasi homo unus, eadem mente, uno consilio.*[375]

---

367. *b* Rot. Parl. 43 Edw. 3. nu. 1. 25. Edw. 3. nu. 15. 50 Edw. 3. nu. 2.

368. *c* Rot. Par. 4 Hen. 6. nu. 12. See the Act of that Parliament.

369. *d* Rot. Par. 3. Hen. 6. nu. 1. & 10.

370. *e* Rot. Parl. 27 H. 6. nu. 18.

371. *f* Rot. Par 2 Hen. 4. nu. 14. 5 Hen. 4. nu. 18, 20.

372. Rot. Parl. 21 Ric. 2. by the Count of Arundell to the D. of Lancast. 4 Hen. 6. nu. 12.

373. [*Ed.:* You would be insuperable if you were inseparable. This proverb, Divide and rule, has been rejected, since the root and the summit of authority are confirmed by the consent of the subjects.]

374. Rot. Parl. anno 11 Hen. 4. nu. 10. the King desired this unity. 20 Judicum.

375. [*Ed.:* As if one man, with one mind, and one counsel.]

For the fifth, the Summons of Parliament is by forty dayes or above before the sitting, to the end that preparations might be had for the arduous and urgent affaires of the realme: and that both the King, according to the example of King David, and likewise the Nobles and Commons should prepare:[376] for *praeparatae meditationes sunt semper saniores & meliores quam properatae,*[377] wherein both Houses may greatly expedite the businesse of the Common-wealth in Parliament if they will pursue the ancient custome of Parliament, viz. in the beginning thereof to appoint a select Committee to consider of the Bils in the two last Parliaments that passed both Houses, or either of them, and such as had been preferred, read, or committed, and to take out of them such as be most profitable for the Common-wealth.

The honour and antiquity of the Parliament.

For the honour and antiquity of the Parliament, see the first part of the In-stitutes, Sect. 164. *Verb. Veigne les Burgesses,* and in the Preface to the ninth Book of my Reports, fo. 1,2,3,4, &c. whereunto you may adde, Int' leges Edwardi regis, cap. 8[378] De decimis Ecclesiae reddendis, Sect. De apibus vero, *&c. Haec enim praedicavit beatus Augustinus, & concessa sunt à rege Baronibus & populo.*[379] A grant by expresse Act of Parliament. *Vide infra, cap. 79. pag.*

The power and jurisdiction of the Parliament.

[a380] Of the power and jurisdiction of the Parliament for making of laws in proceeding by Bill, it is so transcendent and absolute, as it cannot be confined either for causes or persons within any bounds. Of this Court it is truly said: [b381] *Si antiquitatem spectes, est vetustissima, si dignitatem, est honoratissima, si jurisdictionem, est capacissima.*[382]

---

376. 1 Chron cap. 28.

377. [*Ed.:* prepared thoughts are always wiser and better than hurried.]

378. 7 Hen. 6. 28. lib. 11. fo. 14. Inter leges Edwardi regis. ca. 8.

379. [*Ed.:* Among the laws of King Edward, chapter 8, concerning tithes to be rendered to the Church, in the section concerning bees, etc.: These things were preached by the Blessed Augustine, and were granted by the king, to the barons and people.]

380. *a* See 13 Eliz. cap. 1. 39 Hen. 6. 15 Vide infra. ca. 79.

381. *b* Fortesc. ca. 18.

382. [*Ed.:* If you consider its antiquity, it is the oldest, if its worthiness, it is the most honourable, if its jurisdiction, it is the most extensive.]

c383 *Huic ego nec metas rerum, nec tempora pono.*384

Yet some examples are desired. d385 Daughters and Heirs apparant of a man or woman, may by Act of Parliament inherit during the life of the Ancestor.

e386 It may adjudge an Infant or Minor of full age.

f387 To attaint a man of treason after his death.

g388 To naturalize a meere Alien, and make him a Subject borne. h389 It may bastard a childe that by law is legitimate viz. begotten by an Adulterer, the husband being within the foure Seas.

To legitimate one that is illegitimate, and born before marriage absolutely. And to legitimate *secundum quid*390 but not *simpliciter.*391 As to take one example for many.

i392 John of Gaunt Duke of Lancaster had by Katherine Swinford before marriage four illegitimate children, *viz.* Henry, John, Thomas, and Joane. And because they were borne at k393 Beaufort in France, they were vulgarly called Henry De Beaufort, &c. John before the 20 year of Richard the Second was Knighted, and Henry became Priest. l394 At the Parliament holden 20 Ric.2. the King by Act of Parliament in forme of a Charter doth legitimate these three sonnes, and Joane the daughter: and the Charter beginneth thus. *Rex, &c. Charissimis consanguineis nostris nobilibus viris*m395 *Johanni Militi:* n396 *Henrico Clerico:* o397 *Thomae* p398 *domicello, ac dilectae nobis nobili mulieri*

383. *c* Virgil.

384. [*Ed.:* To this I set neither boundaries nor periods. (Virgil, *Aeneid,* i. 278.)]

385. *d* Rot. Par 12 Edw. 4. nu. 20, 21, 22. the case of the wives of the Duke of Clarence and Glocester.

386. *e* 12 Edw. 4. nu. 34. Duke of Buckingham.

387. *f* 21 Ric. 2. nu. 27. Sir Ro. Plesington. 31 Hen. 6. cap. 1.

388. *g* This is usuall in many Parliaments.

389. *h* Rot. Par. 5 & 6. Edw. 6 the Lo Marquisse of Winchesters case.

390. [*Ed.:* conditionally.]

391. [*Ed.:* absolutely (i.e. without qualification).]

392. *i* Rot. Pat. Anno 10 Ric. 2. m. 6.

393. *k* Beaufort came to the House of Lanc. by mariage between *Blanch* of Arcois, and *Edmond* first Earle of Lancast.

394. *l* Rot. Pat. 20 Ric. 2. membr. 7.

395. *m* This *John* in Anno 21 Ric. 2. was created Earle of Somerset, and Marquisse Dorset. But in 1 Hen. 4. the Marquiship was taken away by Parliament.

396. *n* This *Henry* was after Bishop of Winchester, Cardinall of S. Ewseby, and Chancellor of England.

397. *o* This *Thomas* was in 21 Ric. 2. created Earle of Dorset.

398. *p* For *Domicellus, &c.* See *Lamb. inter leges Edw. fo. 139. b. Nos indiscrete domicellos de pluribus dicimus, quia Baronum filios vocamus domicellos, Angli vero nullos, nisi natos regum.*

q399 Johannae Beaufort domicellae Germanis praecharissimi avunculi nostri, Jo-
hannis Ducis Lancastriae natis ligeis | nostris Salutem, &c. Nos dicti avunculi [37]
nostri genitoris vestri precibus inclinati, vobiscū qui (ut asseritur) defectū nataliū
patimini, ut hujusmodi defectu (quae ejusq; qualitatis quascunq: praesentibus
habere volumus pro sufficienter expressis) non obstante ad quaecunque honoris
dignitates, (excepta dignitate regali) praeheminencias, status, gradus, & officia Note.
publica & privata tam perpetua quam temporalia, atq; feudal' ac nobil' qui-
buscunque nominibus nuncupantur, etiamsi ducatus, principat', comitat', Bar-
onia, vel alia feuda fuerint, etiamsi mediate, vel immediate vel à nobis dependeant
seu teneantur, praefici, promoveri, eligi, assumi & admitti, illaq; recipere, retinere,
perinde libere & licite valeatis, ac si de legitimo thoro nati existeretis, quibuscunq;
statutis seu consuetudinibus regni nostri Angliae in contrarium editis seu observatis
(quae hic habemus pro totaliter expressis) nequaquam obstantibus; de plenitudine
nostrae regalis potestatis, ac de assensu Parliamenti nostri tenore praesentium dis-
pensamus, vosque & vestrum quemlibet Natalibus restituimus, & legitimamus.
In cujus rei testimonium. Teste Rege apud Westm. 9 die Febr. Per ipsum regem
*in Parliamento.*400

In this Act are divers things worthy of observation. 1. The names whereby
they were legitimated. 2. That this legitimation was not *simpliciter,* but *se-*
cundum quid: for they were legitimated and made capable of all dignities,
except the Royall Dignity: so as this legitimation extended not to make them

---

399. q *Joane* was first married to *Ralph* the first Earle of Westmerland, and after to *Robert Ferrers* Lo.
of Owseley.

400. [*Ed.:* The king, etc. to our beloved and noble kinsmen John, knight, Henry, clerk, Thomas,
servant, and our beloved noblewoman Joan Beaufort, maid, being brothers and sisters born of our most
beloved uncle, John, duke of Lancaster, and our lieges, greeting. We, being inclined to the prayers of our
said uncle, your begetter, since you suffer from a defect of birth (as is asserted), so that notwithstanding
such defect (which we will take of the same quality as if sufficiently expressed in the premises) you may
be appointed, promoted, chosen, received and admitted to whatsoever dignities of honour (excepting the
royal dignity), preeminences, estates, degrees, and offices both public and private, both perpetual and
temporary, feudal and noble, by whatever names they are called, even if they are duchies, principalities,
earldoms, baronies or other fees, and whether they are mediate or immediate or are held of us, and that
you should be able to receive and retain them as freely and lawfully as if you had been born in lawful
wedlock, notwithstanding in any way any statutes or customs whatsoever of our realm of England (which
we take here as if fully expressed) have been published or observed to the contrary: by the fullness of our
royal power, and with the assent of our parliament, by the tenor of the presents, we dispense, restore and
legitimate you and each of you. In witness whereof [etc.] Witness the king at Westminster on the ninth
day of February [etc.] By the king himself in parliament.]

or their posterities inheritable to the Crowne,[401] but to all other dignities. 3. That before their legitimation, they were not created to any of their dignities. 4. The briefe and artificiall penning of this ligitimation, with generall words, as if the particularity were expressed, and with a brief *non obstante*,[402] and with as little blemish as may be. 5. And hereby it appeareth, that Henry the Seventh being son of Edmond of Hadham E. of Richmond, & Margaret his wife, daughter & heir of John de Beaufort D. of Somerset: which Margaret lineally descended from the said John de Beaufort, legitimated & made capable of all dignities, as is aforesaid. *excepta regali dignitate*,[403] that the best title of Henry the Seventh to the Crown, was by Elizabeth his wife, eldest daughter of Edward the Fourth. Yet before this mariage the Crown was by Act of Parliament in-tayled to Henry the Seventh and to the heirs of his body, the right of the Crowne then being in the said Elizabeth, eldest daughter of Edward the Fourth 6. In this Act, the said Thomas before his legitimation could not be called Esquire, and therefore he hath this addition of *Domicello*,[404] either derived of the French word *Domoicell*, which signifieth a young souldier not yet knighted, or signifieth nobly borne. And note, Johan, the daughter, had the addition of De Beaufort and Domicella in that sense also.

[b405] And albeit I finde an attainder by Parliament of a subject of High Treason being committed to the Tower, and forth-comming to be heard, and yet never called to answer in any of the Houses of Parliament, although I question not the power of the Parliament, for without question the attainder standeth of force in law: yet this I say of the manner of the proceeding, *Auferat oblivio, si potest; si non, utcunque silentium tegat:*[406] for the more high and absolute the jurisdiction of the Court is, the more just and honourable it ought to be in the proceeding and to give example of justice to inferiour Courts. But it is demanded, since he was attainted by Parliament, what should be the reason

Note pro corona.

401. Rot. Parl. *Anno* 1 Hen. 7. not in print. 7 Hen. 4. cap. 2. the like to Hen. 4. the right of the Crowne being then in the descent from *Philip* daughter and heir of *Lionel* Duke of Clarence. Vid. 1 Hen. 7. 12 13 25 Hen. 8. cap. 12. repeal by 28 Hen. 8. cap. 7. & 1 Mar. Parl. 1. cap. I. See 13 Eliz. ca. 1. *in principio.*

402. [*Ed.:* Not withstanding, a writ or clause in a document or order excusing the performance of a duty.]

403. [*Ed.:* excepting the royal dignity,]

404. *See Hovenden, pag. 608. for this word *Domicel.*

405. *b* Rot. Parl. 22 Hen. 8. The attainder of *The Cromwell* Earle of Essex.

406. [*Ed.:* Let oblivion sweep it away, if possible; if not, let it be covered in silence:]

that our Historians do all agree in this that he suffered death by a law which he himself had made. For answer hereof, I had it of Sir Thomas Gawdye Knight, a grave and reverend Judge of the Kings Bench, who lived at that time, that King Henry the Eighth commanded him to attend the chiefe Justices, and to know whether a man that was forth comming might be attainted of High Treason by Parliament, and never called to his answer. The Judges answered, that it was a dangerous question, and that the High Court of Parliament ought to give examples to inferiour Courts for proceeding according to justice, and no inferiour Court could do the like; and they thought that the High Court of Parliament would never do it. But being by the expresse commandment of the king and pressed by the said Earle to give a direct answer: they said, that if he be attainted by Parliament, it could not come in question afterwards whether he were called or not called to answer. | And albeit their [38] opinion was according to law, yet might they have made a better answer, for by the Statutes of Mag. Cart. ca. 29. 5 Edw.3. cap. 9. & 28 Edw.18. 3. cap. 5. No man ought to be condemned without answer, &c. which they might have certified, but *facta tenent multa, quae fieri prohibentur*[407] the act of Attainder being passed by Parliament, did bind, as they resolved. The party against whom this was intended, was never called in question, but the first man after the said resolution, that was to attainted, and never called to answer, was the said Earl of Essex; whereupon that erroneous and vulgar opinion amongst our Historians grew that he died by the same law which he himself had made. The reheresall of the said Attainder can work no prejudice, for that I am confidently perswaded, that such honourable and worthy members shall be from time to time of both Houses of Parliament, as never any such Attainder, where the party is forth comming, shall be had hereafter without hearing of him.

[a]408 *Nunquid lex nostra judicat hominem, nisi prius audierit ab ipso, & cognoverit quid faciat?*[409] Doth our law judge any man, before it hear him and know what he doth? [b]410 It is not the manner of the Romans to deliver any

---

407. [*Ed.:* Deeds contain many things which are prohibited to be done.]

408. *a* Lex Divina. John 7. v. 15. Deut. c. 17. v. 10. & ca. 19. v. 15. Mat. par. 18. Johannis 273. *Incivile videtur et contra Canones in hominem absentem non vocatum, non convictum nec confessum ferre sententiam.* Hereof see *paulo postea.*]

409. [*Ed.:* Does our law judge a man before it has first heard him and knows what he does?]

410. *b* Acta 25. 16. Gen. 3. 9. *Dixit dominus, Adam ubi es. Vide* Gen. 18. 21. Ecclesiasticus 11 7. 8.

man to die, before that he which is accused have the accusers face to face, and have licence to answer for himself concerning the crime laid against him.

[c411] *Ait Josua ad Acab, Fili mi, da gloriam domino Deo Israel, & confitere mihi quid feceris, ne abscondas.*[412]

[d413] *Interrogatus Levita maritus mulieris interfectae quomodo tantum scelus perpetratum esset, &c.*[414] And the conclusion is after hearing and discerning the cause, consider, consult, and then give sentence.

[e415] And as evil was the proceeding in Parliament against Sir John Mortimer, third son of Edmond the second Earl of March (Descended from Lionell Duke of Clarence) who was indicted of high Treason for certain words, in effect, that Edmond Earl of March should be King by right of inheritance, and that he himself was next rightfull heir to the Crown after the said Earl of March; wherefore if the said Earl would not take it upon him, he would: and that he would goe into Wales, and raise an Army of 20000. men, &c. which indictment (without any arraignment or pleading) being meerly faigned to blemish the title of the Mortimers, and withall being insufficient in law, as by the same appeareth, was confirmed by Authority of Parliament; & the said Sir John being brought into the Parliament without arraignment or answer, judgement in Parliament was given against him upon the said indictment; That he should be carried to the Tower of London, and drawn through the City to Tiborn, and there hanged, drawn and quartered, his head to be set on London bridge, and his four quarters on the four gates of London, as by the Record of Parliament appeareth.

The proceeding in Parliament against Absents.

The ancient law and custome of the Parliament was, that when any man was to be charged in Parliament with any crime or offence, or misdemeanour, the Kings Writ was directed to the Sherif to summon and injoin the party to appear before the King in the next Parliament. For example.

---

411. *c* Praxis Sanctorum Josua 7. 19. 22, 23., etc.

412. [*Ed.:* Joshua said to Acab, My son, give glory to the Lord God of Israel, and confess to me what you have done, do not conceal it.]

413. *d* Jud. 20. 3.

414. [*Ed.:* The Levite who was the husband of the slain woman, when asked how so wicked a crime had been committed, etc.]

415. *e* Rot. Par. 2. Hen. 6. nu. 18.

Dominus Rex mandavit Vic' quod assumptis secum quatuor de discretioribus & leg'
militibus Com' sui in propria persona sua accederet ad Nicholaum de Segrave,[416]
& ipsum in praesentia praedictorum militum summon' & ex parte domini regis
firmiter ei injungeret quod esset coram domino rege in proximo Parliament' suo apud
Westm' in primo adventu domini regis ibidem ad audiendam voluntatem ipsius
domini regis super hiis, quae tunc ibidem proponere intenderet vers. eum, & ad
faciendum & recipiendum ulterius quod curia domini regis consideraret in prae-
missis. Et Vic' modo mandavit quod assumptis secum Thoma Wale, Waltero filio
Roberti | de Daventry, Roberto de Gray de Wollaston, & Radulpho de Normavill   [39]
quatuor milit', & in propria persona sua accessit apud Stowe ad manerium praedicti
Nicholai, et in praesentia eorundem militum summon' praedictum Nicholaum, &
ei firmiter injunxit quod esset coram domino rege in isto Parliamento nunc juxta
formam & tenorem mandati praed', &c.

    Almaricus de Sancto Amando, Magister Johannes de Sancto Amando, Willielmus
de Monte Acuto, Richardus Attehaw constabularius castri Oxon',[417] *Ricūs de Hurle,*
Thomas de Carleton capellanus, Iohannes de Ros, Iohannes de Trenbrigg, Willielmus
Attewarde frater ejus, & Philippus de Wigenton attachiat' fuerunt per Vic' in castro
Oxon' per praecept' domini regis responsur' eidem domino regi in Parliamento suo
in Crastino Sancti Mathaei Apostoli Anno regni sui xxxiii. super quibusdam cri-
minibus & transgresionibus infra scriptis, & inde per manucaptionem sufficient'
adjornat' coram ipso domino rege hic ad hunc diem, scilicet a die Paschae in xv.
dies, &c.[418]

---

416. *Placita in Parliamento Domini Regis, Anno* Edw. 1. 33. Northampt.

417. *Placita coram domino rege,* Pas. 33 Edw. 1. Rot. 19. Oxon.

418. [*Ed.:* The lord king commanded the sheriff to take with him four discreet and lawful knights of
his county, and to go in person to Nicholas de Segrave, and in the presence of said knights to summon
him, and firmly enjoin him on behalf of the king to appear before the lord king at his next parliament at
Westminster upon the lord king's arrival there, that he might hear there the will of the lord king himself
concerning those charges that the king was intending to lay against him, and that he might do and receive
besides what the court of the lord king decided regarding the same. And the sheriff now gave orders, and
he took with him the four knights Thomas Wale, Walter the son of Robert de Daventry, Robert de Gray
de Wollaston, and Ralph de Normanville, etc., and went in person to the manor of the aforesaid Nicholas
at Stowe, and in the presence of these same knights summoned said Nicholas, and firmly enjoined him
to appear before the lord king at the next parliament, according to the said form and tenor, etc.

    Almaric de Sancto Amando, Master John de Sancto Amando, William de Monte Acuto, Richard At-
tehaw the constable of Oxford Castle, Richard de Hurle, the chaplain Thomas de Carleton, John de Ros,
John de Trenbrigg, William Attewarde his brother, and Philip de Wigenton were attached by the sheriff
in Oxford Castle, by order of the lord king, to answer to the same lord king at his Parliament on the
morrow of St. Matthew the Apostle, in the 33rd year of his reign, concerning certain crimes and trespasses
specified below. Then through sufficient mainprise they were given a day to appear before the lord king
himself, namely the 15th day following Easter.]

Or a writ might be directed to the party himself, when any complaint was made against him, *De injuriis, gravaminibus, ut molestationibus,*[419] to appear in his proper person before the King and his Councell, etc. As for example:

Dominus Rex mandavit breve suum Roberto de Burghersh in haec verba.[420] *Edwardus Dei gratia, &c. Dilecto et fideli suo Roberto de Burghersh constabular' castri sui Dover et custod' suo quinque portuum. Salutem. Quia dilectus nobis in Christo Abbas de Faveresham & Robertus de Gurne balivus suus ejusdem villae coram concilio nostro apud Eborum existente de diversis injuriis, gravaminibus et molestationibus eis per vos voluntar' et absq; causa rationabili multipliciter illatis graves querimonias deposuerunt, petentes instanter ut eis super hoc fieri faceremus remedium opportunum; propter quod dedimus eis diem coram nobis et concilio nostro a die Pasch. in xv. dies, &c. ad querelas suas predictas tunc ostendend', et ad faciend' super hoc ulterius et recipiend' quod Iustitia suaderet: Vobis mandamus, quod in propria persona vestra sitis coram nobis et concilio nostro ad diem praedict' praefatis Abbati et balivis suis super praemissis respons', factur' et receptur' quod curia nostra consideraverit in hac parte, & ab injuriis, gravaminibus, molestationibus et districtionibus indebitis praefatis Abbati et balivis suis interim inferendis penitus desistendo. Et habeatis ibi hoc breve. Teste me ipso apud Linliscu xxx. die Januarii, Anno regni nostri xxx. Virtute cujus brevis praedictus Robertus venit, et breve illud protulit ad diem in eodem contentum. Et praedictus Abbas venit et querelas suas protulit in quodam rotulo scriptas, et quas in curia hic querelando ostendit et legere fecit, de quibus prima est haec, &c.*[421]

---

419. [*Ed.:* concerning injuries, burdens, or hardships.]

420. *Placita coram rege apud Cantuar' de termino Pasc. anno regni regis* E. 1. 30. *Consimile breve ubi supra eidem Roberto de Burghersh ad sectam majoris et baronum quinque portuum.*

421. [*Ed.:* The lord king sent his writ to Robert de Burghersh in the following words: "Edward by the grace of God, etc., to his beloved and faithful Robert de Burghersh, constable of his castle at Dover and his warden of the Cinque Ports, greetings. Because our dearly beloved in Christ the Abbot de Faversham, and his bailiff Robert de Gurne of the same vill, before our council at York have made grave complaints concerning various wrongs, burdens and hardships which you, voluntarily and without reasonable cause, have inflicted on them, and because they earnestly ask that we provide them with suitable relief in this matter, we accordingly have set a date for them to appear before us and our council, 15 days after Easter. . .that they might present their aforementioned complaints, and do and receive besides whatever justice recommends. We command you to appear before us and our council on said day, to respond to said abbot and his bailiffs on these matters, and to do and receive what our court decides in this case, and in the meantime you shall completely desist from inflicting unjustified injuries, burdens, hardships and distress on said abbot and his bailiffs. And you shall present there this writ. Witness: myself. At Lincoln(?), on January 30 in the 30th year of our reign." On the strength of this writ said Robert came and presented the writ on the day specified in it. And said abbot came and produced his complaints written on a certain

Now they which absent themselves shall be proceeded withall, Vide 50 Edw.3. nu.37. Adam Buries case, 2. parte Patent. 21 Ric.2. nu.15, 16. Rot. Par. 17 Ric.2. nu.28. 11 Hen.4. nu.37, 38. 15 Hen.6. fo.17. Sir John Pilkingtons case.

And where by order of law a man cannot be attainted of high treason,[422] unlesse the offence be in law high treason, he ought not to be attainted by generall words of high treason by Authority of Parliament (as sometime hath been used) but the high treason ought to be specially expressed, seeing that the Court of Parliament is the highest and most honourable Court of Justice, and ought (as hath been said) give example to inferiour Courts.

There was an Act of Parliament made in the 11 year of King Hen.7. which had a fair flattering preamble, pretending to avoid divers mischiefs,[423] which were, 1. To the high displeasure of Almighty God. 2. The great let of the | [40] Common law, and 3. The great let of the wealth of this land: And the Purvien of that Act tended in the execution contrary, *ex diametro,* viz. to the high displeasure of Almighty God, the great let, nay the utter subversion of the Common law, and the great let of the wealth of this land, as hereafter shall manifestly appear. Which Act followeth in these words:

> The King our Soveraign Lord calling to his remembrance[424] that many good Statutes and Ordinances be made for the punishment of riots, unlawfull assemblies, reteinders in giving and receiving of liveries, signs and tokens unlawfully, extortions, maintenances, imbracery, excessive taking of wages contrary to the Statute of Labourers and Artificers, the use of unlawfull games, inordinate Apparell, and many other great enormities and offences, which been committed and done daily contrary to the good statutes, for many and divers behoofull considerations severally made and ordained, to the displeasure of Almighty God, and the great let of the Common law, and wealth of this land, notwithstanding that generally by the Justices of the Peace in every shire within this Realm in the open Sessions is given in charge to enquire of many offences committed contrary to divers of the said Statutes, and divers enquests thereupon there straitly sworn, and charged before the said Justices to enquire of the premisses,

---

roll, and he presented these complaints in his suit and had them read here in court, the first of which was as follows, etc.]

422. 25 Hen. 8. ca. 12. Eliz. Barton, and others. And see the Act of the Attainder of the Lord Cromwell, *Anno* 32 Hen. 8. *ubi supra.*

423. A mischievous Act with a flattering Preamble in 11 Hen. 7.

424. 11 Hen. 7. ca. 3.

and therein to present the troth which any letted to be found by imbracery, maintenance, corruption and favour; by occasion whereof the said Statutes be not, nor cannot be put in due execution: For reformation whereof, for so much that before this time the said offences, extortions, contempts, and other the premisses might not, nor as yet may be conveniently punished by the due order of the law, except it were first found and presented by the verdict of twelve men there to duly sworn, which for the causes afore rehearsed will not find nor yet present the truth: Wherefore be it by the advice and assent of the Lords Spirituall and Temporall, and the Commons in this present Parliament assembled, and by authority of the same enacted, ordained and established, that from henceforth as well the Justices of Assise in the open Sessions to be holden afore them, as the Justices of Peace in every County of the said Realm,[425] upon information for the King before them to be made, have full power and authority[426] by their discretion to hear and determine all offences and contempts committed and done by any person or persons against the form, Ordinance and effect of[427] any statute made and not repealed, and that the said Justices upon the said information have full power and authority to award and make like processe against the said offenders and every of them, as they should or might make against such person or persons as been present and indicted before them of trespasse done contrary to the Kings peace, and the said offender, or offenders duly to punish according to the purport, form, and effect of the said Statutes. Also be it enacted by the said Authority, that the person which shall give the said information for the King shall by the discretion of the said Justices content and pay to the said person or persons against whom the said information shall be so given his reasonable costs and dammages in that behalf sustained, if that it be tried or found against him, that so giveth or maketh | any such information. Provided always, that any such information extend not to treason[428] murder, or felony, nor to any other offence, wherefore any person shall lose life, or member, nor to lose by nor upon the same information any lands, tenements, goods or chattels to the party making the same information. Provided also that the said informations shall not extend to any person dwelling in any other shire, then there, as the said information shall be given or made, saving to every person and persons,

[41]

425. *a* Upon information with out any indictment.

426. *b* By their discretion, and not *secundum legem & Consuetudinem Angl.* as all proceedings ought to be.

427. *c* Obsolete statutes and all, and specially such as time had so altered from the originall cause of the making thereof, as either they could not at all, or very hardly be observed and kept.

428. But it extended to a Premunire, misprision of treason, &c.

cities, and towns, all their liberties and franchises to them and every of them of right belonging and appertaining.

By pretext of this law Empson and Dudley did commit upon the Subject unsufferable pressures and oppressions, and therefore this statute was justly soon after the decease of Henry the Seventh repealed at the next Parliament after his decease, by the statute of 1. Hen.8. ca. 6.[429]

A good caveat to Parliaments to leave all causes to be measured by the golden and streight metwand of the law, and not to the incertain and crooked cord of discretion.

It is not almost credible to foresee,[430] when any Maxime, or Fundamentall law of this Relam is altered (as elsewhere hath been observed) what dangerous inconveniences doe follow, which most expressly appeareth by this most unjust and strange Act of 11 Hen.7. for hereby not only Empson and Dudley themselves, but such Justices of Peace (corrupt men) as they caused to be authorized, committed most grievous and heavy oppressions and exactions, grinding of the face of the poor Subjects by penall laws (be they never so obsolete or unfit for the time) by information only without any presentment or triall by Jury being the ancient birthright of the Subject, but to hear and determine the same by their discrtion, inflicting such penalty, as the statutes not repealed imposed: These and other like oppessions and exactions by or by the means of Empson and Dudley and their instruments, brought infinite treasures to the Kings Cofers, whereof the King himself in the end with great grief and compunction repented, as in[431] another place we have observed.

The danger ensuing by alteration of any of the Maximes of the law.

This statute of 11 Hen.7 we have recited, and shewed the just inconveniences thereof, to the end, that the like should never hereafter be attempted in any Court of Parliament. And that others might avoid the fearfull end of those two time-servers, Empson and Dudley, *Qui eorum vestigia insistunt, eorum exitus perhorrescant.*[432]

See the statute of 8 Edw.4. ca. 2 the Statute of Liveries, an Information, &c. by the discretion of the Judges to stand as an originall, &c. This Act is deservedly repealed.

---

429. 1 Hen. 8 ca. 6.

430. See the 2. part of the Institutes, W. 1. ca 26. See the Preface to the 4. part of the Report.

431. In the Chapter of the Court of Wards and Liveries.

432. [*Ed.:* Let those who follow in their footsteps be affrighted by their end.]

Vide 12 Ric.2. cap. 1. Punishment by discrtion &c. Vide 5 Hen.4. ca. 6. 8. See the[433] Comission of Sewers, Discretion ought to be thus described, *Discretio est discernere per legem quid sit justum.*[434] And this description is proved by the Common law of the land, for when a Jury doe doubt of the law, and desire to doe that which is just, they find the speciall matter, and the entry is, *Et super tota materia, &c. petunt discretionem Justiciariorum,*[435] and sometime, *advisamentum & discretionem Justiciariorum in praemissis, &c.*[436,437] that is, they desire that the Judges would discern by law what is just, and give judgement accordingly.

[42] | Acts against the power of the Parliament subsequent bind not.

An Article of the Statute made in 11 Ric.2. cap.5. is, that no person should attempt to revoke any Ordinance then made, is repealed,[438] for that such restraint is against the jurisdiction and power of the Parliament, the liberty of the subject and unreasonable. And likewise the last Will and Testament of king Richard the Second. under the Great Seal, Privy Seal, and Privy Signet, whereby the devised certain mony, treasure, &c. to his successors upon condition to observe all the Acts and orders at the Parliament holden in Anno 21 of his reign, was holden unjust and unlawfull, for that it restrained the Soveraign liberty of the Kings his Successors.

Sundry Lords of Parliament (but no Bishops) or six of them,[439] and certain knights of shires of the Commons or three of them are authorised by Authority of Parliament to examine answer, and plainly determine all the Petitions, exhibited in that Parliament, and the matters contained in the same by their good advice and discretion, &c.[440] The high power of a Parliament to be committed to a few is holden to be against the dignity of a Parliament and that no such Commission ought to be granted.[441]

433. Lib. 5. fo. 100. Rooks case. Lib. 10. fo. 128. &c.
434. [*Ed.:* Discretion is to know through law what is just.]
435. [*Ed.:* And concerning the entire matter, etc., they seek the discretion of the judges,]
436. Pl. Com. 348. Barnards case.
437. [*Ed.:* the advisement and discretion of the judges in said matters, etc.]
438. 1 Hen. 4. nu. 144. 21 Ric. 2. nu. 20. repealed by 1 Hen. 4. ca. 3. 1 Hen. 4. nu 48. Vid. 7 Hen. 4. nu. 37.
439. 21 Ric. 2. ca. 16. 21 Ric. 2. nu. 44.
440. 1 Hen. 4. nu. 70.
441. 2 Hen. 4. ca. 22. Vide 21 R. 2. nu. 44.

An Act in 11 Ric.2. ca.3. that no man against whom any judgment, or forfeiture was given should sue for pardon or grace, &c. was holden to be unreasonable without example, and against the law and custome of Parliament, and therefore that branch by Authority of Parliament was adnichaled, and made void.[442]

Also I find that in times past the Houses of Parliament have not been clearly dealt withall, but by cunning artifice of words utterly deceived, and that in cases of greatest moment, even in case of High Treason, as taking one example for a warning in like cases hereafter.

King Henry the Eighth after the Clergy of England had in their Convocations acknowledged him Supream Head of the Church of England, thought it no difficult matter to have the same corroborated and confirmed by Authority of Parliament, but withall secretly and earnestly desired that the impugners and deniers thereof, though it were but by word, might incur the offence of High Treason, and finding the one, that is, the acknowledgement of his Supremacy likely to have good passage, and having little hope upon that which he found to effect the other concerning High Treason, sought to have it passe in some other Act by words closely cowched, though the former Act of Supremacy had been the proper place.[443] And therefore in the Act of recognition of his Supremacy it is enacted, that he should have annexed and united to the Crown of this Realm the Title and Stile thereof:[444] and afterwards towards the end of the Parliament, a bill was preferred whereby many offences be High Treason, and thereby it is enacted, "That if any person or persons by [a445] word or writing, 1. practise or attempt any bodily harm to the King, the [b446] Queen or their heirs apparant, 2. or to [c447] deprive them or any of them, of their dignity, [d448] title, or name of their royall estates, 3. or that the King should be an [e449] Heretique, Schismatique, Tyrant, Infidell, or Usurper

Acts of Parliament ought to be plainly, and clearly, and not cunningly and darkly penned, specially in criminal causes.

442. 26 Hen. 8. ca. i.

443. 26 Hen. 8. ca. i.

444. 26 Hen. 8. ca. 13.

445. *a* By word, &c. this by construction referres to the 2. clause.

446. *b* Shadowed with the Queen or Prince.

447. *c* Deprive, an obscure word.

448. *d* Note this word [title] in the former Act.

449. *e* Parker B. of *Cant. Lib. de Antiquitate Brit. Ecclesiae. Clerus animo toto obstupuit, nondum enim quid sibi hic novus vellet titulus, aut quorsum tenderit, prospexit, &c.*

of the Crown, &c. that every such persons so offending should be adjudged Traytors, &c." So as now by this latter Act, he that by word or writing attempts to deprive the King of the title of his royall estate is a Traytor, but the former Act had annexed to the Crown the title of the stile of Supremacy, and therefore he that should by word of writing attempt to deprive the King thereof should be a Traytor. And [f450] upon this law of 26 Hen.8. ca.13. for denying of the Kings Supremacy divers suffered death as incase of High Treason, whereas all laws, especially penall, and principally those that are penall in the highest degree [g] ought to be so plainly and perspicuously penned, as every Member of both Houses may understand the same, and according to his knowledge and conscience give his voice. [h451] *Erit autem lex honesta, justa, possibilis, secundum naturam & secundum conseutudinem patriae, temporique conveniens, necessaria & utilis, manifesta quoque, ne aliquid per obscuritatem incautum cap-|-tione contrudat, nullo privato commodo, sed pro communi civium utilitate conscripta, ideo in ipsa constitutione ista consideranda sunt, quia cum leges institutae fuerint non erit liberum arbitrium judicare de ipsis, sed oportebit judicare secundum ipsas,*[452] which be excellent rules for: all Parliaments to follow.[453] But the Statute of 5 Eliz. ca. 1.[454] hath concerning the Supremacy dealt plainly and perspicuously as by the same appeareth.

And albeit it appeareth by these examples, and many other that might be brought, what transcendent power and authority this Court of Parliament hath, yet though divers Parliaments have attempted to barre, restrain, suspend, qualifie, or make void subsequent Parliaments, yet could they never effect it, for the latter Parliament hath ever power to abrogate, suspend, qualifie, ex-

What qualities laws ought to have.

[43]

---

450. *f* But this Act lived not long, for twice it was repealed viz. by 1 Edw. 6. c. 12. & 1 Mar. c. 1.

451. *h* Isidor. 2 Etymol.

452. [*Ed.:* Moreover, the law shall be honest, just, able to be complied with, in accordance with nature and custom, suited to the time and country, necessary and useful, also clear, lest through obscurity it deceive the unwary, and it shall be written not for private advantage, but for the general benefit of the citizens. These things must be considered when the law is being formulated, because once laws have been passed one will not have the freedom to judge them, but rather will be obliged to base his judgements on them.]

453. 5 Eliz. ca. 1.

454. Exod. 4. 16. *Tu, i. Moses eris ei, i. Aaron, in hiis quae ad deum pertinent, &c.* Exod 32. 15, 16. *Moses custos utriusque tabulae.* Numb. 10. 1, 2. *Moses custos utriusque tabulae.* Joshua 24. 1. *Congregavit Josua, &c.* 28. *dimisit.* 1 Chron. 15. 4. 1 Chron. 16. 43. Rex David. 2 Chron. 5. 2. Rex Solomon. 2 Chron. 29. 15. &c. Ezekias. Nota. 1 Sam. 15. 17. *Et ait Samuel ad Saul, nonne cum parvulus esses caput in tribubus factus es?* and the tribe of Levi was one. 1 Maccab. 14. 44. See hereafter ca. 74.

plain, or make void the former in the whole or in any part thereof, notwith-standing any words of restraint, prohibition, or penalty in the former:[455] for it is a maxime in the law of the Parliament, *quod leges posteriores priores con-trarias abrogant.*[456]

Subsequent parliaments cannot be restrained by the former.

Acts of Parliament enrolled in other Courts.

For the better observation of any Act of Parliament enacted for the Com-monwealth, or of a Petition of right, or Judgment in Parliament, or the like, and to incourage the Judges that the same may be duly executed, the same may be inrolled in the Courts of Justice in this manner.[457] The tenor of the Record must be removed into the Chancery by writ of *Certiorari*[458] and de-livered into the Kings Bench by the hands of the Chancelor or Lord Keeper and sent by *Mittimus*[459] to the Court of Common pleas, and by like *Mittimus* into the Exchequer and the King by his writ may command any Court to observe and firmly to keep such an Act of Parliament, as it appeareth by these two precedents. *Ex Rotulo Claus. Anno 28 Edw.1. m.2. Dors. Rex Thesaurar' & Baronibus suis de Scaccar' Salutē. Quia volumus quod Magna Carta domini Henrici quondam Regis Angliae patris nostri de libertatibus Angliae quam con-firmavimus & etiam innovavimus in omnibus & singulis articulis suis firmiter & inviolabiliter observetur. Vobis mandamus quod Cartam praedictam in om-nibus & singulis suis articulis quantum in vobis est coram vobis in dicto Scaccario observari faciatis firmiter & teneri. T.R. apud Dunfres 23. die Octobris.*

Rex Justic' suis de Banco Salutem: Cum in alleviationem gravaminum quae populus regni nostri occasione guerrarum hactenus toleravit, ac in emendationem status ejusdem populi, nec non ut ex hoc se exhibeat ad nostra servicia promptiorem, nobisque in agendis nostris libentius subsidium faciat in futurum, quosdam ar-

---

455. 43 Edw. 3. ca. 1. 11 Hen. 7. ca. 1. 28 Hen. 8. ca. 17. 1 Edw. 6. ca. 11. Lib. 4. fo. 46. the B. of Cant. case.

456. [*Ed.:* Later laws abrogate prior laws that are contrary to them.]

457. Int. Placita Parl. 18 Edw. 1. rot. 18. Ibid. 20 Edw. 1. Magnum Placitum int. Com. Gloc' & Com. Heref. & Essex irr. Rot. Claus. An. 28 Edw. 1. in Dors. irr. le Magna Carta. Pasch. 33 Edw. 1. rot. par. Nich. Segraves case. Rot. 22. Tr. 12 Edw. 2. Ro. 60. *de irr Petition in Parliament, al banke le Roy.*

458. [*Ed.:* To be informed of. A writ of common law origin issued by a superior to an inferior court requiring the better to produce a certified record of a particular case tried therein.]

459. [*Ed.:* Writ enclosing a record sent to be tried in a court palatine; it derives its name from the Latin word *mittimus,* "we send."].

*ticulos eidem populo plurimum (annuente Domino) profuturos de gratia nostra
speciali duxerimus concedendos. Vobis mandamus quod dictos articulos quos vobis
mittimus sigillo nostro consignatos coram vobis in banco praedicto quantum in
vobis est juxta vim, formam & effectum eorundem observari faciatis firmiter &
teneri. T. R. apud Dunfres 30. die Octobris.*[460]

Every Member of the Parliament ought to come.

Every Lord Spirituall and Temporall, and every Knight, Citizen and Burgesse
shall upon Summons come to the Parliament, except he can reasonably, and
honestly excuse himself, or else he shall be amerced &c.[461] that is, respectively,
a Lord by the Lords, and one of the Commons by the Commons.

By the Statute of 6 Hen.8. ca.16 no Knight, Citizen or Burgesse of the
House of Commons shall depart from the Parliament without licence of the
Speaker and Commons, the same to be entred of record in the book of the
Clerk of the Parliament, upon pain to lose their wages.

[44] ❦ If a Lord depart from Parliament without license, it is an offence done
out of the Parliament, and is finable by the Lords:[462] and so it is of a Member
of the House of Commons, he may be fined by the House of Commons. *Vide*
1 & 2 Ph. & Mar. *coram rege*. Rot.48. divers informations by the Attorny
Generall for departing without license, *ut supra*.

---

460. [*Ed.: From the close roll of the 28th year of the reign of Edward I, membrane 2, in the dorse*. The
king to his treasurer and barons of the Exchequer, greetings. It is our desire that the Magna Carta of the
liberties of England of our father Lord Henry once King of England, which we have confirmed and reissued,
be strictly and inviolably observed in each and all of its articles. Accordingly, we command that you see
to it that to the best of your ability said charter be strictly observed and obeyed before you in said Exchequer
in each and all of its articles. Witness: the king. At Dumfries, October 23.

The king to his justices of the bench, greetings. In order to relieve the burdens which the people of
our realm have heretofore suffered on the occasion of war, and to improve the condition of these same
people, that they might thereby in the future prove readier to serve us, and more willingly lend us aid in
our enterprises, we have decided that by our special grace said people should be granted certain articles,
which will (God willing) be of great profit to them. We therefore command you to see to it that the
aforementioned articles which we are sending to you under our seal be strictly observed before you in said
bench, to the best of your ability, according to the force, form and intent of the same. Witness: the king.
At Dumfries, October 30.]

461. 5 Ric. 2. Stat. 2. c. 4 Rot. par. 31 Hen. 6. nu. 46. fines were set, &c. If any of the Lords or Commons
come not, &c. they shall be fined.

462. Vi. 3. Edw. 3. 13. sup. If any of the Lords of Commons depart. &c. they shall be fined 1 & 2 Ph.
& M. Rot. 48. *ut sup*.

*[463] The punishment of Sheriffes for their negligence in retorning of Writs or for leaving out of their retorns any City or Borough which ought to send Citizens and Burgesses.

Advice concerning new and plausible projects and offers in Parliament.

When any plausible project is made in Parliament to draw the Lords and Commons to assent to any Act[464] (especially in matters of weight and importance) if both Houses do give upon the matter projected and promised their consent, it shall be most necessary, they being trusted for the Commonwealth, to have the matter projected and promised (which moved the Houses to consent) to be established in the same act, lest the benefit of the Act be taken, and the matter projected and promised never performed, and so the Houses of Parliament performe not the trust reposed in them. As it fell out (taking one example for many) in the reigne of Hen.8. On the Kings behalfe the Members of both Houses were informed in Parliament, that no King or Kingdome was safe, but where the King had three abilities. First, To live of his own, and able to defend his kingdome upon any sudden invasion or insurrection. 2. To aide his confederates, otherwise they would never assist him. 3. To reward his well deserving servants. Now the project was, that if the Parliament would give unto him all the Abbies, Priories, Friories, Nunneries, and other Monasteries, that for ever in time then to come, he would take order that the same should not be converted to private use: But first, that his Exchequer for the purposes aforesaid should be enriched. Secondly, the kingdome strengthened by a continuall maintenance of 40 thousand well trained souldiers with skilfull Captains and Commanders, Thirdly, for the benefit and case of the Subject, who never afterwards (as was projected) in any time to come should be charged with Subsidies, Fifteenths, Loanes, or other common aides. Fourthly, lest the honour of the Realme should receive any diminution of honour by the dissolution of the said Monasteries there being 29 Lords of Parliament of the Abbots and Priors (that held of the King *per Baroniam* whereof more in the next lease) that the King would create a number of Nobles, which we omit. The said Monasteries were given to the King by authority of

463. *5 Ric. 2. stat. 2. ca. 4.
464. See before pa. 14 Rot. par. 13 Edw. 3.

divers Acts of Parliament,[465] but no provision was therein made for the said project, or any part thereof;[466] only ad *faciend, populum*[467] these possessions were given to the King his heirs and successors to do and use therewith his and their own wils to the pleasure of Almighty God, and the honour and profit of the Realme.

Now observe the Catastrophe; in the same Parliament of 32 Hen.8. when the great and opulent Priory of Saint Johns of Jerusalem was given to the King, he demanded and had a Subsidie both of the Clergie and Laity. And the like he had in 34 H.8 and in 37 H.8. he had another Subsidie.[468] And since the dissolution of the said Monasteries he exacted divers loanes, and against law received the same.

Whom the King may call to the Lords House of Parliament.

If the king by his Writ calleth any Knight or Esquire to be a Lord of the Parliament,[469] he cannot refuse to serve the King there in *communi illo concilio,*[470] for the good of his country. But if the King had called an*[471] Abbot, Prior, or other regular Prelate by Writ to the Parliament to the Common Councell of the Realme, if he held not of the King *per Baroniam,*[472] he might
[45] refuse to serve in | Parliament, because *quoad secularia* he was *mortuus in lege,*[473] and therefore not capable to have place and voice in Parliament[474] unlesse he did hold *per Baroniam* and were to that Common Councell called by Writ, which made him capable: and though such a Prelat Regular had been often called by Writ, and had *de facto* had place & voice in Parliament, yet if in *rei*

---

465. 27 Hen. 8. demonsteries, & 31 Hen. 8 cap. 13. 33 Hen. 8. cap. 14.

466. 27. Hen. 8. cap. 28.

467. [*Ed.:* for the purpose of persuading the people.]

468. 32 Hen. 8. ca. 23. 50. 34 Hen. 8. cap. 16. & 27. 37 Hen. 8. cap. 24.

469. Rot. Claus. in dors. 10 Hen. 7. 20 Septemb. Writs to divers *ad ordinem militiqe de Balneo suscipiend. juxta antiquam consuetudinem in creatione usitatam.*

470. [*Ed.:* in that common council.]

471. *Of regular Prelats that hold *per Baroniam.*

472. [*Ed.:* by baronage (by a heritable barony).]

473. [*Ed.:* in regard to secular things. . . . dead in law.]

474. And so was it adjudged in the Parliament at York, An. 12. Edw. 2 in the case of the Abbot of S. James extra Northamp. Stanf. pl. cor. 153. a.

veritate[475] he held not *per Baroniam,* he ought to be discharged of that service, and to sit in Parliament no more.

[a476] For that the Abby of Leicester was founded by Robert Fitz-Robet Earle of Leicester (albeit the patronage came to the Crowne by the forfeiture of Simon de Mountford Earle of Leic.) yet being of a subjects foundation, it could not be holden *per Baroniam,* and therefore the Abbot had no capacity to be called to the Parliament and thereupon the King did grant, *quod idem Abbas & successores sui de veniendo ad Parliamenta & concilia nostra vel haeredum nostrorum quieti sint & exonerati imperpetuum.*[477]

[b478] *De jure & consuetudine Angliae ad Archidiaconatum Cantuariensem, &c. Abbates, Priores, aliosq; Praelatos quoscunque per Baroniam de domino rege tenentes pertinet in Parliamentis regiis quibuscunque ut Pares regni praedicti personaliter interesse, ibiq; de regni negotiis ac aliis tractari consuetis cum caeteris dicti regni Paribus ac aliis ibidem jus interessendi habentibus consulere & tractare, ordinate, statuere, & diffinire, ac caetera facere quae Parliamenti tempore ibid. immunient faciend.*[479]

No man ought to sit in that High Court of Parliament, but he hath right to sit there: for it is not only a personall offence in him that sitteth there without authority, but a publick offence to the Court of Parliament, and consequently to the whole Realme. But all the cases abovesaid, and others that might be remembered touching this point, as little Rivers, do flow from the fountaine of *Modus tenendi Parliamentum,* where it is said.[480] *Ad Parliamentum summoneri & venire debent ratione tenurae suae omnes & singuli Archiepisc', Episcopi, Abbates, Priores & alii majores cleri qui tenent per comitatum vel bar-*

---

475. [*Ed.:* in the truth of the thing; in actual truth.]

476. [*Ed.: a* Rot. pat. An. 26 Edw. 3. part. 1. no. 22 See Rot. claus. in dors. 11 Edw. 3. part 2. m. 11. *Religious que teignont per Barony sent tenus de venier an Parliament* Vid. ibid. 13 Edw. 3. part 2. m. 28 & 1.

477. [*Ed.:* That said abbot and his successors shall be forever free and exempt from coming to parliaments and councils, both our own and those of our heirs.]

478. *b* Rot. pat. 11 Ric. 2. part 1. m. 2. Artic. 34.

479. [*Ed.:* Concerning the law and custom of England to the Archdeaconate of Canterbury, etc. It is the duty of all abbots, priors, and other prelates who hold of the king by barony, to attend in person all royal parliaments as peers of the realm, and, with the rest of the peers of said realm and others who have the right of attendance there, to consult, deliberate, ordain, rule and decide on matters of state and the other matters customarily treated there, and to perform there at the time of parliament all the other tasks required.]

480. *Modus tenendi* Parl. ca. 2. This is *infra* explained by the Assise of Clarendon.

oniam ratione hujusmodi tenurae, & nulli minores, nisi eorum praesentia ne-cessaria vel utilis reputetur, &c.[481]

One rare and strange creation of a Lord regular to Parliament we cannot passe over, which was, That King Hen.8. in the fifth year of his reign, by his Letters Patents under the Great Seale, did grant unto Richard Banham Abbot of Tabestock in the County of Devon, being of his patronage, and to the successors of the said Abbot, *ut eorum quilibet, qui pro tempore ibidem fuerit Abbas, sit & erit unus de spiritualibus & religiosis dominis Parliamenti nostri, haeredum & successorum nostrorum, gaudend' honore, privilegio & libertatibus ejusdem.*[482]

By that which hath been said, it appeareth that this creation of a regular Lord of Parliament was voide, for that the Abbot was neither *Baro,* nor had *Baroniam,* &c. And if the King might create Abbots or Priors Lords of Par-liament, in this manner, by the same reason he might create Deans and Arch-deacons Lords of Parliament, which without question he cannot.

By the Act of Parliament of 10 Hen.2. called the Assise of Clarendon,[483] it is declared, *Ut pars consuetudinum & libertatum antecessorum Regis, viz. Henrici primi & aliorum, quae observari debent in regno & ab omnibus teneri, viz. Archiepiscopi, Episcopi, & universae personae regni, qui de rege tenent in capite habeant possessiones suas de rege sicut baroniam, & inde respondeant Justiciariis & ministris regis, & sequantur & faciant omnes consuetudines regias, & sicut caeteri barones debent interesse judiciis Curiae regis cum baronibus, quousq; per-veniatur ad diminutionem membrorum vel ad mortem.*[484,485] So as by this Act a tenure of the king in chiefe was in equipage with a Barony.

---

481. [*Ed.:* There should be summoned and come to parliament by reason of their tenure all and singular archbishops, bishops, abbots, priors, and other major clergy who hold by barony or county, and no minor clergy, unless their presence be thought useful or necessary, etc.]

482. [*Ed.:* That whoever of these serves for a time there as abbot, is and shall be one of the spiritual and religious lords of parliament, both our own and those of our heirs and successors, and he shall enjoy the honor, privilege and liberties of the same.]

483. 10 Hen. 2. cap. 11. Mat. par. 97. Assisa de Clarendon.

484. Rot. Parl. 11 & 21 Ric. 2.

485. [*Ed.:* As part of the customs and liberties of the king's predecessors, namely Henry I and others, which should be observed in the kingdom and binding on all, the archbishops, bishops and all persons of the realm who hold from the king in chief should hold their possessions from the king by baronial tenure, and accordingly should answer to the justices and ministers of the king, and observe and perform all royal customs, and like other barons are obliged to attend the trials of the Royal Court, unless it is a case involving death or loss of limb.]

And King John by his great Charter of liberties made *Anno* 17 of his reigne[486] granteth, *Quod faciemus summoneri Archiepiscopos, Episcopos, Abbates, Comites, & Majores Barones regni singulatim per literas nostras.*[487] Out of this Clause we are to observe these things: First, that these Barons called here *Majores,* were Lords of Parliament, and called thereunto by the Kings Writs, Secondly, that they were called *Majores* comparatively, and that was in respect | of others which were called *Barones minores,* or *Nobiles minores,* and were freeholders that[488] hold by Knights Service and Escuage, i. *Servitium scuti,* of three sorts, viz. *Milites, Armigeri, & Generosi,* knights, Esquires, and Gentlehomes, or Gentlemen. These *Barones minores* were Lords of Mannors, and had not the dignity of Lords, but had Courts of their Freeholders, which to this day are called Court Barons, *Curiae Baroniar'.* Of this Baron it is said in that law made by King Edward before the Conquest: *Barones qui suam habent*[*489] *Curiam de suis hominibus, videant ut sic de eis agant, quatenus erga deum reatum non incurrant, & regem non offendant.*[490]

Baro à Bar, Germanica lingua liberum & sui juris significat,[491] 1. Which agreeth well with that which hath been said. 2. That *Baro major* was called *Baro major regni.* 3. That every greater Baron was severally summoned by the Kings Writ, which continueth to this day.

[46]

Nota, a Knights fee is the service of a Knight, that is of a man at Arms, or of War.

The fees of the Knights, Citizens, and Burgesses of Parliament.

First, for the Knight of any County it is 4 s. *per diem,* and so it hath been time out of mind, which is particularly expressed in many Records, but let us take one in *haec verba. Johannes Shordich unus militum comitatus Middlesex venientium ad Parliamentum tent' apud Westm' in Cro. Animarum ultim' prae-terit' habet allocationem 4 li. & 4 s. pro 21 diebus pro expensis suis veniendo ad*

---

486. Cart. *libertat. a Rege Johanne Anno 17 regni sui concess.* Mat. Par. 343.

487. [*Ed.:* That we shall cause to be summoned individually by our writs the archbishops, bishops, abbots, earls, and greater barons of the realm.]

488. Hereof see the second part of the Instit. cap.de Militibus. 1 Edw. 2. *Inter leges* Edw. cap. 21. Ib. ca. 9.

489. *1. Curiam Baronis. Glanv. li. 8. cap. 11. acc Bract. li. 3. 154. b. Camd. Brit. 121.

490. [*Ed.:* The barons who have their own court of their own men should see that they deal with them in such a way as to do no offense to God nor offend the king.]

491. [*Ed.:* Baro is derived *bar,* and in the German tongue means a man who is free and under his own authority.]

Parliament' praedict' ibid. morando, & exinde ad propria redeundo, capiendo per diem 4 s. Teste Rege apud Westm' 24 die Novemb. Anno 46.[492,493] Every Citizen and Burgesse is to have 2 s. *per diem, ut supra, mutatis mutandis.*[494]

[a495] *Nota* the Writ *De expensis militum,* on the expenses of soldiers &c. both comprehend the summe according to the abovesaid computation, and a commandment to the Sheriffe to levie the same [b496] *De communitate comitatus praedict' tam infra libertates, quam extra (Civitatibus & Burgis de quibus cives & burgenses ad Parliamentum nostrum, &c. venerunt duntaxat exceptis.)*[497] The like Writs to the Sheriffes *De expensis civium & Burgensium* to levie the same in Cities and Boroughs.

[c498] An. 1 Ric.2. nu.11. The Commons petitioned in Parliament, that all persons having Lay fee might contribute to the charge of the Knights, and to all tallages. The King answered, [The Lords of the Realm will not lose their old liberties,] Note the Writ is *De communitate.*

[d499] Also there is a Writ in the register *De expensis militis non levandis ab hominib' de antiquo dñco nec ab nativis.* [e500,501] Other discharges *De expensis militū.*

[f502] For the wages of the knights of the Shire of Cambridge see the statute of 34 Hen. 8. cap.24. *Consimile pro Insula de Ely,* &c.[503]

---

492. Indors. claus. An. 46 Edw. 3. nu. 4. Rot. claus. 7 Ric. 2. nu. 1. *de expensis milit. Regist.* fo. 192. 2. acc *Diota. Veniendo, Morando, Redeundo, per diem* 4 s. Par. 51 Edw. 3. nu. 45 35 Hen. 8. cap. 1. See the ancient Treatise, *De modo tenendi Parl.*

493. [*Ed.:* (let us take one) in the following words: John Shordich, one of the knights of the county of Middlesex who came to the parliament held at Westminster on the morrow of All Souls last, has a 21-day allowance of 4 pounds 4 shillings, to cover his expenses in coming to parliament and staying here and then returning home, receiving 4 shillings per day. Witness: the king. At Westminster, on November 24, in the 46th year of his reign.]

494. [*Ed.:* two shillings per day, as above, making the necessary changes.]

495. *a* Regist. f. 192. 2 See the stat. of 12 R. 2. ca. 12 & see 23 H. 6. ca. 11. how the Sheriffe shall levie the same. See 8 R. 2. tit. Avowrie 260. what the Common law was.

496. *b Nota, de communitate.* Vid. sup. pa. 1. For the legall understanding of this word Commons.

497. [*Ed.:* from the community of said county both within liberties and without (excepting only the cities and boroughs which have sent citizens and burgesses to our parliament).]

498. *c* Rot. Par. 1 R. 2 nu. 11.

499. *d* Regist. 261 7 H. 6. 35 b. F. N. B. 14 E.

500. [*Ed.:* On not levying a knight's expenses from men of the ancient demesne, nor from naifs.]

501. *e* Regist. 191, 192. 12 R. ca. 12.

502. *f* 34 H. 8. ca. 24. 9 H. 6. nu. 46.

503. [*Ed.:* A similar one for the Isle of Ely, etc. (the opening words of the statute cited).]

[504] Hen. 4. An.14. of his reigne summoned a Parliament *Cro. Purifica-tionis*,[505] On the morrow of the Purification and he deceased 20 Martii following, so as the Parliament was dissolved by his decease. Thereupon it was a question, whether the Knights and Burgesses should have their wages seeing nothing passed in that Parliament. And it was resolved, that if upon view of the Kings [h506] Records any like presidents may be found, allowances of their fees shall be made. [i507] Also the Clergy were contributory by reason of their Benefices to the expenses of the procurators of the Clergy.

[k508] But Chaplains which are Masters of the Chancery and attendants at the Parliament, shall not be contributory by reason of their Benefices to the expenses of the Clergy, as by the Register *ubi supra* above appears: and this was by an Act of Parliament made in*[509] 4 Edw. 3 which in generall words is recited in the Writ directed to the Arch-deacon for their discharge.

Who be eligible to be a Knight, Citizen, or Burgesse of Parliament.

A Knight Baneret being no Lord of Parliament is eligible to be Knight, Citizen, or Burgesse of the House of Commons being under the degree of a Baron, who is of the lowest degree of the Lords House. But Thomas Camois was not only a Knight Baneret, but a Baron and Lord of Parliament in *Anno* 7 Ric. 2 and served in that Parliament as a Baron of the Realme,[510] and therefore as of a thing notorious he was discharged. One under the age of 21 years is not eligible, neither can any Lord of Parliament sit there untill he be of the full age of 21 years.   [47]

An Alien cannot be elected of the Parliament, because he is not the Kings liege subject, and so it is albeit he be made Denizen by Letters Patents, &c.[511]

504. *g* Rot. Par. 1 H. 5nu. 26.
505. [*Ed.*: on the morrow of the Purification.]
506. *h Nota*, for presidents.
507. *i* Regist. 261. F. N. B. 229. 2.
508. *k Vid. sup.* pa. 4,5.
509. *Parl. An. 4 Edw. 3. *apud* Winton. whereof there is no Roll now retaining.
510. See the stat. of 5 R. 2 cap. 4. Vid. sup. pa 4. 5. Rot. brev. 7 R. 2. Dors. claus. 7 R. 2 m. 10. & 37.
511. Vi. stat. der Mar. cap.

for thereby he is made *quasi, seu tanquam ligeus;*[512] but that will not serve, for he must be *ligeus revera,*[513] and not *quasi,* &c. And we have had such an one chosen and disallowed by the House of Commons, because such a person can hold no place of judicature: but if an Alien be naturalized by Parliament, then he is eligible to this or any other place of judicature.

But it is objected that Gilbert de Umphrevill Earle of Andgos in Scotland, was called by the Kings Writ to the Parliament in 39 Edw. 3. by the name of Gilbert Earle of Andgos:[514] and in a Writ of Ravishment of Ward brought against him, by the name of Gilbert Umphrevill Chivaler he pleaded to the Writ, that he was Earle of Andgos not named in the Writ: and for that he was summoned to every Parliament by the name of the Earle of Andgos, and the King sent to him a Writ of Parliament under the Great Seale, as to a Peer of the land, by judgement of the Court the Writ did abate. We have searched for the truth of this case, and do finde it in the Plea Rols in this manner.

Richard de Umphrevill Baron of Prodhowe and Redesdale in the County of Northumberland, had issue Gilbert, who after the death of his Father was a Baron of this Realm, and in the reign of Hen. 3. married with Mawde daughter and heir of the Earl of Andgos in Scotland, who by her had issue Gilbert, who was Earle of Andgos as heir to his mother, and Baron of Prodhow and Redesdale as heir to his father: he sat in Parliament upon summons by Writ in 27 Edw. 1. 28 Edw. 1. 30 Edw. 1. 35 Edw. 1. 1 Edw. 2. and 2 Edw. 2. by the name of Gilbert Earle of Andgos. Robert his sonne sat in Parliament, Anno 12 Edw. 2. by the same name of dignity, and so forth, all E. the Seconds reign. And Gilbert his sonne sat in Parliament in 6 Edw. 3. and in every Parliament following untill, and in 4 Ric. 2. by the same name. And in Gilbert his sonne (who deceased in *Anno* 15 Hen. 6) that surname of Umphrevil ceased. Hereby it appeareth that the said Richard Umphrevil and his posterity, from whence soever they originally descended, were liege Englishmen: for if they had been Aliens, they could not have enjoyed the Lordships of Prodhowe, Otterborne, Harbottle, and Redesdale in England, nor the Barony of Kime

All this doth appear in the Rols of Parliament in all the severall time.

512. [*Ed.:* as if a liege, or a quasi-liege.]
513. [*Ed.:* a true liege.]
514. 39 Edw. 3. 35,36.

in Lancashire, which the two last Gilberts enjoyed, And note, the Book in 39 Edw. 3. concludeth, that Gilbert Umphrevil was summoned to the Parliament under the Great Seale, *Come un Pier del Realme*.[515]

A Bishop elect may sit in Parliament as a Lord thereof.[516]

These two were commonly called the Erles of Kime.

Of Knights, Citizens and Burgesses of Parliament.

None of the Judges of the Kings Bench, or Common Pleas. or Barons of the Exchequer that have judiciall places can be chosen knight, Citizen, or Burgesse of Parliament, as it is now holden, because they be assistants in the Lords House; and yet you may reade in the*[517] Parliament Roll, An. 31 Hen. 6. that Thorp Baron of the exchequer was Speaker of the Parliament. But any that have judiciall places in the Court of Wards, Court of Duchie, or other Courts Ecclesiasticall, or Civill, being no Lord of Parliament, are eligible.[518]

None of the Clergy, though he be of the lowest Order, are eligible to be Knight, Citizen, or Burgesse of Parliament, because they are of another body, viz. of the Convocation.

A man attainted of treason or felony, &c. is not eligible: for concerning the election of two Knights, the words of the Writ be, *Duos milites gladiis cinctos magis idoneos, & discretos eligi fac.*[519] And for the election of Citizens & Burgesses, | the words of the Writ be, *Duos, &c. de discretioribus & magis sufficientibus,*[520] which they cannot be said to be, when they are attainted of treason or felony, &c. [48]

Maiors and Bailiffes of Townes Corporate are eligible against the opinion in Brook, *Anno* 38 Hen.8. tit' Parliament.

Any of the profession of the Common Law, and which is in practice of the same, is eligible. For he which is eligible of common right cannot be disabled by the said Ordinance in Parliament in the Lords House in 46 Edw.3.[521] unlesse

515. [*Ed.:* as Peer of the Realm]
516. Hil. 18 Edw. 1. fo. 4. nu. 105.
517. *Rot. Par. 31 Hen. 6 nu. 26, 27, 28. Note, he could not be speaker unlesse he were Knight of the shire &c. in the book of Burgesses of the House of Commons.
518. *a* Alexan. Nowels case, who after was Deane of Pauls being a Prebend. 1 Mar.
519. [*Ed.:* Select two of the more suitable and discreet knights armed with swords.]
520. [*Ed.:* two, etc., of the more suitable and discreet.]
521. Rot. Par. 46 Edw. 3. nu. 10.

it had been by Act of Parliament: and if it had been by authority of Parliament, yet had the same been abrogated by the said statues of 5 Ric. 2. stat. 2. cap. 2. and 7 Hen. 4. cap. 15.[522] which are generall lawes without any exception, as hath been said.

At a Parliament holden at Coventry *Anno* 6 Hen. 4. the Parliament was summoned by Writ (and by colour of the said Ordinance) it was forbidden, that no Lawyer should be chosen Knight, Citizen, or Burgesse, by reason whereof this Parliament was fruitlesse, and never a good law made thereat, and therefore called *Indoctum Parliamentum,*[523] or Lack-learning Parliament.[524] And seeing these Writs were against law, Lawyers ever since (for the great and good service of the Common-wealth) have been eligible: for, as it hath been said, the Writs of Parliament cannot be altered without an Act of Parliament: and albeit the prohibitory clause had been inserted in the Writ, yet being against law, Lawyers were of right eligible, and might have been elected Knight, Citizen, or Burgesse in that Parliament of 6 Hen. 4.

By speciall order of the House of Commons the Attorny Generall is not eligible to be a Member of the House of Commons.

At the Parliament holden 1 *Caroli Regis,* the Sheriffe for the County of Buckingham was chosen Knight for the County of Norff. and returned into the Chancery: and having a Subpena out of the Chancery served upon him, at the suit of the Lady C. *pendente Parliamento,* upon motion, he had the priviledge of Parliament allowed unto him by the judgement of the whole House of Commons.

Who shall be Electors of Knights, Citizens, and Burgesses, how and when: and of Elections.

Who shall be electors, and who shall be chosen, and the time, place, and manner of election, and therein the duty of the Sheriffe, you may read in the positive lawes of 7 Hen. 4. cap.15. 11 Hen. 4. cap.1. 1 Hen. 5. cap.1. 8 Hen.

---

522. 5 R. 2. stat. 2. ca. 4. 7 Hen. 4. ca. 15.

523. [*Ed.:* Lack-learning Parliament.]

524. Rot. Claus. Anno 6 Hen. 4. See before pa. 10. 4 Petty Acts passed at this Parliament of little or no effect, as by the same appears. Rot. Parl 50 Edw. 3. nu. 83. an Ordinance that no Sheriffe should be Justice of peace, &c. bound not the subject untill a statute made 1 Mar. c. 8.

6. cap.7. 10 Hen. 6. ca.2. 23 Hen. 6. cap.15. 6 Hen. 6. cap.4. &c. which need not here be particularly rehearsed.

No Knight, Citizen or Burgesse can sit in Parliament before he hath taken the Oath of Supremacy.[525]

Vide. Rot. Claus. 7 Ric. 2. 7 Octobris in Dors. Sir Thomas Moreville elected one of the Knights for the County of Hertford, *Ibid.* James Berners chosen to serve in Parliament, and both of them discharged. See the Record.

No election can be made of any Knight of the Shire but between 8 and 11 of the clock in the forenoone: but if the election be begun within that time, and cannot be determined within those hours the election may be made after.

For the election of the Knights, if the party or the Freeholders demand the Poll, the Sheriffe cannot deny the scrutiny for he cannot discerne who be Freeholders by the view: and though the party would wave the Poll yet the Sheriffe must proceed in the scrutiny.

If the King doth newly incorporate an ancient Borough (which sent Burgesses to the Parliament) and granteth that certain selected Burgesses shall make election of the Burgesses of Parliament, where all the Burgesses elected before, this Charter taketh not away the election of the other Burgesses. And so, if a City, &c. hath power to make Ordinances, they cannot make an Ordinance that a lesse number shall elect Burgesses, for the Parliament then made the election | before; for free elections of Members of the high Court of Parliament are *pro bono publico,* and not to be compared to other cases of election of Mayors, Bailiffes, &c. of Corporations, &c.   [49]

If one be duly elected Knight, Citizen, or Burgesse, and the Sheriffe returne another, the returne must be reformed, and amended by the Sheriffe[526] and he that is duly elected must be inserted: for the election in these cases is the foundation, and not the return.

By originall grant or by custome, a selected number of Burgesses may elect and binde the residue.

Concerning Charters of Exemption.

The King cannot grant a Charter of exemption to any man to be freed from election of Knight, Citizen, or Burgesse of the Parliament (as he may do of

---

525. 5 Eliz. cap. 1.
526. Rot. Parl. 5 Hen. 4. nu. 38.

some inferiour Office or places) because the elections of them ought to be free, and his attendance is for the service of the whole Realme[527] and for the benefit of the King and his people, and the whole Common-wealth hath an interest therein: and therefore a Charter of exemption that King Henry the sixth had made to the Citizens of York of exemption in that case[528] was by Act of Parliament enacted and declared to be voide. And though we finde some presidents that Lords of Parliament have sued out Charters of exemption from their service in Parliament,[529] yet those Charters are holden to be void: for though they be not eligible, as is aforesaid, yet their service in Parliament is for the whole Realme, and for the benefit of the king and his people, of which service he cannot be exempted by any Letters Patents. And if he hath *laesam phantasiam*[530] or be extremely sick, or the like, these be good causes of his excuse in not comming, but no cause of exemption, for he may recover his memory and health, &c. So as the said presidents were grants *de facto,* not *de jure.*[531] for if the King cannot grant a Charter of exemption from being of the grand Assise in a Writ of right, or of a Jury in an Attaint for the mischiefe that may follow in those private actions, *à fortiori,* he cannot grant any exemption to a Lord of Parliament; for his service in Parliament is publick for the whole Realme. But if any Lord of Parliament be so aged, impotent, or sick, as he cannot conveniently without great danger travell to the High Court of Parliament, he may have license of the King under the Great Seale to be absent from the same during the continuance or prorogation thereof: but if the rehearsall be not true, or if he recover his health, so as he become able to travell, he must attend in Parliament. Or without any such license obtained, if he be so aged, impotent, or sick, as is aforesaid, and yet is amerced for his absence, he may reasonably and honestly excuse himselfe by the statute of 5 Ric. 2.[532]

After the precept of the Sheriffe directed to the City or Borough for making of election, there ought *secundum legem & consuetudinem Parliam.*[533] to be

---

527. Pasch. 3 E. 3. fo. 19 tit. coron. F. 161.

528. 29 Hen. 6. cap. 3.

529. Rot. pat. 1 part. 11 Edw. 3. Rot. pat. 4 part. 1 Edw. 4. m. 15. pro Do. Beauchamp. Rot. pat. 2 Edw. 4. part 2. m. 2. pro Dom. Vesey.

530. [*Ed.:* a diseased imagination.]

531. 39 Edw. 3. 15. 34 Hen. 6. 25. 35 Hen. 6. 42.

532. 5 Ric. 2. c. 4. stat. 2.

533. [*Ed.:* according to the law and custom of parliament.]

given a convenient time for the day of the election; and sufficient warning given to the Citizens or Burgesses that have voices, that they may be present: otherwise the election is not good, unlesse such as have voyces doe take notice of themselves and be present at the election.

Any election or voyces given before the precept be read and published, are void and of no force: for the same electors after the precept read and published may make a new election and alter their voyces, *secundum legem & consuetudinem Parliamenti.*

Thus much have we thought good to set down concerning Knights, Citizens, and Burgesses, because much time is spent in Parliament concerning the right of elections, &c. which might more profitably be imployed *pro bono publico.*[534]

Now to treat more in particular (as it hath been much desired) of the lawes,[535] customes, liberties and priviledges of this Court of Parliament (which are the very heartstrings of the Common-wealth, whereof we have remembered some: and you may see some.[536] few other examples in the margent too long here to be | rehearsed) would take up a whole Volume of it selfe: certain it is,   [50] as hath been said, that *Curia Parliamenti suis propriis legibus subsistit.*[537]

All the Justices of England and Barons of the Exchequer are assitants to the Lords to informe them of the Common law, and thereunto are called severally by Writ.[538] Neither doth it belong to them (as hath been said) to judge of any law, custome, or priviledge of Parliament. And to say the truth, the lawes, customes, liberties, and priviledges of Parliament are better to be learned out of the Rols of Parliament, and other Records, and by presidents and continuall experience, then can be expressed by any one mans pen.

> *Per varios actus legem experientia fecit.*
> *Multa multo exercitamentis facilius, quam regulis percipies.*[539]

---

534. [*Ed.:* for the public good; for the welfare of the whole.]

535. See before pag. 24, 25.

536. 16 Ric. 2. Rot. Claus. in dors. Rot. Parl. 11 Ric. 2. nu. 7. 1 Hen. 5. nu. 9. cap. 1.

537. [*Ed.:* The court of Parliament is governed by its own laws.]

538. *a* Rot. Parl. 5 Hen. 4 nu. 12. 23 Hen. 6. nu 45. 27 Hen. 6. nu 18. 31 Hen. 6. nu. 26, 27 Lamb. *Inter leges Edw. Confessoris, ca. 3. Ad synodos, ad capitula venientibus, sive summoniti sunt, sive per se quid agendum habuerint, sit summa pax.*

539. [*Ed.:* Through the manifold activities [of life] experience created law. You will learn many things much more easily from experience than from rules.]

Consultations in Parliament for maintenance of the Navie.

In many Parliaments consultations have been had for the maintenance of the Navie of England, and remedies provided against decay of the same: as taking one example for many. In the Parliament holden in *Anno* 45 Edw.3. the Commons amongst their petitions do affirme, that the decay of the Navy doth arise by three causes.[540] First, for that sundry mens ships are seised for the King, long before they serve, whereby the owners are driven at their charges to find their Mariners, to their undoing. Secondly, for that Merchants, the nourishers of the Navy, are oft restrained in their shipping, whereby Mariners are driven to seek other trades and livings. Thirdly, for that the Maisters of the Kings ships do take up Masters of other ships as good as their selves are, whereby the most of those ships do lye still, and the Mariners enforced to seek new livings: whereof they prayed remedy. To this petition of right the Kings royall answer was, That he would provide remedy.

The decay of the Navy.

The Kings Navy exceeds all others.

    The Kings Navy exceeds all others in the world for three things, viz. beauty, strength, and safety. For beauty, they are so many Royall Palaces: for strength (no part of the world having such Iron and Timber as England hath) so many moving Castles and Barbicans: And for safety, they are the most defensive wals of the Realm. Amongst the ships of other Nations, they are like Lions amongst silly Beasts, or Falcons amongst fearfull fowle.

    In the reign of Queen Elizabeth (I being then acquainted with this bussinesse there were 33 besides Pinnaces; which so garded and regarded the navigation of the Merchants, as they had safe vent for their commodities, and trade and traffick flourished. A worthy subject for Parliaments to take into consideration and to provide remedy as often as need shall require. For navigation, see *Gen.6. 14. Sapient. 14. 6.*[541] *Remp. quasi navem existimare debemus, quae omnium manibus officioq; indiget, &c.*[542] A leak in a ship is timely to be repaired: For as it is in the naturall body of Man, so it is in the politick body of the Common -wealth. *Non morbus in plerisqe sed morbi neglecta curatio corpus interficit.*[543]

---

540. Rot. Parl. 45 H. 3. nu. 32.

541. Patricius, lib. 5. *De institutione reipublicae.*

542. [*Ed.:* We ought to regard the commonwealth as a ship, which requires the labors and services of everyone.]

543. [*Ed.:* In most cases it is not the disease that kills the body, but the failure to treat the disease.]

And thus much for consultations in Parliament concerning the Navy of England.

See the first part of the Institutes. Sect. 164. verb. [*Veigne les Burgesses al Parliament.*] And there have been since the Conquest about 300 Sessions of Parliament whereof divers are not printed.

In perusing over the Rols of Parliament we find First divers Acts of Parliament in print that are not of Record in the Roll of Parliament. Secondly, many acts of Parliament that be in the Rols of Parliament, and never yet printed. Thirdly, divers Clauses omitted in the print which are in the Parliament roll. Fourthly, more in the print then in the Record. Fifthly, many variances between the print and the Roll. Sixthly, Statutes repealed or disaffirmed, and yet printed, &c. Seventhly, whole Parliaments omitted out of the print. Eighthly, whole Parliaments repealed, or a great part.

And of every of these taking some examples; for to handle all at large would require a whole Treatise, which (we having broken the Ice) some good man and | lover of his countrey (we hope) will undertake to wade thorow.

As to the first, These are in print, and not of Record. 20 Edw. 3. the oath of the Judges. 27 Edw. 3. cap.4, 5, 6, 7, 8. concerning the Alneger and Gascoigne Wines. 37 Edw. 3. cap.7. touching silver vessell. 37 Edw. 3. cap.19. of Hawkes 2 Ric. 2. cap.5. of Newes. Vid. 11 R.2. 11. 2 R.2. cap.3. of fained guifts 7 R.2. cap.15. against maintenance. 9 Ric.2. cap.3. of error and attaint. 11 Ric.2. cap.4, 5, & 6. not of Record. 13 Ric.2. cap.11. touching Clothes. 13 Ric.2. cap.19. concerning Salmons. 13 Ric.2. cap.2. touching Pilgrims. 13 Ric.2. cap.15. concerning the Kings Castles and Gaoles. 14 Ric.2. ca.7. concerning tinne 17 Ric.2. cap.8. of unlawfull Assemblies. 17 Ric.2. cap.9. concerning Salmons. 27 Hen. 6. cap.3. touching imployments, &c.

As to the second:[544] These Acts of Parliament are of Record, and not in print. An.11 Edw. 3. the creation of the D. of Cornwall, &c. by authority of Parliament. 3. Ric. 2. nu. 39 concerning Justices of Peace, a profitable law for them. 8. Ric. 2. nu.31. concerning the jurisdiction of the Constable & Marshall. 20 R.2. concerning the legitimation of the children of John of Gaunt D. of Lanc. by Kath. Swinford. 5. Hen. 4. nu.24. a Commission or Act of Parliament for arraying & mustering of men. 8 Hen. 4. nu.12. Clergy exempted from arraying and mustering of men. 11 Hen. 4. nu.28. against Bribery and Brocage

Of the Burgesses of Parliament. About 300 sessions of parliament since the conquest.

[51]

To the first. *De corrupto Judice.*

To the second.

544. See the Princes case lib. 8. fo. 1

in great Officers Judges, &c. 11 Hen. 4. nu.63. concerning Attornies, &c. 6 Hen. 6. nu.27. that a Queen of England Dowager shall not contract her selfe or marry without the Kings license. 9 Hen. 6. nu.25. concerning fees of Privy Counsellors, and other head Officers. And very many others.

To the third.
As to the third: In these Acts of Parliament divers clauses are omitted out of the print, which are in the Parliament Roll. 36 Edw. 3. cap.3. in the Act of Purveyors, &c. in the clause of the penalty, the Steward, Treasurer, and Controller are expressly named, but omitted in the print. 2 Ric. 2. stat.2. cap.4. in confirmation of liberties, &c. saving the Kings regality, is omitted. 13 Ric. 2. cap. 1. concerning presentations of the King, the last clause, concerning ratifications of the King, is omitted. 13 Ric. 2. cap. 2. touching provisions. 14 Ric. 2. cap.4. nu.9. concerning Regrators of wools, high prices omitted in the print. 17 Ric. 2. cap.4. of Malt, leaveth out Hertfordshire. 2 Hen. 5. cap.3. nu.38. concerning enquests. 2 Hen. 5. ca.1. nu. 30. concerning Justices of peace. 9 Hen. 4. cap.8. nu.43. concerning provisions. 8 Hen. 6. nu. 50. cap.10. concerning proces during the Kings will, omitted in the print.

To the fourth.
As to the fourth: In these there is more in the print then in the Record, 9 Hen. 4. cap.9. nu. 43. touching provisions. 2 Hen. 5. stat.2. cap.3. nu.38. touching Jurors, &c.

To the fifth.
The fifth: In these the print vary from the Record in some materiall thing. Generally in all the statutes made concerning provisions, or other the usurpations of the Pope, the biting and bitter words are left out in the print. As to take an examples or two. Vi. 38 Edw. 3. in print. cap.1, 2, 3, 4. and in the Roll, nu.9. &c. 3 Ric. 2.cap.3. in print. Rol, nu. 37. &c. the Bishops being Lord Chancellors. 9 Ric. 2. nu.1, the print mistake the beginning of the Parliament, viz. Monday after &. Luke, for Friday. 9 Hen. 4. cap.2. nu.26. concerning Attornies. &c. A Roll of Parliament intituled 14 Edw. 4. where it should be 13 Edw. 4. 9 Hen. 5.cap. 2 & 3. printed as perpetuall in some Books, where they were to endure but untill the next Parliament.

To the sixth.
The sixth: Statutes pretended to be enacted, and after disaffirmed, and yet printed. 5 Ric. 2. cap. stat.2. touching inquiries of Heresies *Anno* 6 Ric. 2. nu.52. disaffirmed by the Commons, for that they protested it was never their meaning to be justified, and to binde themselves and their successors to the Prelats no more then their ancestors had done before them. Robert Braibroke Bishop of London was then Lord Chancellor. By this and that which followes, it appeareth how necessary it was in those dayes to have some of the Commons to be (as hath been said) at the ingrossing of the Parliament Rols, as appeareth

Rot. Parl. *Anno* 6 Hen. 4. nu.56.7. Hen. 4. nu.65. &c. & *Modo tenend' Parl.*
cap.8. 2 Hen. 4. | cap.15. disavowed by the Commons, and yet the pretended [52]
Act printed 2 Hen. 5. cap.6. against Preachers, disavowed the next Parliament
by the Commons, for that they never assented, and yet the supposed Act
printed.[545]

The seventh: Whole Parliaments omitted out of the print, wherein there   To the
be many notable things to be observed. *An.* 3 Edw. 2. a Parliament holden at   seventh.
Westm. 3 Sept. Dors. Claus. 2 Edw. 2.m. 14. &. 22. *Annis 4 Edw. 2. apud*
London. 5 Edw. 2. apud Westm. 6 Edw. 2.ib. bis.7 Edw. 2.ib.8 Edw. 2.apud
Eborum. 11 Edw. 2. apud Westm. 16 Edw. 2. apud Edw. 2. apud Rippon, & postea
apud Eborum.[546] *An.6 Edw. 3.* a Parliament holden at Westminister the monday
after the feast of S. Gregory. *Anno* 8 Edw. 3. a Parliament holden at York the
day before the feast of S. Peter in Cathedra *Anno* 11 Edw. 3. at Westm. whereat
the Prince was created Duke of Cornwall, &c. *An.* 13 Edw. 3. holden at Westm.
in 15 Mich. 22 Edw. 3. at Westm. the Monday next after the week in the
middest of Lent. 29 Edw. 3.a Parliament holden at Westm the day after S.
Martin. 40 Edw. 3.; at Westm. the Monday after the invention of the Crosse.
7 Ric. 2. at Westm. the Friday after the Feast of S. Mark, &c.

The eighth: whole Parliaments repealed and made void by subsequent Par-   To the
liaments. 1 Hen. 4. cap.3. repealed. 21 Ric. 2. which had repealed the Parliament   eighth.
of 11 Ric. 2. and reviveth the same. By 39 Hen. 6. cap.1.a Parliament holden
at Coventry *Anno* 38 Hen. 6. is wholly repealed. Rot. Par. 12 Edw. 4. nu. A
whole Parliament holden *Anno* 49 Hen. 6. *& readeptionis regni sui primo,*[547]
is repealed and reversed. [a548] Vide the Parliament of 15 Edw. 3. repealed. Rot.
Parl. *anno* 17 Edw. 3. nu. 23. For there it is agreed that the statute of 15 Edw.
3. shall be utterly repealed, and lose the name of a statute, as contrarie to the
laws and prerogative: and for that some Articles there made are reasonable,

545. Rot. Parl. 11 Hen. 4. nu. 12. vide 7 Hen. 4. nu. 11.

546. [*Ed.:* . . . at Westminster on September 3 (*Clause Roll from the 2nd year of Edward II, membranes 14 and 22, in the dorse*); in the 4th year of Edward II at London; in the 5th year at Westminster; in the 6th year twice at Westminster; in the 7th year at Westminster; in the 8th year at York; in the 11th year at Westminster; in the 16th year at Rippon, and later at York. In the 6th year of Edward III . . .]

547. [*Ed.:* in the first year upon regaining his throne.]

548. *a* Where the printed book suppose that there was another Parliament in *Anno* 15 Edw. 3. whereby the former statute was repeated, the truth is, the Parliament was holden at Westm. 15 Pasc. *Anno* 17 Edw. 3.

it is agreed, that such Articles and others agreed in this Parliament shall be made into a statute by the advice of the Justices.

b Histories
sometime
explaine
Records of
Parliament.
ᵇ Many Records of Parliament can hardly be understood, unlesse you joyne thereunto the History of that time. For example: ᶜ⁵⁴⁹ The Cardinall of Winchester Uncle of the King, declareth in open Parliament, that he being in Flanders, in his journey to Rome, returned back of his own will to purge himselfe of a bruit that he should be a Traytor to the Realm, whereof (no accusation being against him) he was easily purged by the Duke of Gloc. Protector, by the Kings commandement. But adde the History thereunto, that the Cardinall having certain of the Kings Jewels in gage, meant to have them brought after him: but these Jewels being arrested and stay'd at Sandwich by the Kings commandement, and the bruit hereof coming to the Cardinals care (he being therewith exceedingly troubled) for the recovery of them, returned in post to the Parliament. Now after he was purged of the bruit of supposed treason; touching the said Jewels stayed at Sandwich to the great hindrance of the Cardinall, as he complained. It was on a motion on his behalfe, ordered that the Cardinall should pay to the King Six thousand pound more for them,

This appeareth in
the same
Parliament
nu 15.
and lend to the King thirteen thousand pound, which was done.

And for a conclusion hereof, and of this Chapter of the High Court of Parliament, it is to be remembred that by the statute of 42 Edw. 3. cap.1. all Statutes are repealed that are against Magna Carta, or Carta de Foresta.

Parliament
in Scot-
land. In
Ireland.
See hereafter cap. 75. how and in what manner Parliaments be holden in Scotland. And cap. 77. how and what manner Parliaments be holden in Ireland, and how Bils shall passe there, never before this time published, as we know.

Cap. VII.
The Court of Kings Bench, *Coram Rege.*[1]

[70] | Bracton doth make in few words at notable expression of this Court.[2] *Habet Rex plures Curias in quibus diversae actiones terminantur, & illarum curiarum*

---

549. *c* Rot. Parl. 10 Hen. 6. nu. 14.
1. [*Ed.:* before the king.]
2. Lib 3. cap. 7. fo. 105. b.

habet unam propriam, sicut Aulam regiam, & Justiciarios capitales qui proprias causas regias terminant. & aliorum omnium, per querelam, vel per privilegium, sive libertatem.[3] And soon after speaking of the Justices of this Court saith:[4] *Item Justiciariorum quidam sunt capitales, generales, perpetui, & majores à latere regis residentes, qui omnium aliorum corrigere tenentur injurias, & errores.*[5]

And Britton saith: *In droit des Justices que sont assignes de nous suer & tener nostre lieu or q nous seons en Angliterre. Voilons que eux eiant conusans de amender faux judgements, & de terminer appeales & auters trespasses faitz enconter nostre peace, &*[6] *enconter nostre jurisdiction, & lour record se esteant solonq; ceo que nous manderons per nostre bře.*[7]   Nota.

Fleta,[8] in describing this Court saith: *Habet & Rex Curiam suam & Justiciarios suos tam milites quam clericos locum suum tenentes in Anglia, coram quibus, & non alibi nisi coram semetipso & concilio suo vel Auditoribus specialibus falsa judicia & errores Justiciariorum revertuntur & corriguntur: ibidem etiam terminantur brevia de appellis, & alia brevia super actionibus criminalibus & injuriarum contra pacem regis illatarum impetrata, & omnia, in quibus continetur ubi tunc fuerimus in Anglia.*[9]

In the Black Book of the Exchequer,[10] it is thus said of the Chief Justice

---

3. [*Ed.:* The king has many courts in which various actions are determined, and of these courts he has one of his own, such as the royal hall, and the chief justices who determine the king's own causes, and those of all others, by plaint or by reason of a privilege or franchise.]

4. Fo. 108. 2.

5. [*Ed.:* Some of the justices are major, general, permanent and of greater importance, remaining at the king's side, whose duty it is to correct the wrongs and errors of all others.]

6. A granter prohibitions.

7. [*Ed.:* In respect of the justices who are assigned to follow us and keep our place wherever we sit in England, we will that they should have knowledge to amend false judgments, and to determine appeals [of felony] and other trespasses done against our peace, and against our jurisdiction, and to record them, according to what we command them by our writ.]

8. [*Ed.:* Fleta: an ancient treatise on the laws of England, founded mainly upon the writings of Bracton and Glanville, and supposed to have been written in the time of Edw. I.]

9. [*Ed.:* The king has his court and his justices, both knights and clerks, keeping his place in England, before whom and not elsewhere—except before the king himself and his council, or special auditors— the false judgments and errors of the justices are overturned and corrected; there also are determined writs of appeals and other writs upon criminal actions and actions for wrongs done against the king's peace, and all things in which it is contained, wherever we shall then be in England.]

10. *Liber, niger in Scaccario,* cap. 4.

of this Court: *Capitalis Justitia praesidet primus in regno.*[11] But of these three ancient Authors we observe these six conclusions.

First, where Bracton saith, *Habet Rex plures curias in quibus diversae actiones* * *terminantur;*[12] Hereby, and in effect by [a] Britton, and this conclusion followeth, that the King hath committed and distributed all his whole power of judicature,[13] to severall Courts of Justice, and therefore the judgement must be *Ideo consideratum est per Curiam.*[14] And herewith do agree divers Acts of Parliament and Book cases, some whereof, for illustration, we will briefly remember; and leave the judicious reader to the rest.

[b][15] *Provisum, concordatum & concessum est, quod tam majores, quam minores justitiam habeant & recipiant in curia Domini Regis.*[16] [c][17] That the lawes Ecclesiastical and Temporall were and yet are administred, adjudged, and executed by sundry Judges, &c. [d][18] *Expedit etiam magistratus reipublicae constitui, quia per eos qui juredicendo praesunt effectus rei accipitur; parum est enim jus in civitate esse, nisi sint qui possunt jura gerere.*[19]

[c] For the pleasure of God & quietnesse of our subjects as to save our conscience, and to keep our Oath, by the assent of our Great men and other of our Councell, we have commanded our Justices, that they shall from henceforth do even law and execution of right to all our Subjects, rich and poor, without having regard to any person, without letting to do right for any Letters or commandement which may come to them from us, or from any other, or by any other cause.

Agreeable to that great Canon of the law *Anno* 3 Edw.1.[20] which we have

Note this word.

---

11. [*Ed.:* The chief justice presides as the first in the kingdom.]

12. [*Ed.:* The king has many courts in which various actions are determined.]

13. [a] See Britton, f. 1. speaking of the King, *Et pur ceo que nous ne suffions in nostre proper-person a oier & terminer touts querels del people. Avomus partie nostre charge en plusore parts come est ordeine, &c.* 20 Edw. 3. cap. 1.

14. [*Ed.:* therefore it is decided by the court.]

15. [b] Stat. de Marlb. 52 Hen. 3. ca. i. Vid. 4. Hen. 4. ca. 22.

16. [*Ed.:* It is provided, agreed and granted that both great men and small shall have and receive justice in the lord king's court.]

17. [c] 24 Hen. 8. cap. 2. in effect.

18. [d] Bract. lib. I. ca 5. fol. 3. b.

19. [*Ed.:* It is also in the interest of the state to appoint magistrates, because by those who are in charge of stating the law the effect of a matter is carried out; for it is not enough to have law in a state unless there are those who can administer the laws.]

20. West. 1. An. 3 Edw. 1. cap. 1. Fleta lib. 1. ca. 29.

translated into Latin:[21] *Rex praecipit quòd pax sacrosanctae Ecclesiae & regni solidè custodiatur & conservetur in omnibus, quodq; justitia singulis tam pauperibus quam | divitibus administratur, nulla habita personarum ratione.*[22] See the second part of the Institutes West. 1. cap.i.

8. H.4.[23] the King hath committed all his power judiciall, some in one Court, and some in another, so as if any would render himselfe to the judgement of the King in such case where the King hath committed all his power judiciall to others, such a render should be to no effect. And 8 H.6.[24] the King doth judge by his Judges (the King having distributed his power judiciall to severall Courts) And the King hath wholly left matters of judicature according to his lawes to his Judges.

And albeit it be enacted that the Delinquent shall be fined at the will of the King,[25] *Non Dominus Rex in camera sua, nec aliter nisi per justiciarios suos (finem imponit) & haec est voluntas regis, viz. per Justiciarios & legem suam, unum est dicere.*[26]

The second conclusion is, that is those dayes this Court of Kings Bench did follow the Court: and therefore Bracton calleth it *Aulam regiam,*[27] because they sat in the Kings Hall. Britton calleth the Justices of this Court, Justices *assignes de nous suer:*[28] and Fleta, *Ubi tunc fuerimus in Anglia.*[29]

The third is, that it is called the Kings Bench, and the Pleas thereof *Coram rege:* because in this Court (as Bracton saith,) those *Capitales justiciarii proprias regis causas terminant,*[30] and therefore the King himselfe cannot be Judge *in propria causa.*[31]

---

21. *e* 20 Edw. 3. cap. I. speaking in the King's person.

22. [*Ed.:* The king commands that the peace of Holy Church and of the realm be firmly kept and preserved in all respects, and that justice be administered to everyone, both poor and rich, having no respect of persons.]

23. 8 Hen. 4. fo. 19.

24. 8 Hen. 6. 20. & tit. Grant. F. 5.

25. 2 Ric. 3. fol. 11.

26. [*Ed.:* The lord king does not impose a fine in his chamber, or anywhere else, except by his justices, and this is the king's will, namely by his justices and his law, which are to say the same thing.]

27. [*Ed.:* The King's hall or palace.]

28. [*Ed.:* justices assigned to follow us.]

29. [*Ed.:* wherever we shall then be in England.]

30. [*Ed.:* the chief justices determine the king's own causes.]

31. [*Ed.:* in his own cause.]

The fourth is, that under these words[32] *proprias causas* are included three things. First, all pleas of the Crowne; as all manner of treasons, felonies, and other pleas of the Crown which *ex congruo,*[33] are aptly called *propriae causae regis,*[34] because they are *placita coronae regis.*[35] Secondly, regularly to examine and correct all and all manner of errors *in fait,*[36] and in law, of all the Judges and Justices of the Realm in their judgments, processe, and proceeding in Courts of record, and not only in pleas of the Crown, but in all pleas, reall, personall, and mixt, (the Court of the Exchequer excepted, as hereafter shall appear.) And this is *proprium quarto modo*[38] to the King in this Court: for regularly no other Court hath the like jurisdiction, and therefore may be well called *propria causa regis.* and these two be of high and soveraign jurisdiction.

[a][39] Thirdly, this Court hath not only jurisdiction to correct errors in judiciall proceeding, but other errors and misdemeanours extrajudiciall tending to the breach of the peace, or oppression of the subjects, or raising of faction, controversy, debate, or any other manner of misgovernment; so that no wrong or injury, either publick or private, can be done, but that this shall be reformed or punished in one Court or other by due course of law. As if any person be committed to prison, this Court upon motion ought to grant an *Habeas corpus,*[40] and upon returne of the cause do justice and relieve the party wronged. And this may be done though the party grieved hath no priviledge in this Court. It granteth prohibitions to Courts Temporall and Ecclesiastical to keep them within their proper jurisdiction. Also this Court may baile any person for any offence whatsoever. And if a Freeman in City, Burgh, or Town corporate be disfranchised unjustly, albeit he hath no priviledge in this Court,

---

32. Of these you may reade in Glanvil lib. I. cap. 2. &c. & lib. 10. cap. 18. and in the third part of the Institutes *per totu,* & Stanf. *per totum.*

33. [*Ed.:* out of congruence.]

34. [*Ed.:* the king's own causes.]

35. [*Ed.:* pleas of the king's crown.]

36. [*Ed.:* in fact.]

37. And in Ireland of errors in the Kings Bench there. Lib. 7. fo. 18. F. N. B. 22. 34 Ass. 7. 39 Edw. 3. Error 88.

38. [*Ed.:* his own to the fourth degree.]

39. *a* Lib. 11. fo. 98. Jam. Bagges case Vid. 10. Edw. 3. ca. 3. Marshalsea.

40. [*Ed.:* the name given to a variety of writs . . . having for their objective to bring a party before a Court or judge particularly to determine the lawfulness of a custody.]

yet this Court may relieve the party, as it appeareth in James Bagges case, *ubi supra, & sic in similibus.*[41]

Fourthly, this Court may hold plea by Writ out of the Chancery,[42] of all trespasses done *Vi & armis*[43] of Replevins, of *Quare impedit*, &c.[44,45]

[b46] See the second part of the Institutes, the 11 Chapter of Mag. Carta, *Communia placita non sequantur curiam nostram.*[47]

Fifthly; this Court hath power to hold plea by Bill for debt, detinue; covenant, promise, and all other personall actions, *ejectione firme,*[48] and the like, against any that is in *custodia Mareschalli,*[49] or any Officer, Minister, or Clerk of the Court: and the reason hereof is, for that if they should be sued in any other Court they should have the priviledge of this Court: and lest there should be a fayler of Justice (which is so much abhorred in law) they shall be impleaded here by Bill though these actions be common pleas, and are not restrained by the said Act | of Magna Carta, *ubi supra*. Likewise the Officers, Ministers, [72] and Clerks, of this Court priviledged by law in respect of their necessary attendance in Court, may implede others by Bill in the actions of foresaid. And all this appeareth by Bracton, who lived when Magna Carta was made, *ubi supra:*[50] where he saith, *Et aliorum omnium per querelam vel per privilegium sive libertatem.*[51] And continuall experience concurreth with antiquity herein.

H. P. captus per querimoniam mercatorum Flandriae & imprisonatus offert domino regi Hus & Haut in plegio ad standum recto, & ad respondendum prae- dictis mercatoribus, & omnibus aliis qui versus eum loqui voluerint, &c.[52] This plea was after the statute of Magna Carta, *Anno 9 H.3.* Of these words *Hus*

Hus & Haut.

---

41. [*Ed.*: as above; and likewise in similar matters.]

42. F. N. B. 89. 92.

43. [*Ed.*: by force and arms.]

44. Tr. 19. Edw. 3. *coram rege* Rot. 56 Linc.

45. [*Ed.*: A real action to recover a presentation.]

46. *b* 2 part of the Institutes, Magna Carta. cap. 11.

47. [*Ed.*: Common pleas shall not follow our court.]

48. [*Ed.*: The name of a writ or action of trespass.]

49. [*Ed.*: in the custody of the marshal.]

50. See the second part of the Institutes, *ubi sup.* 27. Hen. 3. *coram Rege.* Rot. 9.

51. [*Ed.*: And those of all others, by plaint or by reason of a privilege or franchise.]

52. [*Ed.*: H. P., taken upon complaint by the merchants of Flanders and imprisoned, offered the lord king "hus" and "haut" in pledge to stand to right and to answer the aforesaid merchants and all others who would speak against him, etc.]

& Haut,[53] two French words. *Hus* signifying an Elder-tree, and *Haut* the staffe of a Halbert, &c. I leave the conjecture that some have made thereof to themselves: we think it was then common bail changed now to *Do* and *Ro*[54] and the rather for this word [*offert.*][55] And it is observable, that then putting in baile at one mans suit, he was in *custodia Mareschalli* to answer all others which would see him by Bill, and this continueth to this day.[56] If any person be *in custodia Mareschalli,* &c. be it by commitment, or by *Latitat*[57] bill of Mid' or other Proces of law, it is sufficient to give the Court jurisdiction: and the rather, for that the Court of Common pleas is not able to dispatch all the subjects causes, if the said actions should be confined only to that Court. And seeing none but Serjeants at law can practise in the Court of Common pleas, it is necessary that in this Court of Kings Bench Apprentices and other Counsellors of law might by experience inable themselves to be called Serjeants afterwards; otherwise Serjeants must want experience, which is the life of their profession. And the proceedings in that Court for so long time, & under so many honourable Judges and reverend Sages of the law, hath gotten such a foundation, as cannot now without an Act of Parliament be shaken. And the errors in the Kings Bench cannot be reversed (but in certain particular actions by the statute of 27 Eliz. cap.8. wherein the jurisdiction of the Court is saved) but in the High Court of Parliament, as before in the Chapter of the Court of Parliament appeareth.

Sixthly, if a Writ in a reall action be abated by judgement in the Court of Common pleas, and in a Writ of Error the judgement is reversed in this Court, and the Writ is adjudged good, this Court shall proceed upon this Writ, and is not restrained by Magna Carta, *ubi supra, ne curia Domini Regis deficeret in justitia exhibenda.*[58,59]

---

53. [*Ed.:* Wood and staff.]
54. [*Ed.:* i.e. John Doe and Richard Roe, the fictitious names of common bail.]
55. [*Ed.:* offers.]
56. 31 Hen. 6. 10. b. adjudge.
57. [*Ed.:* Writ which issued in personal actions, on the return of *non est inventus* to a bill of Middlesex.]
58. 1 Hen. 7. 12. 14 Hen. 7. 14. 21 Edw. 3. 46. 11 Hen. 4. 49 *in nativo habendo.*
59. [*Ed.:* lest the lord king's court should be deficient in doing justice.]

This Court may hold plea in Assise *of novel disseisin*[60] without any patent[61] for it is *querela*[62] and not *placitum,*[63] and so not within these words *communia placita,*[64] as it hath been expounded and warranted by continuall experience.

A *Scire fac'*[65] to repeal a Patent of the King may be brought in this Court. And where Fleta saith, *Nisi coram semetipso & concilio suo, vel Auditoribus specialib' falsa judicia ac errores justiciariorum revertuntur:*[66] It is to be known that all the Common law errors in the Court of Exchequer (being the proper Court of the King for his revenue and profit) were examinable before Commissioners appointed by the Kings Writ under his Great Seal, which Fleta here calleth *Auditores speciales.*[67] But now by the statute of 31 Edw.3.[68] the Chancelour and Treasurer taking to them the Justices and other sage persons, such as to them seemeth to be taken, shall examine the errors in the Exchequer, &c.

[69] In ancient time, when pleas were holden in Parliament, when the parties descended to issue, the Record was adjourned into the Kings Bench to be tried there.

[70] See the statute of West. I. against preposterous hearings in this Court, and the exposition of the same in the second part of the Institutes.

[71] By the statute of *Artic' super Cart.* the Chancelour and the Justices of

---

60. [*Ed.:* A writ of assise which lay for the recovery of lands or tenements, where the claimant had been lately disseized.]

61. 3 Hen. 4. 7.

62. [*Ed.:* An action preferred in any court of justice. complaint]

63. [*Ed.:* A public assembly at which the king presided, and which comprised men of all degrees, met for consultation about the great affairs of the kingdom.]

64. [*Ed.:* common pleas.]

65. [*Ed.:* A judicial writ, founded upon some matter of record, such as a judgment or recognizance, and requiring the person against whom it is brought to show cause why the party bringing it should not have advantage of such record, or . . . why the record should not be annulled and vacated.]

66. [*Ed.:* except before himself and his council, or special auditors, the false judgments and errors of the justices are reversed.]

67. [*Ed.:* special auditors]

68. See more hereof in the Chapter of the Exchequer. 31 Edw. 3. cap. 12.

69. *a* Rot. Par. 18 Edw. i. nu. 97. *Placit. Int. Jo. de novo Burgo & Regman, &c.*

70. *b* West. I. cap. 14. Against preposterous hearings.

71. *c* Art. sup. cart. 28. Edw. i. cap. 5. Glan. temps. H. 2. lib. 2. ca. 6. & lib. II. ca. I. *Coram Justiciis Domini Regis in Banco sedentibus. Vid. Adjudicat' coram Rege* in every Terme, from I Edw. I. during all his

[73] the Kings Bench were to follow the Court: but notwithstanding both the Chancery and the Kings Bench were at this time setled Courts, during the severall | Terms of the year, as by infinite records both before and after this statute doth appear. So as at this time they did not attend in the Kings Court, but when they were called, yet were accounted as parcell of the Kings houshold as long as they followed the Court: But this cumbersome attendance wholly ceased in the reign of Edward the third and yet the Lord Chancelour would have had his purveyance, as if he had continued still as one of the houshold, until he and all others, but those of the Kings, Queens, or Princes houshold only, were restrained by Act of Parliament. 34 Edw.3. cap.2.[72]

Also upon perusall of the Records in the reign of Henry the third from the beginning of his reign until the ending of it, this Court sat in the Term time where the other Courts of Justice did sit.[73] And the pleas were stiled to be holden *Coram Rege* as to this day they are: and this appeareth by Fitzh. Abridgment, in the titles of *Corone,* of Brief, of Wast &c. and by Bracton who in many places voucheth Judgments in the reign of Henry the third in Terms *Coram Rege.* And this appeareth also in elder times: but hereof thus much shall suffice to prove, that at the making of the said Act of 28 Edw.1. and long before, this Court in Term times sat with the Kings other Courts, and specially for Pleas of the Crown, &c. and that the said Act is to be intended, that the Chancelour and the Judges of this Court should attend the King and follow the Court when they were required.

It is truly said that the Justices *De banco Regis* have supream authority, the King himself sitting there as the law intends.[74] They be more then Justices in Eire.[75]

The Justices in this Court are the soveraign Justices of Oier and Terminer, Gaol-delivery,[76] conservators of the peace, &c. in the Realm. See the books

---

reign in every severall Term in the yeare. And in all those times and Termes the Court of Chancery did sit.

72. 34 Edw. 3. c 1. 2.

73. And so did the Chancery both of them being to some purposes but one Court as it appeareth in the Chapter of the Court of Chancery.

74. 3 El. Dier 187.

75. 27 Ass. p. 1.

76. 7 Edw. 4. 18. 4 Hen. 7. 18. 14 Hen. 7. 21. i: 9. fo. 118. a & b. Segnior Sanchers case.

in the margent, you shall find excellent matter of learning concerning the supream jurisdiction of this Court.[77]

In this Court the Kings of this Realm have sit in the High Bench, and the Judges of that Court on the lower Bench at his feet; but Judicature only belongeth to the Judges of that Court, and in his presence they answer all motions, &c.

The Justices of this Court are the soveraign Coroners of the land, and therefore where the Sherif and Coroners may receive appeals by bill, *è Fortiori*[78] the Justices of this Court may doe it.[79]

So high is the authority of this Court, that when it comes and sits in any County, the Justices of Eire,[80] of Oier and Terminer, Gaol-delivery, they which have conusance, &c. doe cease without any writing to them. But if any indictment of Treason or Felony in a forain County be removed before certain Commissioners of Oier and Terminer in the County where this Court sits, yet they may proceed, because this Court (for that this indictment was not removed before them) cannot proceed for that offence. But if an indictment be taken in Midd. in the Vacation, and after this Court sit in the next Term in the same County (if this Court be adjourned) then may special Commissioners of Oier and Terminer, &c. in the interim proceed upon that indictment, but the more usuall way is by speciall Commission.[81] And all this was resolved by all the Judges of England at Winchester Term, *Anno 1 Jacobi Regis,*[82] in the case of Sir Everard Digby and others: and so had it been resolved, Mich. 25 & 26 Eliz. in the case of Arden and Somervile, for this kind of speciall Commission of Oier and Terminer: and herewith agreeth Pl. Com. in the Earl of Leic' case, *Anno 1 Mar. reginae.*[83]

And so supream is the jurisdiction of this Court,[84] that if any Record be removed into this Court, it cannot (being as it were in his center) be remanded

---

77. 17 Edw. 3. 13. a. Lib. 4. fo. 57. in the Sadlers case. Pl. Com. 262.
78. [*Ed.:* Thinking beforehand.]
79. *a* 21 Ass. 12. 27 Ass. 1. 28 Ass. 52. 21 Hen. 7. 29.
80. *b* Pasch. 12 Edw. 3. *Coram Rege,* Ro. 99. Chichest. W. 1. ca. 3. Lib. 9. fo. 118. *Ubi Supra.*
81. Hil. 1. Jac. Sir Walter Raleighs case, & c.
82. [*Ed.:* First year of the Reign of James I.]
83. Pl. Com. fo. 388. Count de Leic' case acc'.
84. 22 Edw. 3. 6. b. 24 Edw. 3. 73 29 Ass. 52 Stanf. pl. cor. 15.

back, unlesse it be by Act of Parliament. And this appeareth by the Judgment of the Parliament in *Anno 6. Hen.* 8.[85] but by the authority of that Act indictments of felonies and murders removed into the Kings Bench may by the Justices of that Court be remanded, and this Court may send down as well the bodies of all Felons and Murderers, as their indictments into the Counties where the same murders or felonies were committed or done, &c. in such manner, &c. as if the indictments had not been brought into the Kings Bench.

[74] | But the Justices of the Kings Bench of their own authority may grant a *Nisi prius*[86] in case of treason, felony, and other pleas; for there they send but the transcript of the Record and not the Record it self, as shall be said in the Chapter of Justices of *Nisi prius.*[87] But if the Justices of the Kings Bench doe perceive that any indictment is to be removed into that Court by practise or for delay, the Court may refuse to receive the same, before it be entered of Record, and remaund the same back again for justice to be done.

By the statute of 2 *Hen.* 4 the Clerk of the Crown of this Court,[88] if fourscore or an hundred men be indicted of felony or trespasse, of one felony, or one trespasse, and they plead to an issue, as not guilty, the said Clerk ought not to take for the *Venire fac'*[89] nor for the entring of the plea but two shillings only, and not two shillings for every one, which Act is made in affirmance of the Common-law,[90] So if one man be indicted of two severall felonies or trespasses, and is acquired, he shal pay but for one deliverance.

---

85. 6 Hen. 8. cap. 6. It extendeth only to Felonies and Murders.

86. [*Ed.:* The *nisi prius* courts are such as are held for the trial of issues of fact before a jury and one presiding judge.]

87. See before cap. Parliam. pag. 21. when a writ of Error is sued of a Judgment, *Coram rege,* they proceed *super tenore recordi,* and the record it self remaineth in this Court.

88. 2 Hen. 4. cap. 10.

89. [*Ed.:* A judicial writ, directed to the sheriff of the county in which a cause is to be tried, commanding him that he "cause to come" before the court, on a certain day, therein mentioned, twelve good and lawful men of the body of his county, qualified according to law, by whom the truth of the matter may be the better known, and who are in no wise of kin either to the plaintiff or to the defendant, to make a jury.]

90. 26 Ass. p. 47.

Out of this Court are other Courts derived, as from one fountain severall springs and rivers, in respect of the multiplicity of causes, which have increased. *Jurisdictio istius curiae est originalis seu ordinaria, & non delegata.*[92] The Justices of this Court have no Commission, Letters Patents or other means to hold pleas, &c. but their power is originall and ordinary. They were called anciently, *Justiciae, Justiciarii, locum tenentes domini regis, &c.*[93] The Chief Justice,[94] *Justitia Angliae, Justitia prima, Justiciarius Angliae, Justiciarius Angliae capitalis, and Justiciarius noster capitalis ad placita coram nobis terminand.*[95] To observe the changes of these names, and the reason and change thereof, is worthy of observation,

Before the reign of Edward the first the Chief Justice of this Court was created by Letters Patents, and the form thereof (taking one example for all) was in these words.

Rex, &c. Archiepiscopis, Episcopis, Abbatibus, Prioribus, Comitibus, Baronibus, Vicecomitibus, Forestariis, & omnibus aliis fidelibus regni Angliae, Salutem.[96] *Cum pro conservatione nostra, & transquillitatis regni nostri, & ad justitiam universis & singulis de regno nostro exhibendam constituerimus dilectum et fidelem nostrum Philippum Basset Justiciarium Angliae quamdiu nobis placuerit capitalem. Vobis mandamus in fide qua nobis tenemini firmiter injungentes, quatenus in omnibus quae ad officium Justiciarii praedicti, nec non ad conservationem pacis nostrae et regni nostri eidem dum in officio praedicto steterit, plenius sitis intendentes. Teste Rege, &c.*[98]

Designatio Justiciariorum est à rege, jurisdictio vero ordinaria à lege.[91]

Capitalis Justiciatius Angliae.[97]

91. [*Ed.:* The title of judge is of the King and its true and ordinary jurisdiction.]

92. Glanvil lib. 1. ca. 6. 13. &c. *Saepenumero.*

93. [*Ed.:* justices, justiciars, the lord king's lieutenants, etc.]

94. *a* Lib. nigro in Scaccario. par. 1. ca. 4 Never in any legall record (which we have seen) they were called *Summi Justiciarii.*

95. [*Ed.:* justice of England, first justice, justicar of England, chief justiciar of England, and our chief justice to determine pleas before ourself.]

96. Rot. Cart. 45 Hen. 3. 13 Aug.

97. [*Ed.:* Chief Justice of England.]

98. [*Ed.:* The king, etc. to the archbishops, bishops, abbots, priors, earls, barons, sheriffs, foresters, and all other faithful subjects of the realm of England, greeting. Since, for our preservation and for the tranquility of our realm, and in order to provide justice to all and singular of our realm, we have constituted our beloved and faithful Philip Basset to be justiciar of England for so long as it pleases us, we command you in the faith which you hold unto us, with firm injunction, that you submit yourselves fully to him, while he remains in that office, with respect to everything touching the office of justiciar aforesaid, and the preservation of our peace and our realm, etc.]

Herein 6. things are to be observed. 1. That the creation of his office was by Letters Patents. 2. That this officer was originally instituted for three things.

1. Pro conservatione nostra. 2. Tranquillitatis regni nostri. 3. * Ad justitiam universis & singulis de regno nostro exhibendam.[99] The third thing to be observed is, that he was *Justiciarius Anglix capitalis.*[100] 4. That Philip Basset was constituted Chief Justice of England, and after made Knight, for he was not Knight at the making of the Letters Patents. This Philip was of Welledby in the County of Northampton, & was excellently learned in the laws of the Realm; he was younger brother of Baron Bassett of Draiton Basset in the County of Staff. 5. That he was constituted *quamdiu nobis placuerit.*[101] Lastly, the clause of attendance, and the persons that are to give attendance, &c. to him, are very remarkable. This Philip Basset was the last of this kind of creation by any like Letters Patents, and he died Chief Justice neer to the end of the reign of Henry the third King Edward the first being a wise and prudent Prince, knowing that *Cui plus licet quam par est, plus vult quam licet,*[102] (as most of these *summi Justiciarii* did) made three alterations. 1. By limitation of his Authority. 2. By changing *Summus Justiciarius,*[103] to *Capitalis Justic'.*[104] 3. By a new kind of creation, viz. by Writ, lest if he had continued his former manner of creation,

[75]   he I might have had a desire of his former Authority, which three doe expresly appear by the Writ yet in use, viz.

Rex. &c. E. C. militi Salutem. Sciatis quod constituimus vos Justiciarium nostrum capitalem ad placita coram nobis tenenda, durante beneplacito nostro. Teste, &c.[105]

Which writ being called *Breve*[106] doth in few words comprehend the sub-

---

99. [*Ed.:* 1. For our preservation. 2. For the tranquility of our realm. 3. To provide justice to all and singular of our realm.]

100. [*Ed.:* chief justiciar of England (N.B. actually the word *capitalis* (chief) is not in the patent as he gives it).]

101. [*Ed.:* for so long as it pleases us.]

102. [*Ed.:* He to whom more is permissible than is fair wants more than is permissible.]

103. [*Ed.:* highest justiciar.]

104. [*Ed.:* chief justiciar.]

105. [*Ed.:* The king, etc. to E[dward] C[oke], knight, greeting. Know ye that we have constituted you our chief justice to hold pleas before ourself during our good pleasure. Witness, etc.]

106. [*Ed.:* A writ. An original writ. A writ or precept of the king issuing out of his courts. A writ by which a person was summoned or attached to answer an action, complaint, etc. . . . , or whereby anything was commanded to be done in the courts, in order to justice, etc.]

stance of the former Letters Patents: for *Capitalis Justiciarius noster and ad placita coram nobis tenenda*[107] includes all that which was truly intended to be granted to him in the former Letters Patents, which alterations were made by Authority of Parliament, though not now extant.[108] For it is a rule in law, that ancient offices must be granted in such forms and in such manner, as they have used to be, unless the alteration were by Authority of Parliament, And continuall experience approveth, that for many succession of ages without intermission, they have been, and yet are called by the said writ, *Et optimus legum interpres consuetudo.*[109] But after the said alteration, viz. in *anno* 25 Edw. 1.[110] Reginaldus de Grey (was stiled) *Justiciarius Angliae,* and he was in legall proceedings called *Capitalis Justiciarius noster,* when his Patent was, *Capitalis Justiciarius Angliae.*

We have seen a Fine in these words:[111] *Haec est finalis concordia facta in curia domini regis apud Westm' à die Sancti Michaelis in tres septimanas, anno Regni Regis Henrici filii regis Johannis 3. coram domino Huberto de Burgo capitali Justiciario Angliae & aliis domini Regis fidelibus tunc ibi praesentibus.*[112]

^a In the writ *De homine replegiand*[113,114] he (which was formerly called *Capitalis Justiciarius Angliae*) is called *Capitalis justic' noster,* and sometime *Cap. Justic' Regis,* The Stile of this Court of kings Bench is Anglia in the margent: and in divers Acts of Parliament he is called Chief Justice of England. 34 Hen. 8. cap. 26. 37 Hen. 8. cap. 12. 2 Edw. 6. cap. 13. 5 Edw. 6. cap. 11.

The Chief Justice in Ireland is called *Capitalis Justiciar' Hiberniae*[115] at this day, Pasch, 13 Edw. 1. (the pleas in this Court are *Coram rege*) then were stiled thus, *Placita coram locum domini regis tenentibus, &c. Ideo venit inde jurata*

---

107. [*Ed.:* our chief justice [and] to hold pleas before ourself.]

108. See in the chapter of the Constable and Marshall for this point.

109. [*Ed.:* and custom is the best interpreter of laws.]

110. Rot. Par. 25 Edw. 1. so named in the Writ of Parliament to him directed.

111. Nota, this fine was levied, *Inter Martinum Abbatem de Missenden querentem, & Thurstanum Basset deforcientem de 3 Carucu' terrae in lega,* before him in the Kings Bench, in 3 Hen. 3. before Mag. Car. and stiled *Capit. Justiciar' Angliae. Lib. de Missenden* fo. 109. divers other fines with the same stile.

112. [*Ed.:* This is the final concord made in the lord king's court at Westminster in three weeks from Michaelmas day in the third year of the reign of King Henry, son of King John, before the lord Hubert de Burgh, chief justiciar of England, and other faithful subjects of the lord king then and there present.]

113. *a* Regist. fo. 77. 24 Edw. 1. stat' de consultat' 3 Edw. 3. Coron. 361. Lib. Int. Co. tit. action sur le case, Sect. 5.

114. [*Ed.:* Order granting bail to one in prison but not for a crime or on order of the King.]

115. [*Ed.:* Chief justiciar (or justice) of Ireland.]

coram rege vel ejus locum tenentibus,[116] 15 Paschae, &c. within which words all the Judges of the kings Bench were included.

[b117] *Anno domini 969.* in the Abby of Ramsey this Epitaph was ingraden, &c. D. *Ailivinus inclyti regis Edgari cognatus totius Angliae Aldermannus, &c.*[118] who was without question Chief Justice of all England. *Inter leges Aluredi*[119] cap. 34. he is called *Cyninger ealdorman,*[120] i. *Regis Aldermannus sive Senator, five Iudex. Vide cap. 3. 15. & 38. Et inter leges Edovardi ca. 35.*

The rest of the Judges of the Kings Bench have their offices by Letters Patents in these words, *Rex omnibus ad quos praesentes literae pervenerint, Salutem. Sciatis quod constituimus dilectum & fidelem Johannem Doderidge militem unum Justiciariorum ad Placita coram nobis tenenda durante beneplacito nostro, Teste, &c.*[121,122] These Justices of the Kings Bench are stiled *1. Capitales. 2. Generales. 3. Perpetui. 4. Majores a latere regis residentes:*[123] but the Chief Justice is only called by the King, *Capitalis Justiciarius noster.*[124] They are called 1. *Capitales,* in respect of their supream jurisdiction. 2. *Generales,* in respect of their generall jurisdiction throughout all England, &c. 3. *Perpetui,* for that they ought not to be removed without just cause. 4. *Majores à latere regis residentes,* for their honor and safety, that they should be protected by the King in administration of justice, for that they be *a latere Regis.*

And where in 5 Edw. 4. it is holden by all the Justices in the Exchequer chamber[125] that a man cannot be Justice by Writ but by Patent or Commission, it is to be understood of all the Judges, saving the Chief Justice of this Court. But both the Chief Justice, and the rest of the Judges may be discharged by Writ under the Great Seal.

---

116. [*Ed.:* pleas before the lord king's lieutenants, etc. Therefore let a jury come therein before the lord king or his lieutenants in the quindene of Easter, etc.]

117. b *Aldermanni Judices dicti sunt in diebus illis.*

118. [*Ed.:* Of Ailwin, kinsman of the excellent King Edgar, ealdorman of all England, etc.]

119. [*Ed.:* in the laws of Alfred cap. 34.]

120. [*Ed.:* the king's ealdorman [in Anglo-Saxon and Latin], or senator, or judge.]

121. [*Ed.:* The king to all those to whom these present letters shall come, greeting. Know ye that we have constituted our beloved and faithful John Doderidge, knight, one of the justices to hold pleas before ourself during our good pleasure. Witness, etc.]

122. c Bract. li. 3. f. 108.

123. [*Ed.:* 1. major (or chief) 2. general 3. Perpetual 4. the greater among the King's companions and residents.]

124. [*Ed.:* Our Chief Justice.]

125. L. 5 Edw. 4. 137.

None can be a Judge of this Court unlesse he be a Serjeant of the degree of the Coif, and yet in the Writ or Patent to them made, they are not named Serjeants.

| If a Writ be returnable *Coram Justiciariis nostris apud Westm'*,[126] it shall   [76] be returned in the Common place; but if it be returnable in this Court, it must be *Coram nobis ubicunque fuerimus in Anglia*.[127] See the Second part of the Institutes, Mag. Cart. cap. 11. and the exposition upon the same.

In former times some ill disposed Clerks of this Court, because they could have no originall [writ] out of the Chancery for debt returnable into this Court, they would sue out an originall action of trespasse (a meer feigned action) returnable into this Court, and so proceed to Exigent, (where in truth the cause of action is for debt) and when the Defendant appeared, &c. all the former proceedings were waved, and a bill filed for the Defendant for debt. This is an unjust practise in derogation of the dignity and honor of this Court, and worthy of severe punishment according to the statute of West. I. c. 29. when it is found out:[128] *Vide* in the Chapter of the Court of Common Pleas in the end thereof.

Now that we may here say somewhat to a vulgar objection of the multi-plication of suits, in law both in this Court, and other of his Majesties Courts at Westm' more then hath been in the reigns of Edw. 3. Ric. 2. Hen. 4. Hen. 5. Hen. 6. Edw. 4. and R.3. It is to be observed, that there be six causes of the increase of them, whereof two be generall, the other four particular. The generall be Peace, and Plenty: The particular, 1. The dissolution of so many Monasteries, Chanteries, &c. and the dispersing of them into so many severall hands. 2. The swarm of Informers. 3. The number of Concealors. 4. The multitude of Atturnies.

For the first generall: In the reigns of Edw. 3. Ric. 2. Hen. 4. Hen. 5. and part of the reign of Hen. 6. in respect of the wars in France, &c. and in the residue of the reign of Hen. 6. and in the reign of Edw. 4. in respect of the bloody and intestine wars, and in almost continuall alarums within the bowels of this kingdome,[129] between the houses of Lancaster and York, there could

(margin notes:) Multipli-cation of suits.

Peace.

Plenty.

Dissolution of Monas-teries, &c.

Informers. Conceal-ors. Attur-nies.

---

126. [*Ed.:* before our justices at Westminster.]

127. [*Ed.:* before us wheresoever we shall then be in England.]

128. West I. ca. 29. Vid. 30 Hen. 6. 37. a. 30 Edw. 3. 32. It is fraud where one thing is pretended, and another done.

129. *Silent leges inter arma.* [*Ed.:* The law says nothing during war.]

not be so many suits in law, as since this kingdome hath enjoyed peace, which
is the first generall cause. Peace is the mother of plenty, (which is the second
generall cause) and Plenty the Nurse of suits. In particular, by the dissolution
of Monasteries, Chanteries, &c. and dispersing of them, &c. Upon the statutes
made concerning the same (there being such a confluence of Ecclesiasticall
possessions) there arose many questions and doubts, whereupon suits were
greatly increased. 2. Informers and Relators raised many suits, by informations,
writs, &c. in the Kings Courts at Westm' upon penall statutes, many whereof
were obsolete, inconvenient, and not fit for those days, and yet remained as
snares upon the subject, so as the subject might justly say with Tacitus, *Prius
vitiis laboravimus, nunc legibus.*[131] 3. Concealors, Helluones,[132] that endeav-
oured to swallow up Cathedrall Churches and the Ecclesiasticall possessions
of Church-men, and the livings of many others of the Kings subjects. Lastly,
the multitude of[133] Atturnies, more then is limited by law, is a great cause of
increase of suits.

But now on the other side, to shew what great hope there is, that suits in
law shall decrease, for that in effect all the particular causes of the increase of
them are taken away, which we have thought good to remember.

[b][134] For the first, the statute of 35 Eliz. cap. 3. hath remedied part, but the
statute of 21 Jac. ca. 2. hath given a plenary salve for the whole mischief, whereof
you may read at large in the Third part of the Institutes, cap. 87. against
Concealors, *turbidum hominum genus.*[135,136] For the second, by the statute of
21 Jac. cap. 4. Informations, &c. upon penall statutes are to be heard and
determined in their proper Counties, and not in the Courts at Westminster,
whereby the vexatious swarm of Informers, who are best trusted where they
are least known, are banished and turned again to their former occupations.[137]
Concerning Atturnies the number are set down, and that they ought to be

Marginal notes:

Concordia parvae res crescunt exopulentialiter.[130]

Possessions of Monast. and Chanteries &c.

Diminution of suits.

Concealors.

Informers.

Atturnies.

---

130. [*Ed.:* Little agreement comes out of plenty.]

131. [*Ed.:* First we have laboured with faults, now with the laws.]

132. [*Ed.:* gluttons.]

133. See the preambles of the stat. of 4 Hen. 4. ca. 18. 33 Hen. ca. 7.

134. *b* 35 El. ca. 3. 21 Ja. cap. 2.

135. [*Ed.:* a troublesome kind of men.]

136. *c* 21 Jac. ca. 4. See the Third part of the Inst. cap. against vexatious relations Informers. &c.

137. *d* Rot. par. 20. Edw. 1. Rot. 4. *De Apprenticiis & Atturnatis* 15 Ric. 2 nu. 28. 4. Hen. 4 ca. 18. 33 Hen. 6. ca. 7. See Rot. Parl. 13 Hen. 4 nu. 63. not in print.

learned and vertuous, and as I understand, the Judges at this time have this matter in consideration. But besides these, there are some other statutes made for avoiding and decreasing of vexatious suits. As an[138] Act in 21 Jac. Regis cap. 16. for limitation of actions and avoiding suits in law, a good and beneficiall law. Another Act at the same Parliament, cap. 13. for the further reformation of Jeo-l-fails, a good law for ending of suits. Another at the same Parliament, [77] cap.8. to prevent and punish abuses in procuring of processe of *Supersedeas*[139] of the peace and good behaviour, out of his Majesties Courts at Westminster, &c. whereby infinite vexatious, troubles and charges of the subjects are prevented. Another at the same Parliament, ca. 23. for avoiding of vexations delays in causes by removing of actions and suits out of inferior Courts, wherein the former abuse was vexatious, grievous, and chargeable to the subject. A branch of an Act at the same Parliament, cap. 16. for pleading of tender of amends in an action of trespasse, *Quare claus. fregit,*[140] for a trespasse by negligence, or involuntary, wherein the Defendant maketh no title, &c, an excellent and necessary law for avoiding of trifling and vexatious suits, especially in Champion Countries. An Act at the same Parliament, cap.2. against Monopolies and new projects, &c.[141] a great quiet for the time to come. *Anno 3 Caroli Regis nunc,* cap. 1. The petition of Right concerning the rights and liberties of all the subjects of this Realm for their repose and quiet. Lastly, the repeal of so many obsolete penall statutes is a great mean of diminution of suits.

For the abovesaid generall causes, viz. Peace and Plenty, long may they happily by the goodnesse of god continue without abuse within this Realm.

The Kings Bench hath authority for great misprisions and offences, to adjudge and inflict corporall punishment, as Pillory, Papers, and the like: whereof you may read many presidents in the Third part of the Institutes, pag. 219, 220.

---

138. *e* 21 jac. ca. 16.

139. [*Ed.:* The name of a writ containing a command to stay the proceedings at law.]

140. [*Ed.:* Wherefore he broke the close. Action of trespass which has for its object the recovery of damages for an unlawful entry upon another's land.]

141. See the 3. part of the Inst cap. against Monopolists and Projectors. 3 Car. Regis c. 1 21 Jac. ca. 28. 3 Car. ca. 4.